econometric methods

m. dutta

Rutgers – The State University of New Jersey

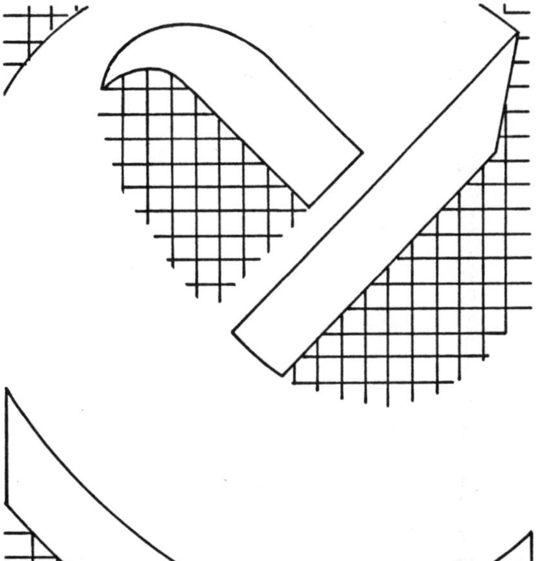

Published by

H88 **SOUTH-WESTERN PUBLISHING CO.**

CINCINNATI WEST CHICAGO, ILL. DALLAS PELHAM MANOR, N.Y.
PALO ALTO, CALIF. BRIGHTON, ENGLAND

ISBN: 0-538-08880-X
Library of Congress Catalog Card Number: 74-18851

2 3 4 5 D 9 8

Printed in the United States of America

To my Mother
and
to the memory of my late Father

preface

This volume is based on my years of teaching econometrics to beginners, some of whom have conquered their fear of the subject matter and have courageously proceeded into the realm of advanced econometrics, while others have remained satisfied with a single exposure to this offshoot of economics. Of the firm believers, by far the majority continue to be doubtful, but fortunately they continue the search.

I have written this book to aid would-be econometricians in preparing themselves for further advanced studies in econometrics. To fulfill this objective, I have drawn heavily upon existing literature. Although direct quotations and footnotes are sparse, the serious reader will find references to source materials throughout the book.

It is my hope that the present volume will adequately satisfy the needs of beginners in econometrics. Even though there are several outstanding advanced treatises on econometrics, the students who take a course in econometrics for the first time often remain baffled. The semester may end in a futile search for lessons in econometrics, while the student is lost between lectures on linear algebra and regression analysis. I have made an attempt here to provide the right mixture of all that should constitute a complete course in econometrics for beginners.

I have followed three specific guidelines. First, I have emphasized the role of economics in econometrics, focusing on how to measure the unknown parameters of models that may be constructed to specify an economic system or a subsystem. Interdependence of economic activities has been underscored right from the beginning.

Secondly, I have made meticulous efforts to explain successive steps relative to the discussion of each subject. Thus inadequate preparation in mathematics and statistical theory, a common phenomenon in classes of introductory econometrics, need not be a complete roadblock in the learning process. In fact students using this book are required to read mathematical and statistical presentations and learn them in the process, even though their basic preparation may leave room for improvement. I have not assumed that students have already done extensive course work in mathematics and statistical theory to prepare themselves for studying this text in their first course in econometrics. All I assume is that they have been exposed to such subject matter in introductory courses and, more importantly, that they are willing to find out for themselves what further preparation in these areas is necessary to continue their studies and to undertake successful research in econometrics should they choose to do so.

Thirdly, problems related to econometric studies, such as heteroscedasticity, serial correlation, multicollinearity, lag structure, instrumental variables, and consistent estimators for an interdependent system, have all been discussed at length, each such topic being treated in an independent chapter. Often beginners in econometrics are not introduced to such topics, or are only marginally introduced. All of these topics have been treated without compromising the basic statistical methods of estimation. In addition to regression and correlation methods, I have introduced fairly extensive discussions regarding the analyses of variance and covariance, orthogonal regression, principal component analysis, prediction, simulation, and Monte Carlo studies.

If the class size is restricted and if its membership is reasonably selective, all of the materials in this book can be covered in one semester (treating sections 3 and 4 of Chapter 9 and the whole of Chapter 13 as optional). The prerequisites for this course are difficult to define. Mathematics and statistics have been used in the text no more than is necessary and should cause no hardship to patient readers; however, some background in mathematics and statistics is clearly a prerequisite. A semester course in statistics and in linear algebra is helpful.

Over the years members of successive classes at Rutgers University have taught me how to teach econometrics, and I am grateful to them. Special mention must be made of Peter D. Loeb, V. Kerry Smith, and Vincent Su, who have given me ungrudging help all through my work on this book. My indebtedness also extends to Lawrence R. Klein, who taught econometrics to me, A. L. Nagar, J. D. Sargan, R. J. Ball, H. O. A. Wold, Ejnar Lyttkens, Murray Brown, Kenneth F. Wallis, Damodar Gujarati, Meghnad Desai, Kanta Marwah, R. F. Kosobud, J. R. Bisignano, G. N. Paraskevopoulos, T. K. Sen, and F. G. Adams. Some of these people have read various parts of the manuscript, and all of them have encouraged me to bring the project to its present status.

My special thanks are due to Mildred Goldberger but for whose extensive editorial help this volume would have been delayed in reaching the readers. I also wish to express my appreciation to Emma L. Wenz, Betty Kaminsky, Myrna Vas, and Irene Matthews for patiently typing successive versions of various parts of the manuscript.

New Brunswick, NJ — m.d.
August, 1974

contents

introduction

what is econometrics?

i.0 MEASUREMENT IN ECONOMICS

Alfred Marshall said: "Qualitative analysis tells the ironmaster that there is *some* sulphur in his ore, but it does not enable him to decide whether it is worthwhile to smelt the ore at all; and if it is, then by what process. For that purpose he needs quantitative analysis, which will tell him *how much* sulphur there is in the ores." [1]

Economists' concern for the measurement of parameters in economic relationships is not new. Students of economic theory (both micro and macro) have been taught at length about such concepts as price elasticity of demand, price elasticity of supply, income elasticity of demand, interest elasticity of investment, marginal propensity to consume, marginal propensity to import, marginal efficiency of capital, multiplier, accelerator, and so on. Quite logically, one of the questions growing out of these studies is how an economist can obtain measurements of such magnitudes.

The task of answering this question can be undertaken only by steps. The first step is to translate the a priori relationships postulated in economic theory in terms of mathematical functions. Once the function is properly defined, the second step is to make use of statistical theory to estimate the function. Broadly speaking, econometrics concerns measurement in economics. It is the study of economic theory in relation to mathematics and statistics.

Obviously, the starting point is economics. Econometric models, if one prefers to use that term, exist on the basis of economic theory, a set of received theorems developed by the teachings of the successive generations of great masters. Jan Tinbergen has aptly said: "An author who does not bind himself to some laws is able to prove anything at any moment he likes. But then he is telling stories, not making theory." [2] Econometricians begin with economic theory, using mathematics and statistics to obtain quantitative values of the parameters that appear in the theory. In the process there is scope for feedback in the sense that econometric research

---

[1] Alfred Marshall, "The Old Generation of Economists and the New," *Quarterly Journal of Economics*, Vol. 11, No. 2 (January, 1897), p. 123.

[2] Jan Tinbergen, "Econometric Business Cycle Research," *Review of Economic Studies*, Vol. 7 (1939-1940), p. 80.

isolates some deficiencies in economic theory, as stated previously, and helps in the reformulation of the theory. This is true in all disciplines where theories have developed by scientific methodology.

Perhaps it is more so in econometrics. The received theorems or maintained hypotheses in economics are not the results of inductive tests based on experimental data. They are primarily derived from deductive reasoning applied to insightful intuition. Econometrics is an exercise in testing such theorems. Indeed the essential contribution of econometrics is constructing models that provide tests of the agreement between theoretical formulations and empirical observations. In the process the theorem may be altered in accordance with the findings observed. Community consumption in real terms, in the pure theory of the Keynesian revolution, depends on the level of community real income and the rate of interest. Subsequently, we learned that consumption depends primarily on the level of income. Still further tests have demonstrated that consumption is dependent functionally not only on the current level of income, but also on some measure of permanent, or normal, income level. Many such illustrations can be provided to indicate how econometric studies contribute to better understanding of the received theorems in economics.

Although intuition is undoubtedly a good guide to the principles of economic behavior, it cannot by itself provide complete answers about given behavior patterns. Intuition, however intelligent, is not based on a systematic methodology. We need methodology to provide meaningful answers to the questions raised. Econometrics provides the systematic methodology for measurements in economics. To suggest that measurement in economics is a one-shot game is nonsense. It has not been so in any science, and it is not so in econometrics. It is a continuous process whose perfection knows no end.

To quote Herman Wold: "Knowledge grows by new models being constructed and then adopted by consensus. And knowledge develops by models being discarded as false or obsolete, and replaced by improved models." [3] To look for final truth in any branch of knowledge is at best a curiosity of the idle mind.

i.1 MATHEMATICS AND STATISTICS IN ECONOMETRICS

Knowledge of mathematics and statistics becomes useful in economics only after the researcher has trained himself in economic theory. Because emphasis is often misplaced, a word of caution is necessary.

You may have heard the famous story that the renowned physicist Max Planck found economics too difficult and became a physics student instead. No one suggested that it was mathematics, or for that matter mathematical statistics, that frightened young Planck. One can only profit by the comments that J. M. Keynes made in reference to this: "The amalgam of logic, intuition,

[3] Herman O. Wold, "Ends and Means of Scientific Method," mimeographed (1968), p. 6.

and wide knowledge of facts, most of which are not precise, which is required for economic interpretation in its highest form" could discourage even the bravest of young learners. Keynes emphasized, "Professor Planck could easily master the whole corpus of mathematical economics in a few days." [4] Rhetoric apart, the basic point to be underscored is that econometrics is an exercise in economics, not in mathematics or statistics as such. Even when the econometrician has performed the mathematical and statistical analysis, forceful intuition and clear understanding of economic facts may prove indispensable in using the results.

This is not to suggest that training in mathematics and statistics can be avoided by one who intends to be a successful econometrician. Keynes made the observation in reference to Planck in 1923. Since then, phenomenal progress has taken place in applying mathematics and mathematical statistics to economic analysis. Indeed, the history of econometrics is the history of this progress in economics, and it dates back to the early 1930s. Oscar Lange writes that the term "econometrics" was introduced in 1926 by Ragnar Frisch. Attempts at a quantitative approach in economic research using statistical methods, which in effect acted as a catalyst for the formal birth of econometrics, go back much further. Tinbergen suggests that econometricians can think of Cournot's works in the 1830s in the same way that economists think of Adam Smith's *Wealth of Nations*. Even earlier, Physiocrats constructed the *Tableau èconomique* to present a quantitative framework of the economic process.

Good knowledge of mathematics and statistics is absolutely indispensable in understanding econometrics and in undertaking econometric research. Suppose that the immediate concern is to study a model of the milk market. The received theorem in economics teaches that the quantity demanded depends on its price, as does the quantity supplied. The econometrician begins with this received theorem and states his proposition in a simple mathematical model, such as:

$$Q^d = \alpha_0 + \alpha_1 P \qquad \textbf{0.1.1}$$

$$Q^s = \beta_0 + \beta_1 P \qquad \textbf{0.1.2}$$

$$Q^d = Q^s \qquad \textbf{0.1.3}$$

where P = price of milk
Q^d = quantity of milk demanded
Q^s = quantity of milk supplied

In these equations α_0, α_1, β_0, and β_1 are *parameters* of the model. A priori theories of economic behavior further suggest that the demand function is negatively sloped, with the quantity demanded increasing as price decreases, whereas the supply function is postively sloped; that is, $\alpha_1 < 0$

[4] J. M. Keynes, "Alfred Marshall, 1842-1924," *Economic Journal*, Vol. 34, No. 3 (September, 1924), p. 333.

and $\beta_1 > 0$. By definition, in equilibrium the quantity of milk demanded is just equal to the quantity supplied; the market is just cleared. In other words the model is closed by the definitional relation 0.1.3.

The three relationships above specify the simple model of the milk market. The econometrician next collects data on the quantity of milk marketed and its equilibrium price and carefully compiles the two series. The researcher should immediately realize that he could not have used only the same two series of observations to estimate the parameters of both the demand and supply functions. He could use the two series to estimate either the demand function or the supply function, but not both. Given the system and the equations describing the system, he must make sure that there exists a logical basis for the autonomy of each relationship and that each equation in the system is identified.[5]

Knowledge of mathematics becomes essential first in specifying the functional form of the received theorem in economics in the context of a given study, and next in securing identification of each of the functional relationships describing the model under investigation. Econometrics, however, must be distinguished from mathematical economics, which deals with exact relationships. Econometrics builds itself on relationships which are stochastic in the sense that unexplained or unexplainable disturbances are not summarily ignored.

The purely mathematical formulation of an economic theory assumes that the relationship is exact. Symbolically,

$$F(X_1, X_2, X_3, \ldots, X_N) = 0 \qquad \textbf{0.1.4}$$

But economics is a social science, and an economic theory is essentially inexact. Such a theory is subject to disturbances which the researcher can hardly control. The above function can be rewritten as follows, using the symbols $U_1, U_2, U_3, \ldots, U_N$ to denote random disturbances:

$$G(X_1, X_2, X_3, \ldots, X_N; \quad U_1, U_2, U_3, \ldots, U_N) = 0 \qquad \textbf{0.1.5}$$

True, there can seldom be a theory that is completely free from such disturbances. In the physical sciences the researcher in his laboratory can build the structure for necessary experimentation with a postulated theory. Disturbances can be, and are, controlled. Such controlled laboratory experiments are difficult if not impossible to design for testing and developing an economic theory. In a class in economic theory, we can consider the effects of a change in the price of milk on the quantity of milk demanded, ceteris paribus, and "prove" or "disprove" the demand theory. Unfortunately, once we leave the classroom, we come to realize that the "other things" are indeed not "equal." In many cases they become quite overwhelming and threaten to

---

[5] This topic will be discussed in Chapter 10. The nature of the problem should be appreciated from the beginning; this is why the problem is introduced at this stage.

demolish our cherished theories. It is important to note that inclusion of the disturbances, U_i, as an independent though unobservable variable in the specific function enforces the irreversibility of economic laws which, in their formal sense, are held reversible.[6] One major problem for measurement in economics is to consider ways and means of appropriately treating these "other things," the disturbances which refuse to remain "equal."

Emphasis on the stochastic nature of an econometric model necessitates extensive use of statistical theory. The milk model, equations 0.1.1 through 0.1.3, in its stochastic form may be restated as follows:

$$Q^d = \alpha_0 + \alpha_1 P + U \qquad \textbf{0.1.6}$$

$$Q^s = \beta_0 + \beta_1 P + V \qquad \textbf{0.1.7}$$

$$Q^d = Q^s \qquad \textbf{0.1.8}$$

The terms U and V refer to the disturbance terms in the respective equations. In other words the quantity of milk demanded or supplied is functionally dependent on the price of milk, but in each case there are disturbances in the functional relationships between the observed variables. The econometrician has to draw upon statistical theory first to impose a plausible form on the distributions of these random terms, since he has no observed data on U and V. He then proceeds to apply the appropriate statistical method of estimation to obtain numerical values for the parameters.

However, it is wrong to assume that statistics is econometrics. To obtain results with economic meaning, econometrics starts with a model given a priori on the basis of economic theory. In estimating the model and in drawing inferences from the estimates, econometricians' indebtedness to mathematical statistics is indeed very great.

i.2 OBJECTIVES OF ECONOMETRICS

What useful purpose does it serve to obtain measurements of economic parameters? How does econometrics contribute to economic analysis? These are pertinent questions. First of all, economic decision making is based on some notion of the future course of events. The businessman wants to know how much merchandise he can expect to sell and at what price. The government of a country wants to follow a policy that results in full employment of the available labor force and full utilization of the existing capacity of the capital stock. At the level of both the firm and the national economy, decision making is based on certain assumptions with respect to the future. An econometrician can provide a systematic model to aid understanding of the future. Indeed prediction or forecasting has often been cited as the prime contribution of econometrics.

A second important contribution is that an econometric model can be used in considering alternatives for the process of decision making. For

[6] Further discussion of this concept will be presented in Chapter 2.

example, it is important to know the consequences on income of alternative taxation policies or of alternative tariff policies. The powerful technique of simulation enables the econometrician to use an appropriate model to analyze the consequences of such alternatives. The policymaker then has the option of basing his decision on this information.

Econometrics is not a mystery box manufacturing numerical values for economic parameters. Rather it has evolved from the pressing need for numerical values of such parameters. The policymaker at the national level, at the company level, and even at the family level needs to have such parameters measured for decision making.

Perhaps the contribution of econometrics in forecasting and in decision making has been overemphasized. Even when econometricians are completely uninterested in prediction or in simulation, interest in analyzing and understanding the structure of the economy remains paramount. Recent research in analyzing the lag structure in economic relationships points to the fact that consumers' responses to changes in income-asset positions and investors' decision-making processes involving planning and appropriation of funds are far from instantaneous. Indeed structural analysis is a prime objective in econometric investigation. Analysis of intersectoral relationships is no less important. Certainly econometricians are interested in knowing what happens in the business sector when some action is taken in the monetary and financial sector, or what happens in the household sector when there is a tax cut. We wish to know not only what happens, but also the intensity of the impact of such events. Econometric research is designed to answer such questions.

Of course, the various objectives of econometric studies are very much interrelated. We are interested in analyzing the structure of the economy and its intersectoral relations partly because we wish to be informed and to decide wisely so that the economy in the future may be what we desire it to be.

i.3 WHITHER ECONOMETRICS?

This introductory chapter concludes with a reference to the often mentioned controversy generated by angry phrases such as "jungleland of facts" and "dreamland of theory." Much empirical research in economics has resulted in the compilation of a huge body of data and the enumeration of certain phenomena on the basis of available data. Compilation of the national income accounts and the census of manufacturers, the collection of family budget data, and the construction of time series of economic observations are not econometric research per se, even though they aid such research. Empirical studies themselves, unless based on economic theory and unless meaningfully treated for disturbances under the ceteris paribus clause, are no guide for positive decision making in economic analysis. On the other hand pure theory is much less interesting to most people unless its operational significance can be tested. Indeed econometrics aspires to provide the link between the land (not "jungle") of facts and the land (not "dream") of theory. Econometric research is very much concerned with positive economics.

Some further confusion can be avoided if we pause one moment at the outset to examine the following statement: Econometric model building is just about writing economic history. In many cases in econometric research, time-series data are used; and this has encouraged some writers to suggest that econometrics is just equationalized economic history. But this statement is inexact and not very helpful. The questions econometricians seek to answer are not those that an economic historian elsewhere would choose to answer. At the other extreme, econometrics is equated with mathematical statistics, mathematics, or statistics. Music is not poetry, nor is biology biochemistry; physics is neither mathematics nor engineering. Even though econometrics draws heavily on mathematics and statistics and also on time-series data, it is what it is in its own right. Indeed econometricians can and do use data that are not historical. One example is cross-sectional data on family budgets. Another example is data from surveys of intended behavior patterns.

The quality of the input (the numerical observations, time series, or cross-sectional data) that goes into econometric research has often invited uncharitable comments from both believers and nonbelievers. Like the researcher in physical science, the econometrician would ideally like to generate experimental data. It is conceivable that in the future we shall be able to generate such data, despite the fact that our subjects of research are human beings and as such are not easily amenable to such experimentation. Who knows that one day we shall not have an electronic gadget to measure the utility that a consumer derives from drinking a cup of tea or coffee?

The use of statistical methods, which are based on the laws of probability, has been questioned since it is hard to describe time-series data as a random sample. For example, the marginal propensity to consume is an important parameter used in macroeconomic studies. If the econometrician has to estimate the parameter with time-series data of the United States, he has two series of observations, one on the aggregate consumption expenditure and one on the aggregate income over the sample years. One heroic assumption he can make is that if there had been a big bowl containing many United States economies in existence at a particular time and if he had succeeded in drawing at random a pair of observations for each of the sample years, he would have drawn the same pairs as the ones recorded by the appropriate data gathering agency.

Much has been said about the uncontrollable factors that exist and continue to effect economic data. The choice is either to work on generating experimental data, with human beings as subjects (or with living beings of a lower order, as is the case with the bioscientists), or to have faith in whatever can be done to decontaminate the body of data collected for research. Indeed, in the process of econometric research over the years, many of the deficiencies of data collected under uncontrolled conditions have been removed.

It has been emphasized that econometric relations are necessarily stochastic. However, extensive research has been done to measure economic parameters by using input-output models or programming models. Such models are usually nonstochastic. Given the technology, a certain output corresponds to certain inputs. The relationship is uniquely determined, and no random disturbing elements are present. Unless econometrics is defined very broadly, such models remain outside the scope of econometric studies. It is interesting to note that attempts to make such programming models stochastic have been reasonably successful.

Finally, recall how desperate the economist was when he came to proclaim, "Economics is what economists do." Indeed it has been hard to define economics. It is no less so when we try to define econometrics. The answer to the question "What is econometrics?" could very well be "It is what econometricians do." Lawrence R. Klein urges that econometrics is not only a matter of studying but one of doing, and invites the curious to "roll up sleeves" and "do a good bit of distasteful work if strong results are to be obtained." [7]

DISCUSSION QUESTIONS

1. How can mathematical economics be distinguished from econometrics? Are econometrics and economic statistics the same?
2. Can econometrics be defined as economic history written in terms of equations?
3. Relate econometrics to the class of programming models.
4. Discuss briefly the contribution of econometrics in terms of prediction, simulation, and structural evaluation.

SUGGESTED READINGS

Haavelmo, Trygve. "The Role of the Econometrician in the Advancement of Economic Theory." *Econometrica,* Vol. 26, No. 3 (July, 1958), pp. 351-357.

Keynes, John M. "Alfred Marshall, 1842-1924." *Economic Journal,* Vol. 34, No. 3 (September, 1924), pp. 311-372.

Koopmans, Tjalling C. "Measurement Without Theory." *Review of Economics and Statistics,* Vol. 29 (1947), pp. 161-172.

Marschak, Jacob. "Economic Structure, Path, Policy and Prediction." *American Economic Review,* Vol. 37, No. 2 (May, 1947), supplement, papers, and proceedings, pp. 81-84.

Marshall, Alfred. "The Old Generation of Economists and the New." *Quarterly Journal of Economics,* Vol. 11, No. 2 (January, 1897), pp. 115-135.

---

[7] Lawrence R. Klein, *An Introduction to Econometrics* (Englewood Cliffs, N.J.: Prentice-Hall, 1962), p. 269.

Schumpeter, Joseph A. "The Common Sense of Econometrics." *Econometrica,* Vol. 1, No. 1 (January, 1933), pp. 5-12.

Stone, J. Richard N. *The Role of Measurement in Economics.* Cambridge, England: Cambridge University Press, 1951.

Tinbergen, Jan. "Econometric Business Cycle Research." *Review of Economic Studies,* Vol. 7 (1939-1940), pp. 73-90.

Wold, Herman O. A. "Econometrics as Pioneering in Nonexperimental Model Building." *Econometrica,* Vol 37, No. 3 (July, 1969), pp. 369-381.

1

the structure and the model; functional forms and stochastic terms

1.0 THE STRUCTURE AND THE MODEL

The term "model" was used in the previous discussion, and indeed it appears very frequently in econometric literature. An economic model relates to a set of structures defined by relationships between economic variables. In econometric research the prime objective is to analyze the behavior pattern of mankind. It is believed that the true or fundamental behavior pattern of mankind is based on postulates of rational and consistent behavior. This pattern is expected to remain stable. This is the basis of a structure and its stability. A structure, however, can and does change over time.

Given the economic phenomenon to be studied, the econometrician defines the relevant structure by a set of equations. In doing so he relies heavily on a priori knowledge in economic theory. In this process four types of relationships may be used:

1. Definitions or identities which need no further proof for their existence,[1] e.g., Sales Revenue = Price × Quantity Sold
2. Technological relationships determined by the "state of the arts" as may be given, e.g., Output = F (Labor, Capital)
3. Institutional or historical relations, which are incorporated by virtue of belonging to the given society, e.g., Sales Tax Revenue = Tax Rate × Volume of Sales where the tax rate is determined by the appropriate governmental institution
4. Behavioral relationships, which describe how particular variables in the economic behavior of an individual or a group respond to changes in other variables, e.g., Aggregate Consumption = F (Aggregate Income)

The structural specification includes a set of variables whose numerical values change through time within the given structure. The variables are usually grouped into two classes—endogenous variables and exogenous

[1] The definitional relation in equation 0.1.3 is a consequence of the definition of market equilibrium in which Q^d is taken to be identically equal to Q^s, but technically this is not an identity.

variables. *Endogenous variables* are variables whose values are determined by the structure, given the values of the exogenous variables. The *exogenous variables* are predetermined, and their values are given for the study. Often in econometric research the lagged value of an endogenous variable, that is, the value of an endogenous variable relative to an earlier time period, is used as an exogenous variable. Insofar as it is predetermined historically, its exogenous character is not open to question. However, the statistical problems relative to the estimation of parameters of such variables will be discussed in Chapter 7. As a matter of fact, current and lagged exogenous variables and lagged endogenous variables are all taken as predetermined. The following presentation may be helpful:

	Current	Lagged
Endogenous	Determined by the model	Predetermined
Exogenous	Predetermined	Predetermined

Exogenous variables are known and affect determination of the endogenous variables, but they themselves are assumed not to be affected by the endogenous variables. That is, there is a flow of influence from the exogenous to the endogenous variables but not vice versa. A more formal statement to be developed later (Chapter 11, page 279) is that a variable is exogenous and predetermined if it is independent of the disturbance term U_i in a stochastic equation. In practice the choice is often arbitrary.

The set of equations describing a structure enables the econometrician to generate the values of the endogenous variables. In econometrics the relationships among the variables are stochastic, and thus the endogenous variables are stochastic variables. A given stochastic structure enables us to determine the conditional probability distribution of the endogenous variables, given the values of the exogenous variables. Or we can say that the expected values of the endogenous variables are determined under explicit assumptions on the joint distributions of the stochastic elements in the behavioral equations of the structure.

Each equation appearing in a given structure must be identified.[2] The concept of identification is important, and failure to satisfy this condition often leads to estimating pseudorelationships. Let us refer to the milk model, which relates to the structure of the milk market. The supply equation refers to the behavior of firms offering supplies of milk in the market, whereas the demand equation refers to the behavior of the households who offer to buy milk. In this simple illustrative model no cognizance is taken of the demand for milk by, say, the cheese industry or of the possibility that milk is withdrawn from the market and stored by the dairy firms. The important point

[2] Identification in econometric models has a technical definition. Chapter 10 will deal with identification.

here is that each autonomous equation should embody the relevant behavior pattern of a specific group of actors in the economy. This property of identification provides the logical foundation for distinguishing the supply equation from the demand equation.

Essentially a model describes a set of structures, all of which have the same set of variables. Each equation in a model explains the corresponding endogenous variable as in the structural specification. (A model is not necessarily stochastic, but this book is concerned with stochastic models.) Notice that in a stochastic structure the parameters of the joint distribution of the stochastic elements appearing in the behavioral relationships are completely specified and thus known. But in a stochastic model no such a priori restriction is necessary. Of course, in practice the assumption of a specific nature of distribution is convenient. Even when the convenient normal distribution appears to be too much of a simplification, certain restrictive assumptions with respect to stochastic terms are essential before estimation of the model can progress.

The distinction between a structure and a model should be noted carefully. Any set of assumptions that approximately describes an economy or a sector of an economy can be used as the basis for the equations of an economic model. A model offers a formal description of the relationships between endogenous and exogenous variables. A structure is defined by a specific "true" description of the same set of relationships, in terms of the "true" values of the parameters.

In its simplest form the following is an exposition of the Keynesian model of aggregate income determination:

$$C = \alpha + \beta Y + U \qquad \textbf{1.0.1}$$

$$Y = C + I \qquad \textbf{1.0.2}$$

$$I = I_0 \qquad \textbf{1.0.3}$$

where C = consumption
I = investment
Y = income
U = the disturbance term, that is, the stochastic element in the behavior equation, which cannot be observed
α and β are the (unknown) parameters

The model has the familiar exposition that the level of consumption in the community depends stochastically on the level of income in the community. The total level of equilibrium income of the community is by definition equal to the sum of consumption and investment expenditures in the community. The level of investment I_0 is determined exogenously, that is, given by knowledge from outside the present model.

A structure relative to this model is, for example,

$$C = 18 + 0.9Y + U \qquad \textbf{1.0.4}$$

$$Y = C + I \qquad \textbf{1.0.5}$$

where the true values of the parameters α and β are fixed (not estimated from a sample) and where the form and parameters of the distribution function relative to the term U in equation 1.0.4 are also fixed. When the structure of the two equations is known, each value of the exogenous variable I can be used to solve these two equations for the values of the endogenous variables C and Y.

In practice the econometrician working with this simple illustrative model collects data on the three variables, say from the historical record of a particular economy, and estimates the parameters, subject to the restrictions imposed on the U term. "True" structural parameters are seldom known to him.[3] Nor does he possess information as to the "true" specification of the U term. His freedom to draw random samples repeatedly and to estimate the parameters repeatedly is also limited.

The rationale for econometric research can be looked at from another aspect, however. The numerical values of the variables observed are in fact believed to be generated by the "true" structure. Given that the specification of the model is valid and that the method of estimation is appropriate, the parameters estimated from these observations are the rewarding output of the pursuit.

Should there exist another structure generating exactly the same set of observations distributed exactly as before, it becomes yet another member of the same model. A serious problem of identification arises when two such structures with different "true" values of the structural parameters belong to the same model and generate the same joint distribution of the given set of endogenous variables.

1.1 SPECIFICATION AND THE FUNCTIONAL RELATIONSHIP OF THE MODEL

Given the structure of an economy or of a sector or even a subsector of it, the econometrician constructs a model and hopes that this model reveals truth about the basic structure. In specifying the equations of the model, as noted in the Introduction, he draws on the teachings of economic theory.

Let us imagine an introductory class in economic theory. The instructor is teaching the theory of demand. Other things being equal, he says, the quantity of a commodity demanded per unit of time is inversely related to its price. The concept of a demand schedule—the change in quantity demanded against the change in price—has provided some very common quiz material. Diagrams have been drawn in Figure 1-1, and for better exposition the axes have been reversed. The evidence is conclusive. "Other things being equal," the familiar demand curve is derived in either case.

By contrast, in an econometrics class the instructor must be careful to pronounce a word of caution. The mathematical function $Q = f(P)$ is

[3] Recall the distinction between "population" and "sample" in statistics. "True" parameters refer to the parameters of the population as distinguished from the values of the parameters estimated from samples.

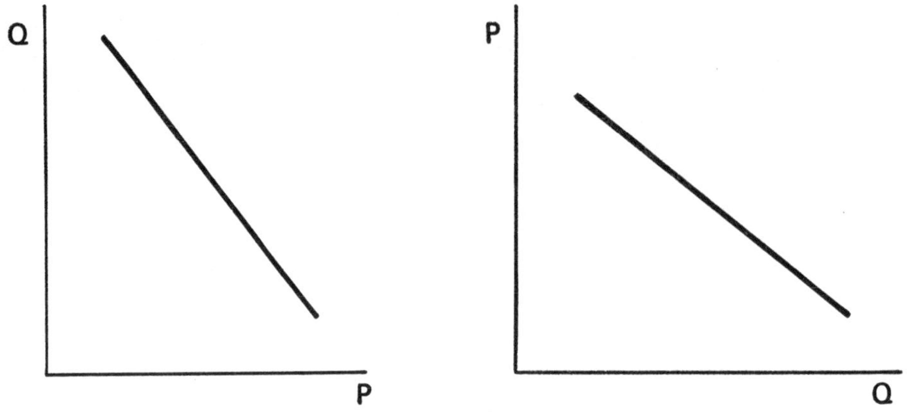

$Q = f(P)$ $\qquad$ $P = g(Q)$

FIGURE 1-1

nonstochastic, exact, and reversible; but in econometrics the equations do not have those properties. There, disturbance terms do appear in the form:

$$Q = F(P, U) \tag{1.1.1}$$

and the function is stochastic and irreversible. The variable U, though we cannot observe it, cannot be excluded. Certain assumptions are made about the unobservable values of the U term and its relationship with P, the independent variable included in the function. If we reverse the function, we cannot at once assume that the same relationship will hold between U and Q.[4] In a stochastic function as such, the direction of functional dependence is specifically given by the maintained hypothesis.

The econometrician is concerned about the direction of functional dependence. Indeed one of the most baffling questions for economic statisticians in the early days of econometric research was: Does quantity depend on price, that is, $Q = f(P)$; or does price depend on quantity, that is, $P = g(Q)$? An appropriately specified model suggests that the quantity offered for market transaction and the price are simultaneously determined, given the free competitive market mechanism. In other words, variables Q and P are endogenous and simultaneously determined by the model, appropriately specified. A model that seeks to explain the joint determination of two endogenous variables usually has two equations. Thus it calls for a multiequation model. Simultaneous-equation-system models will be discussed in Chapters 11 through 13.

[4] This subject has been referred to on page 5. Further discussions appear on page 43 and in section 4.3.

This is not to suggest that there is no room for single-equation models in econometric research. Appropriate specification of a single equation may enable the researcher to fulfill the objective of his particular study. Consider the demand function for milk and let it be respecified as follows:

$$
\begin{aligned}
Q^d &= f(P, Y, U) \\
Q^d &= \text{quantity of milk demanded} \\
P &= \text{price of milk} \\
Y &= \text{income of the community consuming milk} \\
U &= \text{disturbance terms}
\end{aligned}
\qquad \textbf{1.1.2}
$$

Economic theory suggests that income of the community should be included as an explanatory variable in the demand function rather than in the supply function. Respecification of the function based on this a priori knowledge reassures the investigator that the function he is estimating relates to the community's demand behavior. Inclusion of one or more additional exogenous variables in the function is thus an improvement. As a matter of fact, if variables with systematic impact on the variations of the dependent variable are not recognized and explicitly introduced in the function to be estimated, the disturbance term U ceases to be truly random. It is important to note that if the function itself is not properly specified, the conditions of specification with respect to the disturbance term as commonly invoked in econometric research do not hold.

Even when the variables of a single-equation model have been carefully enumerated, the form of the function needs to be specified. If economic theory has been found to be inadequate in the former case, it has been found to be more so in the latter. Often the econometrician is left with the trial-and-error method. At times, given a specific function, he experiments with alternative specifications of the form.

Econometric research is largely restricted to using linear functions or nonlinear functions which can be appropriately transformed to linear ones. The assumption of a linear relationship is for convenience. The estimation methods discussed in this text will be useful as long as the relations are linear with respect to the parameters to be estimated, even if the variables appearing are in nonlinear forms, such as:

$$Y = \alpha_0 + \alpha_1 X + \alpha_2 X^2 + U$$

or

$$Y = \alpha_o + \alpha_1 X + \alpha_2 X^2 + \alpha_3 X^3 + U \qquad \textbf{1.1.3}$$

It is also true that for small-sample time-series studies the linearity assumption is inoffensive. But if we have models where nonlinearity involves the parameter, the usual methods of estimation can still be useful if a linear transformation of the function can be made.

There is a wide spectrum of choice for the econometrician in specifying the functional form of his models. In what follows a description of a set of choices is offered.

Equation 1.1.4 and Figure 1-2 are suggested by the Keynesian model, where C is aggregate consumption and Y is aggregate income of an economy. The term α is a positive intercept, and β is the positive slope $dC/dY > 0$ in a simple two-variable consumption function.

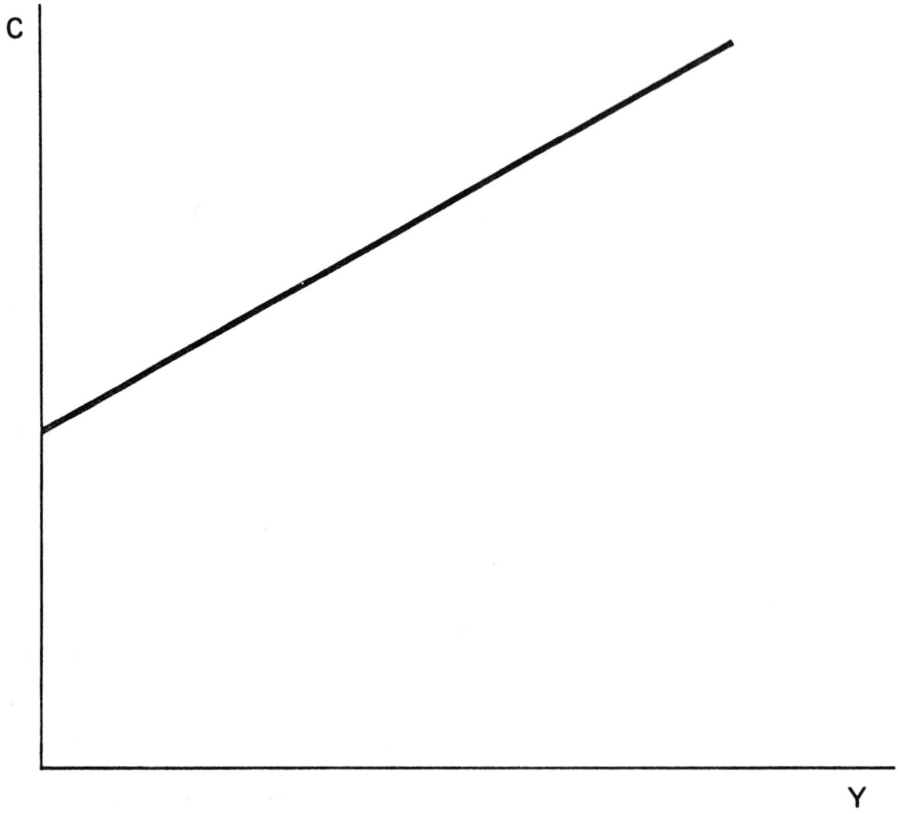

FIGURE 1-2

$$C = \alpha + \beta Y \qquad \textbf{1.1.4}$$

Figure 1-3 illustrates the consumption function 1.1.5, with $\alpha = 0$ and $\beta = dC/dY_p > 0$. If consumption C is based on permanent income Y_p as proposed by Friedman (that is, Y_p is not just the aggregate income at the given time), the consumption function will pass through the origin. The linear model illustrated in Figure 1-4 and in equation 1.1.6 is the familiar downward-sloping demand curve, where P is the price of the given commodity, Q is the quantity of the commodity demanded, $\alpha > 0$, and $\beta = dQ/dP < 0$.

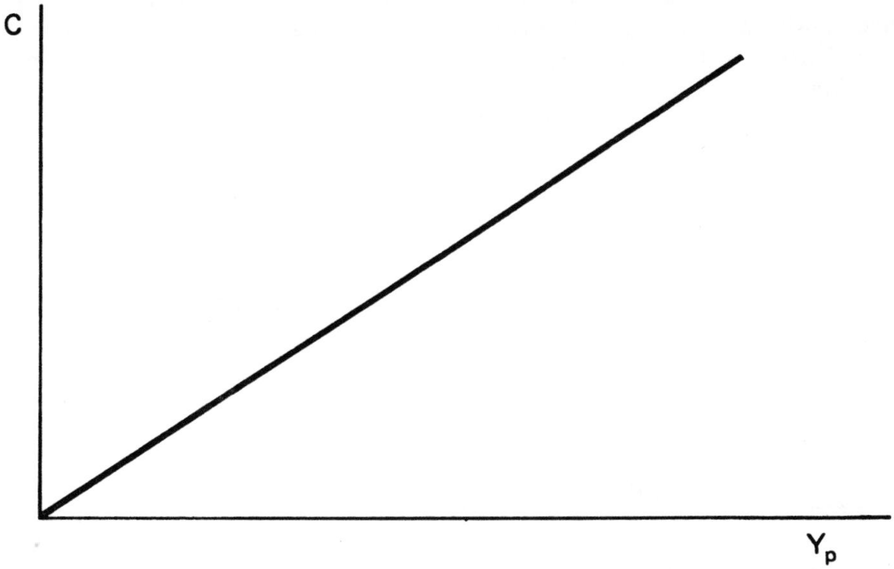

FIGURE 1-3

$$C = \beta Y_p \qquad 1.1.5$$

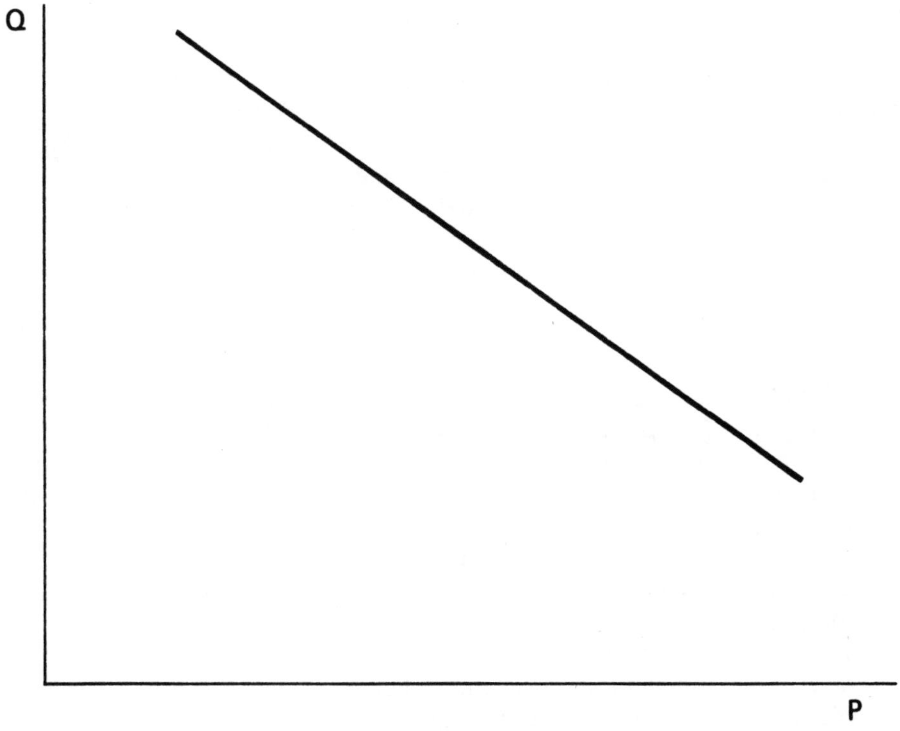

FIGURE 1-4

$$Q = \alpha + \beta P \qquad 1.1.6$$

Consider Figure 1-5 and equation 1.1.7 as the linear aggregate savings model, where S is aggregate savings and Y is aggregate income, and with $\beta = dS/dY > 0$, but $\alpha < 0$. This says that the economy's aggregate savings function has a negative intercept.

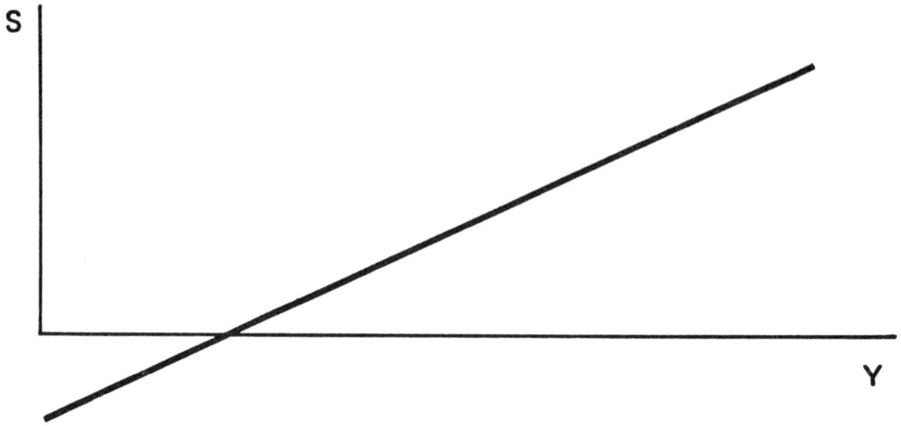

FIGURE 1-5

$$S = \alpha + \beta Y \qquad \textbf{1.1.7}$$

There are many illustrations of linear models with varying a priori restrictions on parameters with respect to their signs and values. Obviously the polynomial model 1.1.8 is nonlinear in variables, as it includes higher powers of Q. For estimation purposes Q and Q^2 may be considered to be two independent regressors. The model in Figure 1-6 is an illustration of the total revenue curve, where total revenue R is functionally dependent on the output sold Q. The curve is a parabola and can be derived as follows:

$$R = PQ$$

Defining $P = \alpha - \beta Q$ as a simple demand relation, we obtain $R = Q(\alpha - \beta Q) = \alpha Q - \beta Q^2$.

The polynomial model 1.1.9 is a good illustration of the total cost function, where Y is total cost and X is output. The function depicts the rising portion of a parabola as shown in Figure 1-7.

With the specification $\beta < 0$ in model 1.1.10, we can have the familiar U-shaped curve shown in Figure 1-8, where Y is marginal cost and X is total output.

Figure 1-9 and model 1.1.11 show a further extension of curvilinear functions. For estimation purposes the higher powers of X can be considered as independent regressors even though in reality there is one exogenous variable X. As long as each regressor in the set (X, X^2, X^3) is not an exact linear combination of one or two of the others, the usual method of estimation will be usable. Intuitively one can see that if one has to estimate one

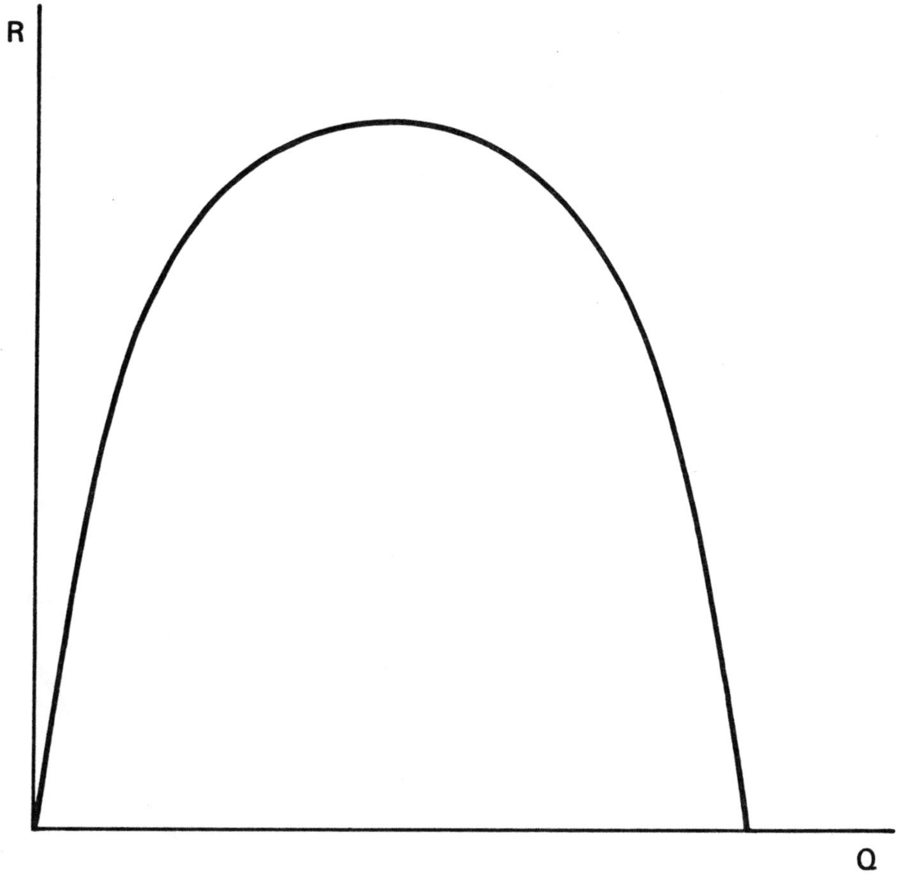

FIGURE 1-6

$$R = \alpha Q - \beta Q^2 \qquad \mathbf{1.1.8}$$

parameter for each of these powers of X, each such expression must contain independent information. Fortunately X^2 and X^3, even if they are expressions in X, cannot in general be linearly dependent in the sense that the values of X^2 or of X^3 could be obtained by multiplying the values of X by a constant.

X	X^2	X^3
3	9	27
2	4	8
5	25	125

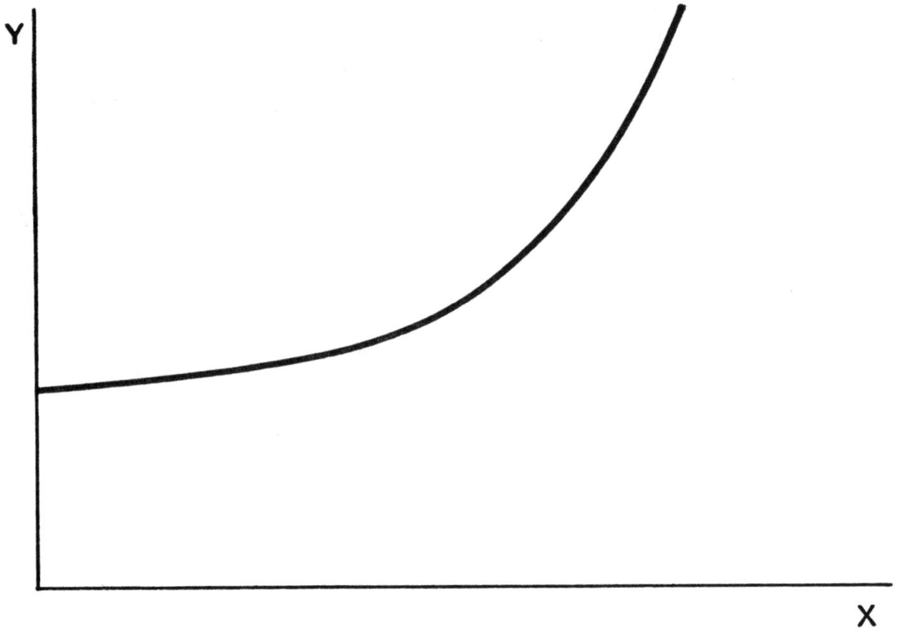

FIGURE 1-7

$$Y = \alpha + \beta X + \xi X^2 \qquad \textbf{1.1.9}$$

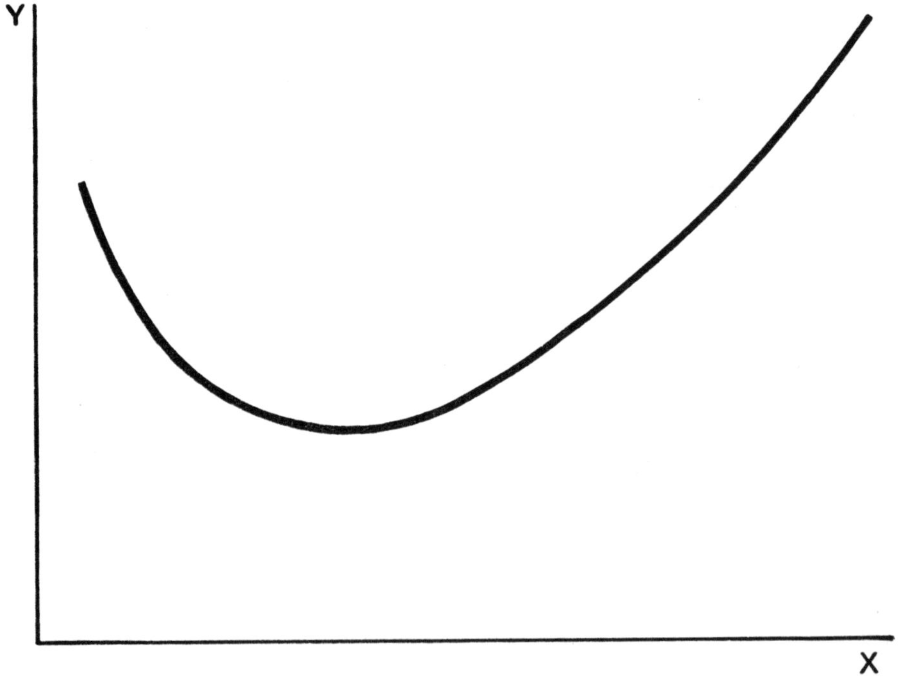

FIGURE 1-8

$$Y = \alpha + \beta X + \xi X^2 \qquad \textbf{1.1.10}$$

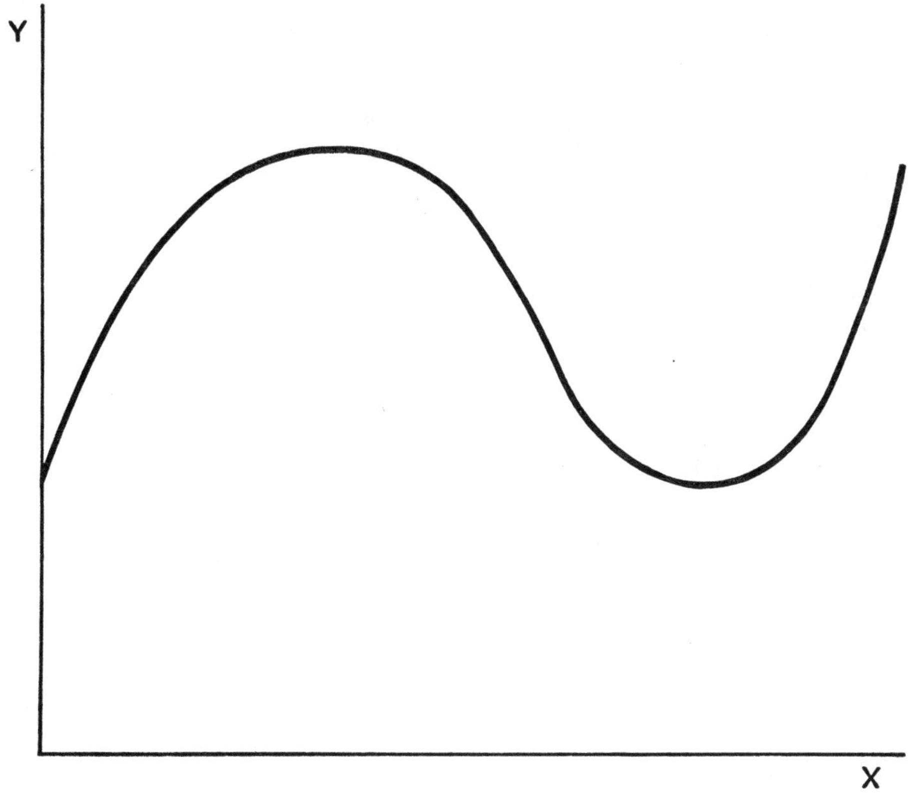

FIGURE 1-9

$$Y = \alpha + \beta X + \xi X^2 + \delta X^3 \qquad \textbf{1.1.11}$$

None of these columns is linearly dependent on any other column. This point will be developed further in Chapter 5.

The curves shown in the left-hand diagrams of Figures 1-10 and 1-11 can be transformed into straight lines by the use of appropriate transformations. For the concave curve of equation 1.1.12.A, the transformation is log $Y = Z$; and for the convex curve of equation 1.1.13.A, the transformation is log $X = W$.

The double-log transformation shown graphically in Figure 1-12 is carried out by taking the logarithm of both sides of the equation to transform the exponential form of equation 1.1.14.A to linear equation 1.1.14.B.

In the case of hyperbolic functions, reciprocal transformations aid nonlinearity problems. Hyperbolas correspond to equations containing terms with the variables $1/X$ or $1/Y$, and such equations can be transformed into linear equations by using the transformations $W = 1/X$ or $Z = 1/Y$ or both. Figures 1-13 and 1-14 illustrate this.

Logarithmic or reciprocal transformations have been widely used in econometric research. For statistical estimation the functions so transformed are linear in the transformed variables. The choice of the actual

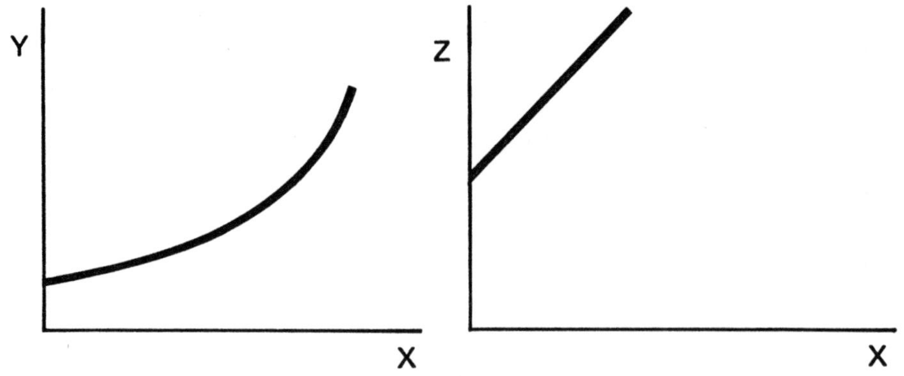

FIGURE 1-10

(A) $\log Y = \alpha + \beta X$ (B) $Z = \alpha + \beta X$ **1.1.12**

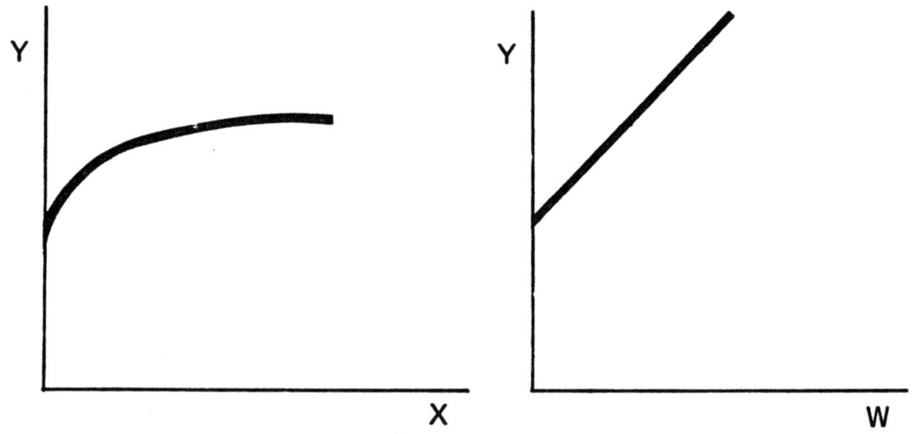

FIGURE 1-11

(A) $Y = \alpha + \beta \log X$ (B) $Y = \alpha + \beta W$ **1.1.13**

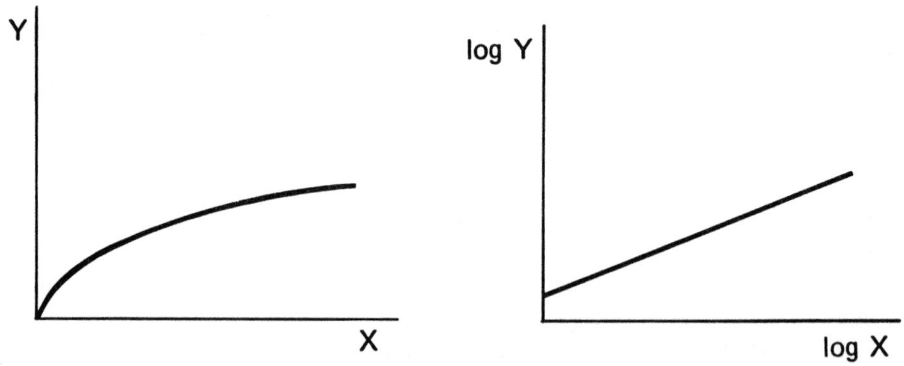

FIGURE 1-12

(A) $Y = \alpha X^{\beta}$ (B) $\log Y = \log \alpha + \beta \log X$ **1.1.14**

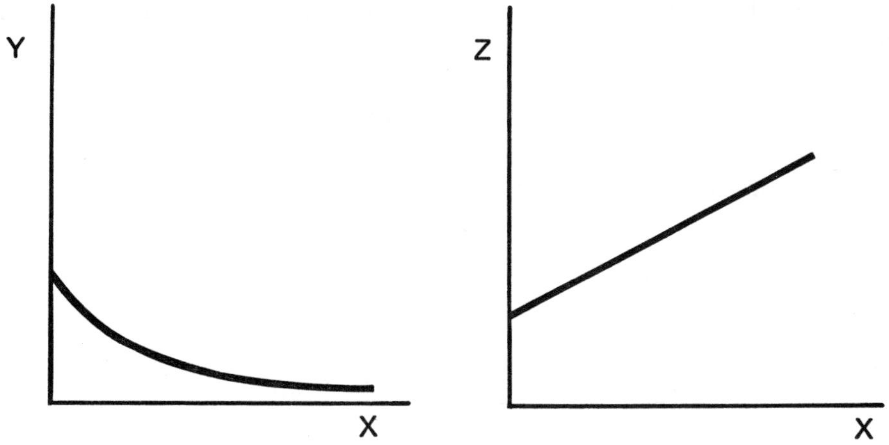

FIGURE 1-13

$$Y = \frac{1}{\alpha + \beta X} \qquad\qquad Z = \alpha + \beta X \qquad \textbf{1.1.15}$$

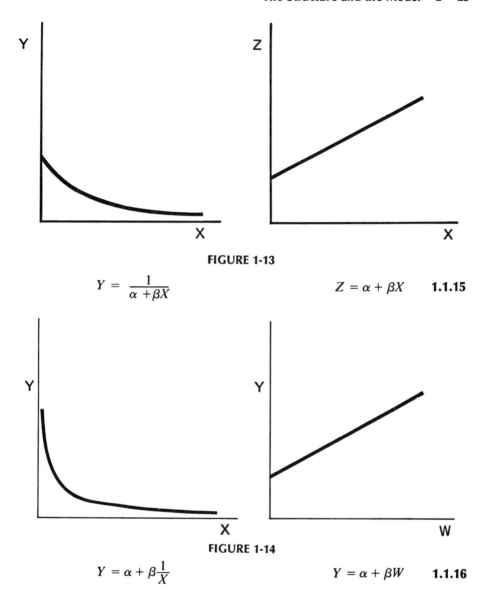

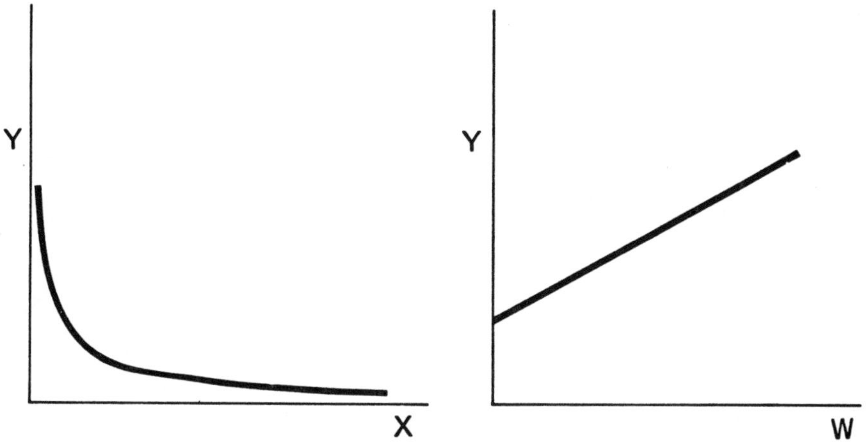

FIGURE 1-14

$$Y = \alpha + \beta \frac{1}{X} \qquad\qquad Y = \alpha + \beta W \qquad \textbf{1.1.16}$$

transformation in the individual case should, of course, depend on the logic of the theory on which the function is based. If not, a close examination of the scatter diagram of the sample data provides an intelligent guide to the appropriate form of the function to be estimated.

The transformations of nonlinear equations into linear ones as described above do not change the fundamental properties of the relationships of the variables. Consider the following form of the demand function:

$$Q = KP^{\alpha} \qquad \textbf{1.1.17}$$

where Q = quantity demanded
P = price
K and α are constants

The above is the exponential form of the familiar demand curve. We can write:

$$\frac{dQ}{dP} = f'(P) = K\alpha P^{\alpha - 1} \qquad \textbf{1.1.18}$$

Note that η, elasticity of demand, can be defined as: [5]

$$\eta = \frac{\frac{d}{d(P)}(\log_e Q)}{\frac{d}{d(P)}(\log_e P)}$$

$$\frac{d(\log Q)}{d(P)} = \frac{d(\log Q)}{d(Q)}\frac{d(Q)}{d(P)} = \frac{1}{Q}\frac{d(Q)}{d(P)}$$

and

$$\frac{d(\log P)}{d(P)} = \frac{1}{P}$$

Therefore,

$$\eta = \frac{d(Q)}{d(P)}\frac{P}{Q}$$

Using equation 1.1.18,

$$\eta = K\alpha P^{\alpha - 1}\frac{P}{Q}$$

Replacing Q by KP^α from equation 1.1.17,

$$\eta = K\alpha P^{\alpha - 1}\frac{P}{KP^\alpha}$$

$$= \alpha \qquad \textbf{1.1.19}$$

which is the coefficient of elasticity, assumed to be constant. The econometrician can estimate the above exponential (nonlinear) function by a double-log transformation as follows:

$$\log Q = \log K + \alpha \log P$$

Note that:

$$\frac{d(\log Q)}{d(\log P)} = \alpha$$

The change in the natural logarithm is approximately the same thing as percentage change. Therefore we can write: [6]

[5] $\log_e$ = log to the base e; $e = 2.71828$.

[6] The symbol $\doteq$ means approximately equal.

$$\frac{\%\text{ change in } Q}{\%\text{ change in } P} \doteq \alpha \doteq \text{elasticity}$$

1.2 SPECIFICATION OF THE MODEL AND THE DISTURBANCE TERM

Specification of the function and its form draws heavily on economic theory and mathematics. Specification of the disturbance term is greatly dependent on statistical theory. Often specification of the disturbance term is considered the central problem of econometrics per se.

Let us continue our discussion with the simplest form of a model of demand: Other things being equal, the quantity of a commodity demanded depends on its price; a single endogenous variable, Q^d, is functionally dependent on a single exogenous variable, P:

$$Q^d = f(P) \qquad \textbf{1.2.1}$$

Since other things are seldom equal and random factors govern human behavior in the real world, a stochastic function is used:

$$Q^d = g(P, U) \qquad \textbf{1.2.2}$$

For simplicity a linear relationship is specified:

$$Q^d = \alpha + \beta P + U \qquad \textbf{1.2.3}$$

The U is a symbolic variable. In this book it is called the disturbance term. "Shock term," "error term," and "stochastic term" are used synonymously.[7] One cannot observe this symbolic variable. That is, there exists no series of observations on this variable that can be used for estimation purposes. It represents the unobservable chance factors, and it does not affect the relationship in any systematic way. A part of the variation in quantity demanded is systematically associated with variation in price. However, some random variation remains unexplained. There may be innumerable chance factors that affect the relationship arbitrarily and contribute to this nonsystematic part of the variation. It is of little concern if there are many of them, but it is harmful if they are interrelated. It is highly probable that if they are so related, they will have systematic impact on the endogenous variable. Assuming innumerable elements of chance in U, we must also assume that none is large enough to develop a dominating and hence systematic pattern of impact on the dependent variable and that none of them are so interlinked as to develop such a pattern.

---

[7] But the distinction should be noted carefully. "Stochastic" is synonymous with "random"; errors belong to stochastic variables and shocks are suffered by relations connecting them. "Disturbances" is the term that covers all.

It would be an error of specification if all other variables that might have systematically explained variations in quantity demanded are not explicitly included in equation 1.2.3. The variable U, the portmanteau variable, conceptually incorporates all such variables; but to the degree they are systematically related to Q, U will not be a random variable. Some variables that might be intuitively important cannot be quantified. Some variables, intuitively considered important and thought to be quantifiable, may not have yet been quantified and no observations on them may be currently available. The variable U cannot be required to carry all these burdens. It is important for good research in econometrics that all non-random variables be quantified if there are a priori reasons to believe that such variables systematically affect human behavior with respect to the problem under investigation. Only then can we expect to ensure the randomness of the unobservable, symbolic variable denoted by U.

One possibility is to make some assumptions on the nature of the probability distribution of the random disturbance terms U_i which we cannot observe. We can, for example, assume that the values of the disturbance terms were generated from a normal distribution with mean, μ, zero and variance, σ_u^2, finite and constant, and that the values were drawn independently from such a distribution. In terms of the model 1.2.3, we can present these assumptions as in Figure 1-15. For any given value of P_i (which is fixed), the distribution of the U_i's and hence of the Q_i^d's, is normal; and the variance of this distribution is constant over different values of P_i.

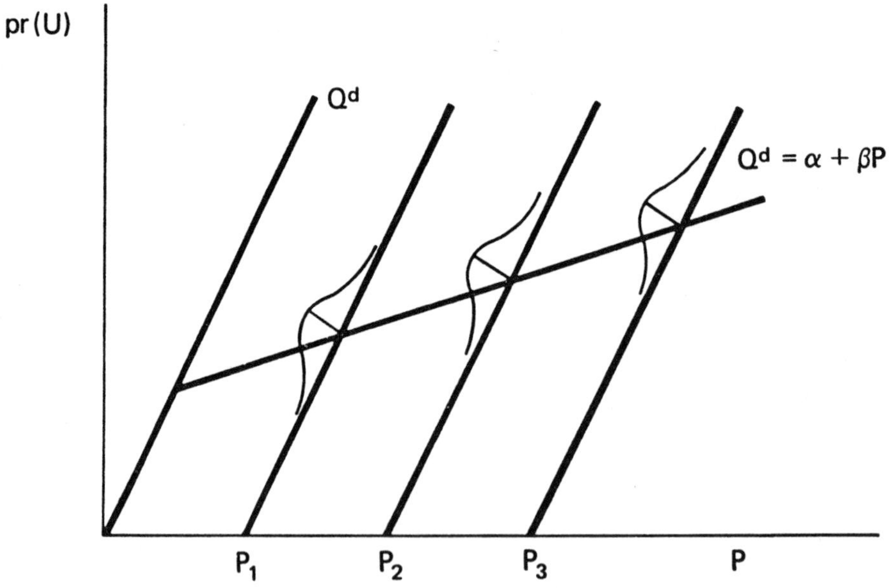

FIGURE 1-15

The above assumption is certainly convenient to provide a rational structure to the otherwise unobservable U_i's. Assuming the normal distribution, the probability density function of U_i can be written as:

$$f(U_i) = \frac{1}{\sqrt{2\pi\sigma_u^2}} \exp[-(U_i - \mu_u)^2/2\sigma_u^2] \qquad \textbf{1.2.4}$$

where μ_u = mean of U
σ_u^2 = variance of U

Knowledge of these two parameters will completely specify the function. The mean of U is assumed to be zero, while the variance of U remains unknown. We can estimate the variance of U. If we know a priori that the variance of U is 9, we can rewrite:

$$f(U_i) = \frac{1}{\sqrt{2\pi 9}} \exp(-U_i^2/18) \qquad \textbf{1.2.5}$$

If the sample size is large, the assumption of the normal distribution becomes appropriate. The fact that much of econometric research is based on small samples limits the scope of this assumption.

However, even without the restrictive assumption of the normal distribution, there exist statistical methods of estimation that yield reliable results. In the absence of any knowledge of the nature of the distribution, it will usually be assumed that the disturbances U_i are random variables with zero mean and constant and finite variance, and that they were drawn independently from this unknown distribution. This argument will be further developed in Chapter 2.

1.3 ADDITIVE DISTURBANCE TERMS

It is widely assumed for simplicity that the disturbance term is additive. Nonadditivity of the term creates a difficult situation. Suppose that the disturbance term is multiplicative:

$$Q = AK^{\alpha} L^{\beta} U \qquad \textbf{1.3.1}$$

One solution is to take its log linear form:

$$\log Q = \log A + \alpha \log K + \beta \log L + \log U \qquad \textbf{1.3.2}$$

where log U satisfies the same set of assumptions as does U. Such a simple solution is, however, not available at all times. In this volume, the discussion is confined to linear models with additive disturbance terms.

DISCUSSION QUESTIONS

1. Carefully define the relationship between a model and a structure.
2. Define the four types of relationships used in econometrics.

3. An econometric relationship is typically stochastic:

$$Q = F(P, U)$$

Why can't the relationship be reversed and written as: $P = G(Q, U)$? Explain the significance of this irreversibility of an equation in an econometric model.

4. It has been suggested that for small-sample time-series studies the assumption of a linear relationship between the dependent and independent variables is inoffensive. Why?

5. Illustrate five a priori hypotheses in economic theory where linear functional dependence between variables has been widely used.

6. Discuss briefly the normal distribution.

7. Often in practice, examination of the scatter diagram provides the basis for the nature of the postulated functional relationship between the variables in economic analysis, linear or otherwise. How good is this approach?

8. Enumerate three common instances where nonlinear relationships between variables are linearized by appropriate transformation.

SUGGESTED READINGS

Allen, R. G. D. *Mathematical Analysis for Economists*. London: Macmillan & Co., 1963.

Ezekiel, Mordecai, and Karl A. Fox. *Methods of Correlation and Regression Analysis: Linear and Curvilinear,* 3d ed. New York: John Wiley & Sons, 1959.

Haavelmo, T. "The Probability Approach to Econometrics." *Econometrica,* Vol. 12, supplement (July, 1944), pp. 1-118.

Lovell, Michael C., and Edward Prescott. "Multiple Regression with Inequality Constraints: Pretesting Bias, Hypothesis Testing and Efficiency." *Journal of the American Statistical Association,* Vol. 65, No. 330 (June, 1970), pp. 913-925.

Malinvaud, Edmond. *Statistical Methods of Econometrics.* Amsterdam: North-Holland Publishing Co., 1966.

Prais, S. J., and H. S. Houthakker. *The Analysis of Family Budgets.* Cambridge, England: Cambridge University Press, 1955.

Schultz, Henry. *The Theory and Measurement of Demand.* Chicago: University of Chicago Press, 1938.

Stone, J. Richard N. *The Measurement of Consumers' Expenditure and Behaviour in the United Kingdom, 1920-1938.* Cambridge, England: Cambridge University Press, 1954.

Theil, H. "Specification Errors and the Estimation of Economic Relationships." *Revue de L'Institut International de Statistique,* Vol. 25 (1957), pp. 41-51.

Theil, Henri. *Economic Forecasts and Policy,* 2d ed. Amsterdam: North-Holland Publishing Co., 1961.

Wold, Herman O. A., and Lars Juréen. *Demand Analysis; A Study in Econometrics*. New York: John Wiley & Sons, 1953.

Wold, Herman O. A., and P. Faxer. "On the Specification Error in Regression Analysis." *Annals of Mathematical Statistics,* Vol. 28, No. 1 (March, 1957), pp. 265-267.

2

regression and correlation models (I)

2.0 THE FRAMEWORK OF THE ORDINARY LEAST SQUARES REGRESSION MODEL

Consider the familiar demand model:

$$Q_i^d = \beta_0 + \beta_1 P_i + U_i, \qquad i = 1, 2, \ldots, N \qquad \textbf{2.0.1}$$

Here Q_i^d is the ith observation on quantity demanded of a given commodity, and it is the endogenous variable. The equation expresses its linear dependence on P_i, the ith observation on the price of the commodity. P is the exogenous variable. U_i is a symbolic variable representing the effects of unobserved and unobservable random variables. We wish to obtain estimates of the unknown parameters β_0 and β_1. As we shall presently see, the *ordinary least squares* (OLS) regression method is a technique that can be fruitfully used in estimating these parameters.

The left-hand variable Q_i^d in equation 2.0.1 is variously described as the endogenous variable, the regressand, the dependent variable, or the explained variable. The variable P_i on the right-hand side of the equation is variously described as the exogenous variable, the regressor, the independent variable, or the explanatory variable.

Equation 2.0.1 can be interpreted as follows: The demand for a commodity varies over time or across different geographical markets. A part of this variation is associated systematically with variation in the price of the commodity, while the rest of the variation in demand is attributed to random factors, U, which cannot be observed but about whose occurrence certain assumptions can be made. To restate:

> Total variation in the dependent variable = Systematic variation associated with variation in the independent variable + Random variation attributed to factors unknown and unknowable.

The random part is symbolized by U_i; the nature of its probability distribution is unknown. We shall see that to obtain the ordinary least squares (hereafter, OLS) results, it is not necessary to assume a normal distribution for U_i. Since U_i is a random variable, so is Q_i^d. The systematic part of the variation is explained by price, P_i, which is, by assumption, a fixed variable and thus has no probability distribution. There is a distribution of Q^d for every such fixed value of P.[1]

If the relationship between Q^d and P were exact, $Q_i^d = \beta_0 + \beta_1 P_i$, the pairs of observations (Q_i^d, P_i) would all lie on the straight line in Figure 2-1, and every U_i would be zero. Suppose that we know the numerical values

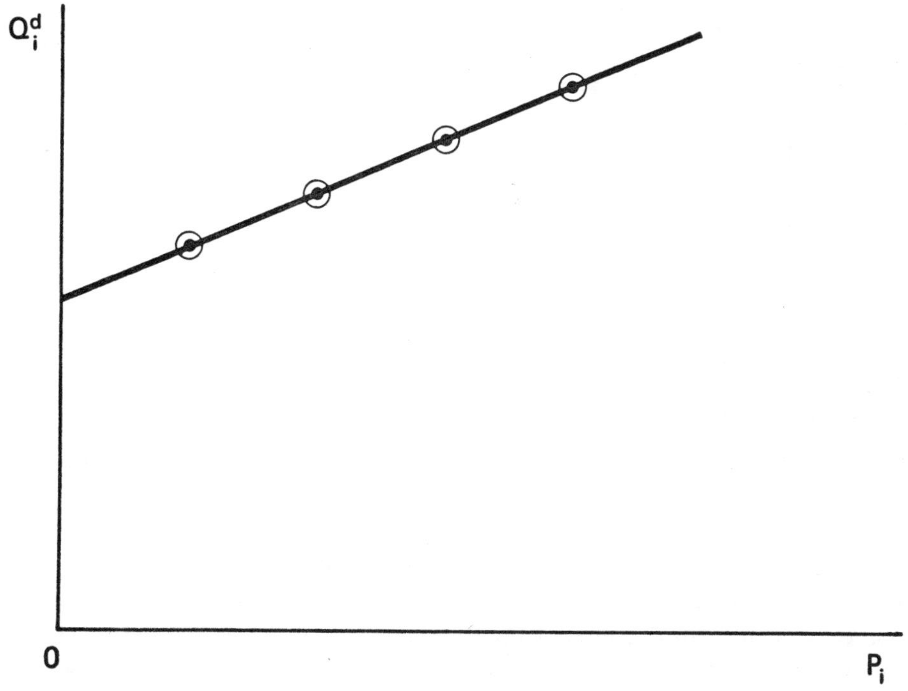

FIGURE 2-1

of the parameters β_0 and β_1 in the equation above and that we have collected a set of ten observations on Q^d and P. This set is the sample and its sample size, N, is ten. Using these values of β_0 and β_1 for each value of P in the sample, we can obtain a calculated value for Q^d. The ten calculated values of Q^d will all lie on a straight line. The observed values of Q^d will not necessarily be the same as the calculated ones. Some of the observed and calculated values may agree, but it is extremely unlikely that they will all agree. In Figure 2-2 the observed and estimated values of the Q_i^d's in a hypothetical situation are plotted.

[1] It will be shown later that it is possible to consider the variable P as random and having a distribution.

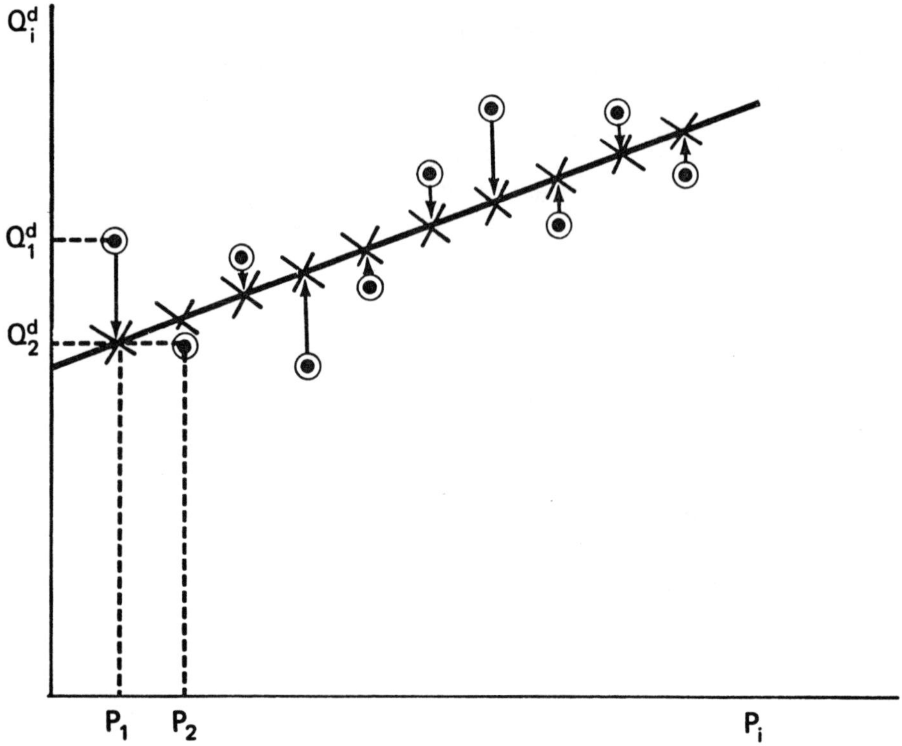

FIGURE 2-2

The points indicated by the crosses on the line, (Q^d_1, P_1), (Q^d_2, P_2), and so on, correspond to the values of Q^d calculated from the equation. The points indicated by the circled dots are the ten observations of Q^d in the sample. The vertical distance between each pair of observed and calculated values of Q^d_i for each P_i is a measure of the deviation of the observed value from the straight line. These deviations are identified as the part of the variation in Q^d associated with random variables. These deviations can then be the estimates of the variable U. The estimated value of U_i, denoted $\hat{U}_i$, can be computed as the *residuals* of each observation Q^d_i when the systematic variation $\beta_0 + \beta_1 P_i$ is subtracted: [2]

$$\hat{U}_i = Q^d_i - \hat{\beta}_0 - \hat{\beta}_1 P_i \qquad \textbf{2.0.2}$$

It is important to notice the direction of the arrows as indicated in the diagram. Each arrow is parallel to the vertical axis representing Q^d. Each estimated value of $\hat{U}_i$ is the vertical deviation between a pair of observed

[2] The caret (^) is used whenever reference is made to the estimated value of a parameter as opposed to its true value. The caret over $\hat{U}_i$ refers to the estimated value of true U_i. The same is true for $\hat{\beta}_0$ and $\hat{\beta}_1$.

and estimated values for Q_i^d.[3] The rationale of the least squares regression method for estimating the parameters is to obtain a straight line that will minimize the sum of the squared vertical deviations ($\Sigma\hat{U}_i^2$).

We could consider minimizing the sum of the residuals $\Sigma\hat{U}_i$, that is, the sum of the vertical deviations $\Sigma(Q_i^d - \hat{Q}_i^d)$ as they are. But for a particular set of observations, many different lines can have a sum of deviations exactly equal to zero; and there is no way of telling which one of the estimated lines corresponds to the true underlying linear relation. Consider the two estimated lines in Figure 2-3. Points indicated by circled dots are the

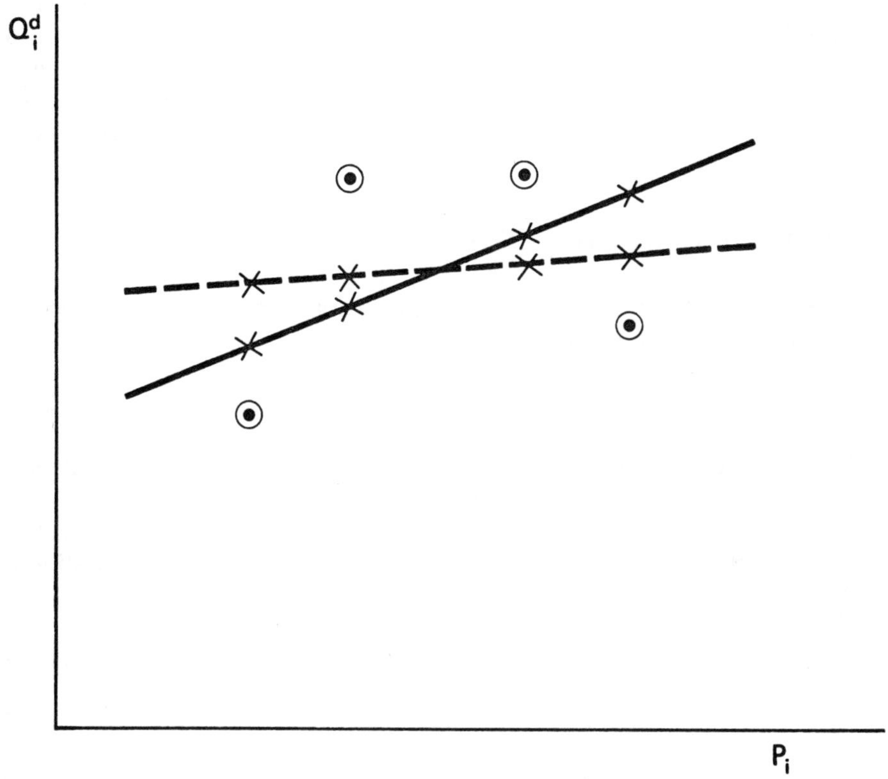

FIGURE 2-3

observed values of Q_i^d. In this diagram the deviations from the solid line are −1, +2, +1, −2, and:

$$\Sigma\hat{U}_i = -1 + 2 + 1 - 2 = 0 \qquad \textbf{2.0.3}$$

Similarly, the sum of deviations from the broken line is:

[3] We could define deviations along the horizontal line, and that would change the direction of functional dependence from $Q = F(P,U)$ to $P = G(Q,U)$. We could consider orthogonal deviations if we were to estimate orthogonal regression parameters. (See Chapter 8.)

$$\Sigma \hat{U}_i = -2 + 1\tfrac{1}{2} + 1\tfrac{1}{2} - 1 = 0 \qquad \textbf{2.0.4}$$

A second alternative is to estimate the line such that the sum of absolute deviations is a minimum:

$$\Sigma \left| \hat{U}_i \right| = \Sigma \left| Q_i^d - \hat{Q}_i^d \right| = \text{min} \qquad \textbf{2.0.5}$$

The signs of the estimated residuals are then always positive, and the sum of the absolute values of the residuals can no longer be zero. It would be preferable to work with deviations from the mean, but absolute deviations from the mean are unsatisfactory measures. It can be shown that if we have to work with absolute values of the deviations, deviations from the median are a better measure. However, the median as a measure of central tendency does not possess the useful mathematical properties of the mean. Thus minimization of the sum of absolute deviations has not generally been considered a useful technique for parameter estimation.

2.1 THE MATHEMATICS OF THE OLS METHOD

It is convenient to denote the dependent variable by Y_i and the independent variable by X_i. Equation 2.0.1 can be written as:

$$Y_i = \beta_0 + \beta_1 X_i + U_i \qquad \textbf{2.1.1}$$

In Figure 2-2 the vertical distances between the observations on Y (the dependent variable) and the regression line are the unexplained deviations or the residuals. There is such a distance, positive above the line and negative below, for each observation Y_i. The algebraic expression for the deviation is given as:

$$\hat{U}_i = Y_i - (\hat{\beta}_0 + \hat{\beta}_1 X_i) \qquad \textbf{2.1.1.A}$$

or

$$\hat{U}_i = Y_i - \hat{\beta}_0 - \hat{\beta}_1 X_i \qquad \textbf{2.1.1.B}$$

We wish to obtain estimates of β_0 and β_1 that make the sum of squared deviations a minimum:[4]

$$\Sigma \hat{U}_i^2 = \Sigma (Y_i - \hat{\beta}_0 - \hat{\beta}_1 X_i)^2 \rightarrow \text{a minimum} \qquad \textbf{2.1.2}$$

Notice that the expression on the right is a function of the two "variables" β_0 and β_1:

---

[4] Throughout the discussion that follows, the symbol Σ means summation over all sample observations. Since $i = 1, \ldots, N$, it is equivalent to $\sum_{i=1}^{N}$.

$$\Sigma \hat{U}_i^2 = S(\beta_0, \beta_1) \qquad \textbf{2.1.3}$$

The values of X_i and Y_i are given from the observations. In other words we can conceivably "fit" various straight lines to the given set of observations on Y_i and X_i by varying the values of β_0 and β_1. And, of course, we wish to estimate the unique straight line that will minimize $\Sigma \hat{U}_i^2$, the sum of unexplained variations in Y. The necessary condition that a function of two variables takes a minimum value is that there are values of these variables, say $\hat{\beta}_0$ and $\hat{\beta}_1$, such that the partial derivatives of the function evaluated at $\hat{\beta}_0$ and $\hat{\beta}_1$ are both zero:

$$\left.\frac{\partial S(\beta_0, \beta_1)}{\partial \beta_0}\right|_{\hat{\beta}_0, \hat{\beta}_1} = 0 \qquad \textbf{2.1.4}$$
$$\left.\frac{\partial S(\beta_0, \beta_1)}{\partial \beta_1}\right|_{\hat{\beta}_0, \hat{\beta}_1} = 0$$

To find these values of β_0 and β_1, we shall partially differentiate the function $\Sigma \hat{U}_i^2 = S(\beta_0, \beta_1)$ with respect to each variable and set each of the two partial derivatives equal to zero. We shall then have two equations in the two unknowns, $\hat{\beta}_0$ and $\hat{\beta}_1$, and we can solve them to get expressions for these values in terms of observations Y_i and X_i.

Carrying out the partial differentiation,

$$\begin{aligned}
\frac{\partial}{\partial \beta_0} S(\beta_0, \beta_1) &= \frac{\partial}{\partial \beta_0}[\Sigma (Y_i - \beta_0 - \beta_1 X_i)^2] \\
&= 2[\Sigma(Y_i - \beta_0 - \beta_1 X_i)] \frac{\partial(-\beta_0)}{\partial \beta_0} \\
&= 2\Sigma(Y_i - \beta_0 - \beta_1 X_i)(-1) \\
&= -2\Sigma Y_i + 2N\beta_0 + 2\beta_1 \Sigma X_i
\end{aligned} \qquad \textbf{2.1.5}$$

Similarly,

$$\begin{aligned}
\frac{\partial}{\partial \beta_1} S(\beta_0, \beta_1) &= \frac{\partial}{\partial \beta_1} [\Sigma(Y_i - \beta_0 - \beta_1 X_i)^2] \\
&= 2[\Sigma(Y_i - \beta_0 - \beta_1 X_i)] \frac{\partial}{\partial \beta_1}(- \beta_1 X_i) \\
&= 2\Sigma(Y_i - \beta_0 - \beta_1 X_i)(-X_i) \\
&= -2\Sigma Y_i X_i + 2\beta_0 \Sigma X_1 + 2\beta_1 \Sigma X_i^2
\end{aligned} \qquad \textbf{2.1.6}$$

Setting each of the expressions for the partial derivatives equal to zero and dividing through by -2, we can write for the OLS estimates of $\hat{\beta}_0$ and $\hat{\beta}_1$:

$$(\Sigma Y_i - N\hat{\beta}_0 - \hat{\beta}_1 \Sigma X_i) = 0 \qquad \textbf{2.1.7}$$

$$\Sigma Y_i X_i - \hat{\beta}_0 \Sigma X_i - \hat{\beta}_1 \Sigma X_i^2 = 0 \qquad \textbf{2.1.8}$$

from which:

$$\Sigma Y_i = N\hat{\beta}_0 + \hat{\beta}_1 \Sigma X_i \qquad \textbf{2.1.9}$$

$$\Sigma Y_i X_i = \hat{\beta}_0 \Sigma X_i + \hat{\beta}_1 \Sigma X_i^2 \qquad \textbf{2.1.10}$$

Solution by Cramer's Rule and by Successive Substitution

Equations 2.1.9 and 2.1.10 are called the *normal equations* of the regression. Notice that each equation is a linear expression in β_0 and β_1; thus we have the familiar problem of solving two linear equations in two unknowns. There are two methods of solution, solution by Cramer's rule using determinants and solution by successive substitution.

We may rewrite the pair of normal equations in matrix form as follows:

$$\begin{bmatrix} \Sigma Y_i \\ \Sigma Y_i X_i \end{bmatrix} = \begin{bmatrix} N & \Sigma X_i \\ \Sigma X_i & \Sigma X_i^2 \end{bmatrix} \begin{bmatrix} \hat{\beta}_0 \\ \hat{\beta}_1 \end{bmatrix} \qquad \textbf{2.1.11}$$

To solve these equations for $\hat{\beta}_1$ with Cramer's rule, we form two determinants:

$$D = \begin{vmatrix} N & \Sigma X_i \\ \Sigma X_i & \Sigma X_i^2 \end{vmatrix} = N\Sigma X_i^2 - (\Sigma X_i)^2$$

and

$$N_1 = \begin{vmatrix} N & \Sigma Y_i \\ \Sigma X_i & \Sigma Y_i X_i \end{vmatrix} = N\Sigma Y_i X_i - \Sigma X_i \Sigma Y_i$$

The value of $\hat{\beta}_1$ that satisfies the two normal equations is:

$$\hat{\beta}_1 = \frac{N_1}{D} = \frac{N\Sigma Y_i X_i - \Sigma X_i \Sigma Y_i}{N\Sigma X_i^2 - (\Sigma X_i)^2} \qquad \textbf{2.1.12}$$

To solve for $\hat{\beta}_0$, we form the determinant N_0 as follows:

$$N_0 = \begin{vmatrix} \Sigma Y_i & \Sigma X_i \\ \Sigma Y_i X_i & \Sigma X_i^2 \end{vmatrix} = \Sigma Y_i \Sigma X_i^2 - \Sigma Y_i X_i \Sigma X_i$$

Dividing by the value of D calculated above, we have:

$$\hat{\beta}_0 = \frac{N_0}{D} = \frac{\Sigma Y_i \Sigma X_i^2 - \Sigma Y_i X_i \Sigma X_i}{N\Sigma X_i^2 - (\Sigma X_i)^2} \qquad \textbf{2.1.13}$$

Since by definition the mean of a set of observations on Y is expressed by $\bar{Y} = \frac{\Sigma Y_i}{N}$ and, similarly, $\bar{X} = \frac{\Sigma X_i}{N}$, we can write:[5]

$$\hat{\beta}_0 = \bar{Y} - \hat{\beta}_1\bar{X} \qquad \textbf{2.1.13.A}$$

The two formulas 2.1.12 and 2.1.13 are OLS estimators of the coefficients in a bivariate equation, with X the independent variable and Y the dependent variable.

It is of course possible to obtain the same result by using the method of substitution. Let us illustrate the case with respect to $\hat{\beta}_1$, using normal equations 2.1.9 and 2.1.10. Multiplying through equations 2.1.9 and 2.1.10 by ΣX_i and N respectively, we obtain:

$$\Sigma X_i \Sigma Y_i = N\beta_0 \Sigma X_i + \beta_1(\Sigma X_i)^2$$

$$N\Sigma Y_i X_i = N\beta_0 \Sigma X_i + N\beta_1 \Sigma X_i^2$$

By subtraction and rearrangement, we can solve for $\hat{\beta}_1$:

$$\hat{\beta}_1 = \frac{N\Sigma Y_i X_i - \Sigma X_i \Sigma Y_i}{N\Sigma X^2 - (\Sigma X_i)^2} \qquad \textbf{2.1.14}$$

and this is the result obtained in equation 2.1.12.

A further interesting result can be obtained from equation 2.1.14 to show:

$$\hat{\beta}_1 = \frac{\Sigma(X_i - \bar{X})(Y_i - \bar{Y})}{\Sigma(X_i - \bar{X})^2} \qquad \textbf{2.1.14.A}$$

To see this, the numerator and the denominator in equation 2.1.14.A will be manipulated separately. Multiply each expression by N.

$$\begin{aligned}
&N\Sigma(X_i - \bar{X})(Y_i - \bar{Y}) \\
&\quad = N\Sigma X_i Y_i - N\bar{X}\Sigma Y_i - N\bar{Y}\Sigma X_i + N^2\bar{X}\bar{Y} \\
&\quad = N\Sigma X_i Y_i - N\frac{1}{N}\Sigma X_i\, \Sigma Y_i - N\frac{1}{N}\Sigma Y_i\, \Sigma X_i \\
&\qquad\qquad + N^2\frac{1}{N}\Sigma X_i \frac{1}{N}\Sigma Y_i \\
&\quad = N\Sigma X_i Y_i - \Sigma X_i \Sigma Y_i - \Sigma Y_i \Sigma X_i \\
&\qquad\qquad + \Sigma X_i \Sigma Y_i \\
&\quad = N\Sigma X_i Y_i - \Sigma X_i \Sigma Y_i
\end{aligned}$$

---

[5] The numerator of the expression for $\hat{\beta}_0$ can be rewritten as: $\Sigma Y_i \Sigma X_i^2 - \left(N\Sigma Y_i X_i \frac{\Sigma X_i}{N} - \Sigma X_i \Sigma Y_i \frac{\Sigma X_i}{N}\right) - \Sigma X_i \Sigma Y_i \frac{\Sigma X_i}{N}$ by adding and subtracting the term $\Sigma X_i \Sigma Y_i \frac{\Sigma X_i}{N}$. The expression in parentheses is equal to the numerator of $\hat{\beta}_1$ multiplied by $\bar{X}$.

The above is the expression for the numerator in equations 2.1.14 and 2.1.12. Again,

$$\begin{aligned} N\Sigma(X_i - \bar{X})^2 &= N\Sigma X_i^2 - 2N\bar{X}\Sigma X_i + N^2\bar{X}^2 \\ &= N\Sigma X_i^2 - 2N\frac{1}{N}\Sigma X_i\,\Sigma X_i \\ &\qquad + N^2\frac{1}{N}\Sigma X_i\frac{1}{N}\Sigma X_i \\ &= N\Sigma X_i^2 - 2(\Sigma X_i)^2 + (\Sigma X_i)^2 \\ &= N\Sigma X_i^2 - (\Sigma X_i)^2 \end{aligned}$$

The above is the expression for the denominator in equations 2.1.14 and 2.1.12. We obtain the results in equation 2.1.14.A, since the N in the numerator and the denominator cancel out.

Recall that the vanishing of the first partial derivatives of a function is a necessary condition only for the existence of an extreme value of a given function. Whether the function is at a minimum or a maximum when both its partial derivatives vanish (both are equal to zero) will depend on whether the second partial derivatives are greater or smaller than zero at the given point. However, in the present situation the normal equations determine the minimum for the sum of squared deviations.[6]

OLS Estimates Expressed in Terms of Deviations from Variable Means

Equation 2.1.14.A shows it is possible to obtain the OLS estimators in terms of the deviations of X_i and Y_i from their respective means $\bar{X}$ and $\bar{Y}$. As we shall see, this result can be derived directly. Define:

$$x_i = X_i - \bar{X}$$

$$y_i = Y_i - \bar{Y}$$

Let us consider equation 2.1.9, the first of the two normal equations. Dividing through by N, we obtain:

$$\bar{Y} = \beta_0 + \beta_1\bar{X} \qquad \textbf{2.1.15}$$

This equation shows that the means of both variables lie on the regression line.

Return to the model 2.1.1:

$$Y_i = \beta_0 + \beta_1 X_i + U_i$$

[6] There is no finite maximum for function 2.1.2. The sum of squared deviations will be maximum only when at least one of the parameters β_0 and β_1 is infinite.

Subtracting equation 2.1.15 from equation 2.1.1, we have:

$$(Y_i - \bar{Y}) = \beta_1(X_i - \bar{X}) + U_i \qquad \textbf{2.1.16}$$

or,

$$y_i = \beta_1 x_i + U_i \qquad \textbf{2.1.17}$$

and for the OLS estimate of β_1,

$$y_i - \hat{\beta}_1 x_i = \hat{U}_i \qquad \textbf{2.1.18}$$

By squaring and summing over N, we obtain the function of the "variable" β_1 to be minimized:

$$\Sigma(y_i - \hat{\beta}_1 x_i)^2 = \Sigma \hat{U}_i^2 \qquad \textbf{2.1.19}$$

Because β_1 is the single variable, this expression is differentiated:

$$\frac{d}{d\beta_1}\Sigma(y_i - \hat{\beta}_1 x_i)^2 = -2\Sigma x_i(y_i - \hat{\beta}_1 x_i) = 0$$

from which:

$$\Sigma x_i y_i - \hat{\beta}_1 \Sigma x_i^2 = 0$$

or,

$$\Sigma x_i y_i = \hat{\beta}_1 \Sigma x_i^2 \qquad \textbf{2.1.20}$$

Finally,

$$\hat{\beta}_1 = \frac{\Sigma x_i y_i}{\Sigma x_i^2} \qquad \textbf{2.1.21}$$

Equation 2.1.21 has been called the basic result of the OLS regression model, perhaps because of the greater concern for the estimate of the slope of the regression line (β_1). The estimates of $\hat{\beta}_0$ of the intercept β_0 can be easily obtained when β_1 has been estimated. From equation 2.1.15 it follows that:

$$\hat{\beta}_0 = \bar{Y} - \hat{\beta}_1 \bar{X} \qquad \textbf{2.1.22}$$

Note that the same result was obtained in equation 2.1.13.A.

It has been shown that the estimates of the parameters β_0 and β_1 make use of the sum of the squares of the disturbances U_i. These terms are random. It follows that the estimates $\hat{\beta}_0$ and $\hat{\beta}_1$ are also random. Therefore, it is important to investigate the statistical properties of the estimates: means, $[E(\hat{\beta}_0), E(\hat{\beta}_1)]$; and variances, $[\text{var}(\hat{\beta}_0), \text{var}(\hat{\beta}_1)]$. To do so we must study the statistical properties assumed for the disturbances. This is the subject of section 2.2.

2.2 THE NATURE OF THE DISTURBANCES

In the derivation of the least squares estimators, as discussed in the previous section, great reliance is placed on the disturbance variable U_i included in the regression model. However, there are no observations on this variable, nor is there any information as to the probability distribution of the U_i's. The econometrician could assume that they are normally distributed and proceed to work with the appropriate mathematical function. Assumption of a normal distribution is often considered too rigorous and restrictive. A particular set of assumptions on the statistical characteristics of the disturbance term U is usually made for the application of the OLS method of estimation. Assumptions of course cannot be proved, but the following will indicate why this set is reasonable.

Assumptions on the Disturbance Term in a Regression Model

The assumptions are:

$$E(U_i) = 0, \qquad i = 1, 2, \ldots, N \tag{2.2.1}$$

$$E(U_iU_j) = 0, \qquad i \neq j \tag{2.2.2}$$

$$= \sigma_u^2, \qquad i = j \tag{2.2.3}$$

$$i, j = 1, 2, \ldots, N$$

$$E(X_iU_i) = 0 \tag{2.2.4}$$

The assumption $E(U_i) = 0$ specifies that the *expected value* of U_i is zero for any value of the independent variable X_i. This is an important assumption. This assumption can be appreciated in terms of model 2.1.1. For any value of X_i which is assumed to be a fixed mathematical variable, we can conceivably repeat the experiment and generate many random observations on Y_i. For the true values of the parameters β_0, β_1, we obtain:

$$E(Y_i) = \beta_0 + \beta_1 X_i \tag{2.2.5}$$

since $E(U_i) = 0$. For the ith value of X, the disturbance term U_i may not be zero. Note that, although the value of an individual disturbance term U_i is sometimes positive and sometimes negative, on an average the term is zero. In other words the random disturbance term U_i in a stochastic equation is important for a single experiment; but for repeated experiments, if it were possible to do such repeated experiments in econometrics, these U_i's are not likely to affect the basic relationship.

The second assumption has two parts. Consider model 2.1.1:

$$Y_i = \beta_0 + \beta_1 X_i + U_i$$

Assume that $i = 1, 2, \ldots, 5$. There will then be five U terms as follows:

$$\begin{aligned}
Y_1 - \beta_0 - \beta_1 X_1 &= U_1 \\
Y_2 - \beta_0 - \beta_1 X_2 &= U_2 \\
Y_3 - \beta_0 - \beta_1 X_3 &= U_3 \\
Y_4 - \beta_0 - \beta_1 X_4 &= U_4 \\
Y_5 - \beta_0 - \beta_1 X_5 &= U_5
\end{aligned} \tag{2.2.6}$$

Taking the column vector of the U_i term **U** and its row vector **U′**, the following arrangements can be obtained:

$$\mathbf{U} = \begin{bmatrix} U_1 \\ U_2 \\ U_3 \\ U_4 \\ U_5 \end{bmatrix} \qquad \mathbf{U}' = [U_1, U_2, U_3, U_4, U_5]$$

$$\mathbf{UU}' = \begin{bmatrix} U_1^2 & U_1U_2 & U_1U_3 & U_1U_4 & U_1U_5 \\ U_2U_1 & U_2^2 & U_2U_3 & U_2U_4 & U_2U_5 \\ U_3U_1 & U_3U_2 & U_3^2 & U_3U_4 & U_3U_5 \\ U_4U_1 & U_4U_2 & U_4U_3 & U_4^2 & U_4U_5 \\ U_5U_1 & U_5U_2 & U_5U_3 & U_5U_4 & U_5^2 \end{bmatrix} \qquad 2.2.7$$

Taking the expected value,

$$E(\mathbf{UU}') = \begin{bmatrix} E(U_1^2) & E(U_1U_2) & E(U_1U_3) & E(U_1U_4) & E(U_1U_5) \\ E(U_2U_1) & E(U_2^2) & E(U_2U_3) & E(U_2U_4) & E(U_2U_5) \\ \cdot & & & & \cdot \\ \cdot & & & & \cdot \\ \cdot & & & & \cdot \\ E(U_5U_1) & \cdot & \cdot & \cdot & E(U_5^2) \end{bmatrix} \qquad 2.2.8$$

By assumptions 2.2.2 and 2.2.3, equation 2.2.8 may be written as follows:

$$E(\mathbf{UU}') = \begin{bmatrix} \sigma_u^2 & 0 & 0 & 0 & 0 \\ 0 & \sigma_u^2 & 0 & 0 & 0 \\ 0 & 0 & \sigma_u^2 & 0 & 0 \\ 0 & 0 & 0 & \sigma_u^2 & 0 \\ 0 & 0 & 0 & 0 & \sigma_u^2 \end{bmatrix} \qquad 2.2.9$$

In compact matrix notation:

$$E(\mathbf{UU'}) = \sigma_u^2 \begin{bmatrix} 1 & 0 & 0 & 0 & 0 \\ 0 & 1 & 0 & 0 & 0 \\ 0 & 0 & 1 & 0 & 0 \\ 0 & 0 & 0 & 1 & 0 \\ 0 & 0 & 0 & 0 & 1 \end{bmatrix} \qquad \textbf{2.2.10}$$

$$= \sigma_u^2 \mathbf{I}_N$$

where **I** is the identity matrix with N rows and N columns ($N \times N$).

The terms on the main diagonal show that for each observation the expected value of each squared disturbance term, $E(U_i^2) = \sigma_u^2$, is constant and finite. This constancy of variance is an important property known as *homoscedasticity*. (This property will be discussed at greater length in the next chapter.)

The zeros in the off-diagonal positions show that the expected values of the products of two different disturbance terms are all zero; that is, $E(U_iU_j) = 0$ when $i \neq j$ as in equation 2.2.9. This means that no two U_i's are correlated. The disturbance or error term associated with one observation is statistically independent of the disturbance or error term associated with another observation. In fact the U terms of all observations are all statistically independent and not interrelated. This assumption of mutual statistical independence of disturbances is described by saying that the disturbances are assumed to be serially noncorrelated or free form serial correlation. (This topic will be covered more extensively in the next chapter.)

Assumption 2.2.4, stated as $E(X_iU_i) = 0$, means that X_i and U_i are statistically independent for all i. Indeed, the assumption of constant variance, equation 2.2.3, would not have been fulfilled without this assumption.

Another way of stating equation 2.2.4 is to use the covariance of X_i and U_i. We can write: $\text{cov}(X_iU_i) = E\{[X_i - E(X_i)]\,[U_i - E(U_i)]\}$.

$$\text{cov}(X_iU_i) = E[\Sigma(X_i - \bar{X})\,(U_i - 0)]$$

since $E(U_i) = 0$ by assumption and $E(X_i) = \bar{X}$ in the sample space. Therefore,

$$\begin{aligned} \text{cov}(X_iU_i) &= E(\Sigma X_iU_i - \bar{X}\Sigma U_i) \\ &= E(\Sigma X_iU_i) \\ &= \Sigma E(X_iU_i) \\ E(X_iU_i) &= \text{cov}(X_iU_i) = 0 \end{aligned} \qquad \textbf{2.2.11}$$

This assumption is easily satisfied when X_i, the independent variable, is a *mathematical variable* and not a stochastic variable. The different values of a mathematical variable are fixed constants that do not change for different samples. One way to think of the characteristics of a mathematical variable is to imagine a piece of experimental equipment that can be set at a series of fixed positions on a dial. In every series of experiments, the values of the variable corresponding to that piece of equipment will have the same fixed constants read from the fixed positions on the dial. The other variable will take on a different set of values in the different series of experiments. If X is a nonstochastic variable, then $E(X_i) = X_i$, and:

$$\begin{aligned} E(X_iU_i) &= X_iE(U_i) \\ &= 0 \end{aligned} \qquad \textbf{2.2.12}$$

since following equation 2.2.1,

$$E(U_i) = 0$$

If X_i is not truly a fixed mathematical variable, the specific assumption is rather arbitrary. By making this assumption, even when the values of X_i are not truly fixed constants, the researcher indicates the direction of functional dependence. In terms of the present model, the implication is that the direction of dependence is from X to Y, and that there is no "feedback" effect from Y to X. This is a strong assumption which may not be realistic. In economic theory we can always turn the relation $Y = f(X)$ around to state $X = g(Y)$. But when the relation is stochastic, $Y = f(X,U)$, it cannot be turned around to yield $X = g(Y,U)$ without violating the assumption of statistical independence between X and U. (The discussion of mutual interdependence between the dependent and independent variables will be postponed until models of simultaneous equations are examined.)

Note that assumption 2.2.4 continues to be made in a regression model where a given dependent variable Y_i depends linearly on more than one X_i. This is the *multiple regression model,* and assumption 2.2.4 is restated to mean that each of the X's in the specified model is statistically independent of the disturbance term U. That is, in a model where there are K different X variables, we have:

$$\begin{aligned} Y_i = \beta_0 + \beta_1X_{i1} + \beta_2X_{i2} + \cdots + \beta_KX_{iK} + U_i& \\ i = 1, 2, \ldots, N& \\ k = 1, 2, \ldots, K& \end{aligned} \qquad \textbf{2.2.13}$$

The assumption is then stated as:

$$E(X_{ik}U_i) = 0$$

or,

$$E(X_{i1}U_i) = E(X_{i2}U_i) = \ldots = E(X_{iK}U_i) = 0 \qquad \textbf{2.2.14}$$

The Rank Condition in a Multiple Regression Model

Before the multiple regression model is discussed in the following section, it is convenient to state another assumption specifically made for such models. The matrix of X_{ik}, the regressors or the independent variables in a multiple regression model, has a rank equal to K plus 1. K is the number of parameters $\beta_1, \beta_2, \ldots, \beta_K$, the estimated coefficients of the K independent variables; and "1" stands for the intercept or the constant term β_0, the other estimated parameter. We further assume that $K + 1$ is less than or equal to the number of observations N. Formally stated, the rank condition is:

$$r(\mathbf{X}) = K + 1 \leq N \tag{2.2.15}$$

where $\mathbf{X}$ is the matrix of observations on the X variables.

A clear understanding of this assumption is important. If the X_{ik}'s are arranged column-wise ($k = 1, 2, \ldots, K$), each column of X's is used to estimate one parameter β_k. We have no observed values with which to estimate β_0; but we can construct a proxy variable X_0 by using a column of elements, all of which have a constant value of 1. The columns $X_1, X_2, \ldots, X_K$ are observed values of the variables included in the model. It is easy to show that we cannot estimate K independent parameters, $\beta_1, \beta_2, \ldots, \beta_K$, from these colunms of information unless the columns themselves are linearly independent.[7] Consider a model, (suppressing the subscript i):

$$Y = \beta_0 + \beta_1 X_1 + \beta_2 X_2 + \beta_3 X_3 + \beta_4 X_4 + U \qquad k = 1, 2, 3, 4 \tag{2.2.16}$$

where:

$$X_4 = \xi X_2 \tag{2.2.17}$$

from which:

$$\begin{aligned} Y &= \beta_0 + \beta_1 X_1 + \beta_2 X_2 + \beta_3 X_3 + \beta_4 \xi X_2 + U \\ &= \beta_0 + \beta_1 X_1 + \gamma X_2 + \beta_3 X_3 + U \end{aligned} \tag{2.2.18}$$

where $\gamma = (\beta_2 + \beta_4 \xi)$. There is no way of disentangling β_2 and β_4 from the combination of the two.

This is the problem of *exact multicollinearity*, which will be treated at length in Chapter 5. The rank condition of the matrix has to do with this problem. For a matrix the rank is given by the number of independent columns or rows, whichever is less. A simple example may help fix the idea:

$$X = \begin{bmatrix} 4 & 2 & 2 & 5 \\ 8 & 4 & 10 & 22 \\ 16 & 8 & 7 & 9 \\ 10 & 5 & 17 & 13 \end{bmatrix}$$

[7] Recall that the definition of linear independence for a set of variables requires that no single variable in the set can be expressed as a linear combination of one or more of the others.

Columns 1 and 2 are linearly dependent since column 1 is equal to the product of column 2 multiplied by a constant. The rank of this 4 × 4 matrix is not 4. Four parameters cannot be estimated from these four columns of observed data, even if they have been collected from four apparently independent sources. Check the rank condition row-wise. Of course we cannot estimate four parameters unless we have at least four linearly independent rows of observations. Fulfillment of rank condition ensures that not only are the columns linearly independent, but the rows are also. Often in econometric research the number of observations is too small. We cannot estimate four parameters unless we have at least four observations in each column. In the case where there are less than four observations in each column, we do not have four rows, let alone four linearly independent rows of observations. The rank condition will not be fullfilled if the linear independence of either rows or columns does not hold.

2.3 Extension of OLS to the Multiple Regression Model

The OLS method of estimation can easily be extended to the case where there is more than one explanatory variable in the model. Let us consider the case where a dependent variable Y_i is a linear function of two independent variables X_{i1} and X_{i2}, and the relationship is stochastic as before:

$$Y_i = \beta_0 + \beta_1 X_{i1} + \beta_2 X_{i2} + U_i, \qquad i = 1, 2, \ldots, N \tag{2.3.1}$$

The U_i's are subject to assumptions 2.2.1, 2.2.2, 2.2.3, 2.2.14, and 2.2.15 as discussed in the previous section. We begin by rewriting equation 2.3.1:

$$Y_i - \hat{\beta}_0 - \hat{\beta}_1 X_{i1} - \hat{\beta}_2 X_{i2} = \hat{U}_i \tag{2.3.2}$$

Squaring and summing over N, we have:

$$\Sigma(Y_i - \hat{\beta}_0 - \hat{\beta}_1 X_{i1} - \hat{\beta}_2 X_{i2})^2 = \Sigma \hat{U}_i^2 \tag{2.3.3}$$

Taking partial derivatives with respect to β_0, β_1, and β_2 and setting them equal to zero, we obtain:

$$\frac{\partial}{\partial \beta_0} \Sigma(Y_i - \beta_0 - \beta_1 X_{i1} - \beta_2 X_{i2})^2$$

$$= -2\Sigma(Y_i - \beta_0 - \beta_1 X_{i1} - \beta_2 X_{i2}) = 0 \tag{2.3.4}$$

$$\frac{\partial}{\partial \beta_1} \Sigma(Y_i - \beta_0 - \beta_1 X_{i1} - \beta_2 X_{i2})^2$$

$$= -2\Sigma X_{i1}(Y_i - \beta_0 - \beta_1 X_{i1} - \beta_2 X_{i2}) = 0 \tag{2.3.5}$$

$$\frac{\partial}{\partial \beta_2} \Sigma(Y_i - \beta_0 - \beta_1 X_{i1} - \beta_2 X_{i2})^2$$

$$= -2\Sigma X_{i2}(Y_i - \beta_0 - \beta_1 X_{i1} - \beta_2 X_{i2}) = 0 \tag{2.3.6}$$

From equations 2.3.4 through 2.3.6 we obtain:

$$\Sigma(Y_i - \hat{\beta}_0 - \hat{\beta}_1 X_{i1} - \hat{\beta}_2 X_{i2}) = 0 \qquad \textbf{2.3.7}$$

$$\Sigma X_{i1} (Y_i - \hat{\beta}_0 - \hat{\beta}_1 X_{i1} - \hat{\beta}_2 X_{i2}) = 0 \qquad \textbf{2.3.8}$$

$$\Sigma X_{i2} (Y_i - \hat{\beta}_0 - \hat{\beta}_1 X_{i1} - \hat{\beta}_2 X_{i2}) = 0 \qquad \textbf{2.3.9}$$

or,

$$\Sigma Y_i = N\hat{\beta}_0 + \hat{\beta}_1 \Sigma X_{i1} + \hat{\beta}_2 \Sigma X_{i2} \qquad \textbf{2.3.10}$$

$$\Sigma X_{i1} Y_i = \hat{\beta}_0 \Sigma X_{i1} + \hat{\beta}_1 \Sigma X_{i1}^2 + \hat{\beta}_2 \Sigma X_{i1} X_{i2} \qquad \textbf{2.3.11}$$

$$\Sigma X_{i2} Y_i = \hat{\beta}_0 \Sigma X_{i2} + \hat{\beta}_1 \Sigma X_{i1} X_{i2} + \hat{\beta}_2 \Sigma X_{i2}^2 \qquad \textbf{2.3.12}$$

Equations 2.3.10 through 2.3.12 are the three normal equations that yield estimates of the three parameters β_0, β_1, and β_2. These results compare with the normal equations 2.1.9 and 2.1.10 in the two-variable case. As in the two-variable case these three normal equations are three linear equations in three unknowns: β_0, β_1, and β_2. We can solve them by Cramer's rule to find the OLS estimators for the $\hat{\beta}_k$ coefficients, ($k = 1, 2, 3$).

The same mechanics can easily be extended to the case where there are K independent variables (X's):

$$Y_i = \beta_1 X_{i1} + \beta_2 X_{i2} + \ldots + \beta_K X_{iK} + U_i, \quad i = 1, 2, \ldots, N \quad k = 1, 2, \ldots, K \qquad \textbf{2.3.13}$$

Notice that we introduce all X_K's as independent regressors and suppress β_0, the parameter relating to the constant term intercept or level of function 2.3.13. This is done for simplicity and to help fix attention on regressors on which we have independent observations. We can begin by specifying a proxy variable, say X_0, which has a constant value of 1 (see section 2.2, equations 2.3.10 through 2.3.12 of this section, and also the numerical examples in section 3.4).

It is convenient to write the more general case in matrix form:

$$\mathbf{Y} = \begin{bmatrix} Y_{11} \\ Y_{21} \\ \cdot \\ \cdot \\ \cdot \\ Y_{N1} \end{bmatrix} \qquad \mathbf{X} = \begin{bmatrix} X_{11} & X_{12} & \ldots & X_{1K} \\ X_{21} & X_{22} & \ldots & X_{2K} \\ \cdot & \cdot & & \cdot \\ \cdot & \cdot & & \cdot \\ \cdot & \cdot & & \cdot \\ X_{N1} & X_{N2} & \ldots & X_{NK} \end{bmatrix}$$

$$\mathbf{U} = \begin{bmatrix} U_{11} \\ U_{21} \\ \cdot \\ \cdot \\ \cdot \\ U_{N1} \end{bmatrix} \qquad \boldsymbol{\beta} = \begin{bmatrix} \beta_1 \\ \beta_2 \\ \cdot \\ \cdot \\ \cdot \\ \beta_K \end{bmatrix}$$

The first subscript refers to the observation and the second subscript to the variable. Y_{N1} indicates the Nth observation on Y_1. (Note that there is only one Y in the model. Also note that this book does not use bold lower case letters for column and row vectors of a given variable. Bold letters are used for matrix notation in general.) Similarly, X_{NK} is the Nth observation on the Kth X; X_{12} is the first observation on the second X; X_{21} is the second observation on the first X; and so forth.

The set of N observations on Y can be written as an $N \times 1$ column vector, and we state that:

$\mathbf{Y}$ is an $N \times 1$ column vector.

The observations on each of the K independent variables form an $N \times 1$ column vector. Combining these K vectors into a matrix yields $\mathbf{X}$, and:

$\mathbf{X}$ is an $N \times K$ matrix.

Similarly,

$\mathbf{U}$ is an $N \times 1$ column vector of disturbance terms

and

$\boldsymbol{\beta}$ is a $K \times 1$ column vector of K different β's.

The basic linear model 2.3.13 can now be expressed as a matrix equation:

$$\begin{bmatrix} Y_{11} \\ Y_{21} \\ \cdot \\ \cdot \\ \cdot \\ Y_{N1} \end{bmatrix} = \begin{bmatrix} X_{11} & X_{12} \ldots X_{1K} \\ X_{21} & X_{22} \ldots X_{2K} \\ \cdot & \cdot \qquad \cdot \\ \cdot & \cdot \qquad \cdot \\ \cdot & \cdot \qquad \cdot \\ X_{N1} & X_{N2} \ldots X_{NK} \end{bmatrix} \begin{bmatrix} \beta_1 \\ \beta_2 \\ \cdot \\ \cdot \\ \cdot \\ \beta_K \end{bmatrix} + \begin{bmatrix} U_{11} \\ U_{21} \\ \cdot \\ \cdot \\ \cdot \\ U_{N1} \end{bmatrix} \tag{2.3.14}$$

In more compact matrix notation,

$$\mathbf{Y} = \mathbf{X}\boldsymbol{\beta} + \mathbf{U} \tag{2.3.15}$$

The sum of squared residuals to be minimized is:

$$\Sigma(Y_i - \hat{\beta}_1 X_{i1} - \hat{\beta}_2 X_{i2} - \ldots - \hat{\beta}_K X_{iK})^2 = S(\hat{\beta}_1, \hat{\beta}_2, \ldots, \hat{\beta}_K) \qquad \textbf{2.3.16}$$

The K normal equations are obtained from the K partial derivatives of the above expression with respect to each of the β's, with each partial derivative set equal to zero. We can illustrate the case with respect to β_1:

$$\frac{\partial}{\partial \beta_1} S = -2\Sigma X_{i1}\,(Y_i - \hat{\beta}_1 X_{i1} - \hat{\beta}_2 X_{i2} - \ldots - \hat{\beta}_K X_{iK}) = 0 \qquad \textbf{2.3.17}$$

Dividing through by -2 and rearranging,

$$\hat{\beta}_1 \Sigma X_{i1}^2 + \hat{\beta}_2 \Sigma X_{i1} X_{i2} + \ldots + \hat{\beta}_K \Sigma X_{i1} X_{iK} = \Sigma X_{i1} Y_i \qquad \textbf{2.3.18}$$

The K normal equations can thus be written, suppressing the subscript i:

$$\begin{array}{ccccccc}
\hat{\beta}_1 \Sigma X_1^2 & + & \hat{\beta}_2 \Sigma X_1 X_2 & + \ldots + & \hat{\beta}_K \Sigma X_1 X_K & = & \Sigma X_1 Y \\
\hat{\beta}_1 \Sigma X_1 X_2 & + & \hat{\beta}_2 \Sigma X_2^2 & + \ldots + & \hat{\beta}_K \Sigma X_2 X_K & = & \Sigma X_2 Y \\
\cdot & & \cdot & & \cdot & & \cdot \\
\cdot & & \cdot & & \cdot & & \cdot \\
\cdot & & \cdot & & \cdot & & \cdot \\
\hat{\beta}_1 \Sigma X_1 X_K & + & \hat{\beta}_2 \Sigma X_2 X_K & + \ldots + & \hat{\beta}_K \Sigma X_K^2 & = & \Sigma X_K Y
\end{array} \qquad \textbf{2.3.19}$$

Then in matrix notation, the set of K normal equations can be rewritten as:

$$\begin{bmatrix} \Sigma X_1^2 & \Sigma X_1 X_2 & \ldots \Sigma X_1 X_K \\ \Sigma X_2 X_1 & \Sigma X_2^2 & \ldots \Sigma X_2 X_K \\ \cdot & \cdot & \cdot \\ \cdot & \cdot & \cdot \\ \cdot & \cdot & \cdot \\ \Sigma X_K X_1 & \Sigma X_K X_2 & \ldots \Sigma X_K^2 \end{bmatrix} \begin{bmatrix} \hat{\beta}_1 \\ \hat{\beta}_2 \\ \cdot \\ \cdot \\ \cdot \\ \hat{\beta}_K \end{bmatrix} = \begin{bmatrix} \Sigma X_1 Y \\ \Sigma X_2 Y \\ \cdot \\ \cdot \\ \cdot \\ \Sigma X_K Y \end{bmatrix} \qquad \textbf{2.3.20}$$

or, $(\mathbf{X'X})\hat{\boldsymbol{\beta}} = \mathbf{X'Y}$. Next we can solve for $\hat{\boldsymbol{\beta}}$:

$$\begin{bmatrix} \hat{\beta}_1 \\ \hat{\beta}_2 \\ \cdot \\ \cdot \\ \cdot \\ \hat{\beta}_K \end{bmatrix} = \begin{bmatrix} \Sigma X_1^2 & \Sigma X_1 X_2 & \ldots \Sigma X_1 X_K \\ \Sigma X_2 X_1 & \Sigma X_2^2 & \ldots \Sigma X_2 X_K \\ \cdot & \cdot & \cdot \\ \cdot & \cdot & \cdot \\ \cdot & \cdot & \cdot \\ \Sigma X_K X_1 & \Sigma X_K X_2 & \ldots \Sigma X_K^2 \end{bmatrix}^{-1} \begin{bmatrix} \Sigma X_1 Y \\ \Sigma X_2 Y \\ \cdot \\ \cdot \\ \cdot \\ \Sigma X_K Y \end{bmatrix} \qquad \textbf{2.3.21}$$

Using the compact matrix notation as in equation 2.3.15, $\mathbf{Y} = \mathbf{X}\boldsymbol{\beta} + \mathbf{U}$, the expression in equation 2.3.21 becomes:

$$\hat{\boldsymbol{\beta}} = (\mathbf{X}'\mathbf{X})^{-1}\mathbf{X}'\mathbf{Y} \qquad \textbf{2.3.22}$$

Writing C_{ij} for the elements of the inverse matrix $(\mathbf{X}'\mathbf{X})^{-1}$, we can obtain:[8]

$$\begin{bmatrix} \hat{\beta}_1 \\ \hat{\beta}_2 \\ \cdot \\ \cdot \\ \cdot \\ \hat{\beta}_K \end{bmatrix} = \begin{bmatrix} C_{11} & C_{12} & \cdots & C_{1K} \\ C_{21} & C_{22} & \cdots & C_{2K} \\ \cdot & \cdot & & \cdot \\ \cdot & \cdot & & \cdot \\ \cdot & \cdot & & \cdot \\ C_{K1} & C_{K2} & \cdots & C_{KK} \end{bmatrix} \begin{bmatrix} \Sigma X_1 Y \\ \Sigma X_2 Y \\ \cdot \\ \cdot \\ \cdot \\ \Sigma X_K Y \end{bmatrix} \qquad \textbf{2.3.23}$$

From equation 2.3.23 the solution for $\hat{\beta}_1$ is:

$$\hat{\beta}_1 = C_{11}\Sigma X_1 Y + C_{12}\Sigma X_2 Y + \ldots + C_{1K}\Sigma X_K Y \qquad \textbf{2.3.24}$$

and the solution for $\hat{\beta}_K$ is:

$$\hat{\beta}_K = C_{K1}\Sigma X_1 Y + C_{K2}\Sigma X_2 Y + \ldots + C_{KK}\Sigma X_K Y \qquad \textbf{2.3.25}$$

2.4 PROPERTIES OF THE OLS ESTIMATORS

Parameters estimated by the least squares regression method have certain important properties. They are (1) linear, (2) unbiased, and (3) "best," and are often summarized as BLUE (that is, Best Linear Unbiased Estimators).

Linearity of OLS Estimators

Let us first consider the property of linearity in a two-variable case. Recall the fundamental result from equation 2.1.21:

$$\hat{\beta}_1 = \frac{\Sigma x_i y_i}{\Sigma x_i^2}$$

Since $y_i = Y_i - \bar{Y}$, this can be written as:

$$\hat{\beta}_1 = \Sigma\left[\frac{x_i}{\Sigma x_i^2}(Y_i - \bar{Y})\right]$$

$$= \Sigma\left(\frac{x_i Y_i}{\Sigma x_i^2}\right) - \bar{Y}\left(\frac{\Sigma x_i}{\Sigma x_i^2}\right) \qquad \textbf{2.4.1}$$

---

[8] Recalling that the expansion of a determinant by "alien cofactors" always equals zero, consider the $K \times K$ matrix $\mathbf{A}$. The product $\mathbf{A} \cdot \text{Adjoint}\ (\mathbf{A}) = |\mathbf{A}|\mathbf{I}$, and thus $\dfrac{\mathbf{A} \cdot \text{Adjoint}\ \mathbf{A}}{|\mathbf{A}|} = \mathbf{I}$ or $\mathbf{A}^{-1} = \dfrac{\text{Adjoint}\ \mathbf{A}}{|\mathbf{A}|}$. For further discussion see G. Hadley, *Linear Algebra* (Reading, Mass.: Addison-Wesley Publishing Co., 1961).

Notice that the second term of the right-hand expression is zero, since Σx_i, which is $\Sigma(X_i - \bar{X})$, is of course zero.[9] Thus we have:

$$\hat{\beta}_1 = \Sigma W_i Y_i \qquad \textbf{2.4.2}$$

or,

$$\hat{\beta}_1 = W_1Y_1 + W_2Y_2 + \ldots + W_NY_N$$

where:

$$W_i = \frac{x_i}{\Sigma x_i^2}$$

Each W_i is a fixed constant since it depends only on the values $X_i - \bar{X}$, values which are assumed to be fixed in repeated samples. This proves that $\hat{\beta}_1$ is a linear function of the sample observations Y_i. By substituting this linear expression for $\hat{\beta}_1$ in the equation for $\hat{\beta}_0$, equation 2.1.22, it can be shown that $\hat{\beta}_0$ is also a linear function of sample observations. From equation 2.1.22 we have:

$$\begin{aligned}\hat{\beta}_0 &= \bar{Y} - \hat{\beta}_1\bar{X} \\ &= \bar{Y} - \bar{X}\Sigma W_iY_i \qquad \textbf{2.4.3} \\ &= \frac{1}{N}\Sigma Y_i - \bar{X}\Sigma W_iY_i \\ &= \Sigma\left(\frac{1}{N} - \bar{X}W_i\right)Y_i \qquad \textbf{2.4.4}\end{aligned}$$

Now consider linearity of OLS estimators for the multiple regression. In the K-variable case it can easily be seen that β_k is a linear expression of Y_i. From equation 2.3.24, using the i subscript, we have:

$$\hat{\beta}_1 = C_{11}\Sigma X_{i1}Y_i + C_{12}\Sigma X_{i2}Y_i + \ldots + C_{1K}\Sigma X_{iK}Y_i \qquad i = 1, 2, \ldots, N \qquad \textbf{2.4.5}$$

Letting $N = 3$ and $K = 2$, we can write:

$$\hat{\beta}_1 = C_{11}\sum_{i=1}^{3} X_{i1}Y_i + C_{12}\sum_{i=1}^{3} X_{i2}Y_i \qquad \textbf{2.4.6}$$

or,

$$\hat{\beta}_1 = Y_1(C_{11}X_{11} + C_{12}X_{12}) + Y_2(C_{11}X_{21} + C_{12}X_{22}) + Y_3(C_{11}X_{31} + C_{12}X_{32}) \qquad \textbf{2.4.7}$$

9
$$\begin{aligned}\Sigma x_i &= \Sigma(X_i - \bar{X}), \qquad i = 1, 2, \ldots, N \\ &= \Sigma X_i - N\bar{X} \\ &= \Sigma X_i - N\frac{1}{N}\Sigma X_i = \Sigma X_i - \Sigma X_i \\ &= 0\end{aligned}$$

and

$$\hat{\beta}_2 = C_{21} \sum_{i=1}^{3} X_{i1}Y_i + C_{22} \sum_{i=1}^{3} X_{i2}Y_i \qquad 2.4.8$$

or,

$$\hat{\beta}_2 = Y_1(C_{21}X_{11} + C_{22}X_{12}) + Y_2(C_{21}X_{21} + C_{22}X_{22}) + Y_3(C_{21}X_{31} + C_{22}X_{32}) \qquad 2.4.9$$

Obviously $\hat{\beta}_k$ is a linear function of Y_i. Each Y_i is multiplied by one of the fixed sets of weights as discussed above.

Unbiasedness of OLS Estimators

It will now be proven that the OLS estimators are *unbiased*. An estimator of a parameter in a stochastic equation is unbiased if the expected value of the estimated parameter is equal to the true value of the parameter,

$$E(\hat{\beta}_1) = \beta_1$$

From equation 2.4.2 we have:

$$\hat{\beta}_1 = \Sigma W_i Y_i$$

Given the model $Y_i = \beta_0 + \beta_1 X_i + U_i$ and substituting for Y_i, we can write:

$$\hat{\beta}_1 = \Sigma W_i(\beta_0 + \beta_1 X_i + U_i)$$
$$= \beta_0 \Sigma W_i + \beta_1 \Sigma W_i X_i + \Sigma W_i U_i$$

To complete the proof we need the following two results on W_i:

$$\Sigma W_i = 0$$

and

$$\Sigma W_i X_i = 1$$

To prove the first of the two results, we begin with the definition of W_i from equation 2.4.2:

$$W_i = \frac{x_i}{\Sigma x_i^2}$$

Therefore,

$$\Sigma W_i = \frac{\Sigma x_i}{\Sigma x_i^2}$$

and

$$\Sigma W_i = 0 \qquad 2.4.10$$

since the numerator $\Sigma x_i = \Sigma(X_i - \bar{X}) = 0$.

To obtain the second of the two results, we begin with $\Sigma W_i x_i$ when $x_i = X_i - \bar{X}$. We can therefore write:

$$\Sigma W_i x_i = \Sigma W_i X_i - \bar{X}\Sigma W_i$$

Since from equation 2.4.10, $\Sigma W_i = 0$,

$$\Sigma W_i x_i = \Sigma W_i X_i$$

Using the definition of W_i, we can write:

$$\begin{aligned} \Sigma W_i X_i &= \Sigma W_i x_i \\ &= \Sigma \frac{x_i}{\Sigma x_i^2} x_i \\ &= \frac{\Sigma x_i^2}{\Sigma x_i^2} \\ &= 1 \end{aligned} \qquad \textbf{2.4.11}$$

We can now make use of these results in the equation:

$$\hat{\beta}_1 = \beta_0 \Sigma W_i + \beta_1 \Sigma W_i X_i + \Sigma W_i U_i$$

Substituting $\Sigma W_i = 0$ and $\Sigma W_i X_i = 1$, we have:

$$\hat{\beta}_1 = \beta_1 + \Sigma W_i U_i \qquad \textbf{2.4.12}$$

Taking the expected value on both sides:

$$E(\hat{\beta}_1) = E(\beta_1) + E(\Sigma W_i U_i)$$

But $E(\beta_1) = \beta_1$ since the expected value of a constant is equal to the constant. And $E(\Sigma W_i U_i) = \Sigma W_i E(U_i)$ because the W_i as shown above takes on a set of fixed values over all samples. Thus we obtain:

$$E(\hat{\beta}_1) = \beta_1 + \Sigma W_i E(U_i) \qquad \textbf{2.4.13}$$

Now since $E(U_i) = 0$,

$$E(\hat{\beta}_1) = \beta_1 \qquad \textbf{2.4.14}$$

This means that although a particular value of $\hat{\beta}_1$ may not be equal to the true value β_1, the expected value of $\hat{\beta}_1$, $E(\hat{\beta}_1)$, will be equal to the true β_1. It can also be shown that:

$$E(\hat{\beta}_0) = \beta_0$$

From equation 2.4.4,

$$\hat{\beta}_0 = \Sigma\left(\frac{1}{N} - \bar{X}W_i\right)Y_i$$

Substituting for Y_i,

$$\hat{\beta}_0 = \Sigma\left(\frac{1}{N} - \bar{X}W_i\right)(\beta_0 + \beta_1 X_i + U_i)$$

$$= \beta_0 - \beta_0\bar{X}\Sigma W_i + \beta_1\bar{X} - \beta_1\bar{X}\Sigma X_i W_i + \Sigma\left(\frac{1}{N} - \bar{X}W_i\right)U_i$$

Using the results $\Sigma W_i = 0$ from equation 2.4.10 and $\Sigma W_i X_i = 1$ from equation 2.4.11, we have:

$$\hat{\beta}_0 = \beta_0 + \Sigma\left(\frac{1}{N} - \bar{X}W_i\right)U_i \tag{2.4.15}$$

Therefore, taking expected values on both sides of this equation,

$$E(\hat{\beta}_0) = \beta_0 + \Sigma\left(\frac{1}{N} - \bar{X}W_i\right)E(U_i)$$
$$= \beta_0 \tag{2.4.16}$$

since $E(U_i) = 0$.

We can now examine unbiasedeness of OLS estimators in the K-variable case. In the K-variable case too the property of unbiasedness can easily be shown. We know from basic rules of linear algebra that for a matrix of rank R,

$$(\mathbf{X}'\mathbf{X})\ (\mathbf{X}'\mathbf{X})^{-1} = \mathbf{I}_R \tag{2.4.17}$$

where $\mathbf{I}_R$ is the identity matrix of rank R.

Continuing the discussion in terms of $K = 2$ and using the notation C_{ij} for elements of $(\mathbf{X}'\mathbf{X})^{-1}$ as before, we can write:

$$\begin{bmatrix} \Sigma X_1^2 & \Sigma X_1 X_2 \\ \Sigma X_1 X_2 & \Sigma X_2^2 \end{bmatrix} \begin{bmatrix} C_{11} & C_{12} \\ C_{21} & C_{22} \end{bmatrix} = \begin{bmatrix} 1 & 0 \\ 0 & 1 \end{bmatrix}$$

Since $C_{12} = C_{21}$, we obtain:

$$\begin{bmatrix} C_{11}\Sigma X_1^2 + C_{12}\Sigma X_1 X_2 & C_{12}\Sigma X_1^2 + C_{22}\Sigma X_1 X_2 \\ C_{11}\Sigma X_1 X_2 + C_{12}\Sigma X_2^2 & C_{12}\Sigma X_1 X_2 + C_{22}\Sigma X_2^2 \end{bmatrix} = \begin{bmatrix} 1 & 0 \\ 0 & 1 \end{bmatrix}$$

from which:

$$C_{11}\Sigma X_1^2 + C_{12}\Sigma X_1 X_2 = 1$$

$$C_{12}\Sigma X_1 X_2 + C_{22}\Sigma X_2^2 = 1$$

and

$$C_{11}\Sigma X_1 X_2 + C_{12}\Sigma X_2^2 = C_{12}\Sigma X_1^2 + C_{22}\Sigma X_1 X_2 = 0 \tag{2.4.18}$$

Suppressing the i subscript and ignoring the constant term β_0 when $K = 2$, we write the model as:

$$Y = \beta_1 X_1 + \beta_2 X_2 + U \qquad \textbf{2.4.19}$$

and using equation 2.3.24,

$$\hat{\beta}_1 = C_{11}\Sigma X_1 Y + C_{12}\Sigma X_2 Y \qquad \textbf{2.4.20}$$

By substituting for Y from equation 2.4.19,

$$\begin{aligned}
\hat{\beta}_1 &= C_{11}\Sigma X_1(\beta_1 X_1 + \beta_2 X_2 + U) + C_{12}\Sigma X_2(\beta_1 X_1 + \beta_2 X_2 + U) \\
&= \beta_1 C_{11}\Sigma X_1^2 + \beta_2 C_{11}\Sigma X_1 X_2 + C_{11}\Sigma X_1 U + \beta_1 C_{12}\Sigma X_1 X_2 \\
&\qquad + \beta_2 C_{12}\Sigma X_2^2 + C_{12}\Sigma X_2 U \\
&= \beta_1(C_{11}\Sigma X_1^2 + C_{12}\Sigma X_1 X_2) + \beta_2(C_{11}\Sigma X_1 X_2 + C_{12}\Sigma X_2^2) \\
&\qquad + C_{11}\Sigma X_1 U + C_{12}\Sigma X_2 U \\
&= \beta_1 + C_{11}\Sigma X_1 U + C_{12}\Sigma X_2 U
\end{aligned}$$

since:

$$C_{11}\Sigma X_1^2 + C_{12}\Sigma X_1 X_2 = 1$$

and

$$C_{11}\Sigma X_1 X_2 + C_{12}\Sigma X_2^2 = 0$$

By taking expected values, we have:

$$E(\hat{\beta}_1) = \beta_1 + C_{11}\Sigma X_1 E(U) + C_{12}\Sigma X_2 E(U)$$

The sets of values X_{i1} and X_{i2} are fixed in repeated samples, and thus $\Sigma X_1 E(U) = E(U)\Sigma X_1$ and $\Sigma X_2 E(U) = E(U)\Sigma X_2$. Since $E(U) = 0$ by assumption, we have:

$$E(\hat{\beta}_1) = \beta_1 \qquad \textbf{2.4.21}$$

Thus the OLS estimator $\hat{\beta}_1$ is an unbiased estimator of β_1. In a similar way it can be shown that $\hat{\beta}_2$ is an unbiased estimator of β_2.

OLS Estimators are "Best": Variance of the OLS Estimators

The least squares estimators are "best" in the sense that their variance is a minimum. To be more precise, they have the minimum variance of the class of linear unbiased estimators. In this sense the OLS estimators are the most efficient in this class. Two estimators may both be unbiased; but if one of them has a larger variance, it is relatively less efficient than the other. It may be easier to comprehend the concept of efficiency by a diagrammatic presentation, Figure 2-4. In the diagrams β is the true value of the estimated

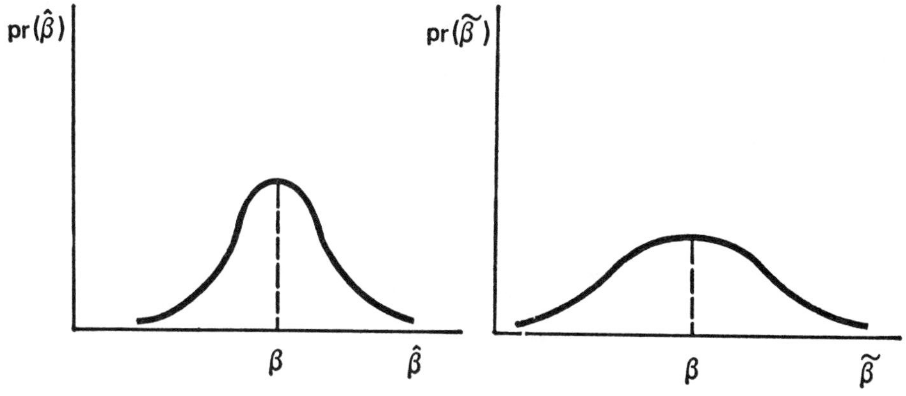

FIGURE 2-4

parameter, and the two bell-shaped curves represent the probability distribution of the values of two different estimators of β obtained in repeated samplings. Both $\hat{\beta}$ and $\tilde{\beta}$ are independent unbiased linear estimators; but $\hat{\beta}$, which has a smaller variance, is relatively more efficient than $\tilde{\beta}$, which is shown with a larger variance.

Efficiency is a relative concept and can be measured by the relative magnitude of variances of the two estimators. That is, the relative efficiency of $\hat{\beta}$ compared to $\tilde{\beta}$ is given by:

$$\frac{\text{var}(\hat{\beta})}{\text{var}(\tilde{\beta})} \gtrless 1 \qquad \textbf{2.4.22}$$

If the ratio of the two variances is exactly equal to 1, the two estimators are equally efficient; if the ratio is greater than 1, $\hat{\beta}$ is relatively less efficient than $\tilde{\beta}$; and if the ratio is less than 1, $\tilde{\beta}$ is relatively less efficient than $\hat{\beta}$.

The definition of *variance* of a parameter is given in terms of the deviation between the estimated parameter $\hat{\beta}_1$ and its expected value $E(\hat{\beta}_1)$:

$$\text{var}(\hat{\beta}_1) = E\{[\hat{\beta}_1 - E(\hat{\beta}_1)]^2\} \qquad \textbf{2.4.23}$$

We have seen that the OLS estimator $\hat{\beta}_1$ is an unbiased estimator of β_1. Thus from equation 2.4.14,

$$E(\hat{\beta}_1) = \beta_1$$

Equation 2.4.23 can be rewritten as:

$$\text{var}(\hat{\beta}_1) = E\ \{[\hat{\beta}_1 - E(\hat{\beta}_1]^2\} = E[(\hat{\beta}_1 - \beta_1)^2] \qquad \textbf{2.4.24}$$

Recall from equation 2.4.12 that:

$$\hat{\beta}_1 = \beta_1 + \Sigma W_i U_i$$

Thus,

$$(\hat{\beta}_1 - \beta_1) = \Sigma W_i U_i$$

Squaring and taking expected values,

$$E[(\hat{\beta}_1 - \beta_1)^2] = E[(\Sigma W_i U_i)^2] \quad 2.4.25$$

$$= \sigma_u^2 \Sigma W_i^2 \quad 2.4.26$$

where $E(U_i^2) = \sigma_u^2$ by assumption. To see this clearly, let us suppose that there are only two terms, U_1 and U_2:

$$E[(\Sigma W_i U_i)^2] = E[(W_1 U_1 + W_2 U_2)^2]$$

$$= E(W_1^2 U_1^2 + W_2^2 U_2^2 + 2U_1 W_1 U_2 W_2) \quad 2.4.27$$

$$= E(W_1^2 U_1^2 + W_2^2 U_2^2)$$

Note that given assumption 2.2.2, $E(U_i U_j) = 0$, $i \neq j$:

$$E(2U_1 W_1 U_2 W_2) = 2W_1 W_2 E(U_1 U_2) = 0$$

Now,

$$E(W_1^2 U_1^2 + W_2^2 U_2^2) = \sum_{i=1}^{2} \left[W_i^2 E(U_i^2) \right]$$

Therefore, since from equation 2.2.3, $E(U_i^2) = E(U_i U_j) = \sigma_u^2$ for $i = j$,

$$\text{var}(\hat{\beta}_1) = \sigma_u^2 \Sigma W_i^2 \quad 2.4.28$$

Recall equation 2.4.2:

$$W_i = \frac{x_i}{\Sigma x_i^2}$$

Therefore,

$$\Sigma W_i^2 = \frac{\Sigma x_i^2}{(\Sigma x_i^2)^2} = \frac{1}{\Sigma x_i^2} \quad 2.4.29$$

Using equation 2.4.29,

$$\text{var}(\hat{\beta}_1) = \sigma_u^2 \frac{1}{\Sigma x_i^2} \quad 2.4.30$$

Note that σ_u^2 is an unknown parameter. An estimate of it will be derived in equation 2.4.71.

$\text{Var}(\hat{\beta}_0)$ can now be defined. As before, $E(\hat{\beta}_0) = \beta_0$ because the OLS estimator $\hat{\beta}_0$ is unbiased (from equation 2.4.16), and thus:

$$\begin{aligned}\text{var}(\hat{\beta}_0) &= E\{[\hat{\beta}_0 - E(\hat{\beta}_0)]^2\} \\ &= E[(\hat{\beta}_0 - \beta_0)^2]\end{aligned}$$

By using equation 2.4.15,

$$(\hat{\beta}_0 - \beta_0) = \Sigma\left(\frac{1}{N} - \bar{X}W_i\right)U_i \qquad \textbf{2.4.31}$$

Therefore,

$$\begin{aligned}\text{var}(\hat{\beta}_0) = E[(\hat{\beta}_0 - \beta_0)^2] &= E\left\{\left[\Sigma\left(\frac{1}{N} - \bar{X}W_i\right)U_i\right]^2\right\} \\ &= \Sigma\left(\frac{1}{N} - \bar{X}W_i\right)^2 E(U_i^2)\end{aligned}$$

Thus,

$$\begin{aligned}\text{var}(\hat{\beta}_0) &= \sigma_u^2\left[\Sigma\left(\frac{1}{N} - \bar{X}W_i\right)^2\right] \\ &= \sigma_u^2\left(\frac{1}{N} - \frac{2\bar{X}}{N}\Sigma W_i + \bar{X}^2\Sigma W_i^2\right)\end{aligned} \qquad \textbf{2.4.32}$$

Recalling that $\Sigma W_i = 0$ and that $\Sigma W_i^2 = 1/\Sigma x_i^2$,

$$\text{var}(\hat{\beta}_0) = \sigma_u^2\left(\frac{1}{N} + \frac{\bar{X}^2}{\Sigma x_i^2}\right) \qquad \textbf{2.4.33}$$

Combining the two numerator terms with a common denominator,

$$\begin{aligned}\text{var}(\hat{\beta}_0) &= \sigma_u^2\left[\frac{(\Sigma x_i^2 + N\bar{X}^2)}{N\Sigma x_i^2}\right] \\ &= \sigma_u^2\left[\frac{\Sigma(X_i - \bar{X})^2 + N\bar{X}^2}{N\Sigma x_i^2}\right]\end{aligned}$$

since $x_i = (X_i - \bar{X})$. Hence,

$$\text{var}(\hat{\beta}_0) = \sigma_u^2\left(\frac{\Sigma X_i^2 - N\bar{X}^2 + N\bar{X}^2}{N\Sigma x_i^2}\right)$$

since $\Sigma(X_i - \bar{X})^2 = \Sigma X_i^2 - N\bar{X}^2$. Therefore,

$$\text{var}(\hat{\beta}_0) = \sigma_u^2\left(\frac{\Sigma X_i^2}{N\Sigma x_i^2}\right) \qquad \textbf{2.4.34}$$

In the general K-variable case, the variance of $\hat{\beta}_K$ can be obtained as follows. Recall the equation for the OLS estimator $\hat{\boldsymbol{\beta}}$ in the K-variable case in equation 2.3.22:

$$\hat{\boldsymbol{\beta}} = (\mathbf{X}'\mathbf{X})^{-1}\mathbf{X}'\mathbf{Y}$$

Substituting for **Y** from the compact matrix expression for basic equation 2.3.15, $\mathbf{Y} = \mathbf{X}\boldsymbol{\beta} + \mathbf{U}$,

$$\begin{aligned}\hat{\boldsymbol{\beta}} &= (\mathbf{X}'\mathbf{X})^{-1}\mathbf{X}'(\mathbf{X}\boldsymbol{\beta} + \mathbf{U}) \\ &= (\mathbf{X}'\mathbf{X})^{-1}\mathbf{X}'\mathbf{X}\boldsymbol{\beta} + (\mathbf{X}'\mathbf{X})^{-1}\mathbf{X}'\mathbf{U} \qquad \textbf{2.4.35} \\ &= \boldsymbol{\beta} + (\mathbf{X}'\mathbf{X})^{-1}\mathbf{X}'\mathbf{U}\end{aligned}$$

since $(\mathbf{X}'\mathbf{X})^{-1}(\mathbf{X}'\mathbf{X}) = \mathbf{I}$. Therefore, taking expected values,[10]

$$\begin{aligned}E(\hat{\boldsymbol{\beta}}) &= \boldsymbol{\beta} + E[(\mathbf{X}'\mathbf{X})^{-1}\mathbf{X}'\mathbf{U}] \\ &= \boldsymbol{\beta} + (\mathbf{X}'\mathbf{X})^{-1}\mathbf{X}'E(\mathbf{U})\end{aligned}$$

Since **X** is by assumption a fixed set of numbers and since $E(\mathbf{U})$ is by assumption zero,

$$E(\hat{\boldsymbol{\beta}}) = \boldsymbol{\beta} \qquad \textbf{2.4.36}$$

Thus $\hat{\boldsymbol{\beta}}$ is an unbiased estimator of $\boldsymbol{\beta}$.

Note that using the above results,

$$\hat{\boldsymbol{\beta}} - E(\hat{\boldsymbol{\beta}}) = (\hat{\boldsymbol{\beta}} - \boldsymbol{\beta}) = (\mathbf{X}'\mathbf{X})^{-1}\mathbf{X}'\mathbf{U} \qquad \textbf{2.4.37}$$

To obtain the variance of the estimated parameters, the following manipulation is carried out:

$$\begin{aligned}\text{var}(\hat{\boldsymbol{\beta}}) &= E[(\hat{\boldsymbol{\beta}} - \boldsymbol{\beta})\,(\hat{\boldsymbol{\beta}} - \boldsymbol{\beta})'] \\ &= E\{[(\mathbf{X}'\mathbf{X})^{-1}\mathbf{X}'\mathbf{U}]\,[(\mathbf{X}'\mathbf{X})^{-1}\mathbf{X}'\mathbf{U}]'\} \\ &= E[(\mathbf{X}'\mathbf{X})^{-1}\mathbf{X}'\mathbf{U}\mathbf{U}'\mathbf{X}(\mathbf{X}'\mathbf{X})^{-1}] \qquad \textbf{2.4.38} \\ &= (\mathbf{X}'\mathbf{X})^{-1}\mathbf{X}'E(\mathbf{U}\mathbf{U}')\mathbf{X}(\mathbf{X}'\mathbf{X})^{-1} \\ &= \sigma_u^2(\mathbf{X}'\mathbf{X})^{-1}(\mathbf{X}'\mathbf{X})\,(\mathbf{X}'\mathbf{X})^{-1}\end{aligned}$$

---

[10] The expected value of the vector $\hat{\boldsymbol{\beta}}$ is the vector of the expected values of its components:

$$E(\hat{\boldsymbol{\beta}}) = \begin{bmatrix} E(\hat{\beta}_1) \\ E(\hat{\beta}_2) \\ \cdot \\ \cdot \\ \cdot \\ E(\hat{\beta}_K) \end{bmatrix}$$

Since $E(\mathbf{UU'}) = \sigma_u^2\mathbf{I}$ by assumption 2.2.10,

$$\begin{aligned} \text{var}(\hat{\boldsymbol{\beta}}) &= (\mathbf{X'X})^{-1}E(\mathbf{UU'}) \\ &= \sigma_u^2(\mathbf{X'X})^{-1} \end{aligned} \qquad \textbf{2.4.39}$$

The OLS Estimates Have the Smallest Variance

Now that the concept of variance has been developed, it remains to be shown that the OLS estimates have the smallest variance of all estimators in the class of linear unbiased estimators. One way this can be shown is by demonstrating that no other linear unbiased estimator has a smaller variance.

From equation 2.4.2,

$$\hat{\beta}_1 = \Sigma W_i Y_i$$

Consider any other linear unbiased estimator:

$$\hat{\beta}_1^* = \Sigma D_i Y_i \qquad \textbf{2.4.40}$$

where:

$$D_i = W_i + V_i \qquad \textbf{2.4.41}$$

V_i being an arbitrary set of weights.

The basic model is, as before,

$$Y_i = \beta_0 + \beta_1 X_i + U_i$$

Therefore, substituting for Y_i,

$$\begin{aligned} \hat{\beta}_1^* &= \Sigma D_i(\beta_0 + \beta_1 X_i + U_i) \\ &= \beta_0 \Sigma D_i + \beta_1 \Sigma X_i D_i + \Sigma U_i D_i \end{aligned}$$

Taking the expected value of both sides of the equation,

$$\begin{aligned} E(\hat{\beta}_1^*) &= \beta_0 \Sigma D_i + \beta_1 \Sigma X_i D_i + \Sigma_i D_i E(U_i) \\ &= \beta_0 \Sigma D_i + \beta_1 \Sigma X_i D_i \end{aligned} \qquad \textbf{2.4.42}$$

since $E(U_i) = 0$. $E(\hat{\beta}_1^*) = \beta_1$ if $\Sigma D_i = 0$ and $\Sigma D_i X_i = 1$.

From equation 2.4.41, $D_i = W_i + V_i$. Therefore,

$$\Sigma D_i = \Sigma W_i + \Sigma V_i \qquad \textbf{2.4.43}$$

For $\hat{\beta}_1^*$ to be an unbiased estimator of β_1, the V_i's must fulfill certain restrictions:

$$\begin{aligned} \Sigma D_i &= \Sigma W_i + \Sigma V_i \\ &= 0 + \Sigma V_i \end{aligned}$$

Because $\Sigma W_i = 0$ from equation 2.4.10, notice that:

$$\Sigma D_i = 0 \text{ if and only if } \Sigma V_i = 0 \qquad \mathbf{2.4.44}$$

Similarly,

$$\begin{aligned} \Sigma D_i X_i &= \Sigma W_i X_i + \Sigma V_i X_i \\ &= 1 + \Sigma V_i X_i \end{aligned}$$

Since from equation 2.4.11, $\Sigma W_i X_i = 1$,

$$\Sigma D_i X_i = 1 \text{ if and only if } \Sigma V_i X_i = 0 \qquad \mathbf{2.4.45}$$

We wish to show that $\text{var}(\hat{\beta}_1^*)$ is no smaller than $\text{var}(\hat{\beta}_1)$. Following equations 2.4.25 and 2.4.26,

$$\begin{aligned} \text{var}(\hat{\beta}_1^*) &= E[\Sigma D_i U_i)^2] \\ &= \sigma_u^2 \Sigma D_i^2 \end{aligned} \qquad \mathbf{2.4.46}$$

Using equation 2.4.43,

$$\begin{aligned} \Sigma D_i^2 &= \Sigma (W_i + V_i)^2 \\ &= \Sigma W_i^2 + \Sigma V_i^2 + 2\Sigma W_i V_i \end{aligned} \qquad \mathbf{2.4.47}$$

$\Sigma W_i V_i = 0$, by the following argument: using $W_i = \dfrac{x_i}{\Sigma x_i^2}$, we can obtain the following result, since the numerator $\Sigma V_i x_i$ is zero:

$$\Sigma W_i V_i = \frac{\Sigma x_i V_i}{\Sigma x_i^2} = 0$$

Note that from equation 2.4.45, $\Sigma V_i X_i = 0$; and $\Sigma V_i = 0$ from equation 2.4.44. Therefore, when $x_i = (X_i - \bar{X})$,

$$\Sigma V_i x_i = \Sigma V_i X_i - \bar{X} \Sigma V_i = \Sigma V_i X_i = 0$$

Thus,

$$\Sigma D_i^2 = \Sigma W_i^2 + \Sigma V_i^2 \qquad \mathbf{2.4.48}$$

We have:

$$\text{var}(\hat{\beta}_1^*) = \sigma_u^2 (\Sigma W_i^2 + \Sigma V_i^2) \qquad \mathbf{2.4.49}$$

Recall equation 2.4.28:

$$\text{var}(\hat{\beta}_1) = \sigma_u^2 \Sigma W_i^2$$

We rewrite:

$$\text{var}(\hat{\beta}_1^*) = \text{var}(\hat{\beta}_1) + \sigma_u^2 \Sigma V_i^2 \qquad \textbf{2.4.50}$$

$\Sigma V_i^2 \geq 0$, since every term is nonnegative.

$$\therefore \text{var}(\hat{\beta}_1^*) \geq \text{var } \hat{\beta}_1 \qquad \textbf{2.4.51}$$

Thus it is established that the estimated parameter $\hat{\beta}_1^*$, or for that matter any other linear unbiased estimator, has a variance no smaller than the variance of $\hat{\beta}_1$. In other words $\text{var}(\hat{\beta}_1)$ is the smallest in the class of linear estimates. (No attempt is made here to develop the argument in terms of the K-variable case.)

A Direct Proof of the Minimum Variance

That the OLS estimators have minimum variance can also be proved more directly by using Lagrange multipliers. This will be shown in terms of $\hat{\beta}_1$ in the two-variable model.

Recall from equation 2.4.2 that $\hat{\beta}_1 = \Sigma W_i Y_i$. Also from equation 2.4.14, $E(\hat{\beta}_1) = \beta_1$ when, as shown in equations 2.4.10 and 2.4.11,

$$\Sigma W_i = 0$$

$$\Sigma W_i X_i = \Sigma W_i x_i = 1$$

We can write:

$$\text{var}(\hat{\beta}_1) = \text{var}(\Sigma W_i Y_i) \qquad \textbf{2.4.52}$$

$$\begin{aligned} \text{var}(\Sigma W_i Y_i) &= \Sigma W_i^2 \text{ var}(Y_i) \\ &= (\Sigma W_i^2)\sigma_u^2 \end{aligned} \qquad \textbf{2.4.53}$$

The result, equation 2.4.53, assumes that the Y_i's are independent and random with finite and constant variance.

$$\text{var}(Y_i) = E\{[Y_i - E(Y_i)]^2\} \qquad \textbf{2.4.54}$$

Given the model,

$$Y_i = \beta_0 + \beta_1 X_i + U_i$$

$$E(Y_i) = E(\beta_0) + E(\beta_1)X_i + E(U_i)$$

we know that $E(\beta_0) = \beta_0$ and $E(\beta_1) = \beta_1$; and β_0 and β_1 are assumed independent. We have also assumed that $E(U_i) = 0$ and $E(X_i U_i) = 0$ since X_i is a fixed mathematical variable. Therefore we can write:

$$E(Y_i) = \beta_0 + \beta_1 X_i \qquad \textbf{2.4.55}$$

from which:

$$\begin{aligned} \text{var}(Y_i) &= E[(Y_i - \beta_0 - \beta_1 X_i)^2] \\ &= E(U_i^2) \qquad \textbf{2.4.56} \\ &= \sigma_u^2 = \text{var}(U_i) \end{aligned}$$

Note that the dependent variable Y_i and the disturbance term U_i have the same variance σ_u^2. But their means are not the same.

$$E(U_i) = 0$$

and following equation 2.4.55,

$$E(Y_i) = \beta_0 + \beta_1 X_i$$

Thus the distribution of U_i is given by zero mean and finite and constant variance σ_u^2. The dependent variable Y_i has the same distribution with mean $\beta_0 + \beta_1 X_i$ and the same variance σ_u^2.

Using the results $E(\hat{\beta}_0) = \beta_0$ and $E(\hat{\beta}_1) = \beta_1$, we can also write:

$$E(Y_i) = E(\hat{\beta}_0) + E(\hat{\beta}_1)X_i \qquad \textbf{2.4.57}$$

Refer to equation 2.4.53; and since σ_u^2 is finite and constant, we need to minimize:

$$(\Sigma W_i^2) \qquad \textbf{2.4.58}$$

subject to constraints 2.4.10 and 2.4.11. We can then set up the following Lagrange function:

$$\begin{aligned} f(W_1, W_2, \ldots, W_N, \lambda_1, \lambda_2) = \Sigma W_i^2 &- \lambda_1 (\Sigma W_i) \\ &- \lambda_2 (\Sigma W_i x_i - 1) \end{aligned} \qquad \textbf{2.4.59}$$

where λ_1 and λ_2 are the Lagrange multipliers. Taking partial derivatives with respect to all the W_i's, λ_1, and λ_2 and setting them equal to zero, we obtain the following results:

$$\frac{\partial f}{\partial W_i} = 0, \quad i = 1, 2, \ldots, N$$

$$2W_i - \lambda_1 - \lambda_2 x_i = 0$$

or,

$$W_i = \frac{\lambda_1}{2} + \frac{\lambda_2}{2} x_i \qquad \textbf{2.4.60}$$

$$\frac{\partial f}{\partial \lambda_1} = 0, \ \Sigma W_i = 0 \qquad \textbf{2.4.61}$$

$$\frac{\partial f}{\partial \lambda_2} = 0, \ \Sigma W_i x_i = 1 \qquad \textbf{2.4.62}$$

Equations 2.4.61 and 2.4.62 are the given constraints. Substituting equation 2.4.60 into equation 2.4.61, we solve for λ_1:

$$\Sigma\left(\frac{\lambda_1}{2} + \frac{\lambda_2}{2}\, x_i\right) = 0 \qquad \textbf{2.4.63}$$

Since $\Sigma x_i = \Sigma(X_i - \bar{X}) = 0$, we can rewrite equation 2.4.63:

$$\begin{aligned} \Sigma\frac{\lambda_1}{2} &= 0 \\ \lambda_1 &= 0 \end{aligned} \qquad \textbf{2.4.64}$$

Substituting equation 2.4.60 into equation 2.4.62, we obtain the following solution for λ_2:

$$\Sigma\left(\frac{\lambda_1}{2} + \frac{\lambda_2}{2} x_i\right) x_i = 1$$

or,

$$\frac{\lambda_1}{2}\Sigma x_i + \frac{\lambda_2}{2}\Sigma x_i^2 = 1 \qquad \textbf{2.4.65}$$

Again, since $\Sigma x_i = 0$,

$$\begin{aligned} \frac{\lambda_2}{2}\Sigma x_i^2 &= 1 \\ \lambda_2 &= \frac{2}{\Sigma x_i^2} \end{aligned} \qquad \textbf{2.4.66}$$

Substituting equations 2.4.64 and 2.4.66 back into equation 2.4.60, we solve for W_i:

$$\begin{aligned} W_i &= 0 + \frac{2}{\Sigma x_i^2}\,\frac{1}{2}\, x_i \\ &= \frac{x_i}{\Sigma x_i^2} \end{aligned} \qquad \textbf{2.4.67}$$

Therefore,

$$\hat{\beta}_1 = \Sigma W_i Y_i$$

which is the OLS estimator. Thus the unbiased linear estimator of β_1 with minimum variance is the OLS estimator.

Mean Square Error

It has been shown that OLS estimators are unbiased and that they have the least variance of all linear estimators, and these two properties help prove that they are also *minimum mean square error estimators*.

The mean square error of an estimator $\hat{\beta}$ for a parameter β is defined as follows:

$$\text{MSE}(\hat{\beta}) = E[(\hat{\beta} - \beta)^2] \tag{2.4.68}$$

Adding and subtracting $E(\hat{\beta})$ inside the brackets,

$$\begin{aligned}\text{MSE}(\hat{\beta}) &= E\big(\{[\hat{\beta} - E(\hat{\beta})] + [E(\hat{\beta}) - \beta]\}^2\big)\\ &= E\{[\hat{\beta} - E(\hat{\beta})]^2 + [E(\hat{\beta}) - \beta]^2\\ &\qquad + 2[\hat{\beta} - E(\hat{\beta})]\,[E(\hat{\beta}) - \beta]\} \qquad \textbf{2.4.69}\\ &= E\{[\hat{\beta} - E(\hat{\beta})]^2\} + E\{[E(\hat{\beta}) - \beta]^2\}\\ &\qquad + 2\{[E(\hat{\beta}) - E(\hat{\beta})]\,[E(\hat{\beta}) - \beta]\}\end{aligned}$$

The last term on the right is zero because it contains a zero factor. The first term is the definition of the variance of the $\hat{\beta}$. The second term is the definition of the bias of the estimate $\hat{\beta}$. Thus,

$$\text{MSE }(\hat{\beta}) = \text{var}(\hat{\beta}) + (\text{bias } \hat{\beta})^2 \tag{2.4.70}$$

The OLS estimator $\hat{\beta}$ has zero bias and minimum variance of linear estimators. Thus it has minimum mean square error.

The implication of the equation expressing the mean square error as the sum of variance and the square of the bias is that neither minimum variance nor minimum (zero) bias is absolutely preferred by itself. Clearly the most desirable property of an estimator is that its calculated value be as close as possible to the true value of the parameter being estimated. Thus an estimator with small variance and small bias may give a parameter value closer to the true value than will an unbiased estimator with a large variance.

Notice that in general we cannot obtain an estimate of the MSE of an estimator because the true value of the parameter is unknown. We can estimate the MSE only when the statistical characteristics are known, as they were in the proof above by our assumptions on the U_i terms and the fixed character of the X_i's.

Estimating the Variance

The variance of the OLS estimators has been defined in terms of σ_u^2. For estimating σ_u^2, residuals computed from regression analysis are used. The OLS estimator of σ_u^2 is given by:

$$\hat{\sigma}_u^2 = \frac{\Sigma s_i^2}{N - K - 1} \tag{2.4.71}$$

where s_i = i^{th} residual computed from the regression

K = number of parameters estimated (one for the constant term β_0)

Consider model 2.1.1 with a single independent variable and two parameters to be estimated. Note that U_i in the model refers to the true disturbance term.

$$Y_i = \beta_0 + \beta_1 X_i + U_i$$
$$\bar{Y} = \beta_0 + \beta_1 \bar{X} + \bar{U}$$

Subtracting,

$$\begin{aligned}(Y_i - \bar{Y}) &= \beta_1(X_i - \bar{X}) + (U_i - \bar{U}) \\ y_i &= \beta_1 x_i + (U_i - \bar{U})\end{aligned} \qquad \textbf{2.4.72}$$

From the definition of computed residual,

$$\hat{U}_1 = Y_i - \hat{\beta}_0 - \hat{\beta}_1 X_i$$

Therefore,

$$\frac{1}{N}\Sigma\hat{U}_i = \frac{1}{N}\Sigma(Y_i - \hat{\beta}_0 - \hat{\beta}_1 X_i)$$

or,

$$0 = \bar{Y} - \hat{\beta}_0 - \hat{\beta}_1 \bar{X}$$

since the sum of the residuals from least squares regression is equal to zero. Therefore, by subtraction,

$$(\hat{U}_i - 0) = (Y_i - \bar{Y}) - \hat{\beta}_1(X_i - \bar{X}) \qquad \textbf{2.4.73}$$

Defining $s_i = (\hat{U}_i - 0) = \hat{u}_i$ in terms of least squares residuals, $y_i = (Y_i - \bar{Y})$ and $x_i = (X_i - \bar{X})$ as before, we can write:

$$s_i = y_i - \hat{\beta}_1 x_i \qquad \textbf{2.4.74}$$

Substituting for y_i from equation 2.4.72 into equation 2.4.74,

$$\begin{aligned}s_i &= \beta_1 x_i + (U_i - \bar{U}) - \hat{\beta}_1 x_i \\ &= -(\hat{\beta}_1 - \beta_1)x_i + (U_i - \bar{U})\end{aligned} \qquad \textbf{2.4.75}$$

We want to obtain an unbiased estimator of σ_u^2 so that $E(\hat{\sigma}_u^2) = \sigma_v^2$. Squaring, summing over all N terms, and taking the expected value,

$$\begin{aligned}E(\Sigma s_i^2) = E[(\hat{\beta}_1 - \beta_1)^2\, \Sigma x_i^2 &+ \Sigma(U_i - \bar{U})^2 \\ &- 2(\hat{\beta}_1 - \beta_1)\, \Sigma x_i\, (U_i - \bar{U})]\end{aligned} \qquad \textbf{2.4.76}$$

For convenience consider the right-hand side of equation 2.4.76 term by term. We can calculate the first term as:

$$E[(\hat{\beta}_1 - \beta_1)^2\, \Sigma x_i^2] = \sigma_u^2$$

since, following equations 2.4.23 through 2.4.30,

$$E(\hat{\beta}_1 - \beta_1)^2 = \sigma_u^2 \frac{1}{\Sigma x_i^2}$$

For the next term we have:

$$E[\Sigma(U_i - \bar{U})^2] = E(\Sigma U_i^2 - 2\bar{U}\Sigma U_i + N\bar{U}^2)$$

$$= E\left[\Sigma U_i^2 - \frac{2(\Sigma U_i^2)}{N} + \frac{(\Sigma U_i^2)}{N}\right]$$

$$= E\left[\Sigma U_i^2 - \frac{1}{N}(\Sigma U_i^2)\right]$$

$$= \Sigma E(U_i^2) - \frac{1}{N}[\Sigma E(U_i^2)]$$

$$= (N - 1)\sigma_u^2$$

The last term on the right in equation 2.4.76 is $E[(\hat{\beta}_1 - \beta_1)\,\Sigma x_i(U_i - \bar{U})]$. From equation 2.4.12, $(\hat{\beta}_1 - \beta_1) = \Sigma W_i U_i$. Thus,

$$E(\hat{\beta}_1 - \beta_1)\,\Sigma x_i(U_i - \bar{U}) = E[\Sigma W_i U_i\,\Sigma x_i(U_i - \bar{U})]$$

$$= E\left[\frac{\Sigma U_i x_i}{\Sigma x_i^2}(\Sigma U_i x_i - \bar{U}\Sigma x_i)\right]$$

The second term inside the bracket is $\left(\frac{\bar{U}\Sigma x_i}{\Sigma x_i^2}\right)$ Since $W_i = \frac{x_i}{\Sigma x_i^2}$ and $\Sigma W_i = 0$,

$$-\left(\frac{\bar{U}\Sigma x_i}{\Sigma x_i^2}\right) = -\,\bar{U}\Sigma W_i = 0$$

Substituting this result above,

$$E(\hat{\beta}_1 - \beta_1)\,\Sigma x_i(U_i - \bar{U}) = E\left[\frac{\Sigma U_i x_i}{\Sigma x_i^2}\,(\Sigma U_i x_i)\right]$$

$$= E\left[\frac{(\Sigma U_i x_i)^2}{\Sigma x_i^2}\right]$$

Expanding the numerator for an illustrative case where $i = (1, 2)$,

$$\left(\sum_{i=1}^{2} U_i x_i\right)^2 = U_1^2 x_1^2 + U_2^2 x_2^2 + 2U_1 x_1 U_2 x_2$$

$$= \sum_{i=1}^{2} (U_i^2)\,x_i^2 + 2U_1 x_1 U_2 x_2$$

Taking expected values and noting that $E(U_1x_1U_2x_2) = x_1x_2E(U_1U_2)$, this expression becomes:

$$E\left(\sum_{i=1}^{2} U_ix_i\right) = \Sigma E(U_i^2)\, x_i^2$$
$$= \sigma_u^2 \Sigma x_i^2$$

since $E(U_iU_j) = 0$ for $i \neq j$ (from equation 2.2.2), and $E(U_iU_j) = \sigma_u^2$ for $i = j$ (from equation 2.2.3). The third term on the right side of equation 2.4.76 can then be written:

$$E(\hat{\beta}_1 - \beta_1)\, \Sigma x_i(U_i - \bar{U}) = \sigma_u^2 \frac{\Sigma x_i^2}{\Sigma x_i^2} = \sigma_u^2$$

Substituting these results into equation 2.4.76,

$$\begin{aligned} E(\Sigma s_i^2) &= \sigma_u^2 + (N - 1)\sigma_u^2 - 2\sigma_u^2 \\ &= (N - 2)\, \sigma_u^2 \end{aligned} \qquad 2.4.77$$

From equation 2.4.77 we take as the estimator for σ_u^2 :

$$\hat{\sigma}_u^2 = \frac{1}{N - 2} \Sigma s_i^2 \qquad 2.4.78$$

The argument above shows that $E(\hat{\sigma}_u^2) = \sigma_u^2$, and this estimator of σ_u^2 is unbiased. In the case of a multiple regression model for which we wish to estimate K parameters in a K-variable model, the estimator derived above can be generalized to yield equation 2.4.71.[11] In matrix notation,

$$\hat{\sigma}_u^2 = \frac{\hat{\mathbf{U}}\hat{\mathbf{U}}'}{N - K - 1} \qquad 2.4.79$$

where:

$$\hat{\mathbf{U}} = \mathbf{Y} - \mathbf{X}\hat{\boldsymbol{\beta}}$$

The *estimated standard deviation* of the error term U is denoted $\hat{\sigma}_u$ and is calculated for both the bivariate and the multivariate regression models as:

$$\hat{\sigma}_u = \sqrt{\hat{\sigma}_u^2} \qquad 2.4.80$$

[11] Note that the intercept β_0 must be counted as an independent parameter, and it should be estimated before residuals are calculated for estimating $\hat{\sigma}_u^2$ with equation 2.4.78.

DISCUSSION QUESTIONS

1. Briefly review the framework of the OLS regression model. Derive the normal equations in a two-variable case.

2.

y	x
5	7
3	8
2	10
1	7
9	8

where $y = (Y_i - \bar{Y})$ and $x = (X_i - \bar{X})$

(a) Given the above data and the model $y_i = \beta x_i$, use the appropriate formula to estimate $\hat{\beta}$.

(b) Compute $\hat{\sigma}^2$ and var($\hat{\beta}$) using the appropriate formula.

(c) Can the intercept of the function be estimated from the given information?

(d) If observations of variable X are always on $\bar{X}$, define $\hat{\beta}$.

3. Use the data to estimate the regression $Y_t = \beta_0 + \beta_1 X_t$.

PERSONAL CONSUMPTION EXPENDITURES AND DISPOSABLE INCOME, 1950-1969
(in billions of 1958 dollars)

Year	Y = Personal Consumption	X = Disposable Income
1950	230.5	249.6
1951	232.8	255.7
1952	239.4	263.3
1953	250.8	275.4
1954	255.7	278.3
1955	274.2	296.7
1956	281.4	309.3
1957	288.2	315.8
1958	290.1	318.8
1959	307.3	333.0
1960	316.1	340.2
1961	322.5	350.7
1962	338.4	367.3
1963	353.3	381.3
1964	373.7	407.9
1965	397.7	435.0
1966	418.1	458.9
1967	430.3	477.7
1968	452.6	497.6
1969	466.0	509.4

4. Given the following:

Y	X
3	19
5	17
7	3

and $Y_i = \beta_0 + \beta_1 X_i$

(a) Compute ΣY_iX_i, ΣY_i, ΣX_i, ΣX_i^2, and $(\Sigma X_i)^2$.

(b) Estimate $\hat{\beta}_1 = \dfrac{N\Sigma Y_iX_i - \Sigma X_i\Sigma Y_i}{N\Sigma X_i^2 - (\Sigma X_i)^2}$

(c) Estimate $\hat{\beta}_0$ by using equation 2.1.13.

(d) Compare the estimate of $\hat{\beta}_0$ with that of (c) above by using $\hat{\beta}_0 = \bar{Y} - \hat{\beta}_1\bar{X}$.

(e) Draw a diagram to show that the means of both variables lie on the regression line.

5. In a stochastic relationship the assumption $E(X_iU_i) = 0$ postulates a unique direction of functional dependence. Explain.

6. Show that in a multiple regression model,

$$\hat{\boldsymbol{\beta}} = (\mathbf{X}'\mathbf{X})^{-1}\mathbf{X}'\mathbf{Y}$$

and

$$\text{var}(\hat{\boldsymbol{\beta}}) = \sigma_u^2\,(\mathbf{X}'\mathbf{X})^{-1}$$

7.

Y	X_1	X_2
3	7	5
7	11	3
5	8	9
9	10	3

Given the model $Y = \beta_0 + \beta_1X_1 + \beta_2X_2$, estimate β_0, β_1, and β_2 and their respective variances.

8. Estimate the model: $Y_t = \beta_0 + \beta_1X_{t1} + \beta_2X_{t2}$

Y	X_1	X_2	Y	X_1	X_2
50.5	52.8	37.8	43.0	45.6	45.4
52.0	57.0	39.0	42.4	44.5	41.7
57.8	66.1	42.7	47.7	51.0	46.0
60.9	66.7	44.5	52.2	56.3	49.9
63.0	70.6	48.3	59.1	65.2	55.1
66.3	73.2	50.6	62.5	69.2	57.3
66.0	73.5	52.2	58.5	62.9	56.6
68.8	75.4	54.7	61.7	67.7	60.9
70.8	79.6	55.2	65.7	72.9	67.0
64.9	70.7	54.4	74.6	88.7	74.2
54.2	59.6	52.9			

9. Review the appropriate rank condition of the $\mathbf{X}$ matrix in a multiple regression model.

10. Enumerate the assumptions made in a usual regression model on the true disturbance terms.

11. Show that the regressand Y_i and the disturbance term U_i have the same variance but different means.

12. Show that the OLS estimates are best, linear, and unbiased. Specify the assumptions you need to make with respect to the disturbance terms in proving each of the properties of the OLS estimates.

13. Show that $E(\hat{\sigma}_u^2) = \sigma_u^2 = \frac{1}{N - K - 1}\Sigma s_i^2$

14. Examine: $E(X_iU_i) = \text{cov}(X_iU_i) = 0$, when X_i is a "fixed" exogenous variable. Show that the OLS estimate is consistent when this assumption is valid. (Hint) Recall the result:

$$\hat{\beta} = \beta + \Sigma W_i U_i$$

$$= \beta + \frac{\Sigma x_i u_i}{\Sigma x_i^2}$$

$$\text{since } W_i = \frac{x_i}{\Sigma x_i^2}$$

To prove consistency, take the probability limit and write:

$$\text{Plim }(\hat{\beta}) = \beta + \text{Plim}\left(\frac{\Sigma x_i u_i}{\Sigma x_i^2}\right)$$

This can be written as:

$$\text{Plim }(\hat{\beta}) = \beta + \frac{\text{Plim }(\Sigma x_i u_i)/T}{\text{Plim }(\Sigma x_i^2)/T}$$

Plim $(\Sigma x_i u_i)/T$ is a consistent estimator of $\text{cov}(X_iU_i)$, and Plim $(\Sigma x_i^2)/T$ is a consistent estimator of $\text{var}(X_i)$. The above is true if, as is assumed, the numerator is zero and the denominator is finite and nonzero. Since Plim $(\hat{\beta}) = \beta$, the OLS $\hat{\beta}$ is seen to be consistent.

SUGGESTED READINGS

Anderson, R. L., and T. A. Bancroft. *Statistical Theory in Research.* New York: McGraw-Hill Book Co., 1952.

Dhrymes, Phoebus J. *Econometrics: Statistical Foundations and Applications.* New York: Harper & Row, Publishers, 1970.

Ezekiel, M., and K. A. Fox. *Methods of Correlation and Regression Analysis: Linear and Curvilinear,* 3d ed. New York: John Wiley & Sons, 1959.

Goldberger, Arthur S. *Topics in Regression Analysis.* New York: Macmillan Co., 1968.

Goldberger, A. S. *Econometric Theory.* New York: John Wiley & Sons, 1964.

Graybill, F. A. *An Introduction to Linear Statistical Models.* Vol. 1. New York: McGraw-Hill Book Co., 1961.

Huang, David S. *Regression and Econometric Methods.* New York: John Wiley & Sons, 1970.

Johnston, J. *Econometric Methods,* 2d ed. New York: McGraw-Hill Book Co., 1972.

Kmenta, Jan. *Elements of Econometrics.* New York: Macmillan Co., 1971.

Malinvaud, E. *Statistical Methods of Econometrics.* Amsterdam: North-Holland Publishing Co., 1966.

Theil, H. *Principles of Econometrics.* New York: John Wiley & Sons, 1971.

Thomas, James J. *Notes on the Theory of Multiple Regression.* Athens, Greece: Center of Economic Research, 1964.

Wold, Herman O. A., and Lars Juréen. *Demand Analysis; A Study in Econometrics.* New York: John Wiley & Sons, 1953.

Wonnacott, Ronald J., and Thomas H. Wonnacott. *Econometrics.* New York: John Wiley & Sons, 1970.

Yule, G. U., and M. G. Kendall. *An Introduction to the Theory of Statistics,* 14th ed. London: Charles Griffin & Co., 1950.

3

regression and correlation models (II)

3.0 SOME FURTHER RESULTS OF REGRESSION ANALYSIS: THE ADDITIONAL ASSUMPTION OF NORMAL DISTRIBUTION OF U_i

In the course of the discussion so far, we have seen how the assumptions on the statistical characteristics of the disturbances are necessary for the OLS properties. These assumptions are: $E(U_i) = 0$; $E(U_iU_j) = 0, i \neq j$; $E(U_iU_j) = \sigma_u^2, i = j$; and $E(U_iX_i) = 0$. Each of these assumptions was used extensively in obtaining unbiased and efficient estimators in the regression model. Also, we used the assumption on the mutual linear independence of the independent variables when there is more than one independent variable in the regression model.

If we assume that the disturbance terms U_i have a normal distribution, certain further results can be deduced. Note that the estimators $\hat{\beta}_k$ obtained by the OLS regression method are *point estimators*. Their specific numerical values estimated from the sample data are given with no indication of a margin of error in the estimates. It would be preferable to be able to determine *confidence intervals* for the estimated parameters and to have the results of *significance tests* for the estimates. Then we could state that, given the size of the sample, the true value of the estimated parameter falls within an error band on either side of the estimated value at some confidence level, say, 95 times out of 100 experiments. Specification of this error band minimizes the chances of the estimates being totally wrong. Fortunately there exists statistical theory on which we can draw for the estimation of confidence intervals and for significance tests on the estimated parameters.

To do this the assumption of normality for the distribution of the disturbance terms is useful. The assumption of a normal distribution is not as offensive as it may appear. Mathematicians have shown that various other distributions approximate the normal distribution in the limit as the sample grows without bound.

If random samples of N observations are drawn from an infinite normal population with a mean μ and a variance σ^2, written as $\mathcal{N}(\mu, \sigma^2)$, the sample means $\bar{X}_N$ will have a normal distribution with the mean μ and the variance

σ^2/N (variance of the population corrected for the sample size), written as $\mathcal{N}(\mu, \sigma^2/N)$. From statistical theory we know that the random variable $X \sim \mathcal{N}(\mu, \sigma^2)$, that is, a normal distribution with mean μ and variance σ^2, can be transformed into the *standardized normal distribution* having zero mean and unit variance, written as $\mathcal{N}(0,1)$. For the original normally distributed variable X,

$$Z = \frac{X - \mu}{\sigma} \text{ and } Z \sim \mathcal{N}(0, 1) \qquad \textbf{3.0.1}$$

where $\sigma = \sqrt{\sigma^2}$.

If a random variable X has mean μ_x and variance σ_x^2, then the means of successive random samples of size N, $\bar{X}_N$, are approximately normally distributed whether or not X is normally distributed. Thus,

$$Z = \frac{\bar{X}_N - \mu_x}{\sigma_x/\sqrt{N}} \text{ and } Z \sim \mathcal{N}(0, 1) \qquad \textbf{3.0.2}$$

This last result, equation 3.0.2, is quite significant and is based on the central limit theorem. A special case of this theorem states that if one draws a random sample of size N from a population that is not necessarily normally distributed but has a finite variance σ^2 and if one repeats the experiment by randomly drawing samples of N observations from the original population whose distribution remains unspecified as before, the distribution of sample means $\bar{X}_N$'s will have the unique property of approximating the normal distribution as the sample size N increases without bound. Thus for many different distributions of the original population, the population composed of the means of the samples from this population will be normally distributed.[1] One can then use this approximate normal distribution to compute probabilities for the estimated mean, to find the confidence interval for the mean, and to test statistical hypotheses without any knowledge of the distribution of the original population.

If the U_i's are assumed to be normally distributed, the least squares regression parameters which have been shown to be linear functions of the U_i's are themselves normally distributed. Hence the Z transformation, following equation 3.0.1:

$$Z = \frac{(\hat{\beta}_k - \beta_k)}{\sqrt{\text{var}(\beta_k)}} \text{ and } Z \sim \mathcal{N}(0, 1) \qquad \textbf{3.0.3}$$

[1] For a review of alternative distribution theories approximating normal distribution, the central limit theorem, and the Z and t distributions, refer to P. G. Hoel, *Introduction to Mathematical Statistics* (3d ed.; New York: John Wiley & Sons, 1962); A. M. Mood and F. A. Graybill, *Introduction to the Theory of Statistics* (2d ed.; New York: McGraw-Hill Book Co., 1963); and Robert V. Hogg and Allen T. Craig, *Introduction to Mathematical Statistics* (2d ed.; New York: Macmillan Co., 1968).

Note that the estimate of $\hat{\beta}_k$ obtained by least squares is a point estimate, a mean point estimated from a given sample. The assumption of normal distribution of U_i's in a given sample, if it is not large enough, may be unwarranted. However, if the experiments can be repeated, the assumption of an approximate normal distribution of the new population of the estimated means is plausible; and following equation 3.0.2, one can obtain the standard normal Z transformation.

The econometrician generally constructs confidence intervals and applies significance tests based on probabilities calculated on the assumption that the transformation to the standard normal distribution is valid for the case in hand.

In econometrics we do not observe the U_i's; we work with the $\hat{U}_i$'s, residuals computed from the regression lines. We have seen before how estimated variances of the estimated parameters can be calculated from the residuals. Because we must work with the computed residuals and have no way of knowing the true value of σ_u^2 it is convenient to use Student's t distribution instead of the Z distribution.[2] (The t distribution table is included in the Appendix, page 376.) The argument of the t distribution is given by:

$$t = \frac{\bar{X} - \mu_x}{\hat{\sigma}_x/\sqrt{N}} \tag{3.0.4}$$

where $\hat{\sigma}_x/\sqrt{N}$ is the estimate of the standard deviation σ_x. This distribution like the standard normal distribution, is symmetric about a zero mean. The t distribution has been shown to be based on the ratio of the standard normal Z distribution and the square root of the quantity $\hat{\sigma}_x^2/\sigma_x^2$ which has an independent χ^2 distribution with appropriate degrees of freedom. This correction for degrees of freedom makes the use of the t distribution in small sample situations especially attractive.

In terms of var($\hat{\beta}_0$) in equation 2.4.34, var($\hat{\beta}_1$) in equation 2.4.30, and $\hat{\sigma}_u^2$ in equation 2.4.71, the argument of the t distribution is given by the following: For β_0,

$$t = \frac{(\hat{\beta}_0 - \beta_0)\sqrt{N\Sigma x_i^2}}{\hat{\sigma}_u\sqrt{\Sigma X_i^2}} = \frac{(\hat{\beta}_0 - \beta_0)}{\sqrt{\text{var}(\hat{\beta}_0)}} \tag{3.0.5}$$

and for β_1,

$$t = \frac{(\hat{\beta}_1 - \beta_1)\sqrt{\Sigma x_i^2}}{\hat{\sigma}_u} = \frac{(\hat{\beta}_1 - \beta_1)}{\sqrt{\text{var}(\hat{\beta}_1)}} \tag{3.0.6}$$

[2] See Hoel, *op. cit.*; or Mood and Graybill, *op. cit.* For a discussion of the χ^2 distribution also see Chapter 8 of this book.

When the above quantities are calculated, they can be used along with the related degrees of freedom to find the probability that the true values of the parameters β_0 and β_1 lie within the intervals $\pm(\hat{\beta}_0 - \beta_0)$ and $\pm(\hat{\beta}_1 - \beta_1)$.

A commonly used test in econometric research is based on the null hypothesis, the assumption that β_0 or β_1 is equal to zero. We set up the null hypothesis for β_0, H_0: $\beta_0 = 0$, against the alternative H_1: $\beta_0 \neq 0$. For $\beta_0 = 0$,

$$t = \frac{\hat{\beta}_0}{s_{\hat{\beta}_0}} \qquad 3.0.7$$

and for $\beta_1 = 0$,

$$t = \frac{\hat{\beta}_1}{s_{\hat{\beta}_1}} \qquad 3.0.8$$

where $s_{\hat{\beta}_0} = \sqrt{\text{var}(\hat{\beta}_0)}$ and $s_{\hat{\beta}_1} = \sqrt{\text{var}(\hat{\beta}_1)}$. In the t table corresponding to the numerical value of t and the number of degrees of freedom, there is a numerical value of a probability. This value is a measure of the probability that the calculated value of t would have been obtained for the true value of the calculated parameter equal to zero. In the case where we test the assumption that β_0 or β_1 is zero, a very small probability corresponding to the given values of t for $N - K$ degrees of freedom indicates that $\beta_0 \neq 0$ or $\beta_1 \neq 0$ with probability close to unity.[3]

The t test can be extended to the general K-variable case as follows: For β_k,

$$t = \frac{(\hat{\beta}_k - \beta_k)}{\sqrt{\text{var}(\hat{\beta}_k)}} \qquad 3.0.9$$

Therefore, for the hypothesis $\beta_k = 0$,[4]

$$t = \frac{\hat{\beta}_k}{s_{\hat{\beta}_k}} \qquad 3.0.10$$

where $s_{\hat{\beta}_k} = \sqrt{\text{var}(\hat{\beta}_k)}$

Notice that tests could be based on a value of the true parameter other than zero. However, in practice most econometric research reports the t test based on the zero critical value. In some cases the standard deviation of the estimated parameter is reported, and one can make a quick test of significance. For the zero critical value of β_k, the test consists of simply dividing the estimated parameter by its standard deviation. One then reads the probability of the computed t ratio from the t table with $N - K$ degrees of freedom (K equals the number of parameters including the β_0). The

[3] Recall that if p is the probability of an event E, then $1-p$ is the probability of "not E."

[4] $s_{\hat{\beta}_k}$ can be read variously as either standard deviation or sampling error of the estimated parameter $\hat{\beta}_k$.

econometrician feels satisfied if his computed t ratio has a value of 2 or more. An examination of the t table shows that for 95 percent probability the value of t decreases from 2.306($N = 10$, $K = 2$) to 1.96 ($N = \infty$). Thus a value of 2 becomes a benchmark irrespective of the sample size. For the 95 percent probability level, the t value of 2 (or more) is thus taken as a general test to refute the hypothesis that the true value of the parameter is zero. Given the 95 percent level of probability, the estimated parameter is thus considered significant if its value is at least twice the value of its standard deviation. Again, even though it is the usual practice to consider the 95 percent probability level, one could design a test for any level of probability.

The t distribution is symmetric about the zero mean. This enables us to construct confidence intervals for the estimated parameters given the probability level. The steps are as follows: First, choose the desired level of probability and then read the appropriate value from the t table for the chosen level of probability. Next solve the following equation:

$$t \text{ value read from the } t \text{ table} = \text{computed } t \text{ ratio}$$

or

$$t \text{ value read from the table} = \frac{\text{Estimated parameter value} - \text{True parameter value}}{\text{Estimated standard deviation of the estimated parameter}} \qquad \textbf{3.0.11}$$

Next, choosing the 95 percent confidence level for, say, β_k, we find the value of the t ratio with the appropriate correction for degrees of freedom $N - K$:

$$(\text{pr} = 0.95) = \frac{\hat{\beta}_k - \beta_k}{s_{\hat{\beta}_k}} \qquad \textbf{3.0.12}$$

or,

$$\beta_k = \hat{\beta}_k \pm t_{0.025}(s_{\hat{\beta}_k}) \qquad (\text{pr} = 0.95) \qquad \textbf{3.0.13}$$

Then,

$$\text{pr}(-t_{0.025} < t < + t_{0.025}) = 0.95 \qquad \textbf{3.0.14}$$

Substituting,

$$t = \frac{(\hat{\beta}_k - \beta_k)}{s_{\hat{\beta}_k}}$$

we obtain:

$$\text{pr}\left[-t_{0.025} < \frac{(\hat{\beta}_k - \beta_k)}{s_{\hat{\beta}_k}} < +t_{0.025}\right] = 0.95 \qquad \textbf{3.0.15}$$

from which,

$$\text{pr}(\hat{\beta}_k - t_{0.025}\ s_{\hat{\beta}_k} < \beta_k < \hat{\beta}_k + t_{0.025}\ s_{\hat{\beta}_k}) = 0.95 \qquad \textbf{3.0.16}$$

3.1 THE ASSUMPTION OF NORMAL DISTRIBUTION OF U_i FURTHER EXAMINED

The assumption of the normal distribution of U_i leads to the result that the OLS estimators are the same as the *maximum likelihood estimators*.

These estimators maximize the likelihood that the observed samples are generated by the structure with parameters equal to the estimated parameters.[5] Begin with the joint probability density function of U_i written as follows:

$$P(U_1, U_2, \ldots, U_N) = \left(\frac{1}{\sqrt{2\pi\sigma_u^2}}\right)^N \cdot \exp\left[-(\tfrac{1}{2}\,\sigma_u^2)\sum_{i=1}^{N} U_i^2\right] dU_1, dU_2, \ldots, dU_N \qquad \textbf{3.1.1}$$

This can be seen as follows: First, consider the probability density of U_1, which is, when U_1 is drawn randomly from a normal distribution as in equation 1.2.4,

$$P(U_1) = \frac{1}{\sqrt{2\pi\sigma_u^2}} \exp[-(\tfrac{1}{2}\,\sigma_u^2)\,(U_1^2)] \qquad \textbf{3.1.2}$$

Note that the mean of U_1 is assumed to be zero. It is known that the two parameters, mean and variance, specify the above probability density function. Consider the simple model:

$$Y_1 = \beta_0 + \beta_1 X_1 + U_1$$

from which,

$$U_1 = Y_1 - \beta_0 - \beta_1 X_1$$

We can then write:

$$P(U_1) = \frac{1}{\sqrt{2\pi\sigma_u^2}} \exp[-(\tfrac{1}{2}\,\sigma_u^2)\,(Y_1 - \beta_0 - \beta_1 X_1)^2] \qquad \textbf{3.1.3}$$

Notice that in this case the mean of Y_1, which is $(\beta_0 + \beta_1 X_1)$, and the variance σ_u^2 respecify function 3.1.2. Y_i and U_i have the same variance, but their means are different. Since each U_i is independent by assumption, the joint probability density function in equation 3.1.1 is obtained by multiplying all the individual probability densities:

$$P(U_1, U_2, \ldots, U_N) = \left\{\frac{1}{\sqrt{2\pi\sigma_u^2}} \exp[-(\tfrac{1}{2}\,\sigma_u^2)\,(Y_1 - \beta_0 - \beta_1 X_1)^2]\right\} \cdot \left\{\frac{1}{\sqrt{2\pi\sigma_u^2}} \exp[-(\tfrac{1}{2}\,\sigma_u^2)\,(Y_2 - \beta_0 - \beta_1 X_2)^2]\right\} \cdots \qquad \textbf{3.1.4}$$

(Continued)

[5] "A maximum likelihood estimator $\hat{\theta}$ of the parameter θ in the frequency function $f(x; \theta)$ is an estimator that maximizes the likelihood function $L(X_1, \ldots, X_N; \theta)$ as a function of θ." P. G. Hoel, *Introduction to Mathematical Statistics* (3d ed.; New York: John Wiley & Sons, 1962), p. 58.

$$\cdots \left\{ \frac{1}{\sqrt{2\pi\sigma_u^2}} \exp[-(\tfrac{1}{2}\sigma_u^2)(Y_N - \beta_0 - \beta_1 X_N)^2] \right\}$$

$$= \prod_{i=1}^{N} \left\{ \frac{1}{\sqrt{2\pi\sigma_u^2}} \exp[-(\tfrac{1}{2}\sigma_u^2)(Y_i - \beta_0 - \beta_1 X_i)^2] \right\}$$

The product in equation 3.1.4 is equal to the sum of the exponentials.[6] Thus we can write:

$$P(U_1, U_2, \ldots, U_N) = \left(\frac{1}{\sqrt{2\pi\sigma_u^2}} \right)^N \exp\left[-(\tfrac{1}{2}\sigma_u^2) \sum_{i=1}^{N} (Y_i - \beta_0 - \beta_1 X_i)^2 \right] \qquad \textbf{3.1.5}$$

This is the *likelihood* function of drawing the sample $(U_1, U_2, \ldots, U_N)$ from a normal distribution on the assumption of the linear regression model.

We can write the likelihood function as follows:

$$L = \frac{1}{(\sigma_u^2 2\pi)^{N/2}} \exp\left[-\frac{1}{2\sigma_u^2} \sum_{i=1}^{N} (Y_i - \beta_0 - \beta_1 X_i)^2 \right] \qquad \textbf{3.1.6}$$

It is convenient to work with the logarithmic transformation:

$$\log L = -\frac{N}{2} \log 2\pi - \frac{N}{2} \log \sigma_u^2 - \frac{1}{2\sigma_u^2} \sum_{i=1}^{N} (Y_i - \beta_0 - \beta_1 X_i)^2 \qquad \textbf{3.1.7}$$

Differentiating with respect to β_0, β_1, and σ_u^2,

$$\frac{\partial(\log L)}{\partial \beta_0} = \frac{1}{\sigma_u^2} \sum_{i=1}^{N} (Y_i - \beta_0 - \beta_1 X_i) \qquad \textbf{3.1.8}$$

$$\frac{\partial(\log L)}{\partial \beta_1} = \frac{1}{\sigma_u^2} \sum_{i=1}^{N} X_i (Y_i - \beta_0 - \beta_1 X_i) \qquad \textbf{3.1.9}$$

$$\frac{\partial(\log L)}{\partial \sigma_u^2} = \frac{N}{2\sigma_u^2} + \frac{1}{2\sigma_u^4} \sum_{i=1}^{N} (Y_i - \beta_0 - \beta_1 X_i)^2 \qquad \textbf{3.1.10}$$

Setting the above results equal to zero and rearranging,

---

[6]The symbol $\prod_{i=1}^{N}$ reads as the product of N factors. Notice that this product is of the form $\prod_{i=1}^{N} ke^{\alpha_i}$. But $\Pi[ke^{\alpha_i}] = (ke^{\alpha_1})(ke^{\alpha_2}) \ldots (ke^{\alpha_N}) = k^N e^{\alpha_1 + \alpha_2 + \cdots + \alpha_N}$.

$$\sum_{i=1}^{N} Y_i = N\beta_0 + \beta_1 \sum_{i=1}^{N} X_i \qquad \textbf{3.1.11}$$

$$\sum_{i=1}^{N} X_i Y_i = \beta_0 \sum_{i=1}^{N} X_i + \beta_1 \sum_{i=1}^{N} X_i^2 \qquad \textbf{3.1.12}$$

$$\sigma_u^2 = \frac{1}{N} \sum_{i=1}^{N} (Y_i - \beta_0 - \beta_1 X_i)^2 \qquad \textbf{3.1.13}$$

We then solve for the maximum likelihood estimates of $\tilde{\beta}_0$, $\tilde{\beta}_1$, and $\tilde{\sigma}_u^2$. As we shall see in the next section, the derivation of the estimators of β_0, β_1, and σ_u^2 from the results above compares exactly with that relative to the case of bivariate distribution when X_i is random and the normality assumption is invoked. Note that the first two equations, 3.1.11 and 3.1.12 , are exactly the same as the pair of normal equations, 2.1.9 and 2.1.10, for the OLS estimators, where U_i is not assumed to be normally distributed.

The assumption of normal distribution of U_i thus makes the OLS estimators identical to the maximum likelihood estimators. The maximum likelihood estimators have certain properties: (1) consistency, (2) efficiency, and (3) sufficiency. Instead of discussing the properties in general terms, this book will review them in reference to the OLS estimators. Recall that the OLS estimators are considered to have certain properties under varying assumptions. If the assumption of zero mean, $E(U_i) = 0$, is fulfilled, the OLS estimators are unbiased in the sense that their expected values are the true values of the estimated parameters, or $E(\hat{\beta}_1) = \beta_1$.

If the assumptions of zero mean, $E(U_i) = 0$; constant and finite variance, $E(U_iU_j) = \sigma_u^2$ where $i = j$; zero covariance, $E(U_iU_j) = 0$ where $i \neq j$; and independence of the disturbance term with respect to the exogenous variable, $E(U_iX_i) = 0$, are all fulfilled, the OLS estimators are consistent.[7] The last assumption is not satisfied when a simultaneous system of equations is considered and an endogenous variable appears as a regressor on the righthand side of one or another equation. The OLS estimators are inconsistent for such a system which calls for a different method of estimation. This point will be discussed further in Chapters 11 through 13.

More formally stated, the estimator $\hat{\beta}_k$ is a consistent estimator if in the probability limit sense,

$$\text{pr}\left[\left| \hat{\beta}_k - \beta_k \right| < \epsilon\right] = 1 \text{ as } N \to \infty \qquad \textbf{3.1.14}$$

[7] There is a further restrictive condition for obtaining consistent estimators. As the sample size tends to infinity, the mean and variance of observations on the exogenous variable must have a finite limit, the limit of the variance being positive. Of course the sample size of economic observations seldom really tends to infinity. At this stage we shall not be concerned about this condition. This point will be developed further in Chapter 7.

This says that as the sample size tends to infinity, the probability approaches unity that the estimated parameter $\hat{\beta}_k$ differs from the true parameter β_k by an arbitrarily small amount, $\epsilon > 0$.

As stated previously, in the formal sense the concept of consistency is tied to sample size tending to infinity ($N \to \infty$). Intuitively it is reasonable that a "good" estimator is one whose difference from the true value becomes smaller as N increases. For example, the estimator ought to give an estimate closer to the true value of the parameter when it is based on $N = 30$ than when it is based on $N = 3$. Figure 3-1 helps illustrate the concept. As the sample size increases, the estimated value of $\hat{\beta}_k$ comes closer and closer to the true value of β_k.

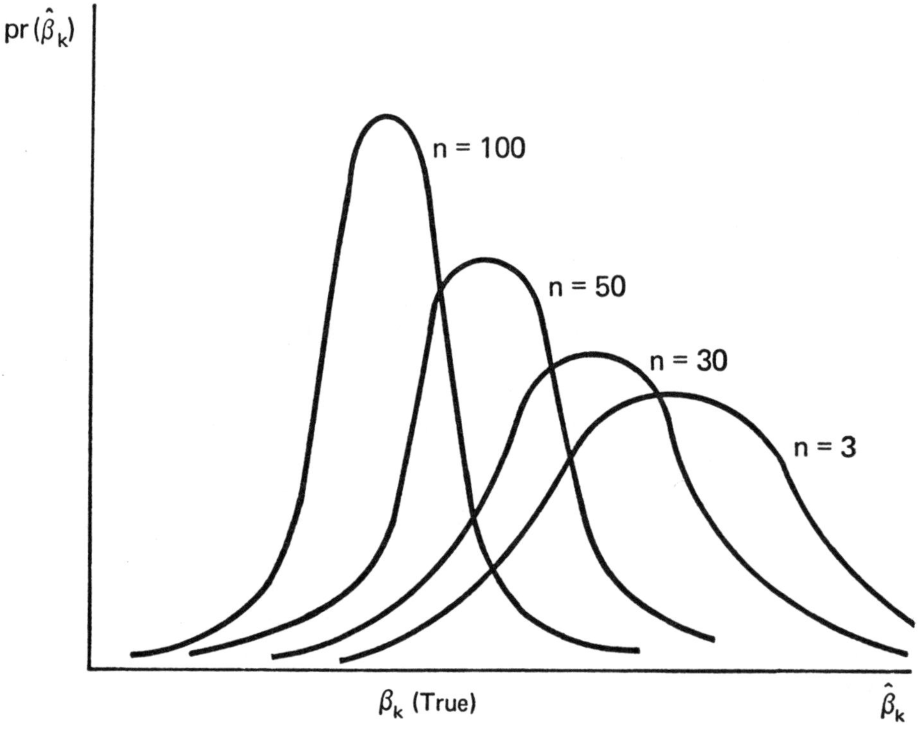

FIGURE 3-1

The OLS estimators have been shown before to be unbiased and to have minimum variance within the class of unbiased linear estimators. Strictly speaking, $\hat{\beta}_k$ is a consistent estimator if its bias and variance approach zero as the sample size approaches infinity. Notice that no assumption as to the nature of the distribution of the U_i's is made to obtain OLS estimators, although it is assumed that the distribution has a finite and constant variance.

To prove that an estimator is efficient involves the assumption of a normal distribution of U_i. In the formal sense the estimated parameter $\hat{\beta}_k$ is an efficient estimator of the true parameter β_k if $\sqrt{N}(\hat{\beta}_k - \beta_k)$ is asymptotically normally distributed with mean zero and variance σ^2 (where N is the sample size), and the variance σ^2 is smaller than the variance of any other estimator that is also asymptotically normally distributed in the same sense. Confined to finite sample size, among all unbiased estimators, the ones with minimum variance are considered efficient. The OLS estimator, as we have seen, has the least variance in the class of linear unbiased estimators and as such is efficient in its class.

The concept of sufficiency is a more difficult one. Given the additional assumption of the normal distribution of U_i, the OLS estimator becomes identical to the maximum likelihood estimator, which is sufficient. An estimator is said to be sufficient if it conveys all the information that the sample of observations contains and if there is no other information that could be obtained by obtaining another estimator. The sufficient estimators are also efficient in the sense that they are of minimum variance among all "regular" unbiased estimators.[8]

3.2 OLS ESTIMATORS IN A BIVARIATE DISTRIBUTION MODEL

It is convenient to assume that the independent variable X_i is fixed and does not vary between samples. As such X_i has no probability distribution. However, the OLS results can be obtained when the X_i's are random and when the pair (Y, X) has a bivariate distribution. Let $f(X_i)$, $i = 1, 2, \ldots, N$, be the probability distribution of X_i. Let us further assume that the conditional probability distribution of Y_i, given X_i, is normal and independent with mean $\beta_0 + \beta_1 X_i$ and constant variance σ_u^2. That is, even if the random X_i has a distribution, it does not depend on β_0, β_1, or σ_u^2. It becomes especially important to emphasize the assumption that the X_i's are statistically independent and that $E(U_i X_i) = 0$. Of course all of the other usual assumptions regarding U_i must also hold.

The likelihood function of the joint distribution of X_i and Y_i can be written as follows:

$$
\begin{aligned}
L &= f(X_1), \ldots, f(X_N) f(Y_1|X_1), \ldots, f(Y_N|X_N) \\
&= f(X_1), \ldots, f(X_N) \frac{1}{(2\pi\sigma_u^2)^{N/2}} \exp\left[-\frac{1}{2\sigma_u^2} \Sigma(Y_i - \beta_0 - \beta_1 X_i)^2\right]
\end{aligned}
\qquad \textbf{3.2.1}
$$

Taking the logarithm of L:

$$
\begin{aligned}
\log L = \log f(X_1) + \ldots + \log f(X_N) - \left(\frac{N}{2}\right) \log 2\pi - \left(\frac{N}{2}\right) \log \sigma_u^2 \\
- \frac{1}{2\sigma_u^2} \Sigma(Y_i - \beta_0 - \beta_1 X_i)^2
\end{aligned}
\qquad \textbf{3.2.2}
$$

[8]A fuller discussion of sufficiency can be found in A.M. Mood and F. A. Graybill, *Introduction to the Theory of Statistics* (2d ed.; New York: McGraw-Hill Book Co., 1963), pp. 167-171.

Differentiating log L with respect to β_0, β_1, and σ_u^2,

$$\frac{\partial \log L}{\partial \beta_0} = \frac{1}{\sigma_u^2} \Sigma(Y_i - \beta_0 - \beta_1 X_i) \qquad 3.2.3$$

$$\frac{\partial \log L}{\partial \beta_1} = \frac{1}{\sigma_u^2} \Sigma X_i (Y_i - \beta_0 - \beta_1 X_i) \qquad 3.2.4$$

$$\frac{\partial \log L}{\partial \sigma_u^2} = \frac{N}{2\sigma_u^2} + \frac{1}{2\sigma_u^4} \Sigma(Y_i - \beta_0 - \beta_1 X_i)^2 \qquad 3.2.5$$

Setting them equal to zero and rearranging, we obtain the estimates of $\tilde{\beta}_0$, $\tilde{\beta}_1$, and $\tilde{\sigma}_u^2$. Thus we obtain the maximum likelihood estimators, as in equations 3.1.11 through 3.1.13. Notice that, in order to show that the OLS estimators are the same as maximum likelihood estimators, we just made the assumption that the conditional probability distribution of Y_i, given X_i, is normal. This is quite a restrictive assumption. Moreover, in econometric analysis observations on X_i and Y_i can seldom be considered as independently drawn from the same bivariate distribution. For the present purpose this book will continue to assume that X_i has no distribution and is fixed.

3.3 CORRELATION MODEL

Its Framework and Computational Design

We would like to know what proportion of the variance of the dependent variable can be associated with the variance of the independent variables. In statistical analysis it is possible to compute R^2, the *coefficient of determination*, and R, the *coefficient of correlation*. (These coefficients corrected for degrees of freedom yield $\bar{R}^2$ and $\bar{R}$.) It is customary to report such statistics in econometric work. However, there is often misdirected emphasis on obtaining a high value of R (or R^2), and a word of caution against "correlation pushing" is important. If the hypothesis based on a priori economic theory is adequately tested, a low value of R is not so bad. Correlation analysis is commonly used to provide the test for what the statistician calls "goodness of fit." The correlation problem arises when the researcher asks whether or not there exists any relationship between the variables under investigation, say, between price and quantity in the two-variable case or between quantity demanded on one hand and the price of the commodity and the income of the purchaser on the other hand in the multivariate case.

A basic difference exists between the regression model and the correlation model. In the regression model it is assumed that the dependent variable is random and has a distribution and that the independent variables are nonrandom, fixed, and, as such, distribution-free. The functional dependence is assumed to be uniquely directed from independent to dependent variables. In the pure correlation model all variables whose correlations are being examined are assumed to be random and to have probability distributions. Strictly speaking, the correlation model assumes that the observed values are random samples from normal bivariate or multivariate populations. Some statisticians have preferred to call the regression model the "determined" case and the correlation model the "undetermined" case. Thus in the context of a regression model measures of correlation have a limited meaning. The populations sampled seldom have two-dimensional or multidimensional normal distributions. This explains the fact that even when the measures of correlation are computed for the regression variables, tests on the significance of these measures are not generally carried out in econometric research. A pure correlation model would warrant such significance tests.

It is important to realize that measures of correlation (R or $\bar{R}$) are measures completely devoid of any cause-effect implications. High values for the correlation measures imply only that the variables "just happen" to vary together, and such variations in both of them may be attributed to or caused by other variables. At best the coefficient of correlation measures the strength of the association or covariation between variables, and it cannot give any information on causation.

The computational aspects of correlation measures are easy to grasp. Two points need to be understood. The measure of statistical association should be: (1) independent of the choice of the origin of the variables, and (2) independent of the scale of measurement of the original variables. To satisfy the first condition, we express the observations on variables in terms of deviations from the mean. To satisfy the second condition, we divide each variable expressed in terms of its mean deviation by its respective standard deviations. Further, the correlation measure should not increase only because more observations are added. Thus we include a correction factor of $1/N - 1$. The simple formula in a two-variable case is:

$$R = \frac{1}{N-1}\Sigma\frac{(X_i - \bar{X})}{s_x}\frac{(Y_i - \bar{Y})}{s_y} \qquad \textbf{3.3.1}$$

Writing $x = X_i - \bar{X}$ and $y_i = Y_i = \bar{Y}$,

$$R = \frac{1}{N-1}\,\frac{\Sigma x_i y_i}{s_x s_y} \qquad \textbf{3.3.2}$$

where:

$$s_x = \sqrt{\frac{\Sigma(X_i - \bar{X})^2}{N-1}} = \sqrt{\frac{\Sigma x_i^2}{N-1}} \qquad \textbf{3.3.2.A}$$

and

$$s_y = \sqrt{\frac{\Sigma(Y_i - \bar{Y})^2}{N-1}} = \sqrt{\frac{\Sigma y_i^2}{N-1}} \qquad \textbf{3.3.2.B}$$

For computation the following formula is often convenient:

$$R = \frac{N\Sigma X_i Y_i - (\Sigma X_i)(\Sigma Y_i)}{\sqrt{N\Sigma X_i^2 - (\Sigma X_i)^2}\ \sqrt{N\Sigma Y_i^2 - (\Sigma Y_i)^2}} \tag{3.3.3}$$

$$= \frac{\Sigma x_i y_i}{\sqrt{(\Sigma x_i^2)(\Sigma y_i^2)}} \tag{3.3.4}$$

where R = the coefficient of correlation
R^2 = the coefficient of determination

One corrects R^2 for the degrees of freedom used up in estimating the parameters as follows:

$$\bar{R}^2 = 1 - (1 - R^2)\frac{N-1}{N-K} \tag{3.3.5}$$

where N is the number of observations, and K is the number of parameters estimated. Obviously the correction will not be significant in the case of a truly large sample or in the case of a value of R^2 very close to one. The statistic R^2 is the measure of association between the two variables X_i and Y_i. In the case of perfect association between X_i and Y_i, both the coefficient of correlation R and the degree of determination R^2 will be unity. Therefore, $\bar{R}^2$ will also be unity. The coefficient of correlation R will be negative when smaller values of one variable are associated with larger values of the other, and positive when smaller values of one are associated with smaller values of the other and larger values with larger. If a linear relation between Y_i and X_i is assumed, a positive value for R will correspond to a positive slope for the conjectured line and a negative value to a negative slope, as in Figure 3-2.

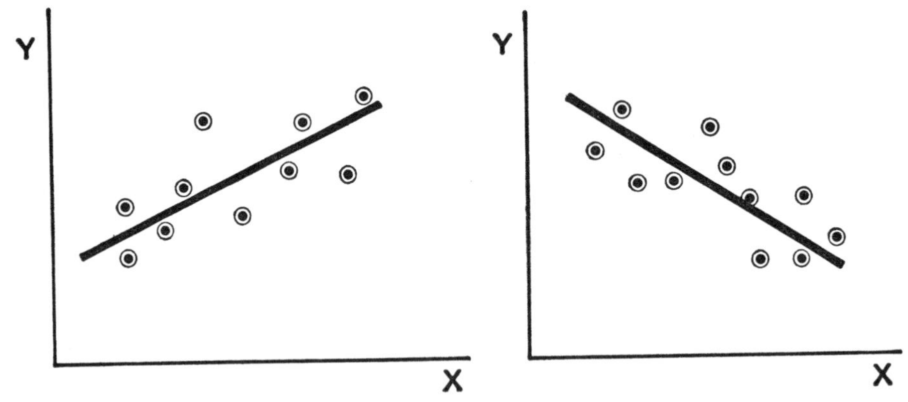

$Y = \beta_0 + \beta_1 X;\ R > 0$ $\qquad$ $Y = \beta_0 - \beta_1 X;\ R < 0$

FIGURE 3-2

The Relationship between the Correlation Coefficient and the Regression Coefficient

Consider model 2.1.1:

$$Y_i = \beta_0 + \beta_1 X_i + U_i$$

or in terms of deviation from the mean,

$$y_i = \beta_1 x_i + U_i$$

Recall equation 2.1.21 for the OLS estimator $\hat{\beta}_1$:

$$\hat{\beta}_1 = \frac{\Sigma x_i y_i}{\Sigma x_i^2}$$

From equation 3.3.2,

$$R = \frac{1}{N-1} \quad \frac{\Sigma x_i y_i}{s_x s_y}$$

Multiplying both sides of equation 3.3.2 by s_y/s_x, we have:

$$R\frac{s_y}{s_x} = \frac{\Sigma x_i y_i}{(N-1)s_x s_y} \; \frac{s_y}{s_x}$$

$$= \frac{\Sigma x_i y_i}{(N-1)s_x^2}$$

Using equation 3.3.2.A,

$$R\frac{s_y}{s_x} = \frac{\Sigma x_i y_i}{(N-1)\left(\frac{\Sigma x_i^2}{N-1}\right)}$$

Therefore,

$$R\frac{s_y}{s_x} = \frac{\Sigma x_i y_i}{\Sigma x_i^2} \qquad \textbf{3.3.6}$$

Notice that the right-hand quantity in equation 3.3.6 is the estimator $\hat{\beta}_1$, exactly as in equation 2.1.21. We can then write:

$$\hat{\beta}_1 = R\frac{s_y}{s_x} \qquad \textbf{3.3.7}$$

The correspondence between the two statistical measures is thus evident. From equation 3.3.7 we can write:

$$\hat{\beta}_1 \frac{s_x}{s_y} = R \qquad \textbf{3.3.8}$$

or,

$$\hat{\beta}_1^2 \frac{s_x^2}{s_y^2} = R^2 \tag{3.3.9}$$

or,

$$\hat{\beta}_1^2 \frac{\Sigma x_i^2}{\Sigma y^2} = R^2 \tag{3.3.10}$$

or,

$$\frac{(\hat{\beta}_1 \Sigma x_i)^2}{\Sigma y_i^2} = R^2 \tag{3.3.11}$$

Since $\hat{y}_i = \hat{\beta}_1 x_i$, we can write:

$$\frac{\Sigma \hat{y}_i^2}{\Sigma y_i^2} = R^2 \tag{3.3.12}$$

Note that $y_i = \hat{y}_i + U_i$, from which $\hat{U}_i = y_i - \hat{y}_i$ and $\hat{U}_i = y_i - \hat{\beta}_1 x_i$.

Total variation in Y is divided into two components, systematic $\hat{y}_i$ and random $\hat{U}_i$ (section 2.0). It follows that:

$$\Sigma y_i^2 = \Sigma \hat{y}_i^2 + \Sigma \hat{U}_i^2 + 2\Sigma \hat{y}_i \hat{U}_i \tag{3.3.13}$$

Since $\Sigma \hat{y}_i \hat{U}_i$ is zero,[9]

$$\Sigma y_i^2 - \Sigma \hat{U}_i^2 = \Sigma \hat{y}_i^2 \tag{3.3.14}$$

Equation 3.3.12 can then be rewritten as:

$$R^2 = \frac{\Sigma y_i^2 - \Sigma \hat{U}_i^2}{\Sigma y_i^2} \tag{3.3.15}$$

9

$$\Sigma \hat{y}_i \hat{U}_i = \hat{\beta}_1 \Sigma x_i (y_i - \hat{\beta}_1 x_i)$$
$$= \hat{\beta}_1 \Sigma x_i y_i - \hat{\beta}_1^2 \Sigma x_i^2$$

Substituting for $\hat{\beta}_1$,

$$\Sigma y_i U_i = \frac{(\Sigma x_i y_i)(\Sigma x_i y_i)}{\Sigma x_i^2} - \left(\frac{\Sigma x_i y_i}{\Sigma x_i^2}\right)^2 \Sigma x_i^2$$

$$= \frac{(\Sigma x_i y_i)^2}{\Sigma x_i^2} - \frac{(\Sigma x_i y_i)^2}{\Sigma x_i^2} = 0$$

or,

$$R^2 = 1 - \frac{\Sigma \hat{U}_i^2}{\Sigma y_i^2} \qquad \textbf{3.3.16}$$

or,

$$R^2 = 1 - \frac{\Sigma(Y_i - \hat{Y})^2}{\Sigma(Y_i - \bar{Y})^2} \qquad \textbf{3.3.17}$$

Therefore,

$$R = \sqrt{1 - \frac{\Sigma(Y_i - \hat{Y})^2}{\Sigma(Y_i - \bar{Y})^2}} \qquad \textbf{3.3.18}$$

What we have under the square root sign is the ratio of the unexplained variation in Y_i and its total variation, subtracted from 1. In other words R^2 is the ratio of the "explained" variation in Y_i, "explained" by its regression on X_i, and the total variation in Y_i.

From equation 3.3.16 we have:

$$R^2 = 1 - \frac{\Sigma \hat{U}_i^2}{\Sigma y_i^2}$$

The above result will help explain the rationale for correcting R^2 as done in equation 3.3.5. Taking expected values,

$$E(R^2) = 1 - \frac{\Sigma E(\hat{U}_i^2)}{\Sigma E(y_i^2)} \qquad \textbf{3.3.19}$$

Using equation 2.4.77, $\Sigma E(\hat{U}_i^2) = (N - 2)\,\sigma_u^2$, so:

$$E(R^2) = 1 - \frac{(N - 2)\hat{\sigma}_u^2}{(N - 1)\hat{\sigma}_y^2} \qquad \textbf{3.3.20}$$

We do not know the true U_i, nor can we compute σ_u^2 as such. In practice the computed residuals from regression analysis are used to estimate $\hat{\sigma}_u^2$. Let us assume that the true U_i are known, and let us rewrite the true R^2 as in equation 3.3.15:

$$R^2 = \frac{\Sigma y_i^2 - \Sigma U_i^2}{\Sigma y_i^2}$$

Taking expected values,[10]

[10] We know that:

$$\Sigma E(Y_i - \bar{Y})^2 = (N - 1)\sigma_u^2$$

Similarly,

$$\Sigma E(U_i - \bar{U})^2 = (N - 1)\sigma_u^2$$

$$E(R^2) = \frac{\Sigma E(y_i^2) - \Sigma E(U_i^2)}{\Sigma E(y_i^2)}$$

$$= \frac{(N-1)\sigma_y^2 - (N-1)\sigma_u^2}{(N-1)\sigma_y^2} \qquad 3.3.21$$

$$= 1 - \frac{\sigma_u^2}{\sigma_y^2}$$

The result of equation 3.3.21 is thus different from that of equation 3.3.20, and a correction factor $(N - 2)/(N - 1)$ needs to be introduced. Hence,

$$\bar{R}^2 = 1 - (1 - R^2)\frac{N-1}{N-2} \qquad 3.3.22$$

The generalized result for the K-variable case is equation 3.3.5.

Multiple Correlation Analysis

Consider model 2.3.15,

$$\mathbf{Y} = \mathbf{X}\boldsymbol{\beta} + \mathbf{U}$$

from which,

$$\hat{\mathbf{Y}} = \mathbf{X}\hat{\boldsymbol{\beta}}$$

when

$$\hat{\boldsymbol{\beta}} = (\mathbf{X}'\mathbf{X})^{-1}\mathbf{X}'\mathbf{Y}$$

and

$$\hat{\mathbf{U}} = \mathbf{Y} - \mathbf{X}\hat{\boldsymbol{\beta}} \qquad 3.3.23$$

Recall the result of equation 3.3.15:

$$R^2 = \frac{\Sigma y_i^2 - \Sigma \hat{U}_i^2}{\Sigma y_i^2}$$

In the context of the above model where we have K different variables X_{i1}, $X_{i2}, \ldots, X_{iK}$ $(i = 1, 2, \ldots, N)$ and we wish to estimate K different β's, the terms in the right-hand expression of equation 3.3.15 can be rewritten as follows:

$$\Sigma y_i^2 = \Sigma Y_i^2 - \frac{1}{N}(\Sigma Y_i)^2$$

$$= \mathbf{Y}'\mathbf{Y} - \frac{1}{N}(\Sigma Y_i)^2 \qquad 3.3.24$$

and

$$\Sigma \hat{U}_i^2 = \hat{\mathbf{U}}'\hat{\mathbf{U}} \tag{3.3.25}$$

Collecting equations 3.3.24 and 3.3.25,

$$\Sigma y_i^2 - \Sigma \hat{U}_i^2 = \mathbf{Y}'\mathbf{Y} - \hat{\mathbf{U}}'\hat{\mathbf{U}} - \frac{1}{N}(\Sigma Y_i)^2 \tag{3.3.26}$$

Notice that what we have is the total sum of the squares in Y, the dependent variable, minus $\hat{\mathbf{U}}'\hat{\mathbf{U}}$, the unexplained sum of the squares, that is, the variation that remains unexplained after Y_i is regressed on the X's. This difference is the explained sum of the squares, and using equations 3.3.23 and 3.3.25,

$$\begin{aligned} \Sigma \hat{U}_i^2 &= \hat{\mathbf{U}}'\hat{\mathbf{U}} \\ &= (\mathbf{Y} - \mathbf{X}\hat{\boldsymbol{\beta}})'(\mathbf{Y} - \mathbf{X}\hat{\boldsymbol{\beta}}) \\ &= \mathbf{Y}'\mathbf{Y} - 2\hat{\boldsymbol{\beta}}'\mathbf{X}'\mathbf{Y} + \hat{\boldsymbol{\beta}}'\mathbf{X}'\mathbf{X}\hat{\boldsymbol{\beta}} \\ &= \mathbf{Y}'\mathbf{Y} - \hat{\boldsymbol{\beta}}'\mathbf{X}'\mathbf{Y} \end{aligned} \tag{3.3.27}$$

since in terms of mathematical manipulation we can write $\hat{\boldsymbol{\beta}}'\mathbf{X}'\mathbf{Y} = \mathbf{Y}'\mathbf{X}\hat{\boldsymbol{\beta}}$ and $\mathbf{X}'\mathbf{X}\hat{\boldsymbol{\beta}} = \mathbf{X}'\mathbf{Y}$ using the OLS estimate of $\hat{\boldsymbol{\beta}}$ as restated in equation 3.3.23. Hence, we rewrite equation 3.3.26 by substituting equation 3.3.27:

$$\Sigma y_i^2 - \Sigma \hat{U}_i^2 = \hat{\boldsymbol{\beta}}'\mathbf{X}'\mathbf{Y} - \frac{1}{N}(\Sigma Y_i)^2 \tag{3.3.28}$$

Next, we rewrite R^2 for the multivariate case:

$$R^2 = \frac{\hat{\boldsymbol{\beta}}'\mathbf{X}'\mathbf{Y} - 1/N\,(\Sigma Y_i)^2}{\mathbf{Y}'\mathbf{Y} - 1/N\,(\Sigma Y_i)^2} \tag{3.3.29}$$

The multiple correlation coefficient is usually written as $R_{y.12\ldots K}$, the multiple correlation between the one dependent variable Y and all the K independent variables $X_1, X_2, \ldots, X_K$.

It is also possible to compute *partial correlation coefficients*. One can reasonably suppose that if the multiple correlation $R_{y.12\ldots K}$ between Y_i and the K different X_i's is measured, it is possible to disentangle the correlation between the Y_i's and each one of the X_k variables in the given relationship. Indeed this measure is easily calculated.

Let us recall the simple result of equation 3.3.1 of the two-variable case as if we were estimating the simple correlation coefficients between Y and X_2, Y and X_3, and so forth. Following equation 3.3.2 we may write, omitting the i subscript:

$$R_{1.2} = \frac{\Sigma x_2 y}{(N-1)s_{x_2}s_y}$$

$$R_{1.3} = \frac{\Sigma x_3 y}{(N-1)s_{x_3}s_y}$$

.

.

.

$$R_{1.K} = \frac{\Sigma x_K y}{(N-1)s_{x_K}s_y}$$

and similarly,

$$R_{2.3} = \frac{\Sigma x_2 x_3}{(N-1)s_{x_2}s_{x_3}} \qquad 3.3.30$$

Without any proof we can write the results for partial correlation coefficients, and it is convenient to do so in terms of two X's, X_2 and X_3. The partial correlation between Y and X_2 with X_3 held constant is, using small r for partial correlation:

$$r_{12.3} = \frac{r_{12} - r_{13}r_{23}}{\sqrt{1-r_{13}^2}\ \sqrt{1-r_{23}^2}} \qquad 3.3.31$$

Similarly,

$$r_{13.2} = \frac{r_{13} - r_{12}r_{23}}{\sqrt{1-r_{12}^2}\ \sqrt{1-r_{23}^2}} \qquad 3.3.32$$

$$r_{23.1} = \frac{r_{23} - r_{12}r_{13}}{\sqrt{1-r_{12}^2}\ \sqrt{1-r_{13}^2}} \qquad 3.3.33$$

The partial correlation coefficients are seldom reported in econometrics. The multiple correlation coefficient $R_{1.23}$ can be shown to be related to simple correlation coefficients as follows:

$$R_{1.23}^2 = \frac{r_{12}^2 + r_{13}^2 - 2r_{12}r_{13}r_{23}}{1 - r_{23}^2} \qquad 3.3.34$$

3.4 NUMERICAL ILLUSTRATIONS

The data at the top of page 91 are used as an illustration of the computations:

Year	Y	X_1	X_2	X_3
1952	12.3	1	263.3	93.1
1953	16.0	1	275.4	93.9
1954	15.7	1	278.3	92.5
1955	21.2	1	296.7	89.2
1956	17.9	1	309.3	91.7
1957	18.8	1	315.8	96.5
1958	15.4	1	318.8	100.0
1959	19.0	1	333.0	103.9
1960	20.0	1	340.2	102.5
1961	18.4	1	350.7	102.5
1962	21.8	1	367.3	102.1
1963	24.1	1	381.3	101.5
1964	25.6	1	406.5	101.2
1965	30.0	1	430.8	99.0

Y = consumer expenditure (in billions of dollars) on automobiles in the United States at constant (1958) prices

X_2 = disposable income (in billions of dollars) in the United States at constant (1958) prices

X_3 = index of automobile prices

From these data we can simply compute:

$$N = 14 \qquad \Sigma Y = 276.2 \qquad \bar{Y} = 19.7285714$$

$$\Sigma X_2 = 4667.4 \qquad \bar{X}_2 = 333.3857142$$

$$\Sigma X_3 = 1369.6 \qquad \bar{X}_3 = 97.8285714$$

$$\Sigma Y^2 = 5{,}725.200$$

$$\Sigma X_2 Y = 94{,}798.116 \qquad \Sigma X_2^2 = 1{,}588{,}428.750$$

$$\Sigma X_3 Y = 27{,}129.199 \qquad \Sigma X_2 X_3 = 458{,}705.406$$

$$\Sigma X_3^2 = 134{,}295.656$$

The standard deviations of Y, X_2, and X_3 are:

$$s_Y = \sqrt{\frac{\Sigma(Y_t - \bar{Y})^2}{N}} = \sqrt{2313.1707851} = 48.0954$$

$$s_{X_2} = \sqrt{\frac{\Sigma(X_{2_t} - \bar{X}_2)^2}{N}} = \sqrt{19.720571430} = 4.44146$$

$$s_{X_3} = \sqrt{\frac{\Sigma(X_{3_t} - \bar{X}_3)^2}{N}} = \sqrt{22.117642860} = 4.70294$$

The general regression model can be written in matrix notation as:

$$\mathbf{Y} = \mathbf{X}\boldsymbol{\beta} + \mathbf{U}$$

where $\mathbf{Y}$ = the vector of the regressand
$\mathbf{X}$ = the matrix of the regressors
$\boldsymbol{\beta}$ = the vector of the unknown parameters
$\mathbf{U}$ = the vector of the disturbance terms

The Simple Regression

In the simple regression of $\mathbf{Y}$ on $\mathbf{X}_2$ we can write:

$$\mathbf{Y} = \mathbf{X}\boldsymbol{\beta} + \mathbf{U}$$

where:

$$\mathbf{Y} = \begin{bmatrix} 12.30 \\ 16.00 \\ \cdot \\ \cdot \\ \cdot \\ 30.00 \end{bmatrix} \quad \mathbf{X} = \begin{bmatrix} 1 & 263.3 \\ 1 & 275.4 \\ \cdot & \cdot \\ \cdot & \cdot \\ \cdot & \cdot \\ 1 & 430.8 \end{bmatrix} \quad \boldsymbol{\beta} = \begin{bmatrix} \beta_1 \\ \beta_2 \end{bmatrix} \qquad \textbf{3.4.1}$$

The first column in $\mathbf{X}$ containing only unity corresponds to the constant term β_1.
Hence, we can compute:

$$(\mathbf{X}'\mathbf{X}) = \begin{bmatrix} N & \Sigma X_2 \\ \Sigma X_2 & \Sigma X_2^2 \end{bmatrix} = \begin{bmatrix} 14 & 4{,}667.4 \\ 4{,}667.4 & 1{,}588{,}428.75 \end{bmatrix}$$

$$|\mathbf{X}'\mathbf{X}| = N\Sigma X_2^2 - (\Sigma X_2)^2 = 453{,}381.0898$$

$$(\mathbf{X}'\mathbf{X})^{-1} = \frac{1}{453381.0898} \begin{bmatrix} 1{,}588{,}428.75 & -4667.4 \\ -4{,}667.4 & 14 \end{bmatrix}$$

$$= \begin{bmatrix} 3.50351787 & -0.01029465 \\ -0.01029465 & 0.00003088 \end{bmatrix}$$

$$\mathbf{X}'\mathbf{Y} = \begin{bmatrix} \Sigma Y \\ \Sigma X_2 Y \end{bmatrix} = \begin{bmatrix} 276.2 \\ 94{,}798.116 \end{bmatrix}$$

$$\mathbf{Y}'\mathbf{Y} = \Sigma Y^2 = 5725.2$$

Estimation

To estimate $\boldsymbol{\beta}$: Using equation 2.3.22, $\boldsymbol{\beta}$ can be estimated as shown in the following:

$$\hat{\boldsymbol{\beta}} = \begin{bmatrix} \hat{\beta}_1 \\ \hat{\beta}_2 \end{bmatrix} = (\mathbf{X}'\mathbf{X})^{-1}\mathbf{X}'\mathbf{Y}$$

$$= \begin{bmatrix} 3.50351789 & -0.01029465 \\ -0.01029465 & 0.00003088 \end{bmatrix} \begin{bmatrix} 276.2 \\ 94{,}798.116 \end{bmatrix} = \begin{bmatrix} -8.2419 \\ 0.0839 \end{bmatrix}$$

To estimate σ^2: By equation 2.4.71 the sampling variance of the model can be written as:

$$s^2 = \frac{1}{N - K} (\mathbf{Y}'\mathbf{Y} - \hat{\boldsymbol{\beta}}\mathbf{X}'\mathbf{Y})$$

$$= \frac{1}{14 - 2} (5725.2 - 5676.9814) = \frac{1}{12} (48.2186)$$

$$= 4.0182$$

The standard deviation of the regression is:

$$s = \sqrt{4.0182} = 2.0046$$

To calculate the variance-covariance matrix of $\hat{\boldsymbol{\beta}}$: According to equation 2.4.39 the variance-covariance matrix of $\boldsymbol{\beta}$ can be written as:

$$\text{var}(\hat{\boldsymbol{\beta}}) = s^2(X'X)^{-1} = 4.0182 \begin{bmatrix} 3.50351789 & -0.01029465 \\ -0.01029465 & 0.00003088 \end{bmatrix}$$

$$= \begin{bmatrix} 14.0779 & -0.0414 \\ -0.0414 & 0.0001 \end{bmatrix}$$

Standard error of $\hat{\beta}_1 = \sqrt{14.0779} = 3.7521$
Standard error of $\hat{\beta}_2 = \sqrt{0.0001} = 0.0111$

To compute R^2: The coefficient of determination can be computed using equation 3.3.29:

$$R^2 = \frac{\hat{\boldsymbol{\beta}}'\mathbf{X}'\mathbf{Y} - \frac{1}{N} (\Sigma Y)^2}{\mathbf{Y}'\mathbf{Y} - \frac{1}{N} (\Sigma Y)^2} = \frac{5676.9814 - 5449.0314}{5725.2000 - 5449.0314} = 0.8254$$

Using equation 3.3.5 to adjust R^2 for degrees of freedom gives:

$$\bar{R}^2 = 1 - (1 - R^2) \frac{N - 1}{N - 2} = 1 - 0.1746 \times \frac{13}{12} = 0.8109$$

Therefore, the statistical results can be presented in the following form:

$$Y = -8.2419 + 0.0839X_2$$
$$(3.7521) \quad (0.0111)$$

$$\bar{R}^2 = 0.8109 \qquad s = 2.0046$$

Testing the Null Hypothesis

Null hypotheses: $\beta_1 = 0$ and $\beta_2 = 0$.

Test: To use the t test we compute:

$$t_1 = \frac{\hat{\beta}_1 - \beta_1}{s_{\hat{\beta}_1}} = \frac{-8.2419}{3.7521} = -2.1966$$

$$t_2 = \frac{\hat{\beta}_2 - \beta_2}{s_{\hat{\beta}_2}} = \frac{0.0839}{0.0111} = 7.5319$$

The table value of t for d.f. = 12 at the 95 percent confidence level is 2.18. Thus the statistical evidence indicates that it is safe to reject the null hypothesis at the 95 percent confidence level for both β_1 and β_2.

Interval Estimation of β

To obtain a 95 percent confidence interval estimate for β_1 and β_2, we write:

$$\text{pr}(-t_{0.025} < t < t_{0.025}) = 0.95$$

Substituting for t gives:

$$\text{pr}\left(-t_{0.025} < \frac{\hat{\beta}_1 - \beta_1}{s_{\hat{\beta}_1}} < t_{0.025}\right) = 0.95$$

and

$$\text{pr}\left(-t_{0.025} < \frac{\hat{\beta}_2 - \beta_2}{s_{\hat{\beta}_2}} < t_{0.025}\right) = 0.95$$

Therefore,

$$\text{pr}(\hat{\beta}_1 - t_{0.025}s_{\hat{\beta}_1} < \beta_1 < \hat{\beta}_1 + t_{0.025}s_{\hat{\beta}_1}) = 0.95$$

and

$$\text{pr}(\hat{\beta}_2 - t_{0.025}s_{\hat{\beta}_2} < \beta_2 < \hat{\beta}_2 + t_{0.025}s_{\hat{\beta}_2}) = 0.95$$

so that the 95 percent confidence limits for β_1 and β_2 are:

$$\hat{\beta}_1 \pm t_{0.025} s_{\hat{\beta}_1} = -8.2419 \pm 2.18\ (3.7521)$$
$$= -8.2419 \pm 8.1045$$
$$= 16.3564,\ 0.1374$$
$$\hat{\beta}_2 \pm t_{0.025} s_{\hat{\beta}_2} = 0.0839 \pm 2.18\ (0.0111)$$
$$= 0.0839 \pm 0.0240$$
$$= 0.1079,\ 0.0599$$

Multiple Regression

To regress Y in both X_2 and X_3, the general model again can be written as:

$$\mathbf{Y} = \mathbf{X}\boldsymbol{\beta} + \mathbf{U}$$

where:

$$\mathbf{Y} = \begin{bmatrix} 12.30 \\ 16.00 \\ \cdot \\ \cdot \\ \cdot \\ 30.00 \end{bmatrix} \quad \mathbf{X} = \begin{bmatrix} 1 & 263.3 & 93.1 \\ 1 & 275.4 & 93.9 \\ \cdot & \cdot & \cdot \\ \cdot & \cdot & \cdot \\ \cdot & \cdot & \cdot \\ 1 & 430.8 & 99.0 \end{bmatrix} \quad \boldsymbol{\beta} = \begin{bmatrix} \beta_1 \\ \beta_2 \\ \beta_3 \end{bmatrix} \qquad \textbf{3.4.2}$$

Before we do estimation and testing, we should first perform the following computations:

$$(\mathbf{X'X}) = \begin{bmatrix} N & \Sigma X_2 & \Sigma X_3 \\ \Sigma X_2 & \Sigma X_2^2 & \Sigma X_2 X_3 \\ \Sigma X_3 & \Sigma X_2 X_3 & \Sigma X_3^2 \end{bmatrix} = \begin{bmatrix} 14 & 4{,}667.4 & 1{,}369.6 \\ 4667.4 & 1{,}588{,}428.75 & 458{,}705.406 \\ 1369.6 & 458{,}705.406 & 134{,}295.656 \end{bmatrix}$$

$$|\mathbf{X'X}| = 78{,}628{,}319$$

$$(\mathbf{X'X})^{-1} = \frac{1}{78{,}628{,}319} \begin{bmatrix} 2{,}098{,}431.50 & 1{,}431{,}379.24 & -34{,}550{,}404.04 \\ 1{,}431{,}379.24 & 4{,}335.02 & -29{,}404.64 \\ -34{,}550{,}404.04 & -29{,}404.64 & 453{,}379.74 \end{bmatrix}$$

$$= \begin{bmatrix} 36.98961821 & 0.01820437 & -0.43941425 \\ 0.01820437 & 0.00005513 & -0.00037397 \\ -0.43941425 & -0.00037397 & 0.00576611 \end{bmatrix}$$

(Continued)

$$\mathbf{X'Y} = \begin{bmatrix} \Sigma Y \\ \Sigma X_2 Y \\ \Sigma X_3 Y \end{bmatrix} = \begin{bmatrix} 276.200 \\ 94{,}798.116 \\ 27{,}129.199 \end{bmatrix} \qquad \mathbf{Y'Y} = 5725.2$$

Estimation of the Parameters

To estimate $\boldsymbol{\beta}$: From equation 2.3.22,

$$\begin{bmatrix} \hat{\beta}_1 \\ \hat{\beta}_2 \\ \hat{\beta}_3 \end{bmatrix} = (\mathbf{X'X})^{-1}\mathbf{X'Y} = \begin{bmatrix} 21.3162 \\ 0.1091 \\ -0.3878 \end{bmatrix}$$

To estimate σ^2: Using equations 2.4.71 and 2.4.79, the sampling variance can be written as:

$$s^2 = \frac{1}{(N-K)} (\mathbf{Y'Y} - \hat{\boldsymbol{\beta}}'\mathbf{X'Y})$$

$$= \frac{1}{14-3} (5725.2 - 5703.0716)$$

$$= 2.0116$$

The standard deviation of regression is:

$$s = \sqrt{2.0116} = 1.4183$$

To calculate the variance-covariance matrix of $\hat{\boldsymbol{\beta}}$:

$$\text{var}(\hat{\boldsymbol{\beta}}) = s^2(\mathbf{X'X})^{-1} = \begin{bmatrix} 74.4095 & -0.0366 & -0.8839 \\ -0.0366 & 0.0001 & 0.0008 \\ -0.8839 & 0.0008 & 0.0116 \end{bmatrix}$$

Standard error of $\hat{\beta}_1 = \sqrt{74.4095} = 8.6261$
Standard error of $\hat{\beta}_2 = \sqrt{0.0001} = 0.0105$
Standard error of $\hat{\beta}_3 = \sqrt{0.0116} = 0.1077$

To compute $\mathbf{R}^2$: The coefficient of determination can be computed by using equation 3.3.29:

$$R^2 = \frac{\hat{\boldsymbol{\beta}}'\mathbf{X'Y} - 1/N\,(\Sigma Y)^2}{\mathbf{Y'Y} - 1/N\,(\Sigma Y)^2} = \frac{5703.0716 - 5449.0314}{5725.2000 - 5449.0314}$$

$$= \frac{254.0402}{276.1686} = 0.9199$$

Using equation 3.3.5 to adjust R^2 for degrees of freedom gives:

$$\bar{R}^2 = 1 - (1 - R^2)\ \frac{N - 1}{N - K} = 1 - 0.0801 \times \frac{13}{11} = 1 - 0.0947 = 0.9053$$

To compute partial correlations: By using equation 3.3.2 the simple correlation coefficients between two variables can be computed as:

$$r_{12} = \frac{\Sigma x_2 y}{(N - 1)s_{x_2} s_y} = \frac{2716.987}{13 \times 4.4415 \times 48.0954} = 0.9085$$

$$r_{13} = \frac{\Sigma x_3 y}{(N - 1)s_{x_3} s_y} = \frac{2100.358}{13 \times 4.7029 \times 48.0954} = 0.6633$$

$$r_{23} = \frac{\Sigma x_2 x_3}{(N - 1)s_{x_2} s_{x_3}} = \frac{108.953}{13 \times 4.4415 \times 4.7028} = 0.3728$$

Of course the cross products in deviation form are calculated by:

$$\Sigma x_2 y = \Sigma(X_2 - \bar{X}_2)\,(Y - \bar{Y}) = \Sigma X_2 Y - N\bar{X}_2\bar{Y}$$

$$= 94798.116 - 14 \times 19.729 \times 333.386 = 2716.987$$

$$\Sigma x_3 y = \Sigma(X_3 - \bar{X}_3)\,(Y - \bar{Y}) = \Sigma X_3 Y - N\bar{X}_3\bar{Y}$$

$$= 27{,}129.199 - 14 \times 97.829 \times 333.386 = 2100.358$$

$$\Sigma x_2 x_3 = \Sigma(X_2 - \bar{X}_2)\,(X_3 - \bar{X}_3) = \Sigma X_2 X_3 - N\bar{X}_2\bar{X}_3$$

$$= 458{,}705.406 - 14 \times 333.386 \times 97.829 = 108.953$$

From equations 3.3.31 through 3.3.33 the partial correlation between Y and X_2 with X_3 held constant is:

$$r_{12.3} = \frac{r_{12} - r_{13}\, r_{23}}{\sqrt{1 - r_{13}^2}\ \sqrt{1 - r_{23}^2}} = \frac{0.9085 - 0.6633 \times 0.3728}{\sqrt{0.5601}\ \sqrt{0.8612}}$$

$$= \frac{0.9085 - 0.2473}{0.7484 \times 0.9283} = \frac{0.6612}{0.6967} = 0.9490$$

The partial correlation between Y and X_3 with X_2 held constant is:

$$r_{13.2} = \frac{r_{13} - r_{12}\, r_{23}}{\sqrt{1 - r_{12}^2}\ \sqrt{1 - r_{23}^2}} = \frac{0.6633 - 0.9085 \times 0.3728}{\sqrt{0.1746}\ \sqrt{0.8612}}$$

$$= \frac{0.6633 - 0.3387}{0.4179 \times 0.9283} = \frac{0.3246}{0.3879} = 0.8368$$

The partial correlation between X_2 and X_3 with Y held constant is:

$$r_{23.1} = \frac{r_{23} - r_{12}\, r_{13}}{\sqrt{1 - r_{12}^2}\;\sqrt{1 - r_{13}^2}} = \frac{0.3728 - 0.9085 \times 0.6633}{\sqrt{0.1746}\;\sqrt{0.5601}}$$

$$= \frac{0.3728 - 0.6026}{0.4179 \times 0.7484} = \frac{-0.2298}{0.3128} = -0.7347$$

In general the statistical results can be presented in the following form:

$$\underset{(8.6261)}{Y = 21.3162} + \underset{(0.0105)}{0.1091X_2} - \underset{(0.1077)}{0.3879X_3}$$

$$\bar{R}^2 = 0.9053 \qquad s = 1.4183 \qquad r_{12.3} = 0.9490 \qquad r_{13.2} = 0.8368$$

Note that usually partial correlation coefficients are not reported.

Test of the Null Hypothesis

Hypotheses: H_0: $\beta_1 = 0$, $\beta_2 = 0$, and $\beta_3 = 0$.

Test: Using the t test we compute:

$$t_1 = \frac{\hat{\beta}_1 - \beta_1}{s_{\hat{\beta}_1}} = \frac{21.3162}{8.6261} = 2.4711$$

$$t_2 = \frac{\hat{\beta}_2 - \beta_2}{s_{\hat{\beta}_2}} = \frac{0.1091}{0.0105} = 10.3552$$

$$t_3 = \frac{\hat{\beta}_3 - \beta_3}{s_{\hat{\beta}_3}} = \frac{-0.3879}{0.1077} = -3.6014$$

The table value of t for d.f. = 11 at the 95 percent confidence level is 2.20. Thus we reject the null hypotheses in all three cases.

Interval Evaluation of β

To obtain 95 percent confidence interval estimates for β_1, β_2, and β_3, we write:

$$\text{pr}(-t_{0.025} < t < t_{0.025}) = 0.95$$

Substituting for t gives:

$$\text{pr}\left(-t_{0.025} < \frac{\hat{\beta}_1 - \beta_1}{s_{\hat{\beta}_1}} < t_{0.025}\right) = 0.95$$

$$\text{pr}\left(-t_{0.025} < \frac{\hat{\beta}_2 - \beta_2}{s_{\hat{\beta}_2}} < t_{0.025}\right) = 0.95$$

$$\text{pr}\left(-t_{0.025} < \frac{\hat{\beta}_3 - \beta_3}{s_{\hat{\beta}_3}} < t_{0.025}\right) = 0.95$$

Therefore,

$$\text{pr}(\hat{\beta}_1 - t_{0.025}s_{\hat{\beta}_1} < \beta_1 < \hat{\beta}_1 + t_{0.025}s_{\hat{\beta}_1}) = 0.95$$

$$\text{pr}(\hat{\beta}_2 - t_{0.025}s_{\hat{\beta}_2} < \beta_2 < \hat{\beta}_2 + t_{0.025}s_{\hat{\beta}_2}) = 0.95$$

$$\text{pr}(\hat{\beta}_3 - t_{0.025}s_{\hat{\beta}_3} < \beta_3 < \hat{\beta}_3 + t_{0.025}s_{\hat{\beta}_3}) = 0.95$$

so that the 95 percent confidence limits for β_1, β_2, and β_3 are:

$$\hat{\beta}_1 \pm t_{0.025}s_{\hat{\beta}_1} = 21.3162 \pm 2.20(8.6261) = 21.3162 \pm 18.6124$$

$$= 2.7038, 39.9286$$

$$\hat{\beta}_2 \pm t_{0.025}s_{\hat{\beta}_2} = 0.1091 \pm 2.20(0.0105) = 0.1091 \pm 0.0227$$

$$= 0.0864, 0.1318$$

$$\hat{\beta}_3 \pm t_{0.025}s_{\hat{\beta}_3} = -0.3879 \pm 2.20(0.1077) = -0.3879 \pm 0.2226$$

$$= -0.6105, -0.1653$$

3.5 INTERPRETATION OF THE REGRESSION RESULTS

Interpretation of the regression results must be done with extreme caution. First, postulated functional dependence cannot mean that the dependence is causal. Consider the multivariate model:

$$Y = \beta_0 + \beta_1X_1 + \beta_2X_2 + \ldots + \beta_KX_K + U \qquad \textbf{3.5.1}$$

As before, equation 3.5.1 states the functional dependence of Y on a set of X's. Explicitly, Y is linearly dependent on K different X's. The disturbance term U is additive in this linear model. Each of these β's (except β_0 which refers to the intercept of the function) measures the marginal variation in Y associated with the marginal variation in the related X variable. Direction of dependence is from the X's to the Y; and by our assumption of the independence of each X from the U term, the postulated direction is irreversible. This is not to suggest that there exists a casual relation between the Y and the X's. It is convenient to discuss the regression results in terms of: (1) the "effects" of the regressors on Y, that is, the regression coefficients $\hat{\beta}_1$, $\hat{\beta}_2$, ... $\hat{\beta}_K$ along with the intercept $\hat{\beta}_0$; (2) the extent of the variability of the estimated $\hat{Y}$, variance $\hat{\sigma}^2_u$, or s^2 or its square root s, commonly referred to as the standard error of the estimate; (3) the statistical significance of the estimated $\hat{\beta}$'s based on the variance of the $\hat{\beta}$'s; and (4) the degree of "goodness of fit" $\bar{R}^2$ corrected for degrees of freedom.

Regression Coefficients

The intercept $\hat{\beta}_0$ estimates the value of Y independent of the X's. In other words when all K of the X's are zero, there exists a value of Y that can be either positive or negative. Recall that in a typical consumption function when aggregate consumption is linearly dependent on aggregate income, the intercept is expected to be positive. Obviously in a typical savings function where savings is defined as income minus consumption, the intercept is generally negative. The intercept $\hat{\beta}_0$ does not vary with the variations in the X's.

The other regression coefficients $\hat{\beta}_1$, $\hat{\beta}_2, \ldots, \hat{\beta}_K$ measure the slope of the function with respect to the X variables in the postulated relation. A marginal change in a given X results in a marginal change in Y; the related $\hat{\beta}_k$ coefficient is an estimate of $\partial Y/\partial X_k$. In a k-dimensional plane, β_k is an estimate of the marginal change in the Y associated with a marginal change in X_k independent of all other X's. Regression coefficients are extensively used for prediction, simulation, or any other operational analyses.

In terms of the example calculated in equation 3.4.1, the intercept of the demand function for automobiles, $\hat{\beta}_1$, is -8.2419; that is, when income is zero, aggregate expenditure on automobiles is $-\$8.24$ billion. The slope of the function, $\hat{\beta}_2$, is 0.0839. For each dollar of additional income of the group, \$0.08 is spent on automobiles. Notice that the intercept of the function is expressed in the original units (in this case billions of dollars). The slope is a ratio of two marginal variations, a marginal change in automobile expenditure in the numerator and a marginal change in income in the denominator. The measure of slope is thus a pure number independent of the units in which the variables of the regression equation are expressed. The value of the slope can, however, be interpreted in terms of the units in which the original variables are measured. In our illustration, equation 3.4.1, units of both variables are in billions of dollars. If income changes by \$1 billion, expenditure on automobiles will change by \$0.08 billion, or \$80 million.

Standard Error of Estimates

The variance of the estimated regression line $\hat{\sigma}_u^2$ $(= s^2)$, another important measure, is related to the concept of an interval estimate as opposed to a point estimate. For the automobile demand equation, equation 3.4.1, the standard deviation of the regression, $\sqrt{s^2} = s$, is 2.00 (in billions of dollars). For a given value of the independent variable, income X_2, estimated model 3.4.1 generates an estimated value of $\hat{Y}_t$. For each such $\hat{Y}_t$ we measure a deviation. Each estimated value $\hat{Y}_t$ will, of course, be on the estimated straight line. Note that the estimate of standard deviation, s, is expressed in original units (in this case billions of dollars). The measure of deviation states that for each such $\hat{Y}_t$ there is a standard deviation. In terms of equation 3.4.1, the value of $\hat{Y}$ in 1952 is $-8.2419 + 0.0839(263.3) = \$13.9$; whereas the observed value of Y in 1952 is \$12.3. The estimated standard deviation of $\pm\$2$ means that the observed value is likely to fall, even if not on the line, within $\$13.9 \pm \$2$. In other words the observed value is likely to fall between \$15.9 and \$11.9 (billion) with a chosen level of probability. Computing the interval estimates for each estimated value $\hat{Y}_t$, we can obtain the pair of broken lines in Figure 3-3.

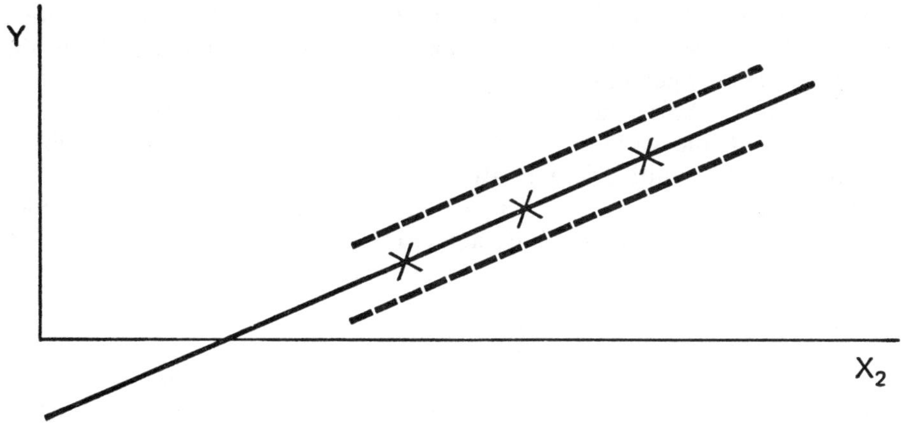

FIGURE 3-3

A 95 percent confidence level is most commonly used. Using the Z table, the appropriate value for Z is 1.96. Rounding off this number, one usually multiplies the estimated standard deviation by a factor of 2 and states that at a 95 percent confidence level the true mean value of Y_t is within the interval given by:

$$Y_t = \hat{Y}_t \pm 2(s) \qquad \textbf{3.5.2}$$

where s is the estimate of σ_u. In terms of equation 3.4.1, we can now say that at a 95 percent confidence level the true mean value of Y in 1952 lies between:

$$\$13.9 \pm 2(2) = 9.9 < Y_t < 17.9 \qquad \textbf{3.5.3}$$

As previously shown it is more appropriate to use the table of t distribution instead of the Z table. The 95 percent confidence interval for Y_t then is:

$$Y_t = \hat{Y}_t \pm t_{0.025}(s) \qquad \textbf{3.5.4}$$

In terms of the above illustration, with $N = 14$, $K = 2$, and degrees of freedom $N - K = 12$,

$$Y_t = \$13.9 \pm (2.179)(2)$$

or,

$$\$9.54 < Y_t < \$18.26$$

The Coefficient of Determination

As pointed out earlier, $\bar{R}^2$ is a statistic that measures concomitant covariation between the dependent variable Y and the independent variable

X or a set of X's. We can say that $\bar{R}^2$ is the coefficient of determination (corrected for degrees of freedom), and in equation 3.4.1 it expresses the degree to which expenditure on automobiles Y and income X_2 vary together. Our calculation shows that as much as 81 percent of the variation in Y is associated with the variation in X_2. Indeed the two variables mostly move together. In the multivariate relationship in equation 3.4.2, $\bar{R}^2$ similarly measures the coefficient of determination; and expenditure on automobiles Y varies with income X_2 and automobile price X_3 together to the extent of 91 percent.

Confidence Interval of Regression Coefficients

The true regression coefficients, often called population parameters, are unknown. In Chapter 1's discussion of the structure and model relationship, it was emphasized that the true parameters of the relationships specifying a structure are fixed. However, we have no knowledge of these true structural parameters. We specify a given model and estimate parameters from the given samples. The estimated parameters thus vary from sample to sample and are seldom fixed. In terms of expected value (over repeated samples), $E(\hat{\beta}_k)$ has been shown to be a BLUE estimator. Because the concept of expected value of a given estimator, $\hat{\beta}_k$, is of limited practical significance, the econometrician computes a confidence interval for the estimated parameter $\hat{\beta}_k$ based on the variance of the estimated parameter $\text{var}(\hat{\beta}_k)$. This says that each estimated parameter $\hat{\beta}_k$ has a standard deviation $s_{\hat{\beta}_k}$ that is obtained from $\sqrt{\text{var}(\hat{\beta}_k)}$ as discussed before. The estimated parameter $\hat{\beta}_k$ has a normal distribution if the disturbance term U_i is assumed to have a normal distribution. Even if in a small sample U_i is not normally distributed, $\hat{\beta}_k$ may be approximately normally distributed under certain assumptions as discussed before. (See Figure 3-4.)

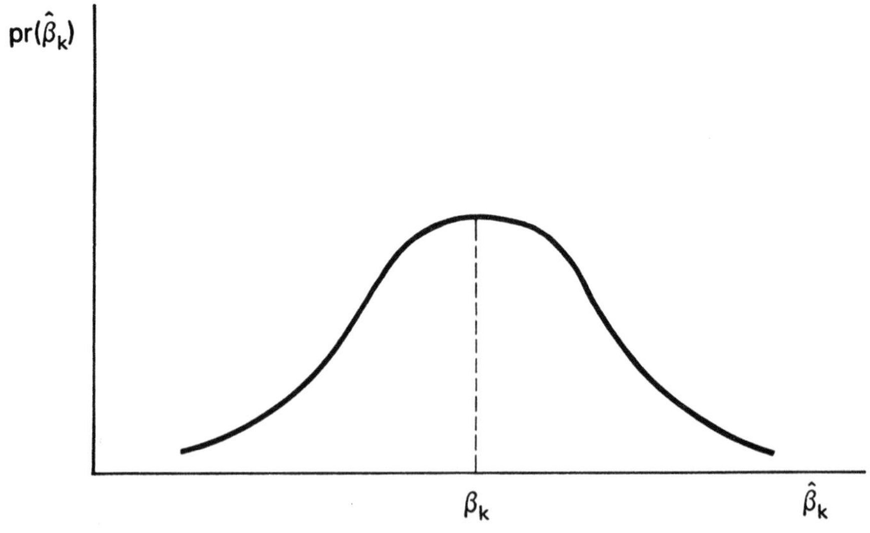

FIGURE 3-4

Once the normal distribution of $\hat{\beta}_k$ is postulated, it can be stated that the estimated value of the parameter $\hat{\beta}_k$ from a given sample lies on the distribution around the true value of the parameter β_k. Using the t distribution, for reasons dicussed before, we calculate a confidence interval for $\hat{\beta}_k$. Again in terms of equation 3.4.1, the estimated standard error of $\hat{\beta}_2$, $s_{\hat{\beta}_2}$ is 0.011. In other words the true value of the parameter lies in the interval at a 95 percent confidence level:

$$\text{pr}(\hat{\beta}_2 - t_{0.025}s_{\hat{\beta}_2} < \beta_2 < \hat{\beta}_2 + t_{0.025}s_{\hat{\beta}_2}) = 0.95 \qquad \mathbf{3.5.5}$$

Alternatively, we can express the same result by saying that for 95 out of every 100 "experiments" the value of β_2 will lie within the calculated interval $\hat{\beta}_2 \pm t_{0.025}\, s_{\hat{\beta}_2}$. Given the sample size (14) and the number of parameters estimated (2) in equation 3.4.1, the appropriate t value is 2.18, and:

$$\begin{aligned} \beta_2 &= 0.0839 \pm 2.18(0.0111) \\ &= 0.0839 \pm 0.0242 \end{aligned} \qquad \mathbf{3.5.6}$$

Thus the true value of β_2 is in the interval between 0.1081 and 0.0597 at a 95 percent confidence level. Similar interpretation can be given all $\hat{\beta}$'s estimated in a regression model.

We can now test the hypotheses. A priori economic theory teaches us that X_2 should have a positive effect on Y; that is, a marginal change in income X_2 should induce a positive marginal change in expenditure on automobiles Y. The a priori constraint is:

$$\frac{dY}{dX_2} > 0 \qquad \mathbf{3.5.7}$$

We set up the null hypothesis:

$$H_0\colon \beta_2 = 0$$

with the alternative hypothesis:

$$H_1\colon \beta_2 \neq 0$$

If the null hypothesis H_0 is true at the 95 percent confidence level, $\hat{\beta}_2$ will approach $\beta_2 = 0$; and there will be only a 5 percent probability of obtaining a t value exceeding 2.18, the critical value from the t table for the problem in equation 3.4.1. In other words the conclusion we draw is not 100 percent certain. If the chosen level of probability is 0.95, we concede that there is a 5 percent probability that the conclusion made will be an error. The computed t value is +7.5319 and falls in the shaded area on the right of the diagram in Figure 3-5, an area known as the *critical region*. Therefore, our conclusion is to reject the null hypothesis $H_0\colon \beta_2 = 0$ and to accept the alternative hypothesis H_1: $\beta_2 \neq 0$; the effect of income on automobile expenditure is not zero. Thus our a priori economic reasoning is found not to be refuted by the evidence.

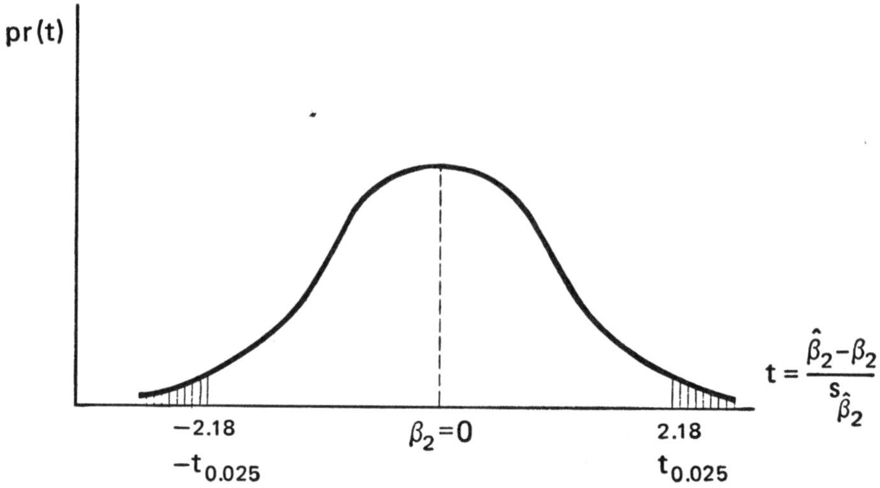

FIGURE 3-5

Following equation 3.5.7 with $\beta_2 > 0$, a one-tail test with a 5 percent critical region on the right can be constructed as in Figure 3-6. Of course the conclusion drawn before (with $t = 0.025$, two-tailed test) is reinforced.

Testing of hypotheses by t tests merits a word of caution. Let us look at the following familiar dilemma of a judge:

	True Situation	
Judge's Verdict	Guilty	Not Guilty
Guilty	+	− −
Not Guilty	−	+

The table expresses the ratings of a judge's verdict as a function of the true guilt or innocence of the defendant. To conclude that a guilty man is guilty and that a not-guilty man is nonguilty is of course to conclude what should be concluded. Otherwise the judge is in error. However, if a guilty man is found not guilty and is allowed to go free, it is considered less of a judicial error than the verdict that pronounces a not-guilty man guilty. The moral of the story is very suggestive.

If from a t test the conclusion is drawn too mechanically, the researcher may err. If a priori reasoning suggests no relationship between the dependent variable Y and the independent variable X_2 or X_3, acceptance of the null hypothesis—that the estimated parameter with respect to X_2 ($\hat{\beta}_2$) or X_3 ($\hat{\beta}_3$) is zero—will not be a mistake. On the other hand if there exists strong a priori reasoning to support the hypothesis of the substantive functional dependence

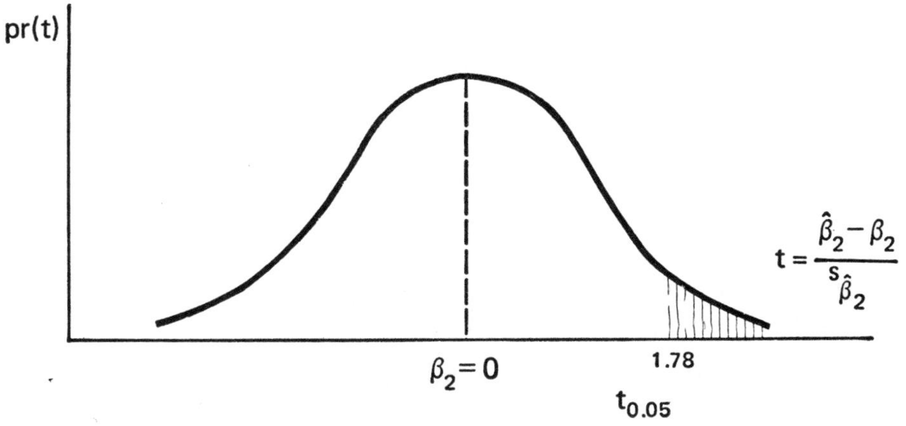

FIGURE 3-6

of Y on X_2 and on X_3 as in equation 3.4.2, lack of evidence from a straightforward t test would not be a strong enough argument to accept the null hypothesis. In equation 3.4.2, t tests sustain the a priori economic reasoning that as income increases, demand for automobiles increases; and as the price of automobiles increases, demand for automobiles decreases. In other words economic theory holds that:

$$\frac{\partial Y}{\partial X_2} > 0 \qquad \frac{\partial Y}{\partial X_3} < 0 \qquad \textbf{3.5.8}$$

If by chance following appropriate testing by t ratios, the null hypothesis with respect to parameters $\hat{\beta}_2$ and $\hat{\beta}_3$ estimated from a given sample were to be accepted, it would involve the repudiation of established economic theories. It is proper not to accept conclusions mechanically, and more so when they are in conflict with the established theory. In other samples the established theory may be upheld.

This is indeed a dilemma for the econometrician. Knowing the relatively weak foundation of economic theory, he is often left with no strong guideline. Nevertheless, firm knowledge of economic theory and understanding of the structure relative to the specific model should help when mechanistic application of statistical tools poses serious questions.

DISCUSSION QUESTIONS

1. The assumption of normal distribution of the disturbance term U_i provides the basis of the t test commonly applied to the regression estimates. Discuss.

2. Compute the correlation coefficient for the following data.

y	x
5	7
3	8
2	10
1	7
9	8

where $y = (Y_i - \bar{Y})$ and $x = (X_i - \bar{X})$

3. Review the rationale behind correcting the coefficient of correlation for the degrees of freedom.

4. Show the relationship between the correlation coefficient computed in question 2 above and the regression coefficient in question 2 of Chapter 2.

5. Compute the $\bar{R}^2$ in the multiple regression model of problem 8, Chapter 2.

6. How is the correlation model different from the regression model? What is meant by correlation pushing?

7.

Y	X
31.50	255.70
30.80	263.30
35.30	275.40
35.40	278.30
43.20	296.70
41.00	309.30
41.50	315.80
37.90	318.80
43.70	333.00
44.90	340.20
43.90	350.70
49.20	367.30
53.70	381.30
59.00	407.90

$$Y_t = \beta_0 + \beta_1 X_t + U_t$$

(a) Estimate β_0 and β_1 and their respective variances. Apply the t test to the estimates of the parameters.
(b) Compute the coefficient of correlation corrected for the degrees of freedom.
(c) Consider Y the expenditure on consumer durables in the country during the period 1951 through 1964, and X the disposable income of the economy (Both variables are in real dollars). How can the economic significance of the statistical findings be interpreted? Compute the elasticity of demand for consumer durables, and see if the empirical findings in the context of the given sample compare with the a priori hypothesis according to economic theory. Explain your answer.

8. Given the assumption that the disturbance terms are normally distributed, in addition to the set of assumptions otherwise given in a regression model, show that the OLS estimator is the maximum likelihood estimator.

9. Apply the t test to the estimates of the parameters of the regression model in problem 8, Chapter 2. Give an explanation of the economic significance of the test findings.

10. Show that the OLS estimators have the minimum variance.

SUGGESTED READINGS

Ezekiel, M., and K. A. Fox. *Methods of Correlation and Regression Analysis: Linear and Curvilinear*, 3d ed. New York: John Wiley & Sons, 1959.

Goldberger, Arthur S. *Topics in Regression Analysis*. New York: Macmillan Co., 1968.

Hoel, P. G. *Introduction to Mathematical Statistics*, 3d ed. New York: John Wiley & Sons, 1962.

Hogg, Robert V., and Allen T. Craig. *Introduction to Mathematical Statistics*, 2d ed. New York: Macmillan Co., 1968.

Huang, David S. *Regression and Econometric Methods*. New York: John Wiley & Sons, 1970.

Mood, A. M., and F. A. Graybill. *Introduction to the Theory of Statistics*, 2d ed. New York: McGraw-Hill Book Co., 1963.

Thomas, James J. *Notes on the Theory of Multiple Regression*. Athens, Greece: Center of Economic Research, 1964.

4

serial correlation and heteroscedasticity

4.0 IMPLICATIONS OF THE OLS ASSUMPTIONS

Chapters 2 and 3 discussed at length the derivation of the ordinary least squares estimators and their properties. These linear estimators are unbiased and have minimum variance in the class of linear estimators. As such, they are efficient and consistent. The proofs of these properties are based on certain assumptions that were spelled out in Chapters 2 and 3. In what follows, these assumptions and the consequences that follow from their violations will be examined.

4.1 SERIAL CORRELATION

Consider the assumption on the expected value of the error term covariances:

$$E(U_i U_j) = 0 \qquad \text{when } i \neq j$$

This assumption specifies the condition of mutual statistical independence for the different disturbance terms U_i. The U_i's are not correlated. This assumption is not met if the model is incorrectly specified and if the variables that have systematic influence on the dependent variable are omitted for convenience (lack of data) or because of inadequate knowledge of the structure.

In econometric studies based on time-series data, this assumption is often violated, an occurrence which presents an obvious problem. But we cannot assume away the existence of this problem even in cross-sectional work. Conceptually, the problem exists in either case. In time-series analysis we are given a set of observations taken in successive time periods. For each time period we assume that the relationship between the dependent and independent variables includes a disturbance term U_t associated with the particular time period. We then further assume that each such term is statistically independent of all other U terms associated with other different time periods. That is, $E(U_t U_{t+\theta}) = 0$ for all θ, where θ refers to all time periods other than the period indicated by t, $\theta = 1, 2, \ldots, T$.

In cross-sectional analysis the observations relate to many different units at a particular given point of time, and each disturbance term is associated with a particular unit. To fulfill the assumption on the disturbance terms, the U_i's related to the individual units must all be statistically independent. The U term related to the Smith family is assumed to be independent of the U term related to the Washington family. That is, $E(U_iU_j) = 0$, $i \neq j$. If the disturbance terms do not fulfill this assumption of mutual independence, they are said to be *autocorrelated* or *serially correlated.*

The assumption of mutual independence of error terms ensures the efficiency of the estimator. Using this assumption we have been able to show that the least squares estimator is "best" in the sense that it has the least variance of the class of linear unbiased estimators. The presence of serial correlation makes the OLS estimators less efficient. Because the variance of the estimator is affected, the estimate of the confidence interval also becomes less reliable. Serial correlation, however, does not affect the property of unbiasedness, nor is the property of consistency necessarily affected.

First-Order Markov Sequence

As a beginning, suppose that the disturbances are linearly dependent in the following pattern:

$$U_t = \rho U_{t-1} + V_t \qquad \textbf{4.1.1}$$

where $|\rho| < 1$, $E(V_t) = 0$, and $E(V_tV_{t+\theta}) = 0$ for all t when $\theta \neq 0$; and $E(V_tV_{t+\theta}) = \sigma_v^2$ for all t when $\theta = 0$. The pattern in equation 4.1.1 is said to follow a first-order Markov sequence. This means that U_t consists of two parts, one that is systematically dependent on U_{t-1} and explained by the coefficient ρ, and one, V_t, that is truly random and fulfills the basic assumptions of zero mean, mutual independence, and constant and finite variance.

Using least squares estimation methods, the estimator of ρ is:

$$\begin{aligned} \hat{\rho} &= \frac{\Sigma U_tU_{t-1}}{\Sigma U_{t-1}^2} \\ &\doteq \frac{\Sigma U_tU_{t-1}}{\Sigma U_t^2} \qquad t = 1, 2, \ldots, T \end{aligned} \qquad \textbf{4.1.2}$$

since $\Sigma U_{t-1}^2 \doteq \Sigma U_t^2$ for a sufficiently large sample.[1] Returning to the first-order Markov condition, it follows that:

$$\begin{aligned} U_t &= \rho U_{t-1} + V_t \\ &= \rho(\rho U_{t-2} + V_{t-1}) + V_t \\ &= \rho^2(\rho U_{t-3} + V_{t-2}) + \rho V_{t-1} + V_t \\ &= \rho^3(\rho U_{t-4} + V_{t-3}) + \rho^2 V_{t-2} + \rho V_{t-1} + V_t \end{aligned}$$

[1] The symbol $\doteq$ denotes approximately equal. In this equation and elsewhere in this section, the symbol t is used for the index of summation to indicate the reference to different time periods. In the previous chapter the summation index used was denoted by i or j.

Continuing the sequence indefinitely,

$$U_t = V_t + \rho V_{t-1} + \rho^2 V_{t-2} + \cdots + \rho^s V_{t-s} + \cdots$$
$$= \sum_{s=0}^{\infty} \rho^s V_{t-s} \qquad \textbf{4.1.3}$$

By assumption, $E(V_t) = 0$. Therefore,

$$E(U_t) = 0 \qquad \textbf{4.1.4}$$

The variance of U_t in terms of the variance of V_t can now be calculated. The expression for U_t^2 in terms of V_t^2 from equation 4.1.3 is:

$$E(U_t^2) = E(V_t^2) + \rho^2 E(V_{t-1}^2) + \rho^4 E(V_{t-2}^2) + \cdots \qquad \textbf{4.1.5}$$

The cross product terms of the form $E(V_t V_{t+\theta})$ vanish because of the assumption in equation 4.1.1. Using the definition of variance, $E(U_t^2) = \sigma_u^2$, we have, ignoring the terms after ρ^s,

$$\sigma_u^2 = (1 + \rho^2 + \rho^4 + \cdots + \rho^s + \cdots)\sigma_v^2 \qquad \textbf{4.1.6}$$

Multiplying this equation by ρ^2, we obtain:

$$\rho^2\sigma_u^2 = (\rho^2 + \rho^4 + \rho^6 + \cdots + \rho^{s+2})\sigma_v^2 \qquad \textbf{4.1.7}$$

Subtracting equation 4.1.7 from equation 4.1.6,

$$\sigma_u^2 (1 - \rho^2) = (1 - \rho^{s+2})\sigma_v^2$$
$$\sigma_u^2 = \frac{1 - \rho^{s+2}}{1 - \rho^2}\sigma_v^2$$

As the index s increases indefinitely, the term ρ^{s+2} approaches zero for $\rho < 1$, and we have:

$$\sigma_u^2 = \frac{1}{1 - \rho^2}\sigma_v^2 \qquad \textbf{4.1.8}$$

Calculating the covariance of the error terms U_t for the first-order Markov scheme of autoregression,

$$E(U_t U_{t-1}) = E[(V_t + \rho V_{t-1} + \rho^2 V_{t-2} + \cdots)(V_{t-1} + \rho V_{t-2} + \rho^2 V_{t-3} + \cdots)]$$
$$= E[V_t + \rho(V_{t-1} + \rho V_{t-2} + \cdots)(V_{t-1} + \rho V_{t-2} + \cdots)]$$
$$= \rho E[(V_{t-1} + \rho V_{t-2} + \cdots)(V_{t-1} + \rho V_{t-2} + \cdots)] \qquad \textbf{4.1.9}$$
$$= \rho E(U_{t-1}U_{t-1})$$
$$= \rho\sigma_u^2$$

Similarly,

$$E(U_tU_{t-2}) = \rho^2\sigma_u^2, \quad E(U_tU_{t-3}) = \rho^3\sigma_u^2$$

And, generally, for any s and t,

$$E(U_tU_{t-s}) = \rho^s\sigma_u^2 \qquad \textbf{4.1.10}$$

We can then write these results in generalized form using matrix notation. The variance-covariance matrix for the disturbance terms when there are only two terms, U_t and U_{t-1}, is:

$$E(\mathbf{UU'}) = \begin{bmatrix} E(U_t^2) & E(U_tU_{t-1} \\ E(U_tU_{t-1}) & E(U_{t-1}^2) \end{bmatrix} \qquad \textbf{4.1.11}$$

Expressing $E(U_t^2)$ and $E(U_tU_{t-1})$ in terms of ρ and σ_v^2 from equations 4.1.8 and 4.1.9,

$$E(\mathbf{UU'}) = \begin{bmatrix} \frac{1}{1-\rho^2}\sigma_v^2 & \frac{\rho}{1-\rho^2}\sigma_v^2 \\ \frac{\rho}{1-\rho^2}\sigma_v^2 & \frac{1}{1-\rho^2}\sigma_v^2 \end{bmatrix} \qquad \textbf{4.1.12}$$

$$= \frac{1}{1-\rho^2}\sigma_v^2 \begin{bmatrix} 1 & \rho \\ \rho & 1 \end{bmatrix}$$

The more generalized expression for $t = 1, 2, \ldots, T$ is:

$$E(\mathbf{UU'}) = \frac{1}{1-\rho^2}\sigma_v^2 \begin{bmatrix} 1 & \rho & \rho^2 & \cdots & \rho^{T-1} \\ \rho & 1 & \rho & \cdots & \rho^{T-2} \\ \rho^2 & \rho & 1 & \cdots & \rho^{T-3} \\ \cdot & \cdot & \cdot & & \cdot \\ \cdot & \cdot & \cdot & & \cdot \\ \cdot & \cdot & \cdot & & \cdot \\ \rho^{T-1} & \rho^{T-2} & \rho^{T-3} & \cdots & 1 \end{bmatrix} \qquad \textbf{4.1.13}$$

Notice that the matrix on the right-hand side of this equation cannot be expressed as a constant multiple of the identity matrix of order T.

$$E(\mathbf{UU'}) \neq k\mathbf{I}_T$$

Compare this equation with equation 2.2.10 derived under the assumption that the disturbance terms are mutually independent. It is obvious that straightforward application of the least squares method will not give a minimum variance estimate of $\text{var}(\hat{\beta}_k)$. Note also that in estimating the sampling variance, given $\text{var}(\hat{\beta}_k) = \sigma_u^2(\mathbf{X}'\mathbf{X})^{-1}$, we make certain assumptions about the distribution of the X's; either they are assumed to be fixed mathematical variables or they have random normal distribution. In the event the X's are autocorrelated, the problem becomes far more intractable.

Durbin-Watson Test

Once we recognize the nature of the problem of serial correlation, we must find out whether it exists in the particular case under investigation. We can use several tests to determine the presence of serial correlation, one of which is the Durbin-Watson test based on the residuals from regression analysis.[2] The test is computed as follows:

$$d = \frac{\sum_{t=2}^{T}(\hat{U}_t - \hat{U}_{t-1})^2}{\sum_{t=1}^{T}\hat{U}_t^2} \qquad \textbf{4.1.14}$$

---

[2] Another well-known test is the von Neumann ratio:

$$\frac{\delta^2}{S^2} = \frac{\sum_{t=2}^{T}(U_t - U_{t-1})^2}{\sum_{t=1}^{T}U_t^2} \quad \frac{T}{T-1}$$

Note that this test is based on random and normal U_t. Since the random observations U_t are not known, the d test (equation 4.1.14), which is based on the regression residuals $\hat{U}_t$, is more directly applicable. For further discussions consult the works of J. von Neumann and I. B. Hart cited in the Selected Readings at the end of Chapter 4.

H. Theil and A. L. Nagar propose a test that is based on an approximate distribution of the Durbin-Watson d which seeks to minimize the region of inconclusive evidence as is the case when d is between d_L and d_u. Refer to the work by Theil and Nagar cited in the Selected Readings at the end of this chapter.

Another test has recently been proposed by R. C. Henshaw. This test is shown to be conclusive but computationally too difficult. For the Durbin-Watson test see J. Durbin and G. Watson, "Testing Serial Correlation in Least Squares Regression Part I," *Biometrika*, Vol. 37 (December, 1950), pp. 409-428; and for Part II, see *Biometrika*, Vol. 38 (June, 1951), pp. 159-178.

Durbin himself has proposed a further test for the inconclusive case which is not discussed here. See J. Durbin, "An Alternative to the Bounds Test for Testing Serial Correlation in Least Squares Regression," *Econometrica*, Vol. 38, No. 3 (May, 1970), pp. 422-429.

Henri Theil has suggested an alternative route. Instead of developing further tests on the least squares residuals, he recommends a new estimator (BLUS) of the residuals. This estimator U will be best, linear, "unbiased" (BLU) and have scalar (S) covariance matrix of the form $\sigma^2 I$. The BLUS estimate $\hat{U}$ can then be used for the autocorrelation test. However, the computational work for the BLUS $\hat{U}$ is more involved. See H. Theil, "The Analysis of Disturbances in Regression Analysis," *Journal of the American Statistical Association*, Vol. 60, No. 312 (December, 1965), pp. 1067-1079.

To analyze it further, expand the expression on the right:

$$d = \frac{\Sigma \hat{U}_t^2 - 2\Sigma \hat{U}_t \hat{U}_{t-1} + \Sigma \hat{U}_{t-1}^2}{\Sigma \hat{U}_t^2}$$

Because $\Sigma \hat{U}_t^2$ is approximately equal to $\Sigma \hat{U}_{t-1}^2$ for a sufficiently large sample, we can write:

$$d \doteq \frac{2\Sigma \hat{U}_t^2 - 2\Sigma \hat{U}_t \hat{U}_{t-1}}{\Sigma \hat{U}_t^2} \qquad \textbf{4.1.15}$$

Rearranging,

$$\begin{aligned} d &= \frac{2\Sigma \hat{U}_t^2}{\Sigma \hat{U}_t^2} - \frac{2\Sigma \hat{U}_t \hat{U}_{t-1}}{\Sigma \hat{U}_t^2} \\ &= 2 - 2\rho \qquad \textbf{4.1.16} \\ &= 2 \end{aligned}$$

if and only if:

$$\rho = \frac{\Sigma \hat{U}_t \hat{U}_{t-1}}{\Sigma \hat{U}_t^2} = 0 \qquad \textbf{4.1.17}$$

Note that the expression for ρ in equation 4.1.17 is just the estimator $\hat{\rho}$ of the coefficient of the first-order Markov sequence 4.1.2.

From this argument we can see that the value of the d statistic depends on the measure of the first-order correlation between U_t and U_{t-1}. The econometrician feels comfortable when his computed d is close to 2. He concludes that the problem of serial correlation is not acute since there is no evidence of significant positive autocorrelation. The d_L and d_U are, respectively, the lower and upper limiting values. Tables computing values of d_L and d_U at various confidence levels are available for different numbers of observations and numbers of parameters estimated. It is important to note that these tables are based on parameters related to truly exogenous variables, excluding the constant term. However, residuals should be computed when the constant along with other parameters has been estimated.

The d_L and d_U values from the tables are used to test the hypothesis of nonautocorrelation of the disturbance terms. If the computed d is above the value of d_U in the table, the conclusion is that the residuals have no positive serial correlation. If it is less than d_L, the hypothesis of no positive serial correlation is rejected. If d is greater than d_L but less than d_U, the evidence is inconclusive.

Note that:

$$\begin{aligned} d &= 2 - 2\rho \\ &= 4 \end{aligned} \qquad \textbf{4.1.18}$$

when $\rho = -1$. Thus it is easy to design a similar test of negative serial correlation by computing a quantity after subtracting the computed d from 4. The quantity $4 - d$ has to be read and compared with the related table values of d_L and d_U. To sum up, for testing the hypothesis $\rho = 0$ against $\rho > 0$, when:

$$\begin{aligned} &d > d_U, \text{ accept } \rho = 0 \\ &d_L \leq d \leq d_U, \text{ no conclusive evidence} \\ &d < d_L, \text{ reject } \rho = 0 \end{aligned} \qquad \textbf{4.1.19}$$

Similarly, for testing $\rho = 0$ against $\rho < 0$, when:

$$\begin{aligned} &4 - d > d_U, \text{ accept } \rho = 0 \\ &d_L \leq 4 - d \leq d_U, \text{ no conclusive evidence} \\ &4 - d < d_L, \text{ reject } \rho = 0 \end{aligned} \qquad \textbf{4.1.20}$$

The quantity d has a possible range of values from 0 to 4. If the residuals are positively serially correlated, then the calculated value of d will be small; alternatively, if the residuals are negatively serially correlated, the calculated value of d will be large. Combining the two sets of rules 4.1.19 and 4.1.20, the two-tailed test can be made as follows. For testing the hypothesis $\rho = 0$ against $\rho \neq 0$, when:

$$\begin{aligned} &d > d_U \text{ or } d < 4 - d_U, \text{ accept } \rho = 0 \\ &d_L \leq d \leq d_U \text{ or } 4 - d_U \leq d \leq 4 - d_L, \text{ no conclusive evidence} \\ &d < d_L \text{ or } d > 4 - d_L, \text{ reject } \rho = 0 \end{aligned} \qquad \textbf{4.1.21}$$

Note that the application of the d test is based on the assumption that the regressors X_i in the equation to be estimated are nonstochastic variables; they are fixed mathematical variables. As such, application of this test when lagged values of Y appear among the regressors will be inappropriate. Chapter 7 will discuss this further. Also note that the d test is good only for first-order autocorrelation. Should there exist any higher order autocorrelation, it is expected that the first-order autocorrelation coefficient will turn out to be significant. With annual time-series data such an assumption has been found to be satisfactory. But with quarterly time-series data, researchers have questioned the usefulness of such an assumption.

Least Squares Estimation in the Presence of Serial Correlation

First difference method: A simple solution for the problem of serial correlation is to select arbitrarily a value for ρ, under the assumption that the disturbances follow a first-order Markov scheme: $U_t = \rho U_{t-1} + V_t$ as in equation 4.1.1. If ρ is assumed to be unity, it follows that:

$$U_t - U_{t-1} = V_t \qquad 4.1.22$$

Consider the regression model:

$$Y_t = \beta_0 + \beta_1 X_t + U_t \qquad 4.1.23$$

Similarly, for the period $t - 1$,

$$Y_{t-1} = \beta_0 + \beta_1 X_{t-1} + U_{t-1}$$

Subtracting,

$$(Y_t - Y_{t-1}) = \beta_1(X_t - X_{t-1}) + (U_t - U_{t-1})$$

or,

$$\Delta Y_t = \beta_1 \, \Delta X_t + V_t \qquad 4.1.24$$

Since V_t is assumed to fulfill the basic assumptions for OLS estimation, the OLS regression estimation in terms of the first differences of the original observations will have the desirable BLUE properties. This method constitutes a shortcut once widely used by econometricians. In general, however, the assumption $\rho = 1$ is of questionable validity. Indeed Kadiyala has recently presented evidence that seriously challenges the validity of the usual procedure of taking the first differences rather than the original variables when the serial correlation coefficient ρ is unity or close to one.[3]

Cochrane-Orcutt method: The Cochrane-Orcutt method is a way of estimating the parameters of a linear equation with autoregressive disturbances that does not assume an arbitrary value of one for ρ.[4] One possibility is to estimate this coefficient by using the residuals obtained from regressing Y on X. Ideally, we can search for a value of ρ.

Let us return to model 4.1.23,

$$Y_t = \beta_0 + \beta_1 X_t + U_t \qquad 4.1.25$$

[3] K. R. Kadiyala, "A Transformation Used to Circumvent the Problem of Autocorrelation," *Econometrica*, Vol. 36, No. 1 (January, 1968), pp. 93-96.

[4] D. Cochrane and G. H. Orcutt, "Application of Least Squares Regression to Relationships Containing Autocorrelated Terms," *Journal of the American Statistical Association*, Vol. 44, No. 245 (September, 1949), pp. 32-61.

J.D. Sargan has shown that the iterative process with values of ρ arbitrarily chosen from -1 to $+1$ will always converge to a stationary value of the residual sum of squares $\Sigma \hat{u}_i^2$. However, in a given situation there may exist several local minima, in which case the process of iteration would converge into one of them depending on the starting value of ρ chosen. See J. D. Sargan, "Wages and Prices in the United Kingdom: A Study in Econometric Methodology," *Econometric Analysis for National Economic Planning*, edited by P. E. Hart, *et al.* (London: Butterworth & Co., 1964), pp. 25-54.

where $U_t = \rho U_{t-1} + V_t$. Writing this equation for period $t - 1$, we have:

$$Y_{t-1} = \beta_0 + \beta_1 X_{t-1} + U_{t-1} \qquad \textbf{4.1.26}$$

We then multiply equation 4.1.26 by ρ, the first-order Markov coefficient, and obtain:

$$\rho Y_{t-1} = \rho\beta_0 + \rho\beta_1 X_{t-1} + \rho U_{t-1} \qquad \textbf{4.1.27}$$

Subtracting equation 4.1.27 from equation 4.1.25,

$$Y_t - \rho Y_{t-1} = \beta_0(1 - \rho) + \beta_1(X_t - \rho X_{t-1}) + (U_t - \rho U_{t-1}) \qquad \textbf{4.1.28}$$

$$= \beta_0(1 - \rho) + \beta_1(X_t - \rho X_{t-1}) + V_t \qquad \textbf{4.1.29}$$

By assumption, the disturbance terms V_t fulfill all the basic conditions for the OLS estimators, and the equation parameters are estimable by the OLS method. But notice that the equation involves transformation of the original observations on Y_t and X_t to $Y_t - \rho Y_{t-1}$ and $X_t - \rho X_{t-1}$ respectively. To carry out this transformation, information on ρ is needed. One solution suggested in this method is to begin with the least squares regression. From the residuals,

$$\hat{U}_t = Y_t - \hat{\beta}_0 - \hat{\beta}_1 X_t$$

we estimate ρ in the regression equation:

$$\hat{U}_t = \rho\hat{U}_{t-1} + V_t$$

and

$$\hat{\rho} = \frac{\Sigma \hat{U}_t \hat{U}_{t-1}}{\Sigma \hat{U}_{t-1}^2} \qquad \textbf{4.1.30}$$

We can then use the estimated coefficient $\hat{\rho}$ in transforming the original observations on Y and X. Construct:

$$X_t^* = X_t - \hat{\rho} X_{t-1}$$

and

$$Y_t^* = Y_t - \hat{\rho} Y_{t-1}$$

and reestimate:

$$Y_t^* = \beta_0^* + \beta_1^* X_t^* + U_t^* \qquad \textbf{4.1.31}$$

We can now apply the Durbin-Watson test to the new set of estimated residuals:

$$\hat{U}_t^* = Y_t^* - \hat{\beta}_0^* - \hat{\beta}_1^* X_t^* \quad \textbf{4.1.32}$$

If the test indicates that autocorrelation persists for this set of residuals, the process can be repeated for another round. In this next round we estimate ρ^* from:

$$\hat{U}_t^* = \rho^* \hat{U}_{t-1}^* + V_t^*$$

and

$$\hat{\rho}^* = \Sigma \hat{U}_t^* \hat{U}_{t-1}^* / \Sigma \hat{U}_{t-1}^{*2} \quad \textbf{4.1.33}$$

We again transform the variables Y_t^* and X_t^* by taking:

$$Y_t^{**} = Y_t^* - \hat{\rho}^*(Y_{t-1}^*)$$

$$X_t^{**} = X_t^* - \hat{\rho}^*(X_{t-1}^*)$$

and estimate:

$$Y_t^{**} = \beta_0^{**} + \beta_1^{**} X_t^{**} + U_t^{**} \quad \textbf{4.1.34}$$

The process can be repeated until the desired results are obtained.

Even though the above method has received much attention, not much is known about its statistical properties. Kadiyala claims that the suggested transformation for the Cochrane-Orcutt method does not necessarily improve the efficiency of the estimators; and that, in fact, there exist cases where it leads to less efficient estimators.[5]

Durbin's method: An alternative method of estimation of the parameter ρ in equation 4.1.35 with appropriate asymptotic properties has been proposed by J. Durbin.[6] To obtain equation 4.1.35, we carry out the following manipulations: Recall equations 4.1.25 through 4.1.27,

$$Y_t = \beta_0 + \beta_1 X_t + U_t$$

$$\rho Y_{t-1} = \beta_0 \rho + \beta_1 \rho X_{t-1} + \rho U_{t-1}$$

Subtracting,

$$Y_t - \rho Y_{t-1} = \beta_0(1 - \rho) + \beta_1 X_t - \beta_1 \rho X_{t-1} + U_t - \rho U_{t-1}$$

or

$$Y_t = \beta_0' + \beta_1' X_t - \beta_2' X_{t-1} + \rho Y_{t-1} + \epsilon_t \quad \textbf{4.1.35}$$

where $\beta_0' = \beta_0(1 - \rho), \beta_1' = \beta_1, \beta_2' = \beta_1 \rho$, and $\epsilon_t = U_t - \rho U_{t-1}$. Use the estimate of $\hat{\rho}$ from the above equation for the transformation of the observed values of Y_t and X_t as discussed above.

---

[5] Kadiyala, *op. cit.*

[6] J. Durbin, "Estimation of Parameters in Time Series Regression Models," *Journal of the Royal Statistical Society*, Vol. 22-B (January, 1960), pp. 139-153.

The search method: Another method of estimating the coefficient ρ is the search method.[7] According to this method, ρ is allowed to take any value between -1 and $+1$ given that the regression model is, as in equation 4.1.31,

$$(Y_t - \rho Y_{t-1}) = \beta_0^* + \beta_1^* (X_t - \rho X_{t-1}) + (U_t - \rho U_{t-1})$$

At each round for each chosen value of ρ, the OLS residual sum of the squares can be calculated. After the search the ρ that makes the residual sum of the squares minimum is selected, and the corresponding estimates of β_0 and β_1 are the recommended estimators.

Generalized least squares method: A. C. Aitken's generalized least squares (GLS) method offers a formal solution to the problem of estimating the parameters of a linear equation with autoregressive disturbance terms.[8] Without proof the outline of the GLS analysis can be described as follows. We shall no longer assume that the expected values of the disturbance terms U_t are mutually independent. Instead we assume that there is mutual dependence. That is,

$$\begin{aligned} E(\mathbf{UU'}) &\neq \sigma_u^2 \mathbf{I} \\ E(\mathbf{UU'}) &= \sigma_u^2 \mathbf{\Omega} \end{aligned} \qquad 4.1.36$$

where $\mathbf{\Omega}$ is the matrix of rows and columns consisting of coefficients of dependence between successive disturbance terms. When the disturbances follow a first-order Markov sequence, (equations 4.1.1 through 4.1.3 and 4.1.8 through 4.1.13), we can write:

$$\mathbf{\Omega} = \begin{bmatrix} 1 & \rho & \rho^2 \ldots \rho^{T-1} \\ \rho & 1 & \rho \ldots \rho^{T-2} \\ \cdot & \cdot & \cdot \quad \cdot \\ \cdot & \cdot & \cdot \quad \cdot \\ \cdot & \cdot & \cdot \quad \cdot \\ \rho^{T-1} & \rho^{T-2} & \rho^{T-3} \ldots 1 \end{bmatrix} \qquad 4.1.37$$

[7] C. Hildreth and J. Y. Lu, *Demand Relations with Autocorrelated Disturbances*, Technical Bulletin No. 276 (East Lansing: University of Michigan Press, 1960); and J. D. Sargan, "Wages and Prices in the United Kingdom: A Study in Econometric Methodology," *Econometric Analysis for National Economic Planning*, edited by P. E. Hart, *et al.* (London: Butterworth & Co., 1964), pp. 25-54.

[8] A. C. Aitken, "On Least Squares and Linear Combinations of Observations," *Proceedings of the Royal Statistical Society of Edinburgh*, Vol. 55 (1935), pp. 42-48.

from which:

$$\boldsymbol{\Omega}^{-1} = (1-\rho^2)^{-1}\begin{bmatrix} 1 & -\rho & 0 & \dots & 0 & 0 \\ -\rho & (1+\rho^2) & -\rho & \dots & 0 & 0 \\ 0 & -\rho & (1+\rho^2) & \dots & 0 & 0 \\ \cdot & \cdot & \cdot & & \cdot & \cdot \\ \cdot & \cdot & \cdot & & \cdot & \cdot \\ \cdot & \cdot & \cdot & & \cdot & \cdot \\ 0 & 0 & 0 & \dots & (1+\rho^2) & -\rho \\ 0 & 0 & 0 & \dots & -\rho & 1 \end{bmatrix} \quad \mathbf{4.1.38}$$

Naturally we must generalize the OLS regression method in a suitable way to take care of this interdependence of disturbance terms. Aitken's method does this job. The GLS estimators of $\boldsymbol{\beta}$ and var($\boldsymbol{\beta}$) for the model:

$$\mathbf{Y} = \mathbf{X}\boldsymbol{\beta} + \mathbf{U}$$

with

$$E(\mathbf{UU}') = \sigma_u^2\boldsymbol{\Omega}$$

are given as:

$$\hat{\hat{\boldsymbol{\beta}}} = (\mathbf{X}'\boldsymbol{\Omega}^{-1}\mathbf{X})^{-1}(\mathbf{X}'\boldsymbol{\Omega}^{-1}\mathbf{Y}) \quad \mathbf{4.1.39}$$

$$\text{var}(\hat{\hat{\boldsymbol{\beta}}}) = \sigma_u^2(\mathbf{X}'\boldsymbol{\Omega}^{-1}\mathbf{X})^{-1} \quad \mathbf{4.1.40}$$

These estimators replace the OLS estimators where:

$$\hat{\boldsymbol{\beta}} = (\mathbf{X}'\mathbf{X})^{-1}(\mathbf{X}'\mathbf{Y})$$

$$\text{var}(\hat{\boldsymbol{\beta}}) = \sigma_u^2(\mathbf{X}'\mathbf{X})^{-1}$$

given $E(\mathbf{UU}') = \sigma_u^2\mathbf{I}$. Notice that the use of the GLS method in this situation requires foreknowledge of the single parameter ρ that enters in the matrix $\boldsymbol{\Omega}$, and that according to equations 4.1.39 and 4.1.40 we must invert this matrix. Not only do we need information about $\boldsymbol{\Omega}$, but the information should be adequate for the necessary mathematical manipulation. The task is difficult but not impossible. An approximation of the true $\boldsymbol{\Omega}$ is considered better than nothing.

The GLS and Cochrane-Orcutt transformation: There exists a relationship between the method of using transformed variables as in equation 4.1.31 and the GLS method. Let us return to the simple model:

$$Y_t = \beta_0 + \beta_1 X_t + U_t$$

and rewrite it in matrix notation:

$$\mathbf{Y} = \mathbf{X}\boldsymbol{\beta} + \mathbf{U}$$

where the vectors of **Y**, **X**, **U**, and $\boldsymbol{\beta}$ are:

$$\mathbf{Y} = \begin{bmatrix} Y_1 \\ Y_2 \\ \cdot \\ \cdot \\ \cdot \\ Y_T \end{bmatrix} \quad \mathbf{X} = \begin{bmatrix} 1 & X_1 \\ 1 & X_2 \\ \cdot & \cdot \\ \cdot & \cdot \\ \cdot & \cdot \\ 1 & X_T \end{bmatrix} \quad \mathbf{U} = \begin{bmatrix} U_1 \\ U_2 \\ \cdot \\ \cdot \\ \cdot \\ U_T \end{bmatrix} \quad \boldsymbol{\beta} = \begin{bmatrix} \beta_0 \\ \beta_1 \end{bmatrix}$$

Suppose that there exists a transformation matrix **W** to operate on the model:

$$\mathbf{W}(\mathbf{Y}) = \mathbf{W}(\mathbf{X}\boldsymbol{\beta} + \mathbf{U}) \qquad \textbf{4.1.41}$$

or,

$$\mathbf{WY} = \mathbf{WX}\boldsymbol{\beta} + \mathbf{WU} \qquad \textbf{4.1.42}$$

where $\mathbf{WY} = \mathbf{Y}^*$

$\mathbf{WX} = \mathbf{X}^*$

$\mathbf{WU} = \mathbf{U}^*$

and

$$E(\mathbf{WUU'W'}) = \sigma_u^2\mathbf{I} \qquad \textbf{4.1.43}$$

The OLS estimator of $\boldsymbol{\beta}$ will thus have the desired properties. Consider the transformation discussed above which transforms X_t, Y_t, and U_t into $X_t - \rho X_{t-1}$, $Y_t - \rho Y_{t-1}$, and $U_t - \rho U_{t-1}$. In matrix notation these transformed variables can be written as:

$$\mathbf{Y}^* = \begin{bmatrix} Y_2 - \rho Y_1 \\ Y_3 - \rho Y_2 \\ \cdot \\ \cdot \\ \cdot \\ Y_T - \rho Y_{T-1} \end{bmatrix} \quad \mathbf{X}^* = \begin{bmatrix} 1-\rho & X_2 - \rho X_1 \\ 1-\rho & X_3 - \rho X_2 \\ \cdot & \cdot \\ \cdot & \cdot \\ \cdot & \cdot \\ 1-\rho & X_T - \rho X_{T-1} \end{bmatrix} \qquad \textbf{4.1.44}$$

$$\mathbf{U}^* = \begin{bmatrix} U_2 - \rho U_1 \\ U_3 - \rho U_2 \\ \cdot \\ \cdot \\ \cdot \\ U_T - \rho U_{T-1} \end{bmatrix}$$

Using the least squares method of estimation, the estimate for $\boldsymbol{\beta}$ is given by:

$$\begin{aligned}\hat{\hat{\boldsymbol{\beta}}} &= [(\mathbf{WX})'(\mathbf{WX})]^{-1}(\mathbf{WX})'\mathbf{WY} \\ &= (\mathbf{X'W'WX})^{-1}(\mathbf{X'W'WY})\end{aligned} \tag{4.1.45}$$

or,

$$\hat{\hat{\boldsymbol{\beta}}} = (\mathbf{X^{*\prime}X^*})^{-1}\mathbf{X^{*\prime}Y^*} \tag{4.1.46}$$

The transformation matrix W is:

$$\mathbf{W} = \begin{bmatrix} -\rho & 1 & 0 \ldots 0 & 0 \\ 0 & -\rho & 1 \ldots 0 & 0 \\ \cdot & \cdot & \cdot & \cdot \\ \cdot & \cdot & \cdot & \cdot \\ \cdot & \cdot & \cdot & \cdot \\ 0 & 0 & 0 \ldots -\rho & 1 \end{bmatrix} \tag{4.1.47}$$

and

$$\mathbf{W'W} = \begin{bmatrix} \rho^2 & -\rho & 0 & \ldots & 0 & 0 \\ -\rho & 1+\rho^2 & -\rho & \ldots & 0 & 0 \\ 0 & -\rho & 1+\rho^2 & \ldots & 0 & 0 \\ \cdot & \cdot & \cdot & & & \cdot \\ \cdot & \cdot & \cdot & & & \cdot \\ \cdot & \cdot & \cdot & & & \cdot \\ 0 & 0 & 0 & \ldots & 1+\rho^2 & -\rho \\ 0 & 0 & 0 & \ldots & -\rho & 1 \end{bmatrix} \tag{4.1.48}$$

Note that the **W′W** matrix in equation 4.1.48 and the $\boldsymbol{\Omega}^{-1}$ matrix in equation 4.1.38 compare closely. They differ by the factor $(1 - \rho^2)^{-1}$ in the $\boldsymbol{\Omega}^{-1}$ matrix and in the element of the first row, first column, which is ρ^2 in the **W′W** matrix and one in the $\boldsymbol{\Omega}^{-1}$ matrix.

There is another less obvious difference between the two estimators. The transformed variables $\mathbf{X}^*$, Y^*, and U^* each contain one row less than the variables X, Y, and U. One observation is "lost" in transforming the variables and with it one degree of freedom. The GLS estimator requires two matrix inversions, $\boldsymbol{\Omega}^{-1}$ and $(\mathbf{X}'\boldsymbol{\Omega}^{-1}\mathbf{X})^{-1}$; and it is thus considerably more difficult to use in applications.

Relative Efficiency of the GLS and OLS Estimators

The GLS estimator is, of course, more efficient than the OLS estimator of the untransformed original regression equation. An approximate measure of this relative efficiency is:

$$\frac{\text{var}(\text{GLS } \hat{\hat{\boldsymbol{\beta}}})}{\text{var}(\text{OLS } \hat{\boldsymbol{\beta}})} = \frac{1 - \rho^2}{1 + \rho^2} \qquad \textbf{4.1.49}$$

where $\hat{\hat{\boldsymbol{\beta}}}$ = GLS estimate of $\boldsymbol{\beta}$, and $\hat{\boldsymbol{\beta}}$ = OLS estimate of $\boldsymbol{\beta}$. This ratio indicates that the efficiency of the OLS estimator relative to the GLS estimator declines in direct proportion to the value of ρ. Table 4-1 shows the loss in efficiency of the OLS estimators when the disturbances are autocorrelated.

TABLE 4-1

Assumed Value of ρ	Relative Efficiency of OLS β in Terms of GLS β Percent
0.2	92 (approximately)
0.4	72
0.8	22

Kadiyala has proposed another transformation matrix which is a $T \times T$ matrix **K** defined as:[9]

$$\mathbf{K} = \begin{bmatrix} \sqrt{1-\rho^2} & 0 & 0 & 0 \ldots 0 & 0 \\ -\rho & 1 & 0 & 0 \ldots 0 & 0 \\ \cdot & & & & \\ \cdot & & & & \\ \cdot & & & & \\ 0 & 0 & 0 & 0 \ldots -\rho & 1 \end{bmatrix} \qquad \textbf{4.1.50}$$

Notice this is equal to the transformation matrix **W** in equation 4.1.47 with an additional row, the first row. We now obtain the following result:

$$\mathbf{KY} = \mathbf{KX}\boldsymbol{\beta} + \mathbf{KU} \qquad \textbf{4.1.51}$$

where

$$\hat{\boldsymbol{\beta}} = [(\mathbf{KX})'(\mathbf{KX})]^{-1}(\mathbf{KX})'(\mathbf{KY})$$

$$E(\mathbf{KUU'K'}) = \sigma_u^2\mathbf{I} \qquad \textbf{4.1.52}$$

It has been shown that the application of the **K** transformation will give a more efficient estimate than the application of the **W** transformation.

---

[9] K. R. Kadiyala, "A Transformation Used to Circumvent the Problem of Autocorrelation," *Econometrica*, Vol. 36, No. 1 (January, 1968), pp. 93-96.

An Illustration of Several Alternative Transformations in the Presence of Serial Correlation

The model is:

$$C_{nd_t} = \beta_0 + \beta_1 Y_t + U_t \qquad \textbf{4.1.53}$$

Based on the data in Table 4-2, a consumption function of nondurable goods in the United States from 1951 to 1966 can be estimated by using ordinary least squares:

$$\begin{aligned} C_{nd} &= 28.0054 + \underset{(0.0048)}{0.3517Y_t} \\ R^2 &= 0.9987 \qquad s = 1.0862 \qquad d = 0.5214 \end{aligned} \qquad \textbf{4.1.54}$$

TABLE 4-2

Year	C_{nd}	Y
1951	116.5	255.7
1952	120.8	263.3
1953	124.4	275.4
1954	125.5	278.3
1955	131.7	296.7
1956	136.2	309.3
1957	138.7	315.8
1958	140.2	318.8
1959	146.8	333.0
1960	149.6	340.2
1961	153.0	350.7
1962	158.2	367.3
1963	162.2	381.3
1964	170.5	406.5
1965	178.2	430.8
1966	185.9	451.5

C_{nd} = consumer expenditure on nondurable goods (in 1958 dollars)
Y = disposable income (in 1958 dollars)

Source: U.S. Department of Commerce, Office of Business Economics, *The National Income and Product Accounts of the United States, 1929-1965* (August, 1966).

From this equation the sample residuals can be calculated by:

$$\hat{U}_t = C_{nd_t} - 28.0054 - 0.3517Y_t \qquad t = 1, 2, \ldots, T \qquad \textbf{4.1.55}$$

Table 4-3 is the table of computation. Therefore we can compute the Durbin-Watson d statistic:

$$d = \frac{\sum_{t=2}^{T} (\hat{U}_t - \hat{U}_{t-1})^2}{\sum_{t=1}^{T} \hat{U}_t^2} = \frac{8.61240369}{16.51773721} = 0.5214 \qquad \textbf{4.1.56}$$

Comparing with the table value, we conclude that there is a high positive serial correlation in this regression equation. To eliminate the serial correlation, the following three methods can be applied.

TABLE 4-3

Year	$\hat{U}_t$	$\hat{U}_{t-1}$	$\hat{U}_t - \hat{U}_{t-1} = \Delta\hat{U}$	$\hat{U}_t^2$	$(\hat{U}_t - \hat{U}_{t-1})^2$
1951	−1.4383			2.06870689	
1952	0.1887	−1.4383	1.6270	0.03560769	2.64712900
1953	−0.4670	0.1887	−0.6557	0.21808900	0.42994249
1954	−0.3870	−0.4670	0.0800	0.14976900	0.00640000
1955	−0.6585	−0.3870	−0.2715	0.43362225	0.07371225
1956	−0.5901	−0.6585	0.0684	0.34821801	0.00467856
1957	−0.3762	−0.5901	0.2139	0.14152644	0.04575321
1958	0.0687	−0.3762	0.4449	0.00471969	0.19793601
1959	1.6744	0.0687	1.6057	2.80361536	2.57827249
1960	1.9420	1.6744	0.2676	3.77136400	0.07160976
1961	1.6491	1.9420	−0.2929	2.71953081	0.08579041
1962	1.0106	1.6491	−0.6385	1.02131236	0.40768225
1963	0.0867	1.0106	−0.9239	0.00751689	0.85359121
1964	−0.4765	0.0867	−0.5632	0.22705225	0.31719424
1965	−1.3231	−0.4765	−0.8466	1.75059361	0.71673156
1966	−0.9036	−1.3231	0.4195	0.81649296	0.17598025
Total				16.51773721	8.61240369

First difference method, equations 4.1.22 and 4.1.24:

$$\Delta C_{nd_t} = 1.3578 + \underset{(0.0416)}{0.2685}\, \Delta Y_t \qquad \textbf{4.1.57}$$

$$R^2 = 0.7440 \qquad s = 1.1492 \qquad d = 2.6603$$

Durbin's method, equation 4.1.35: From equation 4.1.53:

$$C_{nd_t} = \beta_0 + \beta_1 Y_t + U_t$$

where $U_t = \rho U_{t-1} + V_t$. V_t is statistically well-behaved in the sense that it fulfills the OLS assumptions.

For the period $t - 1$ we write equation 4.1.53 as follows:

$$C_{nd_{t-1}} = \beta_0 + \beta_1 Y_{t-1} + U_{t-1} \qquad \textbf{4.1.58}$$

Multiplying equation 4.1.58 through by ρ and subtracting from equation 4.1.53, we obtain:

$$C_{nd_t} - \rho C_{nd_{t-1}} = \beta_0(1 - \rho) + \beta_1 Y_t - \beta_1 \rho Y_{t-1} + V_t \quad \textbf{4.1.59}$$

Rewriting,

$$C_{nd_t} = \beta_0(1 - \rho) + \beta_1 Y_t - \beta_1 \rho Y_{t-1} + \rho C_{nd_{t-1}} + V_t \quad \textbf{4.1.60}$$

Applying the least squares method to equation 4.1.60 will yield a consistent estimate of $\hat{\rho}$. This point will be developed in terms of autoregressive models in Chapter 7. We can then substitute it back into equation 4.1.59 and apply OLS to obtain estimates of β_0 and β_1.

In terms of the numerical illustration,

$$\begin{aligned} C_{nd_t} &= 9.9076 + \underset{(0.0358)}{0.3049Y_t} - \underset{(0.0813)}{0.1896Y_{t-1}} + \underset{(0.1827)}{0.6717C_{nd_{t-1}}} \\ R^2 &= 0.9987 \qquad s = 0.7040 \qquad d = 1.6488 \end{aligned} \quad \textbf{4.1.61}$$

$$\therefore \hat{\rho} = 0.6717$$

At the next step, we estimate:

$$\begin{aligned} (C_{nd_t} - 0.6717C_{nd_{t-1}}) &= 10.7403 + \underset{(0.0081)}{0.3394}(Y_t - 0.6717Y_{t-1}) \\ R^2 = 0.9921 \qquad s &= 0.6769 \qquad d = 1.3015 \end{aligned} \quad \textbf{4.1.62}$$

Cochrane-Orcutt iterative method: Returning to model 4.1.53.

$$C_{nd_t} = \beta_0 + \beta_1 Y_t + U_t$$

where $U_t = \rho U_{t-1} + V_t$. As before, V_t is statistically well-behaved. The OLS residual $\hat{U}_t$ is an estimate of U_t. We can then estimate:

$$\hat{U}_t = \rho \hat{U}_{t-1} + V_t$$

Using equation 4.1.54, we calculate $\hat{U}_t$ as follows:

$$\hat{U}_t = C_{nd_t} - 28.0054 - 0.3517Y_t \quad \textbf{4.1.63}$$

Using $\hat{U}_t$, we now obtain an estimate of $\hat{\rho}$ from equation 4.1.30:

$$\hat{\rho} = 0.6827 \quad \textbf{4.1.64}$$

Then following equation 4.1.31, we construct transformed variables:

$$\begin{aligned} C^*_{nd_t} &= C_{nd_t} - 0.6827C_{nd_{t-1}} \\ Y^*_t &= Y_t - 0.6827Y_{t-1} \end{aligned}$$

and regress,

$$C^*_{nd_t} = 2.9638 + \underset{(0.0128)}{0.4033Y^*_t}$$

$$R^2 = 0.9860 \qquad s = 1.7261 \qquad d = 1.0968$$

In this illustrative case the process will not be continued any further. Table 4-4 presents the results of the three different methods of dealing with serial correlation.

TABLE 4-4

Table of Comparison of Different Methods

	OLS Estimates from Original Data	First Difference	Durbin	Cochrane-Orcutt
β_0	28.0054	1.3578	10.7403	2.9638
β_1	0.3517	0.2685	0.3394	0.4033
d	0.5214	2.6603	1.3015	1.0968

Note that for the number of observations equalling 16 and the number of parameters estimated equalling 1 (excluding β_0), from the table of distribution of the Durbin-Watson d, the 5 percent significance points of d_L and d_U are 1.10 and 1.37 respectively. Evidently any form of transformation gives better results. Because the calculated value of d in this illustration is small, a positive serial correlation ($\rho > 0$) is suspected; and as such, a one-tailed test with the above values of d_L and d_U is recommended. Zvi Griliches and P. Rao have reported a comprehensive Monte Carlo study evaluating relative performances of five alternative estimators.[10] Their findings, among others, point to the fact that the OLS estimates in the context of autocorrelated errors is less efficient than the other estimates.

4.2 HETEROSCEDASTICITY

Heteroscedasticity occurs when the assumption of constant variance of the disturbances is violated. Recall the assumptions $E(U_iU_j) = \sigma_u^2$ for $i = j$ or $E(U_tU_{t+\theta}) = \sigma_u^2$ for $\theta = 0$.

When the variances of the disturbances tend to increase or decrease with increasing values of the regressors, the disturbances are said to be heteroscedastic. They may be heteroscedastic when they are in some way dependent on the regressors appearing in the specified equation or when the equation fails to include all relevant regressors. Failure to make a correct specification by way of explicitly including the relevant regressors to estimate independently all systematic variations in the regressand contributes to making the U term nonrandom; and, as such, the U term is very likely heteroscedastic. Indeed the assumption that the U term is purely random is crucial in meeting the assumption of constant variance.

By plotting the disturbances against a given independent variable X_i or against the estimated value of $\hat{Y}_i$, the heteroscedasticity problem can be visualized as follows. Because the true disturbances U_i are not observed,

[10] Zvi Griliches and P. Rao, "Small-Sample Properties of Several Two-Stage Regression Methods in the Context of Autocorrelated Errors," *Journal of the American Statistical Association*, Vol. 64, No. 325 (March, 1969), pp. 253-272.

one can only plot the residuals $\hat{U}_i$ estimated from the regression, as in Figure 4-1.

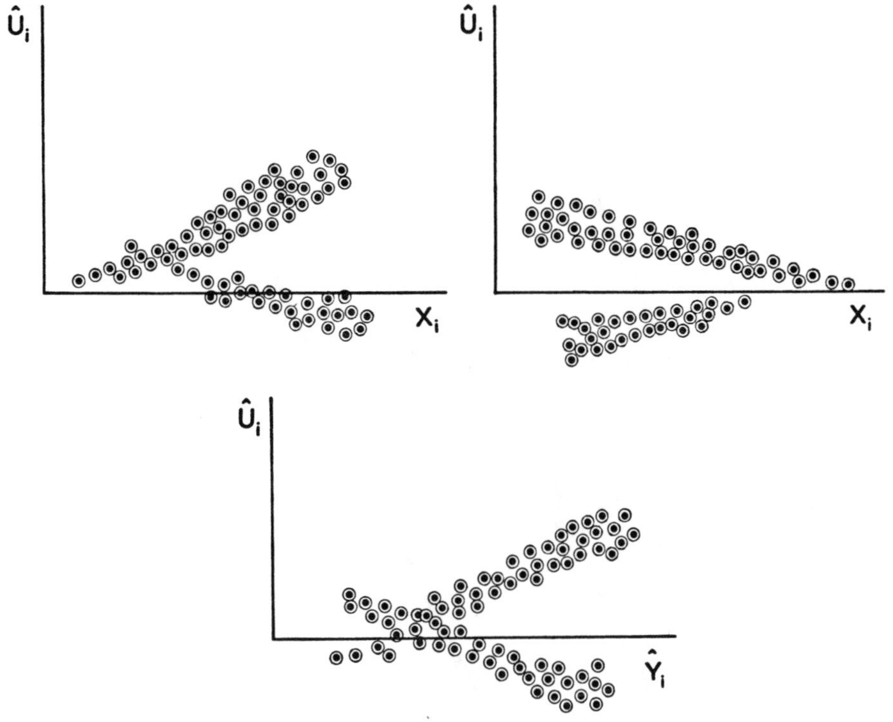

FIGURE 4-1

The problem of heteroscedasticity is more acute in cross-sectional data. It is relatively safe to assume homoscedasticity (the absence of heteroscedasticity) in studies based on aggregative time-series data, since the variables are of a similar magnitude for successive time-period observations. In data for particular individual units, the relative magnitudes of individual observations vary by large amounts. For example, in a time-series study of aggregate consumption C and income Y, the C_t's and Y_t's related to the tth time period are usually of the same magnitude for all t. In studies based on individual family budget data, the consumption of a particular family C_j and its income Y_j may be of very similar magnitudes; whereas the consumption of another family C_k may be only half the magnitude of that family's income Y_k.

It is easy to see that different individual families may spend very different fractions of family income during a particular time period. Newly married couples will be making purchases for new homes, but in older families grown children will be leaving; some families will have the extra expenses of moving or of medical and dental fees, and others will have reduced expenses in the same period. If all family incomes were the same and all other things were equal, these random disturbances would have a distribution with a constant variance. But incomes vary over a considerable range at any one period, and thus the variance of the disturbance terms is likely to vary between different income groups. Figure 4-2 illustrates the situation.

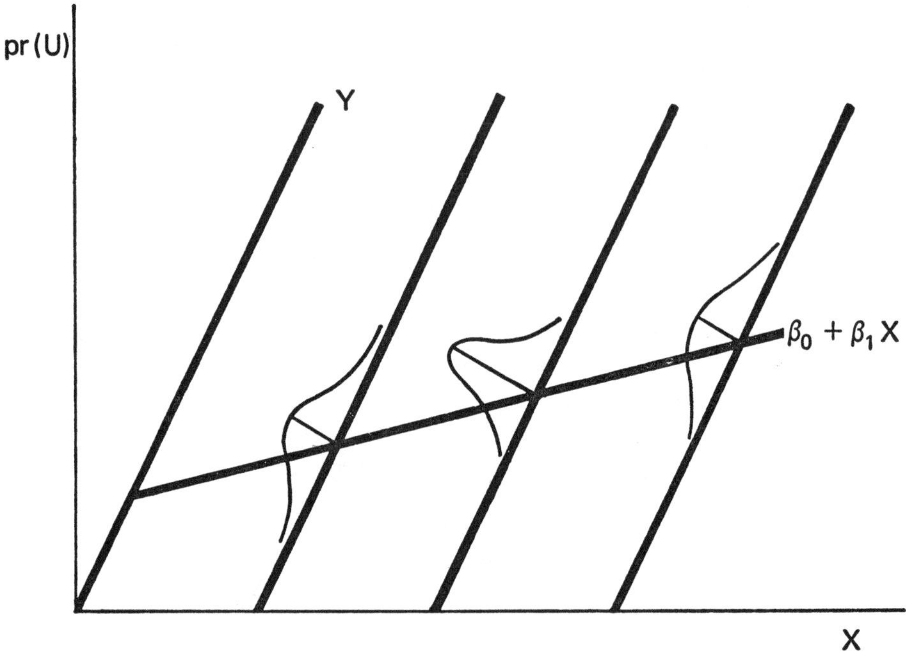

FIGURE 4-2

The presence of heteroscedasticity makes the OLS estimator inefficient in that the property of least variance no longer applies to these estimates. However, they continue to be unbiased and generally consistent. Since heteroscedasticity affects the estimation of the variance of the parameters, significance tests of the parameters are unreliable. This compares with what the previous section stated to be the consequences of the presence of serial correlation in the OLS estimators. Thus the confidence limits and the tests of significance developed in Chapter 3 cannot be applied.

A formal statement of the presence of heteroscedasticity can be expressed as follows. Consider the model in matrix notation:

$$\mathbf{Y} = \mathbf{X}\boldsymbol{\beta} + \mathbf{U} \qquad \textbf{4.2.1}$$

where

$$E(\mathbf{U}\mathbf{U}') = \sigma_u^2\boldsymbol{\Omega} \neq \sigma_u^2\mathbf{I} \qquad \textbf{4.2.2}$$

The expression in equation 4.2.2 expands to:

$$E(\mathbf{UU}') = \sigma_u^2 \begin{bmatrix} 1/\lambda_1 & 0 & 0 \ldots & 0 \\ 0 & 1/\lambda_2 & 0 \ldots & 0 \\ \cdot & \cdot & \cdot & \cdot \\ \cdot & \cdot & \cdot & \cdot \\ \cdot & \cdot & \cdot & \cdot \\ 0 & 0 & 0 \ldots & 1/\lambda_N \end{bmatrix}$$

$$\neq \sigma_u^2 \begin{bmatrix} 1 & 0 & 0 \ldots & 0 \\ 0 & 1 & 0 \ldots & 0 \\ \cdot & \cdot & \cdot & \cdot \\ \cdot & \cdot & \cdot & \cdot \\ \cdot & \cdot & \cdot & \cdot \\ 0 & 0 & 0 \ldots & 1 \end{bmatrix}$$

Notice that there are zeros in the off-diagonal elements, and thus the assumption of mutual independence of disturbances and absence of serial correlation is maintained. The diagonal elements are reciprocals of the different λ_i values, not unity as we would like to assume them to be. Evidently if we knew the values of the λ_i's, we could obtain the least squares estimator in two steps. In the first step heteroscedasticity could be removed by the application of a suitable transformation of all variables in the ith observation. Prior knowledge about the λ_i's becomes important. The reason is quite straightforward: λ_i expresses information about the relationship of one sample point to another. It provides us with a ranking scheme for the variances of every sample point. The transformation then incorporates this ranking into the data point, weighting each one according to its relative position in the ranking.

Once this transformation has been accomplished, at the next step the OLS method can be applied to the transformed variables. Recall that the treatment of serial correlation (without heteroscedasticity) involved transformation of all variables in the ith observation and that the transformation parameter ρ was used. This parameter had to be estimated one way or another before the transformation could be used. The problem in the present case, heteroscedasticity without serial correlation, also essentially relates to transformation of the original variables involving the parameter λ, which is unknown. Here again, results can be obtained only by assuming some knowledge of this unknown parameter.

An Approach to Estimation in the Presence of Heteroscedasticity

The discussion above suggests that one approach to estimation in the presence of heteroscedasticity is to apply the weighted least squares method of estimation instead of the ordinary least squares method. This method has not been used much, and it is not presented here.

Instead let us rewrite model 4.2.1 as follows (in nonmatrix form):

$$Y_i = \beta_0 + \beta_1 X_i + U_i, \qquad i = 1, 2, \ldots, N \tag{4.2.3}$$

Suppose as in equation 4.2.2 that U_i displays heteroscedasticity of the form:

$$E(U_i U_i) = \frac{\sigma_u^2}{\lambda_i} \tag{4.2.4}$$

We can express the terms U_i as:

$$U_i^* = \sqrt{\lambda_i} U_i \tag{4.2.5}$$

The U_i^* will then have a constant variance:

$$\begin{aligned} E(U_i^* U_i^*) &= E[(\sqrt{\lambda_i} U_i)\ (\sqrt{\lambda_i} U_i)] \\ &= \lambda_i E(U_i U_i) \\ &= \lambda_i \frac{\sigma_u^2}{\lambda_i} \qquad \text{(using equation 4.2.4)} \\ &= \sigma_u^2 \end{aligned} \tag{4.2.6}$$

Multiplying Y_i and X_i by $\sqrt{\lambda_i}$, we obtain Y_i^* and X_i^*. Then we obtain the OLS estimator β_0 and β_1 by regressing Y_i^* on X_i^*, and this estimator will be efficient. Of course, if the λ_i's were known, the straightforward application of generalized least squares estimators (GLS) would be preferred. Although the λ_i's are usually not known, some assumptions can be made about estimating them.

If we divide through equation 4.2.3 by X_i, we have a special case:

$$\left(\frac{Y}{X}\right)_i = \beta_0 \left(\frac{1}{X}\right)_i + \beta_1 + \left(\frac{U}{X}\right)_i \tag{4.2.7}$$

Suppose that the disturbance term $(U/X)_i$ is homoscedastic, even if U_i is heteroscedastic. That is,

$$E\left[\left(\frac{U}{X}\right)_i^2\right] = \sigma_u^2 \tag{4.2.8}$$

where σ_u^2 is a finite constant.

The variance of $(U/X)_i$ is:

$$E\left[\left(\frac{U}{X}\right)_i \left(\frac{U}{X}\right)_i\right] = \frac{E(U_i)^2}{X_i^2} \tag{4.2.9}$$

The X_i's are fixed mathematical variables by assumption 2.2.4 in the usual regression model.

It follows that:

$$\frac{E(U_i)^2}{X_i^2} = \sigma_u^2$$

or,

$$E(U_i)^2 = \sigma_u^2 X_i^2 \qquad \textbf{4.2.10}$$

Note that β_1 in the original equation is obtained from the intercept β_1 in equation 4.2.7, that is, the constant term of the transformed equation. If the assumption is made that the disturbances U_i have the variance-covariance matrix as in equation 4.2.2 and that quotient U_i/X_i has constant variance as in equation 4.2.8, it follows that:

$$\sqrt{\lambda_i} = \frac{1}{X_i} \qquad \textbf{4.2.11}$$

This equation provides the link we need to estimate the λ_i's for transforming the original equation into an equation whose disturbances have constant variance. This does not suggest that such an estimate of the λ_i's will always be valid.

A Less Restrictive Procedure

A less restrictive procedure has recently been proposed by R. E. Park.[11] Instead of the simple relationships in equations 4.2.8 through 4.2.10, it is supposed that the nonconstant disturbance variances are a more realistic and thus more complicated function of the independent variable X_i. Let us postulate the following relationship:

$$\sigma_{u_i}^2 = \sigma^2 X_i^\gamma e^v \qquad \textbf{4.2.12}$$

Taking the natural logarithm of both sides, we write:

$$\ln \sigma_{u_i}^2 = \ln \sigma^2 + \gamma \ln X_i + V_i \qquad \textbf{4.2.13}$$

where V_i is a well-behaved disturbance term.

First, estimate $\hat{U}_i$ by applying the OLS method to the original equation 4.2.3. Next, using $\hat{U}_i^2$ as an estimate of $\sigma_{u_i}^2$ from these regression residuals, the parameters γ and σ^2 can be estimated by regressing $\ln \hat{U}_i^2$ on $\ln X_i$ from equation 4.2.13. We can then transform the original equation by dividing both sides of equation 4.2.3 by $X_i^{\hat{\gamma}/2}$ instead of dividing by X_i as in equation 4.2.7. We can then apply OLS to the equation in transformed variables as follows:

$$\left(\frac{Y_i}{X_i^{\hat{\gamma}/2}}\right) = \beta_0 \left(\frac{1}{X_i^{\hat{\gamma}/2}}\right) + \beta_1 X_i^{1-\hat{\gamma}/2} + V^* \qquad \textbf{4.2.14}$$

Notice that if $\hat{\gamma}$ is not significantly different from zero, the transformation proposed will leave the regression equation unchanged. If $\hat{\gamma}$ is not significantly different from 2, this transformation is equivalent to the preceding

[11] R. E. Park, "Estimation with Heteroscedastic Error Terms," *Econometrica*, Vol. 34, No. 4 (October, 1966), p. 888.

one in equation 4.2.7 where we divided each original variable by X_i for the transformation operation.

Goldfeld-Quandt Test

In econometric research the Durbin-Watson test discussed in section 4.1 has been extensively used to find out whether or not the assumption of mutual independence of the U_i term holds for the given sample. No such test for heteroscedasticity has achieved comparable popularity. A pure statistical test, Bartlett's test, is well known, but its theoretical assumptions are too rigorous to warrant its use in econometric research.[12]

A test for heteroscedasticity has been proposed by S. M. Goldfeld and R. E. Quandt.[13] Let us call this the G test. The steps in applying the G test are outlined as follows:

Step 1: Arrange the observations on all variables in order of increasing magnitude. Obviously the choice has to be made as to which variable's magnitude determines the order. For an equation with only one independent variable, the choice is obvious. The choice is not so obvious when there is more than one regressor.

Step 2: Arbitrarily choose the number of central observations to be omitted (C) and decompose the sample into two subsamples in arranged sequence, where:

---

[12] Bartlett's test defines the ratio Q/L, where:

$$Q = N \log \left[\sum_{i=1}^{k} \frac{N_i}{N} (\hat{\sigma}_u^2)_i \right] - \sum_{i=1}^{k} N_i \log (\hat{\sigma}_u^2)_i$$

$$L = 1 + \frac{1}{3(k-1)} \left(\sum_{i=1}^{k} \frac{1}{N_i} - \frac{1}{N} \right)$$

and where $N = \sum_{i=1}^{k} N_i$

$i = 1, 2, \ldots, k$

N = total number of observations in the sample

k = number of subsamples, chosen arbitrarily

N_i = number of observations in the ith subsample

$(\hat{\sigma}_u^2)_i$ = disturbance variance as estimated from the regression residuals from the ith subsample

Given that U is normally distributed and nonautocorrelated (independently distributed), Q/L has the chi square distribution with $k - 1$ degrees of freedom. See R. L. Anderson and T. A. Bancroft, *Statistical Theory in Research* (New York: McGraw-Hill Book Co., 1952), section 12.7, pp. 141-144. This test has not been used in econometrics because one of the basic assumptions of the test is that we have been able to break our sample into *k independent* subsamples. The analytical procedure to determine the optimal groupings of the residuals presented in the test is not useful for econometric research. For a modified test, refer to J. B. Ramsey, "Tests for Specification Errors in Ciassical Linear Least Squares Regression Analysis," *Journal of the Royal Statistical Society*, Vol. 31-B (1969), pp. 350-371.

[13] S. M. Goldfeld and R. E. Quandt, "Some Tests of Homoscedasticity," *Journal of the American Statistical Association*, Vol. 60 (September, 1965), pp. 539-547.

N_1 = the subsample consisting of the first $(N\text{-}C)/2$ observations
N_2 = the subsample consisting of the last $(N\text{-}C)/2$ observations
N = total number of observations in the sample
C = number of central observations omitted arbitrarily

Step 3: Apply least squares regression to N_1 and N_2 independently. Note that such application of the regression method can work if and only if $(N\text{-}C)/2$ is greater than the number of parameters K to be estimated in each case. One can, of course, save degrees of freedom by restricting C to the minimum.

Step 4: Calculate separately the residuals from the two above regressions $(\hat{U}_i)_1$ and $(\hat{U}_i)_2$, square them, and sum the squared residuals for each set separately, $(\Sigma\hat{U}_i^2)_1$ and $(\Sigma\hat{U}_i^2)_2$.

Step 5: In the final step, the test is based on the ratio of the two sums of squared residuals:

$$G = \frac{\text{sum of squared residuals from } N_2}{\text{sum of squared residuals from } N_1}$$

or,

$$G = \frac{(\Sigma\hat{U}_i^2)_2}{(\Sigma\hat{U}_i^2)_1} \qquad \textbf{4.2.15}$$

The summations are over all i in the first $(N\text{-}C)/2$ observations in the denominator and over all i in the last $(N\text{-}C)/2$ observations in the numerator.

Note that G has been shown to have an F distribution with $(N\text{-}C\text{-}2K)/2$ degrees of freedom for both the numerator and the denominator of the ratio.[14] Using the F table, one can determine the critical region at the appropriate level of significance to test whether or not heteroscedasticity is present. If the calculated G value exceeds the critical value from the F table, the evidence indicates that heteroscedasticity is present. One can apply the same test using the residuals $\hat{U}_i^*$ from the regression of the transformed equation 4.2.7 to find out if the transformation of the variables has been an aid in correcting heteroscedasticity. The steps of the test are as before; however, the observations should now be arranged in order of magnitude of $1/X$, not X, as in the case of equation 4.2.3.

The G test holds in the case of pure heteroscedasticity when there exists no serial correlation. The test also assumes normal distribution of the U_i term.

[14] So far there has been no discussion of the F distribution. It will be examined in Chapter 8. At this stage we need know only how to find critical values of this statistic at various levels of significance.

An Illustration of the *G* Test

The model is:

$$Y_i = \beta_1 + \beta_2 X_i + U \qquad i = 1, 2, \ldots 25 \qquad \textbf{4.2.16}$$

where Y= import of merchandise, column 5 in Table 4-5
X= GNP, column 2 in Table 4-5

To test for heteroscedasticity, we first rearrange the sample in order of the ascending values of X and group them into two subsamples as in Table 4-6, omitting the thirteenth observation as the central observation.

TABLE 4-5

GNP and Merchandise Import in 1966 by 25 Countries

(1) Countries	(2) GNP at Market Price (Millions of U.S. Dollars)	(3) Exchange Rate Units of Nation (Currency Per U.S. Dollar)	(4) Import of Merchandise (Millions of National Currency)	(5) Import of Merchandise (Millions of U.S. Dollars)
Argentina	18,733	214.180	224,200	1,047
Australia	25,135	0.893	2,843	2,184
Austria	10,019	26.000	62,100	2,388
Belgium	18,129	50.000	275,500	5,510
Canada	53,328	1.081	10,102	9,345
China (Taiwan)	3,138	40.000	24,801	620
Denmark	11,133	6.907	19,575	2,834
Finland	8,604	3.200	5,542	1,732
Germany, Fed. Rep. of	119,575	4.000	71,400	17,850
Greece	6,578	30.000	34,600	1,153
Ireland	2,930	0.357	364	1,020
Italy	61,435	625.000	4,735,000	7,576
Jamaica	950	0.357	116	325
Japan	97,477	360.000	2,652,000	7,367
Korea, Rep. of	3,901	264.535	184,460	697
New Zealand	5,474	0.719	724	1,007
Norway	7,585	7.143	16,746	2,344
Phillippines	9,269	2.410	3,335	1,384
Puerto Rico	3,360	1.000	1,784	1,784
South Africa	11,944	0.714	1,678	2,350
Spain	24,568	60.000	217,500	3,625
Sweden	21,329	5.173	22,729	4,394
Switzerland	14,744	4.373	17,005	4,889
United Kingdom	105,356	0.357	5,262	14,739
United States	756,490	1.000	26,800	26,800

Source: *Yearbook of National Accounts Statistics*, 1967, Department of Economic and Social Affairs, United Nations.

TABLE 4-6

Y	X	Y	X
325	950	4,889	14,744
1020	2,930	5,510	18,129
620	3,138	1,047	18,733
1784	3,360	4,394	21,329
697	3,901	3,625	24,568
1007	5,474	1,047	25,135
1153	6,578	9,345	53,328
2344	7,585	7,576	61,435
1732	8,604	7,367	97,477
1384	9,269	14,739	105,356
2388	10,019	17,850	119,575
2834	11,133	26,800	756,409

We estimate two independent linear regressions from the two subgroups of sample data and compute the sums of the squares of estimated residuals from the two regression lines so estimated. Thus we obtain:

$$G = \frac{184{,}828{,}208}{2{,}295{,}606} = 80.5139$$

Since in each equation we have estimated two parameters β_1 and β_2, since the number of central observations omitted is 1, and since the total number of observations in the sample is 25, the degrees of freedom are $(25 - 1 - 4)/2 = 10$.

Comparing the calculated value of G with the related value from the F table when $N_1 = 10$, $N_2 = 10$, and $F = 2.97$ at the 95 percent confidence level, the evidence indicates the presence of heteroscedasticity.

In the next stage we respecify the model as follows:

$$\frac{Y}{X} = \beta_1 \frac{1}{X} + \beta_2 + U \qquad \textbf{4.2.17}$$

To test for heteroscedasticity, given the respecified model, we again apply the G test. As before we rearrange the sample into two subsamples in terms of the ascending values of $1/X$, each subsample consisting of 12 observations, with the thirteenth observation again omitted as the central value (Table 4-7). Computing the residuals from the two estimated regressions, we then obtain:

$$G = \frac{0.112}{0.052} = 2.1538$$

With degrees of freedom $N_1 = 10$ and $N_2 = 10$ as before, the comparison of the computed value of G with the corresponding value from the F table indicates the absence of heteroscedasticity at the same confidence level.

TABLE 4-7

Y/X	1/X	Y/X	1/X
3,542,677	132	25,455,852	8,982
14,927,870	836	23,834,714	9,981
13,989,711	949	14,930,982	10,789
7,569,613	1026	20,130,172	11,623
12,331,733	1628	30,903,098	13,184
17,523,672	1875	17,528,124	15,202
12,667,595	3979	18,396,054	18,268
14,754,966	4070	17,867,214	25,634
20,601,060	4688	53,095,238	29,762
5,589,067	5338	19,757,808	31,867
30,393,293	5516	34,812,287	34,130
33,159,251	6782	34,210,526	105,263

Analysts' Pragmatic View of the Heteroscedasticity Problem

Even when the assumption of constant variance is not explicitly stated, econometric analysts have some awareness of the fact that heteroscedasticity presents a real problem. This awareness is manifest in the extensive use of sociodemographic variables (race, religion, caste, color, education, sex, age, marital status, family size, and so forth) in family budget studies. Such variables are included in the hope that, as more of the observed variance is explained by these additional variables included as regressors, the remaining unexplained variance of the disturbance terms is more nearly constant.[15] To the extent that inclusion of such variables in the model corrects for variations in the relative magnitudes of the observations, it is an aid to minimizing heteroscedasticity. This is not to suggest that their inclusion may not create other problems and make the OLS estimators inefficient in other ways.

In practice the researcher has to use judgment. Thus in a model explaining family expenditure on food, we may choose to regress the ratio between family expenditure on food and family size on the ratio between family income and family size if the different families in the sample are found to be of varying size. Similarly, in a model explaining investment of business firms, the ratio between firm investment and sales may be regressed on the ratio between earnings and sales if the firms in the sample have widely varying sales volumes. Implicit in all such cases is the assumption that the chosen form of the equations will be estimable by the OLS method, since the problem of heteroscedasticity is expectedly circumvented by the suggested transformations of the original observations.

4.3 INDEPENDENCE OF THE DISTURBANCE TERMS AND THE REGRESSORS

We have assumed that the exogenous variables appearing as regressors in the estimating equation take on a set of fixed, predetermined values. If

[15] Often nonquantifiable phenomena are quantified by the use of dummy variables (see Chapter 6).

we think of each sample of observations on the variables in a regression equation as a single "experiment," the values of the exogenous variables will be exactly the same set of constant numbers no matter how many times the experiment is repeated. By contrast the assumption that the disturbance term is a stochastic variable implies that it can take on a different set of values, drawn randomly from some unknown probability distribution, each time the experiment is repeated. We have also assumed that $E(U_i X_i) = 0$ from equation 2.2.4 and that $E(U_i X_{iK}) = 0$ from equation 2.2.14. Given the assumption that the exogenous variables are nonrandom fixed values and that the disturbance terms U_i are random, these assumptions have been shown to be valid (Chapter 2).[16]

Failure to meet this important assumption of independence will make the OLS estimators biased, even for very large samples. The degree of bias will depend on the magnitude of the covariance between the disturbance term and the regressors. The OLS estimator will no longer be consistent. Recall that the least squares method of estimation is based on a design which enables us to partition the total variation in the regressand into two separate independent parts: (1) explained variation, that is the part of variation attributed to the regressors, and (2) the residual variations which remain unexplained and are attributed to other random factors, denoted by U_i. When the regressors and the U_i are correlated, the least squares method fails. A more formal argument will be made in Chapter 7. However it can be shown that the OLS estimators will have the desired properties if the assumption is approximately fulfilled.

When actual observations of economic variables are used to estimate the parameters of the equations of econometric models, the assumption that the regressors have only fixed predetermined values or that they are truly independent of disturbance terms even if not fixed is not likely to be very reasonable. For one thing, the observations on exogenous variables appearing as regressors are likely to have observational errors just as those of the endogenous variable have, and these will vary between samples if the experiment is repeated. Furthermore economic theory indicates that in any set of economic variables several different relationships may hold among the variables in even a single observation on them. Models containing more than one equation are likely to give more realistic descriptions of economic phenomena than single-equation models. Thus a variable that appears as an independent variable or as a regressor in one relation may appear as the dependent variable or regressand in another equation in the same model. For these reasons it is important to investigate the effects on the OLS estimators of the violation of the assumption that the exogenous variables and disturbance terms are truly independent.

Indeed we have a serious problem. The true value of the OLS parameters is not known, and neither are the true values of the disturbances. Thus there

---

[16] When the exogenous variables are stochastic (not fixed) but statistically independent of the disturbances, it can be easily shown that the OLS estimators will remain unbiased, consistent, and asymptotically efficient.

is no way of estimating the covariance of regressors and disturbances. The only way to know whether or not the problem of mutual dependence between regressors and disturbances appears in a particular model is by analysis based on the underlying economic theory. Baffled, econometricians have suggested various working solutions for dealing with this problem.

One approach to resolve the problem is found in the work done on demand studies for many agricultural commodities. Consider the linear model stating that the quantity of meat Q is a function of its price P. Writing each variable in terms of deviations from its means and denoting each by its corresponding lowercase letter as before, we write:

$$q_t = \beta p_t + u_t \qquad \textbf{4.3.1}$$

Then the OLS estimate of β is:

$$\hat{\beta} = \frac{\Sigma p_t q_t}{\Sigma p_t^2} \qquad \textbf{4.3.2}$$

and $\hat{\beta}$ is an unbiased estimator of β, that is, $E(\hat{\beta}) = \beta$. But the assumption that $E(p_t u_t) = 0$ is questionable. The quantity of meat demanded and its price are simultaneously determined. But if we do not wish to estimate a set of two equations to determine the two variables Q and P jointly, we may replace the original demand equation with a new demand function as follows:

$$p_t = \beta^* q_t + u_t^* \qquad \textbf{4.3.3}$$

where $E(q_t u_t^*) = 0$.

$$\hat{\beta}^* = \frac{\Sigma p_t q_t}{\Sigma q_t^2} \qquad \textbf{4.3.4}$$

The OLS estimate $\hat{\beta}^*$ from equation 4.3.4 is claimed to be unbiased. The rationale for this process is as follows. Meat is an agricultural product, and the quantity in the market at any time is "given," determined in the previous period; and the variations in price in the current period depend on the variations in quantity so given. If you accept this as a plausible way of designing an experiment, you believe that the assumption of independence of disturbances with respect to the exogenous variable (q_t in this case) holds in this respecification of the model; that is, $E(q_t u_t^*)$ is unquestionably zero.

Another example of a working solution for the problem at hand is the following. Suppose that we wish to compute the marginal propensity to consume from (again all variables in terms of mean deviations):

$$c_i = \beta y_i + u_i \qquad \textbf{4.3.5}$$

$$\frac{\Sigma c_i y_i}{\Sigma y_i^2} = \hat{\beta} \qquad \textbf{4.3.6}$$

and

$$E(\hat{\beta}) = \beta \text{ when } E(u_i y_i) = 0$$

When the observations on C and Y are aggregate time-series data, the plausibility of the last assumption is questionable, since at any given time period t aggregate income of the economy and aggregate consumption are likely to be interdependent and as such jointly determined. But it is plausible to assume that the individual family first receives income and then proceeds to spend it on consumption. If the income of the ith family is thus given, it becomes a fixed variable; and the assumption of zero covariance between this variable and the disturbance term is more likely to be fulfilled. Thus the use of cross-sectional data is often suggested as a helpful way of circumventing the problem at hand.

However, this problem continues to press. Later chapters will discuss the use of instrumental variables and the simultaneous system models proposed to handle this problem. The implication of this assumption in a typical lag model which is autoregressive in variables will also be examined in Chapter 7.

DISCUSSION QUESTIONS

1. Briefly discuss the problem of serial correlation.

2. Define the Durbin-Watson test. How does it differ from the von Neumann test? Can the Durbin-Watson test be applied when the lagged values of the regressand variable appear as regressors in the model?

3. Apply the Durbin-Watson test to problem 8, Chapter 2. (Obtain the series on estimated residuals of the regression from the computer printout, calculate the value of the Durbin-Watson statistic, and compare it with the value of the computer printout.)

4. Review the Cochrane-Orcutt method of estimating a linear regression when disturbances are autoregressive or serially correlated. Compare the method with the Generalized Least Squares method. How do these two methods differ from the transformation proposed by Kadiyala?

5. The text has reviewed Durbin's proposed method of correction. Is the OLS estimate of the parameter in the first stage of the two-stage method of estimation proposed by Durbin unbiased and consistent? (Hint: Chapter 7 gives an appropriate answer to this question.)

6. Heteroscedasticity is often a serious problem in econometric research. Why?

7. Review suggested approaches to estimation of a regression model in the presence of heteroscedasticity.

8. Apply the Goldfeld-Quandt test to problem 3, Chapter 2, and make comments on your findings.

SUGGESTED READINGS

Aitken, A. C. "On Least Squares and Linear Combinations of Observations." *Proceedings of the Royal Statistical Society of Edinburgh,* Vol. 55 (1935), pp. 42-48.

Cochrane, D., and G. H. Orcutt. "Application of Least Squares Regression to Relationships Containing Autocorrelated Terms." *Journal of the American Statistical Association,* Vol. 44, No. 245 (September, 1949), pp. 32-61.

Durbin, James. "Testing for Serial Correlation in Systems of Simultaneous Regression Equations." *Biometrika,* Vol. 44 (December, 1957), pp. 370-377.

———. "Estimation of Parameters in Time Series Regression Models." *Journal of the Royal Statistical Society,* Vol. 22-B (January, 1960), pp. 139-153.

———. "An Alternative to the Bounds Test for Testing Serial Correlation in Least Squares Regression." *Econometrica,* Vol. 38, No. 3 (May, 1970), pp. 422-429.

Durbin, James, and G. Watson. "Testing Serial Correlation in Least Squares Regression Part I." *Biometrika,* Vol. 37 (December, 1950), pp. 409-428.

———. "Testing Serial Correlation in Least Squares Regression Part II." *Biometrika,* Vol. 38 (June, 1951), pp. 159-178.

Goldberger, A. S. *Econometric Theory.* New York: John Wiley & Sons, 1964.

Goldfeld, S. M., and R. E. Quandt. "Some Tests of Homoscedasticity." *Journal of the American Statistical Association,* Vol. 60 (September, 1965), pp. 539-547.

Griliches, Zvi, and P. Rao. "Small-sample Properties of Several Two-Stage Regression Methods in the Context of Autocorrelated Errors." *Journal of the American Statistical Association,* Vol. 64, No. 325 (March, 1969), pp. 253-272.

Hart, I. B. "Significance Levels for the Ratio of the Mean Square Successive Differences to the Variance." *Annals of Mathematical Statistics,* Vol. 13 (1942), pp. 445-447.

Hart, I. B., and J. von Neumann. "Tabulation of the Probabilities for the Ratio of the Mean Square Successive Difference to the Variance." *Annals of Mathematical Statistics,* Vol. 13 (1942), pp. 207-214.

Henshaw, R. C. "Testing Single-Equation Least Squares Regression Models for Autocorrelated Disturbances." *Econometrica,* Vol. 34, No. 3 (July, 1966), pp. 646-660.

Hildreth, C., and J. Y. Lu. *Demand Relations with Autocorrelated Disturbances,* Technical Bulletin No. 276. East Lansing: University of Michigan Press, 1960.

Johnston, J. *Econometric Methods,* 2d ed. New York: McGraw-Hill Book Co., 1972.

Kadiyala, K. R. "A Transformation Used to Circumvent the Problem of Autocorrelation." *Econometrica,* Vol. 36, No. 1 (January, 1968), pp. 93-96.

Lyttkens, Ejnar. "Standard Errors of Regression Coefficients by Autocorrelated Residuals." *Econometric Model Building; Essays in the Causal Chain Approach,* edited by H. O. A. Wold. Amsterdam: North-Holland Publishing Co., 1964, pp. 169-228.

Park, R. E. "Estimation with Heteroscedastic Error Terms." *Econometrica,* Vol. 34, No. 4 (October, 1966), p. 888.

Ramsey, J. B. "Tests for Specification Errors in Classical Linear Least Squares Regression Analysis." *Journal of the Royal Statistical Society,* Vol. 31-B (1969), pp. 350-371.

Sargan, J. D. "The Maximum Likelihood Estimation of Economic Relationships with Autoregressive Residuals." *Econometrica,* Vol. 29, No. 3 (July, 1961), pp. 414-426.

———. "Wages and Prices in the United Kingdom: A Study in Econometric Methodology." *Econometric Analysis for National Economic Planning,* edited by P. E. Hart, *et al.* London: Butterworth & Co., 1964, pp. 25-54.

Theil, H., and A. L. Nagar. "Testing the Independence of Regression Disturbances." *Journal of the American Statistical Association,* Vol. 56, No. 296 (December, 1961), pp. 793-806.

Theil, Henri. "The Analysis of Disturbances in Regression Analysis." *Journal of the American Statistical Association,* Vol. 60, No. 312 (December, 1965), pp. 1067-1079.

———. "A Simplification of the BLUS Procedure for Analyzing Regression Disturbances." *Journal of the American Statistical Association,* Vol. 63, No. 321 (March, 1968), pp. 242-251.

von Neumann, John. "Distribution of the Ratio of the Mean Square Successive Difference to the Variance." *Annals of Mathematical Statistics,* Vol. 12, No. 4 (1941), pp. 367-395.

Zellner, Arnold. "Econometric Estimation with Temporally Dependent Disturbance Terms." *International Economic Review,* Vol. 2, No. 2 (May, 1961), pp. 164-178.

5

multicollinearity

5.0 THE NATURE OF THE PROBLEM

If we wish to estimate the parameters of a demand equation with the quantity demanded of a given commodity Y expressed as a function of price and price alone X, we write:

$$Y_t = \alpha_0 + \alpha_1 X_t + U_t \qquad t = 1, 2, \ldots, T \tag{5.0.1}$$

And using the OLS method from equation 2.1.21, we can obtain the estimate of α_1 as:

$$\hat{\alpha}_1 = \frac{\Sigma x_t y_t}{\Sigma x_t^2} \tag{5.0.2}$$

However, if all $X_t = \bar{X}$, that is, all observations of X_t fall on its mean value, then $x_t = (X_t - \bar{X})$ will be zero for all t, and Σx_t^2 also will be zero. As a result the estimator $\hat{\alpha}_1$ above will be indeterminate. The problem is due to the fact that all observations of X are bunched together with no variation. This is not quite the problem of multicollinearity, but it suggests a way of approaching the problem.

Consider a model containing two or more regressors. Even though the observations on each regressor vary, the set of observations on one regressor does not necessarily vary independently of the set of observations on another regressor. Multicollinearity arises from the presence of interdependence, or lack of independence among the regressors in a multivariate equation. Thus we have multicollinearity when the assumption that each of these regressors is linearly independent of all others or of any linear combination of all or some others is violated. Such independence means regressors are orthogonal to each other. Thus "departures from orthogonality" in the set of regressors is a measure of multicollinearity.

The simple model of demand, equation 5.0.1, is often found inadequate, and economic theory shows that other explanatory variables ought to be included. We respecify the model, omitting the t subscript:

$$Y = \beta_0 + \beta_1 X_1 + \beta_2 X_2 + U \tag{5.0.3}$$

If this equation is a model of the demand for automobiles, then both regressors, the price of automobiles X_1 and disposable income X_2, may be subject to the common influence of business cycle fluctuations. The regressors will then be highly correlated, each one reflecting the common set of economic influences; and a high degree of linear dependence between them is very likely. If X_1 is exactly linearly dependent on X_2, then the parameters β_1 and β_2 cannot be disentangled and their independent estimates cannot be obtained.[1] Ragnar Frisch indicated the problem of multicollinearity as early as 1934 and suggested that many economic time series, subject as they are to a common set of economic influences, move together over time and are thus highly collinear.[2]

Let us return to demand model 5.0.3. The OLS estimation of the model involves fitting a plane to a three-dimensional scatter of observation points. Refering to Figure 5-1, suppose there exists a high degree of linear dependence between X_1 and X_2 and that the correlation between them is close to one. Depending on the severity of interdependence, there will be few observations in the X_1, X_2 plane because all the sample points are concentrated in the limiting case of perfect collinearity between X_1 and X_2 in a single vertical plane through which passes the line, say, $X_1 = \delta_0 + \delta_1 X_2$. In effect this means that the hypothesized three-dimensional scatter has collapsed into a two-dimensional one. Any number of planes can pass through this two-dimensional linear scatter of points and the line of best fit will lie in each one of them. There is not enough information to locate the slope of the plane independently if X_1 and X_2 are exactly linearly dependent.

Exact linear dependence is an extreme case. We shall presently see that if a linear relationship between X_1 and X_2 is inexact, the OLS method of estimation may be usable.

Multicollinearity and Specification

Multicollinearity may contribute to serious specification error. Suppose that we wish to estimate the aggregate consumption function and that we specify the model a priori as follows:

$$C = \beta_0 + \beta_1 Y + \beta_2 L + U \qquad \textbf{5.0.4}$$

where C = aggregate consumption
Y = aggregate income
L = liquid assets

Suppose that L is exactly linearly dependent on Y, expressed as:

$$L = \zeta Y \qquad \textbf{5.0.5}$$

[1] For an illustrative case see page 44.

[2] R. Frisch, *Statistical Confluence Analysis by Means of Complete Regression Systems* (Oslo, Norway: University Economics Institute, 1934).

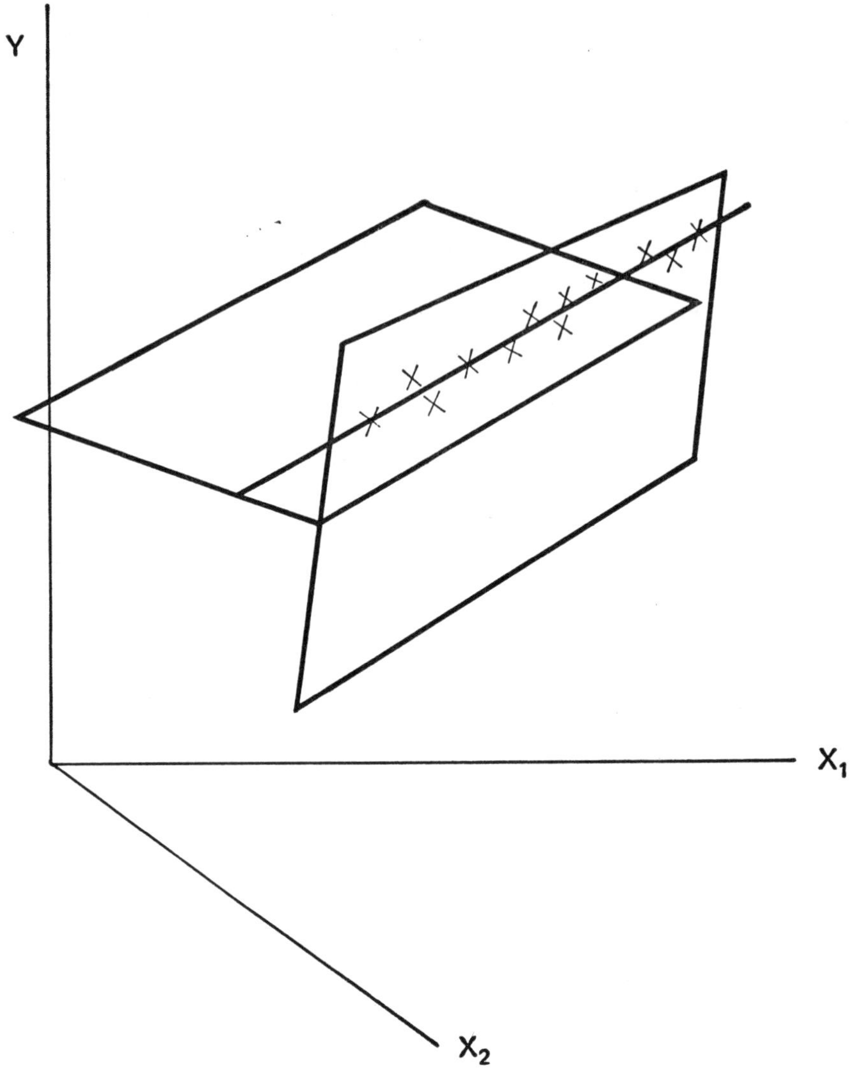

FIGURE 5-1

The OLS regression method of estimating β_1 and β_2 independently as has been shown before will fail. One quick solution often adopted is to drop one variable, say L, from the list of regressors and reestimate the following equation:

$$C = \beta_0 + \beta_1 Y + U^* \quad \mathbf{5.0.6}$$

This solution may very well serve an immediate purpose for the regression, such as forecasting, but the two equations may not relate to the same structure. To the extent that arbitrary exclusion of certain variables from the list of explanatory variables contributes to misspecification of the structure, the problem is very serious. In the example above, exclusion of the variable L means that in the structural relation the coefficient of the variable is zero; that is, $\beta_2 = 0$. This is too strong an assertion to make for the purpose of rescuing the OLS method of estimation. If β_2 is not truly zero, then U^* in equation 5.0.6 is equal to $\beta_2 L + U$ as in equation 5.0.4; and U^* and the exogenous variable retained in the model (Y in this case) will no longer be independent ($\text{cov}YU^* \neq 0$) because of the presence of L in U^*. Nor will U^* be a truly random variable to fulfill the assumption $E(U^*) = 0$. Then the estimators obtained from equation 5.0.6 will be biased.[3]

Consider equation 5.0.4 in terms of mean deviations:

$$c_t = \beta_1 y_t + \beta_2 \ell_t + u_t \qquad \textbf{5.0.7}$$

To deal with the presence of multicollinearity, it may be convenient to drop ℓ_t and estimate the following equation:

$$c_t = \beta_1 y_t + v_t \qquad \textbf{5.0.8}$$

Then,

$$\hat{\beta}_1 = \Sigma c_t y_t / \Sigma y_t^2$$

Using equation 5.0.7 and taking the expected value,

$$\begin{aligned} E(\hat{\beta}_1) &= E\left[\frac{\Sigma y_t(\beta_1 y_t + \beta_2 \ell_t + u_t)}{\Sigma y_t^2}\right] \\ &= \beta_1 + \beta_2\, \Sigma y_t \ell_t / \Sigma y_t^2 \qquad \textbf{5.0.9} \\ &= \beta_1 + \beta_2 \zeta \end{aligned}$$

since $E(u_t) = 0$ and since $\hat{\zeta} = \Sigma y_t \ell_t / \Sigma y_t^2$. Obviously $E(\hat{\beta}_1) \neq \beta_1$, and the estimate $\hat{\beta}_1$ is shown to be biased. Of course if β_2 were truly zero, the specification of equation 5.0.4 would have to be different to begin with.

Multicollinearity and Interaction

The fact of interdependence among the regressors must not be confused with the fact that they have an "interaction effect" on the regressand. It is one thing to say that income Y and liquid assets L are collinear, resulting in the extreme case of exact linear dependence where β_1 and β_2 cannot be estimated independently. But it is quite another thing to say that not only do Y and L have effects on C, but that there also exists an interaction effect of the two variables on consumption. The latter statement implies that, in addition to the linear terms in Y and L, the specification of an equation for C requires a multiplicative interaction term YL.

---

[3] If multicollinearity among the independent variables is severe in a correctly specified model, the choice may be to trade some bias for a smaller variance of the estimator.

$$C = \beta_0 + \beta_1(Y) + \beta_2(L) + \beta_3(YL) + U^{**} \qquad \textbf{5.0.10}$$

The problem at hand is to obtain independent estimators of β_1 and β_2, when Y and L are perfectly or "seriously" collinear. How to obtain an estimator of β_3 is a different issue and one with which this book will not be concerned.

Rank Condition of the X Matrix and Multicollinearity

Let us continue to investigate the problem of multicollinearity. Recall that one of the basic assumptions with respect to the K-variable regression model is that the rank of the **X** matrix should be equal to $1 + K$, the number of parameters to be estimated plus one, with the extra "unit" relating to the "variable" that remains invariant, and the **X** matrix is used to obtain the estimator of the constant term (β_0 in this case). Furthermore, the assumption requires that $1 + K$ should be less than the number of observations in the sample T.[4] If the data matrix for the X's satisfies this rank condition, the regressors are free of multicollinearity. This apparently difficult mathematical condition is really not too difficult to comprehend.

Returning to model 5.0.3, we can see that variables X_1 and X_2 enter the estimates of β_1 and β_2 respectively. To satisfy the rank condition for this case, the rank of the **X** matrix must be $1 + 2 = 3$; and the number of observations T must be greater than or at least equal to $1 + K = 3$ in this case. First, we check that the columns of data representing X_1 and X_2 are independent; neither can be a multiple of another. If there are more than two regressors, one regressor cannot be a linear combination of two or more of the other regressors in the equation. Second, we check the independence of rows. As stated before, rank of a matrix is determined by the number of independent columns or rows, whichever number is less.

In the discussion above, the term "linear combination of regressors" has been used. An illustration may help further understanding of the problem involved here. Consider:

C_1	C_2	C_3
8	−10	14
−4	12	0
2	0	6

5.0.11

Note that $3C_1 + 1C_2 - 1C_3 = 0$, or $C_3 = 3C_1 + C_2$. Column C_3 is a linear combination of columns C_1 and C_2, and the three columns are not linearly independent. The next step is to compute determinants of all square submatrices of the above 3-column × 3-row matrix. One of them turns out to be:

[4] If $T = 1 + K$, then β is not stochastic. Review the discussion on pages 18 and 19 and also pages 44 and 45.

$$\begin{vmatrix} 8 & -10 \\ -4 & 12 \end{vmatrix} = 96 - 40 \neq 0 \qquad \textbf{5.0.12}$$

The calculation in equation 5.0.12 shows that the rank of the above matrix is two, not three. The rank of the matrix is determined by the largest such nonzero subdeterminant of the given matrix.

5.1 MULTICOLLINEARITY AND THE OLS ESTIMATORS

It is instructive to begin with the consideration of the polar case where multicollinearity is totally absent. If the X's in a K-variable multiple regression model are not at all collinear, that is, they are mutually uncorrelated, the $\mathbf{X'X}$ matrix becomes simply a diagonal matrix. Continuing to write all variables in terms of deviations from their respective means,

$$(\mathbf{X'X}) = \begin{bmatrix} \Sigma x_1^2 & 0 \dots & 0 \\ \cdot & \cdot & \cdot \\ \cdot & \cdot & \cdot \\ \cdot & \cdot & \cdot \\ 0 & 0 \dots & \Sigma x_K^2 \end{bmatrix} \qquad \textbf{5.1.1}$$

Its inverse $(\mathbf{X'X})^{-1}$ is also diagonal with elements given by the reciprocals of these diagonal elements. Then we can calculate,

$$\hat{\beta}_k = \frac{\Sigma x_k y}{\Sigma x_k^2}$$

and

$$\text{var}(\hat{\beta}_k) = \frac{\hat{\sigma}_u^2}{\Sigma x_k^2} \qquad \textbf{5.1.2}$$

Notice that these are the OLS estimates we would have obtained by regressing Y on each X_k separately. However, the estimate of $\text{var}(\hat{\beta}_k)$ will not be exactly the same. This can be seen intuitively from the fact that $\hat{\sigma}_u^2$ from the multiple regression of Y on $X_1, X_2, \dots, X_K$ will be different from that obtained by regressing Y on any one of these X's in a simple regression model. The off-diagonal elements in $(\mathbf{X'X})^{-1}$ are zero, and thus will not affect the estimate of the variance in equation 5.1.2.

Let us examine the problem further. Consider model 5.0.3, writing all variables in terms of deviations from their respective means and omitting the t subscript:

$$y = \beta_1 x_1 + \beta_2 x_2 + U \qquad \textbf{5.1.3}$$

Recall equation 2.3.22:

$$\hat{\beta} = (\mathbf{X'X})^{-1}\mathbf{X'Y}$$

Examine the $(\mathbf{X'X})^{-1}$ factor of the expression on the right-hand side. Following the model, the determinant of $\mathbf{X'X}$ is:

$$|\mathbf{X'X}| = \begin{vmatrix} \Sigma x_1^2 & \Sigma x_1x_2 \\ \Sigma x_1x_2 & \Sigma x_2^2 \end{vmatrix} \qquad 5.1.4$$

$$= \Sigma x_1^2\Sigma x_2^2 - (\Sigma x_1x_2)^2$$

If there is an exact linear relationship between x_1 and x_2 such that:

$$x_2 = \delta x_1 \qquad 5.1.5$$

then equation 5.1.4 can be rewritten:

$$|\mathbf{X'X}| = \begin{vmatrix} \Sigma x_1^2 & \delta\Sigma x_1^2 \\ \delta\Sigma x_1^2 & \delta^2\Sigma x_1^2 \end{vmatrix}$$

$$= (\Sigma x_1^2\delta^2\Sigma x_1^2) - (\delta\Sigma x_1^2)(\delta\Sigma x_1^2) \qquad 5.1.6$$

$$= \delta^2(\Sigma x_1^2)^2 - \delta^2(\Sigma x_1^2)^2$$

$$= 0$$

If $|\mathbf{X'X}|$ is zero, the matrix $(\mathbf{X'X})^{-1}$ is not defined. In the language of linear algebra, this is the problem of matrix singularity, and a singular matrix has no inverse.[5]

The situation may improve if the assumed linear relationship between x_1 and x_2 is not exact. Suppose that we have a relation such that:

$$x_2 = \delta x_1 + V \qquad 5.1.7$$

where V is a small but finite residual term such that $\Sigma x_1V = \Sigma V = 0$. We then write:

$$|\mathbf{X'X}| = \begin{vmatrix} \Sigma x_1^2 & \Sigma x_1(\delta x_1 + V) \\ \Sigma x_1(\delta x_1 + V) & \Sigma(\delta x_1 + V)^2 \end{vmatrix}$$

$$= \begin{vmatrix} \Sigma x_1^2 & \delta\Sigma x_1^2 + \Sigma x_1V \\ \delta\Sigma x_1^2 + \Sigma x_1V & \delta^2\Sigma x_1^2 + 2\delta\Sigma x_1V + \Sigma V^2 \end{vmatrix} \qquad 5.1.8$$

$$= \delta^2(\Sigma x_1^2)^2 + 2\delta\Sigma x_1V\Sigma x_1^2 + \Sigma x_1^2\Sigma V^2$$
$$-[\delta^2(\Sigma x_1^2)^2 + 2\delta\Sigma x_1^2\Sigma x_1V + (\Sigma x_1V)^2]$$

[5] Nonsingularity is defined only for square matrices, with the same number of rows as there are columns. A square matrix is nonsingular if the determinant containing all the elements of the matrix has a nonzero value.

$$|\mathbf{X}'\mathbf{X}| = \Sigma x_1^2 \Sigma V^2 - (\Sigma x_1 V)^2 \qquad 5.1.9$$

Since the second term is expected to be zero,

$$|\mathbf{X}'\mathbf{X}| = \Sigma x_1^2 \Sigma V^2 \qquad 5.1.10$$

Since $V^2 > 0$ and $\Sigma x_1^2 > 0$, $|\mathbf{X}'\mathbf{X}|$ will itself be finite and nonzero; and we can proceed to compute $(\mathbf{X}'\mathbf{X})^{-1}$.

To see that a very small numerical value of $\Sigma V^2 \Sigma x_1^2$ (which is the value of the determinant $|\mathbf{X}'\mathbf{X}|$) tends to increase the variance of $\hat{\beta}$, we need to compute $(\mathbf{X}'\mathbf{X})^{-1}$ and then the variance of $\hat{\beta}$. From matrix algebra we can compute the inverse of a matrix as:

$$(\mathbf{X}'\mathbf{X})^{-1} = \frac{\operatorname{adj}(\mathbf{X}'\mathbf{X})}{|\mathbf{X}'\mathbf{X}|} \qquad 5.1.11$$

Using equation 2.4.39, the variance of the estimated vector of coefficients $\hat{\boldsymbol{\beta}}$ is:

$$\operatorname{var}(\hat{\boldsymbol{\beta}}) = \hat{\sigma}_u^2 (\mathbf{X}'\mathbf{X})^{-1}$$

and from equation 2.4.71,

$$\hat{\sigma}_u^2 = \frac{\Sigma S^2}{T - K - 1}$$

where T is the number of observations and $K + 1$ is the number of parameters estimated, including the constant term.

Thus in estimating $\operatorname{var}(\hat{\boldsymbol{\beta}})$, the determinant $|\mathbf{X}'\mathbf{X}|$ plays a crucial part. If this determinant is zero as in equation 5.1.6, elements of the inverse matrix $(\mathbf{X}'\mathbf{X})^{-1}$ will be infinite and the resulting estimator of $\operatorname{var}(\hat{\boldsymbol{\beta}})$ will "explode." If $|\mathbf{X}'\mathbf{X}|$ is not exactly zero, it may be possible to obtain OLS estimators of the coefficients, significant at a chosen confidence level. Otherwise the increase in $\operatorname{var}(\hat{\boldsymbol{\beta}})$, as $|\mathbf{X}'\mathbf{X}|$ approaches zero because of high degree of collinearity between explanatory variables, results in an impasse. What good is a coefficient whose variance is extremely large if not infinite? Thus in a linear model, if the relationship among independent variables is not exact but contains an error term that is small but finite as in equation 5.1.7, the OLS estimation method may continue to yield reliable results. The estimates are still unbiased if the X's, the exogenous variables, are fixed mathematical variables. However, they become less reliable as their variances and covariances increase.

5.2 THE PRESENCE AND SEVERITY OF MULTICOLLINEARITY

Seldom do we find that multicollinearity is either present or absent indisputably. In most cases, especially in economic data, multicollinearity exists in varying degrees. Hence the real issue is how severe it is in a specific case. Note that multicollinearity is not a problem of the method of estimation; it is a problem of the data, a problem basic to the process by which sample observations are "generated" in nonexperimental sciences.

The more exact is the dependence between X_1 and X_2, the closer to one will be the coefficient of correlation r between them. Consider equation 5.1.3, $y = \beta_1 x_1 + \beta_2 x_2 + U$, where $x_2 = \delta x_1 + V$ as in equation 5.1.7. Assuming $\Sigma V = 0$, $\Sigma V x_1 = 0$, and $\Sigma x_1^2 = \Sigma x_2^2 = 1$, (a procedure followed for normalization when variables are taken in terms of deviations from their respective means, and their respective sums of the squares are set equal to unity), we obtain:

$$\delta = r_{x_1 x_2} = r_{12}$$

Thus the coefficient of correlation r_{12} becomes the coefficient of multicollinearity between x_1 and x_2, denoted by δ in the present case. Note that we can now write:

$$(\mathbf{X}'\mathbf{X}) = \begin{bmatrix} \Sigma x_1^2 & \Sigma x_1 x_2 \\ \Sigma x_1 x_2 & \Sigma x_2^2 \end{bmatrix} = \begin{bmatrix} 1 & \delta \\ \delta & 1 \end{bmatrix} = \begin{bmatrix} 1 & r_{12} \\ r_{12} & 1 \end{bmatrix} \qquad 5.2.1$$

It follows that:

$$\text{var}(\hat{\beta}_1) = \text{var}(\hat{\beta}_2) = \frac{\sigma_u^2}{1 - \delta^2} = \frac{\sigma_u^2}{1 - r_{12}^2} \qquad 5.2.2$$

and

$$\text{cov}(\hat{\beta}_1 \hat{\beta}_2) = \frac{-\delta \sigma_u^2}{1 - \delta^2} = \frac{-r_{12}\sigma_u^2}{1 - r_{12}^2} \qquad 5.2.3$$

Obviously as the value of $\hat{\delta}$ or the correlation coefficient r_{12} increases, variance of the estimates increases, as does their covariance. Consequently the estimates become less reliable when serious multicollinearity exists. An investigation of the zero-order correlation matrix of the explanatory variables is thus considered helpful.

Lawrence R. Klein suggests that multicollinearity is severe if:

$$r_{ij} > R_y \qquad 5.2.4$$

where r_{ij} is the zero-order correlation between the independent variables X_i and X_j $(i \neq j)$, and R_Y is the multiple correlation coefficient between the dependent variable Y and the set of independent variables X in the multiple regression equation.[6] This follows the rationale presented in equations 5.2.1 through 5.2.3.

---

[6] L. R. Klein, *An Introduction to Econometrics* (Englewood Cliffs, N. J.: Prentice-Hall, 1962), pp. 64 and 101.

However, zero-order correlation is not a true index of linear dependence when there are more than two X's (independent variables) in the equation. Perfect multicollinearity within a set of three or more explanatory variables is quite possible with very small zero-order pairwise correlations between members of the set. Whenever there are three or more members in the X set, zero-order pairwise correlations by themselves cease to be a meaningful guide. Note that, taking the matrix of such pairwise correlations as a whole, the multiple correlation coefficient for a particular X_k with respect to the others is not just a sum of simple pairwise correlations.[7]

A pragmatic approach to "localize multicollinearity" has been presented in a computer regression program package by Beaton and Glauber.[8] This method suggests the following procedure.

Compute the matrix of zero-order pairwise correlation coefficients where the element r_{ij} is the zero-order correlation coefficient of observations on the variables X_i and X_j.

$$\mathbf{R} = \begin{bmatrix} r_{11} & r_{12} \ldots r_{1K} \\ r_{21} & r_{22} \ldots r_{2K} \\ \cdot & \cdot \quad\quad \cdot \\ \cdot & \cdot \quad\quad \cdot \\ \cdot & \cdot \quad\quad \cdot \\ r_{K1} & r_{K2} \ldots r_{KK} \end{bmatrix} \quad k = 1, 2, \ldots, K \qquad \textbf{5.2.5}$$

Define r^{kk} as the diagonal element of the inverse of the above matrix, $\mathbf{R}^{-1}$, corresponding to the kth variable. It can be shown that:

$$r^{kk} = \frac{|\mathbf{R}_k|}{|\mathbf{R}|} \qquad \textbf{5.2.6}$$

where $|\mathbf{R}_k|$ is the determinant of the correlation matrix of the X variables excluding the kth variable X_k, and $|\mathbf{R}|$ is the determinant of equation 5.2.5.

To illustrate, the following displays the calculation above in terms of the regressor X_2, where $k = 1, 2, 3, 4$.

---

[7] If we assume that the X's have a multivariate, normal distribution, an assumption we seldom can make, Bartlett's test for multicollinearity can be applied. For this test the natural logarithm of the determinant of the correlation matrix is computed from a sample over all X's and multiplied by the factor $-[N - 1 - 1/6\,(2K + 5)]$. This expression will have approximately the chi square distribution with $\mathcal{V} = 1/2\,[K(K - 1)]$ degrees of freedom, where K is the number of X's considered, and N is the sample size. M. S. Bartlett, "Test of Significance in Factor Analysis," *British Journal of Psychology*, Statistics Section, Vol. 3 (1950), p. 83.

[8] E. A. Beaton and R. R. Glauber, "Statistical Laboratory Ultimate Regression Package Programming" (Cambridge, Massachusetts: Harvard Statistical Laboratory, 1962).

$$\mathbf{r}^{22} = \frac{\begin{vmatrix} r_{11} & r_{13} & r_{14} \\ r_{31} & r_{33} & r_{34} \\ r_{41} & r_{43} & r_{44} \end{vmatrix}}{\begin{vmatrix} r_{11} & r_{12} & r_{13} & r_{14} \\ r_{21} & r_{22} & r_{23} & r_{24} \\ r_{31} & r_{32} & r_{33} & r_{34} \\ r_{41} & r_{42} & r_{43} & r_{44} \end{vmatrix}} \qquad 5.2.7$$

If X_2 is perfectly independent of (orthogonal to) the variables X_1, X_3, and X_4, the determinants in the numerator and the denominator in equation 5.2.7 will be the same, and r^{22} will be equal to unity.[9] At the other extreme, should X_2 be exactly dependent on other X's, the denominator will vanish; while the numerator, not containing X_2, remains unaffected. Thus r^{22} becomes infinite. Even though the spectrum $1 < r^{22} < \infty$ remains unexplored, a crude diagnostic technique is available.

A test of the severity of multicollinearity recently proposed by Farrar and Glauber is to compare two different correlation coefficients.[10] One of these

---

[9]Perfect independence of X_2 from X_1, X_3, and X_4 implies that:

$$r_{12} = r_{21} = 0$$

$$r_{22} = 1$$

$$r_{23} = r_{32} = 0$$

$$r_{24} = r_{42} = 0$$

Thus,

$$|\mathbf{R}| = \begin{vmatrix} r_{11} & 0 & r_{13} & r_{14} \\ 0 & 1 & 0 & 0 \\ r_{13} & 0 & r_{33} & r_{34} \\ r_{14} & 0 & r_{43} & r_{44} \end{vmatrix}$$

Expanding $|\mathbf{R}|$ in terms of the elements of the second row, we have:

$$|\mathbf{R}| = -(0)\begin{vmatrix} 0 & r_{13} & r_{14} \\ 0 & r_{33} & r_{34} \\ 0 & r_{43} & r_{44} \end{vmatrix} + (1)\begin{vmatrix} r_{11} & r_{13} & r_{14} \\ r_{13} & r_{33} & r_{34} \\ r_{14} & r_{43} & r_{44} \end{vmatrix}$$

$$-0\begin{vmatrix} r_{11} & 0 & r_{14} \\ r_{13} & 0 & r_{34} \\ r_{14} & 0 & r_{44} \end{vmatrix} + (0)\begin{vmatrix} r_{11} & 0 & r_{13} \\ r_{13} & 0 & r_{33} \\ r_{14} & 0 & r_{43} \end{vmatrix}$$

All terms except the second vanish and:

$$|\mathbf{R}| = |\mathbf{R}_2|$$

Thus for the case when X_2 is perfectly independent, $r^{22} = 1$.

[10] D. E. Farrar and R. R. Glauber, "Multicollinearity in Regression Analysis: The Problem Revisited," *Review of Economics and Statistics*, Vol. XLIX (February, 1967), pp. 92-107. Defining multicollinearity in terms of departures from orthogonality in the set of regressors and assuming X is multivariate normal, Farrar and Glauber use certain known distributional properties to develop their argument. Thus the F test these authors recommend will be useful only when the assumption of multivariate normal distribution of the regressors is fulfilled.

is the correlation coefficient R_y, as estimated for the multiple regression and as defined in equation 5.2.4. The other is the correlation coefficient for the regression of one independent variable, say X_1, on the set of all others, $X_2, X_3, \ldots, X_K$. More generally, we estimate the multiple correlation coefficient of a particular independent variable X_k with respect to all other members in the X set and denote this by R_{x_k}. To test whether X_k is seriously collinear with other X's, form the ratio:

$$\frac{R_{x_k}}{R_y} > 1 \qquad \textbf{5.2.8}$$

Note that although multicollinearity is viewed as a property of the set of independent variables alone, the test depends partly on the multiple correlation between Y and the given X set, as indicated by R_y. Evidently it is possible that some level of collinearity with respect to X_k in a given set of X will not be considered harmful when R_y in the denominator changes following a change of the dependent variable. That is, if R_{x_k} remains invariant to the specification of the dependent variable, but $R_{y_1 \cdot x} \neq R_{y_2 \cdot x}$, the evidence of harmfulness of multicollinearity as indicated by equation 5.2.8 is different for the two regressions. Suppose that $R_{x_k} = 0.8$ in two separate cases, whereas R_y is 0.4 in case A when Y_1 is regressed on the set of X's and 0.9 in case B when Y_2 is regressed on the same set of X's. Even though the independent variable set X is not less multicollinear if related to Y_1 rather than to Y_2, its effects may be more serious in case A than in case B.

$$\frac{0.8}{0.4} > 1 \qquad \text{(case A)}$$

$$\frac{0.8}{0.9} < 1 \qquad \text{(case B)} \qquad \textbf{5.2.9}$$

By the ratio test criterion in equation 5.2.8, case A is serious but case B is not. The test, then, judges not in terms of the existence of multicollinearity, but in terms of its severity in relation to a given case.

Yoel Haitovsky suggests that replacement of the multiple correlations of the set of explanatory variables R_{x_k} in the numerator by "the partial correlation coefficients between all pairs of the explanatory variables" (not zero-order pairwise correlation) may be a better test of multicollinearity.[11] Thus the test can be written as:

$$\frac{r_{12.3\ldots K}}{R_y} > 1$$

or,

$$\frac{r_{ij.1\ldots K}}{R_y} > 1 \qquad (i \neq j, \quad i, j = 1, \ldots, K) \qquad \textbf{5.2.10}$$

---

[11] Yoel Haitovsky, "Multicollinearity in Regression Analysis: Comment," *Review of Economics and Statistics*, Vol. LI (November, 1969), pp. 486-489.

The denominator is as before. The numerator is the partial correlation coefficient between X_1 and X_2, or X_i and X_j, when all other X's of the total K of them remain constant.

At what point the severity of multicollinearity becomes harmful still remains an open question. The econometrician follows the rule of thumb and is satisfied if the t test applied to the estimates of the regression coefficients (other than the constant) is found to be significant at the 95 percent confidence level.

5.3 ESTIMATION IN THE PRESENCE OF MULTICOLLINEARITY

The Pooling Technique

Continuing the illustration of demand analysis, we hypothesize that the quantity demanded of food Y by a country is a function of the price of the commodity X_1 and the income of the country X_2. We have, as before,

$$Y = \beta_0 + \beta_1 X_1 + \beta_2 X_2 + U \qquad \textbf{5.3.1}$$

What can we do if serious multicollinearity is present between X_1 and X_2? Regardless of the degree of severity of multicollinearity (even in the extreme case of exact linear dependence between X_1 and X_2), we can find a solution if β_1 is known a priori or from extraneous sources. Then we have:

$$(Y - \beta_1 X_1) = \beta_0 + \beta_2 X_2 + U \qquad \textbf{5.3.2}$$

This is relatively a simple case. It is clear that we need to have information with respect to a coefficient of an observed variable (X_1 or X_2 in this case). A priori information with respect to the parameter β_0 (related to the constant) will not be useful.

In any case, there remains the problem of how to get information about β_1. Intuition or guess apart (the Bayesian approach is not considered in this volume), a method that has been widely used is the technique of pooling of observations.[12] This technique is so named because it is based on pooling information from both time-series and cross-sectional data.

Suppose that we have information on a cross section of N families and a time series of T time periods. We collect family budget data and assume that all families pay the same price for the particular commodity at any given time. This assumption is based on the presence of a free competitive market. We estimate variations in quantity demanded Y in terms of variations in income X_2 with price assumed invariant, using cross-sectional data collected at time t:

---

[12] J. Tobin, "A Statistical Demand Function for Food in the USA," *Journal of the Royal Statistical Society*, Vol. 113-A (1950), pp. 113-141; H.O.A. Wold and Lars Juréen. *Demand Analysis: A Study in Econometrics* (New York: John Wiley & Sons, 1953), pp. 192-195; and J.R.N. Stone, *The Measurement of Consumers' Expenditure and Behaviour in the United Kingdom, 1920-1938* (Cambridge, England: Cambridge University Press, 1954).

$$Y_i = \beta_0 + \beta_2 X_{i2} + U_i \qquad 5.3.3$$

The subscript i refers to the individual families, and $i = 1, 2, \ldots, N$.

In the next step, we construct the variable Y^*:

$$Y^* = \sum_{i=1}^{N} Y_i - \hat{\beta}_2 \sum_{i=1}^{N} X_{i2} \qquad 5.3.4$$

This is the quantity demanded in the given time period after correction for the effect of variations in income X_2. Now, using the time-series data, the variable Y^* is constructed for each time period. The rationale is that price X_1 of the commodity Y varies over time t, though it is invariant for different families at a given time. The estimating equation then becomes:

$$(Y^*)_t = \beta_0 + \beta_1 (X_1)_t + U_t^* \qquad t = 1, 2, \ldots, T \qquad 5.3.5$$

The estimated coefficients, $\hat{\beta}_1$ from equation 5.3.5 and $\hat{\beta}_2$ from equation 5.3.3, are estimates of β_1 and β_2 respectively in the original equation 5.3.1.

Even though the pooling technique has been extensively used by econometricians, there remain some problems of interpretation.[13] The cross-sectional data are taken at a point of time, say 1960, if family budget data for 1960 is used. In the next step, there may be time-series data for, say, 1946 to 1966. With the pooling method we would be using the coefficient $\hat{\beta}_2$ estimated on the basis of 1960 cross-sectional data to compute our dependent variable Y_t^* at the second stage over all the years 1946 to 1966. Questions arise as to whether the econometrician can satisfactorily distinguish between the two structures and interpret his estimators accordingly. Does cross-sectional analysis refer to purely long-run parameters? Does time-series analysis necessarily refer to purely short-term parameters? What are the roles of sociodemographic variables in a cross-sectional study? How can we isolate them and obtain an unbiased and efficient estimator of the income coefficient? What are the problems involved in aggregation for relating "micro" studies based on cross-sectional data to "macro" studies based on aggregated time-series data? These questions show that although the mechanics of pooling cross-sectional and time-series samples make it appear a relatively simple and attractive solution, the technique leaves many questions in the process unanswered.

Other Solutions

Confronted with the baffling situation of serious multicollinearity, we may find that another solution is to collect new information. The variables that appear to be multicollinear in a given sample may not be so if a new

[13] J. Meyer and E. Kuh, "How Extraneous are Extraneous Estimates?" *Review of Economics and Statistics,* Vol. 39 (1957), pp. 380-393; and E. Kuh, "The Validity of Cross-Sectionally Estimated Behavior Equations in Time-Series Applications," *Econometrica,* Vol. 27, No. 2 (April, 1959), pp. 197-214.

sample is obtained. Thus instead of throwing out collinear variables rather arbitrarily from the set of explanatory variables, it may be proper to collect new sample observations on such variables. Of course the problem of data collection in econometric research is too difficult to make this suggestion very attractive.

Some researchers working with time-series data have sought to resolve the multicollinearity problem by transforming the observed data to first differences. Even when it may help to reduce the multicollinearity problem, the gain may be offset by the fact that such transformations often make disturbances autocorrelated even if they were not so when the original observations were used in the regression.

The purely statistical solution, "to get rid of multicollinearities" in a set of variables appearing jointly as regressors, is available in *component analysis*.[14] In this technique the set X is decomposed into two subsets: (1) a set of statistically significant orthogonal component factors F, and (2) a set of residual components W. By construction the components in F are not collinear and are used in subsequent steps of estimation, and residual components in W are neglected.

The approach has not been appealing to econometricians because each component in F, which turns out to be an artificial linear combination of the original variables in the set X, is difficult to interpret directly as an observed economic variable. In addition what is thrown out in W, the residual component, is regretted by some as loss of available information. The principal component analysis will be discussed in Chapter 8.

DISCUSSION QUESTIONS

1. Write an essay on multicollinearity, bringing out clearly its bearing on: (a) specification error, (b) interaction effect, and (c) the rank condition of the regressor-matrix.
2. Show that if there is an exact linear relationship between X_1 and X_2, the OLS estimator in the following model is indeterminate:

$$Y = b_0 + b_1X_1 + b_2X_2 + U$$

3. (a) The zero-order correlation between X_1 and X_2 in the above model can be used as a test of multicollinearity. Discuss.
   (b) Why can't the same correlation coefficient be effectively used as a test of multicollinearity when there are more than two X's in the model?
   (c) Review briefly the alternative tests recently proposed by (1) Farrar and Glauber and (2) Haitovsky.
4. Briefly describe the pooling technique. What are the limitations of this technique?

---

[14] M. G. Kendall, *A Course in Multivariate Analysis* (New York: Hafner Publishing Co., 1957), pp. 70-75.

5. Consider the case in question 2 above when the linear relationship between the two variables X_1 and X_2 is not exact. Can the parameters of the above model be estimated now by the least squares method?

SUGGESTED READINGS

Balestra, P., and M. Nerlove. "Pooling Cross-Section and Time-Series Data in the Estimation of a Dynamic Model: The Demand for Natural Gas." *Econometrica,* Vol. 34, No. 3 (July, 1966), pp. 585-612.

Farrar, D. E., and R. R. Glauber. "Multicollinearity in Regression Analysis: The Problem Revisited." *Review of Economics and Statistics,* Vol. XLIX (February, 1967), pp. 92-107.

Frisch, R. *Statistical Confluence Analysis by Means of Complete Regression Systems.* Oslo, Norway: University Economics Institute, 1934.

Haavelmo, T. "Remarks on Frisch's Confluence Analysis and Its Use in Econometrics." *Statistical Inference in Dynamic Economic Models,* edited by T. C. Koopmans. New York: John Wiley & Sons, 1950, Chapter 5.

Haitovsky, Yoel. "Multicollinearity in Regression Analysis: Comment." *Review of Economics and Statistics,* Vol. LI (November, 1969), pp. 486-489.

Kendall, M. G. *A Course in Multivariate Analysis.* New York: Hafner Publishing Co., 1957.

Klein, L. R. *An Introduction to Econometrics.* Englewood Cliffs, New Jersey: Prentice-Hall, 1962.

Klein, L. R., and Mitsugu Nakamura. "Singularity in the Equation System of Econometrics: Some Aspects of the Problem of Multicollinearity." *International Economic Review,* Vol. 3, No. 3 (September, 1962), pp. 274-299.

Kuh, E. "The Validity of Cross-Sectionally Estimated Behavior Equations in Time-Series Applications." *Econometrica,* Vol. 27, No. 2 (April, 1959), pp. 197-214.

Meyer, J., and E. Kuh. "How Extraneous Are Extraneous Estimates?" *Review of Economics and Statistics,* Vol. 39 (1957), pp. 380-393.

Sonquist, J. A., and J. N. Morgan. *The Detection of Interaction Effects,* Survey Research Center, Monograph No. 35. Ann Arbor, Michigan: University of Michigan Press, 1964.

Stone, J. R. N. "The Analysis of Market Demand." *Journal of the Royal Statistical Society,* Vol. 108 (1945), Parts III and IV, pp. 286-382.

———. *The Measurement of Consumers' Expenditure and Behaviour in the United Kingdom, 1920-1938.* Cambridge, England: Cambridge University Press, 1954.

Tintner, Gerhard. "A Note on Rank, Multicollinearity and Multiple Regression." *Annals of Mathematical Statistics,* Vol. 16 (1945), pp. 304-308.

Tobin, J. "A Statistical Demand Function for Food in the USA." *Journal of the Royal Statistical Society,* Vol. 113-A (1950), pp. 113-141.

Toro-Vizcarrondo, C., and T. D. Wallace. "A Test of Mean Square Error Criteria for Restrictions in Linear Regression." *Journal of the American Statistical Association,* Vol. 63 (1968), pp. 558-572.

Wallace, T. D., and A. Hussain. "The Use of Error Component Models in Combining Cross-Section with Time-Series Data." *Econometrica,* Vol. 37, No. 1 (January, 1969), pp. 55-72.

Wold, Herman O.A., and Lars Juréen. *Demand Analysis: A Study in Econometrics*. New York: John Wiley & Sons, 1953.

6

dummy variables

6.0 THE ROLE OF DUMMY VARIABLES

In econometric research qualitative variables are often relevant. In a time-series study political events exercise influence on the aggregative data relating to a national economy. Economic policies pursued by a national government may differ with the party in power, and the consequences of different policies are likely to be different. War and peace have impact on the economic behavior, as have national calamities or political crises within the national borders. If we are studying quarterly data, seasonal adjustment may be a problem. In our economic behavior we do respond to a seasonal pattern for reasons many and varied—weather, religion, cultural patterns, and so forth.

In cross-sectional data sociodemographic phenomena contribute a great deal to the diversity of behavior of the microunits, be they families or firms. Religion, education, sex of the head of the family, race, location, home ownership, marital status of the head of the family, family size, ethnic background, political affiliation, trade union membership, all sorts of variables have been experimented with by econometric researchers. Of course prima facie the claim of such qualitative variables for inclusion in a research design is hard to dispute.

6.1 THE TECHNIQUE OF DUMMY VARIABLES: SHIFTS IN THE LEVEL OF A FUNCTION

First we consider how to measure the impact of qualitative variables. The technique of using *dummy variables* has been widely adopted, and the result is the straightforward inclusion of qualitative variables in regression models. This technique uses the value 1 for the presence of the qualitative attribute that is assumed to have an impact on the dependent variable and 0 for the absence of the given attribute. For example it may be hypothesized that the income of a wage earner depends on hours of work and the racial background of the worker (white or nonwhite). We then have:

$$Y = \beta_1' + \beta_2' X_2 + \beta_3' X_3 + \beta_4' X_4 + U' \qquad \textbf{6.1.1}$$

where Y = income of the wage earner
X_2 = hours of work
X_3, X_4 = racial background of the worker

We wish to estimate the parameters β_k', where $k = 1, 2, 3, 4$.

We have quantitative data on Y and X_2, in dollars and hours respectively. As to racial background, we know only whether the individual wage earner in the sample is white or nonwhite. We use the binary dummy variables:

$$\begin{aligned} X_3 &= 1 \quad \text{white} \\ &= 0 \quad \text{nonwhite} \end{aligned}$$

$$\begin{aligned} X_4 &= 1 \quad \text{nonwhite} \\ &= 0 \quad \text{white} \end{aligned}$$

The OLS estimates of $\boldsymbol{\beta}$ are $\hat{\boldsymbol{\beta}} = (\mathbf{X}'\mathbf{X})^{-1}\mathbf{X}'\mathbf{Y}$ from equation 2.3.22, so it is important to examine the character of the $(\mathbf{X}'\mathbf{X})$ matrix carefully. Does the use of the dummy variable technique raise any special problem?

One problem is critical and can be readily seen. Let us elaborate the model as follows. Suppose that there are five individual wage earners in the sample, A, B, C, D, and E, and that two of them, B and C, are nonwhite.

	X_1	Hours of Work X_2	White X_3	Nonwhite X_4
Wage earner A	1	X_{12}	1	0
B	1	X_{22}	0	1
C	1	X_{32}	0	1
D	1	X_{42}	1	0
E	1	X_{52}	1	0

6.1.2

(Recall that X_1 assumes a constant value of 1 to obtain the estimate of the constant term β_1'.)

It follows that :[1]

$$(\mathbf{X}'\mathbf{X}) = \begin{bmatrix} \Sigma X_1^2 & \Sigma X_1X_2 & \Sigma X_1X_3 & \Sigma X_1X_4 \\ \Sigma X_1X_2 & \Sigma X_2^2 & \Sigma X_2X_3 & \Sigma X_2X_4 \\ \Sigma X_3X_1 & \Sigma X_3X_2 & \Sigma X_3^2 & \Sigma X_3X_4 \\ \Sigma X_4X_1 & \Sigma X_4X_2 & \Sigma X_4X_3 & \Sigma X_4^2 \end{bmatrix} \qquad 6.1.3$$

(Continued)

---

[1] The symbol $\sum_{j=1}^{W+NW} Z$ indicates that the variable Z is summed over all individuals in the sample; the symbol $\sum_{j=1}^{W} Z$ indicates that the variable is summed over only the W individuals; and the symbol $\sum_{j=1}^{NW} Z$ indicates that Z is summed only over the NW individuals.

$$= \begin{bmatrix} \sum_{j=1}^{W+NW} 1 & \sum_{j=1}^{W+NW} X_2 & \sum_{j=1}^{W} 1 & \sum_{j=1}^{NW} 1 \\ \sum_{j=1}^{W+NW} X_2 & \sum_{j=1}^{W+NW} X_2^2 & \sum_{j=1}^{W} X_2 & \sum_{j=1}^{NW} X_2 \\ \sum_{j=1}^{W} 1 & \sum_{j=1}^{W} X_2 & \sum_{j=1}^{W} 1 & 0 \\ \sum_{j=1}^{NW} 1 & \sum_{j=1}^{NW} X_2 & 0 & \sum_{j=1}^{NW} 1 \end{bmatrix}$$

We can then write:

$$(\mathbf{X'X}) = \begin{bmatrix} 5 & \sum_{j=1}^{5} X_2 & 3 & 2 \\ \sum_{j=1}^{5} X_2 & \sum_{j=1}^{5} X_2^2 & \sum_{j=1}^{3} X_2 & \sum_{j=1}^{2} X_2 \\ 3 & \sum_{j=1}^{3} X_2 & 3 & 0 \\ 2 & \sum_{j=1}^{2} X_2 & 0 & 2 \end{bmatrix} \qquad \textbf{6.1.4}$$

Notice that column 1 of the $(\mathbf{X'X})$ matrix can be obtained by adding columns 3 and 4. If one column of a matrix is equal to the sum of two other columns, the condition of nonsingularity does not hold, and the matrix cannot be inverted. If the matrix $(\mathbf{X'X})$ cannot be inverted, the estimator $\hat{\beta}'_k$ cannot be obtained, and we are caught in what has been known as the *dummy variable trap*.[2]

Fortunately a solution for this problem has been suggested. We rewrite the model as:

$$Y = \beta_1 + \beta_2 X_2 + \beta_3 X_3 + U \qquad \textbf{6.1.5}$$

Only one aspect of the attribute race is included in the dummy variable, in this case X_3, or white. The impact of the attribute nonwhite may then be discerned from β_1. When we wish to obtain a measure of nonwhite impact, we have:

$$X_3 = 0 \text{ and } E(Y) = \beta_1 + \beta_2 X_2 \qquad \textbf{6.1.6}$$

Similarly, for the white,

---

[2] Daniel B. Suits, "Use of Dummy Variables in Regression Equations," *Journal of the American Statistical Association,* Vol. 52, No. 280 (December, 1957), pp. 548-551.

$$X_3 = 1, \qquad E(Y) = (\beta_1 + \beta_3) + \beta_2 X_2 \qquad \textbf{6.1.7}$$

A general rule to use to avoid the dummy variable trap is that whenever dummy variables are included using the zero-one technique and there is an intercept term in the equation such as β_1 in the present case, the number of such dummy variables should be one less than the number of different ways the dummy variable under consideration is expected to affect the dependent variable. In our example we had only two such values of the chosen qualitative variable, race—white and nonwhite—and thus we include just one dummy variable.

Suppose we have dummy variables for religion: Protestant, Catholic, Hindu, Jewish, and Moslem. The technique will be as shown in Table 6-1.

TABLE 6-1

$X_3 = 1$ Protestant
$\quad = 0$ otherwise

$X_4 = 1$ Catholic
$\quad = 0$ otherwise

$X_5 = 1$ Hindu
$\quad = 0$ otherwise

$X_6 = 1$ Jewish
$\quad = 0$ otherwise

$X_7 = 1$ Moslem
$\quad = 0$ otherwise

X_3	X_4	X_5	X_6	X_7
1	0	0	0	0
0	1	0	0	0
0	0	1	0	0
0	0	0	1	0
0	0	0	0	1

Then, with all the dummy variables included explicitly,

$$Y = \beta_1' + \beta_2' X_2 + \beta_3' X_3 + \beta_4' X_4 + \beta_5' X_5 + \beta_6' X_6 + \beta_7' X_7 + U' \qquad \textbf{6.1.8}$$

As before,

$$Y = \text{income of the wage earner}$$
$$X_2 = \text{hours of work}$$

and the estimating equation is:

$$Y = \beta_1 + \beta_2 X_2 + \beta_3 X_3 + \beta_4 X_4 + \beta_5 X_5 + \beta_6 X_6 + U \qquad \textbf{6.1.9}$$

and β_7' is analyzed from β_1.

When the sample observations relate to Moslems only, β_3, β_4, β_5, and β_6 become zero, and we have:

$$E(Y) = \beta_1 + \beta_2 X_2 \qquad \text{for Moslems} \qquad \textbf{6.1.10}$$

$$E(Y) = (\beta_1 + \beta_3) + \beta_2 X_2 \qquad \text{for Prostestants} \qquad \textbf{6.1.11}$$
$$E(Y) = (\beta_1 + \beta_4) + \beta_2 X_2 \qquad \text{for Catholics} \qquad \textbf{6.1.12}$$
$$E(Y) = (\beta_1 + \beta_5) + \beta_2 X_2 \qquad \text{for Hindus} \qquad \textbf{6.1.13}$$
$$E(Y) = (\beta_1 + \beta_6) + \beta_2 X_2 \qquad \text{for Jews} \qquad \textbf{6.1.14}$$

Notice that β_2 and β_1 appear in each of the equations above and that β_3, β_4, β_5, and β_6 are estimated only for subsets of the original total sample.

The interpretation of such results requires great care. Each value of the dummy variable indicates a parallel shift in the regression line since it affects the intercept, holding the coefficient with respect to hours of work β_2 constant. Figure 6-1 expresses this diagrammatically from model 6.1.5. Similarly, Figure 6-2 applies model 6.1.9 to religion.

It is now clear that this use of dummy variables corresponds to some important assumptions about the impact of the attributes represented this way. One assumption is that the impact on the dependent variable of the nondummy variables is the same for all subsets of the sample. In this case we are assuming that the change in income produced by a change in hours of work is the same for all workers and independent of race or religion. Another assumption in the above use of dummy variables is that the attributes corresponding to the dummy variables have impact only on the level

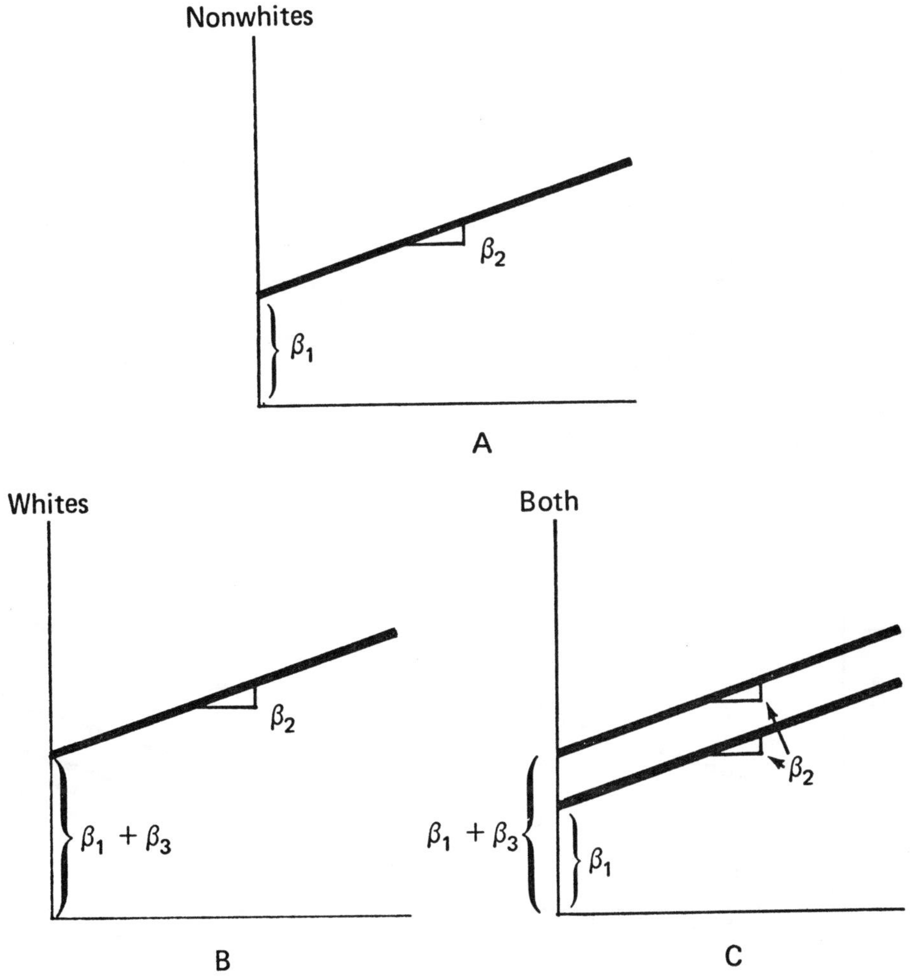

FIGURE 6-1

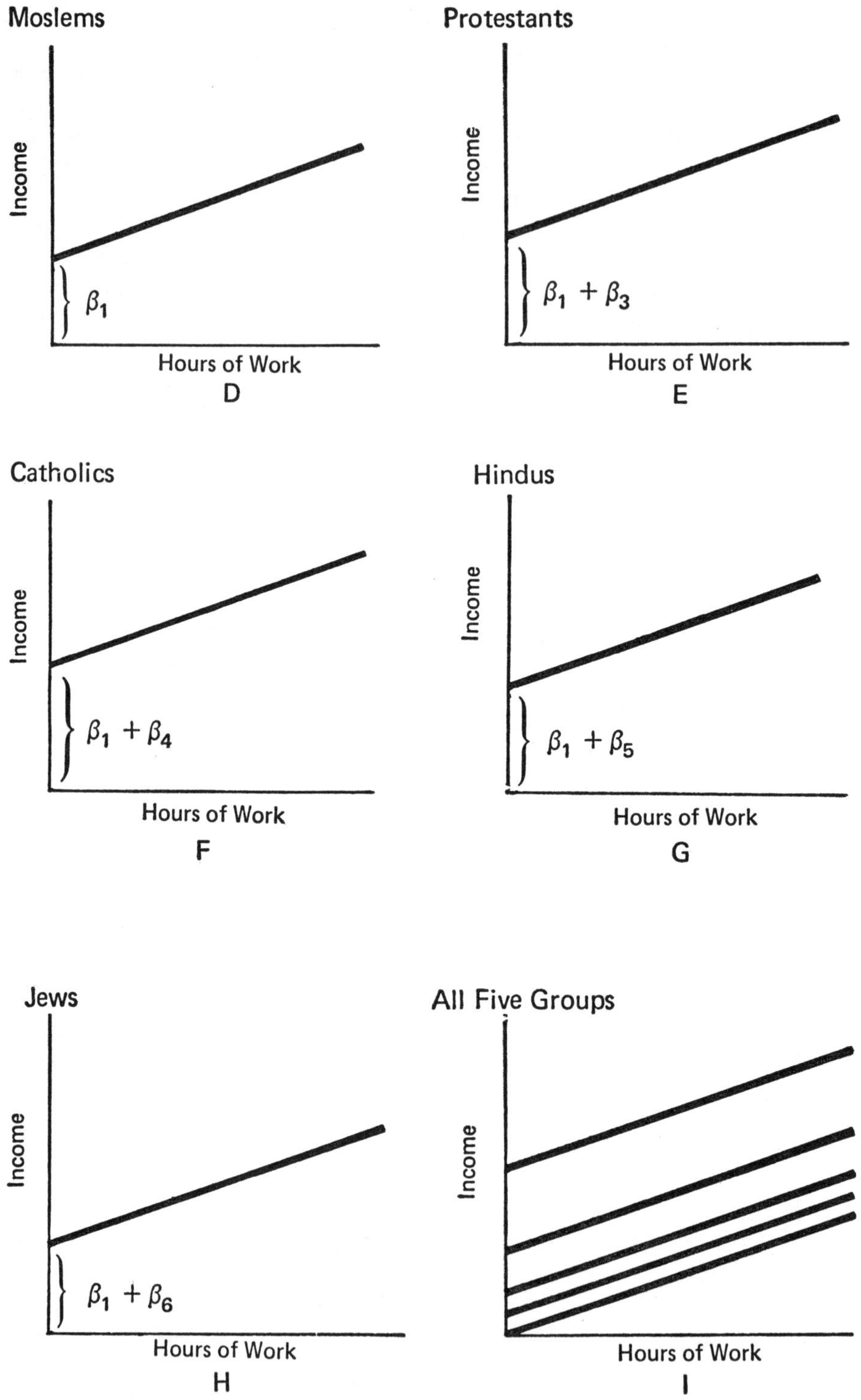
Moslems
Income
β_1
Hours of Work
D
Protestants
Income
$\beta_1 + \beta_3$
Hours of Work
E
Catholics
Income
$\beta_1 + \beta_4$
Hours of Work
F
Hindus
Income
$\beta_1 + \beta_5$
Hours of Work
G
Jews
Income
$\beta_1 + \beta_6$
Hours of Work
H
All Five Groups
Income
Hours of Work
I

FIGURE 6-2

of the dependent variable represented by the intercept of the equation. The third assumption is the linear additivity of these constant terms.

Let us now investigate the situation when we introduce both attributes, race and religion, into the same model. We assume that the income of the wage earner depends on hours of work and on his race and religion.

$$Y = \beta_1' X_1 + \beta_2' X_2 + \zeta_1' X_3 + \zeta_2' X_4 + \delta_1' X_5 + \delta_2' X_6 + \delta_3' X_7 + \delta_4' X_8 + \delta_5' X_9 + U' \qquad \textbf{6.1.15}$$

where Y = income of the wage earner
X_1 = 1 always
X_2 = hours of work
X_3 = 1 white, 0 otherwise
X_4 = 1 nonwhite, 0 otherwise
X_5 = 1 Protestant, 0 otherwise
X_6 = 1 Catholic, 0 otherwise
X_7 = 1 Hindu, 0 otherwise
X_8 = 1 Jewish, 0 otherwise
X_9 = 1 Moslem, 0 otherwise

It is easy to show that we face the same problem of singularity if we wish to estimate the equation in this form. One can easily confirm that columns $X_3 + X_4$ add up to column X_1; similarly, columns $X_5 + X_6 + X_7 + X_8 + X_9$ add up to column X_1. Following the rule noted before, the equation to be estimated is:

$$Y = \beta_1 + \beta_2 X_2 + \zeta_1 X_3 + \delta_1 X_5 + \delta_2 X_6 + \delta_3 X_7 + \delta_4 X_8 + U \qquad \textbf{6.1.16}$$

The function can be interpreted as follows:

Nonwhite + Moslem	$E(Y) = \beta_1 + \beta_2 X_2$	**6.1.17**
White + Moslem	$E(Y) = (\beta_1 + \zeta_1) + \beta_2 X_2$	**6.1.18**
Nonwhite + Protestant	$E(Y) = (\beta_1 + \delta_1) + \beta_2 X_2$	**6.1.19**
White + Prostestant	$E(Y) = (\beta_1 + \zeta_1 + \delta_1) + \beta_2 X_2$	**6.1.20**
Nonwhite + Catholic	$E(Y) = (\beta_1 + \delta_2) + \beta_2 X_2$	**6.1.21**
White + Catholic	$E(Y) = (\beta_1 + \zeta_1 + \delta_2) + \beta_2 X_2$	**6.1.22**
Nonwhite + Hindu	$E(Y) = (\beta_1 + \delta_3) + \beta_2 X_2$	**6.1.23**
White + Hindu	$E(Y) = (\beta_1 + \zeta_1 + \delta_3) + \beta_2 X_2$	**6.1.24**
Nonwhite + Jewish	$E(Y) = (\beta_1 + \delta_4) + \beta_2 X_2$	**6.1.25**
White + Jewish	$E(Y) = (\beta_1 + \zeta_1 + \delta_4) + \beta_2 X_2$	**6.1.26**

Notice that this analysis assumes linear additivity for the coefficients of the dummy variables; that is, it is assumed that the income level for nonwhite

Catholics is the sum of the income level for nonwhites and the income level for Catholics.

But the situation may not always be so tractable. Consider a case where we have two racial characteristics, nonwhite and white, and two sex characteristics, male and female:

$$Y = \beta_1 + \beta_2 X_2 + \zeta_3 X_3 + \delta_4 X_4 + U \qquad \textbf{6.1.27}$$

where Y, X_2, and X_3 are as above
$X_4 = 1$ male, 0 otherwise

Assume that the data are as follows:

Sample	X_1	X_2	X_3	X_4
A	1	X_{12}	1	1
B	1	X_{22}	1	1
C	1	X_{32}	0	0
D	1	X_{42}	0	0
E	1	X_{52}	1	1

6.1.28

Columns 3 and 4 are indistinguishable. This is the problem of perfect multicollinearity between race and sex. All whites are males, and all nonwhites are females. If that is the sample, we cannot obtain independent estimates of ζ_3 and δ_4. In using a number of dummy variables in one regression, the researcher must be careful because, should there be two such collinear variables, multicollinearity may be exact and the $(\mathbf{X}'\mathbf{X})$ matrix truly singular.

6.2 SHIFTS IN BOTH LEVEL AND SLOPE OF A FUNCTION

Now consider the case when the coefficient of the nondummy variable does not remain constant. Should only the level of the dependent economic variable be affected by qualitative attributes? Not necessarily. We can design our model to measure the slope of the functions that may vary with the differences in such qualitative variables.

We write the model:

$$Y = \beta_1 + \beta_2 X_2 + \zeta_3 X_3 + \delta_4 X_4 + \beta_5 X_5 + \beta_6 X_6 + U \qquad \textbf{6.2.1}$$

where now $X_5 = X_2 X_3$

$X_6 = X_2 X_4$

The variables Y, X_2, X_3, and X_4 remain as before, and:

$$X_5 = 0 \text{ when } X_3 = 0 \text{ (nonwhite)} = X_3X_2$$

$$X_6 = 0 \text{ when } X_4 = 0 \text{ (female)} = X_4X_2$$

$\Sigma X_5 = \Sigma X_2$ The sum is over all X_2's when $X_3 = 1$ (white)

$\Sigma X_6 = \Sigma X_2$ The sum is over all X_2's when $X_4 = 1$ (male)

The estimated equation may be interpreted as follows:

Case A. White and male:

$$E(Y) = (\beta_1 + \zeta_3 + \delta_4) + (\beta_2 + \beta_5 + \beta_6)X_2 \tag{6.2.2}$$

Case B. Nonwhite and male:

$$E(Y) = (\beta_1 + \delta_4) + (\beta_2 + \beta_6)X_2 \tag{6.2.3}$$

Case C. White and female:

$$E(Y) = (\beta_1 + \zeta_3) + (\beta_2 + \beta_5)X_2 \tag{6.2.4}$$

Case D. Nonwhite and female:

$$E(Y) = \beta_1 + \beta_2X_2 \tag{6.2.5}$$

Figure 6-3 expresses equations 6.2.2 through 6.2.5 diagrammatically. Notice that this use of dummy variables also assumes linear additivity.

6.3 SOME PROBLEMS RELATED TO THE USE OF DUMMY VARIABLES

A Dummy Dependent Variable

Consider the model:

$$Y_i = \beta_0 + \beta_1X_i + U_i \tag{6.3.1}$$

where Y_i = 1 if the ith family is interracial and/or interfaith by way of martial status
= 0 otherwise
X_i = number of years of college-level education of the couple

This model states that interracial and/or interfaith marriage is functionally dependent on the college-level education of the individuals involved.

From equation 6.3.1,

$$E(Y_i) = \beta_0 + \beta_1X_i$$

and

$$U_i = Y_i - \beta_0 - \beta_1X_i \tag{6.3.2}$$

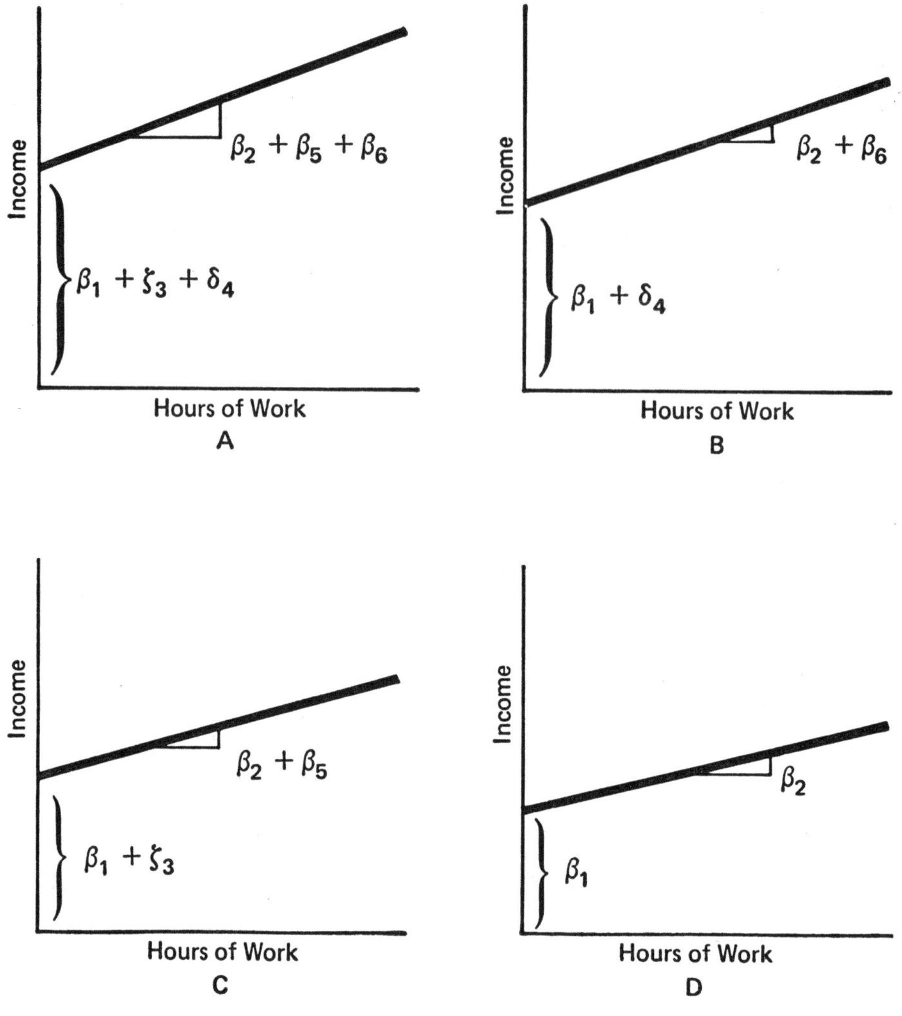

FIGURE 6-3

Note that since Y_i is either 1 or 0, U_i is either $-\beta_0 - \beta_1 X_i$ or $1 - \beta_0 - \beta_1 X_i$. Evidently U_i is not normally distributed. It has a discrete distribution. To be sure, we continue to assume $E(U_i) = 0$. Hence the distribution of U_i must be:[3]

U_i	$f(U_i)$
$-\beta_0 - \beta_1 X_i$	$1 - \beta_0 - \beta_1 X_i$
$1 - \beta_0 - \beta_1 X_i$	$\beta_0 + \beta_1 X_i$

6.3.3

[3] See A. S. Goldberger, *Econometric Theory* (New York: John Wiley & Sons, 1964), pp. 249-250.

Note that $f = 1 - \beta_0 - \beta_1 X_i$ and $1 - f = \beta_0 + \beta_1 X_i$, and the sum is 1. Goldberger has shown that the usual assumption of homoscedasticity of the U_i cannot be maintained in this case. The variance of U_i is:

$$
\begin{aligned}
E(U_i^2) &= (-\beta_0 - \beta_1 X_i)^2 (1 - \beta_0 - \beta_1 X_i) + (1 - \beta_0 - \beta_1 X_i)^2 (\beta_0 + \beta_1 X_i) \\
&= (\beta_0 + \beta_1 X_i)(1 - \beta_0 - \beta_1 X_i) \qquad \textbf{6.3.4} \\
&= E(Y_i)\,[(1 - E(Y_i)]
\end{aligned}
$$

Thus U_i is heteroscedastic since its variance is shown to be systematically dependent on $E(Y_i)$, and therefore also on X_i. The presence of such heteroscedasticity, as we have seen in Chapter 4, makes the OLS estimates of $\hat{\beta}_0$ and $\hat{\beta}_1$ less reliable. They are not efficient, even though they continue to be unbiased. The method of estimation considered for the presence of such heteroscedastic U_i is a possible option. Also note that the U_i in this model has been shown to have a discrete distribution. Thus the assumption of normal distribution is ruled out. Consequently the application of significance tests to the estimates (t tests) is ruled out.

A Dummy Variable with Arbitrary Scales

The use of arbitrary scales for the dummy variables is also known. For example if we assign values such as:

Northeast	= 1
Midwest	= 2
West	= 3
South	= 4

and want to measure the impact of regional location on the behavior pattern, say of consumption, we have to be careful about interpreting the estimated parameters.

Consider the following model:

$$C_i = \beta_0 + \beta_1 R_i + U_i \qquad \textbf{6.3.5}$$

where C_i = consumption of foreign cars by the ith family
R_i = region or residence of the ith family, when regions are indexed 1, 2, 3, 4 as above

From equation 6.3.5,

$$
\begin{aligned}
E(C_i) &= \beta_0 + \beta_1 \quad \text{when the } i^{th} \text{ family belongs to } R = 1 \\
E(C_i) &= \beta_0 + 2\beta_1 \quad \text{when the } i^{th} \text{ family belongs to } R = 2 \\
E(C_i) &= \beta_0 + 3\beta_1 \quad \text{when the } i^{th} \text{ family belongs to } R = 3 \\
E(C_i) &= \beta_0 + 4\beta_1 \quad \text{when the } i^{th} \text{ family belongs to } R = 4
\end{aligned}
\qquad \textbf{6.3.6}
$$

The above results point to the fact that the regional impact on the consumption of foreign cars is uniquely proportional, and the proportionality factor is β_1. This factor is the same between regions one and two, between two and three, and again between regions three and four. Without a priori information this involves an arbitrary assumption.

The problem can be avoided by using binary dummy variables. We rewrite the model as follows:

$$C_i = \beta_0 + \beta_1 R_i(1) + \beta_2 R_i(2) + \beta_3 R_i(3) + U_i \qquad 6.3.7$$

where $R_i(1) = 1$ if the ith family belongs to region 1
$= 0$ otherwise

$R_i(2) = 1$ if the ith family belongs to region 2
$= 0$ otherwise

$R_i(3) = 1$ if the ith family belongs to region 3
$= 0$ otherwise

From equation 6.3.7,

$E(C_i) = \beta_0$ when $R_i(1) = R_i(2) = R_i(3) = 0$, that is, the ith family belongs to region 4
$E(C_i) = \beta_0 + \beta_1$ when the ith family belongs to region 1 **6.3.8**
$E(C_i) = \beta_0 + \beta_2$ when the ith family belongs to region 2
$E(C_i) = \beta_0 + \beta_3$ when the ith family belongs to region 3

Evidently in the interpretation of the above results, no arbitrary assumption with respect to interregional impact on the consumption of foreign cars is involved.

Too Many Dummies

In recent times the attempt to quantify nonquantifiable qualitative variables has become too fashionable. It has been suggested that often the emphasis on qualitative attributes is misplaced. They are sometimes called "nuisance" variables, implying that they give more trouble than information. For example in a cross-sectional study of a consumption function, consumption of the jth family C_j may be regressed not only on the income of the jth family Y_j, but also on race Z_{2j}, religion Z_{3j}, education Z_{4j}, marital status Z_{5j}, family size Z_{6j}, and so forth. Then all Z's are introduced as dummy variables.

Notice that the suggestion is not that the socioeconomic variables are unimportant by any means. However, if the impacts of such variables are random, they will cancel each other out on an average. If the test shows that they do, the econometrician can be sure that omitting these variables from the regression model does not cause the loss of any information about the sources of systematic variation in the dependent variable. Interestingly enough, most econometric studies have shown that family income is the single most important variable in explaining consumption with cross-sectional data.

Another suggestion is worth considering:[4]

$$C_{jt} = \beta_0 + \beta_1 Y_{jt} + \beta_2 Z_{2jt} + \beta_3 Z_{3jt} + \ldots + \beta_K Z_{Kjt} + U_t$$
$$C_{jt+1} = \beta_0 + \beta_1 Y_{jt+1} + \beta_2 Z_{2jt+1} + \beta_3 Z_{3jt+1} + \ldots + \beta_K Z_{Kjt+1} + U_{jt+1} \qquad \textbf{6.3.9}$$

Subtracting,

$$\Delta C_j = \beta_1 \Delta Y_j + \beta_2 \Delta Z_{2j} + \beta_3 \Delta Z_{3j} + \ldots + \beta_K \Delta Z_{Kj} + V_j \qquad \textbf{6.3.10}$$

where $V_j = U_{jt} - U_{jt+1}$. Under the assumption that the attributes of race, religion, education, marital status, and family size of the jth family have not changed over the given time period, the variables:

$$\Delta Z_{2j} = Z_{2jt+1} - Z_{2jt},\ \Delta Z_{3j} = Z_{3jt+1} - Z_{3jt},\ \ldots,\ \Delta Z_{Kj} = Z_{Kjt+1} - Z_{Kjt}$$

will all be zero. The equation then reduces to:

$$\Delta C_j = \beta_1 \Delta Y_j + V_j \qquad \textbf{6.3.11}$$

In a real situation all of them need not remain invariant. The set of dummy variables, the Z's, usually nonquantifiable and qualitative, can be grouped into two subsets. If we take intertemporal cross-sectional samples, the observations on one of these subsets will remain invariant; and thus in the regression equation expressed in terms of first differences, the number of dummy variables will be fewer. For a given model over a given interval between t and $t + 1$, race, religion, and even education may remain invariant, while marital status and family size may change. Of course the use of this model is more expensive since it involves the collection of two surveys over the same sample of individual units at two time periods. However, if observations over the same sample of individual units at successive time points are available, interesting research possibilities open up.

6.4 SEASONAL ADJUSTMENT BY USING DUMMY VARIABLES

An important use of the dummy variable technique (zero-one scale) in time-series data is seasonal adjustment.[5] Given the assumption of linearity

---

[4] Jean Crockett, "A New Type of Estimate of the Income Elasticity of the Demand for Food," *Proceedings of the American Statistical Association, Business and Economic Statistics Section* (1957), pp. 117-122; and H. S. Houthakker and J. Haldi, "Household Investment in Automobiles: An Intertemporal Cross-Section Analysis," *Proceedings of the Conference on Consumption and Saving*, Vol. 1, edited by I. Friend and Robert Jones (Philadelphia: University of Pennsylvania, 1960).

[5] M. C. Lovell, "Seasonal Adjustment of Economic Time Series and Multiple Regression Analysis," *Journal of the American Statistical Association*, Vol. 58, No. 304 (December, 1963), pp. 993-1010; and L. R. Klein *et al.*, *An Econometric Model of the United Kingdom* (Oxford, England: Basil Blackwell & Mott, 1961), pp. 40-51.

and additivity on the dummy variables, this method of seasonal adjustment may be less arbitrary than the traditional ones. Table 6-2 constructs a case using quarterly data.

TABLE 6-2

$Q_1 = 1$ if the observation is of the first quarter
$= 0$ otherwise

$Q_2 = 1$ if the observation is of the second quarter
$= 0$ otherwise

$Q_3 = 1$ if the observation is of the third quarter
$= 0$ otherwise

$Q_4 = 1$ if the observation is of the fourth quarter
$= 0$ otherwise

Q_1	Q_2	Q_3	Q_4
1	0	0	0
0	1	0	0
0	0	1	0
0	0	0	1

Consider a model:

$$P_t = \alpha_0' + \alpha_1' S_t + \beta_1' Q_{1t} + \beta_2' Q_{2t} + \beta_3' Q_{3t} + \beta_4' Q_{4t} + U_t' \qquad \textbf{6.4.1}$$

where P_t = profit at time t
S_t = sales at time t

For reasons discussed earlier, the estimating equation becomes:

$$P_t = \alpha_0 + \alpha_1 S_t + \beta_1 Q_{1t} + \beta_2 Q_{2t} + \beta_3 Q_{3t} + U_t \qquad \textbf{6.4.2}$$

The interpretation is, as before,

for Q_1, $$E(P_t) = (\alpha_0 + \beta_1) + \alpha_1 S_t \qquad \textbf{6.4.3}$$

for Q_2, $$E(P_t) = (\alpha_0 + \beta_2) + \alpha_1 S_t \qquad \textbf{6.4.4}$$

for Q_3, $$E(P_t) = (\alpha_0 + \beta_3) + \alpha_1 S_t \qquad \textbf{6.4.5}$$

for Q_4, $$E(P_t) = \alpha_0 + \alpha_1 S_t \qquad \textbf{6.4.6}$$

The slope $\alpha_1 = \partial P/\partial S$ remains constant. This system is shown in Figure 6-4. We could introduce variables based on cross products of S and Q_i and estimate variations in the slope, as before, if such a hypothesis were considered useful.

6.5 THE USE OF DUMMY VARIABLES IN TESTING STRUCTURAL DIFFERENCES

In econometric research sample observations over time or across individual units are collected for testing a given model. Suppose that time series of observations on Y and X are collected over 50 years. It may appear

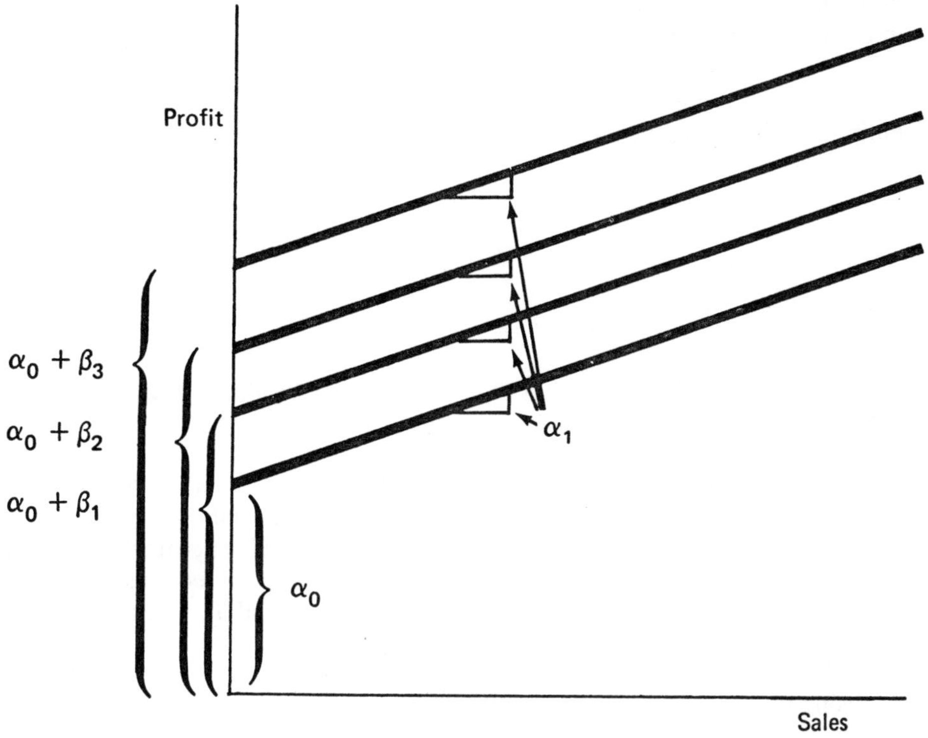

FIGURE 6-4

advantageous to maximize degrees of freedom by lengthening the series. But over this stretch of time, the basic structure that the model seeks to explain may have undergone important changes. Even over a shorter period such structural changes may take place for one reason or another—a war or a revolution. Again, in cross-sectional studies sample observations, even though related to a given time point, may not belong to the same structure. The consumption pattern of farmers in rural areas is likely to be structurally different from that of urban workers. To dramatize the point, suppose that a large cross-sectional sample including families in the United States and the Peoples Republic of China is collected to analyze the savings behavior of households. The data obviously belong to two different economic structures. The problem is how to test the existence of such structural differences. That is, we want to determine whether or not a particular sample belongs to one structure or to two or more. In the latter case true regression coefficients for the different structures are likely to be different, and the coefficients estimated from the unified sample will not be reliable.

The Chow Test

The Chow test is designed to test whether the regression coefficients estimated by assigning subsets of a given set of observations to two or more different structures do in fact belong to the same structure.[6] This test is applied in the following steps:

Step 1: Obtain the least squares estimates of $\hat{\beta}_0$ and $\hat{\beta}_1$ from the entire sample, using the sample observations on Y and X, in the model:

$$Y_t = \beta_0 + \beta_1 X_t + U_t \qquad t = 1, 2, \ldots, T \tag{6.5.1}$$

Then calculate:

$$\Sigma \hat{U}_t^2 = \Sigma(Y_t - \hat{\beta}_0 - \hat{\beta}_1 X_t)^2 \tag{6.5.2}$$

This sum of squared residuals has $T - K$ degrees of freedom. (Note that $K = 2$ is the number of parameters estimated in this case.)

Step 2: Group the sample observations into two separate subsamples, corresponding to the two different structures hypothesized. The sizes of the two subsamples need not be the same. Of course each subsample must be large enough to yield estimates of the parameters involved (again in this case, two). We shall designate the subsamples by T_1 and T_2 when $T = T_1 + T_2$.

Obtain least squares estimators separately for each subsample T_1 and T_2, using two separate regression equations:

$$Y_{t1} = \beta_{01} + \beta_{11} X_{t1} + U_{t1} \tag{6.5.3}$$

$$Y_{t2} = \beta_{02} + \beta_{12} X_{t2} + U_{t2} \tag{6.5.4}$$

where the second subscript refers to the subsample: subscript 1 refers to subsample T_1, and subscript 2 refers to subsample T_2. Calculate:

$$\Sigma \hat{U}_{t1}^2 = \Sigma(Y_{t1} - \hat{\beta}_{01} - \hat{\beta}_{11} X_{t1})^2 \tag{6.5.5}$$

and

$$\Sigma \hat{U}_{t2}^2 = \Sigma(Y_{t2} - \hat{\beta}_{02} - \hat{\beta}_{12} X_{t2})^2 \tag{6.5.6}$$

which will have $T_1 - K$ and $T_2 - K$ degrees of freedom respectively. Obtain the sum $\Sigma \hat{U}_{t1}^2 + \Sigma \hat{U}_{t2}^2$, and this sum of squared residuals will have $T_1 + T_2 - 2K$ or $T - 2K$ degrees of freedom. Calculate:

$$\Sigma \hat{U}_t^{*2} = \Sigma \hat{U}_t^2 - (\Sigma \hat{U}_{t1}^2 + \Sigma \hat{U}_{t2}^2) \tag{6.5.7}$$

Step 3: In the final step apply the F test to the following calculated ratio:

[6] Gregory C. Chow, "Tests of Equality Between Sets of Coefficients in Two Linear Regressions," *Econometrica*, Vol. 28, No. 3 (July, 1960), pp. 591-605.

$$F = \frac{\Sigma \hat{U}_t^{*2}/K}{\Sigma \hat{U}_{t1}^2 + \Sigma \hat{U}_{t2}^2)/T - 2K} \qquad \textbf{6.5.8}$$

with numerator degrees of freedom K and denominator degrees of freedom $T - 2K$. This calculated value of F is compared to the value in the F table at the appropriate level of significance for the same degrees of freedom, K of the numerator and $T - 2K$ of the denominator.

The null hypothesis is the equality of the estimated coefficients of the two different subsample structures:

$$H_0\colon (\hat{\beta}_{01}, \hat{\beta}_{11}) = (\hat{\beta}_{02}, \hat{\beta}_{12})$$

or,

$$H_0\colon (\hat{\beta}_{01}, \hat{\beta}_{11}) - (\hat{\beta}_{02}, \beta_{12}) = 0 \qquad \textbf{6.5.9}$$

If the calculated value of the ratio is less than the tabular value, the difference between the estimated coefficients is not statistically significant and the conclusion is to accept the null hypothesis that the two structures are the same at the chosen significance level. If the calculated ratio exceeds the value found in the F table, the null hypothesis is rejected, the difference between estimated regression coefficients is statistically significant, and the two structures are inferred to be different at the chosen level of significance.

Illustration of the Chow Test: Table 6-3 is a set of example data to which the Chow test can be applied.

TABLE 6-3

Time	Y	X
1946	0.36	8.8
1947	0.21	9.4
1948	0.08	10.0
1949	0.20	10.6
1950	0.10	11.0
1951	0.12	11.9
1952	0.41	12.7
1953	0.50	13.5
1954	0.43	14.3
1955	0.59	15.5
1956	0.90	16.7
1957	0.95	17.7
1958	0.82	18.6
1959	1.04	19.7
1960	1.53	21.1
1961	1.94	22.8
1962	1.75	23.9
1963	1.99	25.2

Source: C. E. V. Leser, *Econometric Techniques and Problems* (New York: Hafner Publishing Co., 1966), Chapter 2, p. 10.

Step 1. The model is as in equation 6.5.1:

$$Y_t = \beta_0 + \beta_1 X_t + U_t$$

$$\Sigma \hat{U}_t^2 = \Sigma(Y_t - \hat{\beta}_0 - \hat{\beta}_1 X_t)^2$$

$$= 0.5722$$

$$\text{d.f.} = T - K = 18 - 2 = 16$$

Step 2.

$$T = T_1 + T_2$$

$$T = 1946 - 1963 = 18$$

$$T_1 = 1946 - 1954 = 9$$

$$T_2 = 1955 - 1963 = 9$$

$$\Sigma \hat{U}_{t1}^2 = \Sigma(Y_{t1} - \hat{\beta}_{01} - \hat{\beta}_{11} X_{t1})^2$$

$$= 0.1396$$

$$\text{d.f.} = T_1 - K = 9 - 2 = 7$$

$$\Sigma \hat{U}_{t2}^2 = \Sigma(Y_{t2} - \hat{\beta}_{02} - \hat{\beta}_{12} X_{t2})^2$$

$$= 0.2167$$

$$\text{d.f.} = T_2 - K = 9 - 2 = 7$$

$$\Sigma \hat{U}_t^{*2} = \Sigma \hat{U}_t^2 - (\Sigma \hat{U}_{t1}^2 + \Sigma \hat{U}_{t2}^2)$$

$$= 0.5722 - (0.1396 + 0.2167)$$

$$= 0.2159$$

Step 3.

$$F = \frac{\Sigma \hat{U}_t^{*2}/K}{(\Sigma \hat{U}_{t1}^2 + \Sigma \hat{U}_{t2}^2)/(T - 2K)}$$

$$= \frac{(0.2159)/2}{(0.3563)/18 - 2(2)} = \frac{(0.2159)/2}{(0.3563)/14} \qquad \textbf{6.5.10}$$

$$= 4.24$$

At the 95 percent significance level for degrees of freedom $K = 2$ and $T - 2K = 14$, the table value of F is 3.74. The computed F value is larger. We therefore reject the hypothesis that the two sets of regression coefficients are the same and that they refer to the same structure. In other words T_1 and T_2 are drawn from two different structures at the 95 percent significance level. Consequently, the general regression model covering the entire sample period does not relate to a stable structure, and its estimated coefficients are unreliable.

The Dummy Variable Test

From the introductory discussion on the role of dummy variables (section 6.0), it was suggested that the use of a dummy variable should be a way to test the same hypothesis of structural unity. This has been demonstrated by Damodar Gujarati.[7] Using the same data series, Gujarati demonstrates that one regression can be estimated for the entire sample by using dummy variables both for the intercept (section 6.1) and the slope (section 6.2). Let the model be as follows:

$$Y_t = \beta_0 + \beta_1 D + \beta_2 X_t + \beta_3 (DX)_t + U_t \qquad t = 1, 2, \ldots, T \qquad \textbf{6.5.11}$$

where $D = 1$ if the observation belongs to the second subsample
$D = 0$ if the observation belongs to the first subsample

(It does not matter if the dummy variable D is reversed, that is, 1 for observations in the first subperiod and 0 for those in the second subperiod.)

$$\begin{aligned} Y_t = \; & -0.2663 \; - \; 1.4839D \; + \; 0.0470X_t \; + \; 0.1034(DX)_t \\ & \;(0.3333) \quad\;\; (0.4703) \quad\;\; (0.0290) \quad\;\; (0.0332) \end{aligned} \qquad \textbf{6.5.12}$$

$$R^2 = 0.9425$$

(Figures in parentheses are standard errors, not t ratios.) Note that the differential intercept and the differential slope coefficients are statistically significant at the 95 percent confidence level. Following the discussions in sections 6.1 and 6.2, the results can be interpreted as follows: For the sample period T_2,

$$\begin{aligned} E(Y_t) &= (-0.2663 - 1.4839) + (0.0470 + 0.1034)X_t \\ &= -1.7502 + 0.1504X_t \end{aligned} \qquad \textbf{6.5.13}$$

and for the sample subperiod T_1,

$$E(Y_t) = -0.2663 + 0.0470X_t \qquad \textbf{6.5.14}$$

Incidentally, the results of two independent regressions for the two subperiods agree with the above results.

To interpret the findings above, we find that both the intercept and slope coefficients differ significantly for the two subperiods. Thus the findings

[7] Damodar Gujarati, "Use of Dummy Variables in Testing for Equality Between Sets of Coefficients in Linear Regressions: A Generalization," *The American Statistician,* Vol. 24, No. 5 (1970), pp. 18-21; and Damodar Gujarati, "Use of Dummy Variables in Testing for Equality Between Sets of Coefficients in Two Linear Regressions: A Note," *The American Statistician,* Vol. 24, No. 1 (1970), pp. 50-52.

confirm the results of the Chow test and uphold the structural divergence hypothesis. The use of dummy variables thus provides a simpler and more straightforward test. It is computationally simpler since only one regression equation instead of three is to be estimated. This dummy variable method also can indicate whether the intercept coefficients or the slope coefficients or both are different.[8]

DISCUSSION QUESTIONS

1. Indicate five important qualitative variables for which dummy variable techniques have been used for quantitative research in recent times.
2. The following estimates have been reported in a recent study:

$$X_t = -211.63 + 0.91(P^{US}/P^{UK})_{t-1} + 2.27Z_{t-1} - 14.86Q_{1t} + 0.53Q_{2t} + 1.00Q_{3t}$$

where X = United Kingdom exports to the United States

P^{US}/P^{UK} = relative prices

Z = level of production in the United States

and Q_{1t} = 1 in first quarter period and 0 in all other periods

Q_{2t} = 1 in second quarter period and 0 in all other periods

Q_{3t} = 1 in third quarter period and 0 in all other periods.

Explain the above results in terms of each of the four quarters of the year.

3. Explain (a) the dummy variable trap, and (b) the linear additivity assumption for the coefficients of the dummy variables.
4. Consider the following consumption function model:

$$C_t = \beta_0 + \beta_1 Y_t + \beta_2 W_t + \beta_3 W_t Y_t + U_t$$

where C = consumption, Y = income, and W = 1 in wartime and 0 in peacetime. (U refers to disturbance terms.)

(a) Compare the consumption functions for war and peace times.

(b) Show that the least squares estimates of the regression coefficients could have been obtained equally well from two separate regressions of C_t on Y_t, one estimated from wartime observations and another from peacetime observations.

---

[8] Extension of the dummy variable technique to a K-variable multiple regression model will be no problem if the test is confined to the intercept coefficient alone. Examining the differential slope coefficients will involve difficulty if no a priori information is available to limit the search to one or two of the independent variables.

5. (a) Define the Chow test.
   (b) Review the technique of using dummy variables for testing structural differences.

SUGGESTED READINGS

Chow, Gregory C. "Tests of Equality Between Sets of Coefficients in Two Linear Regressions." *Econometrica,* Vol. 28, No. 3 (July, 1960), pp. 591-605.

Crockett, Jean. "A New Type of Estimate of the Income Elasticity of the Demand for Food." *Proceedings of the American Statistical Association, Business and Economic Statistics Section* (1957), pp. 117-122.

Gujarati, Damodar. "Use of Dummy Variables in Testing for Equality Between Sets of Coefficients in Two Linear Regressions: A Note." *The American Statistician,* Vol. 24, No. 1 (1970), pp. 50-52.

———. "Use of Dummy Variables in Testing for Equality Between Sets of Coefficients in Linear Regressions: A Generalization." *The American Statistician,* Vol. 24, No. 5 (1970), pp. 18-21.

Houthakker, H. S., and J. Haldi. "Household Investment in Automobiles: An Intertemporal Cross-Section Analysis." *Proceedings of the Conference on Consumption and Saving,* Vol. 1, edited by I. Friend and Robert Jones. Philadelphia: University of Pennsylvania, 1960.

Klein, Lawrence R., R. J. Ball, A. Hazelwood, and P. Vandome. *An Econometric Model of the United Kingdom.* Oxford, England: Basil Blackwell & Mott, 1961.

Lovell, Michael C. "Seasonal Adjustment of Economic Time Series and Multiple Regression Analysis." *Journal of the American Statistical Association,* Vol. 58, No. 304 (December, 1963), pp. 993-1010.

Orcutt, Guy H., Martin Greenberger, John Korbel, and Alice M. Rivlin. *Microanalysis of Socioeconomic Systems: A Simulation Study.* New York: Harper & Row, Publishers, 1961.

Suits, Daniel B. "Use of Dummy Variables in Regression Equations." *Journal of the American Statistical Association,* Vol. 52, No. 280 (December, 1957), pp. 548-551.

7

autoregressive and lag models

7.0 AUTOREGRESSIVE MODELS

In economics, as in other studies of human behavior, it is sometimes necessary to take account of the fact that what happens today very much depends on what happened yesterday. For a particular period the quantity demanded of durable goods such as automobiles or furniture is determined partly by incomes and prices in the current period and partly by the quantities of such goods already on hand, that is, quantities purchased in previous periods. Even the consumption demand for nondurable goods or services, such as tea, coffee, and orchestra or ball game tickets, may be partly determined by patterns of consumption in previous periods. Indeed this is the basis of the "habit formation" hypothesis on consumption.

When these relationships between present and past values of economic variables are expressed as the estimating equations for econometric research, the observations that appear in the equations will include both current values Y_t, X_t and values for one or more previous periods, $Y_{t-1}, X_{t-1}, X_{t-2}, \ldots$. The latter values are described as *lagged values* of the variables. A model in which lagged values of the dependent variable appear as regressors is termed an *autoregressive model.* A model in which a dependent variable is explained by the current value and a series of past values of an independent variable is also essentially an autoregressive model, as we shall see in this chapter. Autoregressive models will often violate one or more of the OLS assumptions and thus require special estimating techniques to make sure that the parameter estimates are unbiased, consistent and efficient.

The simplest case of an autoregressive model can be expressed as a single equation:

$$Y_t = \alpha + \beta Y_{t-1} + U_t \qquad t = 1, 2, \ldots, T \qquad \textbf{7.0.1}$$

Writing all variables in terms of deviations from their respective means and using the OLS regression method of estimation, we obtain for the estimate of β:

$$\hat{\beta} = \frac{\Sigma y_t y_{t-1}}{\Sigma y_{t-1}^2} \qquad \textbf{7.0.2}$$

If we express the estimator $\hat{\beta}$ in terms of weights as in equation 2.4.2, we have:

$$\hat{\beta} = \Sigma W_t Y_t \tag{7.0.3}$$

where

$$W_t = \frac{y_{t-1}}{\Sigma y_{t-1}^2}$$

Substituting into equation 7.0.1,

$$\begin{aligned}\hat{\beta} &= \Sigma W_t(\alpha + \beta Y_{t-1} + U_t)\\ &= \alpha \Sigma W_t + \beta \Sigma W_t Y_{t-1} + \Sigma W_t U_t\end{aligned}$$

Since $\Sigma W_t = 0$ from equation 2.4.10 and $\Sigma W_t Y_{t-1} = 1$ from equation 2.4.11,

$$\hat{\beta} = \beta + \Sigma W_t U_t \tag{7.0.4}$$

Taking expected values on both sides of this equation, we have:

$$E(\hat{\beta}) = \beta + E(\Sigma W_t U_t) \tag{7.0.5}$$

and if $E(\Sigma W_t U_t) = \Sigma W_t E(U_t)$, then, since $E(U_t) = 0$,

$$E(\hat{\beta}) = \beta \tag{7.0.6}$$

As we shall see, in the present case the assumption $E(\Sigma W_t U_t) = \Sigma W_t E(U_t)$ is not likely to hold, and therefore the OLS estimator $\hat{\beta}$ is biased. Note that, following the definition of the weights W_t, we have for the present model:[1]

$$\Sigma W_t U_t = \frac{\Sigma U_t y_{t-1}}{\Sigma y_{t-1}^2} \tag{7.0.7}$$

In the usual regression model the regressor is assumed to be a mathematical variable fixed in repeated sampling, and it is thus independent of U_t, the disturbance term. Recall that $E(U_t) = 0$ by assumption. Thus in equation 7.0.5, $\Sigma W_t E(U_t) = 0$. However, in any autoregressive model, as in the present case, the regressor Y_{t-1} cannot be considered a truly mathematical variable and is not fixed. The variable Y_t is endogenous, determined within the system. According to the model specification, Y_t is dependent on Y_{t-1}

[1] Throughout this chapter the summation Σ is over all t, that is, 1, 2, . . . ,T, and should be read as $\sum_{t=1}^{T}$.

and U_t. The variable y_{t-1} includes Y_t, and Y_t is not independent of U_t.[2] Hence we cannot write $E\left(\frac{\Sigma y_{t-1}U_t}{\Sigma y_{t-1}^2}\right) = \frac{\Sigma y_{t-1}}{\Sigma y_{t-1}^2} E(U_t)$. Therefore,

$$E(\Sigma W_t U_t) \neq 0 \qquad \textbf{7.0.8}$$

Then

$$E(\hat{\beta}) = \beta + E(\Sigma W_t U_t) \neq \beta \qquad \textbf{7.0.9}$$

and the OLS estimator is thus biased.[3]

However, the estimate of $\hat{\beta}$ can be shown to be consistent.

$$\hat{\beta} = \beta + \frac{\Sigma y_{t-1}U_t}{\Sigma y_{t-1}^2}$$

Taking the probability limit,[4]

$$\text{Plim } \hat{\beta} = \beta + \frac{\text{Plim}(\Sigma y_{t-1}U_t)/T}{\text{Plim}(\Sigma y_{t-1}^2)/T} = \beta \qquad \textbf{7.0.10}$$

Note that $\text{Plim}(\Sigma y_{t-1}U_t)/T$ is a consistent estimator of the covariance between Y_{t-1} and U_t and becomes zero in the probability limit. In an autoregressive model, the terms Y_{t-1} and U_t are *contemporaneously uncorrelated*. This means that Y_{t-1} depends on Y_0, the value of Y at the initial period, and on $U_1, U_2, \ldots, U_{t-1}$, but not on U_t. This point will be developed further. Also, note that $\text{Plim}(\Sigma y_{t-1}^2)/T$ is a consistent estimator of the variance Y_{t-1}, which is assumed to be finite and nonzero. This proves that $\hat{\beta}$ is a consistent estimator of β in the given model.

Let us continue with model 7.0.1:

$$Y_t = \alpha + \beta Y_{t-1} + U_t$$

Consider that the subscript t refers to the calendar years beginning with 1898:

$$\begin{aligned} Y_{1899} &= \alpha + \beta Y_{1898} + U_{1899} \\ Y_{1900} &= \alpha + \beta Y_{1899} + U_{1900} \\ Y_{1901} &= \alpha + \beta Y_{1900} + U_{1901} \\ Y_{1902} &= \alpha + \beta Y_{1901} + U_{1902} \end{aligned} \qquad \textbf{7.0.11}$$

---

[2] To see that y_{t-1} includes Y_t, examine the calculation of y_{t-1}, wherein $y_{t-1} = Y_{t-1} - \bar{Y}_{t-1}$, and the mean term $\bar{Y}_{t-1}$ includes the series on Y_t.

[3] Zvi Griliches, "A Note on the Serial Correlation Bias in Estimates of Distributed Lags," *Econometrica*, Vol. 29, No. 1 (January, 1961), pp. 65-73.

The bias will be positive if the disturbances are positively autocorrelated and negative if the disturbances are negatively correlated. Griliches has estimated the asymptotic bias of the OLS estimators when lagged values of the dependent variable appear as a regressor in the equation and the disturbances are autocorrelated. The OLS estimator continues to be biased even if the disturbances are not autocorrelated.

[4] Equation 7.0.10 is obtained by using the result that, given two random variables, X_1 and X_2, Plim (X_1/X_2) = Plim X_1/Plim X_2.

By considering Y_{1898} the initial period and rearranging the successive terms, we obtain:

$$\begin{aligned} Y_{1900} &= \alpha + \beta\alpha + \beta^2 Y_{1898} + \beta U_{1899} + U_{1900} \\ Y_{1901} &= \alpha + \beta\alpha + \beta^2\alpha + \beta^3 Y_{1898} + \beta^2 U_{1899} + \beta U_{1900} + U_{1901} \\ Y_{1902} &= \alpha + \beta\alpha + \beta^2\alpha + \beta^3\alpha + \beta^4 Y_{1898} + \beta^3 U_{1899} + \beta^2 U_{1900} \\ &\quad + \beta U_{1901} + U_{1902} \end{aligned} \tag{7.0.12}$$

In the year 1902 model 7.0.1 is:

$$Y = \alpha^* + \beta^* Y_{1898} + U^* \tag{7.0.13}$$

where $\alpha^* = \alpha + \beta\alpha + \beta^2\alpha + \beta^3\alpha$

$\beta^* = \beta^4$

$U^* = \beta^3 U_{1899} + \beta^2 U_{1900} + \beta U_{1901} + U_{1902}$

If the assumption $E(U_t U_{t-1}) = 0$ holds, then the U_t's of the successive years are mutually independent and nonautocorrelated, that is, $U^* = U_{1899}$, and all other terms vanish. Even then it is evident that unless Y_{1898} is "given" and is truly independent of U_{1899}, the assumption $E(Y_{1898}U_{1899}) = 0$ is not satisfied. This is the assumption of zero covariance between the regressor and the disturbance term. If there is an initial point in time when the observation on the dependent variable can be considered as exogenously given, the econometrician has a pragmatic solution. In an econometric study of demand for color television sets, for example, the year when sales of color television sets first reached 1,000 can be taken as such an initial period. Similarly, regression analysis applied to industrial data may make use of the dates of incorporation of firms to determine the initial fixed observation.

It is convenient to rewrite equation 7.0.12 in general terms:

$$\begin{aligned} Y_t = \alpha(1 + \beta + \beta^2 + \cdots + \beta^{t-1}) + \beta^t Y_0 + U_t + \beta U_{t-1} \\ + \beta^2 U_{t-2} + \cdots + \beta^{t-1} U_1 \end{aligned} \tag{7.0.14}$$

Considering $-1 < \beta < 1$, and as t approaches infinity,

$$Y_t = \frac{\alpha}{1 - \beta} + U_t + \beta U_{t-1} + \beta^2 U_{t-2} + \cdots \tag{7.0.15}$$

This equation shows that Y_{t-1}, the regressor in equation 7.0.1, is not correlated with U_t since it depends on Y_0 and the disturbance terms $U_1, U_2, \ldots,$ U_{t-1}. It is independent of, and not correlated with, $U_t, U_{t+1}, U_{t+2}, \ldots$. We assume that Y_0 is fixed. Thus Y_2 depends on Y_0 and U_1, and Y_3 depends on Y_2 and U_2; that is, Y_t depends on Y_{t-1} and U_t. By assumption $E(Y_0U_1) = 0$, and thus $E(Y_{t-1}U_t) = 0$.

The situation will, however, be complicated if the U_t's are not independent. Then the assumption of nonautocorrelation of the U term fails to hold. As we have seen before, if the disturbances are serially correlated, the OLS estimators are not "best." The estimators are then inefficient as well as biased. Indeed the serial correlation of the disturbance terms is generally common in an autoregressive model with the lagged value of the dependent variable as a regressor.

Consider the U terms in equation 7.0.13. The expression for the disturbance term at each successive time period contains contributions from disturbances of all preceding periods. More generally,

$$U_t = \rho U_{t-1} + \rho^2 U_{t-2} + \cdots + \rho^s U_{t-s} + V_t \qquad \textbf{7.0.16}$$

For a first-order autoregressive scheme,

$$U_t = V_t + \rho U_{t-1} \qquad |\rho| < 1 \qquad \textbf{7.0.17}$$

To show that the OLS estimate in equation 7.0.1 is inconsistent, assume there exists autocorrelation among disturbances as in equation 7.0.17.[5] In terms of mean deviation, we rewrite equation 7.0.1 as:

$$y_t = \beta y_{t-1} + u_t \qquad \textbf{7.0.18}$$

Lag equation 7.0.18 one time period and multiply through by ρ:

$$\rho y_{t-1} = \rho\beta y_{t-2} + \rho u_{t-1} \qquad \textbf{7.0.19}$$

By subtracting equation 7.0.19 from equation 7.0.18, we obtain:

$$y_t = (\rho + \beta)y_{t-1} - \rho\beta y_{t-2} + v_t \qquad \textbf{7.0.20}$$

where $v_t = u_t - \rho u_{t-1}$

Multiplying equation 7.0.20 by y_{t-1} and summing over all t, we have:

$$\Sigma y_t y_{t-1} = (\rho + \beta)\, \Sigma y_{t-1}^2 - \rho\beta \Sigma y_{t-1} y_{t-2} + \Sigma v_t y_{t-1} \qquad \textbf{7.0.21}$$

Dividing through by Σy_{t-1}^2, we obtain:

$$\frac{\Sigma y_t y_{t-1}}{\Sigma y_{t-1}^2} = (\rho + \beta) - \rho\beta \frac{\Sigma y_{t-1} y_{t-2}}{\Sigma y_{t-1}^2} + \frac{\Sigma v_t y_{t-1}}{\Sigma y_{t-1}^2} \qquad \textbf{7.0.22}$$

Note that the left-hand quantity above is the OLS estimate of β in equation 7.0.18.

---

[5] E. Malinvaud, *Statistical Methods of Econometrics* (Chicago: Rand-McNally & Co., 1966), pp. 459-461.

To determine consistency, we take the probability limit and obtain the following result:

$$\text{Plim } \hat{\beta} = (\rho + \beta) - \rho\beta \text{ Plim } \hat{\beta} + \frac{\text{Plim}(\Sigma v_t y_{t-1})/T}{\text{Plim}(\Sigma y_{t-1}^2)/T} \qquad \textbf{7.0.23}$$

When Plim $(\Sigma v_t y_{t-1})/T$ is zero, and Plim $(\Sigma y_{t-1}^2)/T$ is finite and nonzero, following equations 7.0.10 and 7.0.15:

$$\text{Plim } \hat{\beta} + \rho\beta \text{ Plim } \hat{\beta} = \rho + \beta$$

or,

$$\text{Plim } \hat{\beta} = \frac{\rho + \beta}{1 + \rho\beta} \qquad \textbf{7.0.24}$$

Obviously, for $\rho \neq 0$, $\hat{\beta}$ is inconsistent. Note that autoregressive models which contain lagged values of the dependent variable in the regressor set need not always have autocorrelated disturbance terms.

7.1 TESTS OF SERIAL CORRELATION REVISED

The tests of serial independence based on the residuals from the regression of Y_t on fixed regressors, the X_t's in Chapter 4, are invalid when applied to models containing the lagged value of the dependent variable as a regressor.[6] Some further tests have been proposed to meet this situation.[7] The authors of the Durbin-Watson test (discussed in Chapter 4 and noted as d) warned researchers against using the test in a situation when the lagged value of the dependent variable appears as a regressor in the equation. However, the warning is seldom heeded by econometricians who perhaps believe that some test is better than no test.

Durbin's proposed test is computationally simple. Recall equation 4.1.14:

$$d = \frac{\sum_{t=2}^{T} (\hat{U}_t - \hat{U}_{t-1})^2}{\sum_{t=1}^{T} \hat{U}_t^2}$$

Also from equation 4.1.2:

$$\hat{\rho} = \frac{\Sigma \hat{U}_t \hat{U}_{t-1}}{\Sigma \hat{U}_t^2}$$

[6] M. Nerlove and K. F. Wallis, "Use of the Durbin-Watson Statistics in Inappropriate Situations," *Econometrica*, Vol. 34, No. 1 (January, 1966), pp. 235-238.

[7] James Durbin, "Testing for Serial Correlation in Least-Squares Regression When Some of the Regressors Are Lagged Dependent Variables," *Econometrica*, Vol. 38, No. 3 (May, 1970), pp. 410-421. See also J. D. Sargan, "Wages and Prices in the United Kingdom: A Study in Econometric Methodology," *Econometric Analysis for National Economic Planning*, edited by P. E. Hart *et al.* (London: Butterworth & Co., 1964), pp. 25-54.

It can be seen that:

$$\hat{\rho} = 1 - \frac{1}{2} d \tag{7.1.1}$$

The estimate $\hat{\rho}$ can be calculated independently or, making use of the value of the d statistic computed as a part of the output for most computer regression programs, we can apply equation 7.1.1 to calculate the value of $\hat{\rho}$ from the value of d. This estimated value $\hat{\rho}$ is then used to compute the value of another statistic h defined as:

$$h = \hat{\rho} \sqrt{\frac{T}{1 - T \operatorname{var}(\hat{\beta})}} \tag{7.1.2}$$

where $\operatorname{var}(\hat{\beta})$ is the estimate of the variance of the OLS estimate of β. Notice that h is not a real number if the second term in the denominator under the square root sign, $T \operatorname{var}(\hat{\beta})$, is greater than one.

It can be shown that the h statistic corresponds to the standardized normal variable z defined in equation 3.0.3. We can thus make use of the z table given in the Appendix to test the null hypothesis that $\rho = 0$ at some preassigned level of statistical significance. The critical value of z at the 95 percent significance level in the z table is $\pm$ 1.96. For the 99 percent significance level the critical value is $\pm$ 2.58. Thus we accept the hypothesis $\rho = 0$ at the 95 percent level of significance, implying that the disturbances are free of first-order correlation when the calculated value of the h statistic lies between +1.96 and −1.96. At the 99 percent level of significance, we accept the hypothesis of no first-order autocorrelation if the h value lies between +2.58 and −2.58.

Note that in a one-tail 5 percent test, the critical value from the z table is $\pm$1.645. If the computed value of h is greater than 1.645, the null hypothesis $\rho = 0$ (no serial correlation) is rejected and the alternative hypothesis $\rho > 0$ is accepted; that is, there exists evidence of positive serial correlation.

The test is asymptotically valid for the large sample case where $T > 30$. It has been shown to be applicable to a model with any number of lagged values of the dependent variable appearing as regressors:

$$Y_t = \alpha + \beta_1 Y_{t-1} + \cdots + \beta_K Y_{t-K} + \gamma_1 X_{1_t} + \cdots + \gamma_M X_{M_t} + U_t \tag{7.1.3}$$

and for such models the test will indicate the presence or absence of first-order autocorrelation of the disturbance terms at a preassigned level of significance. For the use of the test, we need the variance of the OLS estimate of $\hat{\beta}_1$. The appearance of the term $\operatorname{var}(\hat{\beta})$ in the expression for h indicates that this test for the presence of first-order autocorrelation is sensitive to sampling errors in $\hat{\beta}$, particularly for samples where T is not sufficiently large.

7.2 DISTRIBUTED LAG MODELS

An example of a particular autoregressive model in extensive use in econometric research is the *distributed lag model*. This model and the set of manipulations that follow were presented by L. M. Koyck and are known as the *Koyck transformation*.[8]

The basic idea of this type model is that one variable reacts to another over a period of time rather than instantaneously. In such a model of consumption demand, consumption in the current time period C_t, for example, depends not only on income of the current time period Y_t, but also on the series of past incomes. Omitting the constant term relative to the intercept of the function, the general autoregressive model can be written as:

$$C_t = \Sigma \beta_i Y_{t-i} \qquad \textbf{7.2.1}$$

Adding the disturbance term U_t,

$$C_t = \beta Y_t + \beta_1 Y_{t-1} + \beta_2 Y_{t-2} + \beta_3 Y_{t-3} + \cdots + U_t \qquad \textbf{7.2.2}$$

In this form there are an indefinitely large number of parameters to be estimated: $\beta, \beta_1, \beta_2, \ldots$. We cannot estimate an infinite series of parameters from a finite sample even if the other problems associated with an autoregressive model disappear. Clearly it is necessary to make some simplifying assumptions.

Suppose that the impact on current consumption of a previous income declines exponentially. Income in period s, Y_s, has impact β on consumption in period s, but only impact $\beta\lambda$ in period $s + 1$, $\beta\lambda^2$ in period $s + 2$, and $\beta\lambda^j$ in period $s + j$. That is, the consumer presumably adjusts his expenditure on consumption according to a weighted sum of his past levels of income, the weights declining over time. Stated formally,

$$C_t = \beta \sum_{i=0}^{\infty} \lambda^i Y_{t-i} \text{ with } 0 \leq \lambda < 1 \qquad \textbf{7.2.3}$$

In terms of the coefficients in equation 7.2.2,

$$\beta_1 = \lambda\beta,\ \beta_2 = \lambda^2\beta,\ \beta_3 = \lambda^3\beta,\ \ldots$$

[8] L. M. Koyck, *Distributed Lags and Investment Analysis* (Amsterdam: North-Holland Publishing Co., 1954). For a general survey see Z. Griliches, "Distributed Lags: A Survey," *Econometrica*, Vol. 35, No. 1 (January, 1967), pp. 16-49.

Koyck's original work was done in the context of investment demand analysis. Milton Friedman used a similar lag structure for his study of consumer behavior: Milton Friedman, *Theory of the Consumption Function* (Princeton: Princeton University Press, 1957).

More generally,

$$\beta_i = \beta\lambda^i \qquad 7.2.4$$

where β is some constant, and the restriction that λ is between zero and one ensures the convergence of the β_i's to zero. If $\lambda < 1$, the weights given to the incomes of previous periods decline in proportion to λ^i. For example, if $\lambda = 0.8$, then $\lambda^2 = 0.64$ and $\lambda^3 = 0.51, \ldots$. If $\beta = 0.9$, then $\beta_1 = (0.9)(0.8) = 0.72$, $\beta_2 = (0.9)(0.8)^2 = 0.58$, and $\beta_3 = (0.9)(0.8)^3 = 0.46$. If the series is continued, the numerical value of the impact in a given period t of previous income from a remote period, say, Y_s, denoted β_s, will approach zero. Hence we can continue our research with a finite sample. Note that if λ is zero, the lag scheme immediately collapses. Any value of λ between zero and one will ensure convergence.

Given $0 \leq \lambda < 1$, expanding equation 7.2.3 for time period t and adding the disturbance term yields:

$$C_t = \beta Y_t + \lambda\beta Y_{t-1} + \lambda^2\beta Y_{t-2} + \lambda^3\beta Y_{t-3} + \cdots + U_t \qquad 7.2.5$$

Therefore we can write for the time period $t - 1$:

$$C_{t-1} = \beta Y_{t-1} + \lambda\beta Y_{t-2} + \lambda^2\beta Y_{t-3} + \cdots + U_{t-1} \qquad 7.2.6$$

Multiplying equation 7.2.6 through by λ, we obtain:

$$\lambda C_{t-1} = \lambda\beta Y_{t-1} + \lambda^2\beta Y_{t-2} + \lambda^3\beta Y_{t-3} + \cdots + \lambda U_{t-1} \qquad 7.2.7$$

By subtracting equation 7.2.7 from equation 7.2.5,

$$C_t - \lambda C_{t-1} = \beta Y_t + U_t - \lambda U_{t-1} \qquad 7.2.8$$

By rearranging and writing $V_t = U_t - \lambda U_{t-1}$,

$$C_t = \beta Y_t + \lambda C_{t-1} + V_t \qquad 7.2.9$$

Returning to model 7.2.3, it is possible to apply the same argument if the original distributed lag model had an intercept term:

$$C_t = \alpha + \beta \sum_{i=0}^{\infty} \lambda^i Y_{t-i} \qquad 7.2.10$$

The final equation to be estimated then is:

$$C_t = \alpha(1 - \lambda) + \beta Y_t + \lambda C_{t-1} + V_t \qquad 7.2.11$$

The value of α can be obtained from the estimated values of the intercept and λ from the above equation.

Note that the transformed model in equation 7.2.9 involves the estimation of only two parameters, β and λ, instead of the infinite sequence of parameters β_i of the untransformed equation 7.2.5 in the distributed lag model. Transformation thus aids in reducing the multicollinearity problem, a problem that would be serious even if we chose to regress current consumption on any arbitrarily chosen finite series of previous incomes:

$$C_t = \beta_1 Y_t + \beta_2 Y_{t-1} + \beta_3 Y_{t-2} + \beta_4 Y_{t-4} + U_t \qquad \textbf{7.2.12}$$

where $i = 1, 2, 3, 4$, and $t = 1, 2, \ldots, T$

Collinearity between various series on Y is a baffling problem for the researcher.

By using equation 7.2.9, we can measure the impact on consumption C due to a marginal change in income Y for both short- and long-run analyses. The *impact multiplier,* measuring the instantaneous effect of a change in income Y on consumption C, is then calculated by using β; and the *equilibrium multiplier,* or long-run multiplier, measuring the change in the equilibrium value of consumption C due to a marginal change in income Y, is then calculated by using:

$$\Sigma\beta_i = \beta\Sigma\lambda^i = \frac{\beta}{1 - \lambda} \qquad \textbf{7.2.13}$$

Obtaining reliable estimates of β and λ remains a problem. If the disturbance term U_t follows a first-order Markov scheme, the simplified model 7.2.9 can be estimated by the OLS method only under a particular condition. Suppose that U_t is serially correlated in a first-order Markov scheme with coefficient λ:

$$U_t = \lambda U_{t-1} + V_t \qquad \textbf{7.2.14}$$

where $E(V_t) = 0$, $E(V_t V_{t-\theta}) = 0$, and $E(V^2) = \sigma^2$ finite and constant

Then equation 7.2.9 has a serially independent disturbance term. Thus if the coefficient of first-order correlation happens to be exactly equal to λ, the lagged variable coefficient in the estimating equation 7.2.9, the OLS estimates of β and λ can be obtained consistently; but the estimators will not be free from small-sample bias. Note that we have no independent information on λ and that we cannot proceed to estimate it from equation 7.2.14 since we have no observations on U_t. (Since λ is an unrestricted real number between zero and unity, the probability that the coefficient of first-order serial correlation for U_t will be exactly equal to the true value of $\lambda > 0$ is identically zero.)

It should be pointed out that $E(V_t V_{t-\theta}) \neq 0$. Rather the disturbance term V_t in the transformed equation 7.2.9 is in general serially correlated. This is true even if the original disturbance terms U_t are serially independent. This can be seen as follows. From equation 7.2.14 we have:

$$V_t = U_t - \lambda U_{t-1}$$

so,

$$V_{t-1} = U_{t-1} - \lambda U_{t-2} \qquad \textbf{7.2.15}$$

Therefore,

$$E(V_t V_{t-1}) = E[(U_t - \lambda U_{t-1})(U_{t-1} - \lambda U_{t-2})]$$
$$= E[U_t U_{t-1} - \lambda(U_{t-1}^2) - \lambda U_t U_{t-2} + \lambda^2 U_{t-1} U_{t-2}]$$

Since $E(U_t U_{t-1}) = E(U_{t-1} U_{t-2}) = E(U_t U_{t-2}) = 0$, when U_t is assumed to be serially independent all cross product terms vanish, leaving:

$$E(V_t V_{t-1}) = E[-\lambda(U_{t-1}^2)]$$
$$= -\lambda E(U_{t-1}^2) \qquad \textbf{7.2.16}$$
$$= -\lambda\sigma_u^2 \neq 0$$

As a result the OLS estimators are not consistent or efficient. The presence of bias, as discussed in section 7.0, together with autocorrelated disturbances, may thus make the OLS estimators unusable.

Koyck suggested the use of a method applying OLS estimation in two steps.[9] In the first step obtain the estimate of $\hat{\beta}$ and $\hat{\lambda}$ by the straighforward application of the OLS method to equation 7.2.9, omitting the constant for the intercept of the equation and taking all variables in terms of deviations from their respective means, denoted by lowercase letters. From this estimate we can calculate:

$$\Sigma \hat{V}_t^2 = \Sigma(c_t - \hat{\beta} y_t - \hat{\lambda} c_{t-1})^2 \qquad \textbf{7.2.17}$$

At the second step consistent estimators β^* and λ^* are obtained by solving the following two equations:

$$\beta^* \Sigma y_t^2 + \lambda^* \Sigma y_t c_{t-1} = \Sigma y_t c_t$$

$$\beta^* \Sigma y_t c_{t-1} + \lambda^* \Sigma c_{t-1}^2 = \Sigma c_{t-1} c_t + \frac{(\lambda^* - \rho)\,\Sigma \hat{V}_t^2}{1 - \rho\lambda^* + \hat{\lambda}(\lambda^* - \rho)} \qquad \textbf{7.2.18}$$

where we assume that the disturbance terms follow a first-order Markov scheme, $U_t = \rho U_{t-1} + V_t$, $0 \leq \rho < 1$. Notice that equations 7.2.18 compare with the usual pair of normal equations for the least squares regression method except for the correction factor ρ added to the second equation. However, ρ is unknown, and the suggestion is to use various values of ρ between zero and unity in successive trials that use pairs of ρ values closer and closer together. At some value of ρ, the values of the parameters $\hat{\beta}^*$ and $\hat{\lambda}^*$ will converge in the sense that their numerical values will remain unchanged in further successive trials.

---

[9] L. M. Koyck, *Distributed Lags and Investment Analysis* (Amsterdam: North-Holland Publishing Co., 1954).

7.3 ADAPTIVE EXPECTATION AND PARTIAL ADJUSTMENT MODELS

Man adapts his current behavior not only to past experience but also to future expectations, and this hypothesis has provided the basis for many autoregressive models. Consider the model, suppressing the intercept term:

$$I_t = \delta E_t^* + U_t \qquad \textbf{7.3.1}$$

where I_t is current investment and E_t^* is expected earnings. A firm, in its investment planning, estimates its earnings for the next period $t+1$ in the current period t. Let E_t^* denote the amount expected in the current period to be earned in the next period, and let E_t be the actual earnings in the current period. Suppose that the firm adapts its current expectations for the next period on the basis of how closely the expectations for the current period are matched by actual earnings. This hypothesis, the *adaptive expectation hypothesis,* is expressed in the following equation:[10]

$$(E_t^* - E_{t-1}^*) = \rho(E_t - E_{t-1}^*) \qquad 0 \leq \rho < 1 \qquad \textbf{7.3.2}$$

The difference between the actual earnings E_t and the earnings expected in the preceding period for the current period, that is, the expected earnings in the previous period E_{t-1}^*, indicates the degree of fulfillment of expectation. Based on this experience, the firm revises its present expectation of earnings E_t^*. Adjustment between this past expectation E_{t-1}^* and present expectation E_t^* *is* assumed to be proportional to the experience with the difference between expectation and actuality in the current period t. From equation 7.3.2,

$$\begin{aligned} E_t^* &= \rho E_t + E_{t-1}^* - \rho E_{t-1}^* \\ &= \rho E_t + (1-\rho)E_{t-1}^* \end{aligned} \qquad \textbf{7.3.3}$$

Repeating this process for the period $t-1$,

$$\begin{aligned} E_{t-1}^* &= \rho E_{t-1} + E_{t-2}^* - \rho E_{t-2}^* \\ &= \rho E_{t-1} + (1-\rho)E_{t-2}^* \end{aligned} \qquad \textbf{7.3.4}$$

---

[10] The adaptive expectation model is sometimes formulated as:

$$(E_t^* - E_{t-1}^*) = \rho(E_{t-1} - E_{t-1}^*)$$

with the same restriction on the reaction coefficient ρ. When E_t is not yet known, expectations need to be adapted by comparing E_{t-1}^* with E_{t-1}, the immediate past experience. Such reformulation of equation 7.3.2 will lead to a slightly different final form of equation 7.3.8 as follows:

$$I_t = \beta E_{t-1} + \lambda I_{t-1} + V_t'$$

where $V_t' = U_t - \lambda U_{t-1}$. Note that E_t is replaced by E_{t-1} on the right-hand side. For the econometrician the estimation problem, however, remains as before.

By repeated substitution,

$$E_t^* = \rho \sum_{i=0}^{\infty} (1 - \rho)^i E_{t-i} \qquad \textbf{7.3.5}$$

Substituting equation 7.3.5 into equation 7.3.1,

$$I_t = \delta \left[\rho \sum_{i=0}^{\infty} (1 - \rho)^i E_{t-i} \right] + U_t \qquad \textbf{7.3.6}$$

Define $\lambda = 1 - \rho$ and $\beta = \rho\delta$. The equation can then be expressed:

$$I_t = \beta \sum_{i=0}^{\infty} \lambda^i E_{t-i} + U_t \qquad \textbf{7.3.7}$$

This equation is the same as equation 7.2.3 plus the U_t term. Thus the adaptive expectation model is equivalent to the Koyck transformation of the distributed lag model. Applying the Koyck transformation developed in the preceding section, we have:

$$I_t = \beta E_t + \lambda I_{t-1} + V_t' \qquad \textbf{7.3.8}$$

where

$$V_t' = U_t - \lambda U_{t-1} \qquad \textbf{7.3.9}$$

Equation 7.3.8 has the same form as equation 7.2.9; therefore, the "best" estimates of the parameters β and λ cannot be obtained by straightforward application of the OLS method. One possibility is to use the method of estimation suggested by Koyck, equation 7.2.13.

While the adaptive expectation model attributes the lags to uncertainty of the future and delay in the process of adjustment between anticipation and realization, another lag model is due to the *partial adjustment hypothesis*. Such a model uses a lag structure to explain technological, institutional, and/or psychological barriers to making adjustment to a change instantaneously. It can also be used to express the desire to phase out the increasing costs of rapid changes.

Suppose that the demand for inventory Y is adjusted over time to some desired target Y^*, and that the process of adjustment is described by a model:

$$Y_t - Y_{t-1} = \rho(Y_{t-1}^* - Y_{t-1}) + U_t \qquad 0 < \rho \leq 1 \qquad \textbf{7.3.10}$$

There exists an institutional pattern for the desired level of inventory at a given time. There are also technological constraints, such as storage facilities, to the rate of adjustment feasible at a given time. Assume that Y_t^* is explained as follows, where X_t is an observable economic variable such as gross sales:

$$Y_t^* = \delta X_t \tag{7.3.11}$$

Substituting equation 7.3.11 into equation 7.3.10, we have the partial adjustment model:

$$\begin{aligned} Y_t &= \delta\rho X_{t-1} + (1-\rho)Y_{t-1} + U_t \\ Y_t &= \beta X_{t-1} + \lambda Y_{t-1} + U_t \end{aligned} \tag{7.3.12}$$

when $\beta = \delta\rho$, $\lambda = (1-\rho)$

Even though equation 7.3.12, not unlike equations 7.3.8 and 7.3.9, belong to the class of autoregressive models, there is no reason to assume the presence of autocorrelation in the partial adjustment model. The disturbance terms U_t can be expected to fulfill the condition of mutual independence in this model, and in this respect this model is different from the others reviewed. The transformation here does not include a term $V_t = (U_t - \lambda U_{t-1})$, as in equation 7.2.9, or a term $V_t' = (U_t - \lambda U_{t-1})$, as in equation 7.3.9.

Roger Waud suggested that the two hypotheses, "adaptive expectations" and "partial adjustment," should be combined, because each model by itself is subject to specification errors.[11] Of course such a transformation will have all the problems of an autoregressive model in estimating the parameters.

Further, it is possible to hypothesize that a given variable Y depends on two independent variables X and Z, and the dependence in each case is based on a certain lag structure.[12] In economics the demand for housing may very well depend not only on expected income but also on the expected price of houses. Consider the model:

$$Y_t = \alpha + \beta X_t + \zeta Z_t + U_t \tag{7.3.13}$$

where the lag pattern is:

$$\begin{aligned} Y_t = \alpha &+ \beta(X_t + \lambda X_{t-1} + \lambda^2 X_{t-2} + \ldots) \\ &+ \zeta(Z_t + \rho Z_{t-1} + \rho^2 Z_{t-2} + \ldots) + U_t \end{aligned} \tag{7.3.14}$$

given, as before,

$$0 \leq \lambda < 1 \text{ and } 0 \leq \rho < 1$$

Suppose we apply the Koyck transformation twice in succession. In the first step we lag equation 7.3.14 by one period:

---

[11] Roger Waud, "Misspecification in the 'Partial Adjustment' and 'Adaptive Expectations' Models," *International Economic Review*, Vol. 9, No. 2 (June, 1968), pp. 204-217.

[12] Vincent Su, "The Specification, Estimation and Evaluation of an Economic Relationship Involving Two Independent Distributed Lags" (Doctoral dissertation, Rutgers University, 1970).

$$Y_{t-1} = \alpha + \beta(X_{t-1} + \lambda X_{t-2} + \lambda^2 X_{t-3} + \cdots) + \zeta(Z_{t-1} + \rho Z_{t-2} + \rho^2 Z_{t-3} + \cdots) + U_{t-1} \quad 7.3.15$$

Multiplying both sides by λ,

$$\lambda Y_{t-1} = \alpha\lambda + \beta(\lambda X_{t-1} + \lambda^2 X_{t-2} + \lambda^3 X_{t-3} + \cdots) + \zeta(\lambda Z_{t-1} + \lambda\rho Z_{t-2} + \lambda\rho^2 Z_{t-3} + \cdots) + \lambda U_{t-1} \quad 7.3.16$$

Subtracting from equation 7.3.14 and rearranging,

$$Y_t = \alpha(1 - \lambda) + \beta X_t + \lambda Y_{t-1} + \zeta[Z_t + (\rho - \lambda)Z_{t-1} + \rho(\rho - \lambda)Z_{t-2} + \rho^2(\rho - \lambda)Z_{t-3} + \cdots] + U_t - \lambda U_{t-1} \quad 7.3.17$$

If we repeat the process with equation 7.3.17, that is, lag equation 7.3.17 by one period, multiply both sides by ρ, and subtract the resulting equation from equation 7.3.17, we obtain:

$$Y_t = \alpha(1 - \lambda)(1 - \rho) + (\lambda + \rho)Y_{t-1} - \lambda\rho Y_{t-2} + \beta X_t - \beta\rho X_{t-1} + \zeta Z_t - \zeta\lambda Z_{t-1} + U_t - (\lambda + \rho)U_{t-1} + \lambda\rho U_{t-2} \quad 7.3.18$$

Obviously the estimation involves still higher order autocorrelation of disturbance terms. Also note that we now have to estimate seven regression coefficients including the intercept, and there exist serious nonlinearity problems in the parameters to be estimated. We can extend the model to include lag structures for many more regressors, but the estimation problem will be further compounded. Of course there is no reason to believe that the same type of transformation would apply in all cases. If we have to combine two or more different lag structures for different regressors in one equation for estimation, the problem will be further complicated. In practice one makes simplifying assumptions and then proceeds to estimate an equation:

$$Y_t = \alpha(1 - \lambda) + \beta X_t + \zeta Z_t + \lambda Y_{t-1} + U_t - \lambda U_{t-1} \quad 7.3.19$$

The simplifying assumptions can be extended to cases where there are many more regressors.

7.4 RATIONAL DISTRIBUTED LAG FUNCTION

Corresponding to the lagged values of a variable, the operation of lagging or applying the *lag operator* to a variable can be described as follows. If X_t is a variable with values $X_1, X_2, \ldots, X_T$, then applying the lag operator L to X_t yields the variable X_{t-1} with values $X_0, X_1, \ldots, X_{T-1}$. The lag operator is written as:

$$L(X_t) = X_{t-1}$$

The operator L has the following properties:

(1) $L[L(X_t)] = L^2X_t = X_{t-2}$

(2) $L^MX_t = X_{t-M}$

(3) $(aL^M + bL^N)X_t = aL^MX_t + bL^NX_t$
$= aX_{t-M} + bX_{t-N}$

The lag operator can be used in a method of estimating a general form of autoregressive models known as the *generalized rational distributed lag function.*[13] Consider equation 7.2.1:

$$C_t = \beta Y_t + \beta_1 Y_{t-1} + \beta_2 Y_{t-2} + \beta_3 Y_{t-3} + \cdots$$

Expressing the right-hand side in terms of the lag operator L, we have:

$$\begin{aligned} C_t &= \beta Y_t + \beta_1 LY_t + \beta_2 L^2 Y_t + \beta_3 L^3 Y_t + \cdots \\ &= (\beta + \beta_1 L + \beta_2 L^2 + \beta_3 L^3 + \cdots)Y_t \qquad 7.4.1 \\ &= \beta(L)Y_t \end{aligned}$$

where $\beta(L)$ is the polynomial in L in parentheses in the equation above. If the sequence β_i has a *rational generating function,* we write:

$$C_t = \beta(L)Y_t = \frac{U(L)}{V(L)}\,Y_t \qquad 7.4.2$$

This corresponds to "generating" an infinite decimal from a rational fraction.[14] The expressions $U(L)$ and $V(L)$ are polynomials in the lag operator:

---

[13] Dale W. Jorgenson, "Rational Distributed Lag Functions," *Econometrica,* Vol. 34, No. 1 (January, 1966), pp. 135-149.

[14] The basic notion corresponds to the use of a fraction with a whole number numerator and denominator to approximate a real number. For example, the number Π, which is not a rational fraction, can be approximated by rational fractions:

$$\Pi = 3.14159\ldots$$

$$\Pi \doteq \frac{22}{7}, \frac{256}{81}, \frac{157}{50}, \ldots$$

Any one of these fractions is closer to the actual value of Π than are the whole numbers 3 and 4.

Jorgenson's method of analyzing the general form of an autoregressive model depends on the observation that the general form of this model, with an indefinitely large number of successive lagged terms, can be approximated more closely by a ratio of two polynomials with a finite number of lagged terms in both the numerator and denominator than by a polynomial with an integral number of lagged terms. Notice the similarity between the rational fractions that approximate a real number and the rational distributed lag functions that approximate an arbitrary lag function.

$$U(L) = U_0 + U_1L + U_2L^2 + \cdots + U_mL^m$$
$$V(L) = V_0 + V_1L + V_2L^2 + \cdots + V_nL^n \qquad 7.4.3$$

where m and n are finite integers. V_0 is normalized at unity. This restriction is imposed to ensure that a rational generating function may be represented in only one way, as the ratio of two polynomials.

Multiplying both sides of equation 7.4.2 by $V(L)$, we have:

$$V(L)C_t = U(L)Y_t \qquad 7.4.4$$

Using equation 7.4.3 and rewriting,[15]

$$(1 + V_1L + V_2L^2 + \cdots + V_nL^n)C_t = (U_0 + U_1L + U_2L^2 + \cdots + U_mL^m)Y_t \qquad 7.4.5$$

The rational distributed lag function becomes:

$$C_t = U_0Y_t + U_1Y_{t-1} + U_2Y_{t-2} + \cdots + U_mY_{t-m} - V_1C_{t-1} - V_2C_{t-2} - \cdots - V_nC_{t-n} \qquad 7.4.6$$

This form of the autoregressive model is more general than those considered above, because it contains the finite lag function and the Koyck distributed lag function as special cases. When $V(L) = 1$ and:

$$U(L) = \beta_0 + \beta_1L + \beta_2L^2 + \cdots + \beta_mL^m$$

we have the finite distributed lag function:

$$C_t = \beta_0Y_t + \beta_1Y_{t-1} + \beta_2Y_{t-2} + \cdots + \beta_mY_{t-m} \qquad 7.4.7$$

Similarly, when $V(L) = 1 - \lambda L$ and $U(L) = 1 - \lambda$, we obtain the Koyck formulation of the geometric distributed lag function:

$$(1 - \lambda L)C_t = (1 - \lambda)Y_t$$

or,

$$C_t - \lambda C_{t-1} = (1 - \lambda)Y_t$$

or,

$$C_t = (1 - \lambda)Y_t + \lambda C_{t-1} \qquad 7.4.8$$

Indeed a distributed lag function is a member of the class of rational distributed lag functions if and only if it has a finite number of lags in both $U(L)$ and $V(L)$.

---

[15] The terms $U_0, U_1, U_2, \ldots, U_m$ are constant coefficients and should not be confused with the same expressions used to denote the disturbance terms in a stochastic equation. The same is true for $V_0, V_1, \ldots, V_n$.

The estimation of a rational distributed lag function, as in equation 7.4.6, continues to be a problem. Obviously the OLS method is inadequate. The Koyck method suggested in equation 7.2.13 has been interpreted as an application of the weighted least squares regression method and may be applied in this case. However, this volume does not discuss this method of estimation, as it does not discuss the various iterative methods suggested to estimate nonlinear parameters also in the face of autocorrelation of disturbance terms.[16] Instead, the following section presents a method of estimation that makes use of the instrumental variable technique and works within the framework of the OLS method of estimation.

7.5 ESTIMATING MODELS WITH LAGGED DEPENDENT VARIABLES AS REGRESSORS AND SERIALLY CORRELATED DISTURBANCE TERMS

Recently Kenneth F. Wallis proposed a two-step estimation scheme to rescue the OLS method in the face of the problems described before.[17] Applied to the model:

$$C_t = \alpha + \beta Y_t + \beta_1 C_{t-1} + U_t \qquad t = 1, 2, \ldots, T \tag{7.5.1}$$

where C_t = aggregate consumption
Y_t = aggregate income

this method consists of the following procedure.

Step 1

Estimate α, β, and β_1 with Y_{t-1} as the instrumental variable for C_{t-1}, a method explained in Chapter 9. In the present application the method of instrumental variables can be easily specified. We know the OLS estimator,

$$\hat{\boldsymbol{\beta}} = (\mathbf{X}'\mathbf{X})^{-1}\mathbf{X}'\mathbf{Y}$$

while the instrumental variable estimator is:

$$\hat{\boldsymbol{\beta}}^* = (\mathbf{Z}'\mathbf{X})^{-1}\mathbf{Z}'\mathbf{Y} \tag{7.5.2}$$

In the context of the present model 7.5.1, $\mathbf{Y}$ is a $T \times 1$ column vector of observations on C_t. The matrix of regressors, $\mathbf{X} = (X_0, Y_t, C_{t-1})$, is a $T \times 3$ matrix of

[16] L. R. Klein, "The Estimation of Distributed Lags," *Econometrica*, Vol. 26, No. 4 (October, 1958), pp. 553-565. P. J. Dhrymes, *Distributed Lags: Problems of Estimation and Formulation* (San Francisco: Holden-Day, 1971). P. J. Dhrymes, "Efficient Estimation of Distributed Lags with Autocorrelated Error Terms," *International Economic Review*, Vol. 10 (February, 1969), pp. 47-67. A. Zellner and M. S. Geisel, "Analysis of Distributed Lag Models with Application to Consumption Function Estimation," *Econometrica*, Vol. 38, No. 6 (November, 1970), pp. 865-888.

[17] Kenneth F. Wallis, "Lagged Dependent Variables and Serially Correlated Errors: A Reappraisal of Three-Pass Least Squares," *Review of Economics and Statistics*, Vol. 49, No. 4 (November, 1967), pp. 555-567. See also, N. Liviatan, "Consistent Estimation of Distributed Lags," *International Economic Review*, Vol. 4, No. 1 (January, 1963), pp. 44-52.

T observations on the three variables in set **X**. Matrix **Z**, given as $\mathbf{Z} = (X_0, Y_t, Y_{t-1})$, is also a $T \times 3$ matrix of T observations on the three variables in set **Z**, where:

$$\mathbf{Y} = \begin{bmatrix} C_1 \\ C_2 \\ \cdot \\ \cdot \\ \cdot \\ C_T \end{bmatrix} \quad \mathbf{X} = \begin{bmatrix} 1 & Y_1 & C_0 \\ 1 & Y_2 & C_1 \\ \cdot & \cdot & \cdot \\ \cdot & \cdot & \cdot \\ \cdot & \cdot & \cdot \\ 1 & Y_T & C_{T-1} \end{bmatrix} \quad \mathbf{Z} = \begin{bmatrix} 1 & Y_1 & Y_0 \\ 1 & Y_2 & Y_1 \\ \cdot & \cdot & \cdot \\ \cdot & \cdot & \cdot \\ \cdot & \cdot & \cdot \\ 1 & Y_T & Y_{T-1} \end{bmatrix} \quad \boldsymbol{\beta} = \begin{bmatrix} \alpha \\ \beta \\ \beta_1 \end{bmatrix}$$

Recall that X_0 in both matrix **X** and matrix **Z** is a column of ones used in the regression scheme to estimate the intercept of the function α. Notice that Y_t is assumed to be a truly exogenous variable in model 7.5.1. We also assume Y_t is a fixed variable, so that $\text{cov}(Y_t U_t) = 0$. By the same token $\text{cov}(Y_{t-1} U_t) = 0$, even when the assumption that $\text{cov}(C_{t-1} U_t) = 0$ is false in the small sample situation.

Calculate the regression residuals $\hat{U}_t$ from step 1, and then estimate the first-order serial correlation coefficient ρ, making a correction for the bias in estimates $\hat{U}_t$:

$$\hat{\rho} = \frac{\left(\frac{1}{T-1}\right)\sum_{t=2}^{T} \hat{U}_t \hat{U}_{t-1}}{\left(\frac{1}{T}\right)\sum_{t=1}^{T} \hat{U}_t^2} + K/T \qquad \textbf{7.5.3}$$

where K is the number of parameters estimated—three in this case.

Step 2

Use the estimate of $\hat{\rho}$ to obtain the matrix $\mathbf{\Omega}$, and from it, the GLS estimators. Recall the GLS estimator from Chapter 4, given as:

$$\hat{\hat{\boldsymbol{\beta}}} = (\mathbf{X}'\mathbf{\Omega}^{-1}\mathbf{X})^{-1}(\mathbf{X}'\mathbf{\Omega}^{-1}\mathbf{Y}) \qquad \textbf{7.5.4}$$

where $\sigma_u^2\mathbf{\Omega}$ is the variance-covariance matrix of the disturbances. In the present case with serially correlated disturbances, $E(\mathbf{UU}') \neq \sigma_u^2\mathbf{I}$, a matrix with all off-diagonal elements zero. The variance-covariance matrix of the disturbance terms has nonzero elements in addition to the diagonal elements, and $E(\mathbf{UU}') = \sigma_u^2\mathbf{\Omega}$. Using the value of $\hat{\rho}$ from step 1, we can construct this $\mathbf{\Omega}$ matrix. Notice that the matrix $\mathbf{\Omega}$ is based on the value of this single parameter; and that once the estimator $\hat{\rho}$ is obtained from equation 7.5.3, the application of the GLS method is no problem.

To apply this two-step estimation method to regressions involving more than one exogenous variable, the choice of a suitable instrumental variable can be resolved as follows. First, using OLS, regress C_t on all the exogenous variables, omitting C_{t-1}. Next use the regression coefficients to obtain the regression estimate $\hat{C}_t$, which is a linear combination of all exogenous variables. Lag $\hat{C}_t$ for a period, and $\hat{C}_{t-1}$ can then be used as the instrumental variable in step 1.

If the true ρ and hence the $\mathbf{\Omega}$ matrix are known, it can be shown that the parameters estimated by the GLS method are consistent and asymptotically efficient. It can also be shown that when GLS is applied using an estimated variance-covariance matrix of the error terms, if the lagged dependent variable appears as a regressor, the resulting estimates are consistent but not asymptotically efficient.

7.6 FLEXIBLE DISTRIBUTED LAGS

The distributed lag model to which the Koyck transformation can be applied is based on the assumptions that an infinite number of past values of the independent variable contribute to the current value of the dependent variable and that the amount of the contribution decreases as the time lag increases. In Figure 7-1 the curve describes the time path of weights for an infinite distributed lag with geometrically declining weights.

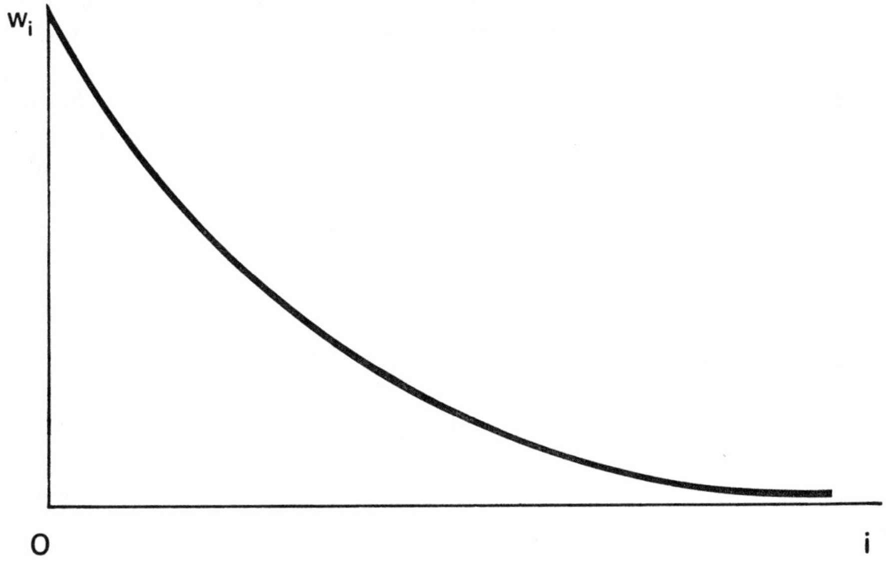

FIGURE 7-1

As we have seen, the infinite distributed lag model can be used to describe several different economic relationships; but there are clearly others for which it does not supply an accurate model. When business firms make investment decisions, there is a lag between the time when the firm appropriates funds for investment projects and the time when expenditures on these projects are actually made; but such a lag is clearly not infinite. Obviously only a finite number of appropriations made in previous periods enter into the investment expenditures at any particular time, even when several different investment projects are being carried out. Appropriations made far back into the past will all have been spent before the present, and thus their impact on current expenditures will be zero. Similarly, appropriations made in the current period are not likely to have any impact on current expenditures for large-scale capital investment projects.[18]

The finite lag model needed to describe the relationship between appropriations and investment expenditures can be applied to other economic relationships also. For example the amount of beef or pork reaching the market at a particular time depends on decisions made on the basis of market conditions in previous periods; but because only animals of specific age are sent to the market, the number of such past periods that have influence is not infinite but finite. Moreover, once the decision has been made to send cattle to the feed lots, the amount of beef that will reach the market a few months later cannot be altered by subsequent decisions.[19]

For models describing these kinds of economic relationships, a particular kind of finite lag structure is needed. These *flexible distributed lag models* have the property that values of the independent variable prior to a particular previous time period do not have any impact on the current value of the dependent variable, and that values of the independent variable after some other later period also have no impact in the current period. The impact of the independent variable during the relevant period can have a variety of forms, as shown in Figure 7-2.

Suppose we know a priori on the basis of economic reasoning that the value of the variable Y_t depends on the values of the variable X in periods $(t-1), (t-2), \ldots, (t-j)$; but that values of X in periods prior to $t-j$ and after $t-1$ have no impact on Y_t. We express this relationship:

$$Y_t = \alpha + \sum_{i=1}^{j} \beta_i X_{t-i} + U_t \qquad \textbf{7.6.1}$$

We can express this relationship in terms of weights w_i as follows:

$$Y_t = \alpha + \beta(w_1 X_{t-1} + w_2 X_{t-2} + \cdots + w_j X_{t-j}) + U_t \qquad \textbf{7.6.2}$$

The coefficients in equation 7.6.1 equal those in equation 7.6.2 ($\beta_i = \beta w_i$). The weights w_i will thus have one of the shapes indicated in the diagrams in

---

18 Shirley Almon, "The Distributed Lag Between Capital Appropriations and Expenditures," *Econometrica*, Vol. 33, No. 1 (January, 1965), pp. 178-196.

19 M. K. Evans, "An Agricultural Submodel for the United States Economy," *Essays in Industrial Econometrics*, Vol. 2, edited by L. R. Klein (Philadelphia: Economics Research Unit, University of Pennsylvania, 1969), p. 95.

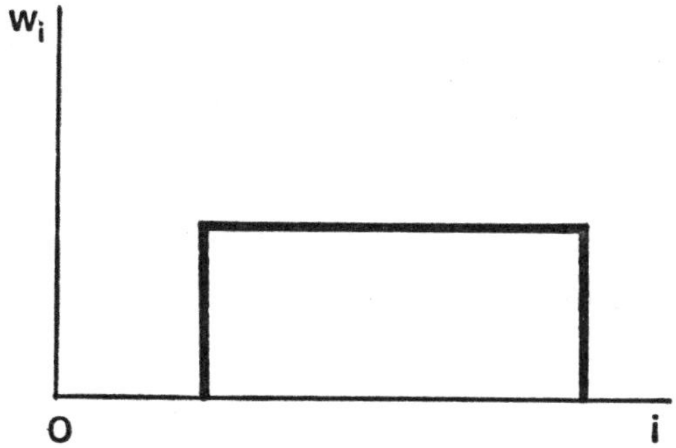

a. Rectangular Lag Structure

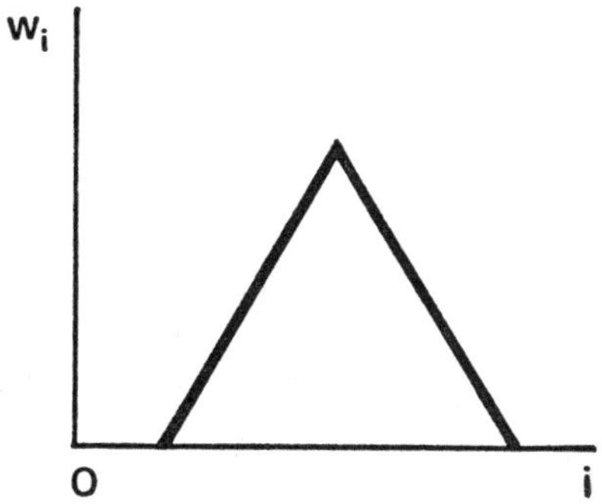

b. Inverted *V* Lag Structure

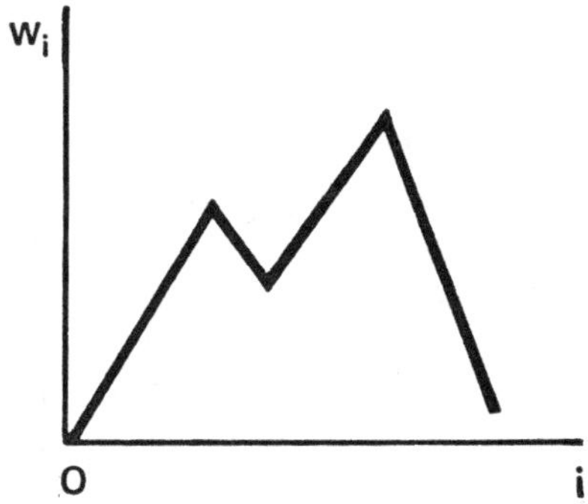

c. Inverted *W* Lag Structure

FIGURE 7-2

Figure 7-2, and this suggests the use of a polynomial expression for w_i as a function of the interval i.[20]

$$w_i = w(i) = \lambda_0 + \lambda_1 i + \lambda_2 i^2 + \cdots + \lambda_r i^r \qquad \textbf{7.6.3}$$

The degree of the polynomial will be determined by the shape that is assumed for the weight function $w(i)$. For the inverted V lag structure of Figure 7-2b, the degree of the polynomial will be at least two; because, as we know from a mathematical argument, the number of maximum or minimum values of a polynomial is at most one less than the degree of the polynomial. Similarly, the polynomial for the weight function corresponding to Figure 7-2c must be of degree at least four.

Suppose that the length of the interval for the finite lag structure was determined a priori to be four periods, and suppose we know that $w(1) = w(6) = 0$, then only values of the independent variable in periods $t - 2$ to $t - 5$ have

[20] A continuous function defined on a closed interval can be approximated to any desired degree of closeness by an appropriate polynomial, according to a theorem of Weirstrasse.

impact on the dependent variable in period t. Substituting these values in equation 7.6.3, we have:

$$\begin{aligned} w(1) &= \lambda_0 + \lambda_1 1 + \lambda_2 1^2 + \lambda_3 1^3 = 0 \\ &\lambda_0 + \lambda_1 + \lambda_2 + \lambda_3 = 0 \\ w(6) &= \lambda_0 + \lambda_1 6 + \lambda_2 6^2 + \lambda_3 6^3 = 0 \\ &\lambda_0 + 6\lambda_1 + 36\lambda_2 + 216\lambda_3 = 0 \end{aligned} \qquad \textbf{7.6.4}$$

Solving these two equations for λ_0 and λ_1 in terms of λ_2 and λ_3, we have:

$$\begin{aligned} \lambda_0 &= 6\lambda_2 + 42\lambda_3 \\ \lambda_1 &= -7\lambda_2 - 43\lambda_3 \end{aligned} \qquad \textbf{7.6.5}$$

These two equations correspond to the two constraints on the polynomial $w(i)$: that it take on the value zero at $i = 1$ and at $i = 6$.

Returning to equation 7.6.3, we can now write the numerical values for the coefficients of the λ's in the polynomial expressions for the weights $w(i)$:

$$\begin{aligned} i = 1 \quad & w(1) = 0 \\ i = 2 \quad & w(2) = \lambda_0 + 2\lambda_1 + 4\lambda_2 + 8\lambda_3 \\ i = 3 \quad & w(3) = \lambda_0 + 3\lambda_1 + 9\lambda_2 + 27\lambda_3 \\ i = 4 \quad & w(4) = \lambda_0 + 4\lambda_1 + 16\lambda_2 + 64\lambda_3 \\ i = 5 \quad & w(5) = \lambda_0 + 5\lambda_1 + 25\lambda_2 + 125\lambda_3 \\ i = 6 \quad & w(6) = 0 \end{aligned} \qquad \textbf{7.6.6}$$

These expressions can now be substituted for the weights w_i in equation 7.6.2, and we have:

$$\begin{aligned} Y_t = \alpha + \beta[&X_{t-2} (\lambda_0 + 2\lambda_1 + 4\lambda_2 + 8\lambda_3) \\ &+ X_{t-3} (\lambda_0 + 3\lambda_1 + 9\lambda_2 + 27\lambda_3) \\ &+ X_{t-4} (\lambda_0 + 4\lambda_1 + 16\lambda_2 + 64\lambda_3) \\ &+ X_{t-5} (\lambda_0 + 5\lambda_1 + 25\lambda_2 + 125\lambda_3)] + U_t \end{aligned} \qquad \textbf{7.6.7}$$

Collecting terms and rearranging, we get an equation with coefficients of the form $\beta\lambda_i$.

$$Y_t = \alpha + \beta\lambda_0 Q_0 + \beta\lambda_1 Q_1 + \beta\lambda_2 Q_2 + \beta\lambda_3 Q_3 + U_t \qquad \textbf{7.6.8}$$

where Q_0, Q_1, Q_2 and Q_3 are linear combinations of the predetermined variables X_{t-2}, X_{t-3}, X_{t-4}, and X_{t-5}:

$$Q_0 = X_{t-2} + X_{t-3} + X_{t-4} + X_{t-5}$$
$$Q_1 = 2X_{t-2} + 3X_{t-3} + 4X_{t-4} + 5X_{t-5} \qquad \textbf{7.6.9}$$
$$Q_2 = 4X_{t-2} + 9X_{t-3} + 16X_{t-4} + 25X_{t-5}$$
$$Q_3 = 8X_{t-2} + 27X_{t-3} + 64X_{t-4} + 125X_{t-5}$$

Notice that although the Q's are linear combinations of the variables X_{t-i}, the Q's will be linearly independent if the X_{t-i}'s are linearly independent.

We can now substitute into equation 7.6.8 the solutions for λ_0 and λ_1 in terms of λ_2 and λ_3 from equation 7.6.5 to get:

$$Y_t = \alpha + \beta\lambda_2 (6Q_0 - 7Q_1 + Q_2) + \beta\lambda_3 (42Q_0 - 43Q_1 + Q_3) + U_t \qquad \textbf{7.6.10}$$

Notice that two of the parameters are nonlinear in this equation, $\beta\lambda_2$ and $\beta\lambda_3$, in which products of the parameter β with λ_2 and λ_3 appear. However, for a particular numerical value of β, the parameters are linear; and since the expressions inside the parentheses are combinations of the observed values of the X_{t-i}'s, the equations can be estimated by OLS. With these estimates for α, λ_2, and λ_3, estimates of λ_0 and λ_1 can be calculated from equation 7.6.5; and these estimates for the λ_i can be substituted into equation 7.6.6 to yield estimates of the weights w_i. In applications of this lag structure, for simplicity, the value of β is taken as one.

Another way to estimate the flexible distributed lag function is to use the Lagrange interpolation formula. In any case application of this method is dependent on a priori knowledge of (1) length of the lag—the lag structure has a finite time horizon, and (2) shape of the time-path of the lag structure, that is, the degree of the polynomial.

DISCUSSION QUESTIONS

1. Consider the model:

$$Y_t = \beta_0 + \beta_1 Y_{t-1} + U_t$$

   (a) Show that the least squares estimates of the regression coefficients are biased.
   (b) Are they consistent? If not, why not?

2. The distributed lag model proposed by Koyck has been extensively used. Take, for example,

$$C_t = \beta_0 + \beta_1 Y_t + \lambda C_{t-1} + U_t$$

   where C = aggregate consumption and Y = aggregate income.
   (a) Review the above model in terms of the well-known permanent income hypothesis.

(b) Discuss the problem in estimating the above model by the least squares method.
(c) Describe the solution proposed by Koyck.

3. Explain the modification of the Durbin-Watson test for a model such as that of question 2.

4. In terms of the problem of estimation of regression coefficients by the least squares method, adaptive expectation models differ from the partial adjustment models. Why?

5. Consider the model:

$$Y_t = \beta_0 + \beta_1 Y_{t-1} + \beta_2 X_t + U_t$$

where $U_t = \rho U_{t-1} + V_t$ and the V_t are independently distributed with a zero mean and a finite variance.
(a) Obtain the Wallis estimator.
(b) Discuss the criteria for choosing the instrumental variable.
(c) How can the method be used when several X variables appear as regressors in the relationship?

6. Review the rational distributed lag function, and show that the Koyck distributed lag function is a special case of the generalized function.

7. Consider the model:

$$Y_t = \alpha + \beta\,(w_0 X_t + w_1 X_{t-1} + w_2 X_{t-2}) + U_t$$

The weights w_i ($i = 0, 1, 2$) are described by a second degree polynomial when:

$$w_0 + w_1 + w_2 = 1 \text{ and } w_{-1} = w_3 = 0$$

Collect suitable economic and/or business data on Y and X, and estimate the above by the least squares method.

SUGGESTED READINGS

Almon, Shirley. "The Distributed Lag Between Capital Appropriations and Expenditures." *Econometrica*, Vol. 33, No. 1 (January, 1965), pp. 178-196.

Alt, F. "Distributed Lags." *Econometrica*, Vol. 10, No. 2 (April, 1942), pp. 113-128.

Ando, Albert, Robert N. Solow, E. Carry Brown, and John Kareken. "Lags in Fiscal and Monetary Policy." *Stabilization Policies*. Englewood Cliffs, N.J.: Prentice-Hall, 1963, pp. 25-30.

Cagan, Phillip D. "The Monetary Dynamics of Hyperinflation." *Studies in the Quantity Theory of Money*, edited by Milton Friedman. Chicago: University of Chicago Press, 1956, pp. 25-117.

De Leeuw, Frank. "The Demand for Capital Goods by Manufacturers: A Study of Quarterly Time Series." *Econometrica,* Vol. 30, No. 3 (July, 1962), pp. 407-423.

Dhrymes, Phoebus J. "On the Treatment of Certain Recurrent Nonlinearities in Regression Analysis." *Southern Economic Journal,* Vol. 33, No. 2 (October, 1966), pp. 187-196.

———. "Efficient Estimation of Distributed Lags with Autocorrelated Error Terms." *International Economic Review,* Vol. 10 (February, 1969), pp. 47-67.

———. *Distributed Lags; Problems of Estimation and Formulation.* San Francisco: Holden-Day, 1971.

Durbin, James. "Testing for Serial Correlation in Least-Squares Regression When Some of the Regressors Are Lagged Dependent Variables." *Econometrica,* Vol. 38, No. 3 (May, 1970), pp. 410-421.

Eisner, Robert. "A Distributed Lag Investment Function." *Econometrica,* Vol. 28, No. 1 (January, 1960), pp. 1-29.

Evans, M. K. "An Agricultural Submodel for the United States Economy." *Essays in Industrial Econometrics,* Vol. 2, edited by L. R. Klein. Philadelphia: University of Pennsylvania, 1969.

Fisher, I. "Note on a Short-Cut Method for Calculating Distributed Lags." *Bulletin of International Institute of Statistics,* Vol. 29 (1937), pp. 323-328.

Friedman, Milton, *Theory of the Consumption Function.* Princeton: Princeton University Press, 1957.

Griliches, Zvi. "A Note on Serial Correlation Bias in Estimates of Distributed Lags." *Econometrica,* Vol. 29, No. 1 (January, 1961), pp. 65-73.

———. "Distributed Lags, A Survey." *Econometrica,* Vol. 35, No. 1 (January, 1967), pp. 16-49.

Hannan, E. J. "The Estimation of Relationships Involving Distributed Lags." *Econometrica,* Vol. 33, No. 1 (January, 1965), pp. 206-224.

Jorgenson, Dale W. "Capital Theory and Investment Behavior." *American Economic Review,* Vol. 53, No. 2 (May, 1963), pp. 247-259.

———. "Rational Distributed Lag Functions." *Econometrica,* Vol. 34, No. 1 (January, 1966), pp. 135-149.

Klein, Lawrence R. "The Estimation of Distributed Lags." *Econometrica,* Vol. 26, No. 4 (October, 1958), pp. 553-565.

Koyck, L. M. *Distributed Lags and Investment Analysis.* Amsterdam: North-Holland Publishing Co., 1954.

Liviatan, N. "Consistent Estimation of Distributed Lags." *International Economic Review,* Vol. 4, No. 1 (January, 1963), pp. 44-52.

Malinvaud, E. "The Estimation of Distributed Lags: A Comment." *Econometrica,* Vol. 29, No. 3 (July, 1961), pp. 430-433.

Nagar, A. L., and Y. P. Gupta. "The Bias of Liviatan's Consistent Estimator in a Distributed Lag Model." *Econometrica,* Vol. 36, No. 2 (April, 1968), pp. 337-342.

Nerlove, Marc. *Distributed Lags and Demand Analysis for Agricultural and Other Commodities,* Department of Agriculture Handbook No. 141. Washington, D.C.: U.S. Government Printing Office, 1958.

———. *The Dynamics of Supply: Estimation of Farmers' Response to Price.* Baltimore: Johns Hopkins University Press, 1958.

Nerlove, Marc, and Kenneth Wallis. "Use of the Durbin-Watson Statistics in Inappropriate Situations." *Econometrica,* Vol. 34, No. 1 (January, 1966), pp. 235-238.

Orcutt, Guy H., and D. Cochrane. "A Sampling Study of the Merits of Autoregressive and Reduced Form Transformations in Regression Analysis." *Journal of the American Statistical Association,* Vol. 44, No. 245 (September, 1949), pp. 356-372.

Sargan, J. D. "The Estimation of Relationships with Autocorrelated Residuals by the Use of Instrumental Variables." *Journal of the Royal Statistical Society,* Vol. B, No. 21 (1959), pp. 91-105.

———. "Wages and Prices in the United Kingdom: A Study in Econometric Methodology." *Econometric Analysis for National Economic Planning,* edited by P. E. Hart *et al.* London: Butterworth & Co., 1964, pp. 25-54.

Solow, Robert M. "On A Family of Lag Distributions." *Econometrica,* Vol. 28, No. 2 (April, 1960), pp. 393-406.

Su, Vincent. "The Specification, Estimation and Evaluation of an Economic Relationship Involving Two Independent Distributed Lags." Doctoral dissertation, Rutgers University, 1970.

Taylor, L. D., and T. A. Wilson. "Three Pass Least Squares: A Method for Estimating Models with a Lagged Dependent Variable." *Review of Economics and Statistics,* Vol. 46, No. 4 (November, 1964), pp. 329-346.

Wallis, Kenneth F. "Lagged Dependent Variables and Serially Correlated Errors: A Reappraisal of Three-pass Least Squares." *Review of Economics and Statistics,* Vol. 49, No. 4 (November, 1967), pp. 555-567.

Waud, Roger. "Misspecification in the 'Partial Adjustment' and 'Adaptive Expectations' Models." *International Economic Review,* Vol. 9, No. 2 (June, 1968), pp. 204-217.

Zellner, Arnold, and M. S. Geisel. "Analysis of Distributed Lag Models with Application to Consumption Function Estimation." *Econometrica,* Vol. 38, No. 6 (November, 1970), pp. 865-888.

8

variance-covariance analysis, principal component analysis, and orthogonal regression

8.0 THE FRAMEWORK: CHI-SQUARE AND F DISTRIBUTIONS

The format of this book precludes an exhaustive discussion of the theories of distribution. In the course of the discussion of the regression model, references have been made to the normal distribution, the standardized normal distribution, and the t distribution. However, in this chapter the chi-square and the F distributions will be discussed, since they provide the foundation of the analysis of variance and covariance.[1]

The Chi-Square Distribution

Suppose that X_i is a random sample of N ($i = 1, 2, \ldots, N$) observations from a normal parent population with mean μ and variance σ^2. Define:

$$z_i = \frac{X_i - \mu}{\sigma} \quad \text{where } z_i \sim \mathcal{N}(0, 1)$$

The variable z_i is a standardized variable normally distributed with mean zero and variance unity. If N such independent, standardized normal variables are squared and summed, we obtain a normalized *chi-square variable* with N degrees of freedom. Formally stated,

$$w = \sum_{i=1}^{N} \frac{(X_i - \mu)^2}{\sigma^2} \qquad \textbf{8.0.1}$$

has a χ^2 distribution with N degrees of freedom.

---

[1] R. L. Anderson and T. A. Bancroft, *Statistical Theory in Research* (New York: McGraw-Hill Book Co., 1952), pp. 68-85.

Note that expression 8.0.1 is a sum of independent and identically distributed variables and is a sum of squares. Note further that the use of the χ^2 distribution involves knowledge of σ^2, which we lack.

The F Distribution

A very useful statistic in hypothesis testing is the F *distribution* which involves the ratio of two variables with chi-square distributions. If χ_1^2 and χ_2^2 are two independently distributed chi-square distributions with N_1 and N_2 degrees of freedom, the F distribution can be written as:

$$F = \frac{N_2\chi_1^2}{N_1\chi_2^2} \qquad \textbf{8.0.2}$$

It is convenient to develop this argument in terms of comparison of two variances. Given the degrees of freedom N_1 and N_2, respectively,

$$\chi_1^2 = \frac{N_1 S_1^2}{\sigma_1^2} \text{ and } \chi_2^2 = \frac{N_2 S_2^2}{\sigma_2^2}$$

where S_1^2 and S_2^2 are two independent sample estimates of σ_1^2 and σ_2^2 respectively. Applying the F statistic for testing the hypothesis $\sigma_1^2 = \sigma_2^2 = \sigma_0^2$ when σ_0^2 is the true variance, we have:

$$F = \frac{S_1^2/\sigma_1^2}{S_2^2/\sigma_2^2} \qquad \textbf{8.0.3}$$

Should the hypothesis that the population variances of the two samples are truly equal and that they are equal to the true variance be valid, the F statistic in equation 8.0.3 becomes the ratio of two sample variances with appropriate degrees of freedom:

$$F = \frac{S_1^2}{S_2^2} \qquad \textbf{8.0.4}$$

with N_1 and N_2 as the degrees of freedom for the numerator and for the denominator respectively.

The F distribution is symmetric and can be used for two-tail tests. A table of F values for N_1 and N_2 degrees of freedom has been computed. The entries in this table are critical values of the F ratio such that at a chosen level of probability the table value of F is the largest value at which the null hypothesis is accepted. In other words there exists a probability that the two random samples from two normal populations yield the same variances. If the computed F value is smaller than the critical value for the appropriate degrees of freedom and the chosen level of probability, we accept the null hypothesis. That is, we conclude from the evidence that there is no significant difference between the two variances given the confidence level.

Two limiting assumptions of the F test can be stated as follows:

1. The F test is based on independent samples drawn randomly from the given normal population. The transformed variables z_i are independent, random normal variables with mean zero and unit variance.
2. Samples drawn from the given normal population have constant variances. That is, the variances are homoscedastic.

We shall see in the following sections that some use may be made of the F test even when the assumptions of normality and homoscedasticity hold only approximately.

8.1 ANALYSIS OF VARIANCE

The analysis of variance is a powerful statistical technique for testing from sample observations whether one variable is truly associated with another variable, or whether the observed association between the two variables is due to sampling fluctuations.[2] The technique is based on partitioning the total variance in a set of data into several component variances, each component representing a different attribute. If the component variance relative to a given attribute is found to be greater than the estimated sampling variance in the data, greater than what can be explained by sampling fluctuations alone, the variable representing the attribute concerned is considered significant.

One-Way Classification

The simplest use of analysis of variance is the case in which observations are classified into groups on the basis of a single attribute. Table 8-1 contains data for family expenditures on consumption. There are observations on 24 family units, and it is assumed that the data are a random sample from a normal

Table 8-1

	$X_{i=1}$ = Married		$X_{i=2}$ = Unmarried		$X_{i=3}$ = Separated or Divorced	
	X_{1j}	$(X_{1j} - \bar{X}_1)^2$	X_{2j}	$(X_{2j} - \bar{X}_2)^2$	X_{3j}	$(X_{3j} - \bar{X}_3)^2$
$j = 1$	$144	9	$140	16	$151	1
$j = 2$	$139	64	$137	49	$147	9
$j = 3$	$133	196	$128	256	$137	169
$j = 4$	$156	81	$153	81	$152	4
$j = 5$	$143	16	$138	36	$142	64
$j = 6$	$156	81	$151	49	$163	169
$j = 7$	$147	0	$145	1	$146	16
$j = 8$	$158	121	$160	256	$162	144
		568		744		576

[2] J. E. Freund, *Modern Elementary Statistics* (3d ed.; Englewood Cliffs, New Jersey: Prentice-Hall, 1967). P. G. Hoel, *Elementary Statistics* (2d ed.; New York: John Wiley & Sons, 1966). H. Scheffé, *The Analysis of Variance* (New York: John Wiley & Sons, 1959). M. G. Kendall, *A Course in Multivariate Analysis* (New York: Hafner Publishing Co., 1957). T. W. Anderson, *An Introduction to Multivariate Statistical Analysis* (New York: John Wiley & Sons, 1958).

distribution with a common variance. The total sample of 24 families is grouped into three classes corresponding to three types of marital status. Calculate:

$$\bar{X}_1 = 147 \quad \bar{X}_2 = 144 \quad \bar{X}_3 = 150 \quad \bar{X} = \frac{\bar{X}_1 + \bar{X}_2 + \bar{X}_3}{3} = 147$$

and using:

$$S_i^2 = \frac{\sum_j (X_{ij} - \bar{X}_i)^2}{N_i - 1}$$

$$S_1^2 = 81.1 \quad S_2^2 = 106.3 \quad S_3^2 = 82.3$$

The variance "within" the classes can now be calculated and denoted by S_2^{*2}.

$$\begin{aligned} S_2^{*2} = \frac{1}{N - C}\sum_i\sum_j (X_{ij} - \bar{X}_i)^2 &= \frac{1}{N - C}(568 + 744 + 576) \\ &= \frac{1}{21}(1888) \\ &= 89.9 \end{aligned} \qquad \textbf{8.1.1}$$

Note that $N = 24$, the total number of observations; and $C = 3$, the number of classes into which the observations have been grouped.

Néxt the variance "between" the classes S_1^{*2} can be calculated as follows:

$$S_1^{*2} = \frac{1}{C - 1}\sum_i\sum_j (\bar{X}_i - \bar{X})^2$$

where $\bar{X}_i$ is the mean of the eight observations in each class i, and $\bar{X}$ is the mean of the total sample.

$$\begin{aligned} S_1^{*2} &= \frac{1}{3 - 1} \times N_i[(\bar{X}_1 - \bar{X})^2 + (\bar{X}_2 - \bar{X})^2 + (\bar{X}_3 - \bar{X})^2] \\ &= \frac{1}{3 - 1} \times 8[(147 - 147)^2 + (144 - 147)^2 + (150 - 147)^2] \\ &= \frac{1}{2}(8)(18) \\ &= 72 \end{aligned} \qquad \textbf{8.1.2}$$

Note that N_i = the number of observations in the ith class. If each class does not contain the same number of observations, as is many times the case in variance analysis, the formula will have to be appropriately adjusted.

Next compute:

$$F = \frac{S_1^{*2}}{S_2^{*2}} = \frac{72}{89.9} = 0.80 \qquad \textbf{8.1.3}$$

We are interested in testing the hypothesis that the differences in the mean consumption expenditures of families with different marital status are not statistically significant. For this purpose we form the null hypothesis in terms of the variances: There is no true difference between the two estimates of variances. Symbolically:

$$H_0\colon \sigma_1^{*2} = \sigma_2^{*2} \qquad \textbf{8.1.4}$$

If this null hypothesis is true, then the numerical difference between the two variance estimates is attributed to sampling chance, and the conclusion is that the two estimates are stochastically the same. In terms of expectation:

$$E(S_1^{*2}) = E(S_2^{*2}) \qquad \textbf{8.1.4.A}$$

To test the null hypothesis we compare the value of F taken from the F distribution table with the calculated value of F. The table gives the value of the ratio of two parameters (two variances) as a function of the degrees of freedom of the numerator and denominator.[3] We calculate the degrees of freedom $N_1 = 2$, the number of classes C minus 1, and $N_2 = 21$, the total number of observations N minus the number of classes C as specified.

At the 5 percent significance level the critical value of F related to $N_1 = 2$ and $N_2 = 21$ is 3.47. Since our computed value is 0.80, which is much smaller, the conclusion is that the null hypothesis is accepted. There is no significant difference between the two estimates of variances. On an average the consumption expenditure of the families is not significantly affected by their marital status.

The Fundamental Identity and the Generalized Result

We can make some useful generalizations of the results. Using the subscript r for rows and c for columns and denoting the jth item in the ith column by X_{ij}, we can construct a general table as follows:

$$\begin{array}{ccccc} X_{11} & X_{21} & X_{31} & \cdots & X_{c1} \\ X_{12} & X_{22} & X_{32} & \cdots & X_{c2} \\ \cdot & \cdot & \cdot & & \cdot \\ \cdot & \cdot & \cdot & & \cdot \\ \cdot & \cdot & \cdot & & \cdot \\ X_{1r} & X_{2r} & X_{3r} & \cdots & X_{cr} \end{array} \qquad \textbf{8.1.5}$$

[3] In reading any F table, be sure that the calculated degrees of freedom for the numerator and denominator correspond to the labeled values in the table. Usually the numerator degrees of freedom are given horizontally, and the denominator degrees of freedom vertically.

The estimate of the natural variance of the data matrix above is:

$$\hat{\sigma}^2 = \sum_i \sum_j \frac{(X_{ij} - \bar{X})^2}{N - 1} \qquad \textbf{8.1.6}$$

Now we get an interesting result known as the *fundamental identity*. Let us write:

$$(X_{ij} - \bar{X}) = (X_{ij} - \bar{X}_i) + (\bar{X}_i - \bar{X}) \qquad \textbf{8.1.7}$$

$$\sum_i \sum_j (X_{ij} - \bar{X})^2 = \sum_i \sum_j (X_{ij} - \bar{X}_i)^2 + \sum_i \sum_j (\bar{X}_i - \bar{X})^2 + 2\sum_i \sum_j (X_{ij} - \bar{X}_i)(\bar{X}_i - \bar{X}) \qquad \textbf{8.1.8}$$

The cross product term vanishes since:

$$2\sum_i \sum_j (X_{ij} - \bar{X}_i)(\bar{X}_i - \bar{X}) = 2\sum_i [(\bar{X}_i - \bar{X}) \sum_j (X_{ij} - \bar{X}_i)] \qquad \textbf{8.1.9}$$

and $\sum_j (X_{ij} - \bar{X}_i) = 0$, being the sum of the deviations from the mean within a group. Therefore we have:

$$\sum_i \sum_j (X_{ij} - \bar{X})^2 = \sum_i \sum_j (X_{ij} - \bar{X}_i)^2 + \sum_i \sum_j (\bar{X}_i - \bar{X})^2 \qquad \textbf{8.1.10}$$

Total sum of squares = sum of squares "within" the classes
+ sum of squares "between" the classes

from which,

$$F = \frac{\text{estimated variance "between" the classes}}{\text{estimated variance "within" the classes}} = \frac{S_1^{*2}}{S_2^{*2}} \qquad \textbf{8.1.11}$$

In terms of the regression model, the "between" sum of squared deviations is the explained deviations of the dependent variable from its mean; and the "within" sum of squared deviation is the residual or unexplained deviations. The simple numerical example illustrated in Table 8-2 will aid in the understanding of the above results.

Table 8-2

Class 1		Class 2		Class 3	
X_{1j}	$(X_{1j} - \bar{X}_1)^2$	X_{2j}	$(X_{2j} - \bar{X}_2)^2$	X_{3j}	$(X_{3j} - \bar{X}_3)^2$
2	4	3	4	6	0
5	1	6	1	5	1
4	0	6	1	6	0
3	1	3	4	6	0
6	4	7	4	7	1
20	10	25	14	30	2

$$\bar{X}_1 = 4 \qquad \bar{X}_2 = 5 \qquad \bar{X}_3 = 6$$

and

$$\bar{X} = \frac{\bar{X}_1 + \bar{X}_2 + \bar{X}_3}{3} = 5$$

We then compute $\sum_i \sum_j (X_{ij} - \bar{X}_i)^2$ and $\sum_i \sum_j (\bar{X}_i - \bar{X})^2$:

$$\begin{aligned}\sum_i \sum_j (X_{ij} - \bar{X}_i)^2 &= \sum_j (X_{1j} - \bar{X}_1)^2 + \sum_j (X_{2j} - \bar{X}_2)^2 + \sum_j (X_{3j} - \bar{X}_3)^2 \\ &= 10 + 14 + 2 \\ &= 26\end{aligned}$$

$$\begin{aligned}\sum_i \sum_j (\bar{X}_i - \bar{X})^2 &= N_i\,[(\bar{X}_1 - \bar{X})^2 + (\bar{X}_2 - \bar{X})^2 + (\bar{X}_3 - \bar{X})^2] \\ &= 5\,[(4 - 5)^2 + (5 - 5)^2 + (6 - 5)^2] \\ &= 5\,[(1 + 0 + 1)] \\ &= 10\end{aligned}$$

To examine the fundamental identity, we need to demonstrate that equation 8.1.10 holds in terms of the numerical example. That is, we must obtain the following result:

$$\sum_i \sum_j (X_{ij} - \bar{X}_i)^2 + \sum_i \sum_j (\bar{X}_i - \bar{X})^2 = \sum_i \sum_j (X_{ij} - \bar{X})^2$$

or

$$26 + 10 = 36$$

Indeed this can be shown to be so since:

$$\begin{aligned}\sum_i \sum_j (X_{ij} - \bar{X})^2 &= 9 + 0 + 1 + 4 + 1 + 4 + 1 + 1 + 4 + 4 + 1 + 0 \\ &\quad + 1 + 1 + 4 \\ &= 36\end{aligned}$$

Correcting for the appropriate degrees of freedom, we have:

$$S_2^{*2} = \text{variance ``within'' the classes}$$

$$\frac{1}{N - C} \sum_i \sum_j (X_{ij} - \bar{X}_i)^2 = \frac{1}{15 - 3}(26) = 2.17$$

$$\begin{aligned}S_1^{*2} &= \text{variance ``between'' the classes} \\ &= \frac{1}{C - 1} \sum_i \sum_j (\bar{X}_i - \bar{X})^2 \\ &= \frac{1}{3 - 1}(10) \\ &= 5\end{aligned}$$

The total variance is:

$$V = \frac{1}{N-1} \sum_i \sum_j (X_{ij} - \bar{X})^2$$

$$= \frac{1}{15-1} \cdot (36)$$

$$= 2.57$$

The F test is, as before:

$$F = \frac{S_1^{*2}}{S_2^{*2}}$$

$$= \frac{\frac{1}{3-1}(10)}{\frac{1}{15-3}(26)} \qquad \textbf{8.1.12}$$

$$= \frac{5}{2.17}$$

$$= 2.3$$

Comparing this value with 3.89, the critical value from the F table at the 5 percent level of significance, with $N_1 = 2$ and $N_2 = 12$, one concludes that there is no significant difference between the two estimates of variances. The observed difference between the two variances is due to random variation in the observations.

We can now construct the analysis of variance table, Table 8-3.

Table 8-3

Analysis of Variance Table

Source	Sum of Squares	d.f.	Estimated Variance
Between	$\sum_i \sum_j (\bar{X}_i - \bar{X})^2$	$C - 1$	$S_1^{*2} = \frac{\text{sum of squares}}{C-1}$
Within	$\sum_i \sum_j (X_{ij} - \bar{X}_i)^2$	$N - C$	$S_2^{*2} = \frac{\text{sum of squares}}{N-C}$
Total	$\sum_i \sum_j (X_{ij} - \bar{X})^2$	$N - 1$	$V = \frac{\text{sum of squares}}{N-1}$

Note: Sum of squares: between + within = total
Degrees of freedom: $C - 1 + N - C = N - 1$

Two-Way Classification

It is possible to design an n-way classification model for the analysis of variance. To illustrate a two-way classification model, we assume that the X_{ij}'s are independent random variables having normal distribution with mean μ_{ij} and variance σ^2. The computational formula may be developed as follows (no proof is presented):

$$\sum_i\sum_j (X_{ij} - \bar{X})^2 = \sum_i\sum_j (\bar{X}_{i\cdot} - \bar{X})^2 + \sum_i\sum_j (\bar{X}_{\cdot j} - \bar{X})^2 + \sum_i\sum_j (X_{ij} - \bar{X}_{i\cdot} - \bar{X}_{\cdot j} + \bar{X})^2 \qquad 8.1.13$$

where columns have the index i, rows have the index j and:

$\bar{X}_{i\cdot}$ = column mean of the ith column

$\bar{X}_{\cdot j}$ = row mean of the jth row

$\bar{X}$ = overall mean

We then compute:

$$S_c^2 = \frac{\sum_i\sum_j (\bar{X}_{i\cdot} - \bar{X})^2}{c-1} = \frac{r\sum_i (\bar{X}_{i\cdot} - \bar{X})^2}{c-1} \qquad 8.1.14$$

$$S_r^2 = \frac{\sum_i\sum_j (\bar{X}_{\cdot j} - \bar{X})^2}{r-1} = \frac{c\sum_j (\bar{X}_{\cdot j} - \bar{X})^2}{r-1} \qquad 8.1.15$$

$$S_0^2 = \frac{\sum_i\sum_j (X_{ij} - \bar{X}_{i\cdot} - \bar{X}_{\cdot j} + \bar{X})^2}{(r-1)(c-1)} \qquad 8.1.16$$

where S_c^2 = column variations or variations due to the property according to which columns are chosen

S_r^2 = row variations or variations due to the property according to which rows are arranged

S_0^2 = other or remaining variations after the variations attributable to column variations and to row variations have been accounted for

We design two F tests:

$$F_r = \frac{S_r^2}{S_0^2} = \frac{c(c-1)\sum_j (\bar{X}_{\cdot j} - \bar{X})^2}{\sum_i\sum_j (X_{ij} - \bar{X}_{i\cdot} - \bar{X}_{\cdot j} + \bar{X})^2} \qquad 8.1.17$$

$$N_1 = r - 1,\ N_2 = (r-1)(c-1)$$

and

$$F_c = \frac{S_c^2}{S_0^2} = \frac{r(r-1)\sum_i (\bar{X}_{i\cdot} - \bar{X})^2}{\sum_i\sum_j (X_{ij} - \bar{X}_{i\cdot} - \bar{X}_{\cdot j} + \bar{X})^2} \qquad 8.1.18$$

$$N_1 = c - 1,\ N_2 = (r-1)(c-1)$$

Consider the following two-way classification model where a test is designed to find out the significance of two nonquantitative variables, religion and color, on average annual income. Let A, B, and C be three religions—Protestant, Catholic, and Jewish—arranged column-wise; and let white and black be the two colors, organized row-wise. (The numbers here are hypothetical.)

	Protestent A	Catholic B	Jewish C	
White	\$8500	\$9100	\$9400	$\bar{X}_{\cdot 1} = 9000$
Black	\$7100	\$6900	\$7000	$\bar{X}_{\cdot 2} = 7000$

$$\bar{X}_{1\cdot} = 7800 \quad \bar{X}_{2\cdot} = 8000 \quad \bar{X}_{3\cdot} = 8200 \quad \bar{X} = 8000$$

$$S_c^2 = \frac{r \sum_i (\bar{X}_{i\cdot} - \bar{X})^2}{c - 1}$$

$$= \frac{2[(7800 - 8000)^2 + (8000 - 8000)^2 + (8200 - 8000)^2]}{3 - 1}$$

$$= 160{,}000/2 = 80{,}000$$

$$S_r^2 = \frac{c \sum_j (\bar{X}_{\cdot j} - \bar{X})^2}{r - 1} = \frac{3[(9000 - 8000)^2 + (7000 - 8000)^2]}{2 - 1}$$

$$= \frac{6{,}000{,}000}{1} = 6{,}000{,}000$$

$$S_0^2 = \frac{\sum_i \sum_j (X_{ij} - \bar{X}_{i\cdot} - \bar{X}_{\cdot j} + \bar{X})^2}{(r - 1)(c - 1)}$$

$$= \frac{(-300)^2 + (100)^2 + (200)^2 + (300)^2 + (-100)^2 + (-200)^2}{(2 - 1)(3 - 1)}$$

$$= \frac{280{,}000}{2} = 140{,}000$$

One can use the following computational formula:

$$\sum_i \sum_j (X_{ij} - \bar{X}_{i\cdot} - \bar{X}_{\cdot j} + \bar{X})^2 = \sum_i \sum_j (X_{ij} - \bar{X})^2 - \sum_i \sum_j (\bar{X}_{i\cdot} - \bar{X})^2 - \sum_i \sum_j (\bar{X}_{\cdot j} - \bar{X})^2$$

and $\sum_i \sum_j (X_{ij} - \bar{X})^2$ can be computed from $\sum_i \sum_j X_{ij}^2 - rcX^2$.

Returning to the illustration,

$$F_c = \frac{80{,}000}{140{,}000} = 0.5714 \qquad \textbf{8.1.19}$$

$$F_r = \frac{6{,}000{,}000}{140{,}000} = 42.8471 \qquad \textbf{8.1.20}$$

The calculated value of F_c (0.5714) is smaller than the critical value $F\ (N_1 = 2, N_2 = 2) = 19.00$ at the 5 percent level, and F_r (42.8471) is greater than $F(N_1 = 1, N_2 = 2) = 18.51$ at the 5 percent level. According to the test, religion has no significance, but color has significance insofar as average annual income differences are concerned. Table 8-4 summarizes the results obtained for this example.

Table 8-4

The Analysis of Variance Table (II)

Source	Sum of Squares	d.f.	Estimated Variance
Between columns	160,000	$2 = (c - 1)$	80,000
Between rows	6,000,000	$1 = (r - 1)$	6,000,000
Residual	280,000	$2 = (r - 1)(c - 1)$	140,000
Total	6,440,000	$5 = (N - 1)$	1,288,000

Note: Sum of squares: between columns + between rows + residuals = total
Degrees of freedom: $(c - 1) + (r - 1) + (r - 1)(c - 1) = N - 1$

Analysis of Variance and the Regression Model

It is easy to see that the two-way classification analysis of variance model can be arranged in terms of a regression model. The observations on the incomes can be designated as Y_i and the observations on religion and color as X_{1i} and X_{2i} respectively. The relationship can then be written in the familiar form:

$$Y_i = \beta_0 + \beta X_{1i} + \beta_2 X_{2i} + U_i \qquad i = 1, 2, \ldots, N \qquad \textbf{8.1.21}$$

The same kind of transformation is possible with the one-way classification model testing the influence of marital status on consumption expenditure. We can write:

$$Y_i = \beta_0 + \beta_1 X_i + U_i \qquad i = 1, 2, \ldots, N \qquad \textbf{8.1.22}$$

where Y = expenditure on consumption
X = marital status

Numerical observations on marital status X are not readily available. However, we have seen that the use of dummy variables (Chapter 6) to represent different kinds of marital status may enable the researcher to carry on the regression analysis straightforwardly. Indeed introduction of the technique of dummy variables has somewhat overshadowed the use of variance analysis in econometric research. However, the F statistic continues to be widely used, at least as a supplementary test of the degree of association between the variables in a postulated relationship. It is also no exaggeration to say that in recent times analysis of variance appears to have been rediscovered in econometric research, particularly when the analyst is anxious to test the significance of nonquantifiable or qualitative variables in a study.

In what follows, the relationship between the regression model and the analysis of variance model will be examined more closely. Let us consider the simple regression model 8.1.22:

$$Y_i = \beta_0 + \beta_1 X_i + U_i$$

or, in terms of mean deviations:

$$y_i = \beta_1 x_i + U_i$$

The analysis of variance model partitions the total variance in y and the total degrees of freedom to identify the sources of variations. Following the analysis of variance model, we can formulate Table 8-5.

Table 8-5

Source	Sum of Squares	Degrees of Freedom	Estimated Variance
Total (observed Y)	Σy_i^2	$N - 1$	$\Sigma y_i^2/(N - 1)$
Regression (estimated $\hat{Y}$)	$\Sigma \hat{y}_i^2$	1	$\hat{\beta}_1^2 \Sigma x_i^2$
Residual ($\Sigma \hat{U}_i^2$)	$\Sigma y_i^2 - \hat{\beta}_1^2 \Sigma x_i^2$	$N - 2$	$\dfrac{\Sigma y_i^2 - \hat{\beta}_1^2 \Sigma x_i^2}{N - 2}$

The total sum of squares is thus decomposed into two components, regression and residual, with degrees of freedom 1 and $N - 2$, respectively. If we add these two, we get a total of $N - 1$ degrees of freedom for the N observations of the data. Notice that the total sum of squares is associated with $N - 1$ degrees of freedom. The regression sum of squares has been associated with 1 degree of freedom. In a K-variable case, it will have K degrees of freedom. The residual sum of squares is associated with $N - 2$ degrees of freedom, since the residuals must satisfy the two least squares conditions in terms of the present model. Clearly, the degrees of freedom of the residual sum of squares depend on the number of parameters estimated in the given model. In this case, residuals are obtained by estimating the two parameters β_0, β_1 with two least squares conditions; while in the K-variable case, the residuals will have $N - K - 1$ degrees of freedom since the residuals satisfy $K + 1$ least squares conditions, one for each estimated parameter plus one for the intercept β_0.

Following the discussion of the standard normal distribution, we can state that the variable:

$$z = \frac{\hat{\beta}_1 - \beta_1}{S_{\hat{\beta}_1}}$$

is normally distributed with zero mean and unit variance, or:

$$\frac{\hat{\beta}_1 - \beta_1}{\sigma_u / \sqrt{\Sigma x_i^2}} \text{ is distributed } \mathcal{N}(0,1) \qquad \textbf{8.1.23}$$

where β_1 is the true (mean) value of β_1 and $S_{\hat{\beta}_1} = \sqrt{\sigma_u^2 / \Sigma x_i^2}$. Next, following equation 8.0.1, this standard normal variable when squared has a chi-square distribution with 1 degree of freedom. That is, $(\hat{\beta}_1 - \beta_1)^2/(\sigma_u^2/\Sigma x_i^2)$ will have a chi-square distribution with 1 degree of freedom. Similarly,

$$\frac{U_i - \bar{U}}{\sigma_u} \text{ is distributed } \mathcal{N}(0,1) \qquad \textbf{8.1.24}$$

where $\bar{U}$ is the true mean value of population U_i. Since $E(U_i) = \bar{U} = 0$, $\Sigma U_i^2/\sigma_u^2$ has a chi-square distribution with $N - 2$ degrees of freedom.

Next, following equation 8.0.2, we use the ratio of the two chi-square distributions and obtain the following F distribution:

$$F = \frac{(\hat{\beta}_1 - \beta_1)^2}{\dfrac{\sigma_u^2}{\Sigma x_i^2}} \cdot \frac{\sigma_u^2}{\Sigma U_i^2} \qquad \textbf{8.1.25}$$

$$= \frac{(\hat{\beta}_1 - \beta_1)^2 \, \Sigma x_i^2}{\Sigma U_i^2}$$

Now we can test the hypothesis that Y is not functionally dependent on X, as postulated in the model; that is, H_0: $\beta_1 = 0$. Under this null hypothesis,

$$F = \frac{\hat{\beta}_1^2 \Sigma x_i^2}{\Sigma U_i^2} \qquad \textbf{8.1.26}$$

or following the analysis of variance table, Table 8-3,

$$F = \frac{\text{regression variance}}{\text{residual variance}} = \frac{\text{explained variance}}{\text{unexplained variance}} \qquad \textbf{8.1.27}$$

We then compare the computed F value with the F value found in the table at a chosen level of significance for the degrees of freedom of the numerator (1 in this case) and of the denominator ($N - 2$ in this case). If the computed F value is smaller than the value in the table, we accept the null hypothesis and conclude that $\beta_1 = 0$. That is, variations in Y are not truly associated with those in X at the given level of significance.

To illustrate from regression model 3.4.1, we can construct Table 8-6.

Table 8-6

Source	Sum of Squares	d.f.	Estimated Variance
Total	$\mathbf{Y'Y} - \frac{(\Sigma Y)^2}{N} = 276.1686$	13	
Regression	$\mathbf{\hat{Y}'\hat{Y}} - \frac{\Sigma(Y)^2}{N} = 227.9500$	1	227.9500
Residual	$\mathbf{Y'Y} - \mathbf{\hat{Y}'\hat{Y}} = 48.2186$	12	4.0182

$$F = \frac{\text{regression variance}}{\text{residual variance}} = \frac{227.9500}{4.0182} = 56.7294 \qquad \textbf{8.1.27.A}$$

The table value of $F(1,12)$ equals 4.75 at the 5 percent level of significance, so we reject the hypothesis that $\beta_2 = 0$. The conclusion is that the association between the two variables is statistically significant.

In terms of the multiple regression used to illustrate model 3.4.2, the analysis of variance table can be written as in Table 8-7.

Table 8-7

Source	Sum of Squares	d.f.	Estimated Variance
Total	$\mathbf{Y'Y} - \frac{(\Sigma Y)^2}{N} = 276.1686$	13	
Regression	$\mathbf{\hat{Y}'\hat{Y}} - \frac{\Sigma(Y)^2}{N} = 254.0402$	2	127.0201
Residual	$\mathbf{Y'Y} - \mathbf{\hat{Y}'\hat{Y}} = 22.1284$	11	2.0117

$$F = \frac{\text{regression variance}}{\text{residual variance}} = \frac{127.0201}{2.0117} = 63.1407 \qquad \textbf{8.1.27.B}$$

The table value of $F(2,11)$ equals 3.98 at the 5 percent level of significance, so we reject the hypothesis that $[\beta_2,\beta_3] = 0$.

We therefore conclude that a significant association, covariation, exists between the three variables included in the model. We can further analyze the significance of the association of Y with X_2 or X_3 separately by applying the F test to a ratio where the numerator is the regression or explained variance in terms of X_2 or X_3 alone, and the denominator is the residual variance as appropriately computed. Table 8-8 illustrates the case.

Table 8-8

Source	Sum of Squares	d.f.	Estimated Variance
Total	276.1686	13	
Regression (X_2)	227.9500	1	227.9500
Regression (X_2 and X_3)	254.0402	2	
Regression (X_3 by subtraction)	26.0902	1	26.0902
Residual	22.1284	11	2.0117

Using the data from Table 8-8, the test for the additional effect of X_3 is then:

$$F = \frac{26.0902}{2.0117} = 12.9692 \qquad \textbf{8.1.28}$$

The table value of $F(1,11)$ equals 4.84 at the 5 percent level of significance, so we reject the null hypothesis. In other words, we conclude that the covariation between Y and X_3 for a given X_2 is statistically significant.

The significance of X_2 alone can be determined as in Table 8-9.

Table 8-9

Source	Sum of Squares	d.f.	Estimated Variance
Total	276.1686	13	
Regression with X_2	227.9500	1	227.9500
Residual	48.2186	12	4.0182

$$F = \frac{227.9500}{4.0182} = 56.7294 \qquad \textbf{8.1.29}$$

Of course, this is the result we obtained in equation 8.1.27.A. The table value of $F(1,12)$ equals 4.75 at the 5 percent significance level. The conclusion is, as before, that the association between Y and X_2 for a given X_3 is statistically significant.

Obviously, an alternative way would be to apply the test directly with respect to X_3 and then to X_2 by subtraction.

The relationship between the linear regression model and the analysis of variance model thus becomes quite easy to see. However, if the regression relation is nonlinear, the F test will not be meaningful.

8.2 ANALYSIS OF COVARIANCE

Basically, *covariance analysis* is an extension of the analysis of variance.[4] It is also based on the F distribution, and as such it is subject to the same limiting assumptions as is the analysis of variance. Covariance analysis permits the analysis of the relationship between certain interdependent variables while testing whether other variables (which may be nonquantifiable) affect the relationship under investigation. For example, consumption expenditure of a family depends on the income of the family, according to economic reasoning. At the same time it is believed that the consumption pattern of a family may vary between different regions in the same national economy and that the estimate of the regression coefficients from national data may be influenced by regional effects. If these effects are not explicitly accounted for in the regression model, the estimates will be biased in unknown ways. The analysis-of-covariance model seeks to analyze the effect of both variables, income and regional pattern, at the same time. Indeed covariance analysis is an attempt to combine the methods of regression and analysis of variance. One would otherwise use two independent analyses—analysis of variance for testing regional impact on consumption pattern and regression analysis for the estimation of income effect.

Consider the model:

$$Y_i = \alpha + \beta X_i + U_i \qquad \textbf{8.2.1}$$

with a priori side conditions:

$$\alpha \geqq 0, \beta > 0, \qquad i = 1, \ldots, N$$

$$Y_i = \text{consumption of the } i^{th} \text{ family}$$

$$X_i = \text{income of the } i^{th} \text{ family}$$

$$U_i = \text{disturbance terms}$$

The U_i's are assumed to be random, normally distributed, and homoscedastic, as in the assumptions of variance analysis. Recall that in the simple regression model, the U_i's were assumed to be random and homoscedastic, but not necessarily normally distributed .

[4] E. Malinvaud, *Statistical Methods of Econometrics* (Amsterdam: North-Holland Publishing Co., 1966), pp. 233-236. R. L. Anderson and T. A. Bancroft, *Statistical Theory in Research* (New York: McGraw-Hill Book Co., 1952), pp. 297-312.

Now consider the problem if the estimated α and β vary between groups of individuals, say from one regional group to another, when the data are taken from family units of diverse regional backgrounds. Assume that there are P such regional patterns. We could estimate α and β for each region from P different regression relations based on data collected separately from each region. Alternatively, we could design an experiment to test the hypothesis that the parameters $\hat{\alpha}_j$ and $\hat{\beta}_j$ estimated for the different regions are equal to the same true α and β respectively, regardless of regional differences. This test can be accomplished by the analysis of covariance, which permits us to evaluate with one calculation the effects on consumption of the quantitative variable, income, as well as the qualitative variable, regional pattern. Table 8-10 illustrates the analysis of covariance.

Table 8-10

Analysis of Covariance Table[5]

Source of Variation	d.f.	Sum of Squares
Within classes with unequal effects	$N - 2P$	$\sum_{j=1}^{P} \Sigma_i^j (Y_i - \bar{Y}_{j\cdot})^2 - \sum_{j=1}^{P} \beta_j^* \Sigma_i^j (Y_i - \bar{Y}_{j\cdot})(X_i - \bar{X}_{j\cdot})$
Differences among the β_j's	$P - 1$	$\sum_{j=1}^{P} (\beta_j^* - \bar{\beta}) \Sigma_i^j (Y_i - \bar{Y}_{j\cdot})(X_i - \bar{X}_{j\cdot})$
Within classes with equal effect	$N - P - 1$	$\sum_{j=1}^{P} \Sigma_i^j (Y_i - \bar{Y}_{j\cdot})^2 - \bar{\beta} \sum_{j=1}^{P} \Sigma_i^j (Y_i - \bar{Y}_{j\cdot})(X_i - \bar{X}_{j\cdot})$

$i = 1, 2, \ldots, N \quad j = 1, 2, \ldots, P.$

Σ_i^j = summation over i for all observations in the jth class. Note that in Table 8-10, Y_i and X_i can be read as Y_{ji} and X_{ji} respectively.

$\bar{Y}_{j\cdot}, \bar{X}_{j\cdot}$ = means of Y_i and X_i respectively in the jth class.

$$\hat{\beta}_j^* = \frac{\Sigma_i^j(Y_i - \bar{Y}_{j\cdot})(X_i - \bar{X}_{j\cdot})}{\Sigma_i^j(X_i - \bar{X}_{j\cdot})^2} \qquad \textbf{8.2.2}$$

[5] E. Malinvaud, *Statistical Methods of Econometrics* (Amsterdam: North-Holland Publishing Co., 1966), p. 234.

$$\hat{\bar{\beta}} = \frac{\sum_{j=1}^{P} \Sigma_i^j (Y_i - \bar{Y}_{j}\cdot)(X_i - \bar{X}_{j}\cdot)}{\sum_{j=1}^{P} \Sigma_i^j (X_i - \bar{X}_{j}\cdot)^2} \quad 8.2.3$$

Note that $\hat{\beta}_j^*$ and $\hat{\bar{\beta}}$ are least squares regression coefficients. Essentially, $\hat{\beta}_j^*$ is the estimated coefficient of β with respect to the jth class, and $\hat{\bar{\beta}}$ is the estimated coefficient β over the entire sample.

$$F = \frac{N - 2P}{P - 1} \frac{\sum_{j=1}^{P} (\hat{\beta}_j^* - \hat{\bar{\beta}}) \Sigma_i^j (Y_i - \bar{Y}_{j}\cdot)(X_i - \bar{X}_{j}\cdot)}{\sum_{j=1}^{P} \Sigma_i^j (Y_i - \bar{Y}_{j}\cdot)^2 - \sum_{j=1}^{P} \hat{\beta}_j^* \Sigma_i^j (Y_i - \bar{Y}_{j}\cdot)(X_i - \bar{X}_{j}\cdot)} \quad 8.2.4$$

where $N_1 = P - 1$

$N_2 = N - 2P$

Given the appropriate level of confidence and the degrees of freedom N_1 and N_2, read the F value from the table. If the computed value of F is greater than the table value of F, reject the null hypothesis that the estimated parameters are the same and equal to the "true" parameter irrespective of regional classification. Table 8-11 provides a numerical example.

TABLE 8-11

Y	X	R
8	12	1
4	6	1
2	6	1
6	8	1
7	12	2
3	7	2
8	8	2

$i = 1, 2, \ldots, 7 (N = 7)$. $j = 1, 2 (P = 2)$.

$\Sigma_i^1 Y_i = 20 \quad \bar{Y}_1\cdot = 5$

$\Sigma_i^1 X_i = 32 \quad \bar{X}_1\cdot = 8$

$\Sigma_i^2 Y_i = 18 \quad \bar{Y}_2\cdot = 6$

$\Sigma_i^2 X_i = 27 \quad \bar{X}_2\cdot = 9$

$$\hat{\beta}_1^* = \frac{(8-5)(12-8)+(4-5)(6-8)+(2-5)(6-8)+(6-5)(8-8)}{(12-8)^2+(6-8)^2+(6-8)^2+(8-8)^2}$$

$$= \frac{20}{24} = 0.83$$

$$\hat{\beta}_2^* = \frac{(7-6)(12-9)+(3-6)(7-9)+(8-6)(8-9)}{(12-9)^2+(7-9)^2+(8-9)^2}$$

$$\doteq \frac{7}{14} = 0.5$$

$$\hat{\bar{\beta}} = \frac{20+7}{24+14} = \frac{27}{38}$$

$$= 0.71$$

$$\Sigma_i^1 (Y_i - \bar{Y}_{1}.)^2 = (8-5)^2 + (4-5)^2 + (2-5)^2 + (6-5)^2$$

$$= 20$$

$$\Sigma_i^2 (Y_i - \bar{Y}_{2}.)^2 = (7-6)^2 + (3-6)^2 + (8-6)^2$$

$$= 14$$

$$\Sigma_i^1 (Y_i - \bar{Y}_{1}.)(X_i - \bar{X}_{1}.) = 20$$

$$\Sigma_i^2 (Y_i - \bar{Y}_{2}.)(X_i - \bar{X}_{2}.) = 7$$

We then calculate the F ratio:

$$\text{Numerator} = (\hat{\beta}_1^* - \hat{\bar{\beta}})\Sigma_i^1 (Y_i - \bar{Y}_{1}.)(X_i - \bar{X}_{1}.)$$

$$+ (\hat{\beta}_2^* - \hat{\bar{\beta}})\Sigma_i^2 (Y_i - \bar{Y}_{2}.)(X_i - \bar{X}_{2}.)$$

$$= (0.83 - 0.71)(20) + (0.50 - 0.71)(7)$$

$$\doteq 1$$

$$\text{Denominator} = \Sigma_i^1 (Y_i - \bar{Y}_{1}.)^2 + \Sigma_i^2 (Y_i - \bar{Y}_{2}.)^2$$

$$- [\hat{\beta}_1^* \Sigma_i^1 (Y_i - \bar{Y}_{1}.)(X_i - \bar{X}_{1}.)$$

$$+ \hat{\beta}_2^* \Sigma_i^2 (Y_i - \bar{Y}_{2}.)(X_i - \bar{X}_{2}.)]$$

$$= 20 + 14 - [(0.83)(20) + (0.50)(7)]$$

$$\doteq 14$$

$$N - 2P = 7 - 4 = 3$$

$$P - 1 = 2 - 1 = 1$$

$$F = \frac{3}{1} \cdot \frac{1}{14} \qquad 8.2.5$$

$$= \frac{3}{14}$$

$$= 0.21$$

The critical value from the F table for $N_1 = 1$, $N_2 = 3$ at the 5 percent level of significance is 10.13. We therefore accept the hypothesis that all the parameters $\hat{\beta}_j^*$ are equal to the same unknown β regardless of the regional differences. In other words $E(\hat{\beta}_1^*) = E(\hat{\beta}_2^*) = \ldots = \beta$, and the observed differences between the regions are due to chance or sampling fluctuations.

Covariance analysis, though well known elsewhere, has not been extensively used in econometric research. Instead the technique of dummy variables has dominated. Using a dummy equal to 1 when the ith family belongs to the jth region and 0 otherwise and introducing a dummy variable for differential slopes, we can rewrite the regression equation and apply regression analysis directly. We then estimate, omitting the subscript i:

$$Y = \beta_0 + \beta_1 X + \beta_2 DX + \beta_3 D + U \qquad 8.2.6$$

$$E\,(Y) = \beta_0 + \beta_1 X \text{ for region 1} \qquad 8.2.7$$

$$E\,(Y) = (\beta_0 + \beta_3) + (\beta_1 + \beta_2)\,X \text{ for region 2} \qquad 8.2.8$$

when $D = 1$ for region 2

$= 0$ for region 1

It should be evident that the test of equality of intercepts can be made by the analysis of variance technique or by introducing differential intercept dummies (section 6.1), while the test of equality of slopes can be made by the analysis of covariance method or by introducing differential slope dummies (section 6.2).

8.3 ORTHOGONAL REGRESSION

The discussion so far has been confined to the regression model developed in Chapters 2 and 3. The framework of that analysis is based on a linear model where the estimated regression line is mathematically so constructed as to minimize the sum of squares of deviations of observed points from the estimated line, deviations to be so minimized being vertically measured.

Suppose, as in Figure 8-1, we choose to measure the deviations along lines perpendicular to the regression line and to minimize the sum of squares of such deviations for the estimation of parameters of the regression line. The estimating equation is given by:

$$\beta_1' X_i + \beta_2' Y_i = \beta_0' + \tilde{U}_i \qquad 8.3.1$$

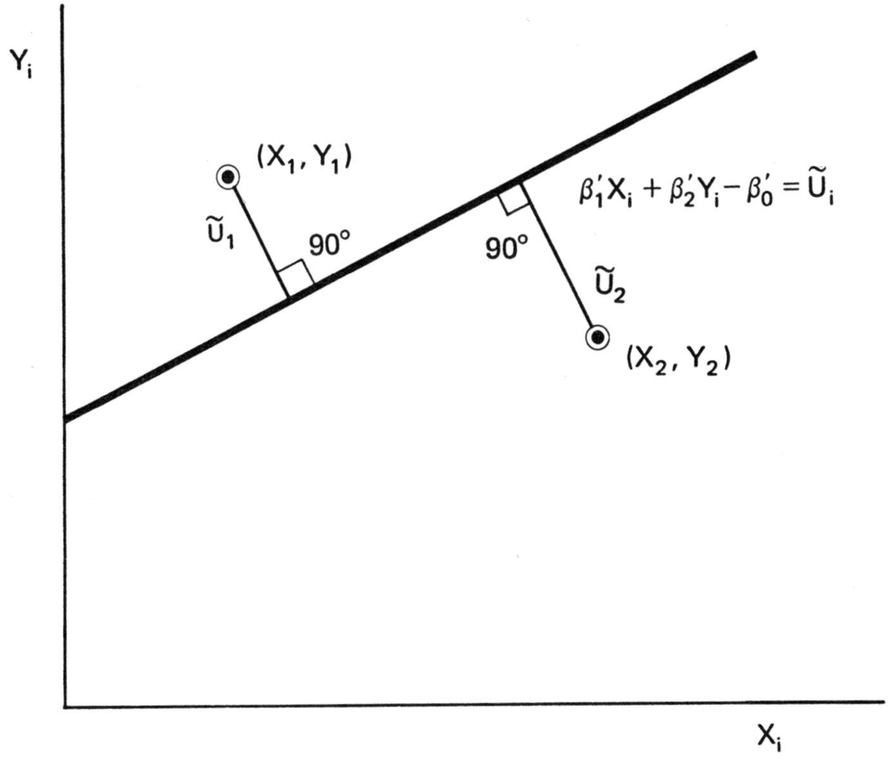

FIGURE 8-1

where $\beta_1'^2 + \beta_2'^2 = 1$. Note that $\tilde{U}_i$ is the perpendicular deviation, distinguished from U_i, which denotes the vertical deviation as before.

This method is *orthogonal regression*.[6] The regression line is obtained by minimizing $\Sigma \tilde{U}_i^2$ instead of ΣU_i^2, subject to the additional restriction that the sum of the squares of the coefficients of the variables describing the function, Y and X, is equal to unity; that is, $\beta_1'^2 + \beta_2'^2 = 1$. Let us examine the case more fully.

In Figure 8-2 where Y_i is linearly dependent on X_i, the slope of the line is β_1, and thus:

$$\tan \theta = \beta_1 \qquad \textbf{8.3.2}$$

The angle between $\tilde{U}_i$ and U_i is θ, as indicated. Thus:

$$\tilde{U}_i = U_i \cos \theta \qquad \textbf{8.3.3}$$

The ordinary least squares equation is given by:

---

[6] E. Malinvaud, *Statistical Methods of Econometrics* (Amsterdam: North-Holland Publishing Co., 1966), pp. 7-10 and 40-44. L. R. Klein, *A Textbook of Econometrics* (Evanston, Illinois: Row, Peterson & Co., 1956), pp. 289-291.

$$Y_i = \beta_0 + \beta_1 X_i + U_i$$

or,

$$Y_i - \beta_0 - \beta_1 X_i = U_i \qquad \textbf{8.3.4}$$

Substituting, we have:

$$\tilde{U}_i = (Y_i - \beta_0 - \beta_1 X_i) \cos \theta \qquad \textbf{8.3.5}$$

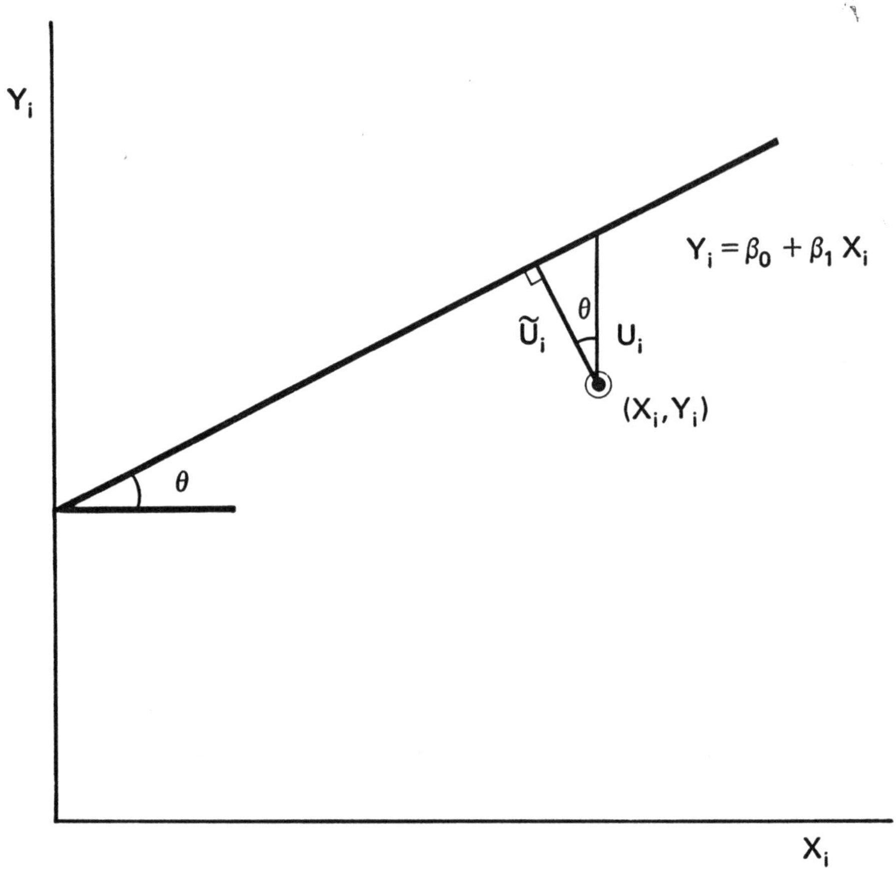

FIGURE 8-2

Using equation 8.3.2 and rearranging,

$$\tilde{U}_i = Y_i \cos \theta - X_i \tan \theta \cos \theta - \beta_0 \cos \theta \qquad \textbf{8.3.6}$$

Since $\tan \theta = \dfrac{\sin \theta}{\cos \theta}$,

$$\tilde{U}_i = Y_i \cos \theta - X_i \frac{\sin \theta}{\cos \theta} \cos \theta - \beta_0 \cos \theta \qquad \textbf{8.3.7}$$

Letting $\cos\theta = \beta_2'$, $-\sin\theta = \beta_1'$, and $\beta_0 \cos\theta = \beta_0'$, we can express the estimating equation for the orthogonal regression with disturbance terms denoted by $\tilde{U}_i$ as:

$$\tilde{U}_i + \beta_0' = \beta_2' Y_i + \beta_1' X_i \qquad \textbf{8.3.8}$$

This is exactly the same equation as equation 8.3.1. This estimating equation must satisfy the condition corresponding to the trigonometric identity:

$$\sin^2\theta + \cos^2\theta = 1 \qquad \textbf{8.3.9}$$

Since $\beta_2' = \cos\theta$ and $\beta_1' = -\sin\theta$, we shall have as the corresponding restriction on β_1' and β_2':

$$\beta_1'^2 + \beta_2'^2 = 1 \qquad \textbf{8.3.10}$$

We are interested in obtaining estimators β_0', β_1', and β_2' as in the case of the OLS regression model. We now work with the function:

$$\mathcal{L} = \Sigma\,(\beta_1' X_i + \beta_2' Y_i - \beta_0')^2 - \lambda(\beta_1'^2 + \beta_2'^2) \qquad \textbf{8.3.11}$$

where λ is the Lagrange multiplier. We take derivatives of this function with respect to β_0', β_1', and β_2' and set them equal to zero. Differentiation with respect to β_0' yields the following result:

$$\beta_0' = \beta_1'\bar{X} + \beta_2'\bar{Y} \qquad \textbf{8.3.12}$$

Alternatively, writing all variables in terms of deviations from their respective means (thus eliminating β_0') and differentiating with respect to β_1' and β_2' and setting them equal to zero, we obtain the following results:[7]

$$\begin{aligned} \beta_1'(\Sigma x_i^2 - \lambda) + \beta_2'\Sigma x_i y_i &= 0 \\ \beta_1'\Sigma x_i y_i + \beta_2'(\Sigma y_i^2 - \lambda) &= 0 \end{aligned} \qquad \textbf{8.3.13}$$

The above equations can be compared with the set of normal equations in the OLS regression model.

Note that equations 8.3.13 are a linear, homogeneous system of (algebraic) equations in β_1' and β_2' and thus will have a nonzero solution if and only if its determinant is zero. Also note that for a nonzero solution of β_1' and β_2', $\Sigma\tilde{U}_i^2$, the

[7] The equation of the regression line expressed in terms of deviations from the mean, x_i and y_i, and with no constant term corresponds to a linear transformation in the XY plane which transforms the regression line into a line parallel to it, passing through the origin. Because $\beta_0' = \beta_1'\bar{X} + \beta_2'\bar{Y}$, the coefficient β_0' can be calculated from the coefficients of the transformed line $\beta_1' x_i + \beta_2' y_i = \tilde{U}_i$.

quantity to be minimized, takes the value λ. This can be seen as follows. Writing in terms of deviations from the means,

$$\Sigma \tilde{u}_i^2 = \Sigma(\beta_1' x_i + \beta_2' y_i)^2 \qquad \textbf{8.3.14}$$
$$= \beta_1'^2 \Sigma x_i^2 + \beta_2'^2 \Sigma y_i^2 + 2\beta_1'\beta_2' \Sigma x_i y_i$$

From equations 8.3.13 we solve for $\beta_1' \Sigma x_i^2$ and $\beta_2' \Sigma y_i^2$ to get:

$$\beta_1' \Sigma x_i^2 = \beta_1' \lambda - \beta_2' \Sigma x_i y_i \qquad \textbf{8.3.15}$$
$$\beta_2' \Sigma y_i^2 = \beta_2' \lambda - \beta_1' \Sigma x_i y_i$$

Multiplying the first equation by β_1' and the second by β_2', we have:

$$\beta_1'^2 \Sigma x_i^2 = \beta_1'^2 \lambda - \beta_1'\beta_2' \Sigma x_i y_i \qquad \textbf{8.3.16}$$
$$\beta_2'^2 \Sigma y_i^2 = \beta_2'^2 \lambda - \beta_1'\beta_2' \Sigma x_i y_i$$

When the right-hand sides of these equations are substituted into equations 8.3.14, we get:

$$\Sigma \tilde{u}_i^2 = \beta_1'^2 \lambda + \beta_2'^2 \lambda \qquad \textbf{8.3.17}$$
$$= \lambda(\beta_1'^2 + \beta_2'^2)$$

since $\beta_1'^2 + \beta_2'^2 = 1$ from equation 8.3.10 yielding the desired result:

$$\Sigma \tilde{u}_i^2 = \lambda \qquad \textbf{8.3.18}$$

Thus to minimize $\Sigma \tilde{U}_i^2$, we need to solve equations 8.3.13 for β_1' and β_2' using λ_1, the smaller root of λ from:

$$\begin{vmatrix} \Sigma x_i^2 - \lambda & \Sigma x_i y_i \\ \Sigma x_i y_i & \Sigma y_i^2 - \lambda \end{vmatrix} = 0 \qquad \textbf{8.3.19}$$

In this simple case the expanded determinant is a quadratic expression in λ, and the smaller root λ_1 is given by:

$$\lambda_1 = \tfrac{1}{2}\left[(\Sigma x_i^2 + \Sigma y_i^2) - \sqrt{(\Sigma x_i^2 - \Sigma y_i^2)^2 + 4(\Sigma x_i y_i)^2}\right] \qquad \textbf{8.3.20}$$

Alternatively, equation 8.3.19 can be expressed as the mathematical problem of finding values of the scalar λ, which satisfy:

$$\mathbf{AX} = \lambda\mathbf{X} \qquad \textbf{8.3.21}$$
$$\text{or } \mathbf{AX} - \lambda\mathbf{X} = \mathbf{0} \qquad \textbf{8.3.22}$$

where $\mathbf{A}$ = a square matrix
$\mathbf{X} \neq \mathbf{0}$ (a characteristic vector)
λ = a characteristic root

We then write:

$$(\mathbf{A} - \lambda\mathbf{I})\mathbf{X} = 0 \tag{8.3.23}$$

There will be a nonzero solution for **X** only if:

$$|\mathbf{A} - \lambda\mathbf{I} = 0| \tag{8.3.24}$$

Following the simple 2 × 2 illustration,

$$\begin{vmatrix} \alpha_{11} - \lambda & \alpha_{12} \\ \alpha_{21} & \alpha_{22} - \lambda \end{vmatrix} = 0 \tag{8.3.25}$$

from which

$$(a_{11} - \lambda)(a_{22} - \lambda) - (a_{12}\,a_{21}) = 0 \tag{8.3.26}$$

or

$$\lambda^2 - (a_{11} + a_{22})\lambda + a_{11}a_{22} - a_{12}a_{21} = 0 \tag{8.3.27}$$

and the roots are:

$$\begin{aligned} \lambda_1 &= \tfrac{1}{2}[(a_{11} + a_{22}) + \sqrt{(a_{11} + a_{22})^2 - 4(a_{11}a_{22} - a_{12}a_{21})}] \\ \lambda_2 &= \tfrac{1}{2}[(a_{11} + a_{22}) - \sqrt{(a_{11} + a_{22})^2 - 4(a_{11}a_{22} - a_{12}a_{21})}] \end{aligned} \tag{8.3.28}$$

In the case of a symmetric matrix, as in regression analysis $\alpha_{12} = \alpha_{21}$, we have the following results:

$$\begin{aligned} \lambda_1 &= \tfrac{1}{2}[(a_{11} + a_{22}) + \sqrt{(a_{11} - a_{22})^2 + 4a_{12}^2}] \\ \lambda_2 &= \tfrac{1}{2}[(a_{11} + a_{22}) - \sqrt{(a_{11} - a_{22})^2 + 4a_{12}^2}] \end{aligned} \tag{8.3.29}$$

Note that since what we have under the square root sign is the sum of two squared quantities, the roots λ_1 and λ_2 are real in the symmetric case. Of course the computation work in a multiple regression (no longer the simple 2 × 2 case) will be quite overwhelming.

It is convenient to approach the problem of orthogonal regression from an alternative route, the route of geometry. Let us denote as in Figure 8-3 the vertical deviation by U_i, as before, the horizontal deviation by U_i', and the perpendicular deviation by $\tilde{U}_i$. The area of a triangle is equal to one half the base times the altitude. Considering the triangle with sides U_i, U_i', and H, we can obtain the following results:

$$\begin{aligned} \tfrac{1}{2}(U_i'U_i) &= \text{area of the triangle} \\ &= \tfrac{1}{2}(H\tilde{U}_i) \end{aligned} \tag{8.3.30}$$

Therefore,

$$\tfrac{1}{2}(H\tilde{U}_i) = \tfrac{1}{2}(U_i'U_i) \tag{8.3.31}$$

Multiplying both sides by two,

$$H\tilde{U}_i = U_i'U_i \tag{8.3.32}$$

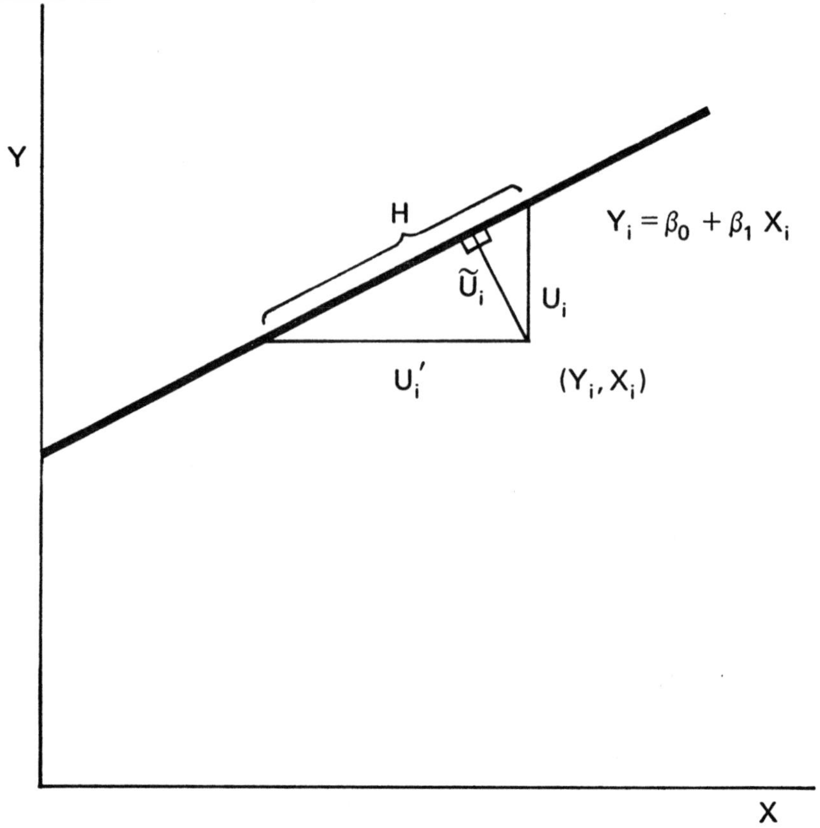

FIGURE 8-3

Orthogonal Regression: A Geometric Exposition

Squaring both sides,

$$H^2\tilde{U}_i^2 = U_i'^2U_i^2 \qquad \textbf{8.3.33}$$

We also know that the sum of the squares of the two sides of a right-angle triangle is equal to the square of the hypotenuse. The triangle under consideration is a right triangle and H is its hypotenuse. Thus we can write:

$$H^2 = U_i^2 + U_i'^2 \qquad \textbf{8.3.34}$$

Therefore,

$$H^2\tilde{U}_i^2 = \tilde{U}_i^2(U_i^2 + U_i'^2) \qquad \textbf{8.3.35}$$

Substituting equation 8.3.35 into equation 8.3.33,

$$\tilde{U}_i^2(U_i^2 + U_i'^2) = U_i^2U_i'^2 \qquad \textbf{8.3.36}$$

β_1 is the slope of the regression line, and:

$$\beta_1 = \frac{U_i}{U'_i} \tag{8.3.37}$$

Therefore,

$$\beta_1^2 = \frac{U_i^2}{U_i'^2} \tag{8.3.38}$$

or,

$$U_i'^2 = \frac{1}{\beta_1^2}\, U_i^2 \tag{8.3.39}$$

Substituting equation 8.3.39 into equation 8.3.36,

$$\tilde{U}_i^2\left(U_i^2 + \frac{U_i^2}{\beta_1^2}\right) = U_i^2\,\frac{U_i^2}{\beta_1^2} \tag{8.3.40}$$

It follows that:

$$\tilde{U}_i^2 U_i^2 + \tilde{U}_i^2\,\frac{U_i^2}{\beta_1^2} = \frac{U_i^2 U_i^2}{\beta_1^2} \tag{8.3.41}$$

Multiplying both sides by β_1^2/U_i^2, we have:

$$\tilde{U}_i^2 U_i^2\,\frac{\beta_1^2}{U_i^2} + \tilde{U}_i^2 = U_i^2 \tag{8.3.42}$$

or,

$$\tilde{U}_i^2\beta_1^2 + \tilde{U}_i^2 = U_i^2 \tag{8.3.43}$$

or,

$$\tilde{U}_i^2(\beta_1^2 + 1) = U_i^2 \tag{8.3.44}$$

or,

$$\tilde{U}_i^2 = \frac{U_i^2}{\beta_1^2 + 1} \tag{8.3.45}$$

Note that U_i is the usual vertical deviation in the OLS regression model, and that:

$$U_i^2 = (Y_i - \beta_0 - \beta_1 X_i)^2$$

Thus if we wish to minimize the orthogonal deviations, the task is to minimize the following expression:

$$\Sigma\tilde{U}_i^2 = \frac{\Sigma(Y_i - \beta_0 - \beta_1 X_i)^2}{1 + \beta_1^2} \tag{8.3.46}$$

The above expression to be minimized is a function of the two parameters β_0 and β_1, and we differentiate $\Sigma\tilde{U}_i^2$ with respect to β_0 and β_1 respectively.

We can rewrite the variables in terms of deviations from their respective means and write:

$$\Sigma \tilde{U}_i^2 = \frac{\Sigma(y_i - \beta_1 x_i)^2}{1 + \beta_1^2} \tag{8.3.47}$$

Differentiating with respect to β_1,

$$\begin{aligned} \frac{\partial \Sigma \tilde{U}_i^2}{\partial \beta_1} &= \frac{\Sigma 2(y_i - \beta_1 x_i)(-x_i)}{1 + \beta_1^2} - \frac{\Sigma(y_i - \beta_1 x_i)^2(2\beta_1)}{(1 + \beta_1^2)^2} \\ &= \frac{\Sigma 2(y_i - \beta_1 x_i)(-x_i)}{1 + \beta_1^2} - \frac{\Sigma 2(y_i^2 - 2\beta_1 x_i y_i + \beta_1^2 x_i^2)\beta_1}{(1 + \beta_1^2)^2} \end{aligned} \tag{8.3.48}$$

Multiplying by $\frac{(1 + \beta_1^2)}{2}$ and setting it equal to zero,

$$(-\Sigma x_i y_i + \beta_1 \Sigma x_i^2) - \frac{(\beta_1 \Sigma y_i^2 - 2\beta_1^2 \Sigma x_i y_i + \beta_1^3 \Sigma x_i^2)}{1 + \beta_1^2} = 0 \tag{8.3.49}$$

Multiplying by $(1 + \beta_1^2)$,

$$\begin{aligned} (-\Sigma x_i y_i + \beta_1 \Sigma x_1^2) + \beta_1^2(-\Sigma x_i y_i + \beta_1 \Sigma x_i^2) - \beta_1 \Sigma y_i^2 \\ + 2\beta_1^2 \Sigma x_i y_i - \beta_1^3 \Sigma x_i^2 = 0 \end{aligned} \tag{8.3.50}$$

Rearranging,

$$\begin{aligned} -\Sigma x_i y_i + \beta_1 \Sigma x_i^2 - \beta_1^2 \Sigma x_i y_i + \beta_1^3 \Sigma x_i^2 - \beta_1 \Sigma y_i^2 \\ + 2\beta_1^2 \Sigma x_i y_i - \beta_1^3 \Sigma x_i^2 = 0 \end{aligned} \tag{8.3.51}$$

or,

$$\beta_1^2 \Sigma x_i y_i + \beta_1(\Sigma x_i^2 - \Sigma y_i^2) - \Sigma x_i y_i = 0 \tag{8.3.52}$$

from which:

$$\beta_1 = \frac{(-\Sigma x_i^2 + \Sigma y_i^2) \pm \sqrt{[(\Sigma x_i^2) - (\Sigma y_i^2)]^2 + 4(\Sigma x_i y_i)^2}}{2(\Sigma x_i y_i)} \tag{8.3.53}$$

Obviously, β_1 has two solutions. We wish to minimize equation 8.3.47, and the condition for minimization is satisfied when the second derivative of equation 8.3.47 with respect to β_1 is positive. Thus we shall take the solution of β_1 that meets this condition.

We then obtain β_0 by differentiating $\Sigma \tilde{U}_i^2$ in equation 8.3.46 with respect to β_0:

$$\frac{\partial \Sigma \tilde{U}_i^2}{\partial \beta_0} = \frac{1}{1 + \beta_1^2} [-2\Sigma(Y_i - \beta_0 - \beta_1 X_i)] \tag{8.3.54}$$

By setting the right-hand expression equal to zero and rearranging, we obtain the appropriate result.

8.4 PRINCIPAL COMPONENT ANALYSIS

Principal component analysis is a method that permits a group of variables to be expressed by a set of orthogonal components.[8] Suppose that K predetermined variables appearing in the given equation are linearly dependent and thus severely collinear, or that the number of variables under consideration is greater than the number of observations. Principal component analysis provides a technique by which the set of K observed variables can be expressed as a linear combination of a smaller set of M principal components which are linearly independent. These principal components are not observable in general. Principal component analysis yields information on these component variables. Indeed they turn out to be the characteristic vectors of the covariance matrix of the regressors. Given K independent observed variables, there will be K such components. The observed variables are then redefined in terms of the linear combination of these components designated as principal components. The first M principal components are calculated as those that explain the greatest part of the variation in the sample observations, while the variation explained by other remaining components, $M + 1, M + 2, \ldots, K$, is negligible. Principal component analysis then replaces the set of observations on the original variables by a linear combination of the first M principal components. "In effect, transforming the original vector variable to the vector of principal components amounts to a rotation of coordinate axes to a new coordinate system that has inherent statistical properties."[9]

We begin by defining a set of linear combinations of the regressor variables $X_i (i = 1, 2, \ldots, K)$ with a particular condition on the coefficients of the X_i's.[10]

$$P_i = \sum_{i=1}^{K} f_i X_i \qquad i = 1, 2, \ldots K \qquad \textbf{8.4.1}$$

and

$$\sum_{i=1}^{K} f_i^2 = 1 \qquad \textbf{8.4.2}$$

The first principal component P_1 is then defined as that P for which the variance is a maximum. The variance of P is:

---

[8] H. Hotelling, "Analysis of a Complex of Statistical Variables into Principal Components," *Journal of Educational Psychology*, Vol. 24 (1933), pp. 417-441. M. A. Girshick, "Principal Components," *Journal of the American Statistical Association*, Vol. 31 (1936), pp. 519-528. W. F. Massy, "Principal Components Regression in Explanatory Statistical Research," *Journal of the American Statistical Association*, Vol. 60, No. 309 (March, 1965), pp. 234-256. G. Tintner, *Econometrics* (New York: John Wiley & Sons, 1952), pp. 102-114. T. W. Anderson, *An Introduction to Multivariate Statistical Analysis* (New York: John Wiley & Sons, 1958). P. J. Dhrymes, *Econometrics: Statistical Foundations and Applications* (New York: Harper & Row, Publishers, 1970).

[9] T. W. Anderson, *An Introduction to Multivariate Statistical Analysis* (New York: John Wiley & Sons, 1958), p. 272.

[10] The index i goes from $1, 2, \ldots K$ and refers to the X's, not to the number of observations on each X_i. To appreciate the restriction in equation 8.4.2, review the previous section on orthogonal regression.

$$\text{var}(P_i) = \sum_{i=1}^{K} f_i^2 \text{ var}(X_i) + \sum_{j=1}^{K} \sum_{i=1}^{K} f_i f_j \text{ cov}(X_i X_j) \qquad 8.4.3$$

$$i, j = 1, 2, \ldots, K, \text{ when } i \neq j$$

To maximize var (P) subject to constraint 8.4.2, we write the expression to be maximized as a Lagrangian:

$$\mathcal{L} = \sum_{j=1}^{K} f_i^2 \text{ var}(X_i) + \sum_{j=1}^{K} \sum_{i=1}^{K} f_i f_j \text{ cov}(X_i X_j) - \lambda \left(\sum_{i=1}^{K} f_i^2 - 1 \right) \qquad 8.4.4$$

where λ is the Lagrange multiplier. Differentiating equation 8.4.4 with respect to each of the f_i's and setting them equal to zero, we obtain:

$$2f_1 (\text{var } X_1 - \lambda) + 2 \sum_{\substack{j \\ j \neq 1}}^{K} f_j \text{ cov } (X_1 X_j) = 0$$

$$2f_2 (\text{var } X_2 - \lambda) + 2 \sum_{\substack{j \\ j \neq 2}}^{K} f_j \text{ cov } (X_2 X_j) = 0 \qquad 8.4.5$$

$$\vdots$$

$$2f_K (\text{var } X_K - \lambda) + 2 \sum_{\substack{j \\ j \neq K}}^{K} f_j \text{ cov } (X_K X_j) = 0$$

For the case $i = 1, 2, 3$, these equations can be written as:

$$2f_1 (\text{var } X_1 - \lambda) + 2f_2 \text{ cov } (X_1 X_2) + 2f_3 \text{ cov } (X_1 X_3) = 0$$

$$2f_1 \text{ cov } (X_1 X_2) + 2f_2 (\text{var } X_2 - \lambda) + 2f_3 \text{ cov } (X_2 X_3) = 0 \qquad 8.4.6$$

$$2f_1 \text{ cov } (X_1 X_3) + 2f_2 \text{ cov } (X_2 X_3) + 2f_3 (\text{var } X_3 - \lambda) = 0$$

from which:

$$f_1 (\text{var } X_1) + f_2 (\text{cov } X_1 X_2) + f_3 \text{ cov } (X_1 X_3) = \lambda f_1$$

$$f_1 (\text{cov } X_1 X_2) + f_2 (\text{var } X_2) + f_3 (\text{cov } X_2 X_3) = \lambda f_2 \qquad 8.4.7$$

$$f_1 (\text{cov } X_1 X_3) + f_2 (\text{cov } X_2 X_3) + f_3 (\text{var } X_3) = \lambda f_3$$

In matrix notation,

$$(\mathbf{V} - \lambda \mathbf{I}) \, \mathbf{f} = \mathbf{0} \qquad 8.4.8$$

where $\mathbf{V}$ is the variance-covariance matrix of X_i, and $\mathbf{f}$ is the vector of coefficients f_i.

$$\begin{bmatrix} \text{var } X_1 & \text{cov } X_1X_2 & \text{cov } X_1X_3 \\ \text{cov } X_1X_2 & \text{var } X_2 & \text{cov } X_2X_3 \\ \text{cov } X_1X_3 & \text{cov } X_2X_3 & \text{var } X_3 \end{bmatrix} \begin{bmatrix} f_1 \\ f_2 \\ f_3 \end{bmatrix} = \lambda \begin{bmatrix} f_1 \\ f_2 \\ f_3 \end{bmatrix} \qquad \textbf{8.4.9}$$

To solve the linear homogeneous system 8.4.8, we observe that the system can have a nonzero solution only if its determinant:

$$|\mathbf{V} - \lambda \mathbf{I}| = 0 \qquad \textbf{8.4.10}$$

The expansion of this determinant will be a polynomial of degree K(= rank of **V**), and it will have three roots, λ_1, λ_2, and λ_3 in this case. Let these be $\lambda_1 > \lambda_2 > \lambda_3$. Replacing λ by λ_1, the largest root, one determines the first principal component P_1 by solving the linear homogeneous system for f_1, f_2, and f_3 and using these values as coefficients in a linear combination of the variables X_1, X_2, and X_3.

The principal components can be obtained from the original observations on the X_i's or from the corresponding standardized variables z_i, where:

$$z_{it} = \frac{(X_{it} - \bar{X}_i)}{s_{X_i}}$$

and $\bar{X}_i$ = the mean of all t observations on the ith X, $t = 1, 2, \ldots T$ for each X_i, and s_{X_i} = standard deviation of the sample observations on X_i. This transformation produces a new set of variables z_i with the individual observation z_{it}. The two results that express the principal components in terms of observations directly or in terms of standardized variable values will not be the same. The discussion will continue in terms of the standardized variables, since these standardized variables are all independent of the original units of measurement. Recall that the standardized variable z_i has an approximate normal distribution with zero mean and unit variance. The mechanics of the principal component analysis are outlined for the case of four explanatory variables in what follows.

Suppose we have X_1, X_2, X_3, and X_4, the sets of observations on the variables, and z_1, z_2, z_3, and z_4, the corresponding standardized variables. We have a set of principal components that explains most of the observed variations in the z_i's. Replacing each set of observations on the variables X_i with the corresponding values of a set of observations on the standardized normal variable z_i, we note that:

$$\text{var }(z_i) = r_{ii} = 1 \qquad \textbf{8.4.11}$$

and $$\text{cov }(z_iz_j) = r_{ij} = \text{cov }(z_jz_i) = r_{ji}$$

Then by appropriate manipulations we obtain:

$$\begin{bmatrix} r_{11} & r_{12} & r_{13} & r_{14} \\ r_{21} & r_{22} & r_{23} & r_{24} \\ r_{31} & r_{32} & r_{33} & r_{34} \\ r_{41} & r_{42} & r_{43} & r_{44} \end{bmatrix} \begin{bmatrix} f_1 \\ f_2 \\ f_3 \\ f_4 \end{bmatrix} = \lambda \begin{bmatrix} f_1 \\ f_2 \\ f_3 \\ f_4 \end{bmatrix} \qquad \textbf{8.4.12}$$

or

$$(\mathbf{R} - \lambda \mathbf{I})\, f = 0 \qquad \textbf{8.4.13}$$

At the next step the system of linear homogeneous equations can be solved. The condition for this system to have a solution is that the determinant below is zero:

$$|\mathbf{R} - \lambda \mathbf{I}| = 0 \qquad \textbf{8.4.14}$$

or,

$$\begin{vmatrix} 1-\lambda & r_{12} & r_{13} & r_{14} \\ r_{12} & 1-\lambda & r_{23} & r_{24} \\ r_{13} & r_{23} & 1-\lambda & r_{34} \\ r_{14} & r_{24} & r_{34} & 1-\lambda \end{vmatrix} = 0 \qquad \textbf{8.4.15}$$

The largest root of equation 8.4.14, λ_1, is determined as in equation 8.4.10. Next, the four homogeneous linear equations in equation 8.4.13 can be solved for f_i, obtaining P_1, the first principal component.

$$P_1 = f_1 z_1 + f_2 z_2 + f_3 z_3 + f_4 z_4 \qquad \textbf{8.4.16}$$

It is possible to write each P_i as a linear expression of the z_i's and then return to the original equation to explain variations in the given dependent variable, say Y_i, in terms of the P_i's instead of the z_i's, or X_i's if the X_i's are the explanatory variables in the model. Note that one can continue the complicated mechanics to find λ_2, λ_3, λ_4 and P_2, P_3, P_4. It turns out that the first several principal components explain most of the variances of the z_i's, and it is generally not necessary to determine all four principal components.

However, there remains the problem of giving economic interpretation to the M principal components that account for most of the variances in the observed samples on the K variables. It is, of course, computationally helpful, as noted before, if M is smaller than K; but then there is still the problem of how M such principal components can be uniquely described in terms of observed economic variables. Should the ith principal component be uniquely correlated with a given observed variable, it is usual to describe that component in terms of the correlated observed variable.

Consider Table 8-12 as the correlation matrix in a given hypothetical situation.

Table 8-12

Correlation Matrix of a Hypothetical Case

	P_1	P_2	P_3	P_4	X_1	X_2	X_3	X_4
P_1	1	0	0	0	0.96	0.02	0.01	0.01
P_2	0	1	0	0	0.15	0.86	0.03	0.01
P_3	0	0	1	0	0.01	0.05	0.02	0.90
P_4	0	0	0	1	0.05	0.04	0.86	0.02

From the table one can conclude that P_1 relates to X_1, P_2 to X_2, P_3 to X_4, and P_4 to X_3, where X_1, X_2, X_3, and X_4 are the four observed variables whose economic description is well defined. But the description in economic terms of the set of principal components is always problematical, since any one of them may have significant correlation with more than one of the observed variables. The researcher then has to use personal judgment to interpret the principal components in terms of the observed economic variables.

DISCUSSION QUESTIONS

1. Discuss the chi-square distribution and the F distribution.
2. Review the analysis of variance model and define the fundamental identity.
3. Show the relationship between the analysis of variance model and the regression model.
4. Covariance analysis permits the analysis of the relationship between certain interdependent variables while testing whether other variables (which may be nonquantifiable) affect the relationship under investigation. Examine the above statement using the analysis of covariance table.
5. (a) Define orthogonal regression.
   (b) Compare the normal equations of the OLS model with equations 8.3.13.
   (c) Review the geometric exposition of the orthogonal regression.
6. (a) Analyze the mechanics of obtaining principal components from a set of observed variables. Are these derived components mutually orthogonal?
   (b) Evaluate the case for obtaining principal components from the corresponding standardized variables instead of from the original observations.
   (c) Interpret the principal components in terms of the observed variables whose economic interpretations are known a priori.

SUGGESTED READINGS

Anderson, R. L., and T. A. Bancroft. *Statistical Theory in Research.* New York: McGraw-Hill Book Co., 1952.

Anderson, T. W. *An Introduction to Multivariate Statistical Analysis*. New York: John Wiley & Sons, 1958.

Adams, F. Gerard. "Consumer Attitudes, Buying Plans and Purchase of Durable Goods: A Principal Component Analysis." *Review of Economics and Statistics*, Vol. 46, No. 4 (1964), pp. 347-355.

Dhrymes, Phoebus J. "On the Measurement of Price and Quality Changes in Some Capital Goods." Discussion Paper No. 67, Economic Research Unit. Philadelphia: University of Pennsylvania, 1967.

Freund, John E. *Modern Elementary Statistics*, 3d ed. Englewood Cliffs, New Jersey: Prentice-Hall, 1967.

Girshick, M. A. "Principal Components." *Journal of the American Statistical Association*, Vol. 31 (1936), pp. 519-528.

Hoel, P. G. *Elementary Statistics*, 2d ed. New York: John Wiley & Sons, 1966.

Hotelling, H. "Analysis of a Complex of Statistical Variables into Principal Components." *Journal of Educational Psychology*, Vol. 24 (1933), pp. 417-441.

Kendall, M. G. *A Course in Multivariate Analysis*. New York: Hafner Publishing Co., 1957.

Klein, Lawrence R. *A Textbook of Econometrics*. Evanston, Illinois: Row, Peterson & Co., 1956.

Malinvaud, E. *Statistical Methods of Econometrics*. Amsterdam: North-Holland Publishing Co., 1966.

Massy, W. F. "Principal Components Regression in Exploratory Statistical Research." *Journal of the American Statistical Association*, Vol. 60, No. 309 (March, 1965), pp. 234-256.

Scheffé, H. *The Analysis of Variance*. New York: John Wiley & Sons, 1959.

Tintner, Gerhard. *Econometrics*. New York: John Wiley & Sons, 1952.

9

instrumental variables

9.0 THE CASE FOR AN INSTRUMENTAL VARIABLE

Ever since Keynes emphasized the importance of the concept of marginal propensity to consume, econometricians have been very concerned with estimating this parameter. The following is the Keynesian model in its simplest form:

$$\begin{aligned} C_t &= \alpha + \beta Y_t \\ Y_t &= C_t + I_t \qquad t = 1, 2, \ldots, T \end{aligned} \qquad \textbf{9.0.1}$$

where C = consumption
I = investment
Y = income

In this model investment I is exogenously determined. This model has only one behavioral equation explaining the consumption pattern of the economy. The equation $C + I = Y$ may be considered an accounting identity, which does not express any hypothesis on economic behavior, but indicates only that the variable Y is calculated as the sum of C and I as an equilibrium condition.

To estimate the parameters α and β in equations 9.0.1, the stochastic equation corresponding to the consumption function is written as follows:

$$C_t = \alpha + \beta Y_t + U_t \qquad \textbf{9.0.2}$$

Using the OLS method of estimation, we obtain:[1]

$$\hat{\beta} = \frac{\Sigma c_t y_t}{\Sigma y_t^2} \qquad \textbf{9.0.3}$$

Note that the estimator $\hat{\beta}$ from equation 9.0.3 is biased and inconsistent in this case. Recall that one of the basic assumptions of the OLS method is that the regressor (Y in this case) should be a truly exogenous variable, so that

[1] The lowercase letters denote deviations from the means, e.g., $c_t = C_t - \bar{C}$, $y_t = Y_t - \bar{Y}$, and $i_t = I_t - \bar{I}$.

$E(YU) = 0$. The direction of causality is then assumed to go from Y to C, without C having any effect on Y. Another way of stating this assumption, as noted on page 42, is to say that the covariance between the regressor and the error term is zero; that is, $\text{cov}(YU) = 0$. According to the present model 9.0.1, the variable I is exogenously determined; and thus the assumption $\text{cov}(IU) = 0$ holds. But $\text{cov}(YU) \neq 0$, since Y is an endogenous variable and jointly determined with C by the two equations of the basic model.

Let us further examine the fact that the OLS estimate $\hat{\beta}$ in equation 9.0.3 is biased and inconsistent. In terms of mean deviations, the model can be written as:

$$c_t = \beta y_t + u_t \tag{9.0.4}$$

Multiplying by y_t and summing over all t,

$$\Sigma c_t y_t = \beta \Sigma y_t^2 + \Sigma y_t u_t$$

Dividing through by Σy_t^2, we have:

$$\frac{\Sigma y_t c_t}{\Sigma y_t^2} = \beta + \frac{\Sigma y_t u_t}{\Sigma y_t^2} \tag{9.0.5}$$

Notice that the left-hand expression is the OLS estimate $\hat{\beta}$. So we write:

$$\hat{\beta} = \beta + \frac{\Sigma y_t u_t}{\Sigma y_t^2} \tag{9.0.6}$$

Taking expected value,

$$E(\hat{\beta}) = \beta + E\left(\frac{\Sigma y_t u_t}{\Sigma y_t^2}\right) \tag{9.0.7}$$

It is interesting to note that in the context of the present model,

$$y_t / \Sigma y_t^2 = W_t$$

a concept introduced in Chapter 2. We can then write:

$$E(\hat{\beta}) = \beta + E(\Sigma u_t W_t) \tag{9.0.8}$$

When the assumption that the regressor is a fixed mathematical variable and as such is uncorrelated with the disturbance term is valid, we can write:

$$E(\Sigma u_t W_t) = \Sigma W_t \, E(u_t) = 0$$

since $E(u_t) = 0$. In the present model the regressor y_t and the regressand c_t are jointly determined endogenous variables. The variable c_t is not independent of u_t, so y_t is not independent of u_t. Hence the above result cannot be obtained. Therefore, $E(\hat{\beta}) \neq \beta$ and $\hat{\beta}$ is biased.

To examine the property of consistency, we take the probability limit. Using equation 9.0.6,

$$\text{plim}(\hat{\beta}) = \beta + \text{plim}\left(\frac{\Sigma y_t u_t}{\Sigma y_t^2}\right) \tag{9.0.9}$$

or,

$$\text{plim}(\hat{\beta}) = \beta + \frac{\text{plim}(\Sigma y_t u_t)/T}{\text{plim}(\Sigma y_t^2)/T} \tag{9.0.10}$$

We know that $\text{plim}(\Sigma y_t u_t)/T$ is the population covariance between y_t and u_t, and that $\text{plim}\Sigma y_t^2/T$ is the population variance of y_t. We assume that this variance exists and is finite and nonzero. The covariance between y_t and u_t cannot be assumed to be zero in this case, since y_t is a jointly determined endogenous variable. If it were a truly exogenous variable, uncorrelated with the disturbance term, the covariance term could be assumed to be zero. Thus, with a zero term in the numerator and a finite, nonzero term in the denominator, the expression would be zero, giving $\text{plim}(\hat{\beta}) = \beta$. We have also seen (Chapter 7) that in an autoregressive model where the regressor is contemporaneously uncorrelated with the disturbance term, the assumption of zero covariance in the limit (asymptotically) is valid. But in the present case when the regressor is a jointly determined endogenous variable, such an assumption is untenable. Hence we cannot write $\text{plim}(\hat{\beta}) = \beta$ and the OLS estimate $\hat{\beta}$ is seen to be inconsistent.

If we are working with a single equation describing consumption functionally dependent on income, it is possible to satisfy the assumption on the exogenous character of Y by assertion. The problem becomes difficult when the complete set of equations describing the given model is taken into consideration. Indeed even in the single-equation case the portion of income dollars spent on consumption is quite substantial, and there is reason to believe that the expenditure on total consumption has impact on the total income level for an entire economy.

If we manipulate both relations of the model, we can get the following results. Using the identity $C + I = Y$,

$$\begin{aligned} C_t &= \alpha + \beta(C_t + I_t) + U_t \\ &= \alpha + \beta C_t + \beta I_t + U_t \\ &= \frac{\alpha}{1-\beta} + \frac{\beta}{1-\beta} I_t + \frac{1}{1-\beta} U_t \end{aligned}$$

or,

$$C_t = \beta_0 + \beta_1 I_t + U_t^* \tag{9.0.11}$$

where

$$\beta_0 = \frac{\alpha}{1 - \beta} \qquad \beta_1 = \frac{\beta}{1 - \beta}$$

and

$$U_t^* = \frac{1}{1 - \beta} U_t \tag{9.0.12}$$

The OLS estimator of β_1 in equation 9.0.11 is:

$$\hat{\beta}_1 = \frac{\Sigma c_t i_t}{\Sigma i_t^2} \tag{9.0.13}$$

Following the arguments just presented, it can be shown that $\hat{\beta}_1$ is unbiased and consistent, since I_t is an exogenous variable and uncorrelated with the disturbance term. Similarly the OLS estimator of β_0 is:

$$\hat{\beta}_0 = \bar{C} - \hat{\beta}_1 \bar{I} \tag{9.0.14}$$

The consistent estimates of α and β in equation 9.0.2 can then be calculated by using equation 9.0.12, and these estimates are unbiased and consistent:

$$\beta = \beta_1(1 - \beta)$$

$$\beta = \beta_1 - \beta_1\beta$$

$$\beta + \beta_1\beta = \beta_1$$

$$\beta(1 + \beta_1) = \beta_1$$

from which:

$$\hat{\beta} = \frac{\hat{\beta}_1}{1 + \hat{\beta}_1} \tag{9.0.15}$$

Using equations 9.0.12 and 9.0.15,

$$\hat{\alpha} = \hat{\beta}_0(1 - \hat{\beta})$$

$$= \hat{\beta}_0\left(1 - \frac{\hat{\beta}_1}{1 + \hat{\beta}_1}\right) \tag{9.0.16}$$

9.1 THE METHOD OF INSTRUMENTAL VARIABLES

The estimate $\hat{\beta}$ from equation 9.0.3 has been shown to be inconsistent; $\hat{\beta}$ from equations 9.0.15 is seen to be the consistent estimate of β in equation 9.0.2. We need a method of estimation that will yield this estimator directly. The method developed to deal with this situation is the *method of instrumental variables*.[2] The first step in using this method is to choose an instrumental

[2] O. Reiersol, "Confluence Analysis by Means of Instrumental Sets of Variables," *Arkiv fur Matematik*, Vol. 32 (1945). O. Reiersol, "Confluence Analysis by means of Lag Moments and Other Methods of Confluence Analysis," *Econometrica*, Vol. 9, No. 1 (January, 1941), pp. 1-23. R. C. Geary, "Determination of Linear Relations Between Systematic Parts of Variables with Errors of Observation the Variance of Which are Unknown," *Econometrica*, Vol. 17, (1949), pp. 38-58. Stefan Valavanis, *Econometrics* (New York: McGraw-Hill Book Co., 1959), pp. 110-117.

variable uncorrelated with the disturbance U. In model 9.0.1 we can use I_t as the instrumental variable in obtaining the consistent estimator of the true parameter of marginal propensity to consume. Notice that by definition I_t is an exogenous variable; it is given independently and not determined by the equations of the model. It has impact on both C_t and Y_t, the variables in the consumption equation, through the identity $I = Y - C$, even though it does not enter directly into the consumption function as specified.

The marginal propensity to consume with respect to income is the coefficient β. It can be directly estimated, and the estimator β^* from the method of instrumental variables is obtained as:

$$\hat{\beta}^* = \frac{\Sigma c_t i_t}{\Sigma y_t i_t} \qquad \textbf{9.1.1}$$

The instrumental variable estimate $\hat{\beta}^*$ is consistent. From equation 9.0.4,

$$c_t = \beta y_t + u_t$$

Multiplying by i_t and summing over all t,

$$\Sigma i_t c_t = \beta \Sigma i_t y_t + \Sigma i_t u_t \qquad \textbf{9.1.2}$$

Dividing through by $\Sigma i_t y_t$,

$$\frac{\Sigma i_t c_t}{\Sigma i_t y_t} = \beta + \frac{\Sigma i_t u_t}{\Sigma i_t y_t} \qquad \textbf{9.1.3}$$

The left hand expression is the instrumental variable estimate $\hat{\beta}^*$ in equation 9.1.1. Taking plim,

$$\begin{aligned} \text{plim}(\hat{\beta}^*) &= \beta + \text{plim}\left(\frac{\Sigma i_t u_t}{\Sigma i_t y_t}\right) \\ &= \beta + \frac{\text{plim}(\Sigma i_t u_t)/T}{\text{plim}(\Sigma i_t y_t)/T} \qquad \textbf{9.1.4} \\ &= \beta \end{aligned}$$

We know that $\text{plim}(\Sigma i_t u_t)/T$ and $\text{plim}(\Sigma i_t y_t)/T$ are consistent estimates of population $\text{cov}(i_t u_t)$ and $\text{cov}(i_t y_t)$ respectively. $\text{Cov}(i_t u_t)$ is zero since i_t is an exogenous variable and uncorrelated with u_t. $\text{Cov}(i_t y_t)$ is finite and nonzero since the instrumental variable I_t is so chosen. Therefore, the instrumental variable estimate is consistent.

Note that if we take the expected value, we obtain:

$$E(\hat{\beta}^*) = \beta + E\left(\frac{\Sigma i_t u_t}{\Sigma i_t y_t}\right) \qquad \textbf{9.1.5}$$

We cannot now write:

$$E\left(\frac{\Sigma i_t u_t}{\Sigma i_t y_t}\right) = \frac{\Sigma i_t}{\Sigma i_t y_t} E(u_t) = 0$$

even if by assumption $E(u_t) = 0$. In the OLS regression situation, the corresponding expression is $(\Sigma i_t / \Sigma i_t^2)E(u_t)$. We can write the expression separating $E(u_t)$ only when the regressor I_t is strictly a fixed mathematical variable as explained before. In the present case the term y_t appears in the expression, and this is known to be a jointly determined endogenous variable. We cannot therefore prove directly that the instrumental variable estimate $\hat{\beta}^*$ is unbiased.

The rationale of the instrumental variable method can, however, be analyzed in a straightforward way. Given model 9.0.1 and the consumption function 9.0.2, suppose we regress C_t on I_t and Y_t on I_t. In the simple linear form,

$$C_t = f_1 + f_2 I_t + V_t \qquad \textbf{9.1.6}$$

and

$$Y_t = g_1 + g_2 I_t + W_t \qquad \textbf{9.1.7}$$

where V_t and W_t are the disturbance terms subject to the usual assumptions.

We then obtain:

$$\frac{dC}{dI} = f_2 \text{ or } dC = f_2 dI \qquad \textbf{9.1.8}$$

and

$$\frac{dY}{dI} = g_2 \text{ or } dY = g_2 dI \qquad \textbf{9.1.9}$$

It is then easy to see that a marginal change in the chosen instrument I, dI, should cause simultaneous marginal changes in both C and Y, and these changes are denoted by dC and dY respectively.

We can write:

$$\frac{dC}{dY} = \frac{f_2 dI}{g_2 dI} = \frac{f_2}{g_2} = \beta^* \qquad \textbf{9.1.10}$$

Now let us obtain the OLS estimates of f_2 and g_2. Given the two linear functions 9.1.6 and 9.1.7, the estimates are:

$$\hat{f}_2 = \frac{\Sigma c_t i_t}{\Sigma i_t^2} \qquad \textbf{9.1.11}$$

$$\hat{g}_2 = \frac{\Sigma y_t i_t}{\Sigma i_t^2} \qquad \textbf{9.1.12}$$

Therefore we can write:

$$\hat{\beta}^* = \frac{\hat{f}_2}{\hat{g}_2} = \frac{\Sigma c_t i_t / \Sigma i_t^2}{\Sigma y_t i_t / \Sigma i_t^2} \tag{9.1.13}$$

or,

$$\hat{\beta}^* = \frac{\Sigma c_t i_t}{\Sigma y_t i_t} \tag{9.1.14}$$

This is the instrumental variable estimator given in equation 9.1.1. It can be shown that the instrumental variable technique gives us the estimator β as in equation 9.0.15.

From equation 9.0.15,

$$\hat{\beta} = \frac{\hat{\beta}_1}{1 + \hat{\beta}_1}$$

By inspection $\hat{\beta}_1 = \hat{f}_2$, as defined in equations 9.0.13 and 9.1.11 respectively.

Rewriting $Y = C + I$ and substituting for Y in the expression for $\hat{g}_2$ in equation 9.1.12, we have:

$$\hat{g}_2 = \frac{\Sigma(Y_t - \bar{Y})(I_t - \bar{I})}{\Sigma(I_t - \bar{I})^2} = \frac{\Sigma(C_t + I_t - \bar{C} - \bar{I})(I_t - \bar{I})}{\Sigma(I_t - \bar{I})^2}$$

$$= \frac{\Sigma(C_t - \bar{C})(I_t - \bar{I}) + \Sigma(I_t - \bar{I})(I_t - \bar{I})}{\Sigma(I_t - \bar{I})^2} \tag{9.1.15}$$

$$= \hat{\beta}_1 + 1$$

Then,

$$\hat{\beta}^* = \frac{\hat{f}_2}{\hat{g}_2} = \frac{\hat{\beta}_1}{1 + \hat{\beta}_1} \tag{9.1.16}$$

Thus $\hat{\beta}^*$ is an estimate of β which has been shown to be related to $\hat{\beta}_1$ which in turn is unbiased and consistent.

From the mathematical point of view, an important restriction is that $\Sigma y_t i_t$ in equation 9.1.1 is finite and nonzero. In the straightforward OLS estimator 9.0.3 the corresponding expression is Σy_t^2, and there is no reason to suspect that Σy_t^2 can ever be zero. The instrumental variable estimate $\hat{\beta}^*$ has $\Sigma y_t i_t$ in the denominator, and $\Sigma y_t i_t$ can be zero if the instrumental variable chosen has little to do with the variation in the regressor in the original equation.

Conditions for the selection of an instrumental variable can be restated as follows:

1. The instrumental variable should be truly exogenous, and the covariance between the error term and the instrumental variable should be zero; that is, $\text{cov}(IU) = 0$. This compares with the original assumption of the OLS model, where the covariance between the regressor and the error term is assumed to be zero.

2. The instrumental variable should vary substantially enough to have its impact on both the regressor and the regressand. That is, the covariance between the instrumental variable and each of the endogenous variables appearing in the estimating equation should be nonzero and finite. In the present case,

$$\text{cov}(CI) \neq 0$$
$$\text{cov}(YI) \neq 0$$

We can then estimate the intercept of the model as follows:

$$\hat{\alpha}^* = \bar{C} - \hat{\beta}^*\bar{Y} \qquad \textbf{9.1.17}$$

Following the line of argument in Chapter 2, equations 2.4.23 through 2.4.30, we can also calculate variances of the instrumental variable estimates $\hat{\beta}^*$, $\hat{\alpha}^*$.

$$\text{var}(\hat{\beta}^*) = E\{[\hat{\beta}^* - E(\hat{\beta}^*)]^2\} \qquad \textbf{9.1.18}$$

Using equations 9.1.3 and 9.1.5, we can write:

$$\text{var}(\hat{\beta}^*) = E\left[\frac{\Sigma(i_t u_t)^2}{\Sigma(i_t y_t)^2}\right] \qquad \textbf{9.1.19}$$

From which:[3]

$$\text{var}(\hat{\beta}^*) = \frac{\sigma_u^{*2}\Sigma i_t^2}{(\Sigma i_t y_t)^2} \qquad \textbf{9.1.20}$$

and

$$\text{var}(\hat{\alpha}^*) = \sigma_u^{*2}\left[\frac{1}{T} + \frac{\bar{Y}^2\Sigma i_t^2}{(\Sigma i_t y_t)^2}\right] \qquad \textbf{9.1.21}$$

where σ_u^{*2} is estimated as:

$$S^{*2} = \frac{1}{T-2}\Sigma(C_t - \hat{\alpha}^* - \hat{\beta}^* Y_t)^2 \qquad \textbf{9.1.22}$$

9.2 AN IMPORTANT CASE STUDY

Using annual data for the United States from 1922 to 1941 with variables measured in constant dollars per capita, T. Haavelmo obtained the following results.[4] Let the model be:

---

[3] Goldberger has shown that these are asymptotic variances. They are used as approximations in finite samples. A. S. Goldberger, *Econometric Theory* (New York: John Wiley & Sons, 1964), pp. 285-286.

[4] T. Haavelmo, "Methods of Measuring the Marginal Propensity to Consume," *Studies in Econometric Methods*, edited by W. C. Hood and T. C. Koopmans (New York: John Wiley & Sons, 1953), pp. 75-91.

$$C_t = \alpha + \beta Y_t + U_t$$
$$Y_t = C_t + I_t \qquad \textbf{9.2.1}$$

Using the OLS method as in equation 9.0.3, he calculated that:

$$\hat{\beta} = \frac{\Sigma c_t y_t}{\Sigma y_t^2} = 0.73 \qquad \textbf{9.2.2}$$

Using the instrumental variable method as in equation 9.1.1, he determined that:

$$\hat{\beta}^* = \frac{\Sigma c_t i_t}{\Sigma y_t i_t} = 0.67 \qquad \textbf{9.2.3}$$

Using equation 9.0.13, he also calculated that:

$$\hat{\beta}_1 = \frac{\Sigma c_t i_t}{\Sigma i_t^2} = 2.048 \qquad \textbf{9.2.4}$$

Recall that:

$$\hat{\beta} = \frac{\hat{\beta}_1}{1 + \hat{\beta}_1}$$

Thus

$$\hat{\beta} = \frac{2.048}{1 + 2.048} = \frac{2.048}{3.048} = 0.67 = \hat{\beta}^* \qquad \textbf{9.2.5}$$

Thus $\hat{\beta}^*$ is the consistent estimate of the marginal propensity to consume.

Recalling from equation 9.0.1 that $C + I = Y$, we rewrite:

$$Y - I = C \qquad \textbf{9.2.6}$$

Using equation 9.0.11 for C_t,

$$Y_t - I_t = \frac{\alpha}{1-\beta} + \frac{\beta}{1-\beta} I_t$$
$$Y_t = \frac{\alpha}{1-\beta} + \frac{\beta}{1-\beta} I_t + I_t \qquad \textbf{9.2.7}$$
$$= \frac{\alpha}{1-\beta} + \left(1 + \frac{\beta}{1-\beta}\right) I_t$$

Therefore,

$$Y_t = \frac{\alpha}{1-\beta} + \frac{1}{1-\beta} I_t \qquad \textbf{9.2.8}$$

The quantity $1/1 - \beta$ is the familiar investment multiplier. To make any use of this concept, we first need to obtain a consistent estimate of the marginal propensity to consume. The use of $\hat{\beta}$ from equation 9.0.3 or $\hat{\beta}_1$ from equation 9.0.13 would be wrong. The consistent estimate of $\hat{\beta}$ in equations 9.0.15, which is equal to $\hat{\beta}^*$ in equation 9.1.1, is then very important.

Regressing Y on I, the OLS result obtained from the same data fitted to the equation is:

$$Y_t = \delta_0 + \delta_1 I_t + W_t \qquad \textbf{9.2.9}$$

$$\hat{\delta}_1 = \frac{\Sigma y_t i_t}{\Sigma i_t^2} = 3.048$$

Solving back, using equation 9.2.8,

$$\begin{aligned}
\delta_1 &= \frac{1}{1-\beta} \\
\delta_1(1-\beta) &= 1 \\
\delta_1 - \delta_1\beta &= 1 \\
\delta_1\beta &= \delta_1 - 1 \qquad \textbf{9.2.10} \\
\beta &= \frac{\delta_1}{\delta_1} - \frac{1}{\delta_1} \\
&= 1 - \frac{1}{\delta_1} \\
\beta &= 1 - \frac{1}{3.048} \\
&= 0.67
\end{aligned}$$

This estimation is equal to $\hat{\beta}^* = 0.67$, the result obtained by the instrumental variable method in equation 9.1.1.

9.3 CHOICE OF THE INSTRUMENT IN SPECIFIC CASES

The previous discussion has been carried out in terms of a model based on two simultaneous equations. Model 9.0.1 contains only one exogenous variable and two endogenous variables. The choice of the instrument was then obvious. Two problems arise: (1) In the case where the model contains more than one exogenous variable, the selection of the instrument is not so obvious. (2) In the situation where the model consists of a single equation, but the assumption is violated that the covariance between the regressor and the disturbance term is zero, the use of an instrument, if available, may be helpful; but again the choice is not obvious.

Let us consider the two problems in order. First we can rewrite model 9.0.1 as follows:

$$C = \alpha + \beta Y + U$$
$$Y = C + I + G + F \qquad 9.3.1$$

where G = government expenditure and F = net foreign balance, and all other variables are defined as before. Note that I, G, and F are, by assumption, exogenously determined. C and Y are again endogenous variables jointly determined. We continue to be interested in estimating the parameter β in the consumption function, the marginal propensity to consume. The straightforward application of the OLS method will again yield an inconsistent and biased estimate of β, since $\text{cov}(YU) \neq 0$. Using equation 9.1.1, it has been shown that:

$$\frac{\Sigma c_t i_t}{\Sigma y_t i_t} = \hat{\beta}^*$$

and $\hat{\beta}^*$ is a consistent estimate. Now each of the two other exogenous variables are also equal candidates for the choice of instrumental variable. Indeed we can obtain:

$$\hat{\beta}^* = \frac{\Sigma c_t i_t}{\Sigma y_t i_t} \qquad 9.3.2$$

or,

$$\hat{\beta}^* = \frac{\Sigma c_t g_t}{\Sigma y_t g_t} \qquad 9.3.3$$

or,

$$\hat{\beta}^* = \frac{\Sigma c_t f_t}{\Sigma y_t f_t} \qquad 9.3.4$$

Obviously all three estimates are not going to be the same. There is no easy way of choosing between the three unless we have a priori information that one of the three exogenous variables has a unique claim to be chosen as the instrument.[5] It is logical to consider whether we could use all three of them together as instruments. Such a solution, as we shall see in Chapter 12, is the basis of a method of estimation known as the two-stage least squares regression method (2SLS).

In the case of a single-equation model, the situation is far different. The choice of an instrument is necessarily arbitrary. Consider the model:

$$D_t = \gamma_0 + \gamma_1 P_t + U_t \qquad t = 1, 2, \ldots, T \qquad 9.3.5$$

where D_t = consumption of milk in the school lunch
P_t = price of milk
U_t = disturbance term as before
γ_0 and γ_1 = parameters to be estimated

[5] J. D. Sargan, "The Estimation of Economic Relationships Using Instrumental Variables," *Econometrica*, Vol. 26, No. 3 (July, 1958), pp. 393-415.

The OLS estimator of γ_1 is:

$$\hat{\gamma}_1 = \Sigma dp/\Sigma p^2 = \frac{\Sigma(D_t - \bar{D})(P_t - \bar{P})}{\Sigma(P_t - \bar{P})^2} \qquad \textbf{9.3.6}$$

Assume that cov $(P\ U) \neq 0$. Hence equation 9.3.6 will give a biased and inconsistent estimate of γ_1.

If we know that the expenditures for the consumption of milk are very closely related to a government subsidy plan to provide inexpensive milk for school children, it is possible to use the variable corresponding to the subsidy as an appropriate instrument in this case. Naturally such a subsidy plan will have an impact on the price of milk as well as on the quantity of milk consumed. Hence:

$$\begin{aligned}\hat{\gamma}^* &= \Sigma ds/\Sigma ps \\ &= \frac{\Sigma(D_t - \bar{D})(S_t - \bar{S})}{\Sigma(P_t - \bar{P})(S_t - \bar{S})}\end{aligned} \qquad \textbf{9.3.7}$$

where S is the amount of the subsidy, expressed in comparable units.

Often, however, it is not easy to find an instrument that can be appropriately used for a particular model unless the endogenous and exogenous variables are well defined. If there is a possible choice for an instrumental variable, the method can be used in obtaining consistent estimators for a single equation when the OLS method fails.

9.4 THE METHOD OF INSTRUMENTAL VARIABLES IN MULTIPLE REGRESSION

We have discussed the use of the instrumental variable in a model where the estimating equation is a simple two-variable regression. The following examines its application to equations containing more than two variables. Consider the model:

$$Y = \beta_0 + \beta_1 X_1 + \beta_2 X_2 + U \qquad \textbf{9.4.1}$$

or,

$$\mathbf{Y} = \mathbf{X}\boldsymbol{\beta} + \mathbf{U}$$

The OLS $\hat{\boldsymbol{\beta}} = (\mathbf{X}'\mathbf{X})^{-1}\mathbf{X}'\mathbf{Y}$, where $\mathbf{X} = (X_0, X_1, X_2)$; and $X_{t0} = 1$ for all t.

We then have:

$$\hat{\boldsymbol{\beta}} = \begin{bmatrix} \hat{\beta}_0 \\ \hat{\beta}_1 \\ \hat{\beta}_2 \end{bmatrix} = \begin{bmatrix} N & \Sigma X_1 & \Sigma X_2 \\ \Sigma X_1 & \Sigma X_1^2 & \Sigma X_1 X_2 \\ \Sigma X_2 & \Sigma X_1 X_2 & \Sigma X_2^2 \end{bmatrix}^{-1} \begin{bmatrix} \Sigma Y \\ \Sigma X_1 Y \\ \Sigma X_2 Y \end{bmatrix} \qquad \textbf{9.4.2}$$

Now suppose that one of the basic assumptions of the OLS method, $E(X_2U) = E(X_1U) = 0$, is not fulfilled; suppose instead that $E(X_2U) \neq 0$, even though $E(X_1U) = 0$. Following the argument for the instrumental variable method, X_2 is replaced by an instrument, appropriately chosen, say, Z_2. Applying the instrumental variable method of estimation to equation 9.4.1, we obtain:

$$\hat{\boldsymbol{\beta}}^* = (\mathbf{Z}'\mathbf{X})^{-1}\mathbf{Z}'\mathbf{Y} \qquad \textbf{9.4.3}$$

where $\mathbf{X} = (X_0, X_1, X_2)$, as before, and $\mathbf{Z} = (X_0, X_1, Z_2)$. We then obtain:

$$\hat{\boldsymbol{\beta}}^* = \begin{bmatrix} \hat{\beta}_0^* \\ \hat{\beta}_1^* \\ \hat{\beta}_2^* \end{bmatrix} = \begin{bmatrix} N & \Sigma X_1 & \Sigma X_2 \\ \Sigma X_1 & \Sigma X_1^2 & \Sigma X_1 X_2 \\ \Sigma Z_2 & \Sigma X_1 Z_2 & \Sigma X_2 Z_2 \end{bmatrix}^{-1} \begin{bmatrix} \Sigma Y \\ \Sigma X_1 Y \\ \Sigma Z_2 Y \end{bmatrix} \qquad \textbf{9.4.4}$$

It is unreasonable to suggest that $E(X_2U) \neq 0$ for an arbitrary variable X_2. A more plausible case is a single-equation model where the lagged value of the endogenous variable appears as a regressor.[6] Let us consider the model:

$$Y_t = \beta_0 + \beta_1 X_t + \beta_2 Y_{t-1} + U_t \qquad \textbf{9.4.5}$$

or,

$$\mathbf{Y} = \mathbf{X}\boldsymbol{\beta} + \mathbf{U}$$

There are many instances of econometric models with such a form as we have seen in Chapter 7. By assumption X_t is a predetermined fixed exogenous variable, and $E(X_tU_t) = 0$. Evidently Y_{t-1} is not a truly predetermined variable. It is the endogenous variable determined one time period earlier. Therefore, the assumption that $E(Y_{t-1}U_t) = 0$ is not likely to be fulfilled. To obtain a consistent estimator when this assumption is violated, we can use the instrumental variable method with X_{t-1} as the chosen instrument.

To see that the choice of X_{t-1} is a reasonable one, recall the criteria for this choice:

1. The instrumental variable is exogenous: $\text{cov}(\mathbf{ZU}) = \mathbf{0}$. Indeed X_{t-1} is an exogenous variable, since X_t is exogenous by assumption; and if $\text{cov}(X_tU_t) = 0$, then $\text{cov}(X_{t-1}U_t) = 0$ also.
2. The instrumental variable is related to both the regressand and the regressor it replaces. The covariance of the instrument with the regressand and with the regressor should be nonzero and finite. Rewriting the estimating equation above for period $t - 1$ in this case, $Y_{t-1} = \beta_0 + \beta_1 X_{t-1} + \beta_2 Y_{t-2} + U_{t-1}$. Thus $\text{cov}(X_{t-1}Y_{t-1}) \neq 0$. Also, Y_{t-1} is a regressor for Y_t. Therefore, $\text{cov}(X_{t-1}, Y_t) \neq 0$.

We proceed to carry out the estimation procedure with X_{t-1} as the instrumental variable. The OLS estimator is:

---

[6] N. Liviatan, "Consistent Estimation of Distributed Lags," *International Economic Review*, Vol. 4, No. 1 (January, 1963), pp. 44-52. N. Liviatan, "Errors in Variables and Engle Curve Analysis," *Econometrica*, Vol. 29, No. 3 (July, 1961), pp. 336-362.

$$\hat{\boldsymbol{\beta}} = (\mathbf{X}'\mathbf{X})^{-1}\mathbf{X}'\mathbf{Y}$$

where $\mathbf{X} = (X_0, X_t, Y_{t-1})$ and $X_{t0} = 1$ for all t.

It follows that:

$$\hat{\boldsymbol{\beta}} = \begin{bmatrix} \hat{\beta}_0 \\ \hat{\beta}_1 \\ \hat{\beta}_2 \end{bmatrix} = \begin{bmatrix} N & \Sigma X_t & \Sigma Y_{t-1} \\ \Sigma X_t & \Sigma X_t^2 & \Sigma X_t Y_{t-1} \\ \Sigma Y_{t-1} & \Sigma X_t Y_{t-1} & \Sigma Y_{t-1}^2 \end{bmatrix}^{-1} \begin{bmatrix} \Sigma Y_t \\ \Sigma X_t Y_t \\ \Sigma Y_{t-1} Y_t \end{bmatrix} \tag{9.4.6}$$

The instrumental variable estimator $\hat{\boldsymbol{\beta}}^*$ can be obtained from equation 9.4.3:

$$\hat{\boldsymbol{\beta}}^* = (\mathbf{Z}'\mathbf{X})^{-1}\mathbf{Z}'\mathbf{Y}$$

where $\mathbf{X} = (X_0, X_t, Y_{t-1})$

$\mathbf{Z} = (X_0, X_t, X_{t-1})$

It follows, as in equation 9.4.4, that:

$$\hat{\boldsymbol{\beta}}^* = \begin{bmatrix} \hat{\beta}_0^* \\ \hat{\beta}_1^* \\ \hat{\beta}_2^* \end{bmatrix} = \begin{bmatrix} N & \Sigma X_t & \Sigma Y_{t-1} \\ \Sigma X_t & \Sigma X_t^2 & \Sigma X_t Y_{t-1} \\ \Sigma X_{t-1} & \Sigma X_{t-1} X_t & \Sigma X_{t-1} Y_{t-1} \end{bmatrix}^{-1} \begin{bmatrix} \Sigma Y_t \\ \Sigma X_t Y_t \\ \Sigma X_{t-1} Y_t \end{bmatrix} \tag{9.4.7}$$

Again, it can easily be seen that the instrumental variable estimate $\boldsymbol{\beta}^*$ in the multiple regression model is consistent. We have from equation 9.4.3:

$$\begin{aligned} \hat{\boldsymbol{\beta}}^* &= (\mathbf{Z}'\mathbf{X})^{-1}\mathbf{Z}'\mathbf{Y} \\ &= (\mathbf{Z}'\mathbf{X})^{-1}\mathbf{Z}'(\mathbf{X}\boldsymbol{\beta} + \mathbf{U}) \quad \text{(substituting for } \mathbf{Y} \text{ from equation 9.4.5)} \\ &= (\mathbf{Z}'\mathbf{X})^{-1}\mathbf{Z}'\mathbf{X}\boldsymbol{\beta} + (\mathbf{Z}'\mathbf{X})^{-1}\mathbf{Z}'\mathbf{U} \\ &= \boldsymbol{\beta} + (\mathbf{Z}'\mathbf{X})^{-1}\mathbf{Z}'\mathbf{U} \end{aligned} \tag{9.4.8}$$

From which,

$$\begin{aligned} \text{plim}(\hat{\boldsymbol{\beta}}^*) &= \boldsymbol{\beta} + \text{plim}\left(\frac{1}{T}\,\mathbf{Z}'\mathbf{X}\right)^{-1} \cdot \text{plim}\left(\frac{1}{T}\,\mathbf{Z}'\mathbf{U}\right) \\ &= \boldsymbol{\beta} + \text{plim}\left(\frac{1}{T}\,\mathbf{Z}'\mathbf{X}\right)^{-1} \cdot 0 \end{aligned} \tag{9.4.9}$$

Note that $\text{plim}\left(\frac{1}{T}\,\mathbf{Z}'\mathbf{U}\right)$ is a consistent estimate of the population cov(**ZU**), and that cov(**ZU**) = **0** when **Z** is the instrumental variable. Indeed **Z** is so chosen. The variance in the multiple regression case can be estimated from:[7]

[7] For a proof of the asymptotic variance-covariance matrix, see A. S. Goldberger, *Econometric Theory* (New York: John Wiley & Sons, 1964), pp. 285-286.

$$\text{var}(\hat{\boldsymbol{\beta}}^*) = \hat{\sigma}_u^{*2}(\mathbf{Z}'\mathbf{X})^{-1}(\mathbf{Z}'\mathbf{Z})(\mathbf{X}'\mathbf{Z})^{-1} \qquad \textbf{9.4.10}$$

where $\hat{\sigma}_u^{*2}$ is estimated as:

$$S^{*2} = \frac{1}{T - K}\,[(\mathbf{Y} - \mathbf{X}\hat{\boldsymbol{\beta}}^*)'(\mathbf{Y} - \mathbf{X}\hat{\boldsymbol{\beta}}^*)] \qquad \textbf{9.4.11}$$

A note of caution is necessary. The instrumental variable estimator $\hat{\boldsymbol{\beta}}^*$ should not be confused with $\hat{\boldsymbol{\beta}}^{**} = (\mathbf{Z}'\mathbf{Z})^{-1}\mathbf{Z}'\mathbf{Y}$. We would use $\hat{\boldsymbol{\beta}}^{**}$ if the variable Y_{t-1} were completely removed from the model and X_{t-1} were introduced instead. The use of the instrumental variable X_{t-1} for Y_{t-1} does have consequences for the form of the estimator $\hat{\boldsymbol{\beta}}^*$, but it does not mean that Y_{t-1} ceases to appear in the model and the estimator. The variable continues to appear as a component of the matrix of exogenous variables in **X**.

Note that the **X′X** matrix is symmetric, while the **Z′X** matrix is not. For that matter the **Z′Z** matrix is symmetric too.

The method of instrumental variables may appear puzzling at a first introduction, but the calculations involved are just a little more complicated than for the method of ordinary least squares. The advantages of this method in obtaining consistent estimates of parameters outweigh the very small amount of extra calculations.

DISCUSSION QUESTIONS

1. State the conditions for the selection of an instrumental variable.
2. Show that the instrumental variable estimator is consistent. Can you show that this estimator is unbiased? Give reasons for your answer.
3. Explain the rationale of the instrumental variable method of estimation.
4. Refer to the case study of Haavelmo and indicate how the estimate of the multiplier would be affected if the OLS method of estimation was used to estimate the marginal propensity to consume.
5. Discuss the case for the selection of the instrumental variable when there is more than one predetermined variable appearing in the model.
6. Consider the model:

$$Y_t = b_0 + b_1 X_t + b_2 Y_{t-1} + U_t$$

   Discuss the case for estimating the above model by the instrumental variable method, using X_{t-1} as the instrumental variable.
7. How would you estimate the variance of the instrumental variable estimator, both in the case of the two-variable regression model and the multiple regression model?

SUGGESTED READINGS

Geary, R. C. "Determination of Linear Relations Between Systematic Parts of Variables with Errors of Observation the Variance of Which are Unknown." *Econometrica,* Vol. 17 (1949), pp. 30-58.

Haavelmo, T. "Methods of Measuring the Marginal Propensity to Consume." *Studies in Econometric Method,* edited by W. C. Hood and T. C. Koopmans. New York: John Wiley & Sons, 1953, pp. 75-91.

Liviatan, N. "Consistent Estimation of Distributed Lags." *International Economic Review,* Vol. 4, No. 1 (January, 1963), pp. 44-52.

———. "Errors in Variables and Engle Curve Analysis." *Econometrica,* Vol. 29, No. 3 (July, 1961), pp. 336-362.

Reiersol, O. "Confluence Analysis by Means of Instrumental Sets of Variables." *Arkiv für Matematik,* Vol. 32 (1945).

———. "Confluence Analysis by Means of Lag Moments and Other Methods of Confluence Analysis." *Econometrica,* Vol. 9, No. 1 (January, 1941), pp. 1-23.

Sargan, J. D. "The Estimation of Economic Relationships Using Instrumental Variables." *Econometrica,* Vol. 26, No. 3 (July, 1958), pp. 393-415.

Valavanis, Stefan. *Econometrics.* New York: McGraw-Hill Book Co., 1959.

10

identification

10.0 THE NATURE OF THE PROBLEM

The *identification* of the equations of an econometric model is a basic problem.[1] The effort to estimate parameters for an economic structure may end as a futile exercise unless the relationships describing the structure are properly identified. Given the data on the exogenous and endogenous variables appearing in the model, and given also the assumptions about the disturbance terms, we wish to estimate uniquely the parameters of the true structure that the model seeks to describe. Recall that Chapter 1 concluded that when the parameters of a given model and the parameters of the probability distribution of the disturbance terms take on specific true values, we have a structure. Many different structures are admissible for a given model, since we have no information about the specific numerical values of the true structural parameters.

Identification is an exercise in logic that relates a specified model to a basic structure. If the specification of the model is correct according to economic theory, the presumption is that the structure is identified in terms of the model. The data used to estimate the parameters of the model are then presumed to have been generated by the true structure. A structure is identified with respect to a given model and given data if there is one and only one structure that is so admissible. In other words given the a priori restrictions for the specification of the model and given the data, the estimated parameters are then the estimates of the true parameters of the basic structure, should the identification condition be fulfilled. If it is a single-equation model of milk demand, for example, it is important to be certain that what we estimate are truly the parameters of the demand structure, as distinguished from those of the supply structure. Even when we are

[1] T. C. Koopmans, "Identification Problems in Economic Model Construction," *Studies in Econometric Method*, edited by W. C. Hood and T. C. Koopmans (New York: John Wiley & Sons, 1953), pp. 27-48. T. C. Koopmans and W. C. Hood, "The Estimation of Simultaneous Linear Economic Relations," *Ibid.*, pp. 112-199. Herbert Simon, "Causal Ordering and Identifiability," *Ibid.*, pp. 49-74. Franklin M. Fisher, *The Identification Problem in Econometrics* (New York: McGraw-Hill Book Co., 1966). T. C. Koopmans, H. Rubin, and R. B. Leipnik, "Measuring the Equation Systems of Dynamic Economics," *Statistical Inference in Dynamic Economic Models*, edited by T. C. Koopmans (New York: John Wiley & Sons, 1950), pp. 69-110. Abraham Wald, "Note on Identification of Economic Relations," *Ibid.*, pp. 238-244.

working with a simultaneous system consisting of, say, both the demand and supply relationships, we must assure ourselves that the parameters estimated relate to the true structure, not to a pseudostructure. Indeed identification is a logical problem and needs to be considered carefully before attempts are made to undertake any estimation work.

The Identification Problem—Geometrically

The nature of the problem of identification is evident when we consider the classroom exposition of the demand and supply schedules. Whether he is treating demand or supply as a function of price, the instructor can offer a hypothetical set of numbers on quantity and price, such as those in Table 10-1.

TABLE 10-1

Quantity Demanded	Price	Quantity Supplied
A^* 100	4	300 A
B^* 200	3	200 B
C^* 300	2	100 C

Geometrically, Figure 10-1 shows the demand schedule given by the three hypothetical points, A^*, B^*, and C^*, and the supply schedule given similarly by the A, B, and C points in a price-quantity, two-dimensional map. It is important to note that these points—representing various price-quantity combinations—are all hypothetical alteratives available at a given point in time. In a market operating under the condition of equilibrium, we are able to observe only the one point where supply is equal to demand. This is the point represented by B^* on the demand curve and B on the supply curve. This point belongs to both curves and represents the choice by both demanders and suppliers of 200 units of the commodity at price 3 per unit from among all the alternatives on the demand and supply schedules. Ideally this is when the transaction takes place and the market is "cleared" in perfect competition equilibrium. The econometrician has no way of obtaining directly any observations for other points on the price-quantity schedules of demand and supply.

If the equilibrium observations are used to estimate an equation of the form $Q = \beta_0 + \beta_1 P + U$, will the econometrician be estimating the demand or the supply equation?[2] Can he distinguish the two equations properly so that he is sure of not confusing one with the other? This is the problem of identification.

Identification and Single-Equation Models

In single-equation models the problem of identification is often assumed away. A demand function is a demand function by assertion. However, the

[2] E. J. Working, "What do Statistical Demand Curves Show?" *Quarterly Journal of Economics*, Vol. 41, No. 2 (February, 1927), pp. 212-235. Ragnar Frisch, "Pitfalls in the Statistical Construction of Demand and Supply Curves," *Veröffentlichungen der Frankfurter Gesellschaft für Konjunkturforschung*, Neue Folge, Heft 5, Leipzig, Hans Buske Verlag (1933).

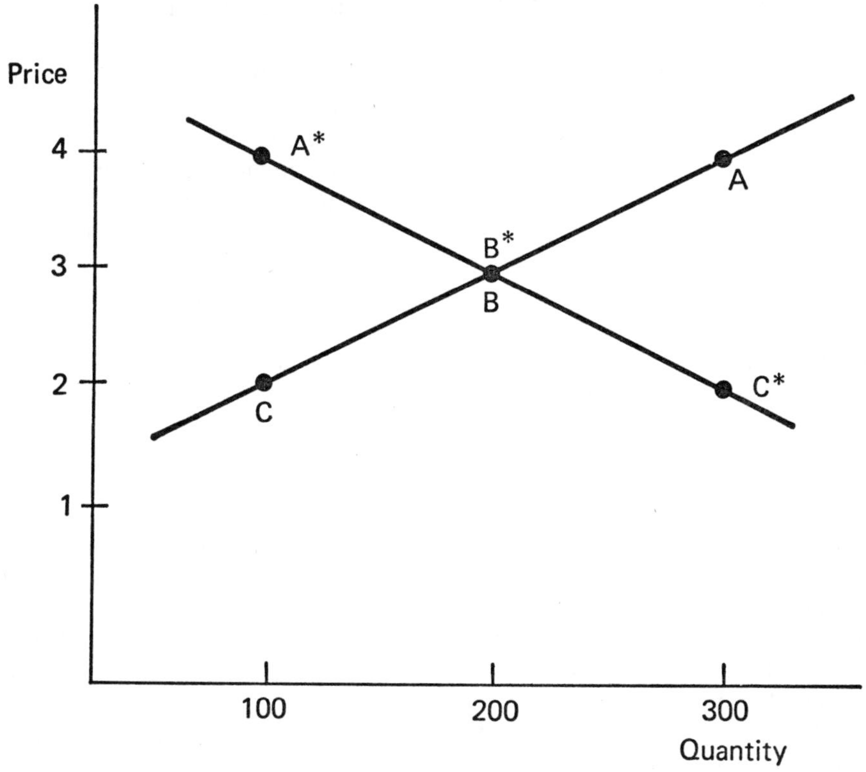

FIGURE 10-1

problem of identification is still important. Henry Schultz used time-series data and estimated demand equations for various commodities.[3] A typical example is his estimated function for wheat demand:

$$\log Q = 1.0802 - 0.2145 \log P - 0.00358T - 0.00163T^2 \qquad \mathbf{10.0.1}$$

where Q = quantity of wheat demanded
P = price of wheat

His data were taken from annual observations on quantity and price from 1921 through 1934. Notice that the variables for quantity and price are expressed as logarithms and that the equation contains terms in T (trend) and T^2. Let us concentrate on the two variables quantity and price in this equation.

The equation happens to be the usual demand function—price and quantity have opposite signs. But Schultz did not obtain the parameters from sets of hypothetical data as used in classroom demonstrations. He collected pairs of observations on quantity and price each year at the given price a specific quantity of wheat demanded or supplied. He had no way of knowing in

[3] Henry Schultz, *Theory and Measurement of Demand* (Chicago: University of Chicago Press, 1938).

advance whether the pairs of observations on price and quantity each year were related to the demand or the supply equation. Fortunately, there is at least one clue that suggests that Schultz really obtained estimates of a demand function. Opposite signs for quantity and price are the sine qua non of a demand function. In a supply function the signs are both expected to be positive. This expectation is based on economic theory, not on mathematics or statistics.

It is possible to identify the estimated equation as the demand equation or the supply equation if there are a priori restrictions on the variance of the disturbance term in each equation. If there is an a priori argument that the variance of the disturbance term U^d in the demand equation is smaller than the variance of the disturbance term U^s in the supply equation, this condition on the disturbance terms may be helpful in identifying the equation when $\text{cov}(U^d U^s) = 0$. Symbolically,

$$\text{var}(U^d) = K\ \text{var}(U^s) \qquad 0 < K < 1 \tag{10.0.2}$$

In words this condition expresses the fact that the demand function is relatively stable and that the supply function is relatively more susceptible to fluctuations. If this condition holds, the equation estimated with price-quantity data will be the demand equation. To obtain estimates for the supply equation, more information is necessary. Clearly with such a priori conditions indicated, price-quantity data can be used to estimate one-equation demand models without any reference to the supply function.

Generally, identification has been discussed in terms of a system model. Emphasis has been on identifying each equation of the model. However, identification of parameter values in a single equation has been shown to be of some consequence, especially in distributed lag models.[4] Remember we have seen in Chapter 7 that an adaptive expectation model and a partial stock adjustment model result in the same final form of the distributed lag model for estimation purposes. The econometrician is baffled and can hardly identify his estimated model with one or the other structure based on the two alternative hypotheses stated above.

10.1 IDENTIFICATION: NECESSARY CONDITION AND NECESSARY AND SUFFICIENT CONDITION

In a model consisting of linear equations, an equation is identified if it is impossible to create another equation in the same variables by any combination of all or some of the other equations in the model or by multiplying any equation by a constant. Consider the model:

$$Q_t^d = \alpha_0 + \alpha_1 P_t + U_t^d \tag{10.1.1}$$

$$Q_t^s = \beta_0 + \beta_1 P_t + \beta_2 R_t + U_t^s \tag{10.1.2}$$

$$Q_t^d = Q_t^s \qquad t = 1, 2, \ldots, T \tag{10.1.3}$$

[4] Jan Kmenta, *Elements of Econometrics* (New York: MacMillan Co., 1971), pp. 442-448.

We have three equations. Equation 10.1.1 expresses the price-quantity demand relationship for an agricultural commodity and α_1 is expected to carry a negative sign, a priori. Equation 10.1.2 describes the supply equation, and the quantity supplied Q^s is expected to depend positively on price P and rainfall R (β_1, $\beta_2 \geq 0$). Equation 10.1.3 is the convenient market-clearing assumption, which states that quantity supplied equals quantity demanded. We wish to obtain independent estimates of the parameters of both the demand and the supply equations.

By substituting supply equation 10.1.2 into market-clearing equation 10.1.3, we have:

$$Q_t^d = \beta_0 + \beta_1 P_t + \beta_2 R_t + U_t^s \qquad \textbf{10.1.4}$$

We multiply equation 10.1.4 by λ and equation 10.1.1 by μ:

$$\lambda Q_t^d = \lambda\beta_0 + \lambda\beta_1 P_t + \lambda\beta_2 R_t + \lambda U_t^s \qquad \textbf{10.1.5}$$

$$\mu Q_t^d = \mu\alpha_0 + \mu\alpha_1 P_t + \mu U_t^d \qquad \textbf{10.1.6}$$

By adding,

$$(\lambda + \mu)Q_t^d = (\lambda\beta_0 + \mu\alpha_0) + (\lambda\beta_1 + \mu\alpha_1)P_t + \lambda\beta_2 R_t + \lambda U_t^s + \mu U_t^d$$

or,

$$Q_t^d = \frac{\lambda\beta_0 + \mu\alpha_0}{\lambda + \mu} + \frac{(\lambda\beta_1 + \mu\alpha_1)}{\lambda + \mu} P_t + \frac{\lambda\beta_2}{\lambda + \mu} R_t + \frac{\lambda}{\lambda + \mu} U_t^s + \frac{\mu}{\lambda + \mu} U_t^d \qquad \textbf{10.1.7}$$

This equation cannot be confused with demand equation 10.1.1, since the original demand equation does not have the R_t variable. A priori rainfall has no effect on demand behavior for this particular commodity. Demand equation 10.1.1 is thus properly identified. By the same token, the supply equation remains unidentified. We have succeeded in creating another equation where quantity is a function of price and rainfall, equation 10.1.7. The estimated parameters of equation 10.1.7 cannot be distinguished from the parameters of structural supply equation 10.1.2. The two structures 10.1.2 and 10.1.7 are seen to be "observationally equivalent." Similar observational equivalence can be seen between the structural equation and its reduced form.

We can further analyze the situation as follows. By substituting equation 10.1.1 into equation 10.1.3, we have:

$$Q_t^s = \alpha_0 + \alpha_1 P_t + U_t^d \qquad \textbf{10.1.8}$$

Multiplying equation 10.1.8 by λ and equation 10.1.2 by μ,

$$\lambda Q_t^s = \lambda\alpha_0 + \lambda\alpha_1 P_t + \lambda U_t^d \qquad \textbf{10.1.9}$$

$$\mu Q_t^s = \mu\beta_0 + \mu\beta_1 P_t + \mu\beta_2 R_t + \mu U_t^s \qquad \textbf{10.1.10}$$

Adding,

$$Q_t^s(\lambda + \mu) = (\lambda\alpha_0 + \mu\beta_0) + (\lambda\alpha_1 + \mu\beta_1)P_t + \mu\beta_2 R_t + \lambda U_t^d + \mu U_t^s$$

or,

$$Q_t^s = \frac{\lambda\alpha_0 + \mu\beta_0}{\lambda + \mu} + \frac{(\lambda\alpha_1 + \mu\beta_1)}{\lambda + \mu} P_t + \frac{\mu\beta_2}{\lambda + \mu} R_t + \frac{\lambda}{\lambda + \mu} U_t^d + \frac{\mu}{\lambda + \mu} U_t^s \quad \textbf{10.1.11}$$

Equation 10.1.11 is indistinguishable from the original supply equation 10.1.2, since in either case Q_t^s is regressed on P_t and R_t.

We shall need a more rigorous expression of the conditions of identification, and two such conditions have been developed. One provides the necessary condition, while the other describes the necessary and sufficient condition. Consider a model:

$$Q_t^d = \alpha_1 + \beta_1 P_t + \gamma_1 Y_t + U_t^d \quad \textbf{10.1.12}$$

$$Q_t^s = \alpha_2 + \beta_2 P_t + \gamma_2 W_t + U_t^s \quad \textbf{10.1.13}$$

$$Q_t^d = Q_t^s \quad \textbf{10.1.14}$$

Equation 10.1.12 says that the quantity demanded of a commodity depends on price P and income Y. Equation 10.1.13 states that quantity supplied depends on price P and workers' attitude W. Equation 10.1.14 is the market-clearing assumption as before. The variables Y_t and W_t are exogenous for this model. The model suggests that Q_t, a unique quantity (demand = supply), and its price P_t are the two endogenous variables determined by the system.

The system can be reduced to two equations. Given Y_t and W_t (exogenous), we then use equation 10.1.14 to obtain a solution for P:

$$\alpha_1 + \beta_1 P_t + \gamma_1 Y_t + U_t^d = \alpha_2 + \beta_2 P_t + \gamma_2 W_t + U_t^s$$

$$\beta_1 P_t - \beta_2 P_t = \alpha_2 - \alpha_1 + \gamma_2 W_t - \gamma_1 Y_t + U_t^s - U_t^d$$

$$P_t = \frac{\alpha_2 - \alpha_1}{\beta_1 - \beta_2} + \frac{\gamma_2}{\beta_1 - \beta_2} W_t - \frac{\gamma_1}{\beta_1 - \beta_2} Y_t + \frac{1}{\beta_1 - \beta_2}(U_t^s - U_t^d)$$

or,

$$P_t = \pi_{11} + \pi_{12} W_t - \pi_{13} Y_t + V_{t1} \quad \textbf{10.1.15}$$

Similarly for Q_t, using equation 10.1.15 in equation 10.1.12 or in equation 10.1.13,

$$Q_t = \frac{\alpha_2\beta_1 - \alpha_1\beta_2}{\beta_1 - \beta_2} - \frac{\gamma_1\beta_2}{\beta_1 - \beta_2} Y_t + \frac{\gamma_2\beta_1}{\beta_1 - \beta_2} W_t + \frac{\beta_1 U_t^s - \beta_2 U_t^d}{\beta_1 - \beta_2}$$

or,

$$Q_t = \pi_{21} - \pi_{22}Y_t + \pi_{23}W_t + V_{t2} \qquad \textbf{10.1.16}$$

where

$$\pi_{11} = \frac{\alpha_2 - \alpha_1}{\beta_1 - \beta_2}, \quad \pi_{12} = \frac{\gamma_2}{\beta_1 - \beta_2}, \quad \pi_{13} = \frac{\gamma_1}{\beta_1 - \beta_2}$$

$$\pi_{21} = \frac{\alpha_2\beta_1 - \alpha_1\beta_2}{\beta_1 - \beta_2}, \quad \pi_{22} = \frac{\gamma_1\beta_2}{\beta_1 - \beta_2}, \quad \pi_{23} = \frac{\gamma_2\beta_1}{\beta_1 - \beta_2}$$

$$V_{t1} = \frac{1}{\beta_1 - \beta_2} \; (U_t^s - U_t^d)$$

and

$$V_{t2} = \frac{\beta_1 U_t^s - \beta_2 U_t^d}{\beta_1 - \beta_2}$$

Equations 10.1.15 and 10.1.16 constitute the *reduced form* of the model. The reduced form of a model consists of one equation for each endogenous variable, with each equation explained entirely by a set of exogenous variables. In other words on the right-hand side of each equation only exogenous variables appear. As we shall see in the following chapter, there is no guarantee that we can obtain a "nice" reduced form for any arbitrary model. If we can, then the estimation of each equation of the model becomes easy. Remember that we wish to estimate the parameters in the original structural equation. Suppose that we wish to estimate β_1 in demand equation 10.1.12. In the reduced form, we estimate π_{12} and π_{23} and then obtain:

$$\pi_{23}/\pi_{12}$$

or,

$$\frac{\gamma_2\beta_1}{\beta_1 - \beta_2} \div \frac{\gamma_2}{\beta_1 - \beta_2} = \beta_1$$

Thus one way of looking at the identification problem is to relate the structural parameters to the reduced form parameters. Some authors have preferred to call the parameters of the structural equations the unrestricted parameters, and those of the reduced form the restricted parameters. Chapter 9 showed that the OLS estimates of the unrestricted parameters in a generally interdependent system model are generally inconsistent since some of the regressors in the equations are jointly determined endogenous variables, and as such the covariance between them and the disturbance terms of the related equations is not uncorrelated in the probability limit. In the reduced form as the manipulations are performed, the regressors appearing in each equation are all exogenous variables; and as such the estimates of restricted parameters are consistent. If we can obtain a unique solution for the unrestricted parameters from the estimates of the restricted parameters, then each equation of the model is just identified. When the number of unrestricted parameters is greater than that of the restricted parameters, we have no unique solution, and the case is one of overidentification. The opposite case is the one of underidentification. Reduced forms will be discussed further in the next chapter.

The necessary condition for identification says that the total number of variables in the model H minus the number of variables appearing in the particular equation H should be equal to the number of endogenous variables in the model K, minus one*. That is,

$$H - H^* = K - 1 \qquad \textbf{10.1.17}$$

Let us check both of the equations for the preceding model. Our model contains four variables, two endogenous variables and two exogenous variables. Three variables appear in equation 10.1.12. Thus,

$$4 - 3 = 2 - 1$$

Supply equation 10.1.13 can be similarly analyzed. Thus each of the equations is *just identified.*

Note that there can be a situation when:

$$H - H^* > K - 1 \qquad \textbf{10.1.18}$$

This is the case of *overidentification.* Should it happen that:

$$H - H^* < K - 1 \qquad \textbf{10.1.19}$$

the equation is *underidentified*, and all methods of estimation fail.

We can distinguish between the exogenous and endogenous variables in the model and redefine the condition of identification. Define:

$K = K^* + K^{**}$ = total number of endogenous variables in the model

$M = M^* + M^{**}$ = total number of exogenous variables in the model

$K^* + K^{**} + M^* + M^{**}$ = total number of variables in the model

$K^* + M^*$ = total number of variables in the ith equation

$K^{**} + M^{**}$ = total number of variables in the model, but not appearing in the ith equation

Notice that the symbols H and H^* are not used in these definitions, but $H = K + M$ and $H^* = K^* + M^*$. Rewriting equation 10.1.17, we have:

$$(K^* + K^{**} + M^* + M^{**}) - (K^* + M^*) = (K^* + K^{**}) - 1$$

or,

$$(K^{**} + M^{**}) = (K^* + K^{**}) - 1$$

or,

$$M^{**} = K^* - 1 \quad \text{(just identified)} \qquad \textbf{10.1.20}$$

$$M^{**} > K^* - 1 \quad \text{(overidentified)} \qquad \textbf{10.1.21}$$

$$M^{**} < K^* - 1 \quad \text{(underidentified)} \qquad \textbf{10.1.22}$$

Thus if the predetermined variables excluded from the ith equation, M^{**}, are equal to the number of endogenous variables appearing in the ith equation, K^*, minus one, the equation is just identified. If the number of such predetermined variables M^{**} is greater than $K^* - 1$, the equation is overidentified; and if the number of predetermined variables in M^{**} is less than the number of endogenous variables appearing in the equation K^*, minus one, the equation is underidentified.

To explain the necessary and sufficient condition, let us return to the supply-demand model. Substituting equation 10.1.13 into equation 10.1.14, we have:

$$Q_t^d = \alpha_2 + \beta_2 P_t + \gamma_2 W_t + U_t^s \qquad \textbf{10.1.23}$$

Multiplying this equation by λ and original demand equation 10.1.12 by μ,

$$\lambda Q_t^d = \lambda\alpha_2 + \lambda\beta_2 P_t + \lambda\gamma_2 W_t + \lambda U_t^s$$

$$\mu Q_t^d = \mu\alpha_1 + \mu\beta_1 P_t + \mu\gamma_1 Y_t + \mu U_t^d$$

Adding,

$$Q_t^d\,(\lambda + \mu) = \lambda\alpha_2 + \mu\alpha_1 + P_t(\lambda\beta_2 + \mu\beta_1) + \lambda\gamma_2 W_t + \mu\gamma_1 Y_t + \lambda U_t^s + \mu U_t^d \qquad \textbf{10.1.24}$$

This equation is indistinguishable from the original demand equation 10.1.12 if γ_2 is zero. Similarly, it can be shown that the original supply equation 10.1.13 is indistinguishable from such a "mongrel" equation if γ_1 becomes zero. Thus if the demand equation is to be identified, it becomes important that the coefficient of the variable that appears in the supply equation but not in the demand equation be nonzero. Alternatively, the coefficient of the variable that appears in the demand equation but not in the supply equation must be nonzero if the supply equation is to be identified.

This condition can be generalized for a situation where the model consists of more than two equations. Make an array of the coefficients of the variables that enter into the system but not into the equation whose identification is being considered. We shall obtain a matrix of coefficients, some elements of which may be zero. The next step is to compute all possible determinants of the order of the number of endogenous variables in the model minus one. At least one of these determinants must be nonvanishing. To illustrate the case, consider an abstract model:

$$\begin{aligned} a_{11}Y_1 + a_{12}Y_3 + a_{13}Y_4 + a_{14}Z_1 &= U_1 \\ a_{21}Y_2 + a_{22}Y_3 + a_{23}Y_4 + a_{24}Z_1 &= U_2 \\ a_{31}Y_1 + a_{32}Y_3 + a_{33}Z_2 &= U_3 \\ a_{41}Y_2 + a_{42}Y_4 + a_{43}Z_3 + a_{44}Z_4 &= U_4 \end{aligned} \qquad \textbf{10.1.25}$$

The Y's are endogenous variables and the Z's are exogenous variables. The a_{ij}'s are coefficients to be estimated. There are four Y's and four Z's, a total of eight variables in the model. Notice that all variables are written on the left-hand side and the residual terms alone on the right-hand side. We need to identify each equation of the model.

To check the necessary condition that the first equation is identified, we have, following equation 10.1.18:

$$(H - H^* = 8 - 4) > (K - 1 = 4 - 1)$$

or, by following equation 10.1.21,

$$(M^{**} = 3) > (K^* - 1 = 3 - 1)$$

Either way, this equation is overidentified. A check will show that each equation in the model is overidentified.

To check the necessary and sufficient condition, let us examine the fourth equation. The first step is to sort out the variables appearing in the model but not in equation 4, as shown in Table 10-2. We have four endogenous variables in the model. Therefore, the determinants we wish to compute are those of the order $4 - 1 = 3$. Possible determinants of this order are:

$$\begin{vmatrix} a_{11} & a_{12} & a_{14} \\ 0 & a_{22} & a_{24} \\ a_{31} & a_{32} & 0 \end{vmatrix}$$

$$\begin{vmatrix} a_{11} & a_{12} & 0 \\ 0 & a_{22} & 0 \\ a_{31} & a_{32} & a_{33} \end{vmatrix}$$

$$\begin{vmatrix} a_{11} & a_{14} & 0 \\ 0 & a_{24} & 0 \\ a_{31} & 0 & a_{33} \end{vmatrix} \qquad \textbf{10.1.26}$$

$$\begin{vmatrix} a_{12} & a_{14} & 0 \\ a_{22} & a_{24} & 0 \\ a_{32} & 0 & a_{33} \end{vmatrix}$$

TABLE 10-2

	Y_1	Y_3	Z_1	Z_2
First Equation	a_{11}	a_{12}	a_{14}	0
Second Equation	0	a_{22}	a_{24}	0
Third Equation	a_{31}	a_{32}	0	a_{33}

The necessary and sufficient condition will be fulfilled if at least one of these determinants is nonzero.

The necessary and sufficient condition cannot, in general, be tested; it depends on the matrix of unknown parameters.[5] Of course it is highly unlikely that all such determinants will be zero unless many of the elements of the matrices are themselves zero. Note that these elements are the parameters of the equations. Should many of them be zero, the necessary condition is also likely to fail. Thus turning the argument around, the sufficient condition is often fulfilled if the necessary condition of identification is satisfied. The truth of this forceful assertation will be easy to appreciate if we again consider the simple model of equations 10.1.12 through 10.1.14.

We have two endogenous variables Q_t and P_t and two exogenous variables Y_t and W_t. For convenience, suppose that we designate the endogenous variables as Y_i's, for example, $Q = Y_1$, $P = Y_2$; and the exogenous variables as Z_i's, for example, $Y_t = Z_1$, $W_t = Z_2$. Let us then rewrite the model:

$$a_{11}Y_1 + a_{12}Y_2 + a_{13}Z_1 = U_1 \qquad \textbf{10.1.27}$$

$$a_{21}Y_1 + a_{22}Y_2 + a_{23}Z_2 = U_2 \qquad \textbf{10.1.28}$$

In both equations we have three out of four variables appearing, and we have only two endogenous variables. Thus using the rule of necessary condition, we have in both cases:

$$4 - 3 = 2 - 1$$

or,

$$M^{**} = 1 = K^* - 1 = 2 - 1$$

Each equation is just identified. If a_{23} is nonzero, the first equation satisfies the necessary and sufficient condition of identification. It is also true with respect to the second equation, if a_{13} is nonzero. If a_{23} is zero, that is, if the coefficient with respect to the variable appearing in the system but not in the equation vanishes, equation 10.1.27 does not satisfy the necessary and sufficient condition of identification. But should this happen, this equation fails to satisfy the test of necessary condition for identification. When a_{23} is zero,

[5] Robert L. Basmann, "On Finite Sample Distributions of Generalized Classical Linear Identifiability Test Statistics," *Journal of the American Statistical Association,* Vol. 55, No. 292 (December, 1960), pp. 650-659.

there are three variables in the model, two endogenous and one exogenous. In this case, the equation fails to satisfy the test of necessary condition:

$$3 - 3 < 2 - 1$$

or,

$$M^{**} = 0 < K^* - 1 = 2 - 1$$

It becomes underidentified. However, fulfillment of the necessary condition does not necessarily ensure fulfillment of the sufficient condition. Of course it is true that fulfillment of the sufficient condition means that the necessary condition has been fulfilled. Once the necessary condition is fulfilled, we can estimate the parameters on the presumption that they are not truly zero, and that the rank condition will have been fulfilled in terms of a priori restrictions of the model.

The Condition Restated: Order and Rank Conditions

A more formal statement of the two conditions of identification discussed can be given in terms of order and rank conditions. The former is a necessary but not sufficient condition. The latter is a necessary and sufficient condition. These conditions involve the concept of the matrix of parameter restrictions, which will be defined below.

The order condition states that:

$$\rho(\varphi) = K - 1 \qquad \textbf{10.1.29}$$

The rank condition is:

$$\rho(\mathbf{A}\varphi) = K - 1 \qquad \textbf{10.1.30}$$

where K is the number of endogenous variables in the model, **A** is the matrix of parameters to be estimated, φ is the matrix of restrictions imposed on a particular equation, and notation ρ indicates the rank of the matrix.

Let us return to the model of equations 10.1.12 through 10.1.14, consisting of the two endogenous variables Q and P and the two exogenous variables Y and W. Using Y_i for the endogenous variables and Z_i for the exogenous variables, the model can be written as before:

$$a_{11}Y_1 + a_{12}Y_2 + a_{13}Z_1 + a_{14}Z_2 = U_1 \qquad \textbf{10.1.31}$$

$$a_{21}Y_1 + a_{22}Y_2 + a_{23}Z_1 + a_{24}Z_2 = U_2 \qquad \textbf{10.1.32}$$

Imposing the restriction on equation 10.1.31 that Z_1 does not appear, we have:

$$a_{13} = 0$$

The matrix **A** is:

$$\mathbf{A} = \begin{bmatrix} a_{11} & a_{12} & a_{13} & a_{14} \\ a_{21} & a_{22} & a_{23} & a_{24} \end{bmatrix}$$

which can be rewritten as:

$$\mathbf{A} = \begin{bmatrix} \mathbf{A}_1 \\ \mathbf{A}_2 \end{bmatrix}$$

where $\mathbf{A}_1$ is the row vector of the coefficients of the first equation and $\mathbf{A}_2$ the row vector of the coefficients of the second equation. We construct the φ matrix so that $\mathbf{A}_1\varphi = a_{13}$, the element restricted to zero value:

$$\varphi = \begin{bmatrix} 0 \\ 0 \\ 1 \\ 0 \end{bmatrix}$$

$$\mathbf{A}_1\varphi = [a_{11} \quad a_{12} \quad a_{13} \quad a_{14}] \begin{bmatrix} 0 \\ 0 \\ 1 \\ 0 \end{bmatrix} = 0 \cdot a_{11} + 0 \cdot a_{12} + 1 \cdot a_{13} + 0 \cdot a_{14} = a_{13} \qquad \textbf{10.1.33}$$

Obviously, the rank of φ is one. The order condition is then fulfilled since the rank of the φ matrix—which is one—is just equal to the number of endogenous variables minus one, or $2 - 1 = 1$.

To examine the rank condition, let us write the $\mathbf{A}\varphi$ matrix:

$$\mathbf{A}\varphi = \begin{bmatrix} a_{11} & a_{12} & a_{13} & a_{14} \\ a_{21} & a_{22} & a_{23} & a_{24} \end{bmatrix} \begin{bmatrix} 0 \\ 0 \\ 1 \\ 0 \end{bmatrix} = \begin{bmatrix} a_{13} \\ a_{23} \end{bmatrix} = \begin{bmatrix} 0 \\ a_{23} \end{bmatrix} \qquad \textbf{10.1.34}$$

since $a_{13} = 0$. Obviously, $\rho(A\varphi) = 1 = K - 1 = 2 - 1 = 1$. The rank condition in this case is fulfilled if and only if a_{23} is nonzero. Equation 10.1.31 is identified. This is the same thing as saying that Z_1 appears in equation 10.1.32 but not in equation 10.1.31, and that equation 10.1.31 is thus identified. Similar results regarding equation 10.1.32 can be obtained by restricting $a_{24} = 0$; that is, Z_2 appears in equation 10.1.31 but not in equation 10.1.32.[6]

Identities and Identification

It is convenient to treat the identities as a part of the basic system for the purpose of identification. Of course the coefficients of an identity is given a priori, typically specified to be 1 or −1. Thus the identification of the identities themselves is no problem. However, they should be taken into account for counting variables and equations in the system for the identification of the stochastic equations in the system. Let us consider the following model:

$$\begin{aligned} Y_{1t} &= \alpha_0 + \alpha_1 Y_{3t} + U_{1t} \\ Y_{2t} &= \beta_0 + \beta_1 Y_{4t} + U_{2t} \\ Y_{3t} &\equiv Y_{4t} - X_{1t} \\ Y_{4t} &\equiv Y_{1t} + Y_{2t} + X_{2t} \end{aligned} \qquad \textbf{10.1.35}$$

where Y_1 = aggregate consumption

Y_2 = aggregate investment

Y_3 = disposable income

Y_4 = net national product

X_1 = taxes minus transfer payments

X_2 = government expenditure

The variables Y_1, Y_2, Y_3, and Y_4 are endogenous; and X_1 and X_2 are exogenous. If the identities are totally ignored, it will be impossible to discuss identification of the two other stochastic equations in this system. Of the six variables in the above model, the two that are exogenous appear in the identities only. Once this information is available, it is possible to show that the other two equations are not underidentified. An alternative approach would be to substitute the identities into the stochastic equations and proceed from there. Obviously such an approach is more complicated. Of course all models are not specified in a way such that exogenous variables appear only in identities.

[6] The discussion of parameter restrictions in this section has been limited to the special case where all restrictions on the parameters are *zero restrictions* of the form $a_{ij} = 0$. A rigorous presentation of the general case can be found in Franklin M. Fisher, *The Identification Problem in Econometrics* (New York: McGraw-Hill Book Co., 1966).

10.2 TO SECURE IDENTIFICATION

Imposition of restriction 10.0.2 that the variance of U^d is a fraction (less than one) of the variance of U^s needs to be further examined. Obviously, if K is equal to unity, the situation is indeterminate, since both var(U_t^d) and var(U_t^s) are equal. It is zero only in the degenerate case when var(U_t^d) is zero. In between the two extreme cases, K takes a value depending on the relative magnitude of the two variance quantities. The smaller the value of var(U_t^d) in relation to the value of var(U_t^s), the smaller is the value of K; and the presumption is that the demand function is identified, or at least "nearly" so. Whether K is known to be small or found to be so, the "smallness" of K by itself is inadequate to resolve the problem of identification satisfactorily.[7] If one had the additional information as to the absolute size of variances, it would be a help. Such information is seldom available.

The following presents a case where it is possible to secure identification by imposing restrictions on the covariance of structural disturbances. Let us return to the simple model:

$$Q_t^d = \alpha_1 + \alpha_2 P_t + \alpha_3 Y_t + U_{t1} \qquad \textbf{10.2.1}$$

$$Q_t^s = \beta_1 + \beta_2 P_t + U_{t2} \qquad \textbf{10.2.2}$$

$$Q_t^d = Q_t^s \qquad \textbf{10.2.3}$$

Equation 10.2.1 is underidentified, and equation 10.2.2 is just identified. Using equation 10.2.3, we obtain the reduced form, as before:

$$Q_t = \pi_{11} - \pi_{12} Y_t + V_{t1} \qquad \textbf{10.2.4}$$

$$P_t = \pi_{21} - \pi_{22} Y_t + V_{t2} \qquad \textbf{10.2.5}$$

where

$$\pi_{11} = \frac{\beta_1\alpha_2 - \beta_2\alpha_1}{\alpha_2 - \beta_2} \qquad \pi_{21} = \frac{\beta_1 - \alpha_1}{\alpha_2 - \beta_2}$$

$$\pi_{12} = \frac{\beta_2\alpha_3}{\alpha_2 - \beta_2} \qquad \pi_{22} = \frac{\alpha_3}{\alpha_2 - \beta_2}$$

$$V_{t1} = \frac{\alpha_2 U_{t2} - \beta_2 U_{t1}}{\alpha_2 - \beta_2} \qquad V_{t2} = \frac{U_{t2} - U_{t1}}{\alpha_2 - \beta_2}$$

Now we wish to solve for the structural parameters in equations 10.2.1 and 10.2.2 in terms of the reduced form estimates of π_{11}, π_{12}, π_{21}, and π_{22}

[7] For further discussions on identification by restrictions on variances and covariances, the basic reference is Franklin M. Fisher, *op. cit.*, pp. 65-125; also J. Johnston, *Econometric Methods* (2d ed.; New York: McGraw-Hill Book Co., 1972), pp. 365-372.

from equations 10.2.4 and 10.2.5. The solution for the β's in equation 10.2.2 is:

$$\beta_2 = \pi_{12}/\pi_{22} \text{ and } \beta_1 = \pi_{11} - \frac{\pi_{12}\pi_{21}}{\pi_{22}} \qquad \textbf{10.2.6}$$

We cannot solve for the α's in equation 10.2.1 without further information.

One such piece of information is the a priori restriction on structural disturbances:

$$E(U_{t1}U_{t2}) = 0 \qquad \textbf{10.2.7}$$

From equations 10.2.4 and 10.2.5 we have:

$$V_{t1} = \frac{\alpha_2 U_{t2} - \beta_2 U_{t1}}{\alpha_2 - \beta_2}$$

and

$$V_{t2} = \frac{U_{t2} - U_{t1}}{\alpha_2 - \beta_2}$$

From which,

$$U_{t1} = V_{t1} - \alpha_2 V_{t2}$$

and

$$U_{t2} = V_{t1} - \beta_2 V_{t2} \qquad \textbf{10.2.8}$$

We impose restriction 10.2.7 in terms of equation 10.2.8:

$$E[(V_{t1} - \alpha_2 V_{t2})(V_{t1} - \beta_2 V_{t2})] = 0 \qquad \textbf{10.2.9}$$

Using the elements of the variance-covariance matrix of the reduced form residuals from equations 10.2.4 through 10.2.5, we can write, suppressing the t subscript:

$$V_{11} - \alpha_2 V_{12} - \beta_2 V_{12} + \alpha_2\beta_2 V_{22} = 0 \qquad \textbf{10.2.10}$$

Using the solution for $\beta_2 = \pi_{12}/\pi_{22}$ from equation 10.2.6, we can write:

$$V_{11} - \alpha_2 V_{12} - \frac{\pi_{12}}{\pi_{22}} V_{12} + \alpha_2 \frac{\pi_{12}}{\pi_{22}} V_{22} = 0 \qquad \textbf{10.2.11}$$

or,

$$\alpha_2 = \frac{\pi_{12}V_{12} - \pi_{22}V_{11}}{\pi_{12}V_{22} - \pi_{22}V_{12}} \qquad \textbf{10.2.12}$$

Next we can solve for α_1 and α_3 in equation 10.2.1:

$$\alpha_1 = \pi_{11} - \alpha_2\pi_{21}$$

and

$$\alpha_3 = \alpha_2\pi_{22} - \pi_{12} \qquad \mathbf{10.2.13}$$

It is obvious that this restriction would not be helpful if β_2 is not identified a priori as in equation 10.2.6. In other words if both equations are under-identified, this type of restriction is no solution.

In practice econometricians have often resolved the identification problem by respecification of the model. For example it is quite reasonable that in a supply-demand model the supply function has a lagged response to price. One then writes the model as:

$$\begin{aligned} Q_t^d &= \alpha_0 + \alpha_1 P_t + U_t^d \\ Q_t^s &= \beta_0 + \beta_1 P_{t-1} + U_t^s \\ Q_t^d &= Q_t^s \end{aligned} \qquad \mathbf{10.2.14}$$

See if the demand and supply functions are identified. Notice that P_{t-1} is a predetermined variable and is therefore considered given or exogenous. If P_t is the regressor in the supply equation, the two equations will not be identified.

Another way of securing identification is to respecify one equation by including a nonlinear function of the variable appearing as the regressor in both equations. Consider the savings-investment model:

$$\begin{aligned} S_t &= \alpha_0 + \alpha_1 Y_t + U_{t1} \\ I_t &= \beta_0 + \beta_1 Y_t + U_{t2} \\ S_t &= I_t \end{aligned} \qquad \mathbf{10.2.15}$$

It is plausible to rewrite the I function as:

$$I_t = \beta_0 + \beta_1 Y_t + \beta_2 Y_t^2 + U_{2t}$$

The nonlinear investment function and the linear savings function can then be easily distinguished from one another.

However, the most generally practiced method of assuring identification has been the imposition of a priori restrictions on the inclusion of variables in an equation. The necessary and sufficient condition corresponding to the existence of a nonvanishing determinant of appropriate order, or to the presence of a nonzero coefficient of a variable appearing in one equation but not in the other of the two-equation model, is generally known as the *zero restriction*.[8] Such a restriction specifies that a certain variable is absent in certain equations. It is pertinent to ask why consumer income Y_t would

---

[8] The restrictions that a specific parameter has a known nonzero numerical value or that some of the parameters are uniquely related in terms of a known nonzero value belong to the same class of restrictions.

ever appear in the demand equation but not in the supply equation for an agricultural commodity, and why the reverse would ever be true for weather conditions W_t. The statistician or mathematician has no answer. We must look back to economic theory to find such support. It is evident that the exclusion of a variable from one or another equation in a system is based on a priori information. The more economic theory is developed to provide a priori information, the more surely will the identification problem be solved. It has been pointed out by some econometricians that variables are often excluded or included in an equation rather arbitrarily, and that most economic relationships are underidentified. This debate can be fully answered only by an evaluation of economic theory and its state of development.

DISCUSSION QUESTIONS

1. If the equilibrium observations are used to estimate an equation of the form:

$$Q_t = b_0 + b_1 P_t + U_t$$

will the econometrician be estimating the demand or the supply equation?

2. Discuss briefly the problem of identification in terms of parameter values in a single-equation model. (Hint: Refer to distributed lag models and also to the discussions relative to dummy variables in models.)

3. (a) Define the conditions of identification in a linear model.
   (b) How can we test the necessary and sufficient conditions for identification?
   (c) What do we mean by overidentification and underidentification?
   (d) Discuss the role of identities in reference to the problem of identification of an equation in a given model.

4. (a) The case for identification by imposing restrictions on the relative size of the variance of structural disturbances of the given equations in a model needs to be carefully examined. Why?
   (b) Discuss the case of identification by imposing restrictions on the covariance of structural disturbances. Can this method work if both equations in a given model are underidentified?

5. Consider the following model:

$$C_t = b_0 + b_1 Y_t + U_t$$

$$Y_t = C_t + I_t$$

where C, Y, and I are aggregate consumption, income, and investment in constant money values; and U refers to the disturbance term as before. Check the identification condition of the relationships of the above model. (Note that C and Y are endogenous and I exogenous.)

6. Rewrite the above model as follows:

$$C_t = b_0 + b_1 Y_t + U_{1t}$$

$$I_t = c_0 + c_1 Y_t + U_{2t}$$

$$Y_t = C_t + I_t$$

Check the identification conditions for both the consumption and investment equations. Use the necessary as well as necessary and sufficient conditions.

7. (a) Refer to the model described in equations 10.1.12 through 10.1.14, and, by using the rank and order conditions, check to see that each equation is just identified.
   (b) How would you know that Y_t appears with a zero coefficient in equation 10.1.13 and a nonzero coefficient in equation 10.1.12? Again, how is it that W_t appears with a nonzero coefficient in equation 10.1.13, but with a zero coefficient in equation 10.1.12?

8. One way of looking at the identification problem is to relate the structural parameters to the reduced form parameters. Examine this statement. (For a fuller discussion of the reduced form, see materials in Chapter 11.)

9. Write out a supply-demand model for a given commodity where both the supply and demand equations are overidentified. Offer a brief justification in terms of economic theory.

10. (a) Is identification a statistical problem or a logical problem?
    (b) If each equation of the given model is underidentified, can the parameters be estimated?
    (c) Is it proper to assume that economic relationships are generally underidentified? Give reasons for your answer.

11. Discuss the identification conditions for each equation in the following model presented by Lawrence R. Klein:

$$C = a_0 + a_1 W + a_2 P + U_1$$

$$I = b_0 + b_1 P + b_2 P_{-1} + b_3 K_{-1} + U_2$$

$$W = g_0 + g_1 Y + g_2 Y_{-1} + g_3 T + U_3$$

$$Y = C + I + G$$

$$Y = P + W$$

$$I = K - K_{-1}$$

Note that C, I, W, P, K, and Y are the endogenous variables in the model; and the exogenous variables are T and G.

12. Review the identification conditions of the following model. (Note that the Y's and X's denote endogenous and exogenous variables respectively).

$$Y_1 = a_0 + a_1(Y_3 + X_1) + a_2 Y_4 + U_1$$

$$Y_2 = b_0 + b_1 Y_4 + b_2 Y_{4-1} + b_3 Y_{5-1} + U_2$$

$$Y_3 = g_0 + g_1(Y_6 + X_2 - X_1) + g_2(Y_6 + X_2 - X_1)_{-1} + g_3 X_3 + U_3$$

$$Y_4 = Y_6 - Y_3 - X_1$$

$$Y_5 = Y_2 + Y_{5-1}$$

$$Y_6 = Y_1 + Y_2 + X_4 - X_2$$

SUGGESTED READINGS

Ando, Albert, Franklin M. Fisher, and Herbert A. Simon. *Essays on the Structure of Social Science Models*. Cambridge, Mass.: Massachusetts Institute of Technology Press, 1963.

Basmann, Robert L. "On Finite Sample Distributions of Generalized Classical Linear Identifiability Test Statistics." *Journal of the American Statistical Association,* Vol. 55, No. 292 (December, 1960), pp. 650-659.

Fisher, Franklin M. *The Identification Problem in Econometrics*. New York: McGraw-Hill Book Co., 1966.

Frisch, Ragnar. "Pitfalls in the Statistical Construction of Demand and Supply Curves." *Veröffentlichungen der Frankfurter Gesellschaft für Konjuncturforschung,* Neue Folge, Heft 5, Leipzig, Hans Buske Verlag (1933).

Haavelmo, Trygve. "The Probability Approach in Econometrics." *Econometrica,* Vol. 12, supplement (1944).

Kmenta, Jan. *Elements of Econometrics*. New York: Macmillan Co., 1971.

Koopmans, T. C., and W. C. Hood. "The Estimation of Simultaneous Linear Economic Relations.". *Studies in Econometric Method,* edited by W. C. Hood and T. C. Koopmans. New York: John Wiley & Sons, 1953, pp. 112-199.

Koopmans, T. C., H. Rubin, and R. B. Leipnik. "Measuring the Equation Systems of Dynamic Economics." *Statistical Inference in Dynamic Economic Models,* edited by T. C. Koopmans. New York: John Wiley & Sons, 1950, pp. 69-110.

Koopmans, Tjalling C. "Identification Problems in Economic Model Construction." *Studies in Econometric Method,* edited by W. C. Hood and T. C. Koopmans. New York: John Wiley & Sons, 1953, pp. 27-48.

Schultz, Henry. *Theory and Measurement of Demand*. Chicago: University of Chicago Press, 1938.

Simon, Herbert. "Causal Ordering and Identifiability." *Studies in Econometric Method,* edited by W. C. Hood and T. C. Koopmans. New York: John Wiley & Sons, 1953, pp. 49-74.

Wald, Abraham. "Note on Identification of Economic Relations." *Statistical Inference in Dynamic Economic Models,* edited by T. C. Koopmans. New York: John Wiley & Sons, 1950, pp. 238-244.

Working, Elmer J. "What Do Statistical Demand Curves Show?" *Quarterly Journal of Economics,* Vol. 41, No. 2 (February, 1927), pp. 212-235.

11

interdependent systems of linear equations

11.0 THE CONCEPT OF INTERDEPENDENCE AND ITS CONSEQUENCE

So far we have considered how to estimate parameters of economic models when the relationship among variables is expressed in a single equation. But the facts of economic life are not so simple that they can all be meaningfully described by single-equation models. This point has been emphasized right from the beginning. The interdependence of economic variables is an important facet in the determination of an economic system. Recall the principles of Marshallian price theory. The quantity demanded as well as the quantity supplied depend on the price of the commodity, and the equilibrium price itself is determined by the "two blades of the scissors" through the market-clearing operation. Symbolically, we can write:

$$\begin{aligned} Q_t^d &= \beta_0 + \beta_1 P_t + U_t^d \\ Q_t^s &= \alpha_0 + \alpha_1 P_t + U_t^s \\ Q_t^d &= Q_t^s \qquad t = 1, 2, \ldots, T \end{aligned} \qquad \mathbf{11.0.1}$$

The quantity exchanged in the market and the price of the commodity are jointly determined by this interdependent system in market operations. Stated more formally, price and quantity are the two endogenous variables jointly determined by this three-equation model. (Check identification!)

The simple Keynesian model of income determination is an example of interdependent relationships in macroeconomics.

$$\begin{aligned} C_t &= \beta_0 + \beta_1 Y_t + U_t \\ Y_t &= C_t + I_t \qquad t = 1, 2, \ldots, T \end{aligned} \qquad \mathbf{11.0.2}$$

In this two-equation macroeconomic model the two variables C (consumption) and Y (income) are endogenous, jointly determined variables, given I (investment) as an exogenous or predetermined variable. Note that only the first equation in the model is a behavioral equation, whereas the second is an equilibrium condition expressed as an accounting identity. The Walrasian theory of general equilibrium takes the student of economics further toward the concept of interdependence and points to the fundamental dictum—"everything depends on everything else."

Economic models constructed to express interdependence in economic relationships are *systems of simultaneous equations*. Each equation in such a system describes a different relationship among a different set of the variables in the system; but all these relationships are assumed to hold at once, that is, *simultaneously*.

For all these interdependent simultaneous equation systems, the classical OLS method of estimation is inadequate. If it is used, it yields biased and inconsistent estimators. The problem in estimating the parameters of multi-equation systems relates to the assumptions on which the properties of the OLS estimators depend. An important assumption states that the disturbance term in each equation is uncorrelated with any of the regressors that appear in the equation; that is, $\text{cov}(XU) = 0$, where X denotes a regressor and U the disturbance term in a particular equation. As discussed in an earlier chapter, this assumption implies that the direction of influence is from the regressors to the regressand. In a single-equation model the variables appearing on the right-hand side of the equation are assumed to be predetermined, and the covariance between the disturbance term and each of these regressors is zero. But in a multiequation model where interdependence among equations is expressed, all variables appearing as regressors in any single equation of the given system cannot be assumed to be predetermined. Indeed one or more of the regressors that appear in each equation of a simultaneous system are endogenous variables jointly determined by the system. When that is the case, the covariance between the disturbance term of the particular equation and the endogenous variables jointly determined by the system and appearing as regressors in the specific equation cannot be assumed to be zero.

Turning the argument around, we can state that a variable is predetermined with respect to the kth equation if and only if it is uncorrelated in the probability limit with the disturbance of the kth equation U_k. As noted before, $\text{plim}(\Sigma XU)/T$ is the consistent estimate of the population $\text{cov}(XU)$. Hence the condition of zero covariance between the regressor and the disturbance of the given equation is important.

In equations 11.0.1, $\text{cov}(P_t U_t^d) \neq 0$ and $\text{cov}(P_t U_t^s) \neq 0$. Similarly, in equations 11.0.2, $\text{cov}(Y_t U_t) \neq 0$. Thus the OLS estimates are seen to be biased and inconsistent, as shown in Chapter 9.

Attempts to solve the problem have received a great deal of attention in econometrics.[1] Two particular attempts will be described in sections 3 and 4 of this chapter: idealized uniequation models and recursive models. As we shall see, neither of these provides a complete solution for the difficulties;

[1] Carl F. Christ, *et al.*, "A Symposium on Simultaneous Equation Estimation," *Econometrica*, Vol. 28, No. 4 (October, 1960), pp. 835-871. T. Haavelmo, "The Statistical Implications of a System of Simultaneous Equations," *Econometrica*, Vol. 11, No. 1 (January, 1943), pp. 1-12.

and econometricians have been led to seek alternatives to the OLS method in order to obtain consistent estimates for models of interdependent systems.

11.1 NOTATIONAL PROBLEMS IN MULTIEQUATION SYSTEMS

Let us examine a familiar model of the market for the commodity wheat:

$$
\begin{aligned}
Q_t &= \alpha_1 + \alpha_2 P_t + \alpha_3 A_t + \alpha_4 N_t + U_{1t} \\
P_t &= \delta_1 + \delta_2 Q_t + \delta_3 W_t + \delta_4 Z_{1t} + \delta_5 Z_{2t} + U_{2t} \\
& \qquad t = 1,2,\ldots,T
\end{aligned}
\qquad \text{11.1.1}
$$

where Q = quantity of the commodity traded
P = price of the commodity
A = aggregate income of the consumers
N = population
W = weather condition
Z_1 = policy variable 1: government wheat subsidy
Z_2 = policy variable 2: government purchases of wheat

Obviously, the first equation is the demand relation and the second is the supply equation. The model is based on the two behavioral equations. The price P and the quantity traded of the commodity Q are the two endogenous variables jointly determined by the two equations of the model. The model uses five exogenous variables—A, N, W, Z_1, and Z_2. These variables are predetermined or determined outside the given model. The specification of the model is based on a priori knowledge of the wheat market.

Denoting the endogenous variables by Y_i and the predetermined variables by X_i, we have:

$$Q_t = Y_{t1} \text{ and } P_t = Y_{t2}$$

and

$$A_t = X_{t1},\ N_t = X_{t2},\ W_t = X_{t3},\ Z_{t1} = X_{t4},\ Z_{t2} = X_{t5}$$

Recall that the constant term (or the parameter relating to the intercept of an equation) can be estimated from a dummy predetermined variable, which assumes the value of 1 for all t. We can include another X variable, say $X_{t6} \equiv 1$, for all t. We can designate the parameters of the Y's by β_{ij} and those of the X's by γ_{ij}. This makes us immediately aware of whether a parameter relates to a jointly determined endogenous variable or to a predetermined variable. It is also convenient to use two subscripts for each such parameter, the first subscript denoting the number of the equation and the second the variable, that is, the ith equation and the jth variable.

If all variables appeared in each equation, model 11.1.1 would be as follows:

$$\begin{aligned}\beta_{11}Y_{t1} + \beta_{12}Y_{t2} + \gamma_{11}X_{t1} + \gamma_{12}X_{t2} + \gamma_{13}X_{t3} + \gamma_{14}X_{t4}\\ + \gamma_{15}X_{t5} + \gamma_{16}X_{t6} + U_{t1} = 0\\ \beta_{21}Y_{t1} + \beta_{22}Y_{t2} + \gamma_{21}X_{t1} + \gamma_{22}X_{t2} + \gamma_{23}X_{t3} + \gamma_{24}X_{t4}\\ + \gamma_{25}X_{t5} + \gamma_{26}X_{t6} + U_{t2} = 0\end{aligned} \qquad \mathbf{11.1.2}$$

Notice, in terms of the equations of wheat model 11.1.1, that we have $\alpha_1 = \gamma_{16}$, $\alpha_2 = \beta_{12}$, $\alpha_3 = \gamma_{11}$, $\alpha_4 = \gamma_{12}$, $\delta_1 = \gamma_{26}$, $\delta_2 = \beta_{21}$, $\delta_3 = \gamma_{23}$, $\delta_4 = \gamma_{24}$, and $\delta_5 = \gamma_{25}$. Following the specification of model 11. 1. 1, the a priori restrictions are $\gamma_{13} = \gamma_{14} = \gamma_{15} = \gamma_{21} = \gamma_{22} = 0$. The first equation can be divided by $-\beta_{11}$ and the second by $-\beta_{22}$, and the form of the equation remains the same. That is, the first parameter in the first equation, β_{11}, can be made equal to -1. Similarly, β_{22}, the second parameter of the second equation, can be made equal to -1. In general we can make $\beta_{ii} = -1$ by dividing the ith equation by the coefficient of Y_i. Obviously, this normalization procedure divides the other parameters in the equation by β_{ii}. Thus the parameters become different from their original form.

Rewriting the above two equations with $\beta_{11} = \beta_{22} = -1$ and rearranging, we obtain the familiar form:

$$\begin{aligned}Y_{t1} &= \beta_{12}Y_{t2} + \gamma_{11}X_{t1} + \gamma_{12}X_{t2} + \gamma_{16}X_{t6} + U_{t1}\\ Y_{t2} &= \beta_{21}Y_{t1} + \gamma_{23}X_{t3} + \gamma_{24}X_{t4} + \gamma_{25}X_{t5} + \gamma_{26}X_{t6} + U_{t2}\end{aligned} \qquad \mathbf{11.1.3}$$

In terms of matrices, we can rewrite these two equations as follows:

$$\begin{bmatrix}\beta_{11} & \beta_{12}\\ \beta_{21} & \beta_{22}\end{bmatrix}\begin{bmatrix}Y_{t1}\\ Y_{t2}\end{bmatrix} + \begin{bmatrix}\gamma_{11} & \gamma_{12} & 0 & 0 & 0 & \gamma_{16}\\ 0 & 0 & \gamma_{23} & \gamma_{24} & \gamma_{25} & \gamma_{26}\end{bmatrix}\begin{bmatrix}X_{t1}\\ X_{t2}\\ X_{t3}\\ X_{t4}\\ X_{t5}\\ X_{t6}\end{bmatrix} + \begin{bmatrix}U_{t1}\\ U_{t2}\end{bmatrix} = \begin{bmatrix}0\\ 0\end{bmatrix} \qquad \mathbf{11.1.4}$$

In a general model with k endogenous and m predetermined variables, the model expands to:

$$\begin{bmatrix} \beta_{11} & \beta_{12} \dots \beta_{1K} \\ \beta_{21} & \beta_{22} \dots \beta_{2K} \\ \cdot & \cdot \quad \cdot \\ \cdot & \cdot \quad \cdot \\ \cdot & \cdot \quad \cdot \\ \beta_{K1} & \beta_{K2} \dots \beta_{KK} \end{bmatrix} \begin{bmatrix} Y_{t1} \\ Y_{t2} \\ \cdot \\ \cdot \\ \cdot \\ Y_{tK} \end{bmatrix} + \begin{bmatrix} \gamma_{11} & \gamma_{12} \dots \gamma_{1M} \\ \gamma_{21} & \gamma_{22} \dots \gamma_{2M} \\ \cdot & \cdot \quad \cdot \\ \cdot & \cdot \quad \cdot \\ \cdot & \cdot \quad \cdot \\ \gamma_{K1} & \gamma_{K2} \dots \gamma_{KM} \end{bmatrix} \begin{bmatrix} X_{t1} \\ X_{t2} \\ \cdot \\ \cdot \\ \cdot \\ X_{tM} \end{bmatrix}$$

$$+ \begin{bmatrix} U_{t1} \\ U_{t2} \\ \cdot \\ \cdot \\ \cdot \\ U_{tK} \end{bmatrix} = \begin{bmatrix} 0 \\ 0 \\ \cdot \\ \cdot \\ \cdot \\ 0 \end{bmatrix} \qquad \textbf{11.1.5}$$

$$k = 1, 2, \dots, K$$
$$m = 1, 2, \dots, M$$
$$t = 1, 2, \dots, T$$

or, in compact matrix notation,

$$\boldsymbol{\beta}\mathbf{Y} + \boldsymbol{\Gamma}\mathbf{X} + \mathbf{U} = 0 \qquad \textbf{11.1.6}$$

where $\boldsymbol{\beta}$ is a $K \times K$ matrix of the coefficients of the jointly determined endogenous variables
$\boldsymbol{\Gamma}$ is a $K \times M$ matrix of coefficients of the predetermined variables
$\mathbf{Y}$ is a $K \times 1$ column vector of K endogenous variables
$\mathbf{X}$ is an $M \times 1$ column vector of M predetermined variables
$\mathbf{U}$ is a $K \times 1$ column vector of K disturbance terms

A single equation, for example the first one, appears as follows, suppressing the t subscript:

$$\beta_{11}Y_1 + \beta_{12}Y_2 + \dots + \beta_{1K}Y_K + \gamma_{11}X_1 + \gamma_{12}X_2 + \dots + \gamma_{1M}X_M + U_1 = 0 \qquad \textbf{11.1.7}$$

Setting β_{11} equal to -1 and rearranging, we obtain the familiar form:

$$Y_1 = \beta_{12}Y_2 + \dots + \beta_{1K}Y_K + \gamma_{11}X_1 + \gamma_{12}X_2 + \dots + \gamma_{1M}X_M + U_1 \qquad \textbf{11.1.8}$$

In matrix notation we can write equation 11.1.7 as:

$$\boldsymbol{\beta}_1\mathbf{Y} + \boldsymbol{\gamma}_1\mathbf{X} + \mathbf{U}_1 = \mathbf{0} \qquad \textbf{11.1.9}$$

where $\boldsymbol{\beta}_1$ is a $1 \times K$ row vector of coefficients of the jointly determined variables appearing in equation 1
$\mathbf{Y}$ is a $K \times 1$ column vector of the jointly determined variables in equation 1
$\boldsymbol{\gamma}_1$ is a $1 \times M$ row vector of coefficients of the predetermined variables appearing in equation 1
$\mathbf{X}$ is an $M \times 1$ column vector of predetermined variables in equation 1
$\mathbf{U}_1$ is a disturbance vector in equation 1

Note that $\boldsymbol{\beta}_1$ is the first row of the $K \times K$ matrix $\boldsymbol{\beta}$, and $\boldsymbol{\gamma}_1$ is the first row of the $K \times M$ matrix in equation 11.1.6.

At times we write:

$$\mathbf{Y}'\boldsymbol{\beta}_1' + \mathbf{X}'\boldsymbol{\gamma}_1' + \mathbf{U}_1 = \mathbf{0}$$

or, suppressing the prime sign,

$$\mathbf{Y}\boldsymbol{\beta}_1 + \mathbf{X}\boldsymbol{\gamma}_1 + \mathbf{U}_1 = \mathbf{0} \qquad \textbf{11.1.10}$$

In equation 11.1.10 the rows and columns of relevant matrices have been transposed, where:

$\mathbf{Y}'$ is a $1 \times K$ row vector of the jointly determined variables in equation 1
$\boldsymbol{\beta}_1'$ is a $K \times 1$ column vector of their coefficients
$\mathbf{X}'$ is a $1 \times M$ row vector of predetermined variables in equation 1
$\boldsymbol{\gamma}_1'$ is an $M \times 1$ column vector of their coefficients
$\mathbf{U}_1$ is a disturbance vector in equation 1

Seldom do all k jointly determined variables and m predetermined variables in the model appear in each equation. To denote that a subset of Y's and X's appear in a particular equation, it is customary to write:

$$\boldsymbol{\beta}_k\mathbf{Y}^* + \boldsymbol{\gamma}_k\mathbf{X}^* + \mathbf{U}_k = 0 \qquad \textbf{11.1.11}$$

or, following equation 11.1.10,

$$\mathbf{Y}^*\boldsymbol{\beta}_k + \mathbf{X}^*\boldsymbol{\gamma}_k + \mathbf{U}_k = 0 \qquad \textbf{11.1.12}$$

where $\mathbf{Y}^*$ and $\mathbf{X}^*$ denote the subset of jointly determined and predetermined variables respectively that appear in equation k, as opposed to $\mathbf{Y}^{**}$ and $\mathbf{X}^{**}$, the subsets of such variables not appearing in equation k.

Note that system 11.1.6 is often written, again ignoring the prime sign, as:

$$\mathbf{Y}\boldsymbol{\beta} + \mathbf{X}\boldsymbol{\Gamma} + \mathbf{U} = \mathbf{0} \qquad \textbf{11.1.13}$$

where **Y** is a $1 \times K$ row vector of the jointly determined variables in the system

- $\boldsymbol{\beta}$ is a $K \times K$ matrix of coefficients of the jointly determined variables in the system
- **X** is a $1 \times M$ row vector of the predetermined variables appearing in the system
- $\boldsymbol{\Gamma}$ is an $M \times K$ matrix of the coefficients of all predetermined variables appearing in the system
- **U** is a $1 \times K$ row vector of disturbance terms of all K equations of the system

In terms of all the observations ($t = 1, 2, \ldots, T$), we can write the **Y**, **X**, and **U** matrices as follows:

$$\mathbf{Y} = \begin{bmatrix} Y_{11} & Y_{12} \ldots Y_{1K} \\ Y_{21} & Y_{22} \ldots Y_{2K} \\ \cdot & \cdot \qquad \cdot \\ \cdot & \cdot \qquad \cdot \\ \cdot & \cdot \qquad \cdot \\ Y_{T1} & Y_{T2} \ldots Y_{TK} \end{bmatrix} \qquad \textbf{11.1.14}$$

$$\mathbf{X} = \begin{bmatrix} X_{11} & X_{12} \ldots X_{1M} \\ X_{21} & X_{22} \ldots X_{2M} \\ \cdot & \cdot \qquad \cdot \\ \cdot & \cdot \qquad \cdot \\ \cdot & \cdot \qquad \cdot \\ X_{T1} & X_{T2} \ldots X_{TM} \end{bmatrix} \qquad \textbf{11.1.15}$$

$$\mathbf{U} = \begin{bmatrix} U_{11} & U_{12} \ldots U_{1K} \\ U_{21} & U_{22} \ldots U_{2K} \\ \cdot & \cdot \qquad \cdot \\ \cdot & \cdot \qquad \cdot \\ \cdot & \cdot \qquad \cdot \\ U_{T1} & U_{T2} \ldots U_{TK} \end{bmatrix} \qquad \textbf{11.1.16}$$

Y is a $T \times K$ matrix of observations on all the jointly determined endogenous variables
X is a $T \times M$ matrix of observations on all the exogenous variables
U is a $T \times K$ matrix of all the disturbance terms

11.2 STRUCTURAL FORM AND REDUCED FORM FOR MULTIEQUATION SYSTEMS

Consider a system of k linear equations involving k endogenous variables, $Y_1, Y_2, \ldots, Y_K$, and m predetermined variables, $X_1, X_2, \ldots, X_M$, as in equations 11.1.5 and 11.1.6.

$$\boldsymbol{\beta}\mathbf{Y} + \boldsymbol{\Gamma}\mathbf{X} + \mathbf{U} = \mathbf{0} \qquad \textbf{11.2.1}$$

To recapitulate,

1. The **Y** is a $K \times 1$ column vector of endogenous variables jointly determined by the system. These variables influence each other, and they are all influenced by the exogenous variables in the system. However, they do not influence the exogenous variables.
2. The **X** is an $M \times 1$ column vector of predetermined variables. These variables are exogenous to the system and assumed to be nonstochastic; that is, they are fixed in repeated sampling.
3. The parameters in the matrices $\boldsymbol{\beta}$ and $\boldsymbol{\Gamma}$ exist, but most of them are unknown. A priori restrictions make some of them equal to zero or unity or make some of them proportional to each other.
4. **U** is a $K \times 1$ column vector of stochastic disturbances. These disturbances have a nondegenerate joint distribution function with zero mean and a variance matrix, denoted $\boldsymbol{\Sigma}$, which is not necessarily diagonal, although it may be diagonal in specific cases.
5. There are T values of each **Y** and **X** corresponding to a random sample of T independently selected observations on all variables. The population from which the sample is drawn is assumed to be infinite. (In econometrics, particularly in time-series data, this assumption is seldom fulfilled.)

The set of equations 11.2.1 is called the *structural form* or *structure* of the model. The term "structure" is used here in a somewhat different context from the earlier discussion relating to the structure and the model (Chapter 2). To avoid confusion, some econometricians prefer the term "primary form." The common usage, the use of the term "structure" in reference to this particular form, is followed here for the equations of the model. From equation 11.2.1 we have the structural form:

$$\boldsymbol{\beta}\mathbf{Y} + \boldsymbol{\Gamma}\mathbf{X} + \mathbf{U} = \mathbf{0}$$

Premultiplying by $\boldsymbol{\beta}^{-1}$, we obtain:

$$\boldsymbol{\beta}^{-1}(\boldsymbol{\beta}\mathbf{Y}) + \boldsymbol{\beta}^{-1}(\boldsymbol{\Gamma}\mathbf{X}) + \boldsymbol{\beta}^{-1}\mathbf{U} = 0 \qquad \textbf{11.2.2}$$

Rearranging,

$$(\boldsymbol{\beta}^{-1}\boldsymbol{\beta})\mathbf{Y} = (-\boldsymbol{\beta}^{-1}\boldsymbol{\Gamma})\mathbf{X} + (-\boldsymbol{\beta}^{-1})\mathbf{U}$$

Let $\boldsymbol{\Omega} = -\boldsymbol{\beta}^{-1}\boldsymbol{\Gamma}$ and $\mathbf{V} = -\boldsymbol{\beta}^{-1}\mathbf{U}$. Then, since $\boldsymbol{\beta}^{-1}\boldsymbol{\beta}\mathbf{Y} = \mathbf{Y}$, we have:

$$\mathbf{Y} = \boldsymbol{\Omega}\mathbf{X} + \mathbf{V} \qquad \textbf{11.2.3}$$

where $\boldsymbol{\Omega}$ is a $K \times M$ matrix of the reduced form coefficients
$\mathbf{V}$ is a $K \times 1$ matrix of reduced form disturbance terms

Equation 11.2.3 is the reduced form of the given structure 11.2.1. Obviously, the reduced form can be obtained only if matrix $\boldsymbol{\beta}$ is nonsingular. If it is singular, the determinant of $\boldsymbol{\beta}$ will be zero, and its inversion will not be possible. In this case there will be no way of obtaining $\boldsymbol{\Omega}$ and $\mathbf{V}$.

Note that in reduced form all the variables appearing on the right-hand side of each equation in the system are X's, which are assumed to be predetermined variables. Thus in estimating parameters for the reduced form equations, the assumption of zero covariance between the disturbance term **V** and the regressors **X** will hold; and the OLS estimators of the reduced form equations will be unbiased and consistent (Chapter 10). We shall presently see that if the model is just identified, the OLS estimators of the reduced form parameters can be useful.

There are several reasons why econometricians prefer to estimate parameters of the equations of a multiequation system in their structural form.[2] First, as we shall presently see in section 11.4, in an overidentified system there exists no unique solution from the reduced form parameters to the structural parameters. In addition, to reach the reduced form by a process of successive substitution, the regressors in all equations add up to a large number even when the structural form of the behavior equations appears to have relatively few regressors.

Next, in moving from the structural form to the reduced form, the essential step is to replace the jointly determined endogenous variables appearing as regressors on the right-hand side of each equation in the system by appropriate combinations of the predetermined variables. Then all the regressors in all the equations in the reduced form are predetermined variables. But in this process the reduced form parameters often become extremely complicated expressions of the structural parameters, and the algebraic manipulation becomes correspondingly difficult.

---

[2] Lawrence R. Klein, "The Efficiency of Estimation in Econometric Models," *Essays in Economics and Econometrics*, edited by Ralph W. Pfouts (Chapel Hill: University of North Carolina Press, 1964), pp. 216-232. H.O.A. Wold, *Econometric Model Building* (Amsterdam: North-Holland Publishing Co., 1967), pp. 5-36.

Furthermore, the process of successive substitution may result in such a combination of regressors appearing in the reduced form equations (even though all are predetermined variables) that the severity of the degree of multicollinearity among this collection of regressors leads to the breakdown of the estimation method. This contingency may arise even when the problem of multicollinearity was not severe in the structural equations.

L. R. Klein shows that direct estimation of the reduced form, not recognizing a priori restrictions that are embedded in the set of structural equations, leads to a loss of efficiency.[3] The optimum use of a priori information requires that the econometrician estimate the structural parameters directly.

11.3 IDEALIZED UNIEQUATION MODELS

Even when the interdependence of economic relationships is recognized, attempts have been made to construct single-equation models that, it is argued, are equally valid. These will be called "idealized uniequation models." It has been claimed that for agricultural commodities, or for perishable goods generally, such models are appropriate.[4]

It is argued that the quantity supplied in the market for these commodities is predetermined. The quantity is partly dependent on factors determined in a previous time period when the activity was initiated; when the crop was planted, for example. The process of producing an agricultural commodity is assumed to continue irreversibly, with each step dependent on previous stages. The quantity that reaches the market is then dependent on purely predetermined variables. If this argument is accepted, it follows that the price of the commodity is determined by the quantity offered in the market, especially when there is a fully competitive market and no withholding of the supply is permitted. This description of the relationships leads to the simple demand model:

$$P_t = \alpha_0 + \alpha_1 Q_t + U_t \qquad \textbf{11.3.1}$$

where $\alpha_1 < 0$
$\alpha_0 \geq 0$

When Q_t is predetermined, $\text{cov}(Q_t U_t) = 0$; and the OLS estimates have been shown to be unbiased and consistent. The equation above expresses a demand relation with a priori restrictions based on economic theory. The econometrician is free to apply the OLS regression method for the estimation of the parameters. Notice that the assumption made here strictly requires his regressing price P_t on quantity Q_t, not Q_t on P_t. The direction of functional dependence is from Q to P, not vice versa.

---

[3] Klein, *loc. cit.*

[4] Karl A. Fox, *Econometric Analysis for Public Policy* (Ames: Iowa State College Press, 1958), pp. 75 and 105.

Some care is necessary at this stage if we wish to compute the price elasticity of demand, which is, algebraically:

$$\frac{dQ/Q}{dP/P} \text{ or } \frac{dQ}{dP}\frac{P}{Q} \qquad \mathbf{11.3.2}$$

from the function $Q = f(P)$. In the present case we have $P = g(Q)$, and the resultant elasticity expression is:

$$\frac{dP/P}{dQ/Q} \text{ or } \frac{dP}{dQ}\frac{Q}{P} \qquad \mathbf{11.3.3}$$

Obviously, this quantity is not the measure of price elasticity but its reciprocal. The above expression is usually called "price flexibility," and price elasticity is then obtained for simplicity by taking its reciprocal.[5]

Even though the argument on which model 11.3.1 is based permits the use of the OLS estimation method, the model is of very limited significance. One can argue that the single-equation demand models based on an a priori restriction that assumes a much smaller variance of the disturbance term in the demand equation compared to that of the variance of the disturbance term of supply equation 10.0.2 are also illustrations of idealized uniequation models. These models recognize the interdependence between demand and supply relations but impose a priori restrictions on their relative disturbance variances. These assumptions make the OLS method for estimating the demand equation applicable without any explicit recognition of its interdependence on the supply function in the form of a second simultaneous equation.

11.4 THE RECURSIVE SYSTEM

Interdependence is a fact of economic life, but one may argue that economic interdependence is not simultaneous but recursive.[6] Model 11.3.1 is essentially an argument for the recursive model. The familiar "cobweb" model of demand and supply is an example of a recursive system.

$$\begin{aligned} Q_t &= a + bP_{t-1} + U_t^s \text{ (supply equation)} \\ P_t &= c + dQ_t + U_t^d \text{ (demand equation)} \end{aligned} \qquad \mathbf{11.4.1}$$

where $b > 0$; $d < 0$; $a, c \geq 0$

[5] Lawrence R. Klein, *An Introduction to Econometrics* (Englewood Cliffs, New Jersey: Prentice-Hall, 1962), p. 52.

[6] R. H. Strotz and H.O.A. Wold, "Recursive vs. Nonrecursive Systems," *Econometrica*, Vol. 28, No. 2 (April, 1960), pp. 417-427. H.O.A. Wold, "A Generalization of Causal Chain Models," *Econometrica*, Vol. 28, No. 2 (April, 1960), pp. 443-463. Ragnar Bentzel and B. Hansen, "On Recursiveness and Interdependency in Economic Models," *Review of Economic Studies*, Vol. 22 (1954), pp. 153-168. Ragnar Bentzel and Herman O.A. Wold, "On Statistical Demand Analysis from the Viewpoint of Simultaneous Equations," *Skandinavisk Aktuarietidskrift*, Vol. 29 (1946), pp. 95-114. For a recent application, see Meghnad Desai, "An Econometric Model of the World Tin Market," *Econometrica*, Vol. 34, No. 1 (January, 1966), pp. 105-134.

This is a dynamic system, and it is assumed to work in a unique time sequence. (The convergence of the system to a single pair of values P and Q depends on the familiar condition on the relative size of the absolute values of parameters b and d.) As we shall see, this assumption implies that the covariance between the disturbance term U and the regressors in each equation is zero; and thus each equation of the system can be estimated by the OLS method to yield unbiased and consistent estimates. For example, in the supply equation above, the variable P_{t-1} is predetermined in the sense that it is known from the previous time period. Thus $\text{cov}(P_{t-1}U_t^s) = 0$. Again, in the demand equation, Q_t is predetermined since it is given from the prior supply equation. Thus $\text{cov}(Q_t U_t^d) = 0$.

The general recursive model can be stated as follows:

$$\begin{array}{lcl} \beta_{11}Y_1 & + & \sum_1^M \gamma_{1M}X_M = U_1 \\ \beta_{21}Y_1 + \beta_{22}Y_2 & + & \sum_1^M \gamma_{2M}X_M = U_2 \\ \vdots & & \vdots \\ \beta_{K1}Y_1 + \beta_{K2}Y_2 + \cdots + \beta_{KK}Y_K & + & \sum_1^M \gamma_{KM}X_M = U_K \end{array} \qquad \textbf{11.4.2}$$

The $\boldsymbol{\beta}$ matrix for this recursive system will thus be as follows:

$$\begin{bmatrix} \beta_{11} & 0 & 0 & 0 \ldots 0 \\ \beta_{21} & \beta_{22} & 0 & 0 \ldots 0 \\ \beta_{31} & \beta_{32} & \beta_{33} & 0 \ldots 0 \\ \cdot & \cdot & \cdot & \cdot \quad \cdot \\ \cdot & \cdot & \cdot & \cdot \quad \cdot \\ \cdot & \cdot & \cdot & \cdot \quad \cdot \\ \beta_{K1} & \beta_{K2} & \beta_{K3} & \beta_{K4} \ldots \beta_{KK} \end{bmatrix} \qquad \textbf{11.4.3}$$

The matrix of coefficients relative to the jointly determined Y endogenous variables is triangular. There is no such restriction on the $\boldsymbol{\Gamma}$ matrix, even though in reality all the X's seldom appear in each equation. Some of the elements of this matrix will be zero by a priori restrictions, so that each equation of the model is identified.

To see that the cobweb model is a recursive system with a triangular $\boldsymbol{\beta}$ matrix, we can rewrite the two equations of the model in structural notation as:

$$\begin{aligned} \beta_{11}Q_t + \beta_{12}P_t + \gamma_{11}P_{t-1} + \gamma_{12} &= U_{t1} \\ \beta_{21}Q_t + \beta_{22}P_t + \gamma_{21} &= U_{t2} \end{aligned} \qquad \textbf{11.4.4}$$

Because P_t does not appear in the first (supply) equation, its coefficient β_{12} equals zero. Thus the $\boldsymbol{\beta}$ matrix for this system is triangular:

$$\boldsymbol{\beta} = \begin{bmatrix} \beta_{11} & 0 \\ \beta_{21} & \beta_{22} \end{bmatrix} \qquad \textbf{11.4.5}$$

The other condition for the recursive system is that the matrix of variance-covariance of error terms in the structural equations, denoted $\boldsymbol{\Sigma}$, is diagonal; that is, the off-diagonal elements in the $\boldsymbol{\Sigma}$ matrix are zero:

$$\boldsymbol{\Sigma} = \begin{bmatrix} E(U_{t1}^2) & 0 & 0 \cdots & 0 \\ 0 & E(U_{t2}^2) & 0 \cdots & 0 \\ \cdot & \cdot & \cdot & \cdot \\ \cdot & \cdot & \cdot & \cdot \\ \cdot & \cdot & \cdot & \cdot \\ 0 & 0 & 0 & E(U_{tK}^2) \end{bmatrix} \qquad \textbf{11.4.6}$$

Let us examine the consequence of the second assumption in terms of the following model:

$$\begin{aligned} \beta_{11}Y_1 + \beta_{12}Y_2 + \gamma_{11}X_1 + U_1 &= 0 \\ \beta_{21}Y_1 + \beta_{22}Y_2 + \gamma_{21}X_1 + U_2 &= 0 \end{aligned} \qquad \textbf{11.4.7}$$

We normalize by setting β_{ii} equal to -1 and rearrange:

$$\begin{aligned} Y_1 &= \beta_{12}Y_2 + \gamma_{11}X_1 + U_1 \\ Y_2 &= \beta_{21}Y_1 + \gamma_{21}X_1 + U_2 \end{aligned} \qquad \textbf{11.4.8}$$

In equation system 11.4.8, U_2 and Y_2 are correlated in the second equation; and in the first equation Y_2 and Y_1 are correlated, as are U_1 and Y_1. It follows that U_2 is correlated with both Y_1 and U_1. Notice neither of the two equations in the system above is identified. If we now apply the a priori restriction that $\beta_{12} = 0$, the first equation is identified and can be estimated by the OLS. The a priori information, however, does not ensure the identification of the second equation; and we cannot therefore estimate the second equation. One solution is to impose the restriction $\beta_{21} = 0$. This restriction makes the two equations identified in the technical sense. However, this development does not resolve the basic problem. Essentially, it seems that the two equations are not at all interdependent. The fallacy of such an argument lies in the fact that we have saved the method of estimation at the cost of understanding the basic interaction of a given economic system. We therefore return to interdependent system 11.4.8 and evaluate the covariance between U_2 and Y_1.[7]

Substituting for Y_2 from the second equation into the first equation,

$$\begin{aligned} Y_1 &= \beta_{12}\,(\beta_{21}Y_1 + \gamma_{21}X_1 + U_2) + \gamma_{11}X_1 + U_1 \\ &= \beta_{12}\beta_{21}Y_1 + \beta_{12}\gamma_{21}X_1 + \beta_{12}U_2 + \gamma_{11}X_1 + U_1 \qquad \textbf{11.4.9} \\ &= \frac{1}{1-\beta_{21}\beta_{12}}(\beta_{12}\gamma_{21} + \gamma_{11})X_1 + \frac{1}{1-\beta_{21}\beta_{12}}(\beta_{12}U_2 + U_1) \end{aligned}$$

From which:

$$\text{cov}(Y_1U_2) = \frac{\beta_{12}\,\text{var}(U_2)}{1-\beta_{21}\beta_{12}} + \frac{\text{cov}(U_1U_2)}{1-\beta_{21}\beta_{12}} \qquad \textbf{11.4.10}$$

Imposition of the a priori restriction $\beta_{12} = 0$ makes the first quantity of the right-hand expression zero and the second quantity of the expression equal to $\text{cov}(U_1U_2)$. Therefore, without the additional restriction that $\text{cov}(U_1U_2) = 0$, $\text{cov}(Y_1U_2) \neq 0$; and we cannot obtain unbiased and consistent estimates by the straighforward application of the OLS. For all practical purposes, we cannot assume that $\text{cov}(Y_1U_2)$ in equation 11.4.10 would be zero, for the two quantities of the right-hand expression would have to cancel each other. Hence it is evident that the restriction $\text{cov}(U_1U_2) = 0$, in addition to the restriction $\beta_{12} = 0$, is crucial in establishing the properties of a recursive system. Note that the restriction $\beta_{12} = 0$ in the context of equations 11.4.8 makes the $\boldsymbol{\beta}$ matrix triangular. The restriction $\text{cov}(U_1U_2) = 0$ can also be generalized to state that the $\boldsymbol{\Sigma}$ matrix is diagonal.

This restriction says that the disturbance term U_1 in equation 1 of model 11.4.1 occurs at time t, and it is independent of the disturbance term U_2 of equation 2 which occurs at time $t + \theta$ in the sequential order of occurrences that supposedly take place in the recursive system. Recall the original OLS assumption that in each equation the U_t's are independent for each t. Nonfulfillment of this assumption leads to a serial correlation problem. For the recursive system we also assume that the U's of each equation are independent of each other. Logically, this is the strict assertion that each equation in the given system, even though connected to other equations in the system as a whole, is strictly independent of any other in the sequence of events. Strict ordering of the equations in terms of time sequence alone can warrant such an assumption. No wonder many economists have expressed serious reservations about such a strong ordering of the time sequence of economic events.

[7] Franklin M. Fisher, *The Identification Problem in Econometrics* (New York: McGraw-Hill Book Co., 1966), pp. 94-96.

The implications of the restrictions on the $\boldsymbol{\beta}$ matrix and the $\boldsymbol{\Sigma}$ matrix are easy to see. The Y's are no longer jointly and simultaneously determined. In each equation there is only one dependent variable. All other variables are predetermined. The Y's appearing in the kth equation as regressors are predetermined by equations appearing earlier in the system, and the X's appearing as regressors in the same equation are also predetermined by assumption. For example, in the first equation Y_1 is the only endogenous variable that appears as the regressand; and $X_1, X_2, \ldots, X_M$ are predetermined. In the second equation, the regressand Y_2 is the only endogenous variable. Among the regressors, Y_1, though endogenous to the system, is predetermined by the first equation, as are the X's by assumption. Similarly, in the kth equation, Y_k is the only endogenous variable appearing as the regressand. The regressors $Y_1, Y_2, \ldots, Y_{k-1}$ are predetermined by prior equations, as are $X_1, X_2, \ldots, X_M$ by assumption. It is evident that the OLS method can be used in estimating the equations in sequence.

The same argument can be extended to the block-recursive system, where blocks are made of subsystems of equations.

$$\begin{bmatrix} \boldsymbol{\beta}_{(11)} & 0 & \ldots & 0 \\ \boldsymbol{\beta}_{(21)} & \boldsymbol{\beta}_{(22)} & \ldots & 0 \\ \cdot & \cdot & & \cdot \\ \cdot & \cdot & & \cdot \\ \cdot & \cdot & & \cdot \\ \boldsymbol{\beta}_{(Q1)} & \boldsymbol{\beta}_{(Q2)} & \ldots & \boldsymbol{\beta}_{(QQ)} \end{bmatrix} \begin{bmatrix} \mathbf{Y}_{(1)} \\ \mathbf{Y}_{(2)} \\ \cdot \\ \cdot \\ \cdot \\ \mathbf{Y}_{(Q)} \end{bmatrix} + \begin{bmatrix} \boldsymbol{\gamma}_{(1)} \\ \boldsymbol{\gamma}_{(2)} \\ \cdot \\ \cdot \\ \cdot \\ \boldsymbol{\gamma}_{(Q)} \end{bmatrix} \begin{bmatrix} \\ \\ \mathbf{X} \\ \\ \\ \end{bmatrix} = \begin{bmatrix} \mathbf{U}_{(1)} \\ \mathbf{U}_{(2)} \\ \cdot \\ \cdot \\ \cdot \\ \mathbf{U}_{(Q)} \end{bmatrix} \qquad 11.4.11$$

That is, the original system is partitioned into $q = (1, 2, \ldots, Q)$ subsystems, each of which is ordered in a well-defined sequence. Of course the assumption is that the variance-covariance matrix of structural disturbances is also block diagonal. The system has the same characteristic as the recursive system described above, except that we are now dealing with a block of equations from a given system. When we estimate the second block of equations, the first block has already been estimated, and the Y_q endogenous variables within the block are therefore predetermined. The same is true for each successive block of equations. In large econometric models the appeal of the block-recursive method is great, since often there are not enough degrees of freedom to obtain simultaneous estimates of the given system as a whole.[8] To design an ordered sequence of blocks of equations from a given system remains a complicated task, however.

---

[8] Franklin M. Fisher, "Dynamic Structure and Estimation in Economy-wide Econometric Models," *The Brookings Quarterly Econometric Model of the United States*, edited by J. S. Duesenberry, *et al.* (Amsterdam: North-Holland Publishing Co., 1965), pp. 589-636. Franklin M. Fisher, "On the Cost of Approximate Specification in Simultaneous Equation Estimation," *Econometrica*, Vol. 29, No. 2 (April, 1961), pp. 139-170.

11.5 INDIRECT LEAST SQUARES

Even when we do not impose any idealized restrictions on the equations of a model or order the equations in a recursive system, we can use the OLS method of estimation to obtain consistent estimators on the condition that each equation of the model is just identified. This is so even when the essential simultaneity of the equations of the model is maintained. The distinction between the structural and reduced forms of a model has been discussed earlier. If each equation of the model is just identified, the reduced form parameters can be estimated by the OLS method; and these in turn can be used to solve for the structural parameters (Chapter 10). But if the system is overidentified, the solutions from the reduced form to the structural form do not yield unique values for the structural parameters. Again, if the system is underidentified, the structural parameters are indeterminate. Thus only if we have a just identified model can the indirect least squares method be used.

Let us illustrate the argument. Consider a two-equation model in which each equation is justified, ignoring the t subscript:

$$\begin{aligned} \beta_{11}Y_1 + \beta_{12}Y_2 + \gamma_{11}X_1 + U_1 &= 0 \\ \beta_{21}Y_1 + \beta_{22}Y_2 + \gamma_{22}X_2 + U_2 &= 0 \end{aligned} \qquad \textbf{11.5.1}$$

where the intercept term is suppressed. Setting $\beta_{11} = \beta_{22} = -1$, we can rewrite:[9]

$$\begin{aligned} Y_1 &= \beta_{12}Y_2 + \gamma_{11}X_1 + U_1 \\ Y_2 &= \beta_{21}Y_1 + \gamma_{22}X_2 + U_2 \end{aligned} \qquad \textbf{11.5.2}$$

The reduced form of equations 11.5.2 can be obtained as follows. Substituting the second equation into the first one, we obtain:

$$\begin{aligned} Y_1 &= \beta_{12}(\beta_{21}Y_1 + \gamma_{22}X_2 + U_2) + \gamma_{11}X_1 + U_1 \\ &= \beta_{12}\beta_{21}Y_1 + \beta_{12}\gamma_{22}X_2 + \gamma_{11}X_1 + U_1 + \beta_{12}U_2 \end{aligned}$$

Collecting $\beta_{12}\beta_{21}Y_1$ on the left-hand side and rearranging,

$$Y_1 = \frac{\gamma_{11}}{1 - \beta_{12}\beta_{21}} X_1 + \frac{\beta_{12}\gamma_{22}}{1 - \beta_{12}\beta_{21}} X_2 + \frac{U_1 + \beta_{12}U_2}{1 - \beta_{12}\beta_{21}} \qquad \textbf{11.5.3}$$

Similarly,

$$\begin{aligned} Y_2 &= \beta_{21}(\beta_{12}Y_2 + \gamma_{11}X_1 + U_1) + \gamma_{22}X_2 + U_2 \\ &= \beta_{21}\beta_{12}Y_2 + \beta_{21}\gamma_{11}X_1 + \gamma_{22}X_2 + U_2 + \beta_{21}U_1 \end{aligned}$$

[9] Notice that the β's and γ's in equations 11.5.2 are not the same as those in model 11.5.1. For example, β_{12} from model 11.5.2 equals $\beta_{12}/-\beta_{11}$ in model 11.5.1. The parameters in model 11.5.2 are more useful to economists than those in equations 11.5.1, so there is no reason to be concerned with the first set.

or,

$$Y_2 = \frac{\beta_{21}\gamma_{11}}{1 - \beta_{21}\beta_{12}} X_1 + \frac{\gamma_{22}}{1 - \beta_{21}\beta_{12}} X_2 + \frac{U_2 + \beta_{21}U_1}{1 - \beta_{21}\beta_{12}} \quad 11.5.4$$

Defining,

$$\delta_{11} = \frac{\gamma_{11}}{1 - \beta_{12}\beta_{21}} \qquad \delta_{21} = \frac{\beta_{21}\gamma_{11}}{1 - \beta_{21}\beta_{12}}$$

$$\delta_{12} = \frac{\beta_{12}\gamma_{22}}{1 - \beta_{12}\beta_{21}} \qquad \delta_{22} = \frac{\gamma_{22}}{1 - \beta_{21}\beta_{12}} \quad 11.5.5$$

$$V_1 = \frac{U_1 + \beta_{12}U_2}{1 - \beta_{12}\beta_{21}} \qquad V_2 = \frac{U_2 + \beta_{21}U_1}{1 - \beta_{21}\beta_{12}}$$

we now rewrite the reduced form:

$$\begin{aligned} Y_1 &= \delta_{11}X_1 + \delta_{12}X_2 + V_1 \\ Y_2 &= \delta_{21}X_1 + \delta_{22}X_2 + V_2 \end{aligned} \quad 11.5.6$$

By applying OLS we can estimate $\hat{\delta}_{11}$, $\hat{\delta}_{12}$, $\hat{\delta}_{21}$, and $\hat{\delta}_{22}$, and then solve "backward" to obtain the structural parameters in equations 11.5.2:

$$\begin{aligned} \hat{\beta}_{12} &= \frac{\hat{\delta}_{12}}{\hat{\delta}_{22}} \\ \hat{\beta}_{21} &= \frac{\hat{\delta}_{21}}{\hat{\delta}_{11}} \\ \hat{\gamma}_{11} &= \hat{\delta}_{11}\left(1 - \frac{\hat{\delta}_{12}}{\hat{\delta}_{22}}\frac{\hat{\delta}_{21}}{\hat{\delta}_{11}}\right) \\ \hat{\gamma}_{22} &= \hat{\delta}_{22}\left(1 - \frac{\hat{\delta}_{12}}{\hat{\delta}_{22}}\frac{\hat{\delta}_{21}}{\hat{\delta}_{11}}\right) \end{aligned} \quad 11.5.7$$

The estimates $\hat{\beta}_{12}$, $\hat{\beta}_{21}$, $\hat{\gamma}_{11}$, and $\hat{\gamma}_{22}$ are the indirect least squares estimates of the corresponding parameters.

Consider the following model in which the first equation is just identified and the second is overidentified:

$$\begin{aligned} Y_1 &= \beta_{12}Y_2 + \gamma_{11}X_1 + \gamma_{13}X_3 + \gamma_{14}X_4 + U_1 \\ Y_2 &= \beta_{21}Y_1 + \gamma_{22}X_2 + U_2 \end{aligned} \quad 11.5.8$$

from which the reduced form is:

$$Y_1 = \frac{\gamma_{11}}{1-\beta_{12}\beta_{21}} X_1 + \frac{\beta_{12}\gamma_{22}}{1-\beta_{12}\beta_{21}} X_2 + \frac{\gamma_{13}}{1-\beta_{12}\beta_{21}} X_3 + \frac{\gamma_{14}}{1-\beta_{12}\beta_{21}} X_4 + \frac{U_1 + \beta_{12}U_2}{1-\beta_{12}\beta_{21}} \qquad 11.5.9$$

$$Y_2 = \frac{\beta_{21}\gamma_{11}}{1-\beta_{12}\beta_{21}} X_1 + \frac{\gamma_{22}}{1-\beta_{12}\beta_{21}} X_2 + \frac{\beta_{21}\gamma_{13}}{1-\beta_{12}\beta_{21}} X_3 + \frac{\beta_{21}\gamma_{14}}{1-\beta_{12}\beta_{21}} X_4 + \frac{\beta_{21}U_1 + U_2}{1-\beta_{12}\beta_{21}}$$

Writing δ_{11}, δ_{12}, δ_{21}, V_1, and V_2 as before, and also,

$$\delta_{13} = \frac{\gamma_{13}}{1-\beta_{12}\beta_{21}} \qquad \delta_{23} = \frac{\beta_{21}\gamma_{13}}{1-\beta_{12}\beta_{21}}$$

$$\delta_{14} = \frac{\gamma_{14}}{1-\beta_{12}\beta_{21}} \qquad \delta_{24} = \frac{\beta_{21}\gamma_{14}}{1-\beta_{12}\beta_{21}} \qquad 11.5.10$$

we rewrite the reduced form:

$$Y_1 = \delta_{11}X_1 + \delta_{12}X_2 + \delta_{13}X_3 + \delta_{14}X_4 + V_1$$
$$Y_2 = \delta_{21}X_1 + \delta_{22}X_2 + \delta_{23}X_3 + \delta_{24}X_4 + V_2 \qquad 11.5.11$$

It is possible to estimate both equations 11.5.11 above by the OLS method. However, concentrating on the second equation, which is overidentified, we see that there is no unique solution for its structural parameters. The coefficients of both X_3 and X_4 are zero in the second equation, and thus we have more a priori information than we need to identify this equation. Indeed it is overidentified, and the problem of estimation by indirect least squares becomes clear. The estimate of the coefficient β_{21} in equation system 11.5.8, for example, can be obtained more than one way:

$$\hat{\beta}_{21} = \frac{\hat{\delta}_{21}}{\hat{\delta}_{11}}$$

or,

$$\hat{\beta}_{21} = \frac{\hat{\delta}_{23}}{\hat{\delta}_{13}} \qquad 11.5.12$$

or,

$$\hat{\beta}_{21} = \frac{\hat{\delta}_{24}}{\hat{\delta}_{14}}$$

It will not generally happen that all these various estimates of β_{21} will be equal, and there is no way of choosing the right one a priori. Thus the indirect least squares method of estimation is of limited use for simultaneous equation models, since such models do not usually consist of a set of simultaneous equations where each one of the equations in the system is just identified. Direct estimation of the parameters of the structural form of the model, as discussed before, is strongly recommended.

DISCUSSION QUESTIONS

1. (a) In general, economic systems are interdependent, leading to the codetermination of several economic variables. Elaborate.
   (b) The OLS estimates of the parameters of generally interdependent systems are seen to be biased and inconsistent. Why? (Hint: Refer to the discussions in Chapter 9.)
2. (a) Describe a multiequation system in its structural form.
   (b) Define the reduced form. Does the reduced form of a multiequation system always exist?
   (c) Why do econometricians prefer to estimate the parameters of the equations of a generally independent system in its structural form?
3. Consider the following model where Y's and X's refer to the sets of codetermined and predetermined variables respectively:

$$b_{11}Y_1 + b_{12}Y_2 + g_{11}X_1 + g_{12}X_2 + g_{10} = U_1$$

$$b_{21}Y_1 + b_{22}Y_2 + g_{21}X_1 + g_{22}X_2 + g_{20} = U_2$$

   where $b_{11} = b_{22} = -1$ and $g_{11} = g_{22} = 0$

   (a) Write the reduced form of the above model.
   (b) Can you specify the condition with respect to the matrix of parameters relative to the b_{ij}'s, i.e.,

$$\begin{bmatrix} b_{11} & b_{12} \\ b_{21} & b_{22} \end{bmatrix}$$

   such that the appropriate reduced form will not be available?
4. Discuss the nature and scope of "idealized uniequation" models in econometric research.
5. (a) Explain the two conditions on which recursive models are based.
   (b) Examine the significance of the assumption that the matrix of the variance-covariance of error terms in the structural equations is diagonal.
   (c) Draw upon economic theory to describe a situation where the recursive model specification is eminently appropriate.
   (d) Comment on the fundamental outline of the recursive models.
6. Briefly describe what is meant by the block-recursive system.

7. (a) Specify a four-equation, interdependent system in which each of the structural equations is stochastic and just identified.
   (b) Obtain the reduced form of the above system and show that from the indirect application of the OLS to the reduced form, consistent estimates of the structural parameters can be obtained.

8. Refer to the above model and respecify one of the four equations to be overidentified. Can the indirect least squares method of estimation be used to obtain determinable solutions for the parameters of the overidentified equation?

SUGGESTED READINGS

Bentzel, Ragnar, and B. Hansen. "On Recursiveness and Interdependency in Economic Models." *Review of Economic Studies,* Vol. 22 (1954), pp. 153-168.

Bentzel, Ragnar, and H.O.A. Wold. "On Statistical Demand Analysis from the Viewpoint of Simultaneous Equations." *Skandinavisk Aktuarietidskrift,* Vol. 29 (1946), pp. 95-114.

Christ, Carl F., Clifford Hildreth, Ta-Chung Liu, and Lawrence R. Klein. "A Symposium on Simultaneous Equation Estimation." *Econometrica,* Vol. 28, No. 4 (October, 1960), pp. 835-871.

Desai, Meghnad. "An Econometric Model of the World Tin Market." *Econometrica,* Vol. 34, No. 1 (January, 1966), pp. 105-134.

Fisher, Franklin M. "On the Cost of Approximate Specification in Simultaneous Equation Estimation." *Econometrica,* Vol. 29, No. 2 (April, 1961), pp. 139-170.

———. "Dynamic Structure and Estimation in Economy-wide Econometric Models." *The Brookings Quarterly Econometric Model of the United States,* edited by J. S. Duesenberry, *et. al.* Amsterdam: North-Holland Publishing Co., 1965, pp. 589-636.

———. *The Identification Problem in Econometrics.* New York: McGraw-Hill Book Co., 1966.

Fox, Karl A. *Econometric Analysis for Public Policy.* Ames: Iowa State College Press, 1958.

Haavelmo, Trygve. "The Statistical Implications of a System of Simultaneous Equations." *Econometrica,* Vol. 11, No. 1 (January, 1943), pp. 1-12.

Klein, Lawrence R. *An Introduction to Econometrics.* Englewood Cliffs, N.J.: Prentice-Hall, 1962.

———. "The Efficiency of Estimation in Econometric Models." *Essays in Economics and Econometrics,* edited by Ralph W. Pfouts. Chapel Hill: University of North Carolina Press, 1964, pp. 216-232.

Strotz, R. H., and H.O.A. Wold. "Recursive vs Nonrecursive Systems." *Econometrica,* Vol. 28, No. 2 (April, 1960), pp. 417-427.

Wold, Herman O.A. "A Generalization of Causal Chain Models." *Econometrica,* Vol. 28, No. 2 (April, 1960), pp. 443-463.

———. *Econometric Model Building.* Amsterdam: North-Holland Publishing Co., 1967.

12

simultaneous system: single-equation methods

12.0 INTRODUCTION

According to one view, behavioral relations in economics are based on very inadequate knowledge and are thus essentially underidentified. In this view the problems of interdependence and simultaneity do not warrant further consideration. One can specify the behavioral relations with as much rigor as the existing knowledge of economic theory permits and estimate the parameters involved in each equation independently by the classical OLS method. It is rather a gloomy view to accept underidentification as the characteristic of relations in economics.

Usually overidentification is considered a serious problem in econometric research. Persistent efforts to develop estimation methods to enable the econometrician to obtain consistent estimators of the parameters in the relations of a simultaneously interdependent system have resulted in two types of results: (1) methods to estimate parameters of each equation separately, even when simultaneous interdependence of the system has been recognized; and (2) methods, such as *full information maximum likelihood* (FIML) and *three-stage least squares* (3SLS), by which all parameters of all the equations are estimated simultaneously.

The present chapter is confined to the discussion of different consistent methods of estimation currently available that estimate each behavioral equation of the system separately.

12.1 THE TWO-STAGE LEAST SQUARES METHOD

The method of *two-stage least squares* (2SLS) has been widely used.[1] This method is relatively simple; in fact it is an extension of the ordinary least squares

[1] H. Theil, *Economic Forecasts and Policy* (2d ed.; Amsterdam: North-Holland Publishing Co., 1961), pp. 335-348. H. Theil, *Principles of Econometrics* (New York: John Wiley & Sons, 1971), pp. 451-460. R. L. Basmann, "A Generalized Classical Method of Linear Estimation of Coefficients in a Structural Equation," *Econometrica*, Vol. 25, No. 1 (January, 1957), pp. 77-83. R. L. Basmann, "The Computation of Generalized Classical Estimate of Coefficients in a Structural Equation," *Econometrica*, Vol. 27, No. 1 (January, 1959), pp. 72-81. R. L. Basmann, "On the Asymptotic Distribution of Generalized Linear Estimators," *Econometrica*, Vol. 28, No. 1 (January, 1960), pp. 97-107.

method. Each equation in the system is estimated independently. However, in estimating each such equation the method makes use of all the predetermined variables appearing in the model even if all of them do not appear in the equation that is currently being estimated. It does so by using a two-stage computational scheme.

To fix the idea firmly, let us consider the following two-equation system with k endogenous variables Y, jointly determined, and m predetermined variables X:

$$\begin{aligned} \beta_{11}Y_1 + \beta_{12}Y_2 + \gamma_{11}X_1 + \gamma_{12}X_2 + \gamma_{13}X_3 + \gamma_{14}X_4 + U_1 = 0 \\ \beta_{21}Y_1 + \beta_{22}Y_2 + \gamma_{21}X_1 + \gamma_{22}X_2 + \gamma_{23}X_3 + \gamma_{24}X_4 + U_2 = 0 \end{aligned} \quad \textbf{12.1.1}$$

where $k = 1,2$ and $m = 1,2,3,4$. Each variable has $t(t = 1,2, \ldots, T)$ observations, and we suppress the subscript t. Next we set $\beta_{ii} = -1$ and specify a priori restrictions:

$$\gamma_{12} = \gamma_{13} = \gamma_{21} = \gamma_{24} = 0$$

We can rewrite the above model as:

$$\begin{aligned} -Y_1 + \beta_{12}Y_2 + \gamma_{11}X_1 + \gamma_{14}X_4 + U_1 = 0 \\ \beta_{21}Y_1 - Y_2 + \gamma_{22}X_2 + \gamma_{23}X_3 + U_2 = 0 \end{aligned} \quad \textbf{12.1.2}$$

from which the familiar format is:

$$\begin{aligned} Y_1 = \beta_{12}Y_2 + \gamma_{11}X_1 + \gamma_{14}X_4 + U_1 \\ Y_2 = \beta_{21}Y_1 + \gamma_{22}X_2 + \gamma_{23}X_3 + U_2 \end{aligned} \quad \textbf{12.1.3}$$

or,

$$\mathbf{Y}\boldsymbol{\beta} + \mathbf{X}\boldsymbol{\Gamma} + \mathbf{U} = \mathbf{0} \quad \textbf{12.1.4}$$

Notice that each of the two equations in the above system is overidentified. Note that $E(\mathbf{XU}) = \mathbf{0}$, since the X_m's are assumed to be predetermined for the system. But $E(\mathbf{YU}) \neq \mathbf{0}$, since the Y_k's are jointly determined endogenous variables, even though they currently appear as regressors.

The first stage of the 2SLS method consists of obtaining $\hat{Y}_k$ as an estimate of Y_k by regressing Y_k on X_1, X_2, X_3, and X_4, that is, on all m predetermined variables appearing in the system. Thus we have:

$$\begin{aligned} Y_1 = \delta_{10} + \delta_{11}X_1 + \delta_{12}X_2 + \delta_{13}X_3 + \delta_{14}X_4 + W_1 \\ Y_2 = \delta_{20} + \delta_{21}X_1 + \delta_{22}X_2 + \delta_{23}X_3 + \delta_{24}X_4 + W_2 \end{aligned} \quad \textbf{12.1.5}$$

from which:

$$\begin{aligned} Y_1 = \hat{Y}_1 + \hat{W}_1 \\ Y_2 = \hat{Y}_2 + \hat{W}_2 \end{aligned} \quad \textbf{12.1.6}$$

In the second stage, the Y_k that appears as the regressor is replaced by $(\hat{Y}_k + \hat{W}_k)$, and the following regression estimates are obtained by OLS:

$$Y_1 = \beta_{12}\hat{Y}_2 + \gamma_{11}X_1 + \gamma_{14}X_4 + U_1 + \beta_{12}\hat{W}_2$$
$$Y_2 = \beta_{21}\hat{Y}_1 + \gamma_{22}X_2 + \gamma_{23}X_3 + U_2 + \beta_{21}\hat{W}_1 \qquad \textbf{12.1.7}$$

The rationale is straightforward. Even though:

$$E(Y_2U_1) \neq 0 \quad E(Y_1U_2) \neq 0$$
$$\sum_t (\hat{Y}_{t2}\hat{U}_{t1}) = 0 = \sum_t (\hat{Y}_{t1}\hat{U}_{t2}) \qquad \textbf{12.1.8}$$

Notice $\hat{Y}_k$ is a linear expression in X_m and $E(X_mU_k) = 0$.

$$E(\hat{Y}_kU_k) = E(\mathbf{X}\hat{\boldsymbol{\delta}}_tU_k) = \boldsymbol{\delta}E(\mathbf{X}U_k) = 0$$

Similarly, $E(Y_kW_k) \neq 0$; but $E(\hat{Y}_k\hat{W}_k) = 0$ since:

$$E(X_mW_k) = 0 \qquad \textbf{12.1.9}$$

by assumption.

Refer to the equation for Y_1. In stage 1, $\hat{Y}_2$ has to be obtained from Y_2, the jointly determined variable appearing as a regressor in this equation, by regressing Y_2 on X_1, X_2, X_3, and X_4. We can write the regression equation for Y_2 as follows:

$$\begin{bmatrix} Y_{12} \\ Y_{22} \\ \cdot \\ \cdot \\ \cdot \\ Y_{T2} \end{bmatrix} = \begin{bmatrix} 1 & X_{11} & X_{12} & X_{13} & X_{14} \\ 1 & X_{21} & X_{22} & X_{23} & X_{24} \\ \cdot & \cdot & \cdot & \cdot & \cdot \\ \cdot & \cdot & \cdot & \cdot & \cdot \\ \cdot & \cdot & \cdot & \cdot & \cdot \\ 1 & X_{T1} & X_{T2} & X_{T3} & X_{T4} \end{bmatrix} \begin{bmatrix} \delta_{20} \\ \delta_{21} \\ \delta_{22} \\ \delta_{23} \\ \delta_{24} \end{bmatrix} + \begin{bmatrix} W_{12} \\ W_{22} \\ \cdot \\ \cdot \\ \cdot \\ W_{T2} \end{bmatrix} \qquad \textbf{12.1.10}$$

or in matrix notation, omitting the t subscript,

$$\mathbf{Y}_2 = \mathbf{X}\boldsymbol{\delta}_2 + \mathbf{W}_2 \qquad \textbf{12.1.11}$$

Notice that we have used an additional regressor, a dummy variable that always remains unity for estimating the intercept of the equation, δ_{20}. Following the OLS method,

$$\hat{\boldsymbol{\delta}}_2 = (\mathbf{X}'\mathbf{X})^{-1}\mathbf{X}'\mathbf{Y}_2 \qquad \textbf{12.1.12}$$

These estimated coefficients can be used to calculate $\hat{\mathbf{Y}}_2$:

$$\hat{\mathbf{Y}}_2' = \mathbf{X}\hat{\boldsymbol{\delta}}_2 \qquad \textbf{12.1.13}$$

where $\hat{\boldsymbol{\delta}}_2$ is the vector of coefficients above, including $\hat{\delta}_{20}$.

Evidently, this regression estimate cannot be obtained when the number of observations T is less than the number of predetermined variables M plus one. That is, the method of estimation can work if and only if:

$$T \geq M + 1 \qquad \textbf{12.1.14}$$

Using equation 12.1.13, we can rewrite equation 12.1.11 as:

$$\mathbf{Y}_2 = \hat{\mathbf{Y}}_2 + \hat{\mathbf{W}}_2$$

or,

$$\mathbf{Y}_2 - \hat{\mathbf{W}}_2 = \hat{\mathbf{Y}}_2$$

This is the result we obtained in equations 12.1.6 before. Note that $\hat{\mathbf{Y}}_2$ is exactly the systematic component of $\mathbf{Y}_2$. In the preceding discussion we isolated and excluded the stochastic component $\mathbf{W}_2$ from the estimated residuals $\hat{\mathbf{W}}_2$.

Let us continue the discussion on estimating the equation for Y_1 in stage 2. Substituting $\hat{Y}_2$ for Y_2 in the equation for Y_1, we can write:

$$Y_1 = \beta_{12}(Y_2 - W_2) + \gamma_{11}X_1 + \gamma_{14}X_4 + U_1 + \beta_{12}W_2 \qquad \textbf{12.1.15}$$

No dummy variable for estimating the intercept is included here.

We have observations on Y_2, but no observations on W_2. In stage 1 we can compute residuals as:

$$\hat{W}_2 = Y_2 - \hat{\delta}_{20} - \hat{\delta}_{21}X_1 - \hat{\delta}_{22}X_2 - \hat{\delta}_{23}X_3 - \hat{\delta}_{24}X_4 \qquad \textbf{12.1.16}$$

and the computed series $\hat{W}_2$ can be used. Alternatively, we can use estimated values of Y_2, that is, $\hat{Y}_2$, immediately. Then we have, using the OLS method, the following estimates:

$$\begin{bmatrix} \hat{\beta}_{12} \\ \hat{\gamma}_{11} \\ \hat{\gamma}_{14} \end{bmatrix} = \begin{bmatrix} \Sigma\hat{Y}_2^2 & \Sigma\hat{Y}_2X_1 & \Sigma\hat{Y}_2X_4 \\ \Sigma X_1\hat{Y}_2 & \Sigma X_1^2 & \Sigma X_1X_4 \\ \Sigma X_4\hat{Y}_2 & \Sigma X_1X_4 & \Sigma X_4^2 \end{bmatrix}^{-1} \begin{bmatrix} \Sigma\hat{Y}_2Y_1 \\ \Sigma X_1Y_1 \\ \Sigma X_4Y_1 \end{bmatrix} \qquad \textbf{12.1.17}$$

We now proceed to the case where there is more than one jointly determined Y variable currently appearing as a regressor in the first equation. Suppose that K^* of the set of K such variables and M^* of the M predetermined variables X appear in the first equation:

$$\mathbf{Y}_1^* = [Y_1, Y_2, \ldots, Y_{K^*}] \text{ and } \mathbf{X}_1^* = [X_1, X_2, \ldots, X_{M^*}]$$

One of the K^* such variables appearing in this equation, such as $\mathbf{Y}_1$, is the regressand; and its coefficient is set equal to -1.

Recall that we can write equation 1 as:

$$\mathbf{Y}^*\boldsymbol{\beta}_1 + \mathbf{X}^*\boldsymbol{\gamma}_1 + \mathbf{U}_1 = \mathbf{0} \qquad \textbf{12.1.18}$$

Thus we have, using equations 12.1.11 and 12.1.12:

$$\mathbf{Y}_2 = \mathbf{X}\hat{\boldsymbol{\delta}}_2 + \hat{\mathbf{W}}_2$$
$$= \mathbf{X}(\mathbf{X}'\mathbf{X})^{-1}\mathbf{X}'\mathbf{Y}_2 + \hat{\mathbf{W}}_2$$

Similarly,

$$\mathbf{Y}_3 = \mathbf{X}\hat{\boldsymbol{\delta}}_3 + \hat{\mathbf{W}}_3$$
$$= \mathbf{X}(\mathbf{X}'\mathbf{X})^{-1}\mathbf{X}'\mathbf{Y}_3 + \hat{\mathbf{W}}_3$$

and for the kth **Y**,

$$\mathbf{Y}_k = \mathbf{X}\hat{\boldsymbol{\delta}}_k + \hat{\mathbf{W}}_k$$
$$= \mathbf{X}(\mathbf{X}'\mathbf{X})^{-1}\mathbf{X}'\mathbf{Y}_k + \hat{\mathbf{W}}_k$$

where

$$\hat{\boldsymbol{\delta}}_k = (\mathbf{X}'\mathbf{X})^{-1}\mathbf{X}'\mathbf{Y}_k$$

and

$$\hat{\mathbf{Y}}_k = \mathbf{X}\hat{\boldsymbol{\delta}}_k;\ \mathbf{Y}_k = \hat{\mathbf{Y}}_k + \hat{\mathbf{W}}_k \qquad \textbf{12.1.19}$$

Taking the entire subset of $\mathbf{Y}^* = (\mathbf{Y}_2, \ldots, \mathbf{Y}_{K^*})$ appearing as regressors in the first equation, we can write:

$$\hat{\mathbf{Y}}^* = \mathbf{X}(\mathbf{X}'\mathbf{X})^{-1}\mathbf{X}'\mathbf{Y}^* \qquad \textbf{12.1.20}$$

$$\mathbf{Y}^* = \mathbf{X}(\mathbf{X}'\mathbf{X})^{-1}\mathbf{X}'\mathbf{Y}^* + \hat{\mathbf{W}} \qquad \textbf{12.1.21}$$

$$\mathbf{Y}^* = \hat{\mathbf{Y}}^* + \hat{\mathbf{W}} \qquad \textbf{12.1.22}$$

$$\hat{\mathbf{Y}}^* = \mathbf{Y}^* - \hat{\mathbf{W}} \qquad \textbf{12.1.23}$$

where

$$\mathbf{W} = \begin{bmatrix} W_{12} & W_{13} & \ldots & W_{1K^*} \\ W_{22} & W_{23} & \ldots & W_{2K^*} \\ \cdot & \cdot & & \cdot \\ \cdot & \cdot & & \cdot \\ \cdot & \cdot & & \cdot \\ W_{T2} & W_{T3} & \ldots & W_{TK^*} \end{bmatrix} \qquad \textbf{12.1.24}$$

Thus in stage 1 we obtain the estimates for members of the **Y*** subset by regressing each Y in the subset on the entire set of X's appearing in the model: $\mathbf{X} = [\mathbf{X}_1, \mathbf{X}_2, \ldots, \mathbf{X}_{M^*}, \mathbf{X}_{M^*+1}, \ldots, \mathbf{X}_M]$. Following the steps as described above in equations 12.1.19 through 12.1.23, we have for equation 1:

$$\mathbf{Y}_1 = (\hat{\mathbf{Y}}^* + \hat{\mathbf{W}})\boldsymbol{\beta}_1 + \mathbf{X}^*\boldsymbol{\gamma}_1 + \mathbf{U}_1 \qquad \textbf{12.1.25}$$

In the second stage the estimating equation is:

$$\mathbf{Y}_1 = \hat{\mathbf{Y}}^*\boldsymbol{\beta}_1 + \mathbf{X}^*\boldsymbol{\gamma}_1 + \mathbf{U}_1 + \hat{\mathbf{W}}\boldsymbol{\beta}_1 \tag{12.1.26}$$

Therefore, it follows that using equation 12.1.23,

$$\mathbf{Y}_1 = (\mathbf{Y}^* - \hat{\mathbf{W}})\boldsymbol{\beta}_1 + \mathbf{X}^*\boldsymbol{\gamma}_1 + \mathbf{U}_1 + \hat{\mathbf{W}}\boldsymbol{\beta}_1 \tag{12.1.27}$$

Using the least squares formula, the estimating equation for the 2SLS can then be written as:

$$\begin{bmatrix} (\mathbf{Y}^* - \hat{\mathbf{W}})'(\mathbf{Y}^* - \hat{\mathbf{W}}) & (\mathbf{Y}^* - \hat{\mathbf{W}})'\mathbf{X}^* \\ \mathbf{X}^{*\prime}(\mathbf{Y}^* - \hat{\mathbf{W}}) & \mathbf{X}^{*\prime}\mathbf{X}^* \end{bmatrix}^{-1} \begin{bmatrix} (\mathbf{Y}^* - \hat{\mathbf{W}})'\mathbf{Y}_1 \\ \mathbf{X}^{*\prime}\mathbf{Y}_1 \end{bmatrix} = \begin{bmatrix} \hat{\boldsymbol{\beta}}_1 \\ \hat{\boldsymbol{\gamma}}_1 \end{bmatrix} \tag{12.1.28}$$

Of course for any solution of equation 12.1.28, the inverse matrix must exist; and the necessary identification condition will be discussed presently. Note that, using equation 12.1.22, we can obtain certain interesting results which will enable us to obtain the 2SLS results at one stroke.

$$\begin{aligned} \hat{\mathbf{W}}'\mathbf{Y}^* &= \hat{\mathbf{W}}'(\hat{\mathbf{Y}}^* + \hat{\mathbf{W}}) \\ &= \hat{\mathbf{W}}'\hat{\mathbf{Y}}^* + \hat{\mathbf{W}}'\hat{\mathbf{W}} \end{aligned} \tag{12.1.29}$$

Since residuals in a regression are uncorrelated with estimated values, $\hat{\mathbf{W}}'\hat{\mathbf{Y}}^* = \mathbf{0}$. Thus,

$$\hat{\mathbf{W}}'\mathbf{Y}^* = \hat{\mathbf{W}}'\hat{\mathbf{W}} \tag{12.1.30}$$

Similarly,

$$\begin{aligned} \mathbf{Y}^{*\prime}\hat{\mathbf{W}} &= (\hat{\mathbf{Y}}^* + \hat{\mathbf{W}})'\hat{\mathbf{W}} \\ &= \hat{\mathbf{Y}}^{*\prime}\hat{\mathbf{W}} + \hat{\mathbf{W}}'\hat{\mathbf{W}} \\ &= \hat{\mathbf{W}}'\hat{\mathbf{W}} \end{aligned} \tag{12.1.31}$$

We now return to equation 12.1.28 and work out the following by using the results in equations 12.1.30 and 12.1.31:

$$\begin{aligned} (\mathbf{Y}^* - \hat{\mathbf{W}})'(\mathbf{Y}^* - \hat{\mathbf{W}}) &= \mathbf{Y}^{*\prime}\mathbf{Y}^* - \hat{\mathbf{W}}'\mathbf{Y}^* - \mathbf{Y}^{*\prime}\hat{\mathbf{W}} + \hat{\mathbf{W}}'\hat{\mathbf{W}} \\ &= \mathbf{Y}^{*\prime}\mathbf{Y}^* - 2\hat{\mathbf{W}}'\hat{\mathbf{W}} + \hat{\mathbf{W}}'\hat{\mathbf{W}} \\ &= \mathbf{Y}^{*\prime}\mathbf{Y}^* - \hat{\mathbf{W}}'\hat{\mathbf{W}} \end{aligned} \tag{12.1.32}$$

It remains to be shown that the new series of residuals W_i are not correlated with the predetermined variables X. By assumption the X's are truly predetermined, and the independence between them and the U's is assumed to be true. Using equation 12.1.21, $\mathbf{Y}^* = \mathbf{X}(\mathbf{X}'\mathbf{X})^{-1}\mathbf{X}'\mathbf{Y}^* + \hat{\mathbf{W}}$,

$$\hat{\mathbf{W}} = [\mathbf{Y}^* - \mathbf{X}(\mathbf{X}'\mathbf{X})^{-1}\mathbf{X}'\mathbf{Y}^*] \tag{12.1.33}$$

$$\begin{aligned} \mathbf{X}'\hat{\mathbf{W}} &= \mathbf{X}'[\mathbf{Y}^* - \mathbf{X}(\mathbf{X}'\mathbf{X})^{-1}\mathbf{X}'\mathbf{Y}^*] \\ &= \mathbf{X}'\mathbf{Y}^* - \mathbf{X}'\mathbf{X}(\mathbf{X}'\mathbf{X})^{-1}\mathbf{X}'\mathbf{Y}^* \end{aligned} \tag{12.1.34}$$

Since $X'X(X'X)^{-1}X'Y^* = X'Y^*$, then:

$$\begin{aligned} X'\hat{W} &= X'Y^* - X'Y^* \\ &= 0 \end{aligned} \qquad 12.1.35$$

If $X'\hat{W}$ is zero, then so is a submatrix of $X'\hat{W}$:

$$X^{*\prime}\hat{W} = 0 \qquad 12.1.36$$

Using these two sets of results, the least squares formula for 2SLS estimates from equation 12.1.28 can be rewritten as follows:

$$\begin{bmatrix} Y^{*\prime}Y^* - \hat{W}'\hat{W} & Y^{*\prime}X^* \\ X^{*\prime}Y^* & X^{*\prime}X^* \end{bmatrix}^{-1} \begin{bmatrix} (Y^* - \hat{W})'Y_1 \\ X^{*\prime}Y_1 \end{bmatrix} = \begin{bmatrix} \hat{\beta}_1 \\ \hat{\gamma}_1 \end{bmatrix} \qquad 12.1.37$$

The variance of the 2SLS estimates can now be computed. Using equation 12.1.26, the second stage equation for estimation is:

$$Y_1 = \hat{Y}^*\beta_1 + X^*\gamma_1 + (U_1 + \hat{W}\beta_1)$$

For convenience we use the notations:

$$\begin{aligned} A &= [\hat{Y}^* \quad X^*] \\ \delta_1 &= \begin{bmatrix} \beta_1 \\ \gamma_1 \end{bmatrix} \end{aligned} \qquad 12.1.38$$

and then rewrite equation 12.1.26:

$$Y_1 = A\delta_1 + (U_1 + \hat{W}\beta_1) \qquad 12.1.39$$

from which the OLS estimate,

$$\hat{\delta}_1 = (A'A)^{-1}A'Y_1 \qquad 12.1.40$$

Returning to equation 12.1.39 and substituting for Y_1, we obtain:

$$\hat{\delta}_1 = \delta_1 + (A'A)^{-1}A'(U_1 + \hat{W}\beta_1) \qquad 12.1.41$$

Notice that:

$$\begin{aligned} A'\hat{W} &= [\hat{Y}^* \quad X^*]'\hat{W} \\ &= 0 \end{aligned} \qquad 12.1.42$$

since equations 12.1.31 and 12.1.36 have shown that $\hat{Y}^{*\prime}\hat{W} = X^{*\prime}\hat{W} = 0$. Therefore,

$$\hat{\boldsymbol{\delta}}_1 = \boldsymbol{\delta}_1 + (\mathbf{A}'\mathbf{A})^{-1}\mathbf{A}'\mathbf{U}_1 \tag{12.1.43}$$

from which:

$$\hat{\boldsymbol{\delta}}_1 - \boldsymbol{\delta}_1 = (\mathbf{A}'\mathbf{A})^{-1}\mathbf{A}'\mathbf{U}_1 \tag{12.1.44}$$

The asymptotic var($\hat{\boldsymbol{\delta}}_1$) can then be obtained from:[2]

$$\text{var}(\hat{\boldsymbol{\delta}}_1) = T^{-1}\sigma_u^2 \text{ plim}\left(\frac{\mathbf{A}'\mathbf{A}}{T}\right)^{-1} \tag{12.1.45}$$

In a finite sample the approximate estimate is:

$$\text{var}(\hat{\boldsymbol{\delta}}_1) = S^2(\mathbf{A}'\mathbf{A})^{-1} \tag{12.1.46}$$

or,

$$\text{var}(\hat{\boldsymbol{\delta}}_1) = S^2 \begin{bmatrix} \mathbf{Y}^{*\prime}\mathbf{Y}^* - \hat{\mathbf{W}}'\hat{\mathbf{W}} & \mathbf{Y}^{*\prime}\mathbf{X}^* \\ \mathbf{X}^{*\prime}\mathbf{Y}^* & \mathbf{X}^{*\prime}\mathbf{X}^* \end{bmatrix}^{-1} \tag{12.1.47}$$

where $\hat{\mathbf{W}}$ is the estimated values of $\mathbf{W}$ and:

$$S^2 = [(\mathbf{Y}_1 - \mathbf{A}\hat{\boldsymbol{\delta}}_1)'(\mathbf{Y}_1 - \mathbf{A}\hat{\boldsymbol{\delta}}_1)]/T - (K^* - 1) - M^* \tag{12.1.48}$$

That is to say, S^2 is the computed residuals from the 2SLS regression corrected for appropriate degrees of freedom.

The 2SLS estimates can be shown to be consistent. Let us use equation 12.1.43 and take the probability limit.

$$\text{plim}(\hat{\boldsymbol{\delta}}_1) = \boldsymbol{\delta}_1 + \text{plim}\left(\frac{\mathbf{A}'\mathbf{A}}{T}\right)^{-1} \cdot \text{plim}\left(\frac{\mathbf{A}'\mathbf{U}_1}{T}\right) \tag{12.1.49}$$

We have always maintained that plim $\left(\frac{\mathbf{A}'\mathbf{A}}{T}\right)$ exists, finite and nonzero. Plim $\left(\frac{\mathbf{A}'\mathbf{U}_1}{T}\right)$ has two components, plim$\left(\frac{\hat{\mathbf{Y}}^*\mathbf{U}_1}{T}\right)$ and plim$\left(\frac{\mathbf{X}^*\mathbf{U}_1}{T}\right)$. The second component is zero by the assumption that the X's are predetermined variables. The first component tends to zero, which can be seen from equation 12.1.8 even if $E(\mathbf{Y}^*\mathbf{U}_1) \neq \mathbf{0}$. Therefore,

$$\text{plim}(\hat{\boldsymbol{\delta}}_1) = \boldsymbol{\delta}_1 \tag{12.1.50}$$

The 2SLS estimates are seen to be consistent.

It is very important to note that the test of consistency is based on the fact that the X's are truly predetermined exogenous variables. If any predetermined variables are lagged endogenous variables, and at the same time the

[2] Arthur S. Goldberger, *Econometric Theory* (New York: John Wiley & Sons, 1964), p. 333.

disturbance term U is autocorrelated, we cannot show that the 2SLS estimator is consistent (review Chapter 7).[3]

The 2SLS Method and Identification Condition

The method of 2SLS yields consistent estimators of the coefficients of an equation only if the equation is just identified or overidentified. If the equation is underidentified, the method cannot be applied since the inverse matrix in equation 12.1.28 or 12.1.37 does not exist. The estimating equation of stage 2 from equation 12.1.39 is:

$$\mathbf{Y}_1 = \mathbf{A}\boldsymbol{\delta}_1 + (\mathbf{U}_1 + \hat{\mathbf{W}}_1\boldsymbol{\beta}_1)$$

and following equation 12.1.40, the estimates of $\boldsymbol{\beta}_1$ and $\boldsymbol{\gamma}_1$ are given as:

$$\hat{\boldsymbol{\delta}}_1 = \begin{bmatrix} \hat{\boldsymbol{\beta}}_1 \\ \hat{\boldsymbol{\gamma}}_1 \end{bmatrix} = (\mathbf{A}'\mathbf{A})^{-1}\mathbf{A}'\mathbf{Y}_1$$

$\mathbf{A}$ is a rectangular matrix with T rows, corresponding to T observations, and $K^* - 1 + M^*$ columns, corresponding to $K^* - 1$ endogenous variables appearing as regressors in this equation and to M^* predetermined regressors in the equation. The matrix $\mathbf{A}'\mathbf{A}$ is then a square matrix with $K^* - 1 + M^*$ rows and columns. The inverse matrix $(\mathbf{A}'\mathbf{A})^{-1}$ exists only if $\mathbf{A}'\mathbf{A}$ is nonsingular, and that is the case only when the rank of $\mathbf{A}'\mathbf{A}$ is equal to the number of rows or columns, whichever is less. The rank of $\mathbf{A}'\mathbf{A}$ cannot be greater than the rank of $\mathbf{A}$, and the rank of $\mathbf{A}$ cannot be greater than the number of columns, $K^* - 1 + M^*$, since that number is generally less than the number of rows in $\mathbf{A}$, rows of T observations. If this situation does not hold, we have the condition stated in equation 12.1.14.

Under what circumstances will the rank of $\mathbf{A}$ be exactly equal to the number of columns? To answer this question, note that the first $K^* - 1$ columns of $\mathbf{A}$ are the estimates $\hat{\mathbf{Y}}_1^*$ of the $K^* - 1$ endogenous variables appearing as regressors in the first equation. Each of these estimates is a linear combination of predetermined variables, and these combinations must be linearly independent of the M^* columns of $\mathbf{A}$ corresponding to the predetermined variables appearing as regressors in this equation. Thus each of the estimates $\hat{\mathbf{Y}}_k^*$ in $\hat{\mathbf{Y}}_1^*$ must contain at least one predetermined variable excluded from the first equation. Since there are $K^* - 1$ columns in $\hat{\mathbf{Y}}_1^*$, there must be at least $K^* - 1$ predetermined variables appearing in these estimates that do not appear

[3] J. D. Sargan, "The Maximum Likelihood Estimation of Economic Relationships with Autoregressive Residuals," *Econometrica,* Vol. 29, No. 3 (July, 1961), pp. 414-426. R. C. Fair, "The Estimation of Simultaneous Equation Models with Lagged Endogenous Variables and First Order Serially Correlated Errors," *Econometrica,* Vol. 38, No. 3 (May, 1970), pp. 507-516. Takeshi Amemiya, "Specification Analysis in the Estimation of Parameters of a Simultaneous Equation Model with Autoregressive Residuals," *Econometrica,* Vol. 34, No. 2 (April, 1966), pp. 283-306.

as one of the M^* predetermined variables appearing in the first equation. In other words at least $K^* - 1$ predetermined variables must be excluded from the first equation. To generalize, the condition of identification is: The number of excluded predetermined variables must be equal to or greater than the number of endogenous variables included in the equation less one if **A** is to have the rank of $K^* - 1 + M^*$. That is,

$$M^{**} \geq K^* - 1 \qquad \textbf{12.1.51}$$

This condition is exactly the necessary condition stated in Chapter 10 that the first equation is either just identified or overidentified.

The 2SLS Method and the Instrumental Variable Method

The 2SLS method is related to the *instrumental variable* method.[4] Consider the simple model:

$$\begin{aligned} C &= \alpha + \beta Y + U \\ Y &= C + I \end{aligned} \qquad \textbf{12.1.52}$$

C and Y are jointly determined, and I is predetermined. Writing all variables in terms of deviations from their respective means and thus eliminating the constant term α, we can obtain the following estimates:

1. The OLS estimate of $\hat{\beta}$:

$$\hat{\beta}_{OLS} = \Sigma cy/\Sigma y^2 \qquad \textbf{12.1.53}$$

2. The instrumental variable estimate of $\hat{\beta}$:

$$\hat{\beta}_{IV} = \Sigma ci/\Sigma yi \qquad \textbf{12.1.54}$$

3. Next, using the 2SLS method, the estimate is:

$$\hat{\beta}_{2SLS} = \Sigma c\hat{y}/\Sigma \hat{y}^2 \qquad \textbf{12.1.55}$$

For the 2SLS method, in stage 1 we regress:

$$y = \delta i + w \qquad \textbf{12.1.56}$$

Thus we have:

[4] For a more detailed discussion refer to Chapter 9. Also see L. R. Klein, "On the Interpretation of Theil's Method of Estimation of Economic Relations," *Meteroeconomica*, Vol. 7, No. 3 (December, 1955), pp. 147-153; and A. S. Goldberger, "An Instrumental Variable Interpretation of *k*-Class Estimation," *Indian Economic Journal*, Vol. 13, No. 3 (1965), pp. 424-431.

$$\hat{y} = \hat{\delta}i \qquad 12.1.57$$

or,

$$y = \hat{y} + \hat{w} \qquad 12.1.58$$

At stage 2 the estimator of β will then be, as in equation 12.1.55:

$$\hat{\beta}_{2SLS} = \Sigma c\hat{y}/\Sigma\hat{y}^2$$

Notice that we can replace $\hat{y}^2$ in the denominator with $y\hat{y}$ by making the following argument:

$$\begin{aligned} E(\Sigma y\hat{y}) &= E[\Sigma(\hat{y} + \hat{w})\hat{y}] \\ &= E(\Sigma\hat{y}^2 + \Sigma\hat{w}\hat{y}) \\ &= \Sigma\hat{y}^2 + \Sigma\hat{w}\hat{y} \end{aligned} \qquad 12.1.59$$

Because $\hat{y}$ is a linear combination of predetermined variables as in equation 12.1.57 (in this specific case we have only one predetermined variable $i = I - \bar{I}$), it is uncorrelated with the estimated residual terms $\hat{w}$, and $\Sigma\hat{w}\hat{y} = 0$. Therefore,

$$\Sigma y\hat{y} = \Sigma\hat{y}^2 \qquad 12.1.60$$

Making the indicated substitution, we rewrite equation 12.1.55 as follows:

$$\begin{aligned} \hat{\beta}_{2SLS} &= \Sigma c\hat{y}/\Sigma\hat{y}^2 \\ &= \Sigma c\hat{y}/\Sigma y\hat{y} \end{aligned} \qquad 12.1.61$$

But $\hat{y} = \hat{\delta}i$ from equation 12.1.57, and substituting we obtain:

$$\begin{aligned} \hat{\beta}_{2SLS} &= \Sigma c\hat{\delta}i/\Sigma y\hat{\delta}i \\ &= \hat{\delta}\Sigma ci/\hat{\delta}\Sigma yi \\ &= \Sigma ci/\Sigma yi \end{aligned} \qquad 12.1.62$$

which is exactly the instrumental variable estimator of β, $\hat{\beta}_{IV}$, given in equation 12.1.54.

The k-Class Estimators

Theil has defined a family of *k-class estimators*.[5] This method can easily be seen by introducing the factor k into equation 12.1.37.

---

[5] Henri Theil, *Economic Forecasts and Policy* (2d ed.; Amsterdam: North-Holland Publishing Co., 1961), pp. 231-236. Note that k in this case does not refer to the number of endogenous variables ($k = 1, 2, \ldots, K$) or to the index denoting the number of X's in the multiple regression model, as indicated elsewhere.

$$\begin{bmatrix} \mathbf{Y}^{*\prime}\mathbf{Y}^* - k\hat{\mathbf{W}}'\hat{\mathbf{W}} & \mathbf{Y}^{*\prime}\mathbf{X}^* \\ \mathbf{X}^{*\prime}\mathbf{Y}^* & \mathbf{X}^{*\prime}\mathbf{X}^* \end{bmatrix}^{-1} \begin{bmatrix} (\mathbf{Y}^* - k\hat{\mathbf{W}})'\mathbf{Y}_1 \\ \mathbf{X}^{*\prime}\mathbf{Y}_1 \end{bmatrix} = \begin{bmatrix} \hat{\boldsymbol{\beta}}_1 \\ \hat{\boldsymbol{\gamma}}_1 \end{bmatrix} \quad \textbf{12.1.63}$$

When $k = 0$, we obtain the OLS estimates. When $k = 1$, the 2SLS estimates are obtained. If k is stochastic and plim $k = 1$, the estimates will converge asymptotically to the 2SLS estimates. It has also been shown that the LISE estimator is a k-class estimator if k is equal to the smallest root L_1 from equations 12.2.34, as the following section will show.[6]

12.2 LIMITED INFORMATION SINGLE-EQUATION METHOD; LEAST VARIANCE RATIO

The *limited information single-equation* (LISE) method also estimates each equation of a simultaneous system independently by using information on all the predetermined variables appearing in the system as a whole.[7] The same results are obtained by the *limited information single-equation maximum likelihood* method (LIML), which is essentially based on the maximum likelihood principle. The *least variance ratio* (LRV) method also obtains the same estimators, given the assumption of normal distribution of the disturbance terms U. The following presents a simplified outline.

Let us consider, as before, the linear model:

$$\mathbf{Y}\boldsymbol{\beta} + \mathbf{X}\boldsymbol{\Gamma} + \mathbf{U} = \mathbf{0} \quad \textbf{12.2.1}$$

We wish to estimate, as before, one equation, for example the first equation of the system:

$$\mathbf{Y}^*\boldsymbol{\beta}_1 + \mathbf{X}^*\boldsymbol{\gamma}_1 + \mathbf{U}_1 = \mathbf{0} \quad \textbf{12.2.2}$$

Given $k = 1, 2, \ldots, K$, this equation has $K^*(k = 1, 2, \ldots, K^*)$ endogenous variables appearing in it; and $K^{**}(k = K^* + 1, K^* + 2, \ldots, K)$ endogenous variables appear in the system but do not appear in this equation. Thus we have:

---

[6] T. W. Anderson and H. Rubin, "The Asymptotic Properties of Estimates of the Parameters of a Single Equation in a Complete System of Stochastic Equations," *Annals of Mathematical Statistics,* Vol. 21, No. 4 (1950), pp. 570-582.

[7] Tjalling C. Koopmans and William C. Hood, "The Estimation of Simultaneous Linear Economic Relationships," *Studies in Econometric Methods,* edited by W. C. Hood and T. C. Koopmans (New York: John Wiley & Sons, 1953), pp. 112-199. Herman Chernoff and Herman Rubin, "Asymptotic Properties of Limited-Information Estimates Under Generalized Conditions," *Studies in Econometric Method,* edited by W. C. Hood and T. C. Koopmans (New York: John Wiley & Sons, 1953), pp. 200-212. Theodore W. Anderson and Herman Rubin, "Estimation of the Parameters of a Single Equation in a Complete System of Stochastic Equations," *Annals of Mathematical Statistics,* Vol. 20, No. 1 (1949), pp. 46-63. Also see Carl F. Christ, *Econometric Models and Methods* (New York: John Wiley & Sons, 1966); Lawrence R. Klein, *A Textbook of Econometrics* (Evanston, Illinois: Row, Peterson & Co., 1956); and P. R. Fisk, *Stochastically Dependent Equations: An Introductory Text for Econometricians* (London: Charles Griffin & Co., 1967).

$$\mathbf{Y}^* = [Y_{t1}, Y_{t2}, \ldots, Y_{tK^*}] \qquad 12.2.3$$

The predetermined variables of the system can likewise be arranged in two separate matrices, $\mathbf{X}^*$ and $\mathbf{X}^{**}$. $\mathbf{X}^*$ is the matrix of predetermined variables appearing in this equation, whereas the variables in $\mathbf{X}^{**}$ do not appear in this equation:

$$\mathbf{X}^* = [X_{t1}, X_{t2}, \ldots, X_{tM^*}] \qquad 12.2.4$$

$$\mathbf{X}^{**} = [X_{tM^*+1}, X_{tM^*+2}, \ldots, X_{tM}] \qquad 12.2.5$$

We wish to estimate the two vectors of coefficients:[8]

$$\boldsymbol{\beta}_1 = \begin{bmatrix} \beta_{11} \\ \beta_{12} \\ \cdot \\ \cdot \\ \cdot \\ \beta_{1K^*} \end{bmatrix} \qquad \boldsymbol{\gamma}_1 = \begin{bmatrix} \gamma_{11} \\ \gamma_{12} \\ \cdot \\ \cdot \\ \cdot \\ \gamma_{1M^*} \end{bmatrix} \qquad 12.2.6$$

The first step is to construct a synthetic variable:

$$\tilde{Y}_{t1} = Y_{t1} + \beta_{12}Y_{t2} + \beta_{13}Y_{t3} + \ldots + \beta_{1K^*}Y_{tK^*} \qquad 12.2.7$$

Note that β_{11} in the first equation is set equal to unity.

Next, the computational scheme involves estimating two regressions:

1. Regress the above synthetic endogenous variable $\tilde{\mathbf{Y}}_1$ consisting of a linear combination of all K^* jointly determined variables appearing in the equation on all the predetermined variables $\mathbf{X}^*$ appearing in the equation.
2. Regress the same synthetic variable $\tilde{\mathbf{Y}}_1$ on all predetermined variables appearing in the system as a whole, $\mathbf{X} = [\mathbf{X}^* \quad \mathbf{X}^{**}]$. That is, the two equations are as follows:

$$\tilde{Y}_{t1} = \gamma_{11}X_{t1} + \gamma_{12}X_{t2} + \ldots + \gamma_{1M^*}X_{tM^*} + W_{t1}$$

$$\tilde{Y}_{t1} = \gamma_{11}X_{t1} + \gamma_{12}X_{t2} + \ldots + \gamma_{1M^*}X_{tM^*} + \gamma_{1M^*+1}X_{tM^*+1} + \ldots + \gamma_{1M}X_{tM} + W_{t1} \qquad 12.2.8$$

Notice that in both equations no jointly determined variable appears as a regressor. All variables appearing as regressors in the two equations above

[8] Recall that β_{11} refers to the coefficient of the jointly determined variable Y_1 in equation 1, and the same pattern applies for $\beta_{12}, \ldots, \beta_{1K^*}$. Similar definitions apply to $\gamma_{11}, \gamma_{12}, \ldots, \gamma_{1M^*}$ as coefficients of predetermined variables appearing in the equation 1.

are predetermined variables only. Thus the condition that the covariance between each regressor and the disturbance term is zero; that is, the condition $E(X_m U_k) = 0$ is fulfilled. By constructing the synthetic variable in equation 12.2.7, we have a way of removing the jointly determined variables (Y_{t1}, $Y_{t2}, \ldots, Y_{tK^*}$) appearing in the equation from the regressors and creating a situation where all of them are combined into one regressand. In this way we avoid the problem that the covariance between each of the jointly determined variables and the U terms is not zero; that is, $E(Y_k U_k) \neq 0$.

$$L = \frac{\text{sum of the squared deviations of } \tilde{\mathbf{Y}}_1 \text{ from its regression on the predetermined variables } M^* \text{ that appear in the equation}}{\text{sum of the squared deviations of } \tilde{\mathbf{Y}}_1 \text{ from its regression on all the predetermined variables } M^* + M^{**} \text{ appearing in the model}} \qquad \textbf{12.2.9}$$

The ratio of the sums of squared deviations cannot be less than one; that is,

$$L \geq 1 \qquad \textbf{12.2.10}$$

This condition holds because the denominator must always be equal to or less than the numerator; the introduction of additional variables in a regression cannot possibly increase the sum of squared deviations. In the numerator the synthetic variable $\tilde{\mathbf{Y}}_1$ is regressed on M^* predetermined variables, whereas in the denominator M^{**} additional predetermined variables are introduced as regressors. Thus the variations in the synthetic variable $\tilde{\mathbf{Y}}_1$ must be explained either to the same extent as in the numerator or more, certainly not less. Indeed we seek to choose a set of β_k's that will make the regression coefficients of these additional regressors M^{**} approximately zero, if not zero, according to the a priori specification of the model. The closer the regression coefficients of the additional M^{**} predetermined variables are to zero, the closer will the variance ratio L be to unity.

The variance ratio can be expressed in the following form:

$$L = \frac{\boldsymbol{\beta}_1 \mathcal{W}^* \boldsymbol{\beta}_1'}{\boldsymbol{\beta}_1 \mathcal{W} \boldsymbol{\beta}_1'} \qquad \textbf{12.2.11}$$

The term "least variance ratio" method comes from the operation of minimizing the variance ratio to derive estimates of $\boldsymbol{\beta}_1$, that is, the β's in equation 1.[9]

[9] The same expression appears in the logarithm of the limited information maximum likelihood (LIML) function, which can be written as, ignoring unnecessary constants:

$$\mathcal{L} = -\frac{1}{2} \log_e \frac{\boldsymbol{\beta}_1 \mathcal{W}^* \boldsymbol{\beta}_1'}{\boldsymbol{\beta}_1 \mathcal{W} \boldsymbol{\beta}_1'}$$

To minimize the L ratio is to maximize the LIML function $\mathcal{L}$. Thus these two methods obtain the same estimators. (This is not proven here.)

Referring to equation 12.2.7, we can write, ignoring the t subscripts:

$$(\beta_{11}, \beta_{12}, \ldots, \beta_{1K^*}) \begin{bmatrix} Y_1 \\ Y_2 \\ \cdot \\ \cdot \\ \cdot \\ Y_{K^*} \end{bmatrix} = \boldsymbol{\beta}_1 \mathbf{Y}_1^{*\prime} = \hat{\mathbf{Y}}_1 \qquad \textbf{12.2.12}$$

To calculate the variance in the numerator of the variance ratio L, each component of the synthetic variable $\tilde{\mathbf{Y}}_1$, that is, each Y in equation 1, is regressed first on the M^* subset of the predetermined variables and then on the complete set of M predetermined variables. The set of regression equations corresponding to equation 1 can be written as follows:

$$\begin{aligned} Y_1 &= g_{11}X_1 + g_{12}X_2 + \ldots + g_{1M^*}X_{M^*} + W_1 \\ Y_2 &= g_{21}X_1 + g_{22}X_2 + \ldots + g_{2M^*}X_{M^*} + W_2 \\ &\quad \cdot \qquad\qquad \cdot \qquad\qquad \cdot \\ &\quad \cdot \qquad\qquad \cdot \qquad\qquad \cdot \\ &\quad \cdot \qquad\qquad \cdot \qquad\qquad \cdot \\ Y_{K^*} &= g_{K^*1}X_1 + g_{K^*2}X_2 + \ldots + g_{K^*M^*}X_{M^*} + W_{K^*} \end{aligned} \qquad \textbf{12.2.13}$$

or,

$$\begin{bmatrix} Y_1 \\ Y_2 \\ \cdot \\ \cdot \\ \cdot \\ Y_{K^*} \end{bmatrix} = \begin{bmatrix} g_{11} & g_{12} \cdots g_{1M^*} \\ g_{21} & g_{22} \cdots g_{2M^*} \\ \cdot & \\ \cdot & \\ \cdot & \\ g_{K^*1} & g_{K^*2} \cdots g_{K^*M^*} \end{bmatrix} \begin{bmatrix} X_1 \\ X_2 \\ \cdot \\ \cdot \\ \cdot \\ X_{M^*} \end{bmatrix} + \begin{bmatrix} W_1 \\ W_2 \\ \cdot \\ \cdot \\ \cdot \\ W_{K^*} \end{bmatrix}$$

or,

$$\mathbf{Y}^{*\prime} = \mathbf{G}^*\mathbf{X}^{*\prime} + \mathbf{W}^{*\prime} \qquad \textbf{12.2.14}$$

where $\mathbf{G}^*$ is the matrix of coefficients. In terms of $\tilde{\mathbf{Y}}_1$, as in equation 12.2.12,

$$\begin{aligned}\tilde{\mathbf{Y}}_1 &= \boldsymbol{\beta}_1 \mathbf{Y}^{*\prime} \\ &= \boldsymbol{\beta}_1(\mathbf{G}^*\mathbf{X}^{*\prime} + \mathbf{W}^{*\prime}) \\ &= \boldsymbol{\beta}_1\mathbf{G}^*\mathbf{X}^{*\prime} + \boldsymbol{\beta}_1\mathbf{W}^{*\prime}\end{aligned} \qquad \mathbf{12.2.15}$$

The estimate of $\tilde{\mathbf{Y}}_1$ is thus obtained from the OLS estimates of the $\mathbf{G}^*$ matrix:

$$\hat{\tilde{\mathbf{Y}}}_1 = \boldsymbol{\beta}_1\hat{\mathbf{G}}^*\mathbf{X}^{*\prime} \qquad \mathbf{12.2.16}$$

The deviations of observed values of $\tilde{\mathbf{Y}}_1$ from estimated values $\hat{\tilde{\mathbf{Y}}}_1$ is then given by:

$$\tilde{\mathbf{Y}}_1 - \hat{\tilde{\mathbf{Y}}}_1 = \boldsymbol{\beta}_1\mathbf{Y}^{*\prime} - \boldsymbol{\beta}_1\hat{\mathbf{G}}^*\mathbf{X}^{*\prime} = \boldsymbol{\beta}_1\hat{\mathbf{W}}^{*\prime} \qquad \mathbf{12.2.17}$$

Squaring and summing over all t to obtain the expression in the numerator of L, we have:

$$\begin{aligned}\sum_t (\boldsymbol{\beta}_1\mathbf{Y}_t^{*\prime} - \boldsymbol{\beta}_1\hat{\mathbf{G}}^*\mathbf{X}_t^{*\prime})^2 &= \sum_t (\boldsymbol{\beta}_1\hat{\mathbf{W}}_t^{*\prime})^2 \\ &= \sum_t (\boldsymbol{\beta}_1\hat{\mathbf{W}}_t^{*\prime}\hat{\mathbf{W}}_t^{*}\boldsymbol{\beta}_1') \\ &= \boldsymbol{\beta}_1\left(\sum_t \hat{\mathbf{W}}_t^{*\prime}\hat{\mathbf{W}}_t^{*}\right)\boldsymbol{\beta}_1'\end{aligned} \qquad \mathbf{12.2.18}$$

Denoting $\sum_t (\hat{\mathbf{W}}_t^{*\prime}\hat{\mathbf{W}}_t^{*})$ by $\mathcal{W}^*$, where:

$$\mathcal{W}^* = \begin{bmatrix} \sum_t \hat{W}_{t1}^{*2} & \sum_t \hat{W}_{t1}^*\hat{W}_{t2}^* & \ldots \sum_t \hat{W}_{t1}^*\hat{W}_{tK^*}^* \\ \sum_t \hat{W}_{t2}^*\hat{W}_{t1}^* & \sum_t \hat{W}_{t2}^{*2} & \ldots \sum_t \hat{W}_{t2}^*\hat{W}_{tK^*}^* \\ \cdot & \cdot & \cdot \\ \cdot & \cdot & \cdot \\ \cdot & \cdot & \cdot \\ \sum_t \hat{W}_{tK^*}^*\hat{W}_{t1}^* & \sum_t \hat{W}_{tK^*}^*\hat{W}_{t2}^* & \ldots \sum_t \hat{W}_{tK^*}^{*2} \end{bmatrix} \qquad \mathbf{12.2.19}$$

we can rewrite to obtain the expression in the numerator of L in equation 12.2.11. That is,

$$\boldsymbol{\beta}_1\left(\sum_t \hat{\mathbf{W}}_t^{*\prime}\hat{\mathbf{W}}_t^{*}\right)\boldsymbol{\beta}_1' = \boldsymbol{\beta}_1\mathcal{W}^*\boldsymbol{\beta}_1' \qquad \mathbf{12.2.20}$$

Similarly, for the denominator of L, regressing each Y of $\mathbf{Y}^*$ on all M predetermined variables X, we have:

$$
\begin{aligned}
Y_1 &= g_{11}X_1 + \ldots + g_{1M^*}X_{M^*} + g_{1M^*+1}X_{M^*+1} + \ldots + g_{1M}X_M + W_1 \\
Y_2 &= g_{21}X_1 + \ldots + g_{2M^*}X_{M^*} + g_{2M^*+1}X_{M^*+1} + \ldots + g_{2M}X_M + W_2 \\
&\quad\vdots \\
Y_{K^*} &= g_{K^*1}X_1 + \ldots + g_{K^*M^*}X_{M^*} + g_{K^*M^*+1}X_{M^*+1} + \ldots + g_{K^*M}X_M + W_{K^*}
\end{aligned}
\qquad 12.2.21
$$

or,

$$
\begin{bmatrix} Y_1 \\ Y_2 \\ \cdot \\ \cdot \\ \cdot \\ Y_{K^*} \end{bmatrix} = \begin{bmatrix} g_{11} & \cdots & g_{1M} \\ g_{21} & \cdots & g_{2M} \\ \cdot & & \cdot \\ \cdot & & \cdot \\ \cdot & & \cdot \\ g_{K^*1} & \cdots & g_{K^*M} \end{bmatrix} \begin{bmatrix} X_1 \\ X_2 \\ \cdot \\ \cdot \\ \cdot \\ X_M \end{bmatrix} + \begin{bmatrix} W_1 \\ W_2 \\ \cdot \\ \cdot \\ \cdot \\ W_{K^*} \end{bmatrix}
$$

or,

$$\mathbf{Y}^{*\prime} = \mathbf{GX}' + \mathbf{W}' \qquad 12.2.22$$

Substituting in the expression for $\tilde{\mathbf{Y}}_1$, we obtain:

$$
\begin{aligned}
\tilde{\mathbf{Y}}_1 &= \boldsymbol{\beta}_1\mathbf{Y}^{*\prime} = \boldsymbol{\beta}_1(\mathbf{GX}' + \mathbf{W}') \\
&= \boldsymbol{\beta}_1\mathbf{GX}' + \boldsymbol{\beta}_1\mathbf{W}'
\end{aligned}
\qquad 12.2.23
$$

As before the estimate of $\tilde{\mathbf{Y}}_1$ is given by:

$$\hat{\tilde{\mathbf{Y}}}_1 = \boldsymbol{\beta}_1\hat{\mathbf{G}}\mathbf{X}$$

and the deviations of observed from estimated values, $\tilde{\mathbf{Y}}_1 - \hat{\tilde{\mathbf{Y}}}_1$, are:

$$\boldsymbol{\beta}_1\mathbf{Y}^{*\prime} - \boldsymbol{\beta}_1\hat{\mathbf{G}}\mathbf{X}' = \boldsymbol{\beta}_1\hat{\mathbf{W}}' \qquad 12.2.24$$

from which the sum of the squared deviations in the denominator of L is calculated as follows:

$$
\begin{aligned}
\sum_t(\boldsymbol{\beta}_1\mathbf{Y}_t^{*\prime} - \boldsymbol{\beta}_1\hat{\mathbf{G}}\mathbf{X}_t')^2 &= \sum_t(\boldsymbol{\beta}_1\hat{\mathbf{W}}_t')^2 \\
&= \sum_t(\boldsymbol{\beta}_1\hat{\mathbf{W}}_t'\hat{\mathbf{W}}_t\boldsymbol{\beta}_1') \\
&= \boldsymbol{\beta}_1\left(\sum_t\hat{\mathbf{W}}_t'\hat{\mathbf{W}}_t\right)\boldsymbol{\beta}_1'
\end{aligned}
\qquad 12.2.25
$$

We then denote $\sum_t (\hat{\mathbf{W}}_t'\hat{\mathbf{W}}_t)$ by $\mathcal{W}$, where:

$$\mathcal{W} = \begin{bmatrix} \sum_t \hat{W}_{t1}^2 & \sum_t \hat{W}_{t1}\hat{W}_{t2} & \cdots & \sum_t \hat{W}_{t1}\hat{W}_{tK^*} \\ \sum_t \hat{W}_{t2}\hat{W}_{t1} & \sum_t \hat{W}_{t2}^2 & \cdots & \sum_t \hat{W}_{t2}\hat{W}_{tK^*} \\ \cdot & \cdot & & \cdot \\ \cdot & \cdot & & \cdot \\ \cdot & \cdot & & \cdot \\ \sum_t \hat{W}_{tK^*}\hat{W}_{t1} & \sum_t \hat{W}_{tK^*}\hat{W}_{t2} & \cdots & \sum_t \hat{W}_{tK^*}^2 \end{bmatrix} \qquad \mathbf{12.2.26}$$

Thus we rewrite equations 12.2.25 as:

$$\boldsymbol{\beta}_1\left(\sum_t \hat{\mathbf{W}}_t'\hat{\mathbf{W}}_t\right)\boldsymbol{\beta}_1' = \boldsymbol{\beta}_1\mathcal{W}\boldsymbol{\beta}_1' \qquad \mathbf{12.2.27}$$

and this is the quantity in the denominator of the ratio in equation 12.2.11.[10]

Of course we do not as yet know the elements of $\boldsymbol{\beta}_1$, but we can now compute $\mathcal{W}^*$ and $\mathcal{W}$ in terms of observed variables:

$$\mathcal{W}^* = \mathbf{Y}^{*\prime}\mathbf{Y}^* - \mathbf{Y}^{*\prime}\mathbf{X}^*(\mathbf{X}^{*\prime}\mathbf{X}^*)^{-1}\mathbf{X}^{*\prime}\mathbf{Y}^* \qquad \mathbf{12.2.28}$$

where $\mathbf{Y}^*$ and $\mathbf{X}^*$ denote the matrices of the observed values of the endogenous and predetermined variables present in the first structural equation. The term $\mathbf{Y}^{*\prime}\mathbf{Y}^*$ is the matrix of the sums of squares and products of the observations on the variables in $\mathbf{Y}^*$. The second term is the matrix of the explained sum of squares and products obtained by regressing $\mathbf{Y}^*$ on $\mathbf{X}^*$. $\mathcal{W}^*$ is then the matrix of the sums of squares and products of the deviations. Recall the least squares estimator for the regression of $\mathbf{Y}^*$ on $\mathbf{X}^*$: $(\mathbf{X}^{*\prime}\mathbf{X}^*)^{-1}\mathbf{X}^{*\prime}\mathbf{Y}^*$. Thus,

$$\hat{\mathbf{Y}}^* = \mathbf{X}^*(\mathbf{X}^{*\prime}\mathbf{X}^*)^{-1}\mathbf{X}^{*\prime}\mathbf{Y}^*$$

from which,

$$\hat{\mathbf{Y}}^{*\prime}\hat{\mathbf{Y}}^* = [\mathbf{X}^*(\mathbf{X}^{*\prime}\mathbf{X}^*)^{-1}\mathbf{X}^{*\prime}\mathbf{Y}^*]'\ [\mathbf{X}^*(\mathbf{X}^{*\prime}\mathbf{X}^*)^{-1}\mathbf{X}^{*\prime}\mathbf{Y}^*]$$

or,

$$\hat{\mathbf{Y}}^{*\prime}\hat{\mathbf{Y}}^* = \mathbf{Y}^{*\prime}\mathbf{X}^*(\mathbf{X}^{*\prime}\mathbf{X}^*)^{-1}\mathbf{X}^{*\prime}\mathbf{Y}^*$$

Similarly, by regressing $\mathbf{Y}^*$ on $\mathbf{X}$,

[10] Notice that in the matrices $\mathcal{W}^*$ and $\mathcal{W}$ the elements are sums involving residuals of the two different regressions of $\tilde{\mathbf{Y}}_1$ even though notationally they look alike.

$$\mathcal{W} = \mathbf{Y}^{*\prime}\mathbf{Y}^{*} - \mathbf{Y}^{*\prime}\mathbf{X}(\mathbf{X}'\mathbf{X})^{-1}\mathbf{X}'\mathbf{Y}^{*} \qquad \textbf{12.2.29}$$

After having obtained estimates of $\mathcal{W}^*$ and $\mathcal{W}$ in terms of observed values of the variables in **Y***, **X***, and **X**, we then differentiate the least variance ratio L in equation 12.2.11 with respect to $\beta_{11}, \beta_{12}, \ldots, \beta_{1K^*}$ simultaneously, temporarily ignoring $\beta_{11} = 1$, and set the results equal to zero for minimization. From equation 12.2.11, omitting the subscript 1 for the vector $\boldsymbol{\beta}$, we can write:

$$L = \frac{\boldsymbol{\beta}\mathcal{W}^*\boldsymbol{\beta}'}{\boldsymbol{\beta}\mathcal{W}\boldsymbol{\beta}'}$$

$$\frac{\partial L}{\partial \beta_i} = \frac{\partial}{\partial \beta_i}\left[\frac{\boldsymbol{\beta}\mathcal{W}^*\boldsymbol{\beta}'}{\boldsymbol{\beta}\mathcal{W}\boldsymbol{\beta}'}\right] = 0 \qquad \textbf{12.2.30}$$

$$= \frac{1}{\boldsymbol{\beta}\mathcal{W}\boldsymbol{\beta}'}[(\mathcal{W}^*\boldsymbol{\beta}')_i - L(\mathcal{W}\boldsymbol{\beta}')_i] = 0,\ i = 1, 2, \ldots, K^*$$

This set of K^* equations can be expressed in compact matrix notation as:

$$\mathcal{W}^*\boldsymbol{\beta}' - L\mathcal{W}\boldsymbol{\beta}' = (0, \ldots, 0) = \mathbf{0} \qquad \textbf{12.2.31}$$

or,

$$(\mathcal{W}^* - L\mathcal{W})\boldsymbol{\beta}' = \mathbf{0}' \qquad \textbf{12.2.32}$$

Because by the specification of the model not all elements of the vector $\boldsymbol{\beta}'$, that is, $\beta_{11}, \beta_{12}, \ldots, \beta_{1K}{}^*$, are zero, the determinant of $\mathcal{W}^* - L\mathcal{W}$ must be zero if $\boldsymbol{\beta}'$ is to have a nonzero solution. Thus,

$$\left|\mathcal{W}^* - L\mathcal{W}\right| = 0 \qquad \textbf{12.2.33}$$

When this determinant is expanded, it yields a polynomial in L of degree K^*, since it is of the order K^*. We can write this polynomial as:

$$a_0L^{K^*} + a_1L^{K^*-1} + \ldots + a_{K^*-1}L + a_{K^*} = 0 \qquad \textbf{12.2.34}$$

This polynomial has K^* numerical roots, which are all real numbers greater than or equal to unity as L is defined. Any one of these roots will make the determinant 12.2.34 zero. Because we wish to minimize the ratio L, we take the smallest of these roots, say L_1, and rewrite equation 12.2.32 as follows:

$$(\mathcal{W}^* - L_1\mathcal{W})\boldsymbol{\beta}' = \mathbf{0}' \qquad \textbf{12.2.35}$$

Given the appropriate condition of identifiability and using the rule $\beta_{11} = 1$, we can solve for the vector of estimates $\hat{\boldsymbol{\beta}}$; and the solutions are indeed unique.

Next we solve for the vector $\boldsymbol{\gamma}$. In terms of a single equation, the first equation, for example, $\boldsymbol{\beta}_1$ is the vector of coefficients of the endogenous variables appearing in the equation, where $\hat{\boldsymbol{\beta}}_1$ is the estimate of $\boldsymbol{\beta}_1$. That is,

$$\hat{\boldsymbol{\beta}}_1 = [\hat{\beta}_{11}, \hat{\beta}_{12}, \ldots, \hat{\beta}_{1K^*}]$$

where $\hat{\beta}_{11} = 1$. When $\hat{\boldsymbol{\beta}}_1$ has been obtained, at the next step $\hat{\gamma}_1 = [\hat{\gamma}_{11}, \hat{\gamma}_{12}, \ldots, \hat{\gamma}_{1M^*}]$ (the coefficients of the predetermined variables appearing in the first equation) can be obtained by regressing $\hat{\boldsymbol{\beta}}_1\mathbf{Y}^{*\prime}$ on $\mathbf{X}^{*\prime}$ as follows. If we write:

$$\hat{\boldsymbol{\beta}}_1\mathbf{Y}^{*\prime} = \boldsymbol{\gamma}_1\mathbf{X}^{*\prime} + \mathbf{U}_1$$

where $\boldsymbol{\beta}_1$ and $\boldsymbol{\gamma}_1$ are column vectors, we have:

$$\hat{\gamma}_1 = \hat{\boldsymbol{\beta}}_1\mathbf{Y}^{*\prime}\mathbf{X}^*(\mathbf{X}^{*\prime}\mathbf{X}^*)^{-1} \qquad \textbf{12.2.36}$$

Let us summarize the steps involved:

1. Calculate $(\mathbf{X}^{*\prime}\mathbf{X}^*)^{-1}\mathbf{X}^{*\prime}\mathbf{Y}^*$ and $(\mathbf{X}'\mathbf{X})^{-1}\mathbf{X}'\mathbf{Y}^*$ after having defined $\mathbf{Y}^*$, $\mathbf{X}^*$, and $\mathbf{X}$ for the particular equation in the system.
2. Calculate $\mathcal{W} = \mathbf{Y}^{*\prime}\mathbf{Y}^* - \mathbf{Y}^{*\prime}\mathbf{X}(\mathbf{X}'\mathbf{X})^{-1}\mathbf{X}'\mathbf{Y}^*$ and $\mathcal{W}^* = \mathbf{Y}^{*\prime}\mathbf{Y}^* - \mathbf{Y}^{*\prime}\mathbf{X}^*(\mathbf{X}^{*\prime}\mathbf{X}^*)^{-1}\mathbf{X}^{*\prime}\mathbf{Y}^*$.
3. Set the determinant $|\mathcal{W}^* - L\mathcal{W}| = 0$ and calculate the numerical coefficients of the polynomial in L. Solve this polynomial for the smallest root L_1.
4. Set up the equation:

$$(\mathcal{W}^* - L_1\mathcal{W})\hat{\boldsymbol{\beta}}_k' = \mathbf{0}'$$

   where the subscript k refers to the kth equation. Solve for the vector $\hat{\boldsymbol{\beta}}_k$ and normalize the results, following the usual rule of setting the $\hat{\beta}_{kk}$ element of the vector of the above coefficients equal to unity, and obtain a unique solution for the vector $\hat{\boldsymbol{\beta}}_k$.
5. Estimate the vector of coefficients of the predetermined variables in the kth equation $\boldsymbol{\gamma}_k$ using the appropriate formula.

Without presenting the proof we shall state that the LISE estimator is consistent and that it has the same asymptotic variance-covariance matrix as the 2SLS estimator. Of course we continue to assume that the system is not underidentified and that the X's are truly exogenous. None of them are lagged endogenous variables; or even if they are, the disturbances are not autocorrelated (review Chapter 7) or the LISE estimator will not be consistent.

12.3 THE FIX-POINT METHOD

The *fix-point* (FP) method, as proposed by Herman Wold, is essentially based on an iterative least squares procedure.[11] It seeks to obtain consistent

[11] Herman O.A. Wold, "A Fix-Point Theorem with Econometric Background, Part I," *Arkiv für Matematik*, Band 6, NR 12 (October, 1964), pp. 209-220; and "A Fix-Point Theorem with Econometric Background, Part II," *Arkiv für Matematik*, Band 6, NR 13 (February, 1965), pp. 221-240. Also see E. J. Mosbaek and H.O.A. Wold (eds.), *Interdependent Systems–Structure and Estimation* (Amsterdam: North-Holland Publishing Co., 1969); and A. Agren, "Extension of the Fix-Point Method: Theory and Application" (Doctoral dissertation, University of Uppsala, Sweden, 1972).

estimators by estimating one equation at a time at each step, as in the 2SLS and LISE methods, and then by using these estimates for the calculation of new proxies for the regressors, repeating this process in successive iterations. It makes no assumption as to the normality of the joint distribution of the U terms, and therefore it is akin to the 2SLS method.

The FP method does not use directly the observations on all the predetermined variables appearing in the system as a whole in estimating the single equation under consideration, as do the 2SLS and LISE methods. This method does make use of restrictions on the structural parameters of the predetermined variables in the system at each stage of successive iterations. Recall that in the 2SLS method, the Y_k's appearing in the particular equation as regressors are replaced in the second stage by their estimated values $\hat{Y}_k$, and that the $\hat{Y}_k$'s are obtained by regressing the observed Y_k's on the complete set of M predetermined variables in $\mathbf{X}$, the matrix of observations on all predetermined variables in the model. If the model has M predetermined variables, we need to fulfill the condition that M is less than T as in condition 12.1.14. The same condition must be satisfied in the LISE/LVR estimation technique, since the expression in the denominator of ratio 12.2.9 is obtained from residuals after regressing all Y_k appearing in the equation concerned on all predetermined variables in the model as a whole. For the FP method, as we shall see, the corresponding condition is $M_i^* + K_i^* \leq T$, with M_i^* and K_i^* being the number of exogenous and endogenous variables in the ith equation of the system.

The rationale of the FP method can be stated as follows. Let us consider a model of two simultaneous equations without the t subscripts:

$$\begin{aligned} Y_1 &= \beta_{12}Y_2 + \gamma_{11}X_1 + \gamma_{12}X_2 + U_1 \\ Y_2 &= \beta_{21}Y_1 + \gamma_{23}X_3 + \gamma_{24}X_4 + U_2 \end{aligned} \qquad \textbf{12.3.1}$$

Note that Y_1 and Y_2 are jointly determined variables and that X_1, X_2, X_3, and X_4 are predetermined variables. There is no explicit constant term in these equations, but one could easily be included in the form $\gamma_{i0}X_0$ with X_0 having the constant value 1. Therefore we state that:

$$\begin{aligned} &E(X_m U_k) = 0 \\ &E(Y_2 U_1) \neq 0 \qquad E(Y_1 U_2) \neq 0 \end{aligned} \qquad \textbf{12.3.2}$$

The immediate problem in estimating the first equation is that $E(Y_2U_1) \neq 0$. For simplicity let us discuss one equation, the first one. In the 2SLS method in its first stage, Y_2 is regressed on all the X's such that:

$$\begin{aligned} Y_2 &= g_1X_1 + g_2X_2 + g_3X_3 + g_4X_4 + g_0 + W_2 \\ \mathbf{Y}_2 &= \mathbf{XG} + \mathbf{W}_2 \end{aligned} \qquad \textbf{12.3.3}$$

Let $\mathbf{G}$ be the OLS estimate of the vector of g coefficients. In the second stage what we have is replacement of Y_2 by its estimate, $\hat{Y}_2 = \mathbf{X}\hat{\mathbf{G}}$, and we have:

$$Y_1 = \beta_{10} + \beta_{12}(\mathbf{X}\hat{\mathbf{G}}) + \gamma_{11}X_1 + \gamma_{12}X_2 + U_1 + \beta_{12}\hat{W}_2 \qquad \textbf{12.3.4}$$

Thus we have only X's as regressors; and since $E(X_m U_1) = 0$ by specification, the problem of $E(Y_2 U_1) \neq 0$ has been circumvented.

In the LISE/LVR ratio, we do a similar exercise. The numerator of the ratio is constructed from residuals obtained by jointly regressing both Y_1 and Y_2 on X_1 and X_2; whereas the denominator is constructed from such residuals by jointly regressing Y_1 and Y_2 on all X's, that is, $X_1, \ldots, X_4$. In both 2SLS and LISE the jointly determined variables appearing as regressors are replaced by X's, that is, predetermined variables, to resolve the problem of nonzero covariance between regressors, the Y's, and disturbance terms, the U's. For theoretical disturbances, we note that:

$$W_1 = U_1 + \beta_{12}W_2$$

In the FP method the idea is to assume that even when $E(Y_2W_1) \neq 0$, it is possible to obtain an estimate for the conditional mean $E(Y_2)$ such that:

$$E[E(Y_2)W_1] = 0 \qquad \textbf{12.3.5}$$

$E(Y_2)$ is determined by adopting an iterative procedure where the initial value of $Y_2^{(0)}$ can be chosen arbitrarily. Rewriting equation 12.3.5 more generally, we can state that with $\mathbf{Y}^*$ denoting the endogenous variables appearing as regressors in the kth equation,

$$\begin{aligned} E(\mathbf{Y}^*\mathbf{W}_k) &\neq \mathbf{0} \\ E[E(\mathbf{Y}^*)\mathbf{W}_k] &= \mathbf{0} \end{aligned} \qquad \textbf{12.3.6}$$

Denote the estimate of $E(\mathbf{Y}^*)$ by $\tilde{\tilde{\mathbf{Y}}}^*$, and let $\mathbf{Y}^{*(s)}$ be the estimate of $\mathbf{Y}^*$ obtained after s iterations. Then:

$$\tilde{\tilde{\mathbf{Y}}}^* = \lim_{s \to \infty} \mathbf{Y}^{*(s)} \qquad \textbf{12.3.7}$$

Successive iterations are expected to converge to a unique limiting value.[12] Should there be such convergence, the FP method is a consistent estimator. Convergence to a secondary parasitic solution can, however, occur in exceptional cases.

The FP method can be explained in terms of a two equation model. Return to model 12.3.1:

$$\begin{aligned} Y_1 &= \beta_{12}Y_2 + \gamma_{11}X_1 + \gamma_{12}X_2 + U_1 \\ Y_2 &= \beta_{21}Y_1 + \gamma_{23}X_3 + \gamma_{24}X_4 + U_2 \end{aligned}$$

[12] The proof that such a limit exists makes use of a theorem called the "fixed point theorem" in mathematics. That is why Wold described this method as "fix-point estimation."

Step 1

In the preliminary step we choose arbitrary sets of values of $Y_1^{(0)}$ and $Y_2^{(0)}$.[13] Substituting $Y_2^{(0)}$ for Y_2 in equation 1 and $Y_1^{(0)}$ for Y_1 in equation 2, we estimate the parameters of each equation by OLS.

$$\begin{aligned} Y_1 &= \beta_{12}Y_2^{(0)} + \gamma_{11}X_1 + \gamma_{12}X_2 + W_1^{(1)} \\ Y_2 &= \beta_{21}Y_1^{(0)} + \gamma_{23}X_3 + \gamma_{24}X_4 + W_2^{(1)} \end{aligned} \qquad \textbf{12.3.8}$$

The parameter estimates are denoted $\hat{\beta}_{12}^{(1)}$, $\hat{\gamma}_{11}^{(1)}$, $\hat{\gamma}_{12}^{(1)}$, and $\hat{\beta}_{21}^{(1)}$, $\hat{\gamma}_{23}^{(1)}$, $\hat{\gamma}_{24}^{(1)}$. In the first iteration the values of $Y_1^{(1)}$ and $Y_2^{(1)}$ are calculated using these parameter estimates.

$$\begin{aligned} Y_1^{(1)} &= \hat{\beta}_{12}^{(1)}Y_2^{(0)} + \hat{\gamma}_{11}^{(1)}X_1 + \hat{\gamma}_{12}^{(1)}X_2 \\ Y_2^{(1)} &= \hat{\beta}_{21}^{(1)}Y_1^{(0)} + \hat{\gamma}_{23}^{(1)}X_3 + \hat{\gamma}_{24}^{(1)}X_4 \end{aligned} \qquad \textbf{12.3.9}$$

Step 2

These values from the first iteration are substituted into the structural equations.

$$\begin{aligned} Y_1 &= \beta_{12}Y_2^{(1)} + \gamma_{11}X_1 + \gamma_{12}X_2 + W_1^{(2)} \\ Y_2 &= \beta_{21}Y_1^{(1)} + \gamma_{23}X_3 + \gamma_{24}X_4 + W_2^{(2)} \end{aligned} \qquad \textbf{12.3.10}$$

The parameters of these equations are estimated by OLS, and the estimates are used to calculate a second set of values of $Y_1^{(2)}$ and $Y_2^{(2)}$.

$$\begin{aligned} Y_1^{(2)} &= \hat{\beta}_{12}^{(2)}Y_2^{(1)} + \hat{\gamma}_{11}^{(2)}X_1 + \hat{\gamma}_{12}^{(2)}X_2 \\ Y_2^{(2)} &= \hat{\beta}_{21}^{(2)}Y_1^{(1)} + \hat{\gamma}_{23}^{(2)}X_3 + \hat{\gamma}_{24}^{(2)}X_4 \end{aligned} \qquad \textbf{12.3.11}$$

At each iteration the calculated values $[Y_1^{(2)}, Y_2^{(2)}]$, $[Y_1^{(3)}, Y_2^{(3)}]$, . . . $[Y_1^{(r)}, Y_2^{(r)}]$ are substituted in the structural equations, and the parameters are estimated by the OLS method. These estimates are then used to calculate a new set of values $[Y_1^{(r+1)}, Y_2^{(r+1)}]$. These iterations are continued until the differences in the values insuccessive iterations become and remain arbitrarily small.

$$\begin{aligned} Y_{t1}^{(r+1)} - Y_{t1}^{(r)} &< \epsilon \\ Y_{t2}^{(r+1)} - Y_{t2}^{(r)} &< \epsilon \end{aligned} \qquad \textbf{12.3.12}$$

---

[13] For an arbitrary choice $Y_1^{(0)}$ and $Y_2^{(0)}$ can be taken as the actual observed values of Y_1 and Y_2. This means that the iteration process starts with a straightforward application of the OLS. Consequently, the parameter estimates at this first round of the iterative process are biased and inconsistent.

where ϵ is an arbitrary small number, $\epsilon > 0$. The values $Y_1^{(r)}$ and $Y_2^{(r)}$ are then taken as the limits $\tilde{\tilde{Y}}_1$ and $\tilde{\tilde{Y}}_2$, as defined by equation 12.3.7:

$$\tilde{\tilde{Y}}_1 = \lim_{s \to \infty} Y_1^{(s)}$$
$$\tilde{\tilde{Y}}_2 = \lim_{s \to \infty} Y_2^{(s)} \tag{12.3.13}$$

To estimate the coefficients of the first equation, the limit values $\tilde{\tilde{Y}}_2 = \tilde{\tilde{Y}}_2^{(r)}$ are substituted for Y_2.

$$Y_1 = \beta_{12}\tilde{\tilde{Y}}_2 + \gamma_{11}X_1 + \gamma_{12}X_2 + \tilde{W}_1 \tag{12.3.14}$$

where:

$$\tilde{W}_1 = Y_1 - \tilde{\tilde{Y}}_1$$

The coefficients are then estimated by OLS, and these estimates are the FP estimates of the coefficients. Given the vectors:

$$\mathbf{Y} = (Y_1 \; Y_2)$$
$$\mathbf{X} = (X_1 \; X_2 \; X_3 \; X_4)$$

and the familiar assumptions with respect to the disturbance terms U_k, the immediate problem is to determine:

$$\tilde{\tilde{\mathbf{Y}}} = (\tilde{\tilde{Y}}_1 \; \tilde{\tilde{Y}}_2) \tag{12.3.15}$$

Let us write:

$$\mathbf{A}Y_1 = \beta_{12}\tilde{\tilde{Y}}_2 + \gamma_{11}X_1 + \gamma_{12}X_2$$
$$\mathbf{A}Y_2 = \beta_{21}\tilde{\tilde{Y}}_1 + \gamma_{23}X_3 + \gamma_{24}X_4 \tag{12.3.16}$$

A is the projection operator; $\mathbf{A}Y_1$ is the projection of Y_1 on the space spanned by $\tilde{\tilde{Y}}_2$, X_1, and X_2; and $\mathbf{A}Y_2$ is the projection of Y_2 on the space spanned by $\tilde{\tilde{Y}}_1$, X_3, and X_4. $\mathbf{A}Y_1$ and $\mathbf{A}Y_2$ coincide with $\tilde{\tilde{Y}}_1$ and $\tilde{\tilde{Y}}_2$ respectively, so that:

$$\mathbf{A}Y_1 = \tilde{\tilde{Y}}_1 = \beta_{12}\tilde{\tilde{Y}}_2 + \gamma_{11}X_1 + \gamma_{12}X_2$$
$$\mathbf{A}Y_2 = \tilde{\tilde{Y}}_2 = \beta_{21}\tilde{\tilde{Y}}_1 + \gamma_{23}X_3 + \gamma_{24}X_4 \tag{12.3.17}$$

The $\tilde{\tilde{Y}}_i$ are defined as in equation 12.3.7. Note that equation 12.3.7 can be estimated when successive iterations converge to the limiting value. In practice the problem of convergence has often been acute.

One way to cope with this problem is the *fractional fix-point* method (FFP). Consider the sth step of iteration. After having obtained the estimate of:

$$\mathbf{Y}_1^{(s)} = \mathbf{Y}^{*(s-1)}\boldsymbol{\beta}^{(s)} + \mathbf{X}^*\boldsymbol{\gamma}^{(s)} \qquad \textbf{12.3.18}$$

the next step is to estimate $\boldsymbol{\beta}^{(s+1)}$ and $\boldsymbol{\gamma}^{(s+1)}$, and regress $\mathbf{Y}_1$ on the values of $\mathbf{Y}^{*(s)}$ and $\mathbf{X}^*$.

$$\mathbf{Y}_1 = \mathbf{Y}^{*(s)}\boldsymbol{\beta}^{(s+1)} + \mathbf{X}^*\boldsymbol{\gamma}^{(s+1)} + \mathbf{W}^{(s+1)} \qquad \textbf{12.3.19}$$

Then with the estimated coefficients $\hat{\boldsymbol{\beta}}^{(s+1)}$ and $\hat{\boldsymbol{\gamma}}^{(s+1)}$, a preliminary value $\mathbf{Y}_{1(0)}^{(s+1)}$ is calculated.

$$\mathbf{Y}_{1(0)}^{(s+1)} = \mathbf{Y}^{*(s)}\hat{\boldsymbol{\beta}}^{(s+1)} + \mathbf{X}^*\hat{\boldsymbol{\gamma}}^{(s+1)} \qquad \textbf{12.3.20}$$

In the next $(s + 2)^{th}$ step, $\mathbf{Y}^{*(s+1)}$ is corrected as follows:

$$\mathbf{Y}^{*(s+1)} = \alpha\mathbf{Y}_{(0)}^{*(s+1)} + (1 - \alpha)\mathbf{Y}^{*(s)} \qquad \textbf{12.3.21}$$

where α is called a relaxation factor and is always greater than zero. Obviously, if $\alpha = 1$, we revert to the FP method in its original form. Thus according to the fractional fix point (FFP) method, at each successive step of iteration a correction is introduced. Attempts have been made to define the optimal value of α. For practical purposes it is claimed that an α close to, but less than unity is a good guess and aids convergence.

The general form for the iteration using the FFP method is:

$$\mathbf{Y}_1^{*(s)} = \alpha[\mathbf{Y}^{*(s-1)}\boldsymbol{\beta}^{(s)} + \mathbf{X}^*\boldsymbol{\gamma}^{(s)}] + (1 - \alpha)\mathbf{Y}^{*(s-1)} \qquad \textbf{12.3.22}$$

12.4 ITERATIVE INSTRUMENTAL VARIABLE METHOD

Another approach proposed to resolve the issue of estimating parameters in an interdependent system is based on the use of the instrumental variable method in an iterative procedure (IIV).[14] At each successive iteration, the estimate of Y^* at the previous iteration, $Y^{*(s-1)}$, is used as an instrument; and the regression is carried out by the instrumental variable method. Thus the IIV method differs from the FP method discussed in section 12.3 even though it works within the framework of iterative least squares in an indirect way.

---

[14] E. Lyttkens, "On the Fix-Point Method and Related Problems: Including an Explicit Treatment of the Estimation Problem of Girshick-Haavelmo Model," Parts I and II (papers presented at the first Blaricum meetings of the Econometric Society, 1967). E. Lyttkens, "Symmetric and Asymmetric Estimation Methods," *Interdependent Systems—Structure and Estimation,* edited by E. J. Mosbaek and H.O.A. Wold (Amsterdam: North-Holland Publishing Co., 1970). M. Dutta and E. Lyttkens, "Iterative Instrumental Variables Method and Estimation of a Large Simultaneous System," Discussion paper No. 7 (New Brunswick, N.J.: Bureau of Economic Research, Rutgers University, May, 1970). G. S. Maddala, "Simutaneous Estimation Methods for Large and Mediumsize Econometric Models," *Review of Economic Studies,* Vol. 38 (1971), pp. 435-445. M. McCarthy, "Notes on the Selection of Instruments for Two Stage Least Squares and *k*-Class Type Estimators for Large Models," *Southern Economic Journal,* Vol. 37, No. 3 (January, 1971), pp. 251-259.

The regressors of the FP method correspond to the instrumental variables of the IIV method; but the parameters are estimated by OLS in the FP method, not by the instrumental variable method. To be sure, the FP and IIV methods do not in general give the same estimates even if both of them converge.

The IIV method, unlike the 2SLS and LISE/LVR methods, can in principle be used in a system where the number of predetermined variables exceeds the number of observations on the variables. In this aspect IIV shares the characteristic of the FP method that the number of observations need not be as great as the number of predetermined variables in the system, but only as great as the largest number of variables, predetermined and endogenous, appearing in a single equation of the system. The problem of undersized models has been approached by several other alternative methods which will not be covered in this book.[15]

The steps for the IIV method will be outlined again in terms of the two-equation model:

$$\begin{aligned} Y_1 &= \beta_{12}Y_2 + \gamma_{11}X_1 + \gamma_{12}X_2 + U_1 \\ Y_2 &= \beta_{21}Y_1 + \gamma_{23}X_3 + \gamma_{24}X_4 + U_2 \end{aligned} \qquad \textbf{12.4.1}$$

In the preliminary step we choose arbitrary values for $Y_1^{(0)}$ and $Y_2^{(0)}$ as in the FP method. For simplicity we can take the observed values on Y_1 and Y_2 and thus begin with the OLS start. Even though this choice means the estimates at the first stage of iteration will be biased and inconsistent under certain assumptions, there can be convergence and the asymptotic properties of the IIV estimators may remain valid.

Step 1

The values $Y_1^{(0)}$ and $Y_2^{(0)}$ are used as instruments for the instrumental variable estimates of the parameters of both equations. Recall that the IV estimates of the parameters of a multivariate regression are given by:

---

[15] Interested readers may consult: T. Kloek and L.B.M. Mennes, "Simultaneous Equation Estimation Based on Principal Components of Predetermined Variables," *Econometrica*, Vol. 28, No. 1 (January, 1966), pp. 45-61; and H. Theil, *Principals of Econometrics* (New York: John Wiley & Sons, 1971), pp. 532-536.

Another alternative is of course the block-recursive method as discussed in Chapter 11. B. Mitchell, "Estimation of Large Econometric Models by Principal Component and Instrumental Variable Methods," *Review of Economics and Statistics*, Vol. 53, No. 2 (May, 1971), pp. 140-146. J. M. Brundy and D. W. Jorgenson, "Efficient Estimation of Simultaneous Equations by Instrumental Variables," *Review of Economics and Statistics*, Vol. 53, No. 3 (August, 1971), pp. 207-224. Brundy and Jorgenson propose a limited iterative method (LIVE) which is consistent as well as efficient. L. R. Klein, "Estimation of Interdependent Systems in Macroeconomics," *Econometrica*, Vol. 37, No. 2 (April, 1969), pp. 171-192. Klein used a set of selected principal components of $(X'X)$ in the 2SLS estimation method. In the first stage of 2SLS, the Y's can be regressed on this set of principal components instead of on all X's in the model. The second stage of the 2SLS can then be solved as before with $\hat{Y}$'s as regressors. P. J. Dhrymes and V. Pandit, "Asymptotic Properties of an Iterate of the Two-Stage Least Squares Estimator," *Journal of the American Statistical Association*, Vol. 67 (1972), pp. 444-447.

$$\hat{\beta} = (\mathbf{Z}'\mathbf{X})^{-1}\mathbf{Z}'\mathbf{Y}$$

where **X** is the matrix of regressors, and **Z** is the same matrix with instruments chosen to replace some original regressors. For equation 1 the **X** matrix of regressors is $[Y_2 \quad X_1 \quad X_2]$. When $Y_2^{(0)}$ is used as an instrument for Y_2, the **Z** matrix is $[Y_2^{(0)} \quad X_1 \quad X_2]$. Thus we have for the IV estimates of the parameters of equation 1:

$$[\hat{\beta}_{12}\ \hat{\gamma}_{11}\ \hat{\gamma}_{12}]' = \{[Y_2^{(0)}\ X_1\ X_2]'\ [Y_2\ X_1\ X_2]\}^{-1}\ [Y_2^{(0)}\ X_1\ X_2]'\mathbf{Y}_1$$

and for the IV estimates of equation 2:

$$[\hat{\beta}_{21}\ \hat{\gamma}_{23}\ \hat{\gamma}_{24}]' = \{[Y_1^{(0)}\ X_3\ X_4]'\ [Y_1\ X_3\ X_4]\}^{-1}\ [Y_1^{(0)}\ X_3\ X_4]'\mathbf{Y}_2 \qquad \textbf{12.4.2}$$

To continue the process of iteration, we then calculate values of $Y_1^{(1)}$ and $Y_2^{(1)}$. These values are obtained from the restricted reduced form of the model, not from structural equation 12.3.1 as in the FP method. The restricted reduced form parameter matrix $\mathbf{\Pi}$ can be calculated directly once the structural parameters have been estimated. For the two-equation model we can use the estimates of the parameters from equation 12.4.2 and then obtain the restricted reduced form $\hat{\mathbf{\Pi}}$ as follows:

$$\hat{\mathbf{\Pi}} = \begin{bmatrix} 1 & -\hat{\beta}_{12} \\ -\hat{\beta}_{21} & 1 \end{bmatrix}^{-1} \begin{bmatrix} \hat{\gamma}_{11} & \hat{\gamma}_{12} & 0 & 0 \\ 0 & 0 & \hat{\gamma}_{23} & \hat{\gamma}_{24} \end{bmatrix} \qquad \textbf{12.4.3}$$

We then calculate estimated values of Y_1 and Y_2 in the restricted reduced form.

$$\mathbf{Y}^{(1)} = \hat{\mathbf{\Pi}}\mathbf{X} \qquad \textbf{12.4.4}$$

or,

$$\begin{bmatrix} Y_1^{(1)} \\ Y_2^{(1)} \end{bmatrix} = \hat{\mathbf{\Pi}} \begin{bmatrix} X_1 \\ X_2 \\ X_3 \\ X_4 \end{bmatrix} \qquad \textbf{12.4.5}$$

Step 2

In the next step the values of $Y_1^{(1)}$ and $Y_2^{(1)}$ are used as instruments for another round of instrumental variable estimation of the parameters of structural equations 12.4.1. These estimated parameters $[\hat{\beta}_{12}^{(2)} \quad \hat{\gamma}_{11}^{(2)} \quad \hat{\gamma}_{12}^{(2)}]$ and $[\hat{\beta}_{21}^{(2)} \quad \hat{\gamma}_{23}^{(2)} \quad \hat{\gamma}_{24}^{(2)}]$ are then used to calculate new values of $Y_1^{(2)}$ and $Y_2^{(2)}$ in the restricted reduced form, as in the first iteration.

The iteration process of using the estimated values $Y_1^{(r)}$ and $Y_2^{(r)}$ as instruments in an IIV estimation of the structural parameters continues until the values obtained from successive iteration become and remain arbitrarily close.

$$
\begin{aligned}
Y_{t1}^{(r+1)} - Y_{t1}^{(r)} &< \epsilon \\
Y_{t2}^{(r+1)} - Y_{t2}^{(r)} &< \epsilon
\end{aligned}
\qquad 12.4.6
$$

where ϵ is an arbitrarily small number, $\epsilon > 0$. The iterative instrumental variable method of estimation is said to converge if these conditions hold for some number of iterations r.

The IIV estimates of the structural parameters of equation 1 are obtained with the values $Y_1^{(r)}$ and $Y_2^{(r)}$ used as instruments in the instrumental variable estimation of these parameters. Notice that, although we have estimated only the parameters of a single equation, say equation 1, we have all the necessary information to obtain IIV estimates of the structural parameters for equation 2. At each successive iteration the structural parameters of the entire system are estimated by using the instrumental variable method.

The method can be easily extended to the general case of k equations with k endogenous variables $(Y_1, Y_2, \ldots, Y_K)$ and m predetermined variables $(X_1, X_2, \ldots, X_M)$.

The IIV Estimates—A Simple Case

An illustrative case may help to clarify the point. Consider the simple Keynesian model denoting all variables in terms of deviations from their respective means:

$$
\begin{aligned}
c_t &= \beta y_t + u_t \\
c_t + i_t &= y_t
\end{aligned}
\qquad 12.4.7
$$

where i_t is predetermined and c_t and y_t are jointly determined. We can observe the iterative procedure following the IIV method as follows. In step 1, using a set of arbitrary values on y_1 denoted $y^{(0)}$, we obtain:

$$\beta^{(1)} = \Sigma c y^{(0)} / \Sigma y y^{(0)} \qquad 12.4.8$$

Alternatively, OLS can be applied straightforwardly, such that:

$$(\text{OLS})\hat{\beta} = \Sigma c y / \Sigma y^2 \qquad 12.4.9$$

This means at the first iteration values on $y^{(0)}$ have been taken as observed, and the OLS $\hat{\beta}$ is used as the $\beta^{(1)}$, the estimate of the structural parameter in the first round of iteration.

Solving equation 12.4.7,

$$y^{(1)} = \frac{1}{1 - \beta^{(1)}} i \qquad 12.4.10$$

Then at the second iteration,

$$(\text{IIV})\beta^{(2)} = \Sigma y^{(1)}c/\Sigma y^{(1)}y \qquad \textbf{12.4.11}$$

from which:

$$Y^{(2)} = \frac{1}{1 - \beta^{(2)}}\, i \qquad \textbf{12.4.12}$$

Again, at the third step of iteration,

$$(\text{IIV})\beta^{(3)} = \Sigma y^{(2)}c/\Sigma y^{(2)}y \qquad \textbf{12.4.13}$$

from which:

$$y^{(3)} = \frac{1}{1 - \beta^{(3)}}\, i \qquad \textbf{12.4.14}$$

Because $y^{(1)}$ and $y^{(2)}$ are proportionate to i, we have:

$$\beta^{(2)} = \beta^{(3)} \qquad \textbf{12.4.15}$$

and

$$y^{(2)} = y^{(3)} \qquad \textbf{12.4.16}$$

which shows that the convergence in this special case is already established at the third step of the iteration. Note that the steps in the IIV method are different from those of the straightforward application of the instrumental variable method as discussed in Chapter 9.

Model 12.4.7 is indeed a very special case where there is only one stochastic equation which is just identified, and we have convergence immediately. In a large overidentified system convergence will take a much longer time, and thus the IIV method is likely to be more expensive.

The IIV method has been shown to yield estimates of parameters different from those obtained by the FP method. This is so because the solutions at each successive stage of iteration are used as regressors in the FP method but as instrumental variables in the IIV method at each stage of iteration.

It is important to note that the IIV estimates will also differ from the 2SLS estimates. In the first stage of the two-stage least squares method, each Y is regressed on the total set of all M predetermined variables in the system. No a priori restrictions are recognized. This unrestricted use of the reduced form in the first stage of the 2SLS method contributes to the difference between the 2SLS estimates of the structural parameters and the IIV estimates of them, since the IIV estimates are obtained by using instruments for each Y from the restricted reduced form solutions of the complete system at each stage of iteration. However, the IIV and 2SLS estimates have the same asymptotic properties.

DISCUSSION QUESTIONS

1. Consider the following model:

$$Y_1 = b_{12} Y_2 + g_{11} X_1 + g_{12} X_2 + g_{10} + U_1$$

$$Y_2 = b_{21} Y_1 + g_{23} X_3 + g_{24} X_4 + g_{20} + U_2$$

Y_1	Y_2	X_1	X_2	X_3	X_4
39.8	2.7	43.7	23.7	180.1	12.7
41.9	−0.2	40.6	20.8	182.8	12.4
45.0	1.9	49.1	21.4	182.6	16.9
49.2	5.2	55.4	22.7	184.5	18.4
50.6	3.0	56.4	23.5	189.7	19.4
52.6	5.1	58.7	25.2	192.7	20.1
55.1	5.6	60.3	25.7	197.8	19.6
56.2	4.2	61.3	25.8	203.4	19.8
57.3	3.0	64.0	26.3	207.6	21.1
57.8	5.1	67.0	26.4	210.6	21.7
55.0	1.0	57.7	25.3	215.7	15.6
50.9	−3.4	50.7	23.3	216.7	11.4
45.6	−6.2	41.3	20.8	213.3	7.0
46.5	−5.1	45.3	19.8	207.1	11.2
48.7	−3.0	48.9	21.4	202.0	12.3
51.3	−1.3	53.3	25.1	199.0	14.0
57.7	2.1	61.8	29.0	197.7	17.6
58.7	2.0	65.0	30.4	199.8	17.3
57.5	−1.9	61.2	30.4	201.8	15.3
61.6	1.3	68.4	33.8	199.9	19.0
65.0	3.3	74.1	39.0	201.2	21.1
69.7	4.9	85.3	45.3	204.5	23.5

(a) Use the data given to obtain the two-stage least squares estimate of the parameters of the above model.
(b) Show that the 2SLS estimates are consistent.
(c) Can the 2SLS estimates be obtained when the sample size is fewer than the number of predetermined variables in the model?
(d) Calculate the variance of the 2SLS estimates.

2. Review the condition of identification in terms of the 2SLS estimates.

3. Show the relationship, if any, between the 2SLS and instrumental variable methods of estimation (Hint: Review Chapter 9).

4. Review Theil's definition of a family of k-class estimators.

5. Obtain the LISE estimates of the parameters of the model in question 1.

6. Briefly review the mechanics of the least variance ratio.

7. Analyze the framework of the fix-point method of estimation. Is this estimator consistent? How is the fractional fix-point method different from the fix-point method?

8. The iterative instrumental variables method combines the principles of iterative method and instrumental variable method. Discuss.

9. Can the fix-point and IIV methods of estimation be used in a situation where the sample size is smaller than the number of predetermined variables in the model?

10. Should the programing facilities permit, obtain the FP and IIV estimates of the model in question 1.

11. Find the ILS, 2SLS, LISE, and IIV estimates of the model in question 5, Chapter 10.

SUGGESTED READINGS

Amemiya, Takeshi. "Specification Analysis in the Estimation of Parameters of a Simultaneous Equation Model with Autoregressive Residuals." *Econometrica*. Vol. 34, No. 2 (April, 1966), pp. 283-306.

Agren, A. "Extension of the Fix-Point Method: Theory and Application." Doctoral dissertation, University of Uppsala, Sweden, 1972.

Anderson, Theodore W., and Herman Rubin. "Estimation of the Parameters of a Single Equation in a Complete System of Stochastic Equations." *Annals of Mathematical Statistics,* Vol. 20, No. 1 (1949), pp. 46-63.

———. "The Asymptotic Properties of Estimates of the Parameters of a Single Equation in a Complete System of Stochastic Equations." *Annals of Mathematical Statistics,* Vol. 21, No. 4 (1950), pp. 570-582.

Basmann, Robert L. "A Generalized Classical Method of Linear Estimation of Coefficients in a Structural Equation." *Econometrica,* Vol. 25, No. 1 (January, 1957), pp. 77-83.

———. "The Computation of Generalized Classical Estimate of Coefficients in a Structural Equation." *Econometrica,* Vol. 27, No. 1 (January, 1959), pp. 72-81.

———. "On the Asymptotic Distribution of Generalized Linear Estimators." *Econometrica,* Vol. 28, No. 1 (January, 1960), pp. 97-107.

Brundy, J. M., and Dale W. Jorgenson. "Efficient Estimation of Simultaneous Equations by Instrumental Variables." *Review of Economics and Statistics,* Vol. 53, No. 3 (August, 1971), pp. 207-224.

Chernoff, Herman, and Herman Rubin. "Asymptotic Properties of Limited-Information Estimates Under Generalized Conditions." *Studies in Econometric Method,* edited by W. C. Hood and T. C. Koopmans. New York: John Wiley & Sons, 1953, pp. 200-212.

Christ, Carl F. *Econometric Models and Methods*. New York: John Wiley & Sons, 1966.

Dhrymes, Phoebus J., and V. Pandit. "Asymptotic Properties of an Iterate of the Two-Stage Least Squares Estimator." *Journal of the American Statistical Association,* Vol. 67 (1972), pp. 444-447.

Dutta, M., and E. Lyttkens. "Iterative Instrumental Variables Method and Estimation of a Large Simultaneous System." Discussion paper No. 7, New Brunswick, N.J.: Bureau of Economic Research, Rutgers University, May, 1970.

Dutta, M., E. Lyttkens, and R. Bergström. "Fix-Point and Iterative Instrumental Variable Methods for Estimating Interdependent Systems." A paper presented at the second World Congress of the Econometric Society, Cambridge, England, September, 1970.

Fair, R. C. "The Estimation of Simultaneous Equation Models with Lagged Endogenous Variables and First Order Serially Correlated Errors." *Econometrica,* Vol. 38, No. 3 (May, 1970), pp. 507-516.

Fisk, P. R. *Stochastically Dependent Equations.* London: Charles Griffin & Co., 1967.

Goldberger, Arthur S. *Econometric Theory.* New York: John Wiley & Sons, 1964.

———. "An Instrumental Variable Interpretation of *k*-Class Estimation." *Indian Economic Journal,* Vol. 13, No. 3 (1965), pp. 424-431.

Johnston, J. *Econometric Methods,* 2d ed. New York: McGraw-Hill Book Co., 1972.

Klein, Lawrence R. "On the Interpretation of Theil's Method of Estimation of Economic Relations." *Meteroeconomica,* Vol. 7, No. 3 (December, 1955), pp. 147-153.

———. "Estimation of Interdependent Systems in Macroeconomics." *Econometrica,* Vol. 37, No. 2 (April, 1969), pp. 171-192.

———. *A Textbook of Econometrics.* Evanston, Illinois: Row, Peterson & Co., 1956.

Kloek, T., and L.B.M. Mennes. "Simultaneous Equation Estimation Based on Principal Components of Predetermined Variables." *Econometrica,* Vol. 28, No. 1 (January, 1966), pp. 45-61.

Koopmans, Tjalling C., and William C. Hood. "The Estimation of Simultaneous Linear Economic Relationships." *Studies in Econometric Methods,* edited by W. C. Hood and T. C. Koopmans. New York: John Wiley & Sons, 1953, pp. 112-199.

Lyttkens, Ejnar. "On the Fix-Point Method and Related Problems: Including an Explicit Treatment on the Estimation Problem of Girshick-Haavelmo Model." A paper presented at the first Blaricum meetings of the Econometric Society, 1967.

———. "Symmetric and Asymmetric Estimation Methods." *Interdependent Systems—Structure and Estimation,* edited by E. J. Mosbaek, and H.O.A. Wold. Amsterdam: North-Holland Publishing Co., 1970.

Maddala, G.S. "Simultaneous Estimation Methods for Large and Medium-size Econometric Models." *Review of Economic Studies,* Vol. 38 (1971), pp. 435-445.

McCarthy, Michael. "Notes on the Selection of Instruments for Two Stage Least Squares and k-Class Type Estimators for Large Models." *Southern Economic Journal,* Vol. 37, No. 3 (January, 1971), pp. 251-259.

Mitchell, B. "Estimation of Large Econometric Models by Principal Component and Instrumental Variable Methods." *Review of Economics and Statistics,* Vol. 53, No. 2 (May, 1971), pp. 140-146.

Mosbaek, E. J., and H.O.A. Wold (eds.). *Interdependent Systems—Structure and Estimation.* Amsterdam: North-Holland Publishing Co., 1970.

Sargan, J. D. "The Maximum Likelihood Estimation of Economic Relationships with Autoregressive Residuals." *Econometrica,* Vol. 29, No. 3 (July, 1961), pp. 414-426.

Theil, Henri. *Economic Forecasts and Policy,* 2d ed. Amsterdam: North-Holland Publishing Co., 1961.

———. *Principles of Econometrics.* New York: John Wiley & Sons, 1971.

Wold, Herman O.A. "A Fix-Point Theorem with Econometric Background, Part I." *Arkiv für Matematik,* Band 6, NR 12 (October, 1964), pp. 209-220.

———. "A Fix-Point Theorem with Econometric Background, Part II." *Arkiv für Matematik,* Band 6, NR 13 (February, 1965), pp. 221-240.

13

full information maximum likelihood method and three-stage least squares method

13.0 SYSTEM METHODS

Several single-equation estimation methods for simultaneous equation systems have been discussed in the previous chapter. These methods recognize the simultaneity of the relations of an interdependent system in a limited sense. In estimating the kth equation with a single-equation method, nothing is assumed to be known about the specification of other equations in the system. In both 2SLS and LISE/LVR no recognition is taken of the *excluded* endogenous variables—those not appearing in the particular equation but appearing in other equations—even though information on all predetermined variables not appearing in the kth equation but appearing in the model is used. These methods thus fail to make use of some a priori information that would improve the estimates. To remedy this, *full information* methods have been developed. The full information methods seek to estimate all the structural equations simultaneously. Thus the complete specification of the model is taken into account explicitly. As one might expect, a method of estimation based on more information yields estimators which are both consistent and efficient.

13.1 THE FULL INFORMATION MAXIMUM LIKELIHOOD METHOD

The *full information maximum likelihood* (FIML) method generally obtains estimators that are consistent, asymptotically normally distributed, and asymptotically efficient.[1] The following discusses this method in general terms without treating the complicated numerical estimation techniques required in very much detail. Consider the model, as before, of k jointly determined Y variables and m predetermined X variables, with $t = 1, 2, \ldots, T$ independent observations on the Y's and X's ($k = 1, 2, \ldots, K$, and $m = 1, 2, \ldots, M$):

$$\mathbf{Y}\boldsymbol{\beta} + \mathbf{X}\boldsymbol{\Gamma} + \mathbf{U} = \mathbf{0} \qquad \textbf{13.1.1}$$

from which the reduced form, as before, is given as:

$$\mathbf{Y} = \boldsymbol{\Omega}\mathbf{X} + \mathbf{V} \qquad \textbf{13.1.2}$$

where $\boldsymbol{\Omega} = -\boldsymbol{\beta}^{-1}\boldsymbol{\Gamma}$ and $\mathbf{V} = -\boldsymbol{\beta}^{-1}\mathbf{U}$. The FIML method seeks to maximize the likelihood function associated with the entire system:

$$L = |\boldsymbol{\beta}|^T \prod_{t=1}^{T} f[(\boldsymbol{\beta}\mathbf{Y}_t + \boldsymbol{\Gamma}\mathbf{X}_t)|\boldsymbol{\Sigma}] \qquad \textbf{13.1.3}$$

where the symbol $\prod_{t=1}^{T}$ indicates the continued product of the terms that follow as the index t runs from one to T: $f[(\boldsymbol{\beta}\mathbf{Y}_1 + \boldsymbol{\Gamma}\mathbf{X}_1)|\boldsymbol{\Sigma}] \cdot f[(\boldsymbol{\beta}\mathbf{Y}_2 + \boldsymbol{\Gamma}\mathbf{X}_2)|\boldsymbol{\Sigma}] \ldots \cdot f[(\boldsymbol{\beta}\mathbf{Y}_T + \boldsymbol{\Gamma}\mathbf{X}_T)|\boldsymbol{\Sigma}]$, and where $\boldsymbol{\Sigma}$ is the variance-covariance matrix of the disturbance terms $E(\mathbf{U}'\mathbf{U})$. The $\boldsymbol{\Sigma}$ matrix is nonsingular. We do not assume it to be diagonal. The assumption that $\boldsymbol{\Sigma}$ is diagonal obviously simplifies the computational design, but such an assumption is unwarranted except for the strictly recursive models. It implies that the error terms of the different equations are uncorrelated, a strong assumption indeed. Of course we continue to assume that error terms associated with a particular equation are serially uncorrelated. Underidentified equations and identities in the system are assumed to have been eliminated.

To appreciate the derivation of the likelihood function, we can begin by concentrating on the stochastic nature of U_t. The likelihood of the sample observations on Y_t, given X_t, can then be written as:

---

[1] Tjalling C. Koopmans, "Statistical Estimation of Simultaneous Economic Relations," *Journal of the American Statistical Association,* Vol. 40, No. 232 Part 1 (December, 1945), pp. 448-466. T. C. Koopmans, R. B. Leipnik, and H. Rubin, "Measuring the Equation Systems of Dynamic Economics," *Statistical Inference in Dynamic Economic Models,* edited by T. C. Koopmans (New York: John Wiley & Sons, 1950), pp. 53-237. Herman Chernoff and Nathan Divinsky, "The Computation of Maximum Likelihood Estimates of Linear Structural Equations," *Studies in Econometric Method,* edited by W. C. Hood and T. C. Koopmans (New York: John Wiley & Sons, 1953), pp. 236-269. T. M. Brown, "Simplified Full Maximum Likelihood and Comparative Structural Estimates," *Econometrica,* Vol. 27, No. 4 (October, 1959), pp. 638-653. Lawrence R. Klein, *A Textbook of Econometrics* (Evanston, Illinois: Row, Peterson & Co., 1956). Carl F. Christ, *Econometric Models and Methods* (New York: John Wiley & Sons, 1966). P. R. Fisk, *Stochastically Dependent Equations.* (London: Charles Griffin & Co., 1967).

$$p(Y_t|X_t) = p(U_t|X_t)\left|\frac{\partial U_t}{\partial Y_t}\right| \qquad \textbf{13.1.4}$$

where $|\partial U_t/\partial Y_t|$ is the absolute value of the determinant formed from the following matrix:

$$\begin{bmatrix} \frac{\partial U_{t1}}{\partial Y_{t1}} & \frac{\partial U_{t1}}{\partial Y_{t2}} & \cdots & \frac{\partial U_{t1}}{\partial Y_{tK}} \\ \frac{\partial U_{t2}}{\partial Y_{t1}} & \frac{\partial U_{t2}}{\partial Y_{t2}} & \cdots & \frac{\partial U_{t2}}{\partial Y_{tK}} \\ \cdot & \cdot & & \cdot \\ \cdot & \cdot & & \cdot \\ \cdot & \cdot & & \cdot \\ \frac{\partial U_{tK}}{\partial Y_{t1}} & \frac{\partial U_{tK}}{\partial Y_{t2}} & \cdots & \frac{\partial U_{tK}}{\partial Y_{tK}} \end{bmatrix} \qquad \textbf{13.1.5}$$

The nature of the above matrix is evident from the examination of one equation of the system, equation 1, say, which we write as follows:

$$U_{t1} = \beta_{11}Y_{t1} + \beta_{12}Y_{t2} + \ldots + \beta_{1K}Y_{tK} + \gamma_{11}X_{t1} + \gamma_{12}X_{t2} + \ldots + \gamma_{1M}X_{tM} \qquad \textbf{13.1.6}$$

from which:

$$\frac{\partial U_{t1}}{\partial Y_{t1}} = \beta_{11}, \quad \frac{\partial U_{t1}}{\partial Y_{t2}} = \beta_{12}, \ldots, \frac{\partial U_{t1}}{\partial Y_{tK}} = \beta_{1K}$$

and this is the first row of matrix 13.1.5. We can obtain the rest of the rows in it if we do similar manipulations in writing out the rest of the equations of the system. So we can see that matrix 13.1.5 is the coefficient matrix $\boldsymbol{\beta}$. Since by assumption $E(X_tU_t) = 0$, we can rewrite equation 13.1.4:

$$\begin{aligned} p(Y_t|X_t) &= p(U_t)\left|\frac{\partial U_t}{\partial Y_t}\right| \\ &= \left|\det \boldsymbol{\beta}\right| p(U_t) \end{aligned} \qquad \textbf{13.1.7}$$

where $t = 1, 2, \ldots, T$. Then the likelihood of the sample observations on the Y's, given the X's, is given by the function:

$$L = \left|\det \boldsymbol{\beta}\right|^T p(U_1)\, p(U_2) \ldots p(U_T) \qquad \textbf{13.1.8}$$

Since $\mathbf{U}_t = \boldsymbol{\beta}\mathbf{Y}_t + \boldsymbol{\Gamma}\mathbf{X}_t$, L is a function of the elements in the $\boldsymbol{\beta}$ and $\boldsymbol{\Gamma}$ matrices. Taking the system of equations as a whole, we obtain the expression in equation 13.1.3 where the matrix **Σ** becomes important. Note that in equation 13.1.3, $|\boldsymbol{\beta}|$ indicates not only the determinant of $\boldsymbol{\beta}$ (as the notation usually does), but also stands for the absolute value of the determinant of the matrix $\boldsymbol{\beta}$, known as the Jacobian.

This method depends on the specification of the function f in equation 13.1.3 in terms of normal distribution.[2] Let $F(\mathbf{U})$, the frequency function relative to all the **U**'s $(U_{t1}, U_{t2}, \ldots, U_{tK})$, be jointly normally distributed. Then the joint probability distribution of the U's is given by:

$$\Psi\,(U_{11}\ldots U_{T1};\ldots;U_{1K}\ldots U_{TK}) = \frac{1}{(2\pi)^{KT/2}\,|\boldsymbol{\Sigma}|^{T/2}} \exp\left(-\frac{1}{2}\sum_{t=1}^{T}\mathbf{U}_t\boldsymbol{\Sigma}^{-1}\mathbf{U}_t'\right) \qquad \textbf{13.1.9}$$

Let us continue to assume that the frequency function relative to the reduced form, $F(\mathbf{V})$, is identical with that relating to the structural equations (normal distribution). Note that:

$$E(\mathbf{V}_t'\mathbf{V}_t) = E(\boldsymbol{\beta}^{-1}\mathbf{U}_t'\mathbf{U}_t\boldsymbol{\beta}^{-1\prime}) = \boldsymbol{\beta}^{-1}E(\mathbf{U}_t'\mathbf{U}_t)\boldsymbol{\beta}^{-1\prime} = \boldsymbol{\beta}^{-1}\boldsymbol{\Sigma}\boldsymbol{\beta}^{-1\prime} \qquad \textbf{13.1.10}$$

By using equations 13.1.2 and 13.1.9, we can write for the reduced form the joint conditional distribution of the Y's, given the X's and the set of reduced form parameters in $\boldsymbol{\Omega}$. This distribution in matrix notation is:

$$\Phi(Y_{11}\ldots Y_{T1};\ldots;Y_{1K}\ldots Y_{TK}|X_{11}\ldots X_{T1};\ldots;X_{1M}\ldots X_{TM}) = \frac{1}{(2\pi)^{KT/2}\left|\boldsymbol{\beta}^{-1}\boldsymbol{\Sigma}\boldsymbol{\beta}^{-1\prime}\right|^{T/2}} \exp\left[-\frac{1}{2}\sum_{t=1}^{T}(\mathbf{Y}_t - \mathbf{X}_t\boldsymbol{\Omega}')\,(\boldsymbol{\beta}^{-1}\boldsymbol{\Sigma}\boldsymbol{\beta}^{-1\prime})^{-1}\,(\mathbf{Y}_t' - \boldsymbol{\Omega}\mathbf{X}_t')\right] \qquad \textbf{13.1.11}$$

We proceed to estimate $\boldsymbol{\Omega}$ by minimizing $(\mathbf{V}'\mathbf{V})$ and, using the OLS method:

$$\hat{\boldsymbol{\Omega}} = (\mathbf{X}'\mathbf{X})^{-1}\mathbf{X}'\mathbf{Y} \qquad \textbf{13.1.12}$$

Note that:

$$\mathbf{V} = \mathbf{Y}'\mathbf{Y} - \mathbf{Y}'\mathbf{X}(\mathbf{X}'\mathbf{X})^{-1}\mathbf{X}'\mathbf{Y} \qquad \textbf{13.1.13}$$

An exactly identified system can be solved row by row, and we can uniquely solve for the structural parameters from the reduced form estimates. If any equations are overidentified, there is no simple solution. Indeed this is the crux of the matter.

Consider the likelihood function expressing the joint conditional distribution of the Y's, given the X's in terms of the structural parameters:

---

[2] A review of the discussion of normal distribution in Chapter 1, pages 26 and 27, and Chapter 3, pages 76 through 78 will be helpful.

$$\Phi(Y_{11}\ldots Y_{T1};\ldots;Y_{1K}\ldots Y_{TK}|X_{11}\ldots X_{T1};\ldots;X_{1M}\ldots X_{TM})$$

$$= \frac{1}{(2\pi)^{TK/2}|\boldsymbol{\beta}^{-1}\boldsymbol{\Sigma}\boldsymbol{\beta}^{-1'}|^{T/2}} \qquad \textbf{13.1.14}$$

$$\exp\left\{-\frac{1}{2}\sum_{t=1}^{T}[\mathbf{Y}_t - \mathbf{X}_t(-\boldsymbol{\beta}^{-1}\boldsymbol{\Gamma})'](\boldsymbol{\beta}^{-1}\boldsymbol{\Sigma}\boldsymbol{\beta}^{-1'})^{-1}[\mathbf{Y}_t' - (-\boldsymbol{\beta}^{-1}\boldsymbol{\Gamma})\mathbf{X}_t']\right\}$$

$$= \frac{1}{(2\pi)^{KT/2}|\boldsymbol{\beta}^{-1}\boldsymbol{\Sigma}\boldsymbol{\beta}^{-1'}|^{T/2}}\exp\left[-\frac{1}{2}\sum_{t=1}^{T}(\mathbf{Y}_t + \mathbf{X}_t\boldsymbol{\Gamma}'\boldsymbol{\beta}^{-1'})\boldsymbol{\beta}'\boldsymbol{\Sigma}^{-1}\boldsymbol{\beta}(\mathbf{Y}_t' + \boldsymbol{\beta}^{-1}\boldsymbol{\Gamma}\mathbf{X}_t')\right]$$

The log likelihood function may now be written as:

$$\log_e\Phi = -\frac{KT}{2}\log_e 2\pi - \frac{T}{2}\log_e|\boldsymbol{\beta}^{-1}\boldsymbol{\Sigma}\boldsymbol{\beta}^{-1'}| \qquad \textbf{13.1.15}$$

$$-\frac{1}{2}\sum_{t=1}^{T}(\mathbf{Y}_t + \mathbf{X}_t\boldsymbol{\Gamma}'\boldsymbol{\beta}^{-1'})\boldsymbol{\beta}'\boldsymbol{\Sigma}^{-1}\boldsymbol{\beta}(\mathbf{Y}_t' + \boldsymbol{\beta}^{-1}\boldsymbol{\Gamma}\mathbf{X}_t')$$

We wish to maximize this function with respect to the unknown parameters $\boldsymbol{\beta}$, $\boldsymbol{\Gamma}$, and $\boldsymbol{\Sigma}$. Obviously, the partial derivatives of the quadratic expression in equation 13.1.15 will contain terms that are nonlinear in $\boldsymbol{\beta}$ and $\boldsymbol{\Gamma}$. For solving such nonlinear equations, the use of an iterative method becomes indispensable. Several such methods have been proposed, but they are not presented here.

A method described as the *linearized maximum likelihood* (LML) method has the same optimal large-sample properties as FIML, and its computation is much simpler.[3] However, this method is computationally more troublesome than the three-stage least squares (3SLS) method, which has the same asymptotic properties and has been more commonly used. The next section will discuss the 3SLS method.

The limited use of the FIML method is not so much due to involved mathematical manipulation, nor should the increased computational difficulties any longer be frightening. Indeed a computer program for computing the FIML estimator is currently available.[4] Instead the problem of appropriate specification of the model, especially of an economic model, is of greater concern. The econometrician does draw on the knowledge of economic theory in stipulating appropriate specification. There is often room for alternative specifications. If a single parameter is wrongly specified, the FIML estimators of all the parameters in the model will be subject to misspecification. One can hope that progress in research on economic

[3] T. J. Rothenberg and C. T. Leenders, "Efficient Estimation of Simultaneous Equation System," *Econometrica*, Vol. 32, No. 1 & 2 (January-April, 1964), pp. 57-76.

[4] Harry Eisenpress, "Note on the Computation of Full-Information Maximum likelihood Estimates of Coefficients of a Simultaneous System," *Econometrica*, Vol. 30, No. 2 (April, 1962), pp. 343-348. Also, Harry Eisenpress and R. J. Foote, "Systems of Simultaneous Equations on IBM 704 and 709," *Journal of Farm Economics*, Vol. 42, No. 5 (1960), pp. 1445-1449.

theory will lead to knowledge that indicates how to make the specification of econometric models unique. We do not yet have that knowledge.

The other serious constraint on the FIML method is that econometricians often have to work with small numbers of observations in which T may not be greater than $K + M$, the minimum number of parameters to be estimated.

13.2 THE THREE-STAGE LEAST SQUARES METHOD

The *three-stage least squares* method (3SLS) uses the two-stage least squares estimates of the moment matrix of the structural disturbances to estimate all coefficients ($\boldsymbol{\beta};\boldsymbol{\Gamma}$) of the complete system simultaneously.[5] Consider the model, ignoring the t subscript, consisting, as before, of K jointly determined and M predetermined variables:

$$\mathbf{Y}\boldsymbol{\beta} + \mathbf{X}\boldsymbol{\Gamma} + \mathbf{U} = \mathbf{0} \qquad \textbf{13.2.1}$$

where the kth equation can be written as it was previously:

$$\mathbf{Y}_k = \mathbf{Y}^*\boldsymbol{\beta}_k + \mathbf{X}^*\boldsymbol{\gamma}_k + \mathbf{U}_k \qquad \textbf{13.2.2}$$

As before, $\mathbf{Y}^*$ and $\mathbf{X}^*$ are matrices of observations on all jointly determined and predetermined variables, respectively, appearing as regressors in the kth equation. Writing:

$$\mathbf{Z}_k = (\mathbf{Y}^* \quad \mathbf{X}^*)_k$$

$$\boldsymbol{\alpha}_k = \begin{bmatrix} \boldsymbol{\beta} \\ \boldsymbol{\gamma} \end{bmatrix}_k$$

we can rewrite equation 13.2.2 as:

$$\mathbf{Y}_k = \mathbf{Z}_k\boldsymbol{\alpha}_k + \mathbf{U}_k \qquad k = 1, 2, \ldots, K \qquad \textbf{13.2.3}$$

Thus for the first equation we have:

$$\mathbf{Y}_1 = \mathbf{Z}_1\boldsymbol{\alpha}_1 + \mathbf{U}_1 \qquad \textbf{13.2.4}$$

---

[5] Arnold Zellner and Henri Theil, "Three-Stage Least Squares: Simultaneous Estimation of Simultaneous Equations," *Econometrica,* Vol. 30, No. 1 (January, 1962), pp. 54-78. Also, A. Zellner, "An Efficient Method of Estimating Seemingly Unrelated Regressions and Tests for Aggregation Bias," *Journal of the American Statistical Association,* Vol. 57, No. 298 (June, 1962), pp. 348-368. A. Zellner, "Estimates for Seemingly Unrelated Regression Equations: Some Exact Finite Sample Results," *Journal of the American Statistical Association,* Vol. 58, No. 304 (December, 1963), pp. 977-992. For an analytical discussion see J. D. Sargan, "Three-Stage Least Squares and Full Maximum Likelihood Estimates," *Econometrica,* Vol. 32, No. 1 & 2 (January-April, 1964), pp. 77-81. A Madansky, "On the Efficiency of Three-Stage Least Squares Estimation," *Econometrica,* Vol. 32, No. 1 & 2 (January-April, 1964), pp. 51-56.

Let us apply 2SLS to this equation in a somewhat different form. Premultiplying both sides of the equation by $\mathbf{X}'$, we have:

$$\mathbf{X}'\mathbf{Y}_1 = \mathbf{X}'\mathbf{Z}_1\boldsymbol{\alpha}_1 + \mathbf{X}'\mathbf{U}_1 \qquad \textbf{13.2.5}$$

where $\mathbf{X} = (X_1, \ldots, X_M)$, the set of all predetermined variables in the model.

Following expression 13.2.5, we next write the complete system.

$$\begin{bmatrix} \mathbf{X}'\mathbf{Y}_1 \\ \mathbf{X}'\mathbf{Y}_2 \\ \cdot \\ \cdot \\ \cdot \\ \mathbf{X}'\mathbf{Y}_K \end{bmatrix} = \begin{bmatrix} \mathbf{X}'\mathbf{Z}_1 & 0 & \ldots & 0 \\ 0 & \mathbf{X}'\mathbf{Z}_2 & \ldots & 0 \\ \cdot & \cdot & & \cdot \\ \cdot & \cdot & & \cdot \\ \cdot & \cdot & & \cdot \\ 0 & 0 & \ldots & \mathbf{X}'\mathbf{Z}_K \end{bmatrix} \begin{bmatrix} \boldsymbol{\alpha}_1 \\ \boldsymbol{\alpha}_2 \\ \cdot \\ \cdot \\ \cdot \\ \boldsymbol{\alpha}_K \end{bmatrix} + \begin{bmatrix} \mathbf{X}'\mathbf{U}_1 \\ \mathbf{X}'\mathbf{U}_2 \\ \cdot \\ \cdot \\ \cdot \\ \mathbf{X}'\mathbf{U}_K \end{bmatrix} \qquad \textbf{13.2.6}$$

The above is a system of $M \times K$ equations. We can apply the generalized least squares method to estimate all the parameters simultaneously if we have information on the variance-covariance matrix of the disturbance vector in system 13.2.6. The variance-covariance matrix of the disturbance vector $\mathbf{X}'\mathbf{U}_1$ can be written as:

$$\begin{aligned} \text{var}(\mathbf{X}'\mathbf{U}_1) &= E(\mathbf{X}'\mathbf{U}_1\mathbf{U}_1'\mathbf{X}) \\ &= \mathbf{X}'E(\mathbf{U}_1\mathbf{U}_1')\mathbf{X} \\ &= E(\mathbf{U}_1\mathbf{U}_1')\,(\mathbf{X}'\mathbf{X}) \\ &= \sigma_{11}\,(\mathbf{X}'\mathbf{X}) \end{aligned} \qquad \textbf{13.2.7}$$

since we assume: (1) predetermined variables are all "fixed" variables, and (2) $E(\mathbf{U}_1\mathbf{U}_1') = \sigma_{11}\mathbf{I}$. (Recall that the structural disturbance terms have zero mean, are serially independent, and are homoscedastic.) We then write:

$$\text{var}\begin{bmatrix} \mathbf{X}'\mathbf{U}_1 \\ \mathbf{X}'\mathbf{U}_2 \\ \cdot \\ \cdot \\ \cdot \\ \mathbf{X}'\mathbf{U}_K \end{bmatrix} = \begin{bmatrix} \sigma_{11}\mathbf{X}'\mathbf{X} & \sigma_{12}\mathbf{X}'\mathbf{X} & \ldots & \sigma_{1K}\mathbf{X}'\mathbf{X} \\ \sigma_{21}\mathbf{X}'\mathbf{X} & \sigma_{22}\mathbf{X}'\mathbf{X} & \ldots & \sigma_{2K}\mathbf{X}'\mathbf{X} \\ \cdot & \cdot & & \cdot \\ \cdot & \cdot & & \cdot \\ \cdot & \cdot & & \cdot \\ \sigma_{K1}\mathbf{X}'\mathbf{X} & \sigma_{K2}\mathbf{X}'\mathbf{X} & \ldots & \sigma_{KK}\mathbf{X}'\mathbf{X} \end{bmatrix} \qquad \textbf{13.2.8}$$

where σ_{ij} denotes the contemporaneous disturbance terms of the ith and j^{th} structural equations. Collecting σ_{ij} in a matrix $\boldsymbol{\Sigma}$, one can write formally var(**XU**) = **Σ** ⊗ (**X′X**), where the symbol ⊗ denotes Kronecker multiplication of matrices. We can write its inverse as:

$$\text{var}^{-1}\begin{bmatrix} \mathbf{X'U}_1 \\ \mathbf{X'U}_2 \\ \cdot \\ \cdot \\ \cdot \\ \mathbf{X'U}_K \end{bmatrix} = \begin{bmatrix} \sigma^{11}(\mathbf{X'X})^{-1} & \sigma^{12}(\mathbf{X'X})^{-1} \ldots & \sigma^{1K}(\mathbf{X'X})^{-1} \\ \sigma^{21}(\mathbf{X'X})^{-1} & \sigma^{22}(\mathbf{X'X})^{-1} \ldots & \sigma^{2K}(\mathbf{X'X})^{-1} \\ \cdot & \cdot & \cdot \\ \cdot & \cdot & \cdot \\ \cdot & \cdot & \cdot \\ \sigma^{K1}(\mathbf{X'X})^{-1} & \sigma^{K2}(\mathbf{X'X})^{-1} \ldots & \sigma^{KK}(\mathbf{X'X})^{-1} \end{bmatrix} = \mathbf{\Sigma}^{-1} \otimes (\mathbf{X'X})^{-1} \qquad \textbf{13.2.9}$$

Note that equations 13.2.8 and 13.2.9 contain σ's that are unknown. The 3SLS method replaces them by their 2SLS estimates, denoted by S^{ii}, where:

$$(s^{ij}) = (s_{ij})^{-1} \qquad \textbf{13.2.10}$$

We then obtain the complete set of estimators in all K equations in the model as follows:

$$\begin{bmatrix} \hat{\alpha}_1 \\ \cdot \\ \cdot \\ \cdot \\ \hat{\alpha}_K \end{bmatrix} = \begin{bmatrix} s^{11}\mathbf{Z}_1'\mathbf{X}(\mathbf{X'X})^{-1}\mathbf{X'Z}_1 & \ldots & s^{1K}\mathbf{Z}_1'\mathbf{X}(\mathbf{X'X})^{-1}\mathbf{X'Z}_K \\ \cdot & \cdot & \cdot \\ \cdot & \cdot & \cdot \\ \cdot & \cdot & \cdot \\ s^{K1}\mathbf{Z}_K'\mathbf{X}(\mathbf{X'X})^{-1}\mathbf{X'Z}_1 & \ldots & s^{KK}\mathbf{Z}_K'\mathbf{X}(\mathbf{X'X})^{-1}\mathbf{X'Z}_K \end{bmatrix}^{-1} \begin{bmatrix} s^{11}\mathbf{Z}_1'\mathbf{X}(\mathbf{X'X})^{-1}\mathbf{X'Y}_1 & + \ldots + & s^{1K}\mathbf{Z}_1'\mathbf{X}(\mathbf{X'X})^{-1}\mathbf{X'Y}_K \\ \cdot & \cdot & \cdot \\ \cdot & \cdot & \cdot \\ \cdot & \cdot & \cdot \\ s^{K1}\mathbf{Z}_K'\mathbf{X}(\mathbf{X'X})^{-1}\mathbf{X'Y}_1 & + \ldots + & s^{KK}\mathbf{Z}_K'\mathbf{X}(\mathbf{X'X})^{-1}\mathbf{X'Y}_K \end{bmatrix} \qquad \textbf{13.2.11}$$

Denoting the column vector on $\boldsymbol{\alpha}_k$ by $\boldsymbol{\alpha}$, we obtain:

$$\text{var}(\hat{\alpha}) = \begin{bmatrix} s^{11}\mathbf{Z}_1'\mathbf{X}(\mathbf{X'X})^{-1}\mathbf{X'Z}_1 \ldots s^{1K}\mathbf{Z}_1'\mathbf{X}(\mathbf{X'X})^{-1}\mathbf{X'Z}_K \\ \cdot \quad \cdot \quad \cdot \\ \cdot \quad \cdot \quad \cdot \\ \cdot \quad \cdot \quad \cdot \\ s^{K1}\mathbf{Z}_K'\mathbf{X}(\mathbf{X'X})^{-1}\mathbf{X'Z}_1 \ldots s^{KK}\mathbf{Z}_K'\mathbf{X}(\mathbf{X'X})^{-1}\mathbf{X'Z}_K \end{bmatrix}^{-1} \qquad \textbf{13.2.12}$$

All the expressions on the right-hand side of equations 13.2.11 and 13.2.12 can be obtained by appropriate calculations with the observed data and the residuals estimated by the 2SLS method at a prior stage.

For computational purposes, we need two groups of numerical results:

1. $\mathbf{Z}_1'\mathbf{X}(\mathbf{X}'\mathbf{X})^{-1}\mathbf{X}'\mathbf{Z}_1$, $\mathbf{Z}_1'\mathbf{X}(\mathbf{X}'\mathbf{X})^{-1}\mathbf{X}'\mathbf{Y}_1$, and so forth.
2. Elements s^{ii} of the inverse of the variance-covariance matrix of structural disturbances estimated by 2SLS.

Compared with 2SLS estimates of structural parameters, the 3SLS estimates are more efficient.

As stated earlier, the prime advantage claimed for the 3SLS method compared with the FIML method is that consistent, asymptotically normally distributed, and asymptotically efficient estimates of all the unknown parameters in the complete system are obtained simultaneously without any iteration. This makes the 3SLS method computationally more attractive.

If some equations are just identified and others overidentified, it is computationally efficient to estimate the two blocks of equations separately. We can apply 3SLS to the block of overidentified equations and obtain estimators just as efficient as when 3SLS is applied to both blocks simultaneously. If there are identities in the system, they are omitted from equation 13.2.11.

However, as argued before, the problem of incorrect specification and the consequent hazards involved in any system method of estimation limit the advantages of such methods. Even if the computational scheme has been simplified, the usefulness of the 3SLS method depends on the correct specification of the complete system, which is a separate and even more difficult problem.

DISCUSSION QUESTIONS

1. What is the logical basis for the full information maximum likelihood and the three-stage least squares methods of estimation?
2. (a) Obtain the 3SLS estimates in question 1, Chapter 12.
   (b) Calculate the variance of these estimates.
   (c) Compare the 3SLS estimates with those of the 2SLS and LISE/LVR estimates.
3. The simultaneous estimation of a simultaneous system in econometrics has met with limited success. Why?

SUGGESTED READINGS

Brown, T. M. "Simplified Full Maximum Likelihood and Comparative Structural Estimates." *Econometrica,* Vol. 27, No. 4 (October, 1959), pp. 638-653.

Chernoff, Herman, and Nathan Divinsky. "The Computation of Maximum Likelihood Estimates of Linear Structural Equations." *Studies in Econometric Method,* edited by W. C. Hood and T. C. Koopmans. New York: John Wiley & Sons, 1953, pp. 236-269.

Christ, Carl F. *Econometric Models and Methods.* New York: John Wiley & Sons, 1966.

Eisenpress, Harry. "Note on the Computation of Full-Information Maximum Likelihood Estimates of Coefficients of a Simultaneous System." *Econometrica*, Vol. 30, No. 2 (April, 1962), pp. 343-348.

Eisenpress, Harry, and R. J. Foote. "Systems and Simultaneous Equations on IBM 704 and 709." *Journal of Farm Economics*, Vol. 42, No. 5 (1960), pp. 1445-1449.

Fisk, P. R. *Stochastically Dependent Equations*. London: Charles Griffin & Co., 1967.

Klein, Lawrence R. *A Textbook of Econometrics*. Evanston, Illinois: Row, Peterson & Co., 1956.

Koopmans, Tjalling C. "Statistical Estimation of Simultaneous Economic Relations." *Journal of the American Statistical Association*, Vol. 40, No. 232, Part 1 (December, 1945), pp. 448-466.

Koopmans, Tjalling C., R. B. Leipnik, and H. Rubin. "Measuring the Equation Systems of Dynamic Economics." *Statistical Inference in Dynamic Economic Models*, edited by T. C. Koopmans. New York: John Wiley & Sons, 1950, pp. 53-237.

Madansky, Albert. "On the Efficiency of Three-Stage Least Squares Estimation." *Econometrica*, Vol. 32, No. 1 & 2 (January-April, 1964), pp. 51-56.

Rothenberg, T. J., and C. T. Leenders. "Efficient Estimation of Simultaneous Equation System." *Econometrica*, Vol. 32, No. 1 & 2 (January-April, 1964), pp. 57-76.

Sargan, J. D. "Three-Stage Least Squares and Full Maximum Likelihood Estimates." *Econometrica*, Vol. 32, No. 1 & 2 (January-April, 1964), pp. 77-81.

Zellner, Arnold. "An Efficient Method of Estimating Seemingly Unrelated Regressions and Tests for Aggregation Bias." *Journal of the American Statistical Association*, Vol. 57, No. 298 (June, 1962), pp. 348-368.

———. "Estimates for Seemingly Unrelated Regression Equations: Some Exact Finite Sample Results." *Journal of the American Statistical Association*, Vol. 58, No. 304 (December, 1963), pp. 977-992.

Zellner, Arnold, and Henri Theil. "Three-Stage Least Squares: Simultaneous Estimation of Simultaneous Equations." *Econometrica*, Vol. 30, No. 1 (January, 1962), pp. 54-78.

14

choice of methods and use of models

14.0 ANY VERDICT YET?

Parameters of an econometric model described by a set of simultaneous equations can be estimated by various alternative methods, as already discussed. The following question is now pertinent: Which of these methods is judged to be most accurate? Note that most econometric models are based on small samples, and thus asymptotic properties belonging to large samples are of little relevance. There has been rather limited theoretical work on the small-sample properties of asymptotically consistent efficient estimators, and proofs of the superiority of one method over another are missing.[1] The following material discusses two different ways researchers have attempted to evaluate the relative merits of various methods: (1) Monte Carlo experiments and (2) tests of predictive power of alternative estimators.

Not only is the choice of an appropriate estimation method an important issue, but it is no less important to determine the appropriate use of an estimated model. Suppose that policymakers can alter values of the X variables that are predetermined in the given model. Can the model demonstrate the alternatives, if one or another of such variables are controlled, so that the policymaker can examine the implications of the options available? Can the model predict the values of the jointly determined endogenous variables? Later sections in this chapter discuss two important uses of an econometric model: (1) simulation and (2) prediction.

---

[1] Interested readers may consult: A. L. Nagar, "The Bias and Moment Matrix of the General k-Class Estimators of the Parameters in Simultaneous Equations," *Econometrica,* Vol. 27, No. 4 (October, 1959), pp. 575-594; A. L. Nagar, "Double k-Class Estimators of Parameters in Simultaneous Equations and Their Small Sample Properties," *International Economic Review,* Vol. 3, No. 2 (May, 1962), pp. 168-188; R. L. Basmann, "On Finite Sample Distributions of Generalized Classical Linear Identifiability Test Statistics," *Journal of the American Statistical Association,* Vol. 55, No. 292 (December, 1960), pp. 650-659; R. L. Basmann, "A Note on the Exact Finite Sample Frequency Functions of Generalized Classical Linear Estimators in Two Leading Overidentified Cases," *Journal of the American Statistical Association,* Vol. 56, No. 295 (September, 1961), pp. 619-636; A. Maeshiro, "A Simple Mathematical Relationship Among k-Class Estimators," *Journal of the American Statistical Association,* Vol. 61, No. 314 (June, 1966), pp. 368-374; and W. Y. Oi, "On the Relationship Among Different Members of the k-Class," *International Economic Review,* Vol. 10 (1969), pp. 36-46.

14.1 MONTE CARLO EXPERIMENTS

If we knew in advance not only the values of the observations on the variables of an econometric model but also the values of the structural parameters and the distributions of the error terms, we could easily compare the estimates obtained by using different methods to learn which method is the best performer. Monte Carlo experiments are a technique for carrying out these comparisons using preassigned values for the predetermined variables and the parameters, using random numbers for the disturbances, and calculating the values of the jointly determined variables.[2] When different estimating methods are applied to the constructed "observations," the resulting estimated parameter values can be compared with the preassigned "true" parameter values.

The design of a Monte Carlo experiment can be described as follows:

1. Describe a model and check the conditions of identifiability. The simultaneous equation model is expressible as:

$$\boldsymbol{\beta}\mathbf{Y} + \boldsymbol{\Gamma}\mathbf{X} + \mathbf{U} = \mathbf{0}$$

   No equation of the system is underidentified.
2. Assign specific values to the elements (structural coefficients) in matrices $\boldsymbol{\beta}$ and $\boldsymbol{\Gamma}$.
3. Specify the probability distribution of the disturbance terms in matrix $\mathbf{U}$. Independent normal distribution is a convenient assumption. Appropriate tables of random numbers can be used for the individual disturbance terms.
4. Specify the values of the predetermined variables. They remain fixed in successive experiments, as is generally assumed in econometric models. A small sample size, say 20 or 30, is useful, since most often it is the hard luck of the econometrician to base his investigations on such small samples.

All these steps imply that the researcher has complete foreknowledge of the structural equations, excepting the value of observations on the jointly determined endogenous variables; that is, matrix $\mathbf{Y}$ is the only unknown. Recall that the econometrician starts with the belief that the values of the jointly determined endogenous variables are generated by the structure he specifies. Once the rest of the model has been assumed to be "known" by design, it is possible to reverse the process to see what values of the endogenous variables are generated.

5. Generate Y values from assumptions 1 through 4 by calculating the systematic component of each Y value from the values of the predetermined variables and the structural parameters and adding the random disturbance.

---

[2] C. F. Christ, *Econometric Models and Methods* (New York: John Wiley & Sons, 1966), pp. 474-481. J. Johnston, *Econometric Methods* (2d ed.; New York: McGraw-Hill Book Co., 1972), pp. 408-420. For a tabular survey see V. Kerry Smith, "A Comparative Tabular Survey of Monte Carlo and Exact Sampling Studies," *Australian Economic Papers*, Vol. 10 (December, 1971), pp. 196-202.

6. Apply the different methods of estimation using the assigned values of the predetermined variables and the generated Y values.
7. Repeat steps 5 and 6. Tabulate the empirical frequency distributions of the estimators, and compare these with the parameters specified in step 2 for the population.

Comparing the parameter values obtained with different estimators yields information on the merits of the estimators in terms of some measure of closeness to the true parameter values.

Examples of Monte Carlo Experiments

Robert Summers carried out Monte Carlo experiments with the following model:[3]

$$\begin{aligned} Y_1 + \beta_{12}Y_2 + \gamma_{11}X_1 + \gamma_{12}X_2 + \gamma_{10} + U_1 &= 0 \\ Y_1 + \beta_{22}Y_2 + \gamma_{23}X_3 + \gamma_{24}X_4 + \gamma_{20} + U_2 &= 0 \end{aligned} \qquad \textbf{14.1.1}$$

A specific parameter combination Summers used to generate samples on the Y's is as follows:

$$\begin{array}{llll} \beta_{12} = -0.7, & \gamma_{11} = 0.8, & \gamma_{12} = 0.7, & \gamma_{10} = -149.5 \\ \beta_{22} = 0.4, & \gamma_{23} = 0.6, & \gamma_{24} = -0.4, & \gamma_{20} = -149.6 \\ \sigma_{11} = 400, & \sigma_{12} = 200, & \sigma_{22} = 400, & \end{array} \qquad \textbf{14.1.2}$$

He then used four different methods—OLS, 2SLS, LISE, and FIML—to estimate the parameters in each sequence of his experiment. He repeated the experiment 50 times, and thus for each parameter he obtained 50 values. In each sample in the experiment, he had 20 observations. He also used another sample of size 40. He specified six different sets of values for the elements in $\boldsymbol{\beta}$ and $\boldsymbol{\Gamma}$ and made alternative specifications regarding the predetermined variables.

Richard Quandt also used Monte Carlo experiments to compare estimation methods.[4] Quandt's model 1, consisting of four Y's and six X's, is specified as:

$$\begin{aligned} Y_1 - 0.2Y_2 + 2.0Y_3 - Y_4 - X_1 - 0.5X_2 + X_3 &= U_1 \\ -Y_1 + Y_2 + 0.5Y_3 + 0.1Y_4 - 2.0X_2 - X_5 &= U_2 \\ 1.5Y_1 - 0.5Y_2 + Y_3 + 0.2Y_4 + 0.5X_3 + X_4 - 2.0X_5 &= U_3 \\ 0.4Y_1 + Y_2 - 0.5Y_3 + Y_4 - X_3 - 0.2X_5 - 3.0X_6 &= U_4 \end{aligned} \qquad \textbf{14.1.3}$$

---

[3] Robert Summers, "A Capital Intensive Approach to the Small Sample Properties of Various Simultaneous Equation Estimators," *Econometrica*, Vol. 33, No. 1 (January, 1965), pp. 1-41.

[4] Richard E. Quandt, "On Certain Small Sample Properties of k-Class Estimators," *International Economic Review*, Vol. 6, No. 1 (January, 1965), pp. 92-104.

The mechanics of Quandt's experiments can be described as follows:

1. Twenty values of the vectors of disturbance terms $\mathbf{U}_1$, $\mathbf{U}_2$, $\mathbf{U}_3$, $\mathbf{U}_4$ are generated using random numbers, where the elements of the vectors are jointly normally distributed with zero mean and covariance matrix:

$$\begin{bmatrix} 1.0 & 0.6 & 0.8 & -1.0 \\ 0.6 & 1.0 & 0 & -0.2 \\ 0.8 & 0 & 2.0 & -0.6 \\ -1.0 & -0.2 & -0.6 & 2.5 \end{bmatrix} \qquad \mathbf{14.1.4}$$

2. The 20 values of each of the six predetermined **X** vectors are assigned.
3. The values of the endogenous variables are calculated from:

$$\mathbf{Y} = -\boldsymbol{\beta}^{-1}\boldsymbol{\Gamma}\mathbf{X} - \boldsymbol{\beta}^{-1}\mathbf{U} \qquad \mathbf{14.1.5}$$

where, as we know from equations 14.1.3,

$$\boldsymbol{\beta} = \begin{bmatrix} 1.0 & -0.2 & 2.0 & -1.0 \\ -1.0 & 1.0 & 0.5 & 0.1 \\ 1.5 & -0.5 & 1.0 & 0.2 \\ 0.4 & 1.0 & -0.5 & 1.0 \end{bmatrix}$$

$$\boldsymbol{\Gamma} = \begin{bmatrix} -1 & -0.5 & 1.0 & 0 & 0 & 0 \\ 0 & -2.0 & 0 & 0 & -1.0 & 0 \\ 0 & 0 & 0.5 & 1.0 & -2.0 & 0 \\ 0 & 0 & -1.0 & 0 & -0.2 & -3.0 \end{bmatrix} \qquad \mathbf{14.1.6}$$

4. In a given run, 100 samples of 20 observations each are generated.
5. Once the data on the **Y** vectors are generated, estimates of $\boldsymbol{\beta}$ and $\boldsymbol{\Gamma}$ are obtained by applying various methods.

Quandt made two alternative specifications of the model and various alternative specifications of the $\boldsymbol{\beta}$ and Σ matrices.

Some Criteria of Evaluation

The different criteria used to compare the relative performances of alternative estimators in a Monte Carlo study need examination. Three important criteria used are the bias, the standard deviation, and the root mean square error of the structural coefficients (review Chapter 3).

To recapitulate,

$$\text{Bias} = E(\hat{\theta}) - \theta$$

$$\text{Variance } (\hat{\theta}) = E\{[\hat{\theta} - E(\theta)]^2\} \qquad \textbf{14.1.7}$$

and

$$\text{MSE} = \frac{\sum_i^N (\hat{\theta}_i - \theta)^2}{N} \qquad \text{RMSE} = \sqrt{\text{MSE}}$$

where θ denotes the true parameter and $\hat{\theta}$ its estimated value. The nearer $\hat{\theta}$ lies to the true value of the parameter, the better is the estimated value. The MSE of the estimates is the average of the sum of the squared deviations of the estimated values from the true value of the parameter concerned. Thus the smaller the RMSE of an estimate, the better the estimate.

Quandt has applied eight measures to evaluate the relative performance of each estimator: (1) The arithmetic mean of the estimates over a run. If the finite sample distribution of an estimator possesses a finite first moment, the comparison of the arithmetic mean with the true value of a parameter provides an estimate of bias. (2) The sample standard deviation, providing an estimate of dispersion about the sample mean. (3) The sample median, calculated as a substitute for the mean. (4) The concentration coefficient C, defined as the relative frequency of estimates falling within 20 percent of the true value of the parameter. (5) A first measure of decentralization D_1, defined as the relative frequency of estimates that have the wrong sign. (6) A second measure of decentralization D_2, defined as the largest deviation of an estimate from the true value. (7) The RMSE, providing an estimate of dispersion about the true value. (8) The mean error of forecast from the equation to be estimated, evaluated at: (a) the mean value of the predetermined variables and (b) a point given by the mean value plus one standard deviation of the predetermined variables.

Given the Σ in matrix 14.1.4, the test results are summarized as follows:

	1	2	3	4	5	6	7	8(a)	8(b)
OLS		√							√
2SLS	√		√	√	√	√	√	√	

A check means that the one estimator is better than the other, using the particular criteria (1, 2, etc.).

However, with the change of specification of Σ, the results do change substantially for OLS.

Summers' one main recommendation, on the basis of root mean square error, seems to suggest the relative inferiority of the OLS method; whereas results as to the relative merit of the LISE, 2SLS, and FIML methods appear to be inconclusive. However, he also seems to suggest that the steadiest method appears to be 2SLS, the one least bothered by misspecification and multicollinearity. Quandt reports that the 2SLS estimates are not unambiguously better than the OLS estimators in small sample situations. He finds that the estimators are relatively poor when there is high multicollinearity among predetermined variables, with 2SLS being relatively more affected. However, OLS is almost always poorer than 2SLS for the less collinear situations. Cragg reports that of the several methods he studies, the full information methods (FIML, 3SLS) rank superior in an interdependent system estimation, and the OLS method ranks lowest; while the other limited information methods (2SLS, LISE, etc.) get intermediate ranking.[5] He also warns that the relative performance of alternative estimators is by no means pronounced. Smith reports that if the $\boldsymbol{\beta}$ matrix of a model is relatively sparse and not quite triangular, the OLS performs better.[6] Indeed the question of what estimator to use in a small-sample situation is far from settled.

It is no longer proper to suggest that computational consideration alone can decide for one method or another, since the hardware of computation technology has made phenomenal progress. In fact OLS has lost some of its former advantage on that score.

14.2 PREDICTION AND SIMULATION EXPERIMENTS

Another line of investigation compares the predictive ability of the estimators obtained by applying various methods to the same model. One can generate forecasts by using the different estimates and testing how closely the predicted values of various methods coincide with actual values of the jointly determined variables. One problem of such an exercise is its inadequate theoretical foundation. If the model specification remains the same, a change in the observations used may be responsible for different results from the application of different methods. The ranking of methods obtained with a model using one set of data may not be the same as the anking obtained using the same model with different data. In other words the ranking of various estimators obtained by testing the same model (same specification) with the Japanese and Australian data may be different just because the two sets of data are different. Nevertheless, such experiments do indicate relative performance of alternative methods, at least in a particular situation. In the absence of fully developed methods for dealing with the problem, such experiments are quite suggestive.

Consideration of Some Results

Fisk's model of the Australian economy has been estimated by various methods of estimation discussed in this volume:[7]

---

[5] J. G. Cragg, "On the Relative Small-Sample Properties of Several Structural Equation Estimators," *Econometrica*, Vol. 35, No. 1 (January, 1967), pp. 89-110.

[6] V. Kerry Smith, "An Economic Evaluation of Several Econometric Estimators for Simultaneous Equation Systems" (Doctoral dissertation, Rutgers University, 1970).

[7] P. R. Fisk, *Stochastically Dependent Equations*. (London: Charles Griffin & Co., 1967).

$$Y_1 + \beta_{12}Y_2 + \gamma_{11}X_1 + \gamma_{14} + U_1 = 0$$
$$Y_1 + \beta_{22}Y_2 + \gamma_{22}X_2 + \gamma_{23}X_3 + \gamma_{24} + U_2 = 0 \qquad 14.2.1$$

The various estimators obtained are presented in Table 14-1. Note that there is a close correspondence between the 2SLS and 3SLS estimates and also between the LISE and FIML estimates, whereas the LML estimates lie between these sets of estimated values. Generally, the OLS estimates are quite different from the others.

TABLE 14-1

	$\hat{\beta}_{12}$	$\hat{\gamma}_{11}$	$\hat{\beta}_{22}$	$\hat{\gamma}_{22}$	$\hat{\gamma}_{23}$
OLS	−0.2685	−0.8896	−0.6053	−0.1307	0.4386
2SLS	0.1662	−1.7176	−0.6409	−0.0948	0.4703
LISE	0.3334	−2.0360	−0.6408	−0.0948	0.4703
3SLS	0.1662	−1.7176	−0.6379	−0.0978	0.4682
LML	0.2733	−1.9215	−0.6457	−0.0898	0.4743
FIML	0.3332	−2.0356	−0.6355	−0.1002	0.4649

Note: LML is the linearized maximum likelihood method.
Source: P. R. Fisk, *Stochastically Dependent Equations* (London: Charles Griffin & Co., 1967), p. 143.

Tatemoto *et al.* have reported their experience with the model of the Japanese economy with many more than two equations.[8] Estimators of parameters in individual equations are in general reported to be relatively stable with respect to the different methods of estimation they used (OLS, 2SLS, LISE). But this is not true of many other models of national economies. We do not know how much of this stability with respect to different estimators is due to chance and how much of it is due to methods of estimation.

Consider the micro model tested by L'Esperance.[9] The model refers to the watermelon market in America and is specified as follows:

$$\begin{bmatrix} 1.0 & \beta_{12} \\ \beta_{21} & 1.0 \end{bmatrix} \begin{bmatrix} Y_1 \\ Y_2 \end{bmatrix} + \begin{bmatrix} \gamma_{11} & \gamma_{12} & 0 & 0 & 0 \\ 0 & 0 & \gamma_{23} & \gamma_{24} & \gamma_{25} \end{bmatrix} \cdot \begin{bmatrix} X_1 \\ X_2 \\ X_3 \\ X_4 \\ X_5 \end{bmatrix} = \begin{bmatrix} U_1 \\ U_2 \end{bmatrix} \qquad 14.2.2$$

[8] Masahiro Tatemoto *et al.*, "A Stabilization Model of the Postwar Japanese Economy 1954-1962," *International Economic Review*, Vol. 8, No. 1 (January, 1967), pp. 13-44.

[9] W. L. L'Esperance, "Further Evidence on the Predictive Power of Various Estimators," *International Economic Review*, Vol. 8, No. 1 (January, 1967), pp. 45-66.

L'Esperance tested Wold's FP estimators as well as the OLS, LISE, and 2SLS estimators by calculating Y values corresponding to the different sets of estimated β's and Γ's and comparing these calculated values with actual Y values.

Table 14-2 presents results based on the root mean square error of forecast for five-year forecasts reported in this experiment. The root mean square error of forecast is defined as follows:

$$(\text{RMSE})_f = \sqrt{\frac{\sum_{i}^{N} (Y_p - Y_a)_i^2}{N}} \qquad \textbf{14.2.3}$$

where $(\text{RMSE})_f$ = root mean square error of forecast
Y_p = predicted value of the jointly determined endogenous variable
Y_a = actual value of the jointly determined endogenous variable
N = number of years in the forecast period

TABLE 14-2

Root Mean Square Error of Forecast

Y_1

F Forecast Period	LISE	2SLS	OLS	FP
1938-1942	0.058	0.054	0.014	0.029
1941-1945	0.086	0.023	0.020	0.094
1948-1952	0.044	0.050	0.039	0.109
1952-1956	0.016	0.017	0.016	0.087
Y_2				
1938-1942	0.154	0.077	0.025	0.043
1941-1945	0.117	0.087	0.113	0.301
1948-1952	0.076	0.083	0.077	0.079
1952-1956	0.051	0.051	0.054	0.140

Source: W. L. L'Esperance, "Further Evidence on the Predictive Power of Various Estimators," *International Economic Review*, Vol. 8, No. 1 (January, 1967), p. 51.

The most significant finding of this study is that when there is a drastic and sustained cyclical change in the jointly determined endogenous Y variables, the use of the estimates derived from simultaneous equation methods is more successful than the use of those derived from OLS estimates in predicting such cyclical changes. The other results reported in general are unfavorable for the FP estimators and are more or less neutral with respect to OLS, LISE, and 2SLS.

Recently, Dutta and Sharma reported further results regarding predictive ability to alternative estimators.[10] They used an econometric model of Puerto Rico, which consists of twenty-three stochastic equations.[11] This model is undersized in the sense that the number of predetermined variables appearing in the model far exceed the number of observations. The findings indicate that the IIV and two-stage principal component method of estimation (a method not discussed in this volume) rank superior to 3SLS, 2SLS, and OLS; while LISE which ranks fairly high comes out with too many wrong signs of parameter estimates. Generally, both OLS and 3SLS are found to do poorly in predictive ability tests.

A Synthetic Approach

The findings of researchers using either of the two alternative approaches need to be brought together. Both Monte Carlo experiments and predictive ability tests are designed to evaluate alternative estimators. If both approaches provide a conformable evaluation of the techniques, then the results of their respective rankings for the estimators should be in agreement. Recently some efforts to reconcile the results of the two alternative methods of research have been reported.[12] Based on the Christ model of the United States economy consisting of four stochastic equations and three identities, the study evaluates OLS, 2SLS, LISE, 3SLS, and IIV.[13] Specification of the coefficient matrices and the disturbance structure for the above model by preassigned values enables the sampling experiments to be performed. In particular twenty-seven observations are generated for each jointly determined variable. The first twenty of these observations are used in obtaining coefficients for the various equations analyzed, while the last seven observations are used for the prediction tests.

It should be noted that these last seven observations come from the same sample space as the first twenty, eliminating the possibility of effects due to structural changes. In other predictive ability tests of alternative estimators, this is not the case. Such tests compare observed values on the jointly determined variables outside the sample period with those predicted by the model estimates. The present design of research appears to

[10] M. Dutta and P. L. Sharma, "Alternative Estimators and Predictive Power of Alternative Estimators: An Econometric Model of Puerto Rico," *Review of Economics and Statistics*, Vol. 55, No. 3 (August, 1973), pp. 381-385. Using several macroeconomic models of the United States, further results have been reported by Sharma. See P. L. Sharma, "Econometric Forecasting with Special Reference to Forecasting Sensitivity of Various Estimators in Aggregate Econometric Models" (Doctoral dissertation, Rutgers University, 1972).

[11] M. Dutta and V. Su, "An Econometric Model of Puerto Rico," *Review of Economic Studies*, Vol. 36, No. 3 (July, 1969), pp. 319-333.

[12] M. Dutta, V. Kerry Smith, and P. D. Loeb, "An Evaluation of Alternative Estimators in the Context of a Simultaneous System with Structural and Predictive Criteria: A Monte Carlo Study" (A paper presented at the European Econometrics Society Meetings, Budapest, Hungary, September, 1972).

[13] C. F. Christ, *Econometric Models and Methods* (New York: John Wiley & Sons, 1966).

be superior to others in this respect. This research design allows the authors to obtain forecasts from each generated sample at each of the seven time periods beyond those used in the estimation of coefficients. Fifty samples, each with twenty-seven observations, have been generated, given:

$$\boldsymbol{\beta} = \begin{bmatrix} -1 & 0 & 0 & 0 & .686 & 0 & 0 \\ 0 & -1 & 0 & 0 & 0 & .490 & 0 \\ 0 & 0 & -1 & 0 & 0 & 0 & .488 \\ 0 & 0 & 0 & -1 & 0 & .189 & 0 \\ 1 & 0 & 0 & -1 & 0 & -1 & 0 \\ 0 & 0 & 1 & 0 & 1 & -1 & 0 \\ 0 & -1 & 1 & 0 & 1 & 0 & -1 \end{bmatrix}$$

$$\boldsymbol{\Gamma} = \begin{bmatrix} 5.679 & 0 & 0 & 0 & 0 & 0 & 0 & 0 & 0 & .246 & 0 & 0 & 0 & 0 \\ 3.489 & 0 & 0 & 0 & 0 & 0 & 0 & 0 & 0 & 0 & .224 & 0 & 0 & 0 \\ -4.886 & 0 & 0 & 0 & 0 & 0 & 0 & 0 & 0 & 0 & 0 & .427 & 0 & -.257 \\ -21.160 & 0 & 0 & 0 & 0 & 0 & .518 & -.352 & -.125 & 0 & 0 & 0 & .296 & 0 \\ 0 & 1.0 & -1.0 & 0 & 0 & 0 & 0 & 0 & 0 & 0 & 0 & 0 & 0 & 0 \\ 0 & 0 & -1.0 & 1.0 & 1.0 & 1.0 & 0 & 0 & 0 & 0 & 0 & 0 & 0 & 0 \\ 0 & 0 & -1.0 & 1.0 & 0 & 0 & 0 & 0 & 0 & 0 & 0 & 0 & 0 & 0 \end{bmatrix} \tag{14.2.4}$$

$$\mathbf{Y} = \begin{bmatrix} Y_{t1} \\ Y_{t2} \\ Y_{t3} \\ Y_{t4} \\ Y_{t5} \\ Y_{t6} \\ Y_{t7} \end{bmatrix} \text{ and } \mathbf{X} = \begin{bmatrix} X_{t1} \\ X_{t2} \\ X_{t3} \\ X_{t4} \\ X_{t5} \\ X_{t6} \\ X_{t7} \\ X_{t8} \\ X_{t9} \\ X_{t10} \\ X_{t11} \\ X_{t12} \\ X_{t13} \\ X_{t14} \end{bmatrix} \qquad t = 1, 2, \ldots T$$

The errors $\mathbf{U}_t$ are drawn from a multivariate normal distribution with zero mean and covariance matrix $\boldsymbol{\Sigma}$.

$$\Sigma = \begin{bmatrix} 6.392 & 1.460 & 1.752 & -2.455 \\ 1.460 & 3.342 & .452 & -2.163 \\ 1.752 & .452 & 2.163 & -1.687 \\ -2.455 & -2.163 & -1.687 & 13.017 \end{bmatrix} \tag{14.2.5}$$

The results with the Christ model indicate that there is appreciable consistency between the estimator rankings provided by the two approaches, Monte Carlo and predictive ability tests. It appears that the 3SLS performs best with the IIV a close second. As for the other estimators, the pattern is not very clear-cut; but it does appear from the structural evaluation that 2SLS and LISE rank marginally higher than OLS.

In recent times the OLS method for a multiequation model has increasingly been considered to be inadequate. The 3SLS and 2SLS methods have found favor with many researchers. The FIML method, particularly under linearized restrictions, can now be applied without great difficulty. Of course the problem of correct and complete specification in a systems method (3SLS and FIML) continues to be bothersome. This is one reason the 2SLS method is very widely used. The FP method is still too new to have provided enough experience for an informed judgment on its merits, and the same is true of the iterative instrumental variable (IIV) method.

14.3 SIMULATION

Simulation is a powerful technique in many kinds of investigations. Simulations of a moon landing, a water-resources system, the reaction to the attack of an antibody, an industrial production process, a traffic jam in a city, a war game, or a happening in the real world in controlled situations are quite well known. In each case the process of simulation uses a particular mathematical model, appropriately designed and fed with as much information as possible, to reproduce the actual response of the modeled system to a set of circumstances. A model is essentially an abstraction and departs from reality in a great number of details. However, an appropriately constructed model may provide the mechanism to reproduce a close simulation of reality.

Suppose that an econometric model of the United States has been constructed with as much care as possible. The model can be put on the computer, and exogenous shocks can be fed in to simulate the actual situations of the United States economy. Why the model itself may not succeed in faithfully generating the time path of the real-world economic dynamism will be discussed presently.

Simulation can also be a useful guide for alternative policy measures to be adopted. A cut in the defense expenditure, a change in the tax rate, and a tightening of the monetary policy are issues of national debate in any country. With an econometric model, policies can be given a trial in the laboratory, so to speak. The econometrician can simulate economic consequences of a policy change by a set of values for the variables and the parameters of the model, and these results can be fruitfully utilized in arriving at the policy decision.

Three major constraints of econometric models, as they are currently constructed, are (1) linearity, (2) assumed knowledge of predetermined variables, and (3) treatment of the disturbance terms. Relationships describing an econometric model are mostly linear or linear approximations of nonlinear relationships. With such built-in linear functions, the time paths of a variable generated in the model can hardly be expected to show the peaks and troughs of actual observations. In the real world smooth uneventful motion of an economic variable is rare, and thus a linear model is likely to show substantial deviation from reality. It is possible to sacrifice simplicity and work with nonlinear relationships themselves. In contrast, a linear model needs to be "shocked" by adding randomly generated disturbances to simulate a realistic time path of the jointly determined endogenous variables.

The second constraint is due to lack of adequate knowledge of the predetermined variables. In most cases some smooth projections of these variables are made over long periods of time by assuming that the values of the variables are constant or changing at a constant rate. These projections of predetermined variables are used to generate the time path of the endogenous variables. In fact in a real situation, the actual observations on the predetermined variables jump rather erratically, deviating substantially from any smooth curve that can be described mathematically. One way to correct for the inability to give an exact mathematical description of the predetermined variable is to restrict the projection of the model to the immediate future when the values of the predetermined variables are known fairly accurately. This rules out any effective simulation providing a meaningful profile or longer time paths of the endogenous variables. Hence the choice is to introduce external shocks to the model so that the erratic pattern of the time sequence of the predetermined variables can be captured.

The third constraint is very significant. Each of the behavior equations in a model has a stochastic disturbance term U_i. Chapter 2 dwelt at length on their nature and statistical properties. However, in practice when one ventures to construct the model of a real economy, some amount of arbitrariness is unavoidable. Recall that theoretically the U term is purely random. To the extent arbitrary considerations fail to satisfy the randomness criteria of the U term, the "dice are loaded." Even if the relationships in a model are based on sound a priori theory of economics and no serious charges of arbitrariness can be maintained, the fact remains that the parameters of an econometric model are estimated from one "given" sample, and sampling errors may be acute. It is indeed a matter of faith that the given sample is truly generated by the structure that the model seeks to describe. Other important sources of error can be attributed to aggregation, index numbers, and sundry data problems involved in constructing a model.

The technique of generating these external shocks is somewhat complicated. It involves the use of random numbers. Numerical values of disturbance terms U are generated by using random number generators and are introduced into the model. Adelman and Adelman, studying the dynamic characteristics of the Klein-Goldberger model of the United States, concluded that in the absence of external shocks their equations generated time paths of the endogenous variables (25 of them) that were mostly monotonic and essentially linear.[14] However, when they introduced random shocks, the time paths became a close representation of the real dynamic situation of the United States economy, as evidenced over time.

Thus, in simulation, use is made of (1) the estimated values of the parameters of the model, (2) the assigned values of the predetermined variables, and (3) the numerical values of random error terms—using random number tables—to generate time paths of the jointly determined endogenous variables in the model. The simulation model is essentially dynamic in nature. Mathematical solutions in terms of difference and/or differential equations of dynamic relationships are well known. These solutions are, however, exact. Simulation in econometrics is essentially stochastic and involves the use of random numbers for generating errors or shocks.

Econometricians have employed the simulation approach to study the effects of the error terms in the behavioral equations of their model, both to examine the prediction potential of the model and to investigate whether errors lead to cumulative deviations from the expected time path generated by the model otherwise.[15] These studies devote much attention to simulating the consequences of alternative economic policy measures, such as improvement of automatic stabilizers, increased unemployment insurance benefits, automatic rate changes in the federal personal income tax, and combinations of these.

Simulation studies are indeed interesting exercises that open new avenues of econometric research. However, much remains to be learned as to the relative merits of the results obtained from simulation studies and the results one could obtain by better specification of the model in terms of linearity, aggregation, and other such problems. We can hope to secure improved specification of a model by better understanding of economic theory. Arbitrariness in the selection of variables in a given function may be greatly reduced. However, with all the improvement we can hope to make in economic theory as well as mathematical and statistical methodology, an econometric model may still remain incapable of generating a real economy in all its great detail. Hence simulation will continue to be a useful tool.

---

[14] Irma Adelman and Frank Adelman, "The Dynamic Properties of the Klein-Goldberger Model," *Econometrica*, Vol. 27, No. 4 (October, 1959), pp. 596-625.

[15] James S. Duesenberry *et al.*, "A Simulation of the United States Economy in Recession," *Econometrica*, Vol. 28, No. 4 (October, 1960), pp. 749-809. G. Fromm and P. Taubman, *Policy Simulations with an Econometric Model* (Washington, D.C.: Brookings Institution, 1968).

14.4 PREDICTION AND PREDICTION ERROR

There is much truth in the popular adage: "The test of the pudding is in its eating." The "goodness" of an econometric model in this sense lies in its predictive power. Indeed much of the efforts at quantifying economic magnitudes and at measuring economic parameters can be attributed to man's concern for predicting the future. It is the imperative need for such measurements that gave birth to econometrics; the needs of "practical" men for reliable prediction and not just the search of academic economists for abstract principle have supported and sustained the growth of this branch of economics. Prediction is by no means the exclusive objective in constructing an econometric model, but it is an important consideration (Chapter 1). Nevertheless, the claim that alternative procedures of estimation are open to the econometrician depending on whether he is interested in structural estimation or predictions is hard to maintain. Econometricians insist that the best forecasts should be made from the best estimate of the structure of the economic system. Intuitively, it is easy to see the logic of this insistence. The family physician may have quick intuitions based on his knowledge of certain quick indices to assure you of your health, but his judgment is scientific only when he has examined your physical system thoroughly. In either case he may turn out to be wrong, as he often does. Your ailment is attributed to factors unknown and unknowable. The econometrician has to study the structure of the economic system to make any methodologically sound prediction, even though uncontrolled and uncontrollable factors may eventually make his predictions go wrong. Naive methods of prediction are based on "experience," and there is no systematized body of knowledge to analyze the expertise of the wise men who do the forecasting, oftentimes successfully.

Econometric predictions are different from those of experienced wise men in that econometric predictions are based on established methods subject to analytic verification. Attempts to compare relative performance of econometric predictions with predictions derived otherwise have not shown that econometric predictions are any worse. Many times they are superior. Almost universally, naive methods are completely inadequate to predict turning points in economic activity. Naive methods are usually of two different kinds: (1) use of the results of an opinion poll in which businessmen or "experts" are asked to express their opinions on the future path of the economy, and the prediction is made from the majority vote; and (2) projection of the future value of a variable based on its past value plus or minus some corrections for errors. Prediction by an econometric model on the other hand is based on (1) specification of a model in terms of economic theory and institutional knowledge, (2) collection of appropriate data on relevant variables, and (3) estimation of the model by well-known statistical methods.

The mechanics of prediction is relatively simple. Consider the model:

$$\beta \mathbf{Y} + \Gamma \mathbf{X} + \mathbf{U} = 0 \qquad \textbf{14.4.1}$$

from which:

$$\mathbf{Y} = \mathbf{\Omega X} + \mathbf{V} \tag{14.4.2}$$

where $\mathbf{\Omega} = -\boldsymbol{\beta}^{-1}\mathbf{\Gamma}$ and $\mathbf{V} = -\boldsymbol{\beta}^{-1}\mathbf{U}$. First, we estimate the matrices $\boldsymbol{\beta}$ and $\mathbf{\Gamma}$ for the structural equations. Next, for prediction we return to the reduced form and construct the $\mathbf{\Omega}$ matrix. Given the knowledge of the members in $\mathbf{X}$, we can now predict values for the members in $\mathbf{Y}$. Notice that prediction necessarily relates to the period outside the sample period originally used for estimation of the coefficients in matrices $\boldsymbol{\beta}$ and $\mathbf{\Gamma}$. Hence the term *extrapolation* is often used.

Note that the alternative method that formulates prediction and estimation as one single problem of statistical decision is not discussed here. Let us translate model 14.4.1 in terms of one of L. R. Klein's early models of the United States.[16] The model consists of six equations referring to six jointly determined endogenous Y variables and eight predetermined variables including lagged endogenous and exogenous variables and a dummy variable always equal to unity for estimating the intercept of the function. There are three stochastic equations, and the remaining three equations are definitional identities. The estimates of structural parameters are obtained by Klein using the FIML method:

$$\begin{bmatrix} -1.0 & 0 & 0.80 & 0 & 0.02 & 0 \\ 0 & -1.0 & 0 & 0 & 0.23 & 0 \\ 0 & 0 & -1.0 & 0.42 & 0 & 0 \\ 1.0 & 1.0 & 0 & -1.0 & 0 & 0 \\ 0 & 0 & -1.0 & 1.0 & -1.0 & 0 \\ 0 & 1.0 & 0 & 0 & 0 & -1.0 \end{bmatrix} \begin{bmatrix} Y_{t1} \\ Y_{t2} \\ Y_{t3} \\ Y_{t4} \\ Y_{t5} \\ Y_{t6} \end{bmatrix}$$

14.4.3

$$+ \begin{bmatrix} 0.23 & 0 & 0 & 0.80 & 0 & 0 & 0 & 16.78 \\ 0.55 & -0.15 & 0 & 0 & 0 & 0 & 0 & 17.79 \\ 0 & 0 & 0.16 & 0 & 0 & 0.13 & 0 & 1.60 \\ 0 & 0 & 0 & 0 & 1.0 & 0 & 0 & 0 \\ 0 & 0 & 0 & 0 & 0 & 0 & -1.0 & 0 \\ 0 & 1.0 & 0 & 0 & 0 & 0 & 0 & 0 \end{bmatrix} \begin{bmatrix} X_{t1} \\ X_{t2} \\ X_{t3} \\ X_{t4} \\ X_{t5} \\ X_{t6} \\ X_{t7} \\ X_{t8} \end{bmatrix}$$

(continued)

[16] L. R. Klein, *Economic Fluctuations of the United States 1921-1941* (New York: John Wiley & Sons, 1950), p. 68.

$$+\begin{bmatrix} U_{t1} \\ U_{t2} \\ U_{t3} \\ 0 \\ 0 \\ 0 \end{bmatrix} = \begin{bmatrix} 0 \\ 0 \\ 0 \\ 0 \\ 0 \\ 0 \end{bmatrix} \qquad t = 1, 2, \ldots T \qquad \textbf{14.4.3 (continued)}$$

where Y_1 = aggregate consumption
Y_2 = net investment
Y_3 = private wage bill
Y_4 = aggregate output
Y_5 = profit share (nonwage income)
Y_6 = capital stock at the end of the year
X_1 = profit share Y_5 lagged for one time period
X_2 = capital stock Y_6 lagged for one time period
X_3 = aggregate output Y_4 lagged for one time period
X_4 = wage bill of the government sector
X_5 = government purchases from the private sector (foreign demand for American goods net of imports is also included)
X_6 = time trend
X_7 = business taxes
X_8 = dummy variable always equal to unity
(All variables are in constant dollars)

By using the matrices $\boldsymbol{\beta}$ and $\boldsymbol{\Gamma}$ above, we obtain $-\boldsymbol{\beta}^{-1}\boldsymbol{\Gamma} = \boldsymbol{\Omega}$ when, suppressing the t subscript:

$$\begin{bmatrix} Y_1 \\ Y_2 \\ Y_3 \\ Y_4 \\ Y_5 \\ Y_6 \end{bmatrix} = \begin{bmatrix} 0.74 & -0.10 & 0.19 & 1.34 & 0.67 & 0.16 & -0.19 & 41.8 \\ 0.86 & -0.16 & -0.06 & 0.90 & 1.12 & -0.05 & -1.28 & 38.1 \\ 0.75 & -0.18 & -0.01 & 0.21 & 0.26 & -0.01 & -0.30 & 26.6 \\ 0.75 & 0.82 & -0.01 & 0.21 & 0.26 & -0.01 & -0.30 & 26.6 \\ 1.49 & -0.28 & 0.17 & 1.54 & 1.93 & 0.14 & -0.48 & 68.4 \\ 0.63 & -0.12 & 0.24 & 0.65 & 0.81 & 0.20 & -0.20 & 30.3 \end{bmatrix} \begin{bmatrix} X_1 \\ X_2 \\ X_3 \\ X_4 \\ X_5 \\ X_6 \\ X_7 \\ X_8 \end{bmatrix} \qquad \textbf{14.4.4}$$

Given values for the X's, we can predict the values of the Y's using the elements in the $\boldsymbol{\Omega}$ matrix. For example, for predicting Y_1 in period $T + 1$ we have to know first $X_1, X_2, \ldots, X_7$ in $T + 1$ (and we know the value X_8, the dummy variable in $T + 1$, as it is always unity). Next we take the elements in the first row of the $\boldsymbol{\Omega}$ matrix and, multiplying through the column of X_{T+1}, we can obtain:

$$Y^P_{1(T+1)} = 0.74X_{1(T+1)} - 0.10X_{2(T+1)} + 0.19X_{3(T+1)} + 1.34X_{4(T+1)} + 0.67X_{5(T+1)} + 0.16X_{6(T+1)} - 0.19X_{7(T+1)} + 41.8 \quad \textbf{14.4.5}$$

Problems in Prediction, Point Prediction, and Interval Prediction

Predicted values of jointly determined variables often deviate from the values actually observed on the Y's. Note that predictions on jointly determined Y variables are conditioned by various factors:

1. Unbiasedness of the parameters estimated is important. The more the estimates differ from the true parameters, the more the predicted values are likely to be off the mark.
2. Distributional properties of the error term, as assumed, need to be satisfied. The more the disturbances deviate from their assumed mean values of zero, the more the predictions are likely to deviate from realized values of the Y's. Indeed the variance of sample residuals becomes a component of the variance of prediction error.
3. Knowledge of the predetermined X variables is used in generating predicted values on the Y's. The deviation of the assigned values of such predetermined variables from the true values subsequently observed contribute to prediction errors.
4. Continuity of the given structure is an important assumption. Major change in political policy, transition from war to peace, and change in social values often effect changes in a given economic structure. It is not bad if we have information on the structural changes that may be forthcoming. Failure to recognize such changes will be sure to contribute to prediction errors.
5. Misspecification of the model often contributes to poor prediction. As pointed out before, a priori zero restrictions may permit the identification of equations in a system from the point of view of pure logic, but it may introduce errors of specification.
6. Constraints of econometric models reviewed in the previous section contribute to prediction errors.

One way to minimize the error in prediction is to construct an interval for the predicted values of the variables concerned. The interval form for prediction states that the prediction will be true plus or minus an estimated interval. This is distinct from *point prediction* where the predicted value is given without any margin for error. If the predicted value is 100, the prediction can be either true or false. In an *interval prediction,* given an interval of plus or minus 10, the prediction is good for any value between 90 and 110. In view of the problems inherent in econometric prediction, construction of an interval for prediction is highly desirable.

Consider the single equation model:

$$Y_t = \beta_0 + \beta_1 X_t + U_t \qquad t = 1, 2, \ldots T \quad \textbf{14.4.6}$$

from which:

$$\hat{Y}_t = \hat{\beta}_0 + \hat{\beta}_1 X_t \quad \textbf{14.4.7}$$

and then the prediction of Y in period $T+1$ is:

$$Y^P_{T+1} = \hat{\beta}_0 + \hat{\beta}_1 X_{T+1} \quad \textbf{14.4.8}$$

The structural relation in period $T+1$ is:

$$Y_{T+1} = \beta_0 + \beta_1 X_{T+1} + U_{T+1} \qquad \textbf{14.4.9}$$

It follows that the prediction error is:

$$Y_{T+1} - Y^P_{T+1} = \beta_0 + \beta_1 X_{T+1} + U_{T+1} - \hat{\beta}_0 - \hat{\beta}_1 X_{T+1} \qquad \textbf{14.4.10}$$

Given that the OLS estimates are best and unbiased, prediction error 14.4.10 is dependent on the component of random disturbances in the disturbance vector U_{T+1}. We assume these random disturbance terms are independent, uncorrelated, and normally distributed. As such the prediction error has a normal distribution with mean zero and a finite variance.

The mean zero can be seen as follows:

$$\begin{aligned} E(Y_{T+1} - Y^P_{T+1}) &= E(\beta_0 + \beta_1 X_{T+1} + U_{T+1}) - E(\hat{\beta}_0 + \hat{\beta}_1 X_{T+1}) \\ &= \beta_0 + \beta_1 X_{T+1} + E(U_{T+1}) - E(\hat{\beta}_0) - E(\hat{\beta}_1) X_{T+1} \qquad \textbf{14.4.11} \\ &= E(U_{T+1}) \end{aligned}$$

since the expected value of a constant or fixed term is the term itself, that is, $E(X) = X$; and the OLS estimates have been shown to have the property $E(\hat{\beta}_k) = \beta_k$. Thus,

$$E(Y_{T+1} - Y^P_{T+1}) = 0 \qquad \textbf{14.4.12}$$

since

$$E(U_t) = 0$$

The variance of the prediction error is:

$$\begin{aligned} \sigma^2_P &= E\{[(Y_{T+1} - Y^P_{T+1}) - E(Y_{T+1} - Y^P_{T+1})]^2\} \\ &= E(Y_{T+1} - Y^P_{T+1})^2 \end{aligned} \qquad \textbf{14.4.13}$$

since we have seen in equations 14.4.11 that $E(Y_{T+1} - Y^P_{T+1}) = 0$.

We can rewrite equations 14.4.13 by subtracting and adding a common term:

$$\begin{aligned} \sigma^2_P &= E\{[Y_{T+1} - E(Y_{T+1}) + E(Y_{T+1}) - Y^P_{T+1}]^2\} \\ &= E\{[Y_{T+1} - E(Y_{T+1})]^2\} + E\{[E(Y_{T+1}) - Y^P_{T+1}]^2\} \end{aligned} \qquad \textbf{14.4.14}$$

since the cross product is zero. Thus,

$$\sigma^2_P = \sigma^2 + \sigma^2_{Y^P_{T+1}} \qquad \textbf{14.4.15}$$

Recall that the dependent variable Y and the disturbance term U have the same variance σ^2. Thus the first term is the variance of the disturbance terms, and the second term depends on the deviations of the estimated parameters $\hat{\beta}_k$ from the true value of the parameters β_k. There are two basic components of the variance of prediction σ_P^2: (1) variance of the disturbances and (2) variance of the estimated parameters, including the intercept estimate. Even if our knowledge of the predetermined variables in the prediction period is correct, the model is truly specified, and the structure remains unchanged, the sampling variability of prediction based on variances of the disturbances and of the estimated parameters persists.

We return to evaluate the term $\sigma^2_{Y^P_{T+1}}$ in equation 14.4.15 by using equations 14.4.8 and 14.4.9:

$$\begin{aligned}
\sigma^2_{Y^P_{T+1}} &= E\{[E(Y_{T+1}) - Y^P_{T+1}]^2\} \\
&= E[(\beta_0 + \beta_1 X_{T+1} - \hat{\beta}_0 - \hat{\beta}_1 X_{T+1})^2] \\
&= E\{[(\beta_0 - \hat{\beta}_0) + (\beta_1 - \hat{\beta}_1)X_{T+1}]^2\} \qquad \textbf{14.4.16} \\
&= E[(\beta_0 - \hat{\beta}_0)^2] + E[(\beta_1 - \hat{\beta}_1)^2 X^2_{T+1}] + 2\,E[(\beta_0 - \hat{\beta}_0)(\beta_1 - \hat{\beta}_1)X_{T+1}] \\
&= \text{var}(\hat{\beta}_0) + \text{var}(\hat{\beta}_1)X^2_{T+1} + 2\,X_{T+1}\,\text{cov}(\hat{\beta}_0\,\hat{\beta}_1)
\end{aligned}$$

By using equations 2.4.30 and 2.4.33 for the estimates of var($\hat{\beta}_1$) and var($\hat{\beta}_0$) respectively and making use of them for cov($\hat{\beta}_0\hat{\beta}_1$), we write:

$$\sigma^2_{Y^P_{T+1}} = \sigma^2\left(\frac{1}{T} + \frac{\bar{X}^2}{\Sigma x_i^2}\right) + X^2_{T+1}\left(\frac{\sigma^2}{\Sigma x_i^2}\right) - 2X_{T+1}\bar{X}\left(\frac{\sigma^2}{\Sigma x_i^2}\right) \qquad \textbf{14.4.17}$$

where $x_i = (X_i - \bar{X})$

or,

$$\begin{aligned}
\sigma^2_{Y^P_{T+1}} &= \frac{\sigma^2}{\Sigma x_i^2}\left(\frac{\Sigma x_i^2}{T} + \bar{X}^2 + X^2_{T+1} - 2X_{T+1}\bar{X}\right) \\
&= \frac{\sigma^2}{\Sigma x_i^2}\left[\frac{\Sigma x_i^2}{T} + (X_{T+1} - \bar{X})^2\right] \qquad \textbf{14.4.18} \\
&= \sigma^2\left[\frac{1}{T} + \frac{(X_{T+1} - \bar{X})^2}{\Sigma x_i^2}\right]
\end{aligned}$$

Substituting equations 14.4.18 into equation 14.4.15, we have:

$$\begin{aligned}
\sigma_P^2 &= \sigma^2 + \sigma^2\left[\frac{1}{T} + \frac{(X_{T+1} - \bar{X})^2}{\Sigma x_i^2}\right] \qquad \textbf{14.4.19} \\
&= \sigma^2\left[1 + \frac{1}{T} + \frac{(X_{T+1} - \bar{X})^2}{\Sigma x_i^2}\right]
\end{aligned}$$

Note that we have no information on σ^2. However, we can estimate it from equation 2.4.78 in this case or from equation 2.4.71 in a K-variable multiple regression situation, and we then rewrite equations 14.4.19:

$$S_P^2 = s^2\left[1 + \frac{1}{T} + \frac{(X_{T+1} - \bar{X})^2}{\Sigma x_i^2}\right] \qquad \textbf{14.4.20}$$

The above formula can be extended to the general K-variable regression model ($k = 1, 2, \ldots K$), and the prediction error can be written as:

$$S_P^2 = s^2\left[1 + \frac{1}{T} + (\mathbf{X}_{T+1_k} - \bar{\mathbf{X}}_k)' \, (\mathbf{X}'\mathbf{X})^{-1}(\mathbf{X}_{T+1} - \bar{\mathbf{X}}_k)\right]$$

where

$$\mathbf{X}_{T+1_k} - \mathbf{X}_k = \begin{bmatrix} X_{T+1,\,1} - \bar{X}_1 \\ X_{T+1,\,2} - \bar{X}_2 \\ \cdot \quad \cdot \\ \cdot \quad \cdot \\ \cdot \quad \cdot \\ X_{T+1,\,K} - \bar{X}_K \end{bmatrix} \qquad \textbf{14.4.21}$$

An inspection of equations 14.4.19 and 14.4.20 indicates how prediction error can become smaller. First, the larger the sample size T, the smaller the fraction $1/T$; and this is why a larger sample size for obtaining estimates of a regression line is always preferred. Secondly, the component $(\mathbf{X}_{T+1} - \bar{\mathbf{X}})^2/\Sigma x_i^2$ merits some scrutiny. The denominator is $\Sigma x_i^2 = \Sigma(X_t - \bar{X})^2$; and the larger is this sum, the smaller the contribution of this component to the total error of prediction, given the numerator. In other words the greater is the dispersion of the observations on the regressor variable in the sample, the larger this sum is likely to be. In the extreme case when all sample observations on X_t are bunched together, that is, not at all dispersed, the sum will be zero and, as we have seen, the regression estimate cannot be defined.

The numerator expression is important too. Of course, the prediction error is a function of the extrapolated values on X_t. As the extrapolated values on X_t move farther from its mean value $\bar{X}$ (which is computed from the sample values on X_t when $t = 1, 2, \ldots T$), the numerator expression most likely becomes larger, and thus contributes to greater prediction error. This is in conformity with the common sense view that to generate predictions for the periods not too far from the sample period is one way to ensure smaller prediction error. Alternatively, predictions for far distant future periods are likely to be far less reliable.

The other contributing factor to the prediction error according to the above formula is the variance of the disturbance σ^2 or its estimate about which we cannot do anything once the given specification of the model is accepted.

Tolerance Interval

There exists a statistical measure that gives a *tolerance interval* for prediction.[17] This interval concept defines a range within which at least a specified proportion p of the observations on Y outside the sample is expected to fall, with probability Γ. The range of k standard deviations measures the tolerance interval. Tables of k for particular values of p and Γ associated with samples of various sizes (normally distributed with constant mean) are available.[18] This interval relates to the expected value of Y in $T + 1$; that is, this defines the interval for the true value of Y in $T + 1$. The choice of k is based on a complicated formula.

Suppose that we predict from a linear k variable single-equation model:

$$Y^P_{T+1} = \mathbf{X}_{T+1}\hat{\boldsymbol{\beta}} \qquad \textbf{14.4.22}$$

given:

$$Y_t = \mathbf{X}_t\boldsymbol{\beta} + U_t \qquad t = 1, 2, \ldots, T \qquad \textbf{14.4.23}$$

where an individual Y is regressed on a set of X's ($k = 1, 2, \ldots K$). $\mathbf{Y}$ is a column vector of T observations, $\mathbf{X}$ is a $T \times M$ matrix of T observations on all M of the X's appearing as regressors in the equation, $\boldsymbol{\beta}$ is a column vector of unknown coefficients (to be estimated), and $\mathbf{U}$ is a column vector of disturbance terms.

The prediction error can be defined as:

$$P = Y_{T+1} - Y^P_{T+1} = \mathbf{X}_{T+1}(\boldsymbol{\beta} - \hat{\boldsymbol{\beta}}) + U_{T+1} \qquad \textbf{14.4.24}$$

The expected value of the prediction error is, as seen before:

$$\begin{aligned} E(P) &= \mathbf{X}_{T+1}E(\boldsymbol{\beta} - \hat{\boldsymbol{\beta}}) + E(U_{T+1}) \\ &= \mathbf{X}_{T+1}\boldsymbol{\beta} - \mathbf{X}_{T+1}E(\hat{\boldsymbol{\beta}}) + E(U_{t+1}) \qquad \textbf{14.4.25} \\ &= 0 \end{aligned}$$

since $E(\hat{\boldsymbol{\beta}}) = \boldsymbol{\beta}$ and $E(U_{t+1}) = 0$. The variance of prediction is as in equation 14.4.15:

$$\begin{aligned} \sigma^2_P &= \mathbf{X}'_{T+1}E(\hat{\boldsymbol{\beta}} - \boldsymbol{\beta})(\hat{\boldsymbol{\beta}} - \boldsymbol{\beta})'\mathbf{X}_{T+1} + E(U^2) \\ &= \sigma^2_{Y^P_{T+1}} + \sigma^2 \end{aligned} \qquad \textbf{14.4.26}$$

[17] W. A. Wallis, "Tolerance Intervals for Linear Regression," *Second Berkeley Symposium on Mathematical Statistics and Probability*, edited by J. Neyman (Berkeley: University of California Press, 1951). L. R. Klein, *A Textbook of Econometrics* (Evanston, Illinois: Row, Peterson & Co., 1956), pp. 252-258.

[18] A. H. Bowker, "Tolerance Limits for Normal Distributions," *Selected Techniques of Statistical Analysis for Scientific and Industrial Research and Production and Management Engineeering*, edited by C. Eisenhart *et al.* (New York: McGraw-Hill Book Co., 1947). Also, W. A. Wallis, *op. cit.*

We assume that $E(\hat{\boldsymbol{\beta}} - \boldsymbol{\beta})U = 0$. An estimate of σ_P^2 is then obtained from the sum of the corresponding estimates of the two quantities on the right-hand side:

$$S_P^2 = S_{Y_{T+1}^P}^2 + s^2 \qquad \textbf{14.4.27}$$

The quantities expressed in equations 14.4.26 are available in ordinary multiple regression analysis; and thus the computation of equation 14.4.27 is rather straightforward.

We can then write the tolerance interval for the value of Y in $T + 1$ as:

$$Y_{T+1} = Y_{T+1}^P \pm k\sqrt{S_{Y_{T+1}^P}^2 + s^2} \qquad \textbf{14.4.28}$$

where k is, as before, defined in Bowker's table.

Prediction Interval Further Considered

Hooper and Zellner propose a test that is based on the familiar t ratio, not on the k table referred to above.[19] However, the prediction interval based on the t statistic should not be confused with the concept of confidence interval in the classical sense, since Y_{T+1}^P is a random variable and the confidence intervals are generally applied to population parameters that are true constants. On the other hand this form of prediction interval is different from the tolerance interval discussed above. This prediction interval is rather akin to the concept of confidence interval of the true parameters, as described in Chapter 3; and it can be interpreted as meaning that at a given level of confidence there is a probability that the value of one future true observation on Y will fall in the interval constructed.

An important limitation of this interval estimate is that any probability statement about the prediction interval is valid only if the vector of exogenous variables **X** used in making the predictions is fixed, not stochastic.

The mechanics of this interval estimate can be easily derived from previous discussions. We can begin with equations 14.4.22:

$$Y_{T+1}^P = \mathbf{X}_{T+1}\hat{\boldsymbol{\beta}}$$

The true relationship in period $T + 1$ is, given the structure specified:

$$Y_{T+1} = \mathbf{X}_{T+1}\boldsymbol{\beta} + U_{T+1}$$

Following equations 14.4.6 through 14.4.20, we can obtain an estimate of the prediction error which is normally distributed with a zero mean and a finite variance, S_P^2.

---

[19] John W. Hooper and Arnold Zellner, "The Error of Forecast for Multivariate Regression Models," *Econometrica*, Vol. 29, No. 4 (October, 1961), pp. 544-555.

We can now obtain the statistic t, where:

$$t = \frac{(Y^P_{T+1} - Y_{T+1})}{\sigma_P} \Bigg/ \frac{S_P}{\sigma_P} \qquad \textbf{14.4.29}$$

and where $\sigma_P = \sqrt{\sigma^2_P}$ and $S_p = \sqrt{S^2_P}$

or,

$$t = \frac{Y^P_{T+1} - Y_{T+1}}{S_P} \qquad \textbf{14.4.30}$$

Note that equation 14.4.30 is the familiar t statistic with $N - K$ degrees of freedom. (There are K of the X's, and K parameters are estimated, including the intercept term.) The numerator is the difference between the estimated value of the prediction on Y and the true value of the variable Y in $T + 1$, and the denominator is the estimate of the standard deviation of prediction. It is now possible to make a probability statement as follows:

$$\Pr(|t| > t_\alpha) = \alpha \qquad \textbf{14.4.31}$$

where t_α is the t value from the t table at the α level of significance. Alternatively, we can state that:

$$\Pr(Y^P_{T+1} - S_P t_\alpha < Y_{T+1} < Y^P_{T+1} + S_P t_\alpha) = 1 - \alpha \qquad \textbf{14.4.32}$$

or, when $\alpha = 0.05$,

$$\Pr(Y^P_{T+1} - S_P t_{0.025} < Y_{T+1} < Y^P_{T+1} + S_P t_{0.025}) = 0.95 \qquad \textbf{14.4.33}$$

Note that the U disturbances are assumed to be random terms normally distributed. Thus the $\hat{\beta}$'s are normally distributed; and since $\hat{Y}_{t+1}$ is a linear combination of $\hat{\beta}$'s, given fixed X's, $\hat{Y}^P_{t+1}$ has a normal distribution. If the prediction-period exogenous variables are stochastic, the predicted variable is not distributed normally for finite samples.

The discussion above has been restricted to single equation models. Attempts have been made to estimate prediction errors for large overidentified systems of simultaneous equations, which are not presented here. Klein has shown that it is relatively simple to estimate prediction errors for a just identified system.[20] Goldberger has shown that predictions using a generalized least squares model require special treatment.[21] Hymans has proposed a prediction error test for overidentified systems of equations that uses the

---

[20] L. R. Klein, *An Introduction to Econometrics* (Englewood Cliffs, N.J.: Prentice-Hall, 1962), pp. 246-250.

[21] A. S. Goldberger, A. L. Nagar, and H. S. Odeh, "The Covariance Matrices of Reduced Form Coefficients and of Forecasts for a Structural Econometric Model, *Econometrica,* Vol. 29, No. 4 (October, 1961), pp. 556-573. A. S. Goldberger, "Best Linear Unbiased Prediction in the Generalized Regression Model," *Journal of the American Statistical Association,* Vol. 57, No. 298 (June, 1962), pp. 369-375.

concept of concentration ellipsoid to determine the joint confidence interval for all the Y's in the system.[22] Pending further investigations into the issues involved, this test has not been commonly used. Theil has offered some practical approaches to the problem.[23]

For more reasons than one, divergences often occur between the predicted values for the Y's and the values subsequently realized for them. As a particular set of estimates is used to predict for periods far outside the sample period, the chances are that predictions will be far less accurate. Intervals have meaning for predictions made for future periods close to the sample period and have less meaning as the future periods move farther from it. Econometric model construction is a continous process. When new observations are obtained, the model may be reestimated, and predictions for the next immediate future period may be generated de novo. This is one way of correcting for structural changes and also for changes in the true values of the predetermined variables. Any estimates of these variables in the far distant future are bound to be only guesses, and predictions based on them will be poor.

In Retrospect

Building econometric models is a relatively new technique in economics. However, it has captured the imagination of many investigators; and efforts to construct such models for the economy as a whole, for a sector of it, for a specific commodity, or for a region or a state have been extensively undertaken. The literature is extensive. There have been several models of the United States. One of the latest, the Brookings Quarterly model, has the giant size of some 300 equations. Several models of states have been reported (California, Michigan, Ohio, Alaska, Hawaii). Attempts to construct models of metropolitan regions or of interstate regions have also been reported. At the commodity level, models are many and varied and cover such diverse items as watermelons, onions, tea, steel, tin, automobiles, and housing. National economic models of the United Kingdom, Canada, Netherlands, Greece, France, Japan, Australia, Israel, India, Jamaica, and Puerto Rico have been constructed. In some cases more than one model of a given country have been reported. Also, an attempt to construct an econometric model of the world as a whole known as the Link model is in progress. Since World War II there has been a phenomenal growth in econometric research.

While research over the last quarter of the century has attempted to answer many questions, it has also revealed that many more questions still remain to be answered. Continuous research alone can succeed in improving methods of econometric research and resolving the issues hitherto unresolved. Critics of econometrics are, on the other hand, becoming impatient.

---

[22] S. H. Hymans, "Simultaneous Confidence Intervals in Econometric Forecasting," *Econometrica*, Vol. 36, No. 1 (January, 1968), pp. 18-36.

[23] H. Theil, *Economic Forecasts and Policy* (2d ed.; Amsterdam: North-Holland Publishing Co., 1961), pp. 10-42.

"Consider your verdict," the King said to the jury.
"Not yet, not yet!" the Rabbit hastily interrupted.
"There's a great deal to come before that!"

—Lewis Carroll

DISCUSSION QUESTIONS

1. Give an outline of the Monte Carlo experiments.
2. The question of what estimator to use in a small-sample situation is far from settled. Review briefly the findings of experiments on the question.
3. Define the root mean square error. How good is this measure for evaluating alternative estimators? What other measures can be used?
4. Evaluation of alternative estimators by predictive ability tests has been undertaken by some researchers. How successful have these undertakings been?
5. What can be done to develop a synthetic approach to relate the Monte Carlo experiments of structural parameters estimates to the predictive ability tests for evaluating alternative estimators?
6. How can an econometric model be used for the simulation of alternative policies?
7. (a) Prediction is a goal of model building in econometrics. Distinguish between naive prediction and econometric prediction.
   (b) List the conditions which can often cause econometric predictions to go wrong. Does the econometrician have control over such conditions?
   (c) Econometric predictions are at best probabilistic. What can be done to obtain an estimate of the prediction error?
   (d) Differentiate between point prediction and interval prediction.
8. Show that the basic components of the variance of prediction are variance of the disturbances and variances of the estimated parameters, including the intercept term.
9. Obtain from question 7, Chapter 3, a prediction for one time period outside the sample period and calculate the variance of prediction. (Hint: Extrapolate the values of X for the out-of-the-sample period.)
10. Discuss the Hooper-Zellner test based on the t ratio.

SUGGESTED READINGS

Adelman, Irma, and Frank Adelman. "The Dynamic Properties of the Klein-Goldberger Model." *Econometrica,* Vol. 27, No. 4 (October, 1959), pp. 596-625.

Ball, R. J. "The Significance of Simultaneous Methods of Parameter Estimation in Econometric Models." *Applied Statistics,* Vol. 12, No. 1 (March, 1963), pp. 14-25.

Basmann, Robert L. "On Finite Sample Distributions of Generalized Classical Linear Identifiability Test Statistics." *Journal of the American Statistical Association,* Vol. 55, No. 292 (December, 1960), pp. 650-659.

———. "A Note on the Exact Finite Sample Frequency Functions of Generalized Classical Linear Estimators in Two Leading Overidentified Cases." *Journal of the American Statistical Association,* Vol. 56, No. 295 (September, 1961), pp. 619-636.

Bowker, A. H. "Tolerance Limits for Normal Distributions." *Selected Techniques of Statistical Analysis for Scientific and Industrial Research and Production and Management Engineering,* edited by C. Eisenhart, M. Hastay, and W. A. Wallis. New York: McGraw-Hill Book Co., 1947.

Brown, T. M. "Standard Errors of Forecast of a Complete Econometric Model." *Econometrica,* Vol. 22, No. 2 (April, 1954), pp. 178-192.

Christ, Carl F. *Econometric Models and Methods.* New York: John Wiley & Sons, 1966.

Cornwall, John. "Economic Implications of the Klein-Goldberger Model." *Review of Economics and Statistics,* Vol. 41, No. 2, Part 1 (May, 1959), pp. 154-161.

Cragg, J. G. "On The Relative Small Sample Properties of Several Structural Equation Estimators." *Econometrica,* Vol. 35, No. 1 (January, 1967), pp. 89-110.

———. "On The Sensitivity of Simultaneous Equation Estimators to the Stochastic Assumptions of the Models." *Journal of the American Statistical Association,* Vol. 61, No. 313 (March, 1966), pp. 136-151.

Duesenberry, James S., Otto Eckstein, and Gary Fromm. "A Simulation of the United States Economy in Recession." *Econometrica,* Vol. 28, No. 4 (October, 1960), pp. 749-809.

Dutta, M., and P. L. Sharma. "Alternative Estimators and Predictive Power of Alternative Estimators: An Econometric Model of Puerto Rico." *Review of Economics and Statistics,* Vol. 55, No.3 (August, 1973), pp. 381-385.

Dutta, M., and Vincent Su. "An Econometric Model of Puerto Rico." *Review of Economic Studies,* Vol. 36, No. 3 (July, 1969), pp. 319-333.

Dutta, M., V. Kerry Smith, and Peter Loeb. "An Evaluation of Alternative Estimators in the Context of a Simultaneous System with Structural and Predictive Criteria: A Monte Carlo Study." A paper presented at the European Econometrics Society Meetings, Budapest, Hungary, September, 1972.

Fisk, P. R. *Stochastically Dependent Equations.* London: Charles Griffin & Co., 1967.

Frisch, Ragnar. "Propagation Problems and Impulse Problems in Dynamic Economics." *Economic Essays in Honour of Gustav Cassel,* edited by J. C. Stamp *et al.* London: George Allen & Unwin, 1933, pp. 171-205.

———. "A Memorandum on Price-Wage-Tax-Subsidy Policies in Maintaining Optimum Employment." United Nations document, partly reproduced in *Meteroeconomica,* Vol. 7 (1955), pp. 111-136.

Fromm, Gary, and Paul Taubman. *Policy Simulations with an Econometric Model.* Washington, D.C.: Brookings Institution, 1968.

Goldberger, Arthur S. *Impact Multipliers and Dynamic Properties of the Klein-Goldberger Model.* Amsterdam: North-Holland Publishing Co., 1959.

———. "Best Linear Unbiased Prediction in the Generalized Regression Model." *Journal of the American Statistical Association,* Vol. 57, No. 298 (June, 1962), pp. 369-375.

Goldberger, A. S., A. L. Nagar, and H. S. Odeh. "The Covariance Matrices of Reduced Form Coefficients and of Forecasts for a Structural Econometric Model." *Econometrica,* Vol. 29, No. 4 (October, 1961), pp. 556-573.

Guetzkow, H. S. (ed.). *Simulation in Social Science: Readings.* Englewood Cliffs, N.J.: Prentice-Hall, 1962.

Hooper, John W., and Arnold Zellner. "The Error of Forecast for Multivariate Regression Models." *Econometrica,* Vol. 29, No. 4 (October, 1961), pp. 544-555.

Hymans, Saul H. "Simultaneous Confidence Intervals in Econometric Forecasting." *Econometrica,* Vol. 36, No. 1 (January, 1968), pp. 18-36.

Johnston, J. *Econometric Methods,* 2d ed. New York: McGraw-Hill Book Co., 1972.

Klein, Lawrence R. *Economic Fluctuations of the United States 1921-1941.* New York: John Wiley & Sons, 1950.

———. *A Textbook of Econometrics.* Evanston, Illinois: Row, Peterson & Co., 1956.

———. *An Introduction to Econometrics.* Englewood Cliffs, N.J.: Prentice-Hall, 1962.

Klein, Lawrence R., and Michael K. Evans. *Econometric Gaming.* New York: Macmillan Co., 1969.

Ladd, George W. "Effects of Shocks and Errors in Estimation: An Empirical Comparison." *Journal of Farm Economics,* Vol. 38, No. 2 (1956), pp. 485-495.

L'Esperance, Wilfred L. "Further Evidence on the Predictive Power of Various Estimators. *International Economic Review,* Vol. 8, No. 1 (January, 1967), pp. 45-66.

Maeshiro, A. "A Simple Mathematical Relationship Among *k*-Class Estimators." *Journal of the American Statistical Association,* Vol. 61, No. 314 (June, 1966), pp. 368-374.

Nagar, A. L. "The Bias and Moment Matrix of the General *k*-Class Estimators of the Parameters in Simultaneous Equations." *Econometrica,* Vol. 27, No. 4 (October, 1959), pp. 575-594.

———. "Double *k*-Class Estimators of Parameters in Simultaneous Equations and Their Small Sample Properties." *International Economic Review,* Vol. 3, No. 2 (May, 1962), pp. 168-188.

———. "A Monte Carlo Study of Alternative Simultaneous Equation Estimators." *Econometrica,* Vol. 28, No. 3 (July, 1960), pp. 573-590.

Oi, W. Y. "On the Relationship Among Different Members of the *k*-Class." *International Economic Review,* Vol. 10 (1969), pp. 36-46.

Orcutt, Guy H., *et al. Microanalysis of Socioeconomic Systems: A Simulation Study*. New York: Harper & Row, Publishers, 1961.

Quandt, Richard E. "On Certain Small Sample Properties of *k*-Class Estimators." *International Economic Review,* Vol. 6, No. 1 (January, 1965), pp. 92-104.

Roos, C. F. "Survey of Econometric Forecasting Techniques." *Econometrica,* Vol. 23 (October, 1955), pp. 363-395.

Sharma, P. L. "Econometric Forecasting with Special Reference to Forecasting Sensitivity of Various Estimators in Aggregate Econometric Models." Doctoral dissertation, Rutgers University, 1972.

Smith, V. Kerry. "An Econometric Evaluation of Several Econometric Estimators for Simultaneous Equation Systems." Doctoral dissertation, Rutgers University, 1970.

———. "A Comparative Tabular Survey of Monte Carlo and Exact Sampling Studies." *Australian Economic Papers,* Vol. 10 (December, 1971), pp. 196-202.

———. *Monte Carlo Methods: Their Role for Econometrics*. Lexington, Mass.: D.C. Heath & Co., 1973.

Summers, Robert. "A Capital Intensive Approach to the Small Sample Properties of Various Simultaneous Equation Estimators." *Econometrica,* Vol. 33, No. 1 (January, 1965), pp. 1-41.

Tatemoto, Masahiro, Tadao Uchida, and Tsunehiko Watanabe. "A Stabilization Model of the Postwar Japanese Economy 1954-1962." *International Economic Review,* Vol. 8, No. 1 (January, 1967), pp. 13-44.

Theil, Henri. *Economic Forecasts and Policy,* 2d ed. Amsterdam: North-Holland Publishing Co., 1961.

———. "Who Forecasts Best?" *International Economic Papers,* Vol. 5 (1954), p. 194.

Wagner, Harvey M. "A Monte Carlo Study of Estimates of Simultaneous Linear Structural Equations." *Econometrica,* Vol. 26, No. 1 (January, 1958), pp. 117-133.

Wallis, W. A. "Tolerance Intervals for Linear Regression." *Second Berkeley Symposium on Mathematical Statistics and Probability,* edited by J. Neyman. Berkeley: University of California Press, 1951.

appendix

THE DURBIN-WATSON TABLE

significance points of d_L and d_U: 5%

n	k' = 1 d_L	k' = 1 d_U	k' = 2 d_L	k' = 2 d_U	k' = 3 d_L	k' = 3 d_U	k' = 4 d_L	k' = 4 d_U	k' = 5 d_L	k' = 5 d_U
15	1.08	1.36	0.95	1.54	0.82	1.75	0.69	1.97	0.56	2.21
16	1.10	1.37	0.98	1.54	0.86	1.73	0.74	1.93	0.62	2.15
17	1.13	1.38	1.02	1.54	0.90	1.71	0.78	1.90	0.67	2.10
18	1.16	1.39	1.05	1.53	0.93	1.69	0.82	1.87	0.71	2.06
19	1.18	1.40	1.08	1.53	0.97	1.68	0.86	1.85	0.75	2.02
20	1.20	1.41	1.10	1.54	1.00	1.68	0.90	1.83	0.79	1.99
21	1.22	1.42	1.13	1.54	1.03	1.67	0.93	1.81	0.83	1.96
22	1.24	1.43	1.15	1.54	1.05	1.66	0.96	1.80	0.86	1.94
23	1.26	1.44	1.17	1.54	1.08	1.66	0.99	1.79	0.90	1.92
24	1.27	1.45	1.19	1.55	1.10	1.66	1.01	1.78	0.93	1.90
25	1.29	1.45	1.21	1.55	1.12	1.66	1.04	1.77	0.95	1.89
26	1.30	1.46	1.22	1.55	1.14	1.65	1.06	1.76	0.98	1.88
27	1.32	1.47	1.24	1.56	1.16	1.65	1.08	1.76	1.01	1.86
28	1.33	1.48	1.26	1.56	1.18	1.65	1.10	1.75	1.03	1.85
29	1.34	1.48	1.27	1.56	1.20	1.65	1.12	1.74	1.05	1.84
30	1.35	1.49	1.28	1.57	1.21	1.65	1.14	1.74	1.07	1.83
31	1.36	1.50	1.30	1.57	1.23	1.65	1.16	1.74	1.09	1.83
32	1.37	1.50	1.31	1.57	1.24	1.65	1.18	1.73	1.11	1.82
33	1.38	1.51	1.32	1.58	1.26	1.65	1.19	1.73	1.13	1.81
34	1.39	1.51	1.33	1.58	1.27	1.65	1.21	1.73	1.15	1.81
35	1.40	1.52	1.34	1.58	1.28	1.65	1.22	1.73	1.16	1.80
36	1.41	1.52	1.35	1.59	1.29	1.65	1.24	1.73	1.18	1.80
37	1.42	1.53	1.36	1.59	1.31	1.66	1.25	1.72	1.19	1.80
38	1.43	1.54	1.37	1.59	1.32	1.66	1.26	1.72	1.21	1.79
39	1.43	1.54	1.38	1.60	1.33	1.66	1.27	1.72	1.22	1.79
40	1.44	1.54	1.39	1.60	1.34	1.66	1.29	1.72	1.23	1.79
45	1.48	1.57	1.43	1.62	1.38	1.67	1.34	1.72	1.29	1.78
50	1.50	1.59	1.46	1.63	1.42	1.67	1.38	1.72	1.34	1.77
55	1.53	1.60	1.49	1.64	1.45	1.68	1.41	1.72	1.38	1.77
60	1.55	1.62	1.51	1.65	1.48	1.69	1.44	1.73	1.41	1.77
65	1.57	1.63	1.54	1.66	1.50	1.70	1.47	1.73	1.44	1.77
70	1.58	1.64	1.55	1.67	1.52	1.70	1.49	1.74	1.46	1.77
75	1.60	1.65	1.57	1.68	1.54	1.71	1.51	1.74	1.49	1.77
80	1.61	1.66	1.59	1.69	1.56	1.72	1.53	1.74	1.51	1.77
85	1.62	1.67	1.60	1.70	1.57	1.72	1.55	1.75	1.52	1.77
90	1.63	1.68	1.61	1.70	1.59	1.73	1.57	1.75	1.54	1.78
95	1.64	1.69	1.62	1.71	1.60	1.73	1.58	1.75	1.56	1.78
100	1.65	1.69	1.63	1.72	1.61	1.74	1.59	1.76	1.57	1.78

Note: k' = number of explanatory variables excluding the constant term.

THE DURBIN-WATSON TABLE

(continued)

significance points of d_L and d_U: 2.5%

n	$k'=1$		$k'=2$		$k'=3$		$k'=4$		$k'=5$	
	d_L	d_U	d_L	d_U	d_L	d_U	d_L	d_U	d_L	d_U
15	0.95	1.23	0.83	1.40	0.71	1.61	0.59	1.84	0.48	2.09
16	0.98	1.24	0.86	1.40	0.75	1.59	0.64	1.80	0.53	2.03
17	1.01	1.25	0.90	1.40	0.79	1.58	0.68	1.77	0.57	1.98
18	1.03	1.26	0.93	1.40	0.82	1.56	0.72	1.74	0.62	1.93
19	1.06	1.28	0.96	1.41	0.86	1.55	0.76	1.72	0.66	1.90
20	1.08	1.28	0.99	1.41	0.89	1.55	0.79	1.70	0.70	1.87
21	1.10	1.30	1.01	1.41	0.92	1.54	0.83	1.69	0.73	1.84
22	1.12	1.31	1.04	1.42	0.95	1.54	0.86	1.68	0.77	1.82
23	1.14	1.32	1.06	1.42	0.97	1.54	0.89	1.67	0.80	1.80
24	1.16	1.33	1.08	1.43	1.00	1.54	0.91	1.66	0.83	1.79
25	1.18	1.34	1.10	1.43	1.02	1.54	0.94	1.65	0.86	1.77
26	1.19	1.35	1.12	1.44	1.04	1.54	0.96	1.65	0.88	1.76
27	1.21	1.36	1.13	1.44	1.06	1.54	0.99	1.64	0.91	1.75
28	1.22	1.37	1.15	1.45	1.08	1.54	1.01	1.64	0.93	1.74
29	1.24	1.38	1.17	1.45	1.10	1.54	1.03	1.63	0.96	1.73
30	1.25	1.38	1.18	1.46	1.12	1.54	1.05	1.63	0.98	1.73
31	1.26	1.39	1.20	1.47	1.13	1.55	1.07	1.63	1.00	1.72
32	1.27	1.40	1.21	1.47	1.15	1.55	1.08	1.63	1.02	1.71
33	1.28	1.41	1.22	1.48	1.16	1.55	1.10	1.63	1.04	1.71
34	1.29	1.41	1.24	1.48	1.17	1.55	1.12	1.63	1.06	1.70
35	1.30	1.42	1.25	1.48	1.19	1.55	1.13	1.63	1.07	1.70
36	1.31	1.43	1.26	1.49	1.20	1.56	1.15	1.63	1.09	1.70
37	1.32	1.43	1.27	1.49	1.21	1.56	1.16	1.62	1.10	1.70
38	1.33	1.44	1.28	1.50	1.23	1.56	1.17	1.62	1.12	1.70
39	1.34	1.44	1.29	1.50	1.24	1.56	1.19	1.63	1.13	1.69
40	1.35	1.45	1.30	1.51	1.25	1.57	1.20	1.63	1.15	1.69
45	1.39	1.48	1.34	1.53	1.30	1.58	1.25	1.63	1.21	1.69
50	1.42	1.50	1.38	1.54	1.34	1.59	1.30	1.64	1.26	1.69
55	1.45	1.52	1.41	1.56	1.37	1.60	1.33	1.64	1.30	1.69
60	1.47	1.54	1.44	1.57	1.40	1.61	1.37	1.65	1.33	1.69
65	1.49	1.55	1.46	1.59	1.43	1.62	1.40	1.66	1.36	1.69
70	1.51	1.57	1.48	1.60	1.45	1.63	1.42	1.66	1.39	1.70
75	1.53	1.58	1.50	1.61	1.47	1.64	1.45	1.67	1.42	1.70
80	1.54	1.59	1.52	1.62	1.49	1.65	1.47	1.67	1.44	1.70
85	1.56	1.60	1.53	1.63	1.51	1.65	1.49	1.68	1.46	1.71
90	1.57	1.61	1.55	1.64	1.53	1.66	1.50	1.69	1.48	1.71
95	1.58	1.62	1.56	1.65	1.54	1.67	1.52	1.69	1.50	1.71
100	1.59	1.63	1.57	1.65	1.55	1.67	1.53	1.70	1.51	1.72

THE DURBIN-WATSON TABLE

(continued)

significance points of d_L and d_U: 1%

n	k' = 1		k' = 2		k' = 3		k' = 4		k' = 5	
	d_L	d_U	d_L	d_U	d_L	d_U	d_L	d_U	d_L	d_U
15	0.81	1.07	0.70	1.25	0.59	1.46	0.49	1.70	0.39	1.96
16	0.84	1.09	0.74	1.25	0.63	1.44	0.53	1.66	0.44	1.90
17	0.87	1.10	0.77	1.25	0.67	1.43	0.57	1.63	0.48	1.85
18	0.90	1.12	0.80	1.26	0.71	1.42	0.61	1.60	0.52	1.80
19	0.93	1.13	0.83	1.26	0.74	1.41	0.65	1.58	0.56	1.77
20	0.95	1.15	0.86	1.27	0.77	1.41	0.68	1.57	0.60	1.74
21	0.97	1.16	0.89	1.27	0.80	1.41	0.72	1.55	0.63	1.71
22	1.00	1.17	0.91	1.28	0.83	1.40	0.75	1.54	0.66	1.69
23	1.02	1.19	0.94	1.29	0.86	1.40	0.77	1.53	0.70	1.67
24	1.04	1.20	0.96	1.30	0.88	1.41	0.80	1.53	0.72	1.66
25	1.05	1.21	0.98	1.30	0.90	1.41	0.83	1.52	0.75	1.65
26	1.07	1.22	1.00	1.31	0.93	1.41	0.85	1.52	0.78	1.64
27	1.09	1.23	1.02	1.32	0.95	1.41	0.88	1.51	0.81	1.63
28	1.10	1.24	1.04	1.32	0.97	1.41	0.90	1.51	0.83	1.62
29	1.12	1.25	1.05	1.33	0.99	1.42	0.92	1.51	0.85	1.61
30	1.13	1.26	1.07	1.34	1.01	1.42	0.94	1.51	0.88	1.61
31	1.15	1.27	1.08	1.34	1.02	1.42	0.96	1.51	0.90	1.60
32	1.16	1.28	1.10	1.35	1.04	1.43	0.98	1.51	0.92	1.60
33	1.17	1.29	1.11	1.36	1.05	1.43	1.00	1.51	0.94	1.59
34	1.18	1.30	1.13	1.36	1.07	1.43	1.01	1.51	0.95	1.59
35	1.19	1.31	1.14	1.37	1.08	1.44	1.03	1.51	0.97	1.59
36	1.21	1.32	1.15	1.38	1.10	1.44	1.04	1.51	0.99	1.59
37	1.22	1.32	1.16	1.38	1.11	1.45	1.06	1.51	1.00	1.59
38	1.23	1.33	1.18	1.39	1.12	1.45	1.07	1.52	1.02	1.58
39	1.24	1.34	1.19	1.39	1.14	1.45	1.09	1.52	1.03	1.58
40	1.25	1.34	1.20	1.40	1.15	1.46	1.10	1.52	1.05	1.58
45	1.29	1.38	1.24	1.42	1.20	1.48	1.16	1.53	1.11	1.58
50	1.32	1.40	1.28	1.45	1.24	1.49	1.20	1.54	1.16	1.59
55	1.36	1.43	1.32	1.47	1.28	1.51	1.25	1.55	1.21	1.59
60	1.38	1.45	1.35	1.48	1.32	1.52	1.28	1.56	1.25	1.60
65	1.41	1.47	1.38	1.50	1.35	1.53	1.31	1.57	1.28	1.61
70	1.43	1.49	1.40	1.52	1.37	1.55	1.34	1.58	1.31	1.61
75	1.45	1.50	1.42	1.53	1.39	1.56	1.37	1.59	1.34	1.62
80	1.47	1.52	1.44	1.54	1.42	1.57	1.39	1.60	1.36	1.62
85	1.48	1.53	1.46	1.55	1.43	1.58	1.41	1.60	1.39	1.63
90	1.50	1.54	1.47	1.56	1.45	1.59	1.43	1.61	1.41	1.64
95	1.51	1.55	1.49	1.57	1.47	1.60	1.45	1.62	1.42	1.64
100	1.52	1.56	1.50	1.58	1.48	1.60	1.46	1.63	1.44	1.65

Source: J. Durbin and G. S. Watson, "Testing Serial Correlation in Least Squares Regression," *Biometrika*, Vol. 38 (June, 1951).

THE F DISTRIBUTION

upper 5% points

n_2 \ n_1	1	2	3	4	5	6	7	8	9	10	12	15	20	24	30	40	60	120	∞
1	161.4	199.5	215.7	224.6	230.2	234.0	236.8	238.9	240.5	241.9	243.9	245.9	248.0	249.1	250.1	251.1	252.2	253.3	254.3
2	18.51	19.00	19.16	19.25	19.30	19.33	19.35	19.37	19.38	19.40	19.41	19.43	19.45	19.45	19.46	19.47	19.48	19.49	19.50
3	10.13	9.55	9.28	9.12	9.01	8.94	8.89	8.85	8.81	8.79	8.74	8.70	8.66	8.64	8.62	8.59	8.57	8.55	8.53
4	7.71	6.94	6.59	6.39	6.26	6.16	6.09	6.04	6.00	5.96	5.91	5.86	5.80	5.77	5.75	5.72	5.69	5.66	5.63
5	6.61	5.79	5.41	5.19	5.05	4.95	4.88	4.82	4.77	4.74	4.68	4.62	4.56	4.53	4.50	4.46	4.43	4.40	4.36
6	5.99	5.14	4.76	4.53	4.39	4.28	4.21	4.15	4.10	4.06	4.00	3.94	3.87	3.84	3.81	3.77	3.74	3.70	3.67
7	5.59	4.74	4.35	4.12	3.97	3.87	3.79	3.73	3.68	3.64	3.57	3.51	3.44	3.41	3.38	3.34	3.30	3.27	3.23
8	5.32	4.46	4.07	3.84	3.69	3.58	3.50	3.44	3.39	3.35	3.28	3.22	3.15	3.12	3.08	3.04	3.01	2.97	2.93
9	5.12	4.26	3.86	3.63	3.48	3.37	3.29	3.23	3.18	3.14	3.07	3.01	2.94	2.90	2.86	2.83	2.79	2.75	2.71
10	4.96	4.10	3.71	3.48	3.33	3.22	3.14	3.07	3.02	2.98	2.91	2.85	2.77	2.74	2.70	2.66	2.62	2.58	2.54
11	4.84	3.98	3.59	3.36	3.20	3.09	3.01	2.95	2.90	2.85	2.79	2.72	2.65	2.61	2.57	2.53	2.49	2.45	2.40
12	4.75	3.89	3.49	3.26	3.11	3.00	2.91	2.85	2.80	2.75	2.69	2.62	2.54	2.51	2.47	2.43	2.38	2.34	2.30
13	4.67	3.81	3.41	3.18	3.03	2.92	2.83	2.77	2.71	2.67	2.60	2.53	2.46	2.42	2.38	2.34	2.30	2.25	2.21
14	4.60	3.74	3.34	3.11	2.96	2.85	2.76	2.70	2.65	2.60	2.53	2.46	2.39	2.35	2.31	2.27	2.22	2.18	2.13
15	4.54	3.68	3.29	3.06	2.90	2.79	2.71	2.64	2.59	2.54	2.48	2.40	2.33	2.29	2.25	2.20	2.16	2.11	2.07
16	4.49	3.63	3.24	3.01	2.85	2.74	2.66	2.59	2.54	2.49	2.42	2.35	2.28	2.24	2.19	2.15	2.11	2.06	2.01
17	4.45	3.59	3.20	2.96	2.81	2.70	2.61	2.55	2.49	2.45	2.38	2.31	2.23	2.19	2.15	2.10	2.06	2.01	1.96
18	4.41	3.55	3.16	2.93	2.77	2.66	2.58	2.51	2.46	2.41	2.34	2.27	2.19	2.15	2.11	2.06	2.02	1.97	1.92
19	4.38	3.52	3.13	2.90	2.74	2.63	2.54	2.48	2.42	2.38	2.31	2.23	2.16	2.11	2.07	2.03	1.98	1.93	1.88
20	4.35	3.49	3.10	2.87	2.71	2.60	2.51	2.45	2.39	2.35	2.28	2.20	2.12	2.08	2.04	1.99	1.95	1.90	1.84
21	4.32	3.47	3.07	2.84	2.68	2.57	2.49	2.42	2.37	2.32	2.25	2.18	2.10	2.05	2.01	1.96	1.92	1.87	1.81
22	4.30	3.44	3.05	2.82	2.66	2.55	2.46	2.40	2.34	2.30	2.23	2.15	2.07	2.03	1.98	1.94	1.89	1.84	1.78
23	4.28	3.42	3.03	2.80	2.64	2.53	2.44	2.37	2.32	2.27	2.20	2.13	2.05	2.01	1.96	1.91	1.86	1.81	1.76
24	4.26	3.40	3.01	2.78	2.62	2.51	2.42	2.46	2.30	2.25	2.18	2.11	2.03	1.98	1.94	1.89	1.84	1.79	1.73
25	4.24	3.39	2.99	2.76	2.60	2.49	2.40	2.34	2.28	2.24	2.16	2.09	2.01	1.96	1.92	1.87	1.82	1.77	1.71
26	4.23	3.37	2.98	2.74	2.59	2.47	2.39	2.32	2.27	2.22	2.15	2.07	1.99	1.95	1.90	1.85	1.80	1.75	1.69
27	4.21	3.35	2.96	2.73	2.57	2.46	2.37	2.31	2.25	2.20	2.13	2.06	1.97	1.93	1.88	1.84	1.79	1.73	1.67
28	4.20	3.34	2.95	2.71	2.56	2.45	2.36	2.29	2.24	2.19	2.12	2.04	1.96	1.91	1.87	1.82	1.77	1.71	1.65
29	4.18	3.33	2.93	2.70	2.55	2.43	2.35	2.28	2.22	2.18	2.10	2.03	1.94	1.90	1.85	1.81	1.75	1.70	1.64
30	4.17	3.32	2.92	2.69	2.53	2.42	2.33	2.27	2.21	2.16	2.09	2.01	1.93	1.89	1.84	1.79	1.74	1.68	1.62
40	4.08	3.23	2.84	2.61	2.45	2.34	2.25	2.18	2.12	2.08	2.00	1.92	1.84	1.79	1.74	1.69	1.64	1.58	1.51
60	4.00	3.15	2.76	2.53	2.37	2.25	2.17	2.10	2.04	1.99	1.92	1.84	1.75	1.70	1.65	1.59	1.53	1.47	1.39
120	3.92	3.07	2.68	2.45	2.29	2.17	2.09	2.02	1.96	1.91	1.83	1.75	1.66	1.61	1.55	1.50	1.43	1.35	1.25
∞	3.84	3.00	2.60	2.37	2.21	2.10	2.01	1.94	1.88	1.83	1.75	1.67	1.57	1.52	1.46	1.39	1.32	1.22	1.00

(table continued on page 373)

upper 1% points

n_2 \ n_1	1	2	3	4	5	6	7	8	9	10	12	15	20	24	30	40	60	120	∞
1	4052	4999.5	5403	5625	5764	5859	5928	5982	6022	6056	6106	6157	6209	6235	6261	6287	6313	6339	6366
2	98.50	99.00	99.17	99.25	99.30	99.33	99.36	99.37	99.39	99.40	99.42	99.43	99.45	99.46	99.47	99.47	99.48	99.49	99.50
3	34.12	30.82	29.46	28.71	28.24	27.91	27.67	27.49	27.35	27.23	27.05	26.87	26.69	26.60	26.50	26.41	26.32	26.22	26.13
4	21.20	18.00	16.69	15.98	15.52	15.21	14.98	14.80	14.66	14.55	14.37	14.20	14.02	13.93	13.84	13.75	13.65	13.56	13.46
5	16.26	13.27	12.06	11.39	10.97	10.67	10.46	10.29	10.16	10.05	9.89	9.72	9.55	9.47	9.38	9.29	9.20	9.11	9.02
6	13.75	10.92	9.78	9.15	8.75	8.47	8.26	8.10	7.98	7.87	7.72	7.56	7.40	7.31	7.23	7.14	7.06	6.97	6.88
7	12.25	9.55	8.45	7.85	7.46	7.19	6.99	6.84	6.72	6.62	6.47	6.31	6.16	6.07	5.99	5.91	5.82	5.74	5.65
8	11.26	8.65	7.59	7.01	6.63	6.37	6.18	6.03	5.91	5.81	5.67	5.52	5.36	5.28	5.20	5.12	5.03	4.95	4.86
9	10.56	8.02	6.99	6.42	6.06	5.80	5.61	5.47	5.35	5.26	5.11	4.96	4.81	4.73	4.65	4.57	4.48	4.40	4.31
10	10.04	7.56	6.55	5.99	5.64	5.39	5.20	5.06	4.94	4.85	4.71	4.56	4.41	4.33	4.25	4.17	4.08	4.00	3.91
11	9.65	7.21	6.22	5.67	5.32	5.07	4.89	4.74	4.63	4.54	4.40	4.25	4.10	4.02	3.94	3.86	3.78	3.69	3.60
12	9.33	6.93	5.95	5.41	5.06	4.82	4.64	4.50	4.39	4.30	4.16	4.01	3.86	3.78	3.70	3.62	3.54	3.45	3.36
13	9.07	6.70	5.74	5.21	4.86	4.62	4.44	4.30	4.19	4.10	3.96	3.82	3.66	3.59	3.51	3.43	3.34	3.25	3.17
14	8.86	6.51	5.56	5.04	4.69	4.46	4.28	4.14	4.03	3.94	3.80	3.66	3.51	3.43	3.35	3.27	3.18	3.09	3.00
15	8.68	6.36	5.42	4.89	4.56	4.32	4.14	4.00	3.89	3.80	3.67	3.52	3.37	3.29	3.21	3.13	3.05	2.96	2.87
16	8.53	6.23	5.29	4.77	4.44	4.20	4.03	3.89	3.78	3.69	3.55	3.41	3.26	3.18	3.10	3.02	2.93	2.84	2.75
17	8.40	6.11	5.18	4.67	4.34	4.10	3.93	3.79	3.68	3.59	3.46	3.31	3.16	3.08	3.00	2.92	2.83	2.75	2.65
18	8.29	6.01	5.09	4.58	4.25	4.01	3.84	3.71	3.60	3.51	3.37	3.23	3.08	3.00	2.92	2.84	2.75	2.66	2.57
19	8.18	5.93	5.01	4.50	4.17	3.94	3.77	3.63	3.52	3.43	3.30	3.15	3.00	2.92	2.84	2.76	2.67	2.58	2.49
20	8.10	5.85	4.94	4.43	4.10	3.87	3.70	3.56	3.46	3.37	3.23	3.09	2.94	2.86	2.78	2.69	2.61	2.52	2.42
21	8.02	5.78	4.87	4.37	4.04	3.81	3.64	3.51	3.40	3.31	3.17	3.03	2.88	2.80	2.72	2.64	2.55	2.46	2.36
22	7.95	5.72	4.82	4.31	3.99	3.76	3.59	3.45	3.35	3.26	3.12	2.98	2.83	2.75	2.67	2.58	2.50	2.40	2.31
23	7.88	5.66	4.76	4.26	3.94	3.71	3.54	3.41	3.30	3.21	3.07	2.93	2.78	2.70	2.62	2.54	2.45	2.35	2.26
24	7.82	5.61	4.72	4.22	3.90	3.67	3.50	3.36	3.26	3.17	3.03	2.89	2.74	2.66	2.58	2.49	2.40	2.31	2.21
25	7.77	5.57	4.68	4.18	3.85	3.63	3.46	3.32	3.22	3.13	2.99	2.85	2.70	2.62	2.54	2.45	2.36	2.27	2.17
26	7.72	5.53	4.64	4.14	3.82	3.59	3.42	3.29	3.18	3.09	2.96	2.81	2.66	2.58	2.50	2.42	2.33	2.23	2.13
27	7.68	5.49	4.60	4.11	3.78	3.56	3.39	3.26	3.15	3.06	2.93	2.78	2.63	2.55	2.47	2.38	2.29	2.20	2.10
28	7.64	5.45	4.57	4.07	3.75	3.53	3.36	3.23	3.12	3.03	2.90	2.75	2.60	2.52	2.44	2.35	2.26	2.17	2.06
29	7.60	5.42	4.54	4.04	3.73	3.50	3.33	3.20	3.09	3.00	2.87	2.73	2.57	2.49	2.41	2.33	2.23	2.14	2.03
30	7.56	5.39	4.51	4.02	3.70	3.47	3.30	3.17	3.07	2.98	2.84	2.70	2.55	2.47	2.39	2.30	2.21	2.11	2.01
40	7.31	5.18	4.31	3.83	3.51	3.29	3.12	2.99	2.89	2.80	2.66	2.52	2.37	2.29	2.20	2.11	2.02	1.92	1.80
60	7.08	4.98	4.13	3.65	3.34	3.12	2.95	2.82	2.72	2.63	2.50	2.35	2.20	2.12	2.03	1.94	1.84	1.73	1.60
120	6.85	4.79	3.95	3.48	3.17	2.96	2.79	2.66	2.56	2.47	2.34	2.19	2.03	1.95	1.86	1.76	1.66	1.53	1.38
∞	6.63	4.61	3.78	3.32	3.02	2.80	2.64	2.51	2.41	2.32	2.18	2.04	1.88	1.79	1.70	1.59	1.47	1.32	1.00

Note: The upper 5 percent and upper 1 percent are values of F that will be exceeded with probability 5 and 1 percent, respectively. n_1 and n_2 are the numbers of degrees of freedom in the numerator and denominator, respectively. *Example:* For 5 degrees of freedom in the numerator and 10 in the denominator, a value of F greater than 3.33 has a probability of 5 percent; and a value of F greater than 5.64 has a probability of 1 percent.

Source: E. S. Pearson and H. O. Hartley, *Biometrika Tables for Statisticians* (New York: Cambridge University Press, 1972).

THE CHI-SQUARE AND THE NORMAL DISTRIBUTION

Degrees of Freedom \ Pb	.995	.990	.975	.950	.900	.750
1	$392704 \cdot 10^{-10}$	$157088 \cdot 10^{-9}$	$982069 \cdot 10^{-9}$	$393214 \cdot 10^{-8}$	.0157908	.1015308
2	.0100251	.0201007	.0506356	.102587	.210720	.575364
3	.0717212	.114832	.215795	.351846	.584375	1.212534
4	.206990	.297110	.484419	.710721	1.063623	1.92255
5	.411740	.554300	.831211	1.145476	1.61031	2.67460
6	.675727	.872085	1.237347	1.63539	2.20413	3.45460
7	.989265	1.239043	1.68987	2.16735	2.83311	4.25485
8	1.344419	1.646482	2.17973	2.73264	3.48954	5.07064
9	1.734926	2.087912	2.70039	3.32511	4.16816	5.89883
10	2.15585	2.55821	3.24697	3.94030	4.86518	6.73720
11	2.60321	3.05347	3.81575	4.57481	5.57779	7.58412
12	3.07382	3.57056	4.40379	5.22603	6.30380	8.43842
13	3.56503	4.10691	5.00874	5.89186	7.04150	9.29906
14	4.07468	4.66043	5.62872	6.57063	7.78953	10.1653
15	4.60094	5.22935	6.26214	7.26094	8.54675	11.0365
16	5.14224	5.81221	6.90766	7.96164	9.31223	11.9122
17	5.69724	6.40776	7.56418	8.67176	10.0852	12.7919
18	6.26481	7.01491	8.23075	9.39046	10.8649	13.6753
19	6.84398	7.63273	8.90655	10.1170	11.6509	14.5620
20	7.43386	8.26040	9.59083	10.8508	12.4426	15.4518
21	8.03366	8.89720	10.28293	11.5913	13.2396	16.3444
22	8.64272	9.54249	10.9823	12.3380	14.0415	17.2396
23	9.26042	10.19567	11.6885	13.0905	14.8479	18.1373
24	9.88623	10.8564	12.4011	13.8484	15.6587	19.0372
25	10.5197	11.5240	13.1197	14.6114	16.4734	19.9393
26	11.1603	12.1981	13.8439	15.3791	17.2919	20.8434
27	11.8076	12.8786	14.5733	16.1513	18.1138	21.7494
28	12.4613	13.5648	15.3079	16.9279	18.9392	22.6572
29	13.1211	14.2565	16.0471	17.7083	19.7677	23.5666
30	13.7867	14.9535	16.7908	18.4926	20.5992	24.4776
40	20.7065	22.1643	24.4331	26.5093	29.0505	33.6603
50	27.9907	29.7067	32.3574	34.7642	37.6886	42.9421
60	35.5346	37.4848	40.4817	43.1879	46.4589	52.2938
70	43.2752	45.4418	48.7576	51.7393	55.3290	61.6983
80	51.1720	53.5400	57.1532	60.3915	64.2778	71.1445
90	59.1963	61.7541	65.6466	69.1260	73.2912	80.6247
100	67.3276	70.0648	74.2219	77.9295	82.3581	90.1332
(Normal)	−2.5758	−2.3263	−1.9600	−1.6449	−1.2816	−.6745

Note: The probability shown at the head of a column is the area in the right-hand tail. The last line of the table shows the value of the standard normal variable that is exceeded with the probability given at the head of the column.

THE CHI-SQUARE AND THE NORMAL DISTRIBUTION

(continued)

Degrees of Freedom \ Pb	.500	.250	.100	.050	.025	.010	.005
1	.454937	1.32330	2.70554	3.84146	5.02389	6.63490	7.87944
2	1.38629	2.77259	4.60517	5.99147	7.37776	9.21034	10.5966
3	2.36597	4.10835	6.25139	7.81473	9.34840	11.3449	12.8381
4	3.35670	5.38527	7.77944	9.48773	11.1433	13.2767	14.8602
5	4.35146	6.62568	9.23635	11.0705	12.8325	15.0863	16.7496
6	5.34812	7.84080	10.6446	12.5916	14.4494	16.8119	18.5476
7	6.34581	9.03715	12.0170	14.0671	16.0128	18.4753	20.2777
8	7.34412	10.2188	13.3616	15.5073	17.5346	20.0902	21.9550
9	8.34283	11.3887	14.6837	16.9190	19.0228	21.6660	23.5893
10	9.34182	12.5489	15.9871	18.3070	20.4831	23.2093	25.1882
11	10.3410	13.7007	17.2750	19.6751	21.9200	24.7250	26.7569
12	11.3403	14.8454	18.5494	21.0261	23.3367	26.2170	28.2995
13	12.3398	15.9839	19.8119	22.3621	24.7356	27.6883	29.8194
14	13.3393	17.1170	21.0642	23.6848	26.1190	29.1413	31.3193
15	14.3389	18.2451	22.3072	24.9958	27.4884	30.5779	32.8013
16	15.3385	19.3688	23.5418	26.2962	28.8454	31.9999	34.2672
17	16.3381	20.4887	24.7690	27.5871	30.1910	33.4087	35.7185
18	17.3379	21.6049	25.9894	28.8693	31.5264	34.8053	37.1564
19	18.3376	22.7178	27.2036	30.1435	32.8523	36.1908	38.5822
20	19.3374	23.8277	28.4120	31.4104	34.1696	37.5662	39.9968
21	20.3372	24.9348	29.6151	32.6705	35.4789	38.9321	41.4010
22	21.3370	26.0393	30.8133	33.9244	36.7807	40.2894	42.7956
23	22.3369	27.1413	32.0069	35.1725	38.0757	41.6384	44.1813
24	23.3367	28.2412	33.1963	36.4151	39.3641	42.9798	45.5585
25	24.3366	29.3389	34.3816	37.6525	40.6465	44.3141	46.9278
26	25.3364	30.4345	35.5631	38.8852	41.9232	45.6417	48.2899
27	26.3363	31.5284	36.7412	40.1133	43.1944	46.9630	49.6449
28	27.3363	32.6205	37.9159	41.3372	44.4607	48.2782	50.9933
29	28.3362	33.7109	39.0875	42.5569	45.7222	49.5879	52.3356
30	29.3360	34.7998	40.2560	43.7729	46.9792	50.8922	53.6720
40	39.3354	45.6160	51.8050	55.7585	59.3417	63.6907	66.7659
50	49.3349	56.3336	63.1671	67.5048	71.4202	76.1539	79.4900
60	59.3347	66.9814	74.3970	79.0819	83.2976	88.3794	91.9517
70	69.3344	77.5766	85.5271	90.5312	95.0231	100.425	104.215
80	79.3343	88.1303	96.5782	101.879	106.629	112.329	116.321
90	89.3342	98.6499	107.565	113.145	118.136	124.116	128.299
100	99.3341	109.141	118.498	124.342	129.561	135.807	140.169
(Normal)	.0000	+.6745	+1.2816	+1.6449	+1.9600	+2.3263	+2.5758

Source: E. S. Pearson and H. O. Hartley, *Biometrika Tables for Statisticians* (New York: Cambridge University Press, 1972).

THE *t* DISTRIBUTION AND THE NORMAL DISTRIBUTION

Degrees of Freedom \ Pb	.25 .5	.1 .2	.05 .1	.025 .05	.01 .02	.005 .01
1	1.000	3.078	6.314	12.706	31.821	63.657
2	.816	1.886	2.920	4.303	6.965	9.925
3	.765	1.638	2.353	3.182	4.541	5.841
4	.741	1.533	2.132	2.776	3.747	4.604
5	.727	1.476	2.015	2.571	3.365	4.032
6	.718	1.440	1.943	2.447	3.143	3.707
7	.711	1.415	1.895	2.365	2.998	3.499
8	.706	1.397	1.860	2.306	2.896	3.355
9	.703	1.383	1.833	2.262	2.821	3.250
10	.700	1.372	1.812	2.228	2.764	3.169
11	.697	1.363	1.796	2.201	2.718	3.106
12	.695	1.356	1.782	2.179	2.681	3.055
13	.694	1.350	1.771	2.160	2.650	3.012
14	.692	1.345	1.761	2.145	2.624	2.977
15	.691	1.341	1.753	2.131	2.602	2.947
16	.690	1.337	1.746	2.120	2.583	2.921
17	.689	1.333	1.740	2.110	2.567	2.898
18	.688	1.330	1.734	2.101	2.552	2.878
19	.688	1.328	1.729	2.093	2.539	2.861
20	.687	1.325	1.725	2.086	2.528	2.845
21	.686	1.323	1.721	2.080	2.518	2.831
22	.686	1.321	1.717	2.074	2.508	2.819
23	.685	1.319	1.714	2.069	2.500	2.807
24	.685	1.318	1.711	2.064	2.492	2.797
25	.684	1.316	1.708	2.060	2.485	2.787
26	.684	1.315	1.706	2.056	2.479	2.779
27	.684	1.314	1.703	2.052	2.473	2.771
28	.683	1.313	1.701	2.048	2.467	2.763
29	.683	1.311	1.699	2.045	2.462	2.756
30	.683	1.310	1.697	2.042	2.457	2.750
40	.681	1.303	1.684	2.021	2.423	2.704
60	.679	1.296	1.671	2.000	2.390	2.660
120	.677	1.289	1.658	1.980	2.358	2.617
(Normal) ∞	.674	1.282	1.645	1.960	2.326	2.576

Note: The smaller probability shown at the head of a column is the area in *one* tail, and the larger probability is the area in *both* tails. *Example:* With 5 degrees of freedom, a positive value of *t* larger than 2.015 has a probability of 5 percent and a value of *t* greater in absolute value than 2.015 has a probability of 10 percent. The distribution is symmetrical.

Source: E. S. Pearson and H. O. Hartley, *Biometrika Tables for Statisticians* (New York: Cambridge University Press, 1972).

index

R

S

T

U